EXCURSIONS, ADVENTURES AND FIELD-SPORTS IN CEYLON

EXCURSIONS, ADVENTURES AND FIELD-SPORTS IN CEYLON

ITS COMMERCIAL AND MILITARY IMPORTANCE

JAMES CAMPBELL

IN TWO VOLUMES

VOL. I

WITH 7 PLATES AND A MAP

Published by

Facsimile Publisher
12 Pragati Market
Ashok Vihar, Ph-2
Delhi-110052
facsimilepublisher.com

Distribution Network
gyanbooks.com
India, USA, Canada, UK, Australia, France

ISBN : 978-93-5324-467-5 (Set)
ISBN : 978-93-5324-468-2 Vol. 1 (HB)
First Published, London, 1843

2nd Impression 2020

Printed at: Gyan Press, Delhi.

Excursions, Adventures and Field-Sports
In
Ceylon
Author: James Campbell

EXCURSIONS,

ADVENTURES, AND FIELD-SPORTS

IN

CEYLON;

Its Commercial and Military Importance,

AND

NUMEROUS ADVANTAGES TO THE BRITISH EMIGRANT.

BY

LIEUT.-COLONEL JAMES CAMPBELL,

FORMERLY OF THE 48TH AND 50TH REGIMENTS,
AND FOR SEVERAL YEARS COMMANDANT OF THE DISTRICTS OF GALLE AND THE SEVEN KORLES, AND JUDICIAL AGENT OF GOVERNMENT.

"There is continual spring, and harvest there
Continual, both meeting at one time."

IN TWO VOLUMES.

VOL. I.

LONDON:
T. AND W. BOONE, 29, NEW BOND STREET.
MDCCCXLIII.

PREFACE.

Conscious that, in publishing these volumes, one of my motives, and that a principal one, is a sincere desire to benefit a very large class of my fellow-countrymen, I should have committed them, unprefaced, to the candid judgment of my readers, had not some circumstances recently occurred, which seem to call for a few additional remarks. As my remarks must be rather of a grave tenor, those persons who prefer lighter themes will have the kindness to pass by my preface, (a fate to which, I believe, prefaces are very subject), and proceed to the work, where, I trust, they will find that I have provided them with a tolerable supply of amusement.

Since the manuscript was prepared for the press, two of the points upon which it treats, those of colonization and emigration, have acquired additional importance. They have, moreover, been brought into Parliamentary discussion, by Mr. C. Buller, who was desirous to ascertain what measures the Colonial Secretary intended to adopt with respect to them. In reply, Lord Stanley ably stated what had been done, and was still doing, for emigrants; but he seemed to wish his hearers to suppose, that no improvement can be made in the system which is at present pursued.

I flatter myself, however, that in the course of my work, I have clearly shewn the contrary to be the case, and that there is "ample room and verge enough" for the most beneficial amelioration. Though it may seem great presumption in me to differ from such an authority as Lord Stanley, I must contend, that the mode of colonizing, so long followed by Great Britain, has been, to say the least, injudicious; for, it has neither benefited the mother country as it ought to have done, nor even the colonies themselves, by any means to such an extent as it ought. In fact, nothing has yet been attempted upon the true principles of colonization; that is to say, to enable settlers to take with them our established religion, our national system of moral and religious instruction, our free institutions, laws, manners, customs, and even our peculiarities, or, as some perhaps would call them, our prejudices. If all this is not looked after, the best national feelings and characteristics soon grow feeble, or are obliterated; so that, instead of becoming integral parts of the empire, and contributing to its strength and prosperity, colonies prove to be only causes of weakness and embarrassment.

I have, likewise, I trust, demonstrated, that the existing system of emigration and colonization has been of advantage only to speculating companies, and land-jobbers, while it has been ruinous not only to the better class of emigrants, but also to artisans and labourers. In short, I have shewn that colonization cannot possibly succeed without cheap labour, and that, as matters are now managed, labour can be cheap only where there are no means of paying for it.

A few words may not be out of place here, with respect to abolishing the mode, so long practised, of supplying New South Wales with convicts, or cheap labour. It might, perhaps, be well to ask ourselves the question, whether, for the sake of experiment, it is advisable to incur the expense of establishing Penitentiary prisons, at Parkhurst and in Van Diemen's Land, merely to ascertain whether a scheme of rewards and punishments will amend vitiated materials; and whether the purpose might not be better effected, in the old way, by sending convicts to Sydney, where they would be either employed in gangs, for the public benefit, or distributed among the respectable settlers, as servants and labourers? Could not the settlers be rendered responsible for the moral and religious instruction of the convicts, under the superintendence of Protectors or Inspectors? Whenever the Protectors found that this essential point had been neglected, they should be authorized to remove the convicts from the service of such unworthy masters, who, of course, should never again be allowed to avail themselves of convict labour. This was nearly all that the old plan wanted to make it work well. The old plan cost the country comparatively nothing; the new one will cost some millions. But why should so great a benefit, as having convicts sent to them, *under proper* regulations, be confined to New South Wales and Van Diemen's Land.

When I suggested that small but sufficient portions of land should be granted for nothing to the poorer class of emigrants—(and I cannot see the necessity, which some theorists insist upon, that they should ultimately be made to pay for it, and for the implements with which they were supplied) —I was not ignorant of the "Canada Act of Union," spoken of by Lord Stanley; nor that it gives up the land revenue to the Provincial Legislature. I knew, too, that such land can only be disposed of by sale; and that a similar system has been adopted in Australia, in several other colonies, and even in Ceylon. But I considered, also, of course, that, if such enactments were found not to work well, they could be repealed or amended; and I am decidedly of opinion, that this must necessarily be the case, if ever Government measures of colonization and emigration are to be expected to afford, to our suffering and redundant population, that relief of which it obviously stands in such urgent need. The time is, perhaps, not far distant, when the prudence of such a course will be manifest to every one.

CONTENTS OF VOLUME I.

CHAPTER I.

CHAPTER II.

CHAPTER III.

PAGE

CHAPTER IV.

CHAPTER V.

CHAPTER VI.

CHAPTER VII.

PAGE

CHAPTER VIII.

CHAPTER IX.

CHAPTER X.

LIST OF PLATES TO VOL. I.

CEYLON.

CHAPTER I.

"Spread the sail," said the King, "seize the winds as they pour from Lena." We rose on the wave with songs. We rushed with joy through the foam of the deep.—OSSIAN.

VOYAGE TO CEYLON COMMENCED — AUTHOR'S REGRET AT HAVING DESTROYED AN OLD JOURNAL — MADEIRA — THE ISLANDS IN THE EAST ATLANTIC—ENTER THE TROPIC—SEA AMUSEMENTS—SUN-SETTING IN THE TROPICS—CAPE VERD ISLANDS—AN ADVENTURE ON LEAVING PORT PRAYA—DOLPHINS AND BONITOS — A MAN OVERBOARD AMONGST SHARKS — A COUP-DE-SOLEIL — DECEPTION ATTEMPTED—DARBY STAR, THE IRISH DANCING MASTER—THUNDER AT THE EQUATOR—AMUSEMENTS AT SEA—NUMBERS OF BIRDS WHICH SURROUND SHIPS APPROACHING THE CAPE OF GOOD HOPE — STORMS AND CALMS — VOYAGE CONTINUED FROM SIMON'S BAY TO CEYLON, ETC.

If it has ever fallen to the reader's lot, to have been sent to a distant part of the world in a troop-ship, or what is commonly called a transport; and, if, during the long period which is usually required for such trying and frequently tedious voyages to many of our foreign possessions, he has had the charge of about three hundred men, most of them, perhaps, never at sea before; he can form an idea of the responsibility which attaches to an officer who is entrusted with such a command.

We had been about three weeks on board a large free-trader, in Cork harbour, bound for Ceylon; but, owing to the dreadful state of the weather, we were not able to put to sea until the latter end of February, 1819, when we at last stood out from the land under a press of sail.

At the time when this narrative commences, we had been four days at sea; and I must say that never, upon any occasion, had I ever witnessed greater wretchedness, or such tragi-comical scenes as were, during that period, enacted on board; but sea-sick people are only laughed at, and told, for their comfort, that there is no danger to be apprehended. Exertion is the best, and, I may say, the only preventive, or cure, for this most depressing of all maladies, which in this instance laid low more able bodied men than I ever remember to have seen its victims. The 1st of March being, however, a tolerably fine day, I at last am able to force out of their lairs every man, woman, and child—I know that I am thought a horrid savage, for insisting upon their coming on deck; but no matter, they will soon begin to forget all their sufferings and annoyances. And, worthy reader, if you should happen to be an emigrant, proceeding upon a voyage to a far distant part of the world, it will be well for you, if the master of the ship, on board of which you may be, should, under similar circumstances, use a little of what may at the time probably seem to you to be most irksome coercion, in order to induce you to exert any energy which is left in you.

As far as I am myself concerned, I have many comforts around me. My books, writing materials, &c., are all within my reach, conveniently and securely placed in my really excellent cabin; but a commanding officer, or an emigrant possessing sufficient means, may look for such comforts in a transport or other vessel,—whilst in such ships, if due precautions are not taken, the lot of people in general is bad enough.

But, reader, before we proceed farther together, I have to acquaint you, that from the time I entered the army, up to the night before the battle of Talavera—and it was an eventful period—I had kept a journal, or rather some brief memoranda of various events or occurrences, with which I happened to be connected, or had witnessed. On the night, however, which was previous to our falling back from the position we occupied beyond the Alberché river, I was sitting over the remains of a bivouac fire, my comrades being all asleep around me. I had, in the course of the afternoon, seen the Spaniards flying in confusion before the French; I felt convinced that we should be attacked next morning by overwhelming numbers of men accustomed to victory; and I was certain that the brunt of the onset would fall upon us. I was then a captain, and commanded a fine company, in a gallant and highly disciplined regiment. I was aware that we should do our duty manfully, and consequently that many of us were likely to bite the dust on the morrow. It was more than probable that I might be amongst the number destined to fall. Thus ruminating, I thought of my note book, and of much that was recorded in it; it was unluckily in my haversack, and I did not like the idea of its falling into any one's hands should I happen to be knocked over. I therefore considered that the best thing I could do was to burn it, before the still reddish embers were entirely extinguished. I did so, taking care that every leaf was consumed; but often, afterwards, I regretted having been so foolish as thus to destroy my book. From that day, until I found myself at sea upon another voyage to an interesting part of the world, I had not kept what I could call a journal; but I now determined once more to do so; and it is from its pages, in many places sadly defaced by white ants, that I am enabled, in a great measure, to compile the following work; and this will, I trust, account for the peculiarities of the style of writing, which must as we proceed be often observable.

Towards evening, on the 2d of March, when we were off Cape St. Vincent, the weather somewhat moderated; and, as we had hitherto made good runs, we were off Gibraltar on the 3d. It has again, however, come on to blow furiously, and a vessel, in company with us, has just been dismasted. Our ship bounds admirably over the huge billows, and shews us that she is equal to the long voyage before us. On the 4th, the gale once more decreased; and, early on the morning of the 5th of March, we were all on deck, sailing delightfully along, and close to the rugged coast of Madeira. The little villages and neat houses, situated in the deep, retired, and finely wooded ravines, have a most picturesque appearance, especially when contrasted with the mountainous and rocky scenery inland.

We did not anchor, it being considered unsafe to do so at this season of the year; but as many of the officers as could be spared from the duties of the ship were allowed to go on shore, where they spent most agreeably the few hours they remained. I had before visited Madeira in its finest season; but though this is the most unfavourable time of the year, we were able to bring off with us a quantity of fine flowers, with some of which my cabin was adorned for some time after. Roses were in full bloom in the open air; and the climate of this much favoured island may certainly be considered as one of the finest in the world. An ample supply of Madeira was procured for present use, and also a considerable quantity for the regimental mess when we should reach Ceylon. The discomforts of the voyage, as I had anticipated, were now almost forgotten, and a day spent on shore had done much towards preparing most of us for what was still before us.

On the 7th of March we were only about twelve miles from the island of Palma. Its lofty mountains were still covered with snow. We also saw at the same time the island of Faro, and, high amidst the clouds, the Peak of Teneriffe, though fully fifty miles distant. But how truly delightful it is to sail gently along among these charming islands; the views, though distance rendered some of them rather indistinct, were in endless variety and magnificence; and the twelve miles which separated us from Palma would have led us, from its great height, to suppose that it was only on the opposite side of a large river. I was once before in nearly the same position as now with regard to these islands; but the weather was then very different, for it was blowing hard, and so cloudy, as almost to conceal the whole of what now so enchantingly presents itself. Sea sickness, since we passed Madeira, has totally disappeared. We have abundance of the good things of this world on board: indeed, it was well for us this was the case, or our now ravenous gentlemen would actually have soon caused a famine. And, worthy reader, if you should happen to be an emigrant proceeding to a distant part of the world, take my advice, and never altogether depend upon your captain, nor his promises, for even indispensable supplies. The loss of our goats, which had all died, from the effects of cold and wet weather, before we reached Madeira—we now felt as a serious misfortune; for few people can, during a long voyage, make up their minds to dispense with milk, and there is no substitute that can make up for it, but the cream prepared in London for long voyages, and sold at only half a guinea a quart.

On the night of the 9th of March, when standing on our course with all sail set, the wind suddenly sprung up right a-head of us, and blew so violently as even to endanger the ship. It continued to blow with equal fury all the 10th, but on the 11th we crossed the tropic of Cancer, and fine weather having returned, we were glad to be able to pursue our course for the Cape Verd islands.

The troops on board are still very healthy; and to do our best to keep them so, (and to what I am going to add, I particularly request the attention of voyagers in general) directions were now given that they were to bathe every morning at daylight. This is always an amusing scene, and greatly liked by every one in tropical climates, as it refreshes the body, braces the nerves, and prepares those who are wise enough to practise it, for the great heat of the day. The soldiers being all dressed in white jackets and trowsers, with neat foraging caps, they looked as well and clean as it is possible to imagine; and, still more to insure cleanliness, they were required to appear at both morning and evening parades without shoes or stockings. We have plenty of drummers and fifers on board; and by good luck, also an Irish fiddler; it was therefore highly amusing to see the different diversions, which were by every means encouraged, going forward—especially in the evenings. In fine weather we have generally two or three groups of dancers, others of singers; and during the whole day and night, our most persevering story tellers or readers are attentively listened to.

Those who have never before been in a tropical climate, are occasionally greatly astonished and delighted with the magnificence of the setting sun. One evening in particular, the almost full moon was ascending to the eastward of the ship, at the moment when the sun was descending below the horizon, enveloped in clouds of various forms, and partaking of many brilliant as well as deep colours, all heaped together in the most picturesque and wonderful manner. They imagined they beheld mountains, promontories, bays, towns, castles, &c., all resplendent in, I may say, golden magnificence ; but what surprised them most was, that the immense objects before them were incessantly assuming new and extraordinary forms, tinged with still greater variety of shades and colouring. I had often seen such scenic imagery in former voyages, but I never had beheld it so diversified, grand and beautiful, as upon this occasion. I have heard persons assert, that in our northern latitudes, they have seen as splendid sun-settings as any ever beheld in the tropics ; but in this opinion I cannot coincide ; or rather, I should suppose, they may not have been so fortunate as I was in opportunities of admiring and wondering at those of the torrid zone, or I am convinced that they would have come to a different conclusion.

How delightful are also the nights in such latitudes; but no person ought upon any account to be allowed to lie down or sleep upon deck; and therefore every half hour, the officer has to rouse up the watch on duty, and make them walk round the masts for a few minutes. This may appear to an inexperienced person, as if it were done merely to annoy; but there is nothing so seriously affects people's health as allowing them to sleep exposed to the night air, and especially to the baneful influence of the moon. If this is permitted, colds, fevers, dysentery, and other diseases, quickly follow, as the certain consequences of such imprudent exposure. This ought always to be carefully attended to by those who have charge of troops or emigrants going to distant parts of the world.

On the 16th of March we made St. Antonio, one of the Cape Verd islands, which, like all those situated in the east Atlantic, is very high—I believe it is about 7,000 feet above the level of the sea. In a former voyage, I spent about three weeks at one of them, St. Jago, and remember well, that it was both hot and unhealthy, and, with the exception of fine fruit and fowls, very little else was to be had there. At the period I allude to, I belonged to one of the regiments forming part of the force under General Robert Crawford, then destined for the west coast of South America, but which was afterwards ordered to the river Plata. Our commanders, it seemed, took it into their heads, that our fleet was pursued by a powerful French squadron, which so outnumbered our escort of line-of-battle ships, frigates, &c. that it was deemed advisable to take refuge in Port Praya. The transports were anchored as near as possible to the shore, and the ships of war were drawn up, in order of battle, from one projecting point of the bay to another on the opposite side, and upon these extremities batteries were erected, and supplied with heavy guns from the shipping, which would have flanked the enemy, had they attacked our fleet. In this position we remained until it was ascertained by a frigate, sent back for the purpose, that our apprehensions were groundless, when we again started for the Cape of Good Hope.

But I can never forget the alarm which I felt the night on which we left Port Praya; for, owing to the number of transports which lay outside of us, it was almost dark before our ship could leave the anchorage and stand out of the bay, which she did under a considerable press of sail; and seeing a very powerful light just before us, it was imagined that we were following in the wake of the Commodore. There was at the time a fine steady breeze, and the night being delightfully cool and refreshing, we were all on deck. The light, however, which we supposed we were following, suddenly neared us; and in an instant we found ourselves just under the bows of a line-of-battle ship, standing in the opposite direction to that which we were pursuing. The captain of our ship was panic struck, and consequently lost all presence of mind. Our destruction, therefore, seemed to be inevitable, as both ships were going at a great rate through the water. The people on board the Theseus (it was that ship carrying a light on her bowsprit end, as she stood back to ascertain the cause of the transports being so long in putting to sea), had fortunately kept a better look out than we had done; and, perceiving our perilous situation, they in a moment altered their course, and by that means were just able to avoid coming in contact with us. So near a thing was it, that their lower rigging and upper ports actually grazed our yard arms; and though our ship was upwards of 700 tons burden, had the Theseus come with her whole force upon us, she must, in all probability, have sent us to the bottom! The breathless silence on board our ship, at the moment of seeming certain contact, cannot be described, nor could the feelings of thankfulness of many of us to Providence be expressed, when we found that we had so narrowly and unexpectedly escaped destruction.

As we continued our voyage, we daily found ourselves more and more surrounded by numbers of fish, such as porpoises, bonitos, dolphins, and flying-fish; several of the latter flew even on board, and constantly into the chains. Our young officers had always their guns ready, and many a ball was fired at the unlucky porpoises, as they rolled along in vast shoals, often within thirty or forty yards of the ship, but with what effect no one could pretend to say, though the practice was always declared to be excellent.

One of the mates was very expert in striking both bonitos and dolphins with the spear. In order to entice these beautiful fish near enough to be within reach of the spear, pieces of scarlet and white cloth were fastened to lines attached to the extremity of the jib-boom, and dragged along upon the surface of the water; and as the fish rose at these lures, the spear was darted at them, and often with effect, so that plenty of both were thus procured. The beauty of the dying dolphin has, however, been far too highly extolled; and in this respect, notwithstanding its fine black and bluish tinge above, and white beneath, I look upon the mackerel-like bonito, though so much inferior in size, as quite its equal. As food, both dolphins and bonitos—at least those caught in the ocean—are dry and insipid; and, although we used different sauces, we could not contrive to make either of them even palatable.

I made many attempts to strike these beautiful shining fish; but I confess that I was not very successful. An Irish soldier, who pretended to know well how to spear salmon,—which art, he said, he had often practised in the sweet Barrow,—in striking at a large dolphin, lost his footing, and, most awkwardly slipping out of the rather too large loop of the rope which enabled us to lean considerably over the side of the ship, he fell into the sea. "A man overboard," in an instant resounded throughout the ship. I was walking the quarter deck at the time with the Captain, who, seizing the wheel, threw the ship up into the wind. A boat fastened to the taffrail was lowered with that rapidity and coolness always evinced by British seamen in moments of necessity or danger. Poor Pat could not swim, and must have been drowned before the boat could possibly have reached him, had not an English drummer, his comrade, instantly stripped and plunged into the sea to his aid—he grasped him just in time, and kept him up with great presence of mind and dexterity, avoiding the attempts of the drowning man to lay hold of him. The seamen in the boat were in the mean time pulling with all their might towards them, now about two hundred yards astern of the ship. But let the reader imagine what must have been my alarm and anxiety, when I saw distinctly through my spy-glass, betwixt them and the ship, floating on the surface of the water, the greater part of the inside of a sheep, attached to a large shark-hook, and which had been for some time towed a long way astern in order to tempt an enormous shark, seen swimming close to us! With the most intense apprehension and watchfulness, we all kept our eyes fixed upon the two men in the water, every moment expecting to see at least one of them taken down by the ferocious monster! The boat however at last reached them, and they were, to our great delight, brought in safety on board.

On the 26th of March we crossed the Equinoctial line, when the thermometer was 83 degrees at noon in the shade—on deck 86°—in the sun 104°, and the temperature of the sea, of which I kept a daily register, 84°. But I should here remark, that, until we approached the line, the weather had been, since we entered the tropic, very agreeable, and by no means oppressively hot. One of the soldiers, however, from going about without his cap, received a coup-de-soleil. In a moment he became delirious, and madly attempted to throw himself into the sea—a number of sharks constantly shewing themselves at the time close to the ship. The surgeon being at hand, he was instantly profusely bled, and powerful medicine being administered, he in a few days entirely recovered, and without suffering from fever, which usually follows a coup-de-soleil.

A few days after this, another soldier was, seemingly, struck in a similar manner by the sun, and also attempted to throw himself into the sea. The surgeon was again sent for; he felt his pulse, then looked steadily at him for a few minutes, and, coming up to me on the quarter deck, said decidedly, that there was nothing the matter with him, and that he firmly believed his madness was only pretended.

Being at once convinced that his object must be to endeavour by this stratagem to obtain his discharge from the regiment, I walked quietly up to him, followed by the same stout drummer, who had saved his comrade's life, to whom I had, in a few words, given directions how to act, and who was moreover cautioned to be sure to lay hold of him if he really attempted to jump into sea. I then desired those holding the apparently determined suicide, to let him go, and to make room for him to spring handsomely out of the ship! "Come, sir, jump!—make haste!—jump, sir!" The fellow seemed astonished, and was evidently much frightened. "Come, drummer, start him with that rope's end—jump sir, jump—there is a shark that has just put his head above water, waiting for you!" The drummer now laid on with all his might—the fellow began to cry like a child, and the surgeon and soldiers to shout and laugh, as the drummer with right good will, and encouraged by me, continued his exercise; so that his cure was thus most ridiculously but speedily effected, and the farce ended in the *madman* getting a sound rope's ending, to the great amusement of every one. He no doubt ought to have been severely punished, but I considered the rope's ending answered quite as well—at all events, we had no more cases of pretended delirium.

I certainly, on this occasion, had taken a hint from what I had witnessed a good many years before. A smart looking fellow, named Darby Star, who had been a country dancing master, somewhere in the south of Ireland, enlisted into the corps to which I was then Adjutant. He soon became a clean, regular, and good looking soldier; but, for some reason or other, was by many suspected of being rather *shy;* and this suspicion was soon confirmed; for when the regiment was upon the point of embarking for service, Darby was taken alarmingly ill; he had pains all over him, especially, as he said, in his bones and in his heart. He was quickly reduced to a mere shadow, so that any one who looked at him, would have thought him in the last stage of a decline. The surgeon, however, and his hospital serjeant, who had been on the watch, in consequence of the number of deceptions of this kind practised in the army about that period, stated openly, that they were both ready to declare before a court-martial, that Darby was an impostor, or as soldiers say, a malingerer. This hint was not lost upon our most zealous commander. Darby was tried, sentenced to receive 500 lashes, tied up to the grating at the gang-way of the ship, and had 50 of the lashes inflicted upon him, in an amazing short space of time. "Stop," said his stern commander. "Will you, Darby Star, confess that you are a malingerer?" Darby was speechless. "Go on,"—and the drum-major was told to see that the drummers did their duty. He received 25 more lashes. "Stop—will you now confess?" In a very weak voice, Darby protested that he was as innocent as the child unborn. "Take him down:"—but all present were told to mark their commanding officer's words; and they well knew his word was never broken—"You, master Darby Star, shall, every Monday morning, receive 50 of the 500 lashes to which you are sentenced, until you acknowledge that you are a malingerer."

Next Monday came. Darby was almost carried up from below, with scarcely an appearance of life in him; his back by no means healed from the effects of the punishment he had received. Without farther ceremony, he was again fastened to the grating. " Drummers, do your duty," sounded in Darby's terrified ears. I confess, I really pitied him; his appearance deceived me, and I knew not what to think—Colonel D——, however, stood determined to go through with what he had begun.

During the infliction of 25 more of the lashes—which I noted with an unsteady hand — Darby called out, in an astonishingly loud voice for so sickly looking a wretch, that he would confess any thing in the wide world, if he would only be forgiven? " Stop!—you confess yourself, then, to have been all along a malingerer?" — " O yes," groaned Darby. " Speak out, sir, so that all on board may hear you distinctly."—" O yes, yes," roared Darby. " Take him down.—Now, sir, you must convince every one present that you are quite recovered; and to shew that you really are so, you must, as an old dancing master, instantly give us a jig." A drummer and fifer were ordered to be in readiness to play a tune for him, as soon as he was dressed.

This was dreadful—for how could an emaciated wretch like Darby be supposed capable of dancing an Irish jig!—" Well, sir, are you ready?" Darby begged, entreated, to be excused; but no excuse would be taken. " Dance, sir:—Drum-major, tie him up again, if he will not dance." Darby began to dance. " Higher, sir, higher!" But Darby now, to the astonishment of every one, got on with his jig in first-rate style: and from that day forward, to the surprise of the whole regiment, his health was *perfectly restored!* Yet he contrived to avoid accompanying us into the streets of Buenos Ayres, in South America; and, under various pretences, often kept out of action in Portugal and Spain. But into the fight at Talavera his Captain was determined that Darby should go. He therefore gave strict orders to his subalterns and non-commissioned officers, that they were to have an eye upon him, and to see that upon no account he quitted the ranks, even for a moment. When he found this to be the case, his alarm when the balls began to fly about him, was truly ridiculous—but in the heat of the action, about two o'clock in the afternoon, when the French in heavy columns attacked our centre; and when the 48th on the one hand, and the 45th on the other, taught them that breaking through an enemy's line in mass, would not answer with a British army, Darby, whilst under strict surveillance, was slightly wounded. He then, to the surprise of every one, became as brave as a lion, stood firm in his place, and fired away into the enemy's dense columns, not thirty yards distant. But, alas! another ball laid poor Darby low for ever. I have more than once seen men made brave by receiving a wound, who had before been labouring under much, of what may be termed, nervous apprehension.

Thunder and lightning in England may be considered as trifling, when compared with those storms which are so constantly raging in tropical regions, especially near the equator. They were at this period both grand and terrible, yet by no means came up to what I had experienced in a former voyage. On that occasion, our commodore, by way of making a short cut, attempted to cross the line much too far to the eastward, and in consequence got into a region of calms, torrents of rain, and the most awful thunder-storms imaginable. The ships, some of which were dismasted, lay with their heads in all directions, and it was even often necessary to lower down boats, to tow them clear of each other; for there was constantly a long rolling sea; so that in this helpless state they floated about, as influenced by the waves or currents, for nearly three weeks. At last, however, through the occasional aid of what sailors call cat's-paws, the fleet contrived to get back to the northward of the equator. When we arrived there, it was deemed requisite to run a few degrees farther to the westward, and, at length, after much severe suffering from intense heat, &c. having taken the track pointed out as the proper one by experienced navigators, we were glad to find ourselves to the southward of the line, bending our course, with a strong breeze, for the coast of South America.

Whilst vessels are propelled by the trade winds through the tropics, sailing is always delightful; and this vast space, being enlivened by a most radiant sun, powerfully influences the mind, and cheers the spirits of the voyager. I had for some nights been watching the north polar star, which had hitherto indicated the quarter of the world which I had now left for many years—perhaps for ever. I looked upon it as a friend from whom I was soon to part; for it was then but a very little way above the horizon—I believe I saw it, for the last time, on the 23d of March.

It has been truly remarked, that men in general are endued with a kind of instinct, which has ever a most powerful influence upon their minds and actions—that is to say the love of country, which nature maintains in their hearts. If this were not the case, mankind would migrate towards the parts of the earth which are most favoured as to climate; leaving the rest of it deserted. To prevent this, the Almighty has wisely established in the heart of every one, an almost invincible attachment to his native land; as powerful in the breast of the inhabitant of the Polar regions, or of the Negro whose home is even the sandy, scorched desert of the torrid zone, as in that of the native of the most delightful country. No one can tell exactly how this attachment is formed, or kept up; but still it is an acknowledged powerful tie. Must we look for its origin in the smile of a mother, of a sister, or of one still more dear to the heart than either? Is it to be traced to the companion of our youth? Or may it probably be caused by the remaining influence of beloved, respected, and pious parents, who did their best to produce in us a love for the Saviour who died for us? It may, perhaps, spring from something even trivial; perhaps from scenery which charmed us in early life; a favourite dog; the field sports in which he accompanied us; the river in which we first used the rod and line—no matter whence it comes, but, however produced, there is found in all men a predominant love of country.

The north polar star, to which the reader is indebted for these remarks, was no longer discernible after the 12th of April, when we discovered that which a few days before we had been on the look out for—that is to say, a small white cloud, which always hangs over the south pole, and also a number of stars forming what is called the great southern cross, which is to this hemisphere what the polar star is to ours. This too plainly told us, that we were fast leaving behind us those homes which so few soldiers, ordered to India, ever see again; yet,

> "Breathes there the man, with soul so dead,
> Who never to himself hath said;
> This is my own, my native land!"

On the 14th of April we crossed the tropic of Capricorn; and had delightful weather until the 17th; but on the night of that day a storm arose, which lasted till the 22d. During the whole of this time the sea ran extremely high; and it blew so furiously, that no sail whatever could be set; and, what was most truly provoking, we were driven by it considerably out of our course. I have long thought that the seas in the Southern hemisphere, are much more boisterous than those in the Northern; and, although I have encountered many a gale in various parts of the world, I have always said, that I had been in only one real storm, and I was exposed to its violence a little to the southward of where we now are. The waves then ran, I may truly say, as high as mountains. Whilst it lasted we kept close to a line-of-battle ship,—one of our convoy—and the enormous waves, which rolled and foamed around and between us, often concealed even her tall masts from our sight; and in an instant after, she appeared, as it were, to hang on the top of a wave, in the act of falling upon us. But how sublimely the Psalmist describes such a storm, when he says—" The sea roared: and the stormy wind lifted up the waves thereof. We were carried up as it were to heaven, and then down again into the deep: our souls melted within us because of trouble."

The expectation of soon falling in with the numbers of birds, of various kinds, which are usually looked for in these latitudes, induced most of the officers to get up their guns and rifles, so as to be ready for the anticipated sport. It is most desirable to have always something going forward—no matter what it is—in order to amuse or occupy the minds of both officers and men during such long voyages; and how necessary also this is in ships conveying emigrants to foreign lands, those who have had most experience can best tell. On this occasion, as I find from my notes, a bottle was hung up to the yard-arm, at which many a single ball was fired, but without effect. The Captain of the ship began to call out to them to have mercy upon his main-yard, as some of the balls seemed to pass rather too close to it, notwithstanding the length of the line by which the bottle was suspended; and which allowed it to swing about with every roll or heave of the vessel. Much laughter and amusement, on the part of both sailors and soldiers, was excited by the number of failures; not a bottle had as yet been touched. I went below, and brought up my gun; and, as soon as I appeared on deck, I heard some of my old companions in arms exclaim—"Now, boys, you will soon see it smashed;" and old Dennis Kelly whispered close behind me, but sufficiently loud for me to hear—"Don't you remember, boys, seeing his Honour tumble the French officer, the very first shot, though many of us had been popping at him, as he dared us, standing up bravely on the ramparts at Ciudad Rodrigo?" I, however, remembered nothing of the kind; nor, afterwards, to give Dennis a glass of grog. The Captain offered to bet any sum that I would not hit the bottle in three attempts. It was, however, at last settled, that whichever of us should lose, was to give a dinner to the officers on board, upon our arrival at the Cape of Good Hope. I was to have two shots. The very first knocked the bottle to pieces, which caused much cheering, whilst the Captain stared in amazement at the feat; for the ship at the time had a great deal of motion. Another bottle was rigged out, and it met with a similar fate. I sent down my gun; having, as Baron Munchausen would have said upon such an occasion, sufficiently displayed my dexterity and superiority; for which I can easily account, though no one else could. The secret was this—along with each ball, I had slipped in, unperceived by any one, a large pinch of No. 6 shot. Of course, the Captain was not allowed to give a dinner at the Cape.

The vastly increased number of birds, which now constantly surrounded the ship, led many to hope that they indicated our approach to land; but, by adverse winds and calms, we were tantalized until the night of the 9th of May, when we at last made it. Unfortunately, the two preceding days had been so cloudy, that we had not obtained an observation of the sun. In consequence, we found ourselves several miles too far to the northward, and were, therefore, obliged to stand out to sea. The wind increased to a strong gale off the land, and soon became so violent as to tear to rags our fore and main sails. The gale still continuing, we had to stand off and on all the 10th, and also until the evening of the 11th, when we made Table Land, and even looked into Table Bay; and vexatious enough it was to us, to see the houses distinctly, and even the people walking about, without our daring to venture in. The night was, moreover, coming on, so that we were again obliged to stand off the shore.

On the 12th, still finding ourselves in the same situation, and the wind continuing against our getting into Simon's Bay, which was our object, I proposed to the Captain to venture into Table Bay, which we could have easily done; but, as his insurance would have thereby been rendered null and void, he refused to do so at that season of the year. He hoped, however, to be able to keep the ship near to where it then was, till the wind should favour us. It moderated on the 13th, but still continued adverse to our reaching Simon's Bay, which was only fifty miles distant.

The number of birds which now flew around the ship really surprised us. Amongst a great many others five albatrosses were shot; the smallest measured about nine feet from the tip of one wing to that of the other. But, having now such excellent sport, our young gentlemen became the less anxious for land; and the 16th found us still farther off the Cape, slaughtering these unfortunate birds. The sailors cooked and ate some of them; but I would not allow the soldiers to do so, being apprehensive that from their oily and fishy nature they might prove unwholesome food.

On the 17th we were completely becalmed close to the Cape. The appearance of the coast, as far as the eye could reach, was very rocky, barren, and apparently uninhabited; consequently a fit abode for the lion and other wild beasts, which we supposed must be numerous there. The Captain having offered me a boat, I had her manned with a crew of soldiers, who were good and able rowers, and, with two other officers, I attempted to land, in the hope of being able to shoot some of the wild animals; but although there was not a breath of wind, the surf which ran and foamed upon the rocky beach, forbade all approach to it.

Whilst looking for a place to land, I shot a very large albatross, which fell almost into the boat. The report of the gun, echoing among the caverns in the rocks, and the, in many places, almost overhanging precipices, brought out such immense flocks of birds as quite astonished us. We could have shot as many of them as we pleased, for they flew around, and within a few yards of us ; thus indicating that they had rarely been disturbed by man.

We had luckily brought fishing lines with us, and the exceeding clearness of the water inducing us to look over the side of the boat, we saw that the bottom was literally covered with fish. Finding it impossible to land, we therefore set to work, using at first, as bait, part of the intestines of the albatross which I had killed, and in a short time we actually loaded the boat, with a reddish fish, very like rock-cod, which when cooked we found to be delicious ;—at least we thought so—perhaps from having been so long deprived of any fish which could be considered as even tolerable.

I had remarked, when rounding the Cape, on a former voyage, that at times there was to be seen a kind of false horizon, which greatly attracted my attention ; and now that we lay becalmed for hours together, this strange visual deception was very striking. I find the following remarks in my journal :—

I have been for some time watching a most beautiful and extraordinary instance of visual deception, which has, I believe, been often seen by voyagers off the southern extremity of Africa, as well as in other parts of the world. There are now (10 A. M.) two distinct horizons—the real and the false—the latter considerably above the former. All the objects, such as two coasting vessels, porpoises, and whales, which are constantly rolling about, and the latter spouting up water, (there being many of the spermaceti genus now in these latitudes)—in short, every large object to be seen on the real horizon, especially to the northward, is distinctly reflected in the false; and as the sun is now labouring, as it were, through a hazy atmosphere, the whole has a very curious and even surprising effect. It appears to me that it might be worthy of the attention of those who understand and are interested in such matters, to endeavour to have this phenomenon closely investigated; as it is ascertained beyond all doubt, that before we captured the Isle of France, a Frenchman there, by some means or other, probably connected with this singular appearance, had, it is well known, the power of seeing objects in the air, though many leagues distant, and still far below the horizon, and was by that means able to acquaint the governor with the exact position of our ships of war, then cruising on the station, though far out of sight of land. He could even announce the approach of ships steering for the island, several days before their arrival. How he did this he kept a profound secret, and when I was at the Isle of France I did not hear that he had divulged it to any one, though I understood that he received a pension from our Government. I am, however, inclined to fancy, as many others did, that it was by means of some kind of reflector, which he might have discovered by accident, that he was enabled to see delineated in the sky objects on the surface of the ocean, though they were a considerable distance off.

On the morning of the 19th we at last got into Simon's Bay, and arrangements were immediately made for the maintenance of discipline whilst in harbour; but, at the same time, with a view to admit of as many officers and men as possible to go on shore in succession. Every thing being thus settled for general convenience and comfort, I set off, accompanied by three of the officers, in a kind of wagon, drawn by four horses, for Cape Town; where we staid and enjoyed ourselves till recalled to embark. But, reader, I have no intention of taking up your time in speaking of the Cape of Good Hope; that has already been done by others, who had much better opportunities than I had of seeing the country, and of forming an opinion of its capabilities of improvement as a British Colony. Here, however, as almost every where else, labour must be found far too expensive for emigrants to prosper.

On the 27th of May, we returned to Simon's Bay, and on the following day we again put to sea; but how ill-timed it would have been had we, in standing out of the Bay, invoked the winds in the beautiful strains of Ossian.—

> "Burst the cloud, O, Wind! that the daughter of night
> may look forth;
> That the shaggy mountain may brighten, and the ocean
> roll its white waves in light;"

for we very soon found the ocean off the southern extremity of Africa as boisterous as usual, especially at this season. It continued to blow furiously, and to rain almost incessantly till we were off the south end of Madagascar; but though we all suffered much from cold, rain, and the sea breaking constantly over the ship, yet, thanks to Providence, we were still without sickness on board. On the 17th of June we saw the Island of Bourbon, and the weather becoming again delightful, we were enabled to resume our former ship-board occupations. Having however, so recently experienced such stormy weather, we could not but remember, that we were still passing through regions subject to the most awful and devastating hurricanes; which I was told at the Isle of France had been known to blow even large vessels out of the water, and force them to some distance upon the land. I was likewise told by a person, upon whose veracity I could depend, that on one occasion a house, inhabited by an old pensioner and his wife, who had the care of a look-out station, was swept away by the irresistible violence of the wind;—neither house, man, nor woman, was ever more seen or heard of!

It is now, however, high time so bring the account of our voyage to a conclusion, and I shall therefore only farther remark, that from Madagascar ships run almost due north till they cross the Equator, which we did on the 27th of June. Our course then lay, I may say, near to the Equinoctial Line, until we passed the Maldive Islands, on the 4th of July; yet, though we were sailing on the torrid zone, we suffered far less from heat than we had expected, for we had constantly fine breezes, and the thermometer in the shade was generally about 82 degrees at noon, and about 80 in the morning and evening. From the Maldive Islands we steered direct for Point de Galle, in Ceylon; as we could not, on account of the monsoon, which then prevailed, proceed to Colombo.

A register of the state of the thermometer was kept throughout the voyage, and it may be thought right, and by some perhaps useful, that it should be laid before the reader. In doing so, I have only to remark, that at noon a quantity of water from a considerable depth was regularly brought up, and its temperature ascertained, as by this means it was expected that our approach to land would be indicated. The tables in which the results are shewn will be found in the Appendix, A.

CHAPTER II.

> "Meanwhile, whate'er of beautiful, or new,
> Sublime or dreadful, in earth, sea, or sky,
> By chance, or search, was offer'd to his view,
> He scann'd with curious and romantic eye."—BEATTIE.

ARRIVAL AT POINT DE GALLE—CEYLON THIEVES—GOVERNMENT REGULATIONS FOR THE GUIDANCE OF TRAVELLERS—HIRE OF LABOURERS OR COOLIES AND CARTS, &c.—THE COUNTRY FROM GALLE TO COLOMBO DESCRIBED.

WITH what intense anxiety all on board were now on the look-out for land! Now and then, those who were most impatient requested a seaman to go aloft, in the hope that he might be able to discover it; but still he descended unsuccessful. Those only who have made such a long voyage as we had done, especially in a troop or emigrant ship, can fully enter into our feelings on an occasion like this. In approaching Ceylon, it is often first seen a great way off; and we had heard and read much of the cooling fragrant breezes, which, having passed over its cinnamon and other spicy groves, are said to perfume the air far into the offing; but, in this instance, at least, we were doomed to be altogether disappointed—nothing of the kind was perceptible. The sun set, as usual, in amazing brilliancy, at which time, or in the morning, objects present themselves most distinctly; nothing, however, but sea and sky met the eye, and the shades of night once more enveloped us, and for that day put an end to our hopes of seeing land. The stately ship, however, under a press of sail, continued to cut her way, in spite of a strong current, through the ocean; causing, as she dashed along, millions of sparkling phosphoric flashes all around her, whilst she left a long and shining train behind her, seemingly composed of myriads of fiery particles.

With the morning's dawn we were all on deck, and in a few minutes land was seen a-head of the ship, and quite close to us; yet none of us could pretend to say, that the fragrant breezes, said to be wafted from the shore, were even then perceptible. But how truly striking were the lofty mountains, and how picturesque the forms of the range of hills, and how finely undulating the surface of the nearer and more level country, which lay before us, and stretched along to the left as far as the eye could reach, beautifully wooded even to the water's edge! Nothing can be more enchantingly lovely and verdant than Ceylon, as it first presents itself to the surprised and worn-out voyager, as he runs in, especially at sun-rise, towards such a bay as that of Galle. We let go our anchor within a short distance of the apparently strong fortifications.

I intend to speak hereafter more particularly of Galle; but, at present, I shall only say, that on landing we found the greater part of the 19th Regiment assembled there, waiting our arrival to relieve them; when, after many years service in the island, they were to return to England. Since that period, great and important changes have taken place in Ceylon; many of which, as well as to what they have led, will be noticed in the course of this work. The voluminous memoranda, however, from which it is in a great measure compiled, were never intended to be submitted to public criticism; on the contrary, they had been kept solely for the author's private use or amusement, when the days should approach when he may probably feel "that he has no pleasure in them." Various reasons and motives now induce him to make use of them; and if, whilst endeavouring to amuse, he is in any respect able to benefit others, to dedicate his pen to the service of religion, or to attract the attention of those who are in power, or are interested in the welfare of a charming part of the East, he will have attained an object which he has long had at heart. By the attainment of that object he is convinced that there would be thrown open a vast field for agriculture, commerce, and civilization, and also for the diffusion of knowledge throughout that interesting part of the world, which is now becoming of vast importance to Great Britain; as, independent of its great value as a colony, it holds out more advantages to a certain description of emigrants from the United Kingdom, than can be met with any where else; for *there* they can employ capital beneficially; *there* they can obtain land on as reasonable terms as in most of our new settlements; and *there*, which is the essential point, they are able to command *labour* at a cheap rate. It is an additional and a great advantage, which cannot be too extensively made known, that the price of food also is equally moderate with that of labour.

The kindness and attention which, as strangers, we experienced from the officers of the 19th Regiment, far exceeded what, under any circumstances, we had ever met with before. There seemed to be a kind of rivalship among them as to whose guests we were to be: indeed, we found before long, that they only most heartily conformed to what was then so liberally exercised throughout the whole island—that is to say, the rites of hospitality. As a matter of course, I fell to the lot of the senior officer, who had only been some forty or fifty years in the service, and who was good enough to assign for my use, apartments in the Government house, in which, as Commandant of the place, he then resided. The soldiers, when landed, were put into barracks; but the officers had to be received into the bungalows of those of the 19th Regiment, there being no barracks for them, nor inns of any kind to accommodate them. Our arrival was reported to Head Quarters, and in a few days orders were received for us to march, on the 23rd of July, 1820, to Colombo, where, as the ships arrived, the Regiment was to be assembled.

It is six days march to Colombo, and we are told that we shall be greatly delighted with the country through which we are to pass; it being represented as not only beautiful, but also remarkably healthy.

We find that, in order to avoid the heat of the day, we must start about two o'clock in the morning, which is the usual hour for the marching of troops in this part of the world; and as there will, on the 23rd, be no moon light, we are to be attended by a number of natives carrying torches. I also find that, excepting his arms and accoutrements, every thing else is here carried for the soldier.

Until the day of our departure from Galle arrived, we spent our time most agreeably with our hospitable friends, from whom we obtained much useful and valuable information about Ceylon, which enabled us to form a pretty correct idea of the ways or doings, not only of the European, but also of the native inhabitants. I therefore flattered myself, that here, as I had previously done elsewhere, I had acquired some little worldly experience; but I was now to be taught a new lesson, and also that I was to pay well for it.

The third night after our arrival at Galle, I retired to bed about eleven in the evening, and, having been rather fatigued, I soon fell fast asleep. While I was in this state, a thief or thieves contrived to get into my room through a window, which for coolness had been left open, and they carried off, I may say, almost every thing I had brought out with me, except my regimentals; those, I imagine, they considered as of no use to them, and even dangerous to meddle with, as they would probably have led to their detection. The various articles which they stole, were in trunks or portmanteaus; and they even got hold of my writing case, which was in one of the latter—carefully locked—out of which, they very quietly, and without in the least disturbing me, took two hundred rix-dollars—considerately returning me the case, and some valuable papers which were in it. Had they robbed me the night before, they would have got a considerable sum of money; but I had fortunately paid it away. I was thus at once convinced, experimentally, of the truth of what I had before heard, that the natives of Ceylon, as well as those of India in general, are as expert thieves as any in the world; and I now record what befel me, as a warning to others, to be more, if possible, on their guard. It was supposed that a native servant, whom I had just hired at the recommendation of the Commandant, in whose service he had been for a short time, must have been concerned in the robbery; or, at least, could easily have prevented it. I was therefore recommended to turn him off, which I accordingly did; but I never was able to recover a single article, and had, at an enormous expense, to replace, as well as I could in Ceylon, what I had lost.

Prepared to look for much which would be new and interesting, and altogether different from what we had been accustomed to in other parts of the world, we commenced our march for Colombo on the 23rd of July, and reached Hiccode the first day. The distance was twelve miles ; of which the first four or five were by torch or chule light. At that period—and I believe the same regulation still exists—the collector, or some of his subordinates, were bound to furnish both torch-bearers and torches, without which no one can travel here at night ; and, in many parts of the island, not only torches, but also drums, or tom-toms, are indispensably necessary to keep off wild beasts, which in several places are very numerous and dangerous. We were, however, informed, that there are none between Galle and Colombo.

Before dawn of day, we crossed a considerable river in boats, which to us were of a new and strange construction. The road was good, though rather sandy, and it ran the whole way close to the sea. It was delightfully shaded by tall palm or cocoa-nut trees, amidst which were occasionally to be seen the neat and clean looking houses of the natives. The strong breeze from the ocean, made travelling as little fatiguing to us as it would have been in England.

A stranger in Ceylon, after a long voyage, during which the imagination, connecting the island with its proximity to the equator, may have pictured to itself only barren hills, parched or stunted trees, and a scorched soil, is agreeably surprised at beholding a most verdant island, whose coasts are skirted by intermingled Palmyra and cocoa-nut trees, even to the verge of the sea. This charming country is highly favoured with continual sea-breezes, which render even its hottest districts much more temperate and agreeable in climate, than any part of the continent of India, excepting, perhaps, its lofty mountainous regions. I find, that the coolest season is during the prevalence of the south-west monsoon, which sets in about the end of April, and lasts till the end of October, when the sun is to the northward of the equator. The change of this monsoon, as I am informed, commences with abundant and refreshing rains, which continue, at intervals, for about ten weeks. The north-east monsoon is of shorter duration. It begins in November, and lasts till March; during which period the sun is to the southward of the Line. It is also attended by heavy rains, especially in the northern parts of the island. Both monsoons are usually ushered in by most tremendous thunder; but thunder storms are common throughout Ceylon at any time of the year, especially amongst and near to the mountains; yet it is surprising how few accidents occur from them.

At Hiccode we were handsomely entertained by Mr. Farrell, to whom I had been previously introduced at Galle; and the friendship then formed between us, I am proud to say, lasted as long as I remained in Ceylon. Soon after, Mr. Farrell, who is without comparison the first sportsman in the island, was removed to that princely station for field sports—Hambentotte.

Next day we marched to Amblangodde—eight

miles. The road lay the whole way close to the sea shore, and was, as the day before, so much shaded or overhung by tall palm and other trees, as to prevent our seeing the country to our right; in which direction it seemed to be densely wooded and thinly inhabited. Though somewhat tired of the uniformity of the objects which presented themselves, we were yet, on the whole, rather pleased than disappointed. At every halting place, there are government rest-houses, where, under good regulations, established by Sir Robert Brownrigg—and which, I believe, are still in force—fish, fowls, eggs, milk, &c. can be procured. But these regulations throw so much light upon the mode of travelling in Ceylon, that I must give them for the reader's amusement and information.*

These regulations are of the utmost importance to an emigrant arriving in Ceylon; for, though some trifling alterations have taken place since they were promulgated, yet they will enable him to make, with what I intend to give hereafter, a tolerably correct estimate of his expenses. I am anxious that every reader should have it in his power to compare them with such charges as must be paid in any of our other new colonies, because when he has made the comparison, the superiority of Ceylon as a country to emigrants, must be obvious.

At Amblangodde there is nothing remarkable to be seen, unless it be a Boodhoo temple; in which, besides the large images of the gods, there are some

* See Appendix B. & C.

strange paintings by native artists. A missionary stationed here was good enough to call upon me; and, judging from what he told me, I concluded, that he had not been by any means successful in converting the natives to Christianity. He attributed his failure more to the people in general being careless about religion of any kind, than to any other cause. He pointed out to me a small temple or Dewalè, dedicated to the Devil, who is much feared there, and indeed, as I found afterwards, throughout Ceylon. He also shewed me a rock, near the temple, upon which dances take place, almost daily, in honour of his Satanic Majesty, whose direful intentions they endeavour to ward off, by even dedicating their children to his service, from their birth. I believe the Dutch, who are not very scrupulous in their modes of proceeding with the natives of their colonies, put an end to these devil-dances during the period they possessed the sea coast; but they have since been revived.

On the 25th, we proceeded to Bentotte, fifteen miles. During this day's journey, the appearance of the country changed considerably, and the scenery also was improved. The lake of Bentotte was frequently to be seen to our right, through openings in the woods, and the sea was almost constantly in view to our left. The trees, though the cocoa-nut still prevailed, were in greater variety, and some of them were of a large size. The spaces, also, between them, were here and there occupied by shrubs and flowers, most of them quite new to us.

The country—and what a country for colonization! seemed to be very thinly inhabited. The houses of the natives were only occasionally visible, yet they invariably had a very neat and cleanly appearance about them, as they were partially seen, encompassed with palm-trees.

The village of Bentotte is delightfully situated close to the sea, and upon the shore of a very fine lake. Enticed by the splendid appearance of its surrounding scenery, and there being a cooling, refreshing breeze from the ocean, immediately after a most plentiful and comfortable breakfast, which our servants knew well how to prepare and set forth, I engaged a boat for a row upon the lake. Accompanied by one of the officers, a head man, and the rest-house keeper, I set off to visit a temple, about four or five miles distant. The shores of the lake are very thickly wooded; but, as usual, the density of the foliage rendered them far too uniform, and consequently uninteresting in appearance. But, if they were partially cleared and cultivated, what enchantingly beautiful settlements could here be formed by Europeans. The temple, to which I was informed, a good deal of the land in its neighbourhood belongs,* stands about two hundred yards from the lake; and, though larger than most of those to be met with in this part of the island, has nothing remarkable in its appearance. I found about half a dozen priests in attendance, who, I understood, are daily engaged in its regularly estab-

* The effects of Veharès, &c., holding so much land as they do in Ceylon, will be shewn hereafter.

lished services. One of them, with whose appearance I was greatly struck, was a very aged and venerable looking man. Through the medium of the rest-housekeeper, who interpreted, I asked him a number of questions; but the answers I received afforded me little information or satisfaction. But to a work recently published by Major Forbes, (of the 78th regiment,) entitled "Eleven Years in Ceylon," I must refer the reader for such information as he may require, respecting the Boodhoo religion, as well as for what is known of the ancient history of this wonderful island, its antiquities, &c.; and also for an account of its princely elephant shooting, all which subjects he has handled in a very able, amusing, and truly interesting manner.

On our return to Bentotte, we frequently crossed from one side of the lake to the other, and wherever we touched at, a very thick and in some places a kind of swampy jungle presented itself, extending quite down to the water's edge. The great want of variety in the scenery was, however, much relieved and enlivened by at least thirty canoes, which were dexterously paddled along by the natives, who were (about 4 P. M.) proceeding to fish in various parts of the tranquil lake. From one of these canoes the head-man took some of the largest and finest fish, which he presented to me. The extraordinary, and as I am told, perpetual verdure of the trees is most striking, especially to a stranger. What a pity it is that such a fine and apparently fertile land, should be allowed to remain in its present wild and uncultivated state! If encouragement were given by a wise government, it may indeed be said that the desert could be made "to blossom like the rose;" for here, it may be supposed, that sugar and other plantations would prosper in the hands of Europeans, though the attempts made at Caltura to bring the cane to perfection may, from what cause I know not, have failed.

Besides the quantities of fine fish to be had, both in the lake and the sea, the coast here is famous for its oysters; which sometimes contain pearls. When they were first shewn to me, I could not imagine what they were; for they only looked like fragments of rock, or rather dirty lumps of coral; and it required hammers to break them to pieces, before the oysters could be got at; but then we found them not only good of their kind, but also well flavoured. These oysters, and shrimps and prawns, are found in quantities all along this shore, and make, perhaps, the very best curries to be met with in any part of India.

On the 26th we proceeded to Caltura, 12 miles. The appearance of the country was much the same as during the former day's march. The village of Caltura is finely and picturesquely situated on the shore of a lake, which the Kaluganga or Black river, has formed at its mouth. It at once struck us all, that this was certainly the most agreeable place to reside in, which we had as yet seen in the island. The sea comes close up to the houses, so that there is always a cool and refreshing breeze from it, rendering the air pure and exhilarating There is a small fort at the end of the village, which commands the point where by means of large ferry boats, the lake is crossed, to the road on the opposite side, leading to Colombo. Mr. A——, the collector of the district, then resided in an excellent house belonging to Government, which had every conveniency attached to it, and was capable of accommodating, comfortably, not only his own family, but a host of visitors. He and Mrs. A—— did every thing in their power to make their delightful abode pleasant to us: indeed hospitality seems to be most liberally dispensed in this part of the world. But Caltura of old, and before we possessed the Kandyan kingdom, was a favourite resort of the Colombo sportsmen, and was therefore always looked upon as a very expensive station for both civil and military.

In order to annoy as little as possible our kind entertainers, I preferred sending my host of servants and coolies to a vacant house in the Fort, where I intended myself to sleep, as it was agreeably situated, and the views from its windows were more extensive and beautiful than from any point which I had as yet visited: even Adam's Peak, I was told, during the north-east monsoon is almost constantly to be seen from it. On leaving this house, about three o'clock next morning, I some way or other contrived to tumble over the rampart into the interior of the Fort; and the wonder is that I was not more seriously injured than I was; for the height is considerable. At first I felt greatly stunned by the fall, but having, with much difficulty, crawled along for some distance, I met a soldier, and sent him to Captain C———, the officer next in command, to request that he would march off the troops, as it would be at least an hour before I was sufficiently recovered from the effects of the fall to be able to follow in my palanquin. It is not a little remarkable, that both Captain C——— and the soldier I had sent to him, fell over the ramparts at the very same spot, and were also much hurt; indeed, the latter nearly broke his neck. The nights in Ceylon are exceedingly dark; so much so, that it is out of the question to think of travelling before the dawn of day without torches, unless there should happen to be moonlight. The troops crossing the lake in boats to reach the Colombo road, amidst such a blaze of light as the number of torches produced, had a very strange and quite a stage effect.

It is necessary here to remark, that the Kaluganga, which has its sources in the lofty region around Adam's Peak, and in the adjacent mountainous district of Saffragam, is a very fine and important river, navigable for large boats to Ratnapora, which is about thirty miles inland. I am told, however, that it is subject, after the heavy periodical rains, to be flooded in a most surprising manner; having been known, in some places, to rise full twenty feet in a few hours; on which occasions it carries all before it into the sea. Up this fine river, and in the adjacent country, there are many excellent situations which settlers might occupy both pleasantly and profitably; and though the cultivation of the sugar cane may have failed in this neighbourhood,—perhaps from want of proper management—there is no reason to apprehend that an agriculturist would be unsuccessful in causing an excellent soil to produce fine crops of grain, coffee, tobacco, &c.

On the 27th we marched to Pantura, 10 miles. The scenery is fully as fine, and the features of the country are much the same, as that we had been passing through for the last two days. There, however, one of the officers had an impressive hint given him that he was no longer in England, but in a country where snakes and reptiles of various kinds may be found. A large black scorpion contrived in the course of the night to get into his bed, and to sting him severely in the pit of the stomach; so severely that he gave tongue lustily, calling out for the surgeon to come immediately to his assistance, as he was sure he was a dead man, being, as he imagined, bitten by a poisonous snake. On a light being procured, the scorpion was found; but it was not until various soothing remedies had been applied, that the violently acute pain which he suffered could, in some degree, be assuaged.

We again marched on the 28th, and, after passing through a very fine and apparently thickly inhabited country, we arrived at Colombo, the capital of the island, and seat of government; having already, though in a cursory way, seen what is considered to be the most delightful part of the maritime provinces.

During this last day's march—15 miles—we saw growing near the road, and throwing out and down to the ground its immense branches, (which on reaching it take root, and thus form, as it were, numerous arches,) one of the finest Bogah trees in Ceylon, or probably in any other part of the world; for I do not exaggerate, when I say, that ten thousand men, if formed in contiguous close columns, could be placed under its shade. These magnificent trees are highly venerated by the worshippers of Boodhoo, as, according to tradition, he usually when on earth sat under one of them.

Short as my experience has been, I must, however, here observe, that I greatly like the climate; but the part of the country—beautiful as it undoubtedly is—which I have just had an opportunity of visiting, has not altogether come up to the expectations I had been led to form of it, from the works of Cordiner, Percival, and other writers; I must nevertheless say, that I was both pleased and delighted with it; and am fully convinced of its vast capabilities of improvement by cultivation, which would take away that too great and therefore tiresome uniformity which every where prevails.

CHAPTER III.

"As the sea,
Far through his azure turbulent domain,
Your empire owns, and from a thousand shores
Wafts all the pomp of life into your ports;
So with superior boon may your rich soil,
Exuberant, Nature's best blessings pour
O'er every land, the naked nations clothe,
And be th' exhaustless granary of the world!"

THOMSON.

FARTHER INTRODUCTORY OBSERVATIONS — COLOMBO AND ITS DOINGS IN 1820 — KANDYAN PRISONERS — TOUGH STORIES — MR. FARRELL'S HUNTING ESTABLISHMENT, AND FIELD SPORTS IN THE HAMBENTOTTE DISTRICT — EXCURSION TO FORT KING — A WATER EXCURSION — STATE OF SOCIETY AT COLOMBO — SIR ROBERT BROWNRIGG'S DEPARTURE — OBSERVATIONS — SIR EDWARD BARNES ASSUMES THE GOVERNMENT OF CEYLON — REMARKS.

WHILST I continue to be, in a great measure, guided by the memoranda, made, I may say upon the spot, as well as by other documents, lately procured, I have no intention of treading in the steps of others, or to touch upon subjects—if I can avoid doing so—which they may have already exhausted; but, though I shall endeavour to render this work amusing, and, if I can, interesting to the general reader, I beg to acquaint him, that my views are at the same time directed to more important matters, connected with the welfare of this fine island. My chief object is, to have it better known, not only as the most desirable part of the world to which persons possessing some capital, and wishing to form new settlements, can emigrate with advantage to themselves and families ; but also to shew what it is capable of being made in an agricultural, commercial, and political point of view. If I can accomplish this, I have no doubt but I must ultimately benefit the people of Ceylon, whilst, at the same time, I may prevent many emigrants from exposing themselves to great hardships and difficulties, which they might, when too late, have found to be insurmountable in our other new colonies, in which they might have been induced to settle, misled by the flattering descriptions given of them, by interested speculators in land.

Already much has been done by many, but particularly by Sir Robert and Lady Brownrigg, to make Colombo pleasant to us. Having brought out letters of introduction to the former, I have every reason to feel truly obliged to both, for the attention they have paid me. Of course, I have been to see everything deserving the notice of a stranger—the too much cried up cinnamon gardens, the lake and its beautiful scenery, the pleasant rides and drives on the Galle face—in short, all that is considered attractive in the neighbourhood. But what delights me most is to find, not only from my own observation, but also from what I am told by others, that Colombo, and the whole of the sea coast, for many miles on both sides of it, are blest with a most agreeable and healthy climate. I also find—but this I had been taught to expect—that society is good: indeed, very superior to what people at home have any idea of. The civil servants of Government and their families, residing in and near Colombo, are not only genteel, but also, in general, well informed; and when to them are added a great number of the military, few parts of the world can surpass this far distant city, and its neighbourhood, in agreeable, hospitable and friendly intercourse.

Some time having now elapsed since I arrived at Colombo, I am beginning to see and understand the listless sort of life led by Europeans in general, both civil and military; and such is the nature of the climate of Ceylon, and the habits it is too often allowed to engender, that from mentioning how one day is spent, a tolerably correct idea may be formed, how months and years steal away, or are lost.

We get out of bed at gun-fire, or soon after five o'clock; and should there be a parade we, military, go to it: if not the morning is devoted to some kind of gentle exercise, such as riding a few miles, until about eight o'clock, when the heat begins to be somewhat oppressive. The roads in the neighbourhood of Colombo are so numerous, that we have great choice in our equestrian excursions; and I may truly say, that in all directions they are so beautiful, that it seems a wonder most people do not seem inclined to extend them farther; yet, though certainly beautiful, I must own they are much too uniform to suit my taste; they having often only tall cocoa-nut trees on both sides, with vistas or openings extending here and there from them, which enable us to see, occasionally, the neat and generally handsome bungalows of European residents, or the plain leaf-thatched cottages of the natives, which are invariably placed in groves of cocoa-nut trees. We now and then, however, come upon larger spaces free from trees of any kind, where commanding views of the sea, and the lake, which adds so much to the admired scenery around Colombo, are extensively spread out before us.

If we take a morning's walk, which is seldom, it is usually in the botanical gardens, which have been lately much improved by Mr. Moon, the superintendant, under the auspices of Lady Brownrigg, and now contain many rare and beautiful trees, shrubs, and flowers; collected throughout the interior, where several new and splendid specimens have been found. The different walks being also tastefully laid out and neatly kept, these gardens bid fair to surpass those at the Cape of Good Hope; and their situation, being all but an island in the lake, renders them in this respect very superior.

After the morning's exercise, we bathe, dress, and sit down about nine to a substantial breakfast; something in the Scotch style, in point of variety of eatables. From breakfast until about two, the hour of tiffin, is usually given up by a few to reading, writing, some interesting study, or indoor occupation; and by too many to downright indolence. From eleven till two is the period of the day allotted for paying visits, when we use our palanquins, or bandies, as gigs are called; for it is then considered too hot for riding or walking. A new arrival here, as at the Presidencies on the continent of India, has to call in state, upon all the respectable residents, a ceremony which cannot be omitted by any one wishing to get into society. Some make a complete dinner at the hour of tiffin; and others, I consider them the most prudent in every sense of the word, are satisfied with fruits of various kinds, which are in great abundance, and bought for a mere trifle. From tiffin till about four o'clock, is usually spent in chat or gossip; our horses are then brought to the door, as all the world soon after turns out for rides or drives, usually upon the Galle face, until sun-set. We all, however, get home about half-past six, then dress and sit down to dinner at seven. Most people, from eating too much at tiffin, or rather as much as they are able, only go through the form of dining; and may, perhaps, condescend to taste some Yorkshire ham, coast mutton—that is, mutton from the continent—hot curry and English cheese. About nine o'clock, unless we have company, we usually rise from table, and by ten most people are in bed. Thus, from the way in which they begin, Europeans in general acquire habits of indolence, which they probably never get rid of as long as they live. A military man is occasionally roused from what may be properly called a state of apathy, by war, or preparations for war; but a civilian is allowed to enjoy permanent, undisturbed, nabob-like repose.

Notwithstanding the facilities for vaccination, which have for years past been afforded by government, their prejudices have hitherto prevented the natives from submitting to it; and in consequence, small-pox is making at this moment the most fearful ravages amongst them; so much so, that many of the unfortunate Moors and Kandyans are flying in the utmost consternation, and are thereby spreading the disease in all directions. About forty or fifty die daily in the Petah, or native town, outside the walls of Colombo; and such is the universal panic, that we can get little or nothing done by the tradespeople. Great as were the sufferings of the Kandyans during the rebellion, which has just been suppressed, (and from all I hear many of them were barbarously treated, and even put to death by our soldiers, when out of sight of their officers; for they had been greatly exasperated by the severe sufferings they had undergone, and the protracted resistance they had met with,) yet the small-pox is far more dreaded and felt by them than even the military punishment inflicted upon them.

We have now in prison here, and I visit him every time I am field officer of the day, the Adikar, who directed the massacre of Major Davie's people, in 1803. I have not heard what our authorities here intend doing with him; but I conclude that he will never again be allowed to return to the interior. Likewise Ehelapola, Maha Nilamè, whose family were so brutally butchered by the last King of Kandy, as shewn in the annexed curious historical picture, by a native artist. Ambitious views tempted him to aspire to the crown; and, as has been too often the case in other parts of the world as well as in this, led to his downfal and his imprisonment. He died some years afterwards in banishment in the Isle of France.

Like all men born and brought up in mountainous regions, the Kandyans are exceedingly attached to their wilds; but though they have the desire, they want the courage and confidence in themselves, and in each other, which are requisite to enable them to stand before our troops, or to defend their country. All the Kandyans I have as yet seen, though in general slender when compared with Europeans, are good-looking men, and very superior to the natives on the coast. For a certain period annually, the Kandyan mountains cannot be seen from Colombo, being hidden by dense clouds constantly hanging over them. This has been the case since our arrival here. The south-west monsoon has, however (3rd November) subsided; and the north-east having sprung up, but being still unsettled, much rain falls daily; at intervals, however, of fine weather, Adam's Peak and other lofty mountains around it, are to be seen far to the eastward; their great height—some of

RAJA SINGHA KING OF KANDY IN THE HALL OF AUDIENCE.

THE MINISTER ADIKAR ON SEEING THE KING PROSTRATES HIMSELF — THE FAMILY OF CHEYLAPOLA ARE BROUGHT BEFORE THE KING

THE KING COMMANDS ONE OF THE SONS TO BE CHOPPED WITH AN AXE

THE CHILDREN'S HEADS ARE CUT OFF, PUT IN A MORTAR, & THE MOTHER IS MADE TO POUND THEM

Published by T. and W. Boone. London, 1843.

THE MOTHER IS MADE TO EAT THE FLESH OF HER SECOND SON

THE MOTHER HER SISTER & DAUGHTER ARE PUSHED INTO THE LAKE

them being considered upwards of 8000 feet above the level of the sea—giving them the appearance of being quite close to us. Yesterday, while going my rounds, I found a few of the unfortunate Kandyan prisoners, with deep anxiety marked in their countenances, gazing intently upon their native mountains, naturally so dear to them. But I trust that most of them will soon be allowed to return to their homes and families; for I suspect that they have now suffered more than enough to put rebellion out of their heads for the rest of their lives.

Few of the wonders of this wonderful land have as yet come under my notice, but I was the other day shewn a frog—reader be not incredulous or alarmed—which had been choked, as I was informed, when trying to swallow a duck! But duck and frog were found lying together on the bank of the river, near my friend Mr. M—'s house, about two miles and a half from Colombo. This was certainly reversing the usual order of such matters; but the great size of this species of frog, in some measure justifies me in believing and telling the story, though I readily admit that it is a tough one. But what I am going to relate, may, I suspect, appear to many to be equally so. A few evenings ago, soon after sun-set, in returning with Captain G— from the cinnamon gardens, we were surrounded by some thousands of bats, at least twice the size of those we have in England, which flew around us, and against us, and seemed so determined to attack us, that we had nothing for it but to lay about us with our walking sticks to keep them off, and in doing so we knocked down several of them. I now, however, whilst dealing in the marvellous, which I must do occasionally, will add, that we had left an officer, Mr. Forbes, at Galle, to take charge of a number of men who had volunteered from the 19th into the regiment; which afforded him an opportunity of visiting that prince of Nimrods, Mr. Farrell, in the Hambentotte district, seventy miles to the eastward of Galle, and of enjoying in perfection the perilous and exciting field sports of that part of Ceylon. The stories he tells—and they may be fully credited—are really wonderful! Therefore, ye home-bred sportsmen, listen, whilst I imperfectly relate what then and there occurred,

He went up, as taught by Mr. Farrell, to within twelve yards of elephants, and shot several of them; also three alligators, or crocodiles, about 20 feet long each; some hundred of pea and jungle fowl, and ducks and other aquatic birds innumerable, besides many deer, elks, buffaloes, wild boars, or hogs, &c. &c. Mr. Farrell's hunting establishment is, indeed, princely; consisting of several fine horses, upwards of eighty greyhounds, besides other dogs of various breeds. Hambentotte, where he reigns and dispenses the most warm-hearted and liberal hospitality, is surrounded by extensive plains, here and there interspersed with large patches of jungle, full of deer, elks, and other animals, which, in the evenings and mornings.

come out in amazing herds, into the open country to feed. Mr. Forbes thought nothing of seeing half-a-dozen stags, with magnificent antlers, at one moment pulled down to the earth by the powerful greyhounds. Well mounted, and armed with guns and spears, they hunted the wild hogs. Herds of these ferocious animals would form a compact body in the midst of the plains, and bid defiance to both hunters and dogs, till their square, to use a military term, was broken from numbers of them being shot. They were then pursued and speared in all directions.

Such manly sports and amusements are, however, attended, as it may be supposed, with considerable danger; for the boars are very fierce and daring animals. An unlucky Singalese, in charge of some of the dogs, was killed close to Mr. Forbes; and they lost several of the finest and most determined greyhounds: some of them being pulled down by alligators, when they pursued the deer into the rivers or ponds. Frequently, both deer and dogs disappeared together under water; but the buffaloes, of which there were great numbers, and of which they shot seven, are by far the most dangerous animals to attack in this island. They likewise—so far did they get into the jungle—fell in with Vedahs, or, as they are called, wild men; who were however, very friendly and obliging, offering them honey and dried deer-flesh, &c., which they had killed with poisoned arrows. In short, there is no end to the wonderful stories he tells of Mr. Farrell's field sports: indeed it will be surprising if even what has been said of them, does not inspire ardour into the heart of many a British sportsman, and induce them, at least to talk of taking a steam trip to Ceylon, for a season's hunting and shooting; and I hope yet to be able to make fishing almost equally attractive.

Almost all the dogs we brought out with us from Ireland (for we expected to have good sport in Ceylon), are already, as is too commonly the case, dead; only one of mine is left, a most powerful animal, named Bran, a present from my friend Mr. Lawe of Cork. He partakes, as I understand, of the blood of the bull and wolf dog, and also of the largest breed of foxhound; and though now scarcely a year and a half old, he already evinces great strength, courage, speed, and sagacity. As it has been intimated to me, that I am to succeed Lieut-Colonel Hook of the 19th regiment, in the command and civil agency of the Seven Korles, one of the most renowned parts of the island for elephant shooting, &c., I intend Bran to be my constant companion there in all my wanderings. As some unaccountable delay, seemed, however, to have taken place in my appointment to that district, and wishing to see some of the island before I proceeded to a station where I was likely to be busily occupied, I made the necessary arrangements for travelling comfortably and expeditiously to Fort King; having been invited by the officer commanding there to spend a few days with him.

I left Colombo in my palanquin, which contained all I could want in the way of clothes, &c. for several days, being advised to travel as unincumbered with superfluous luggage as possible. I took only one native servant with me, who occasionally carried my gun; as I was informed that, after passing Hanwellé, it was very likely I might frequently fall in with elephants. Having started long before dawn of day, I reached Hanwellé by nine o'clock, where I halted to breakfast. This is a small military post, situated upon the beautiful Kalany-ganga, about fourteen miles from Colombo. As I went along, and as the day dawned, I found myself in the midst of the most enchanting scenery imaginable; which increased in loveliness as the sun rose above the trees, shedding greater lustre upon the objects which were distinctly reflected in the broad river, upon the bank of which the road lay almost the whole way. I had travelled the greater part of the distance under the agreeable shade of tall palm-trees, which, however, by no means impeded the views of the finely wooded country, which lay to the northward and upon the opposite bank of the, in some places, lake-like river.

The scenery, after leaving Hanwellé, becomes wilder, and of an entirely different and more rugged character; it was then, also, far more striking as well as fascinating in richness and variety of magnificent forest, intermingled with many fine shrubs and thick jungle. It maintained much the same appearance till I arrived at Avisahavellè, situated among rounded hills and, dark coloured rocks, rising amidst a great expanse of rich foliage. Near the rest-house, there was formerly a small fort, now quite neglected, though some years ago it was a point of importance, as Sittawakka, a royal residence, once stood not far from it; but in the present day, no traces of it remain—at least, none worthy of a traveller's notice. After allowing the bearers of my palanquin about an hour's rest, I next proceeded (travelling, as I had occasionally done before, on foot) to the strongly fortified post of Ruwenwellè; where I remained for the night with Major B——, the commandant, who not only paid me every possible attention, but also gave me much useful information about the surrounding country.

Next morning, we found the road tolerably good and level, running through paddy fields, on leaving which, and passing through a difficult and wilder district, I arrived at Arandenè, where the country improves in appearance, is much better cultivated and more thickly inhabited. Throughout the country I had travelled, since leaving Colombo, there are to be seen the ruins of several forts, which had been of importance when the Portuguese and Dutch possessed the sea-coast; as, during that period, it had almost constantly been the scene of warfare between them and the Kandyans. A wild almost mountainous country intervenes to Hettemulè, a small village, from whence we had to hurry on, as sunset approached rapidly, through a hilly tract, abounding in fine views of splendid and picturesque scenery, to Fort King; which station we did not reach until it had become dark. Fortunately we met with no obstruction from elephants or other animals, though the road, as we learned afterwards, between Fort King and Hettemulè, had of late been much infested by them.

I have no intention of describing more particularly than I have done, the fine tract of land through which I had passed so rapidly, and of which I had, in fact, seen so little; but it struck me, that it was indeed a country which European settlers might well covet; for all it wanted was improved cultivation and better roads, carried in various directions, to render it truly desirable. I remained a day at Fort King; and on the next set off, long before day, attended by a number of torch-bearers and tom-tom beaters, on my return, by the same road to Colombo; where I arrived in safety, highly gratified with this, the first excursion of the kind which I had made in Ceylon; during which it had in many respects risen greatly in my estimation, as a most valuable colony of Great Britain.

Hearing nothing more of my proceeding to the Seven Korles; towards the end of December, I arranged with two very agreeable brother officers—Lieut.-Colonel J. M. S—— and Mr. W——, that, attended by some of our servants, we should set off upon an excursion into the interior; for what I had seen, in my journey to Fort King, made me more anxious than ever, to see more of a country, of which we daily heard so much.

We therefore—anticipating much enjoyment—started from Colombo; and after a pleasant morning's ride of thirteen miles, got to Marotta, on the Galle road; and from thence sent back our horses with their keepers, having no further occasion for them; as we were to embark near that place in boats, which were in waiting for us; and in order to be saved all trouble or annoyance of any kind with boatmen, &c., we had previously settled that we were to take a Modeliar's son with us, a fine intelligent young man, who spoke English tolerably well, and who was to manage every thing. The two boats were each about thirty feet long, and being almost new, and completely covered with thatch, we had nothing to apprehend from vermin, nor of being exposed to the sun, or any rain which might fall. One boat was for ourselves, and the other for our servants. In ours was a couch for each of us; also a table, chairs, and every thing requisite to insure comfort; for we intended never to sleep on shore, or to be indebted to the natives for hospitality; and we were also in hopes of thus avoiding dangers from snakes or reptiles, as well as of escaping the consequences of damp from the ground, in any swampy part of the country, which we might visit in our progress. Our servants' boat was fitted up principally as a cooking place; and in it were safely stowed away the necessary supply of bread, rice, tea, coffee, sugar, wines, &c.; but it was to our guns that we were to look for the greater part of our food.

Ascending a winding sluggish river, which empties itself into the sea at Pantura, we arrived at a village called Balgoddè, about ten or twelve miles from where we had embarked. It was at times from a hundred to four or five hundred yards, or even more, in width; but occasionally, as we proceeded, it became narrow like a canal, (indeed it had of old been used as such by the Dutch), and again opening out, it was so broad and land-locked, as to assume the appearance of an extensive lake; the very thickly wooded banks rendering the scenery on the whole agreeable, though rather too uniform. This monotony was, however, in some measure, relieved by the country in the distance, or back ground, being composed of some lofty blue coloured mountains. Such a continued mass of foliage, beheld in all the brilliancy of a tropical sun, had a truly striking and fascinating effect. But all these attractions disappeared when we landed; for then little else but jungle, and in some places swamps, covered with tall reeds or flags, presented themselves, tenanted, it may be supposed, since the flood, by numerous kinds of waterfowl.

Wherever the ground rose, which it seldom did, we were sure to find the cottages of the natives, surrounded, as usual, by palm trees; under the shade of which, or of the low projecting roofs that form what may be called verandahs to their dwellings, they seemed to pass their lives in the enjoyment of indolence and idleness. Rice cakes, curry, and the fruits which the trees produced, I may say spontaneously, were almost their only food, and appeared to bound their wants and wishes; yet, I by no means looked upon them as a happy people; unless seeming indifference as to surrounding objects, and about the world or its doings, can be said to constitute happiness. Let me, however, indulge in the hope, that this extensive and well watered tract, which is at present almost unoccupied by man, will one day be drained, cleared of superabundant woods, cultivated, and thus rendered healthy and productive by European settlers. The banks of these—I may call them lakes—are already adorned by nature, with tall, spreading, and finely blossoming trees of various kinds, and of different shade of green, brown, and purple coloured leaves, as also with splendid shrubs and flowers; the latter—chiefly of the aquatic kinds—are in general large, brilliant in colours, and strikingly beautiful.

The Dutch, when they held the maritime provinces, did every thing in their power, to prevent strangers from knowing any part of the interior; and they were equally careful to prevent their own people from publishing accounts of what they might have seen there. They took little interest in the history of Ceylon, or of its inhabitants; the acquisition of wealth was their ruling passion; and while they could carry on their commerce in the towns on the sea coast, they cared not for the interior of the island: indeed, they gave it out, that except for a few miles inland, the country was generally very unhealthy, and totally unfit for Europeans to reside in. Even this prejudice, at the time I wrote these memoranda, had not been got over; and I had been warned, before I set out upon this excursion, of what might be the consequences of my anxiety to see what wise people were contented to hear of.

It would be useless to name or describe the places—consisting chiefly of a few native huts—which we visited in succession, or where we fastened our boats for the night; but day after day presented the same description of scenery, and nearly the same objects. The pleasant mornings and evenings were devoted to shooting; and we killed far more birds than were wanted to supply our table amply. They were almost all of the aquatic kinds, such as wild-ducks, teal, &c., also snipe and plover; and in the woods, when not swampy, we found hundreds of pigeons and turtle-doves, which answered very well for pies or curries. We also shot several beautiful birds, the names of which were unknown to us; and among them a few resembling, in plumage, the bird of paradise—there were others, the feathers of which were as white as snow, and most of them like horse-hair.

Our servants being good cooks, no gourmands could have desired better fare than was daily placed upon the board; and there was no lack of good wines, which were cooled in bags, kept wet and hung up in a current of air, under the shade of a tree, till wanted. In short, taking into account the sport we had, many may think that we were much more to be envied than pitied. During the

the heat of the day, the boats were rowed along on the placid surface of the water, amidst perpetual verdure. Reading in turn, playing backgammon, talking over the feats we had performed, and describing what we had individually seen, planning excursions in new directions, and preparing our guns, killed the time most agreeably, when not engaged in shooting.

We saw during our excursion but two snakes, and they were harmless; and the only wild animal we met with was a solitary hare. We were daily moving from place to place, but at the farthest, I think that we were never more than twenty-five or perhaps thirty miles from Colombo. There were abundance of fish in the lakes; a few of which were offered to us by the natives, but we would not use them, as they are looked upon by Europeans as insipid, and sometimes unwholesome; yet many of the lower castes eat them constantly, as I often did afterwards, in my delightful fishing excursions inland from Galle, as well as in the Kandyan territory. We were told that in these sluggish waters there were alligators, but we saw none of them. I shot two amphibious creatures, somewhat like them, called by the Modeliar's son Cobra coy. They were about six feet in length, and had very long tongues, which they constantly and quickly darted from their mouths, in a surprising and threatening manner—they are, however, quite harmless, and I believe they belong to the guana or lizard tribe. I understand that Dr. Davy (who afterwards wrote the account of his travels in the interior) has procured one of them, which I hear, he intends taking to England with him.

On the day appointed, our horses were brought to us at Marotta, and we returned to Colombo, greatly pleased with our week's excursion, into a part of the country rarely visited. We met with no mishaps or adventures; but, soon after our return, one of my companions, Lt.-Colonel S——, had a feverish attack, which confined him to his room for about ten days. Every one said—though I am convinced it was nothing more than a seasoning fever—that he had caught it in the swampy jungle, in which we had, so foolishly, been amusing ourselves.

Being still uncertain how long I might remain at Colombo, I hired a house, very pleasantly situated, on what is called Slave Island, situated nearly in the middle of the lake, which I before mentioned, as constituting the chief ornament of Colombo and its neighbourhood. I was induced to take up my abode there, because there were some very agreeable families, with whom I had become intimate, residing upon the shores of the lake, and whom I could, when so inclined, easily and pleasantly visit by means of a light skiff, which I had always at my command, and which I paddled along without assistance from any one. And how much did I enjoy returning home at night by water; and how beautiful it was, even when the moon did not afford her beams, to behold the shore of the lake one blaze of light, emitted from thousands and tens of thousands of fire-flies, which flitted incessantly from bush to bush!

When the latitude of Colombo and the climate are considered, it will scarcely be believed, that ladies here seem to be fonder of dancing than in England. Wherever I dine, the sound of the fiddle or piano calls the gentlemen, at a proper hour, from their wine to the dance; and, with few exceptions, ladies, whether young or old, married or single (and there were plenty of pretty girls, both English and Dutch), apparently delight in it; and it is often kept up till sunrise. On such occasions, they have always suppers, consisting of every thing in season, with one invariable accompaniment—very hot mulligatani soup; but the crowd of servants in attendance is certainly a great annoyance; for every person has one, and some two, standing behind his chair; and when there is not a punkah, a kind of large fan, suspended over our heads, and pulled backwards and forwards to create a current of air, the heat is sometimes very oppressive. What renders this the more unpleasant is, that the natives anoint themselves all over with cocoa-nut oil, which, when so applied, has to most Europeans a disagreeable effluvia. In other respects the Singalese are very cleanly, bathing at least once a day; and as servants have now been made to dress very neatly in white calico jackets, ornamented with silver buttons,

&c. and not as formerly, with only a piece of that stuff wrapt round their bodies, they look remarkably well when in attendance at table.

The dinner parties, in general, are far too large. I sat down at table, the other day, with no less than fifty-one gentlemen and ladies; but the houses are mostly so contrived, as fully to admit the prevailing breezes; and the punkahs being also kept constantly at work, I do not find the heat so inconvenient as I expected. They always on these occasions give various kinds of wine, such as Madeira, Champagne, Claret, &c., and it is the custom to ask ladies to take ale with us, in the same way we did wine formerly in England.

In order to illustrate in some degree the ways of Ceylon at that period, (and I do not find that they have since greatly changed), I must take the liberty of mentioning, that on the last evening of December, the Regiment gave a ball and supper to all the fashionable world. I was one of the stewards upon the occasion, and was requested to make it as brilliant an affair as Colombo had ever beheld. With the able assistance of my coadjutors, especially that of Captain J—, it was admitted by every one that we were completely successful. We issued upwards of a hundred and fifty invitations, to officers of other corps, civilians, their wives and daughters—in short, to every one admitted into society. This is a point to which I would call the attention of respectable persons, who may intend to settle in Ceylon; for without introductions to some of the first people, they will have little chance of getting into genteel society, or, at all events, into the first circle. Even the Singalese entertain strange notions with regard to the different classes in England. It was in some way or other reported, that one of their Governors had a brother in the wine trade in London; and their indignation was highly excited, at the idea of the King of England having sent out the brother of a person who kept a *wine bazaar* to be their governor.

I hope I shall be pardoned this digression, but, to finish the subject of the ball, I must add, that the transparencies and decorations—which are so easily procured in this land of beautiful flowers and shrubs—were really splendid and much admired. The whole of the company sat down, comfortably, in a large, magnificent bungalow, built for the occasion, and tastefully adorned with the finest foliage, to a most excellent and well laid out supper; after which dancing recommenced, and was kept up till sunrise. We also gave a dinner to the Governor, and about eighty gentlemen, and no delicacy was wanting but *English cheese*, of which we could not procure a morsel in Colombo.

This gaiety had been chiefly occasioned by the approaching departure of Sir Robert and Lady Brownrigg from the island; and, a few days after, the civil servants of government, in conjunction with the military, gave them a farewell dinner, ball and supper, on the eve of their embarkation. Many regretted their departure; but all soon began to worship the rising sun, in the person of Sir Edward Barnes, who now assumed the government.

During Sir Robert Brownrigg's reign, a period of about eight years, great and important changes had taken place in Ceylon. He had dethroned the Kandyan King, and annexing his territories to our former possessions on the sea coast, conquered from the Dutch, had thus extended and consolidated the dominion of the British Sovereign over the whole of this most beautiful and valuable island. Such events had not been accomplished without his having had to encounter and overcome many difficulties; the greatest of which was his suppressing a rebellion —as it was styled— which had raged for about three years in the Kandyan Provinces; during which, it was universally allowed, that he evinced great talent, perseverance, and unshaken firmness. These vast acquisitions are already beginning to cause considerable changes in people's opinions, as to what Ceylon is likely to become as an appendage of Great Britain; especially if they can be permanently secured in a country so very difficult of access as the Kandyan Kingdom. All agree, however, that the necessity of scattering still more both civil and military over the whole island, must have a considerable effect upon society. Points or stations in the maritime provinces, formerly considered of the first importance, are now, I fear injudiciously, no longer looked upon in that light, the consequences of which may hereafter be felt in a commercial point of view at most of the seaports; and new posts are established, or about to be so, in the Kandyan Districts, to insure our conquests there, and to facilitate the collection of the revenue. Some already perceive a considerable change in society at Colombo, Galle, and other stations, and do not hesitate to declare that it has greatly fallen off, and become inferior to what it was in the times of Mr. North or Sir Thomas Maitland; those who remember them tell us, that it was then truly delightful, and perhaps superior to what is to be met with in any of our foreign possessions.

In the Ceylon Calendar, published at Colombo. is a list of Portuguese, Dutch, and British Captains-General and Governors of Ceylon, from an early epoch—that is, from about the year 1590, down to the present day; but if the reader is desirous of obtaining historical information, as to the times of the Portuguese and Dutch, (subjects which I do not intend to touch upon), I must refer him to a work published in 1816, by an author styling himself "Philalethes." The Singalese themselves possess, as I am informed by those who have acquired a sufficient knowledge of their language, many curious documents, or ancient records, which are supposed to contain the history of the country, and of its kings, from a very remote period; but my informants find that where truth is obvious, so much of what is fabulous has been mixed up with it, as to render it difficult, if not hopeless, to attempt to separate the one from the other, so as to make the true portion of it available. I find these remarks in my note book; but the difficulty to which I allude is now got over, and this desirable object has been ably accomplished by Major Forbes, in his "Eleven Years in Ceylon."

CHAPTER IV.

"Should Fate command me to the farthest verge
Of the green earth, to distant barbarous climes,
Rivers unknown to song; where first the sun
Gilds Indian mountains; . . . .
. . . . 'tis nought to me:
Since God is ever present, ever felt,
In the void waste as in the city full."—THOMSON.

REMARKS ON LEAVING COLOMBO—THE MONSOONS AND THE CLIMATE—AUTHOR ARRIVES AT GALLE, AND ASSUMES THE COMMAND OF THE FORTRESS AND DISTRICT—KANDYAN PRETENDER—THE CHARACTER OF THE KANDYANS IN 1820—GALLE AS AN ESSENTIAL LINK IN THE STEAM NAVIGATION OF THE INDIAN OCEAN—PASSAGE BETWEEN CEYLON AND THE CONTINENT EXAMINED—OLD CUSTOMS AT GALLE—REMARKS UPON THE COUNTRY FROM NEGOMBO TO HAMBENTOTTE—AGRICULTURAL LABOURERS—FRUITS OF CEYLON; THEIR CHEAPNESS—PRICES OF ARTICLES OF FOOD AT GALLE VERY MODERATE; AND GIVEN TO ENABLE INTENDING EMIGRANTS TO REGULATE THEIR EXPENDITURE, AND TO COMPARE CEYLON WITH ANY OTHER PART OF THE WORLD AS A POINT FOR EMIGRATION.

BEFORE his departure for England, Sir Robert Brownrigg was pleased to appoint me to the command of the extensive and most desirable district of Galle. I confess that I felt a good deal disappointed at not going at once to the Seven Korles; but Galle, I am told, is a much more pleasant, though by no means so lucrative a command. But before I, for the present, leave Colombo, it is necessary I should remark, that though it may, in some respects, be conveniently situated, as the capital of the Island, in a delightful country, blessed with as fine a climate as any part of the world; though its neighbourhood abounds in beautifully diversified scenery; though the eye is gratified by the sight of a vast expanse of surface, covered with tall cocoa-nut trees, interspersed with handsome bungalows, and the humble but usually neat cottages of the natives; though Colombo itself is a handsome town, with streets running parallel to each other, shaded by beautiful tulip trees; and though many of the houses are large and commodious; yet it must not be forgotten, that, in a commercial point of view, it has one serious disadvantage—that is to say, it has only open roads for shipping, which afford secure anchorage for only about half the year—from the beginning of October to the end of March. At other times, the wind blows frequently from the westward with such violence as to render intercourse with the shore very unsafe; so much so, indeed, that no insurance can be effected upon vessels touching there during that stormy period. In the inner road only small vessels can anchor. Seeing the disadvantages under which, as a sea-port, Colombo was placed, the Dutch turned their attention for many years to Galle; but why it was afterwards neglected, and abandoned as the seat of Government, and a preference again given to Colombo, I have not as yet been able to ascertain.*

* Though it is of importance to persons intending to settle in

In the Month of January, I left Colombo for Galle, in a free-trader, in charge of about two hundred and fifty men, intended to form part of the garrison of the latter place, where we landed on the following morning. I do not remember ever to have experienced finer weather at sea, or to have had a more pleasant passage than upon this occasion.

It is very difficult to form a correct idea of the climate of Ceylon, or of the weather which may be looked for in various parts of it. Indeed, the remarks which I am about to make upon both (and they are chiefly intended for the information of new-comers) are so scattered throughout my notes, that I think it will be best, and will obviate the necessity of recurring to the subject, for me to consolidate here the obser-

Ceylon, especially to those who may have commercial speculations in view, yet I do not wish unnecessarily to occupy space, or to take up too much of the reader's time in speaking of pilotage, harbour dues, &c. I, however, give, in the Appendix, an official statement of the quantity and value of various articles of merchandise imported into Ceylon in 1835; and also an ordinance enacted by the Governor, with the advice and consent of the Legislative Council, for establishing a new Tariff of duties on goods exported and imported. I am not aware that since the year 1837, when this ordinance was promulgated, any further changes have taken place, yet Mr. Bennett, in his "Manual of Useful Information," just published, informs us that duties upon exports amount to about sixteen per cent,—and he adds, "the great difference between the rate duty levied on imports and exports (nearly 250 per cent against the produce of the island) cannot fail to excite attention." Of this I think there cannot be a doubt.—See Appendix D. E. F. G.

vations I made at various periods afterwards, assisted by those of others who have given their attention to this point, but especially Dr. Davy, who is by far the best authority in such matters.

Ceylon being situated between the sixth and tenth degrees of north latitude, that succession of seasons is unknown in it, with which the year is varied in the temperate zone; and the transition of weather from dry to rainy, and from rainy to dry, is rarely diversified. Over most of the island the wind blows for a certain period of the year from the south-west, and a certain period from the north-east. These winds are considerably modified by local circumstances, and prevail with surprising regularity, over a great part of the continent of India, and the Indian Ocean. The south-west monsoon is felt all over the island, and blows more steadily than the north-east: thus at Colombo and Trincomalie, on the opposite shores, the south-west wind prevails constantly for about five months; but the north-east not half the time at the former that it does at the latter place; it being at Colombo confined chiefly to December and January, while at Trincomalie it extends to the month before and the month after. In consequence, on the Colombo side of the island, the period of variable winds is longer than on the Trincomalie side. In the one instance being about five months, comprehending February, March, April, October, and November, during which time the wind is generally from the sea during the day, and from the land at night. In the other instance, it is limited to the middle months, and observes nearly the same diurnal change.

On the state of the winds in the interior, it is very difficult to speak with any degree of certainty. Over the level parts of it, the winds differ but little from what they are on the sea coast. But amongst the mountains it is otherwise; there they vary greatly, according to the features of the country, the direction of the valleys, and the ridges of the more lofty mountains; and according to central situation, or proximity to one or other side of the island; the country on the western side partaking more of the peculiarities of wind of Colombo, that on the eastern of Trincomalie, and that nearly central amongst the mountains, or near their base, having its own peculiarities.

As might be expected from its inter-tropical situation, the quantity of rain that falls in Ceylon is immense; exceeding, I would say, fully four times what falls in England. The parts of the country in which much the largest proportion of rain is looked for, are the mountainous tracts and the maritime provinces, that are most exposed to the force of the monsoons. The parts where there is least rain are those at some little distance from the mountains, and so situated as to render both monsoons land winds. Tangalle in the Megampattoo, to the eastward of the most southern point of the island, is thus situated, and the same may be said of the part of the country for some distance to the northward of the Seven Korles, where a drought has been known to last more than a year at a time, uninterrupted by the fall of a single drop of rain. At the northern extremity, and in the northern low land division of the island, and on the eastern shore, the rainy season commences about the time of the setting in of the north-east monsoon. It lasts about two months, with great violence, flooding all the low parts of the country, and some districts almost entirely. During the other ten months of the year, the weather is in the opposite extreme, being almost constantly dry, showers rarely refreshing the parched soil, excepting about the beginning of the south-west monsoon. On the western side of the island (and to this I particularly beg the attention of settlers who have agricultural pursuits in view), most rain falls about the time of the setting-in of the south-west monsoon. But it is not confined to this period, nor is it so violent, or so continued, as on the opposite side. A whole day of constant rain is very uncommon; all the year round showers are frequent, so that it is very unusual for a month to elapse without them, and it is in consequence of this peculiarity that the western coast of Ceylon is, I may say, never parched, and that its aspect is always so delightfully fresh and green, exciting the admiration of strangers from less favoured parts of India. Owing to the frequency of rains amongst the mountains, the interior is uncommonly well watered; not a valley is without a stream.

From what has just been said, it must be evident, that no kind of comparison, which a person at home would understand, can be drawn between the heat of summer in England, and in this island. Here the heat, if I may so express myself, is pure like the atmosphere, for the winds which, during the continuance of the two monsoons, blow from the ocean in opposite directions, reach Ceylon in a state of the greatest freshness and purity. In England, when the weather is really hot, the air becomes, as it were, a kind of warm oppressive vapour; and I verily believe, if such a state of atmosphere were to exist, for even a day, in a tropical country, to be acted upon by the powerful rays of the sun, it would seriously affect the health of man and beast. Thus we see, how wisely Providence provides what is suitable for various parts of the world; and has rendered almost the whole of it habitable, even from what is supposed by many to be the burning equinoctial line, to the always frozen poles.

The influences of the climate of Ceylon, though seemingly so delightful, are occasionally trying to some constitutions; but, with the exception of Trincomalie and a few other dreaded places, which are well known and carefully avoided, the greater part of the island may be said to be healthy. Yet ladies, (and the truth ought to be told), who set a high value upon their personal charms, especially upon the freshness and fairness of their complexions, ought to be very cautious; for I grieve to say, that they may discover, and that too before they have been long in Ceylon, (and it is far worse on the continent of India), that its climate, though charming, cannot revive once-faded bloom, and that it is very different in its effects upon their looks, to what it is upon the leaves of the trees ; which, as fast as they wither and fall, are replaced by new ones of the most lively and fascinating colours. Alas! on the contrary, even a few years are sometimes sufficient to efface that bewitching bloom, which they will find it impossible to restore, by—what cannot be used in any hot country—the most delicate rouge.

I had only just taken over the command of the Galle district from Lieut.-Colonel Macdonald of the 19th regiment, when information reached us, that another pretender to the throne of Kandy, (certainly not to Lieut.-Colonel Macdonald's surprise), had made his appearance in the province of Wellassè, to the eastward of Badulla, and about 200 miles from this, where a friend of mine, Major H——, 83d regiment, commands. He expected to have been joined by the people of that country, and by the Vedahs, or wild men ; but Lieut.-Colonel Macdonald, who long had the charge of that district, had taught them that rebellion was neither allowable nor profitable. The Pretender's shewing himself there, caused, however, a great sensation throughout the island: but, through the prompt and energetic measures adopted by Sir Edward Barnes, the poor devil was soon caught, and I conclude, will ere long meet the fate of those who are found guilty of unsuccessful rebellion; which of course becomes treason—and

> "Treason does never prosper : What's the reason ?
> Why, when it prospers, none dare call it treason."

He is, of course, represented to be an impostor; but Lieut.-Colonel Macdonald believes that he may have some claims to the crown; not as the son of the dethroned king, but of his predecessor, Rajah Singha. His escaping so long the vigilance of our people, proves, at all events, that, whatever his right to the throne may be, he had many friends in the Kandyan provinces, and those men of influence; as large rewards had long been offered for his apprehension.

An officer has just arrived here, who left Badulla only three days ago; I asked him if he had seen the Pretender. He replied that he had, and that when he set out for Galle, he left him in the *stocks*—perhaps the last of a long line of kings in the stocks!—into which the Commandant had ordered him to be put. He added, that the Pretender is a good-looking young man, with prepossessing manner and address; and that he has acquired a good deal of general information, especially as to what is connected with the affairs of Ceylon. He was commanded to account for his having dared to style himself, or allowing himself to be styled by others, King of Kandy. He replied, in a tone and spirit worthy of admiration, "because it is my birthright." He was further asked, why he had presumed to appoint a native chief second Adikar of the kingdom? "I am king," said he, "and if I reign an hour, a day, or a week, I have a right to appoint the most fit persons to be my ministers." His bearing is represented to be manly and dignified. My informant also adds, that it is the general opinion of those who have seen and conversed with him, that had he once been able to assemble a sufficient force around him, in such a strong and almost inacessible country as that about and beyond Badulla, he would certainly have given us a vast deal of trouble to put him down. Being quite unknown to any of our people, or to the natives in the maritime provinces, he was very lately walking in the streets of Colombo, Trincomalie, and Galle, dressed in the simplest attire. When taken, he had assumed the dress which he considered suitable to his rank; and in this, to make him appear the more ridiculous in the eyes of the Kandyans, he now sits in the stocks. Since his arrival from the continent of India, where, it is understood, he was brought up and educated by a Singalese priest, he had isited many parts of Ceylon; and his remarks upon the state of the country are represented to have been judicious; it is therefore the more surprising how he could have committed such a blunder, as to claim, publicly, the throne, at a time like this, when the people and the country are totally unable to aid or support him and his adherents.

It should here be remarked, that those who suppose the upper classes or castes of Kandyans or Singalese to be either ignorant or altogether illiterate, are greatly deceived. For, on the contrary, their manners are even refined; and they possess much useful knowledge of mankind, deep

KATUBURALE MOHOTHOLE.

Published by T and W Boone London 1843

A MODELIAR

Published by T and W Boone, London, 1843

artifice and great tact: indeed, I have met with few men of any country, who come into, or go out of, a room with more grace and ease than they do; and those who are versed in the more recent history of Ceylon, must have observed, that the Kandyans generally contrived to outwit most of our would-be politicians. In fact, so often was this the case, that Lieut.-Colonel Macdonald, (as he confessed to me and others), latterly thought it best not to treat at all with them—the blow before the word being found to be by far the wisest policy. In proof of this being the general opinion, I must take the liberty of mentioning a remark of Sir Robert Brownrigg's, when I called to take leave of him before he sailed for England, and to thank him for having appointed me to the Galle district. "You have at an early period of life attained," said he, "what officers so much aim at—high rank in the army; and you have already seen much service. If there should ever be another war in the Kandyan provinces, you may expect to be actively employed there. Should that happen, and the force under your orders be such as at all to justify you in doing so, always attack your enemy the moment you can get at him, and never trust to the word or promises of a Kandyan."

The dresses of all the Headmen are remarkably handsome; the figures of two are given here—the one carved in ivory, and the other in wood, by native artists. But a particular description of their dresses and appointments, given in the Ceylon

Calendar, to which I have before alluded, will, I think, astonish the reader.

The Port of Trincomalie, as is well known, is very superior, in many respects, to any other in the island: indeed, there are none to be compared with it in the east, but its great unhealthiness reduces considerably its value. Galle having a harbour safe for ships of the largest size, I may say, for the whole year, and so situated with regard to the monsoons, that they can get in and out at all times, which is not the case with any other port in the island, the prudent and commercial Dutch made it a place of considerable strength and importance, from whence the produce of the maritime provinces, at least on this side of the island, and of the western half of the interior, should be chiefly shipped. With this view, a canal was made, or attempted, which, passing through the country towards Colombo, connects, or was intended to connect, several long and often narrow lakes or pieces of water, and also to communicate with rivers, by which goods can be sent for a considerable distance into the interior. Whether the views of the Dutch were as extensive as they are said to have been, or whether they found the canal to answer their expectations, I cannot pretend to say; but it has been much neglected, and almost all traffic in that direction has long ceased. I was, however, assured by a respectable and intelligent Headman, that though there were some impediments, yet small sized boats could still ply upon it. I fear, however, that the high duties, exacted by us upon almost every kind of goods, have very seriously injured, not only Galle, but also the whole island; and until these are greatly modified, or altogether taken off, permanent improvement in commerce cannot be looked for. But, considering Galle to be the point to which I would direct the attention of those intending to settle in Ceylon, I must, as I proceed, speak a good deal of it, and of the country around and even at some distance from it.

I am, moreover, glad to see that Galle, or, as it is commonly called, Point de Galle, has become an object of great importance in the eyes of Government and of the British nation, as a connecting link in the steam navigation of the Indian ocean. It has been shewn by official documents, and information obtained from the best sources, that there is no difficulty whatever, notwithstanding the strong currents—50 miles in 24 hours—which run off the southern extremity of Ceylon, and the violent gales which at times prevail in the eastern part of the Indian ocean, in making the voyage from Calcutta to Galle against the south-west monsoon; nor from thence to Socotra, near the entrance of the Red Sea, the vessel taking her course through what is called the one and-a-half degree channel.

It has also been shewn, that if there were a sufficient number of good, convenient, and powerful steamers stationed upon this route, that they would be more than constantly filled; and if this communication were established, it could be easily extended to any part of our Colonial possessions to the eastward of India, and with New South Wales: indeed, some of the first Australian merchants in London are anxious to have the passage established to Calcutta by the line alluded to, intending to take on the communication from Galle to Australia. Already a company has been formed in England for communicating by steamers with Ceylon, anticipating that the main stem will be carried out. It is obvious that it would be much more convenient for the Australians to come to Galle than to Calcutta, as it would be only half the distance; and this line would be equally convenient for Sumatra, Java, and the whole of the Australian Archipelago. It is likewise in contemplation to carry steam communication to Melville Island, the most northern point of Australia, there to have a depot, leaving it to local companies to carry it to other parts.

It has been proposed (and, I trust, acceded to) that four steamers should be employed in rotation, as follows:—

No. 1. To leave Socotra January 1; arrive at Calcutta January 19.

No. 2. To leave Socotra February 1; arrive at Calcutta February 19.

No. 3. To leave Calcutta January 1; arrive at Socotra January 19.

No. 4. To leave Calcutta February 1; arrive at Socotra February 19.

Thus, in succession, four steam vessels will ply between Socotra, Ceylon, Madras, and Calcutta;

steaming at most (making every allowance for monsoons, &c.) one hundred and fourteen days each year. And in the event of accident to a boat, by this system, the three would keep up the communication during the repairs of the inefficient boat.

The estimate of the annual disbursements will be nearly as stated in the article (H) of the appendix.

I am aware that the attention of the Madras Government has been given to find or make a convenient and safe passage betwixt Ceylon and the Continent, with the view of facilitating steam and other communication between the Presidencies; but this appears to me to b altogether a hopeless business, (and I am confirmed in this opinion by what I learned from my late friend Captain Dawson, alluded to in the following report) as any opening through Adam's Bridge, which might be effected, would almost to a certainty be closed up, or rather brought back to its present state, by the storms which usually prevail at the commencement of the monsoons, especially that which blows from the southwest. It is, however, necessary to give part of Major Sim's published report, which will be found in the appendix (I).

I have been partly anticipating what is contained in my notes. I, however, considered it necessary to do so; for thus Galle is shewn, at once, to stand pre-eminent as a point of vast importance, and indispensable as a link in the chain of steam navigation over the Indian ocean; circumstances which must ultimately promote not only its welfare as a commercial city, but also that of the whole island.

I have as yet made but one trip upon the canal, extending from Galle; but what I have seen of it, even in a state of decay, convinces me that there has been some very impolitic neglect, on our part, of this seemingly wise plan of the Dutch. The country I passed through, in ascending it in a small boat which I keep for the purpose of making such excursions, is apparently rich in soil, very beautiful, and was continually reminding me of some of our own rivers, though the surprisingly ever-luxuriant and verdant foliage of the trees, told me where I was. Plantains, oranges, custard apples, and other tropical fruits, also grow in considerable quantities upon and near to its banks, which are here and there ornamented with shrubs and wild flowers, the latter chiefly of the aquatic kinds, and if introduced into Great Britain would improve our collections.

The land to some extent around Galle was, at the period I speak of, retained by Government; and the natives allowed to live upon it were removeable at pleasure. Some of those residing in the immediate neighbourhood of the place, are bound to perform certain services. One has to supply the Commandant's table with vegetables, in consideration of his being permitted to hold part of what was formerly a Government garden. Others, for being allowed to fish around the rocks upon which Galle stands, are obliged (or rather were of old) to supply him with fish, which can there be caught in great quantities. The wet ditches of the fortress, upwards of a mile in extent, are full of fish of an inferior description, used only by the natives; but my predecessors in the command have allowed them to become quite choked up with various kinds of water plants, which grow here in great beauty and profusion. The Moormen, for being allowed to live within the walls, are bound to keep the ditches clear of these weeds, or else they are liable to be fined. I am now, however, getting the vast mass of obstructive matter removed, but chiefly by the labour of a large body of convicts, allowed for such purposes. I found parts of the fortifications gone into decay, as well as some of the large public buildings; I am now, at Sir Edward Barnes' desire, repairing them as well as the means placed at my disposal will admit of. We are also getting the streets properly lighted, by replacing and repairing the numerous broken lamps, and we are besides busily occupied in planting trees (chiefly those of the tulip kind, which grow from cuttings), wherever they can afford shade or tend to ornament the city, which, being encompassed by high ramparts, is not so cool as it would otherwise be. Galle, which has many good houses in it, that are let by the Dutch inhabitants at low rents, is delightfully situated on a rocky promontory, projecting some distance into the sea; and behind it there are some finely wooded hills but one in particular stands so near to the fortifications, as in some measure to command part of them, and, for the safety of the place, it ought to have a strong redoubt constructed upon it.

For several years, and whilst the Dutch held the

sea coast only, the Governors, as I have before stated, resided at Galle, and therefore did much to improve and embellish it; but it has for a long time past been greatly neglected, and its importance may probably not be remembered until it is apprehended that it might fall into the hands of an enemy, who would consider its conquest as a first step towards the reduction of the whole island; or till its value as a station for steamers, and its consequent increasing commerce may bring it into notice.

I have made the first of these remarks in the hope of attracting attention to a matter of such vast importance as that of our continuing to possess the dominion of Ceylon; for I fully coincide in opinion with that enlightened and judicious writer, "Philalethes," that, perhaps, the territorial sovereignty of India may hereafter be wrested from this country, in the fluctuations to which that part of the world has always been more particularly liable; but should ever this catastrophe occur, still the possession of Ceylon will, in a commercial and maritime point of view, be no inadequate compensation for the loss. For as commercial superiority must always be associated with that of maritime preponderance in the great Indian ocean, the loss of our Indian commerce would not follow that of the territorial sovereignty. As long as we possess that great naval power in the west, which is likely to be coeval with our present free government, the harbours of Trincomalie and Galle will, more than any thing else, favour the permanence of the same power in the east. The dominion of the land may be more gratifying to the thirst of military distinction, but it is dominion of the sea which alone can afford security to commercial enterprise. The Portuguese might covet Ceylon, from the wide field which it offered for the propagation of the Romish religion; the Dutch might grasp at the possession with no less avidity, from its inexhaustible supply of cinnamon, spices of all kinds, and precious stones; but in a political point of view, it must be more particularly valuable to Great Britain, from its tendency to perpetuate her maritime superiority in the east. But, at the same time, I trust that, in the wise councils and magnanimous policy of Great Britain, moral considerations will not be overlooked in the midst of great colonial or political views, and that she will make her sovereignty of Ceylon contribute to the increase of civilization, to the encouragement of knowledge, the diffusion of Christian benevolence, and the consequent augmentation of the general happiness.

The district of Galle is certainly one of the finest parts of this valuable island; its climate is particularly good and pleasant; and the same may be said of the country extending from Negombo even to Hambentotte; a vast tract, containing soil of different qualities, and well adapted for various kinds of agricultural pursuits; but almost all of it towards Hambentotte may be looked upon as a desert, being covered chiefly with low-growing jungle, infested by wild beasts. The former once cleared, and the latter expelled, what an extent of land is here for settlers possessing some capital to covet; for here they can get men, not slaves, to work or labour for them at a cheap rate; say for coolies employed as porters, &c. twenty-seven shillings per month, and those for agricultural purposes still less, they finding themselves in every thing; and if additional numbers of work people are required at a future period, and as the country advances in agriculture and commercial improvements, why should not the hardy natives of Africa, especially those captured in slavers, and those to be had on the coasts of Mozambique and Zanguebar, be encouraged and assisted by Government to improve their condition in life, by emigrating to Ceylon; and let the Christian and philanthropist contemplate the benefit they would be conferring upon these poor creatures, in thus liberating them from that slavery and wretchedness to which they are subjected in their own land, and in giving them an opportunity of becoming free indeed, by embracing Christianity, surrounded in Ceylon by what to them would be comparative comforts and abundance. As these men require to be better and more substantially fed than the natives of Ceylon, it would, therefore, be necessary that their wages or hire should be higher, and in proportion to the work or labour which they are capable of performing.

The thermometer in this part of the island, as I am informed by those who have long resided here, had been noted as low as 73 degrees, and it was never known to have been higher than 85° or 86°. Fruits of all kinds were even at that period in great abundance, but various other kinds have been added, and the cultivation of most of them much improved, as I find from Mr. Bennett's Manual of Useful Information, already spoken of; he mentions the *mangosteen*, originally introduced by the Dutch; the *ramboutan; nam-nam*, introduced from Malacca; *rose apple*, from Java, partaking of the smell and flavour of a moss-rose; *sour-sop; roussail grapes*, purple and white; of these Mr. Bennett introduced seven sorts, from Teneriffe and Mauritius. In my time, they could only be brought to perfection at Jaffna, where even now they make wine little inferior to the best Madeira. *Lo-quat*, of an agreeable sub-acid flavour, the flower has the exquisite perfume of the hawthorn blossom; *star apple; limonia trifoliata;* English and Persian *melons; Canary almond*, a sweet and delicious nut; *lemons*, not indigenous; limes were, however, always abundant; *bladder cherry*, brought from the Cape of Good Hope; *pomegranate; figs*, they were abundant indeed in the Government-house garden at Galle, but, from my not knowing how to manage them, they were good for nothing; *lovi-lovi; strawberries* and *mulberries; stripe-leaved pine apple*, introduced by Mr. Bennett, from the Mauritius; *the Mandarin orange, the wampi*, and *the Marsan apple.*

The following are indigenous—*pine apple*, of which there are several varieties; the *orange*, the rind is of a deep green-colour, when perfectly ripe, and in flavour this most cooling and delicious fruit is quite equal to the best St. Michael or Barbary orange; the *shaddock* or *pumplenose*, an excellent fruit; a smaller species of shaddock is the forbidden fruit of the West Indies; the *Guava* grows wild, and is in the greatest abundance; *papaw, jar plum, wood apple, mangoes; custard apple*, very like an artificial custard; the *sweet sop, bilimbeing, koang, tamarind, Pharaoh's fig*, and *jack fruit*, a very large fruit, the pulp used in curries, and the seeds, when roasted, are not unlike chesnuts; *rattan fruit*, the *kattamba*, generally liked; the *wiereloo* or olive, very like the common olive; *Caffrarian lime*, used by the natives for cleansing their hair; *Cachew apple;* and *plantain*, of which there are several kinds, most of them excellent, and greatly prized as most wholesome fruit.

The whole of the indigenous fruits of Ceylon are produced in the greatest abundance, and can be purchased for a mere trifle. I ought here, however, also to mention that poultry at Galle are very cheap, viz. geese (taking the rix-dollar at 1*s*. 9*d*.), usually sell for 1*s*. each; ducks, 1*s*. per pair; Muscovy ducks, 1*s*. 2*d*. per pair; turkies (most of which come from Matura, and are very large and fine) about 8*d*. each; pea-fowl, 1*s*. 3*d*. per pair; common fowl, 8*d*. per pair; there are some other kinds of fowls, such as the Malay, &c. &c.; also several kinds of pigeons, all sold at equally cheap rates. Mr. Bennett also mentions, in his very useful Manual, that Ceylon bullocks, which are very small, may be purchased for about thirty to forty shillings each, and cows for less; (we always looked upon buffalo beef as detestable, and scarcely fit for making soup). Jaffna sheep (seldom good) at three, four, or five shillings each; Bengal sheep (which, after being well and expensively fed on grain, afford delicious mutton), and kids vary in price according to the demand for them; but I have known the former, when brought, on great occasions, to table, to have cost the entertainer, between the original price and feeding, fully half-a-guinea per pound. Now, however, sheep, especially those from the Cape of Good Hope, which thrive remarkably well, have been greatly multiplied in Ceylon, so that mutton for common use can be had on very reasonable terms; and I perfectly agree with Mr. Bennett, that too much cannot be said in favour of the fish of Ceylon, particularly of the Seir-fish and soles; to make sauce for which, prawns, from six to eight inches in length, and oysters and shrimps, are in great abundance, excellent of their kinds, and very cheap.

I have dwelt more particularly upon these heads than I intended, but my object in doing so is to shew persons intending to become settlers in Ceylon, how they may regulate their expenditure according to their means, or the capital they may take out with them; and they can thus be enabled to draw their conclusions, whether America, Australia, New Zealand, or Ceylon, holds out most advantages to emigrants, especially of a better class.

CHAPTER V.

"As when a weary traveller, that strays
By muddy shore of broad seven-mouthed Nile,
Unweeting of the perilous wandering ways,
Doth meet a cruel crafty crocodile."—SPENSER.

NATIVE WORKPEOPLE AT GALLE—AMUSEMENTS—GOVERNMENT HOUSES AT GALLE—TIGERS CLOSE TO THE WALLS—SUBMERGED CITIES—CORAL GATHERERS—ADVENTURES IN THE WILDERNESS BEYOND HAMBENTOTTE—ORANGE TREES—REMARKS—WHITE ANTS—FURTHER ACCOUNT OF THE PRETENDER—HE IS SENT OFF TO THE ISLE OF FRANCE—IMPORTANT OFFICIAL DOCUMENTS.

IT ought now to be mentioned, that the Singalese are very neat and ingenious workmen, and that they can imitate, with great exactness, any thing given them as a pattern, especially in ivory, brass, iron, or wood. Of the latter they have several excellent and valuable kinds, (for an account of them I have again to refer the reader to Mr. Bennett's Manual) particularly what is called calamander; the roots of which are very hard and more beautifully variegated than any other wood I have ever seen. Of this they make handsome dressing and work boxes, inlaid with ivory, tortoise-shell, or ebony; which are so well known that the crews and passengers of vessels touching at Galle always purchase them as presents for their friends at home; this they can the better afford to do, as they are usually sold at very reasonable prices. Quantities of jewellery and unset precious stones are also to be procured here from the Moormen, who are the principal dealers in them; such as catseye, ruby, topaz, sapphire, tourmalin, and cinnamon-stone—all of them found in Ceylon. Their gold work is well executed in appearance, but it is by no means durable, and most of the stones sold to strangers have flaws in them, or are otherwise imperfect. There are, however, elegant and expensive rose chains, as they are called, of very pure gold, made, I believe, in the province of Jaffna only, which are always got from thence by persons who intend to make handsome presents. It would surprise a European artist to see the few, simple, yet efficient tools and apparatus used by Singalese artisans.

There can also be had many really good articles of furniture, which are manufactured here by the natives, of different kinds of wood, but chiefly from that of the Jack-tree, which looks like inferior mahogany—they are sold very cheap, so much so, that it would be absurd to think of bringing out furniture to Ceylon from England.

The Singalese are, besides, excellent tailors, ladies' dress-makers, washermen, &c. &c.

I hope I may be excused for likewise mentioning, that I believe no people in the world have so few amusements as the Singalese; indeed they are not worth describing: but the Moormen are the most surprisingly expert people I ever heard of, in flying paper kites; and here this is not the amusement of children only, but also of men. They never, as we do, put long tails to them, yet they contrive to make them ascend to a great height, and to perform many curious but particularly circular evolutions, and to dart with surprising velocity in all directions, even coming down almost to the ground, and instantly going up again as high as before, and there remaining perfectly steady. These people make also what are called pellet-bows; with which, after a little practice, almost any one can shoot with great precision. I have seen a small ball of dried clay, sent from a considerable distance by one of them, go through a large earthen chatty or pitcher, full of water, carried upon a girl's head; and the water, to her great surprise, pour all over her very lightly attired person, without her being aware what could have been the cause, until she saw the aperture made in her chatty. This was sometimes the amusement of our young gentlemen, particularly during the heat of the day; but I never knew an instance when the poor girl was allowed to go home without being more than sufficiently paid for her chatty.

At Galle there are two excellent Government houses, with good gardens attached to them, of which the Commandant has his choice. One of them is called the King's house, and the other the Commandant's. I at present occupy the former, which is large, and contains several spacious and lofty rooms. The room in which I now sit is 132 feet long by 38 wide; but it can be divided, by large folding doors, into three apartments, yet it is only one quarter of the basement of the building; which, like many other old mansions in other parts of the world as well as in this, is said to be haunted. Here, the reputed ghost is that of an old fat Dutch Colonel, who died many years ago, when Commandant of Galle; and his spurs (he having been a knight) still hang up in the church upon a finely decked escutcheon. I have not as yet had a visit from M[eer] Von Hagel; but I attribute this to its being known, that I have always loaded pistols in my bed-room, which is that in which he is said to have died. My servants are, however, sadly alarmed at the stories they have heard, and talk of strange noises, which I know are occasioned by the large bats, which, as we sleep with our windows open, fly in and out of the rooms all night long. I have stated that I always keep loaded pistols in my bed-room to scare away ghosts, and I have good reason for so doing; as I once upon a time, got a sound drubbing from a strong flesh and blood ghost at Charles Fort, Kinsale, in Ireland, where there is a famous ghost-room, of which it became my lot to be the occupant. I also have not forgotten how completely I was plundered by thieves in this very house, soon after my arrival in the island.

Being desirous of making the reader still better acquainted—especially should he intend to be a settler—with what he has to make up his mind to encounter in this most interesting country; (and I must say that the more I see of it, the more I am pleased;) I ought to inform him, that the months of February and March are here the hottest of the year; for the winds do not blow so steadily as during the other ten. Almost daily, during these two months, dark and heavy looking clouds gather around us, and the sky assumes every appearance of a coming thunder-storm. Usually we have a few loud peals, succeeded by a fall of rain such as would astonish any one who was never before in an inter-tropical country; and it should be remembered, that Galle is little more than six degrees from the equator. The air, if it had before been over-heated, is thus instantly reduced to an agreeable temperature. The nights also continue to be cool and pleasant, and the mornings and evenings admit of our taking our usual exercises or amusements.

I was the other day much surprised when told, that a Tiger was caught, in a trap which had been set for him, not quite a mile from the walls of Galle; for I had no idea, though the jungle comes in some places to within half a mile of them, that they would venture so near in such a populous country. The natives, who came to acquaint me with what had occurred, requested that I would go along with them to see the animal, as, according to their account, he had carried off, within the last three weeks, no less than six children. The tigers, or as they are called, chittaws, are not by any means to be compared with the Royal Tigers of the continent of India, either in size or courage , yet they must be formidable foes to encounter. I am also informed by respectable persons, that they are constantly carrying off children, young cattle, or buffaloes, when they can do so unobserved; and that not less than twenty children have been snatched away, within the last fifteen months, in this neighbourhood. The people are, in consequence, always on the alert, to shoot or take them in pits or traps, which they prepare with much ingenuity, baiting them with pariah or almost wild dogs; but they have the humanity to place them in the traps or pits so secured that the tigers cannot get at them to devour them; the dogs are, however, known to have sometimes died from terror alone.

We are given to understand, that under the sea, and to the westward of Galle, there have at times been seen the ruins of towns, &c. long submerged: at all events, vast quantities of whitish coral, growing in the form of flowers, and branches or roots of trees, most of them being very beautiful in appearance under water, may be found in that direction. But, according to tradition, some thousands of years ago, a vast portion of Ceylon, containing many large and populous cities, sunk down in a great convulsion of nature; which cities, it is pretended, may still at times be seen under water. This, most probably, ought only to be looked upon as a perverted or fabulous account of the occurrences at the deluge, orally conveyed from one generation to another since that period. I am, however, told by my friend Mr.

M—, who has long resided in the island, that there are in the possession of the priests of a few of the more ancient temples, memorials written upon almost imperishable talipot leaves, in an old character, which are descriptive of this wonderful event. These, if rendered into English, would amuse the curious and credulous, and be suitable to the taste of the present day, when tales of awful and strange occurrences of all kinds, are so greedily swallowed by the reading multitude. I find these remarks among my memoranda, taken at this time, and I accordingly give them here; but the legend of the submerged cities is repeated in Major Forbes' "Eleven Years in Ceylon."

Some natives had, for weeks past, been requesting that I would allow them to procure a quantity of the beautiful coral to which I have just alluded, to make what is here called chunam; which is lime produced by burning the coral. Part of this they sell to be chewed along with tobacco, betel, and areka nuts; and part to be used as common lime to white-wash their houses, which gives them a remarkably clean and neat appearance. Having a boat at my command, I often, and very successfully, amuse myself in fishing around the rocks; but for some days past I have gone out in the morning with the coral gatherers; who thus proceed in gathering it, and in this method I think it likely that they were originally instructed by the Dutch or Portuguese. The coral being seen some feet beneath in the water, with its head, as it were, turned downwards, two strong pieces of wood, crossing each other at right angles, are let down with a heavy lump or bar of iron fixed at the centre, or part where the pieces of wood meet ; and at the end of the pieces of wood there is a sort of net, made of strong cord. The gatherers move about from place to place, in order that the nets may come in contact with the branches of coral, which are broken off by the wood or iron bar, when they usually fall into or become entangled in the nets. Where the water is not deep, long poles are used with the same kind of net-work at their ends ; and thus they contrive to bring up a considerable quantity in the course of a few days. According to an ancient Dutch custom, they offered to pay me, as commandant, a certain sum ; (and no doubt, they had supposed I went out to look after my share) ; but I begged leave, on this occasion, to decline exercising my right.

The following story will give the reader a correct idea of a part of Ceylon ; but, unless I had known the officer who met with such wonderful mishaps, and were fully convinced of the truth of what I am about to relate, I would not have ventured to do so. The hero of my tale is Lieut.-Colonel Hardy, Deputy-Quarter-Master-General of Ceylon, who, after a residence of eighteen years in the island, has just returned to England.

A short time before his departure, (according to my memoranda), he went to Galle to superintend the removal of detachments to Trincomalie in country boats, and as the soldiers composing them were volunteers from the regiments ordered home, and were very drunken and disorderly, he thought it requisite to accompany them part of the way, in one of the boats which he had reserved for himself. Towards sunset, when he found that the soldiers had become in some degree sober and more quiet, he made for the shore, intending to land at a place about five or six miles to the eastward of Hambentotte—Mr. Farrell's abode—and to walk thither. He went on shore with a bottle of brandy in his hand, which he had brought with him, and having also a small valise, which held a change of clothes, he wanted one of the native boat-men to accompany him, for the purpose of carrying it; but, to his surprise, not one of them would do so; and pushing off the boat, they left the greatly astonished Colonel alone on the sea shore, to shift for himself. But in place of being, as he supposed, only five miles from Hambentotte, he was, as they well knew, five-and-twenty, and in one of the wildest and least frequented parts of the island.

Having no idea where he was, he set off, bottle in hand, and carrying his valise under his arm. The sun was about to set in its usual splendour; it soon did so, and in a few minutes it became almost dark. He did not recollect the features of the country through which he was passing—he had not come, as he expected, to a river which he knew lay in his way; nor could he imagine, well as he was acquainted with the geography of Ceylon, where he was. The night now became quite dark, and he heard all around him the roaring or growling of wild beasts, and the howling and barking of jackals or of pariah dogs. Before he had gone far, the moon arose, giving only an uncertain light, but which enabled him to see, though indistinctly, from the thickness of the jungle, and the obstruction of a few tall trees, that the path before him was occupied by elephants. To retrace his steps, from where he supposed himself to be, was out of the question, and to remain all night where he was, he felt convinced would be certain destruction. Having therefore nothing else for it, he made up his mind to endeavour to pass them. While he was doing so they perceived and pursued him ; but, fortunately, he had then got farther than the part of the path in which they were ; yet as they run fast, and easily make their way through the thickest jungle, he was obliged, in order to escape, to throw away his valise ; and he was delighted to see that they stopped to look at, and turn it over with their trunks—thus giving him an opportunity to make off.

After several strange adventures, and very narrow escapes from buffaloes, other gigantic elephants, &c. (but how he had succeeded in doing so he could not well tell), he now perceived through the trees two large black objects, moving in the very narrow path just before him ; and here he had again no alternative, but if possible to pass in the same way that he had passed the elephants. They soon saw or heard him ; and to his horror he found himself in a moment almost within the grasp of two large terrific bears, which instantly made at him, and in so furious a manner, that he had scarcely time to call upon God to save him! By some means or other, he eluded the hug of the first bear: but he was hopeless of being able to avoid or escape from the claws and frightful teeth displayed in the extended jaws of the second,—when a kind of impulse, for which he could not account, caused him to raise his arm, and to aim a blow at the monster with the bottle which he still held in his hand. This, striking against the teeth of the animal, was dashed to pieces with a great crash, and the brandy flying into the mouth and eyes of the astonished bear, so frightened him as well as his companion, that, growling loudly, they both made off into the jungle.

Thus wonderfully preserved, he again set off, and ran and walked as fast as his legs could carry him; but after many equally narrow escapes, especially from some terrific buffaloes, which he fell in with near a pond, he could not perceive, to his greatly increased astonishment and alarm, (for he expected to have reached Hambentotte long before), any likelihood of a termination to his dangers and labours. He was now, moreover almost naked; his clothes and even his flesh being torn off him in forcing his way through the thick, prickly, and in many places almost impassable jungle. At length, having walked or run, as he calculated, more than twenty miles, he came to the bank of a large river or pond, of which he had by moonlight but a faint recollection; and, being completely exhausted in both body and mind, he threw himself down in despair and covered with blood, close to the root of a large tree, which stood very near the water's edge, and which, from weakness, he was unable to ascend. But, strange to say, he there fell into a profound sleep; and God only knows, how he could have been preserved from the wild animals, snakes, &c. which must have seen him lying in such a helpless state, upon the ground, during the remainder of the night; yet the greatest wonder is, that the alligators, with which the large pond or rather lake abounds, did not devour him!

He awoke—or, what is more likely, recovered from a kind of swoon—about sun-rise; soon found the path that leads to the ford, about half a mile higher up the Mallellè river, (it was upon the bank of the lake which it forms at its mouth that he had thrown himself down), where he crossed it, and, after about two hours walk, through a country with which he was well acquainted, he at last reached Mr. Farrell's house. But, unlike men in general who have been so awfully situated, and exposed to such imminent dangers, he said but little of what had happened to him, and only begged for a bath and clothes; and that a Dhooly (or sort of palanquin used for the removal of sick soldiers), might be got ready for him, in which, after a few hours rest, he returned to Galle, on his way to Colombo.

I hope I may be pardoned for observing, that nature, even in her simplest garb, is, in my opinion, far more engaging than the finest specimens of art to be seen in the largest manufactories or commercial cities. We soon become tired of constantly looking at what science enables men to produce, and of mixing in the gayest scenes in society; but in a country like this, wherein nature displays herself in such wonderful magnificence and endless variety, whether in animals, insects, birds, or vegetable productions, new objects are constantly presenting themselves to our view and admiration. It however requires, that we should possess an innate taste for such lofty enjoyments, or else, like the creations of art, they become to a certain degree tiresome, at least to a soul-less person. I remember an old mercantile friend of mine assuring me, that he considered the busy, bustling crowd, moving to and fro, and mixing with carriages, waggons, carts, &c. in Argyle-street, Glasgow, especially about noon, as the finest sight in the world—such is taste produced by habit.

Among the many beautiful and splendid trees * to be seen in this neighbourhood, there are none that delight me more than the orange; not so much on account of their fine fruit, as for their beautiful sweet-smelling flowers, and the agreeable verdure of their leaves; and in no part of the world have I beheld them in greater perfection than here. We read of an orange tree, which was growing in France, in youthful vigour, and covered with

* For a list of Ceylon trees, see Mr. Bennett's Manual.

flowers after it had been in the ground for many centuries. There was another shewn at Versailles before the Revolution,—and I believe it is there still,—called the Great Bourbon. It was seized with the estates of the Constable of Bourbon in the year 1523, and was then the finest tree in France, and supposed to have been at the time sixty or seventy years old. There were then, also, at Fontainebleau some other orange trees, that were fine even in the time of Francis the First. But when I look around me here, and make all due allowance for the superior vegetative powers of the climate of Ceylon, I am in amazement at the beauty and splendour of many of them, now bearing ripe and unripe fruit, the most fragrant flowers and verdant leaves, all at the same time. I observe, however, that they seem to have arrived at the greatest perfection in situations where they are partially protected or shaded by more lofty trees of a different kind, but apparently of the same age as themselves. The other day, I asked a respectable Singalese the age of some of the orange trees growing near his house. He replied, that he could not tell, nor could his father or grandfather; that formerly they made a good deal of money by selling oranges to the ships which came regularly to Galle; but at present they were of little or no value to him, as he had not been able to dispose of them for several years past, and it had been much the same with all kinds of fruit. Would it not be well to inquire if commerce has increased at Colombo, or elsewhere, in proportion as that of Galle has diminished?—I find this question in my note-book, and I feel convinced it would be most desirable that it were answered in the present day; and also, whether it be wise policy to exact high port and other charges or duties upon exports and imports?

Much as has been said by able writers respecting those wonderful and instructive insects, ants; and although I do not pretend to be able to add any thing new or more interesting, yet I hope I may be excused for observing, that I have for days past been amused in watching the termination of the career of communities of white ants, which here do such incalculable mischief to houses, &c. They are now taking flight from their curious abodes, in amazing swarms; but, after a very short enjoyment of their wings, they fall to the ground in thousands, and die; indeed, many of them seem to be dead even before they reach it. It is really wonderful to see how soon this description of ants disappear after they take wing; in doing which, if seen at a short distance from where they issue from the ground, they more resemble a cloud of dark coloured smoke than any thing else to which I can compare them. They ascend to a considerable height; there they apparently delight in the power their wings have conferred, but it is for a very brief period; for down they soon fall to the ground. Hundreds of birds, attracted to the spot, and other kinds of insects, devour multitudes of them; so that by the following morning, scarcely a vestige of the enormous swarm is to be seen! How wonderfully, I may truly say, are the ways and works of the Almighty displayed in this strange and most interesting country:—and how much I have cause to regret that the thieves who stole my clothes, &c. on my first landing here, deprived me also of my microscope, from which I expected to have derived so much instruction and amusement. I have been obliged to send to England for another.

I am informed, that a certain caste of the natives of Ceylon, as well as in some parts of India, make curries of white ants, and consider them a great treat. I have eaten and even relished frogs; I have tasted snails at the strong recommendation of a French lady, without being much disgusted with them; but I have not as yet taken a fancy for ants.

I before mentioned, that a Pretender to the crown of Kandy had been put into the stocks at Badulla; but I then little expected, that he was to be brought from thence under a strong guard, and delivered into my charge, in order to his being sent to the Isle of France. He was sentenced to die by a Court-martial; but the Governor had no intention of carrying the sentence into effect. It being, however, most desirable towards insuring public tranquillity, that correct information should be obtained from him upon certain points, I received instructions to announce his pardon; but previously to do every thing I could to elicit the truth from him.

Knowing that state or pomp has great effect

upon the people of the East, I assembled at the King's house most of the military in garrison, a number of native Headmen, &c. to be present when he should be brought before me out of the prison, in which he had the previous day been lodged under a guard of Malays. I now, therefore, ordered a British guard to take charge of and escort him to the large room, where I, with such attendants as were thought necessary, was to receive him. He seemed to have suspected what the sentence of the Court-martial was, and most likely concluded that he was now brought out to go through the last scene in which he was to perform a part in this world. He, however, continued firm, and did not betray the slightest fear or weakness.

He was a well looking man, about twenty-eight years of age, with an expressive countenance, and most penetrating eyes; and though he was in irons, and had only a dirty cotton cloth tied round his waist, reaching down to his knees, yet he looked a person of consequence.

I first directed every one but the Garrison Staff Officer, the interpreter and prisoner, to withdraw. I then asked him if he would faithfully answer such questions as were put to him; for upon his doing so his living or dying might depend. He said he was willing and ready to answer any questions put to him. I acquainted him that there was a ship lying at anchor in the bay; and asked him whether he would prefer going a certain distance in her, to a country where he would be well treated, or to undergo the sentence of death pronounced by the Court-martial. His fate, however, entirely depended upon his being candid, and telling the whole truth. He again said that he was ready to answer all my questions.

My instructions from Colombo contained those that were most essential, which being put to him, he seemed delighted, and expressed the greatest willingness to reply to them. My surprise, however, was great, when he told me, that the person I seemed so anxious to find—that is to say, the old Pretender, (who, it was believed, had caused the late rebellion of nearly three years duration, and who had hitherto eluded our search and vigilance) was, when he was sent off from Badulla, actually a prisoner there in charge of a military guard. He at the same time solemnly declared, it was that very man who had encouraged him to assume what he had been taught to consider as his birth-right; but he was now well aware that he had induced him to do so in order to ruin him, as he knew well his claims to the Kandyan throne; for he—the prisoner—was the nephew of Ramissami, &c. whom, he said, the British had endeavoured to make king of Kandy, about the period when Major Davie's people were massacred. He then entered minutely into particulars, to prove all he said of the old Pretender to be correct; and also named two Kandyan ladies, and two Headmen, employed by us in the Kandyan Provinces, who could prove beyond a doubt that Wilbawè, as he called the prisoner at Badulla, was the old Pretender. In conclusion, he added, that he had now told the whole truth, and that he was greatly influenced to do so, in order to be revenged upon the villain who had induced him to set himself up as king, with the treacherous intention of betraying and ruining him. That this Wilbawè is the illegitimate son of Rajah Singha; that he has a younger brother in Bintenè, who, he has no doubt, if even the elder is cut off, will one day set himself up as king.

How far this story may be true or false, I cannot pretend to say, but I have just sent off a copy of his deposition; and by daylight to-morrow morning the unlucky prisoner, Coomarasami, starts for the Isle of France; from whence he is not likely ever to return.

Whatever claim any of these men may have had to the Kandyan throne, the extraordinary documents, which the reader will find in the Appendix,* had completely annulled them. They will therefore, I think, be read with interest by many, even in the present day. It is, however, well known that there were two or three of the great Headmen who had signed the proclamation, but especially Eyhelapola, who expected to have been made king by Sir Robert Brownrigg, in place of Rajah Singha, who was dethroned for his cruelties to his subjects, and for barbarously mutilating some people claiming our protection; and it is more than probable, that Eyhelapola might have accomplished his object, had he only possessed some degree of firmness. It would have been easy for him to have taken the Governor,

* See Appendix J. K. L.

Lady Brownrigg, and all their attendants, prisoners, while they were travelling for pleasure, and to see various parts of the interior, without, I may say, any kind of escort, when the rebellion suddenly broke out. They were at the time only a few miles from where Eyhelapola, having assembled around him about three thousand armed Kandyans, had commenced the insurrection, by depriving a Dissave of his high appointment; but in place of proceeding with the requisite determination, he became alarmed at what he had done, and went in pretended humility, but, numerously attended, to submit himself to the Governor, who, it may well be supposed, under such circumstances, had to appear perfectly satisfied with what he had done. But had this really clever and influential Chief only acted in this instance as he might, and ought for his own interest and views to have done, and taken Sir Robert and Lady Brownrigg prisoners; and then dictated, as the condition of their liberation, his being raised to royalty, it is impossible to say what might have been the result of such a bold, and, in his case, necessary a measure.

CHAPTER VI.

"The sun has lost his rage: his downward orb
Shoots nothing now but animating warmth,
And vital lustre, that, with various ray,
Lights up the clouds, those beauteous robes of heaven.
. . . .
. . . . . . Broad below,
Cover'd with ripening fruits, and swelling fast
Into the perfect year, the pregnant earth,
And all her tribes rejoice. Now the soft hour
Of walking comes: for him who lonely loves
To seek the distant hills, and there converse
With Nature. . . . . ."—THOMSON.

SUBALTERN'S LIFE IN THE INTERIOR, IN 1820—REMARKS UPON THE STATE OF RELIGION, AND THE EDUCATION OF THE SINGALESE — PALM TREES, THEIR GREAT USEFULNESS—STRANGE EFFECTS OF LAND-WIND—TOUGH STORIES—MATURA, A DESCRIPTION OF IT—DONDRA HEAD, RUINS THERE—NOON AND EVENING IN A TROPICAL COUNTRY—CEYLON NIGHTINGALE—FIRE-FLIES—REMARKS.

IN order farther to illustrate the ways or doings of, as well as the life led by some Europeans in this interesting country, I must treat the reader with a few extracts from a letter, which I have just received from a worthy sub., a friend of mine, who commands a post in the interior, where he has been stationed for some time past. The soldiers he has under him are all Caffres, of the 2d Ceylon Regiment, except one European, his servant. He tells me he cannot spend money, as nothing can be procured for it from the Kandyans, who seem scarcely to know its use or value. The only expense he incurs, is in purchasing wine, brandy, tea, and sugar, which are sent up to him from Colombo, by a Parsee merchant, every two months. What he gets as rations, and the presents he receives from the kind and obliging people, amply supply his table; and a few minutes walk with his gun, attended by a pariah dog, which he has tamed, enables him to bring home pea and jungle fowl; but if he is at any time very particular, he can without much difficulty, shoot a deer or elk in the forest. The only returns he can make the Kandyans are presents of long pieces of white calico, of which he occasionally gets up several webs from Colombo, parts of which form complete dresses for both ladies and gentlemen, by being simply rolled round their waists, and allowed to hang down to their knees. Yet, without being influenced by such presents, they almost daily bring him plenty of fowls for curries, &c. and eggs and buffalo milk; so that in point of eating and drinking he is not by any means to be pitied.

He is obliged to deny himself the pleasure of reading much at a time, lest he should get too fast through his very limited supply of books; and as every thing has to be carried up the country to him, a distance of about eighty miles, by coolies, the weight of books becomes a serious matter. His principal amusement, as he is but little of a sportsman, is the cultivation of his garden, in which he grows potatoes, and various kinds of vegetables; but what he chiefly piides himself upon is, that he can sometimes treat himself to a well-rounded cabbage, raised from Cape or English seed. When, however, he wants a superior kind to what his garden produces, he has only to cut down a cocoa-nut tree, the top of which affords him a large dish of excellent cabbage; but he considers it a pity to destroy so valuable a tree for such a purpose. He represents the scenery around him to be both wild and beautiful, and he has plenty of time for contemplation. Some of his amusements are even boyish and laughable; such as pelting sticks and stones at the large bearded monkeys, that often stare at him in surprise from the tops of lofty trees. While he thus impertinently contrives to irritate them, which it is not difficult to do, they, in revenge for the insult, throw down at him cocoanuts, by which means he can usually command a supply. Those mischievous and determined plunderers, the jungle-crows, also amuse and plague him, as they boldly enter his room, stare and caw at him; and then, before he can prevent them, snatch away any thing on which they can lay hold. Their plunder they often carry to the tops of trees, to which he, or a Kandyan, has to ascend, to recover the articles which the barefaced thieves have stolen.

Though he always takes good care to be provided with loaded fire-arms, and to be fully prepared for whatever may happen, he is constantly at night roused and really seriously alarmed by the wild elephants, which have the presumption to come even to the door, and attempt to pull down the cocoa-nut trees, which grow around and even hang over his sylvan abode; thus threatening him and his people with instant destruction. But, besides the tops of the cocoa-nut palms, another strong temptation, which they cannot withstand, is the produce of his garden, especially his cabbages and lettuces. Of these they are so fond, that he is sometimes literally besieged by the animals; and they can seldom be beaten off, before they have eaten, or trampled under their enormous feet, almost every thing in his neatly kept garden. Upon such occasions, he and all his detachment have to get up, and put them to flight, by firing at them, lighting large fires (the materials for which they have always ready), shouting, and making all kinds of noises. He concludes the account of his situation and avocations, by saying, that the attacks of his nocturnal visitors are becoming so frequent, that he fears he must give up his garden; the produce of which is so enticing to them as to be irresistible.

Some subalterns are kept at such stations for perhaps two or three years: indeed, many of them, like Robinson Crusoe, become such "rurals," that when relieved, they greatly regret leaving the solitudes and occupations to which they have become habituated. My friend, however, liked his isolated retreat from the first; but, fortunately for him, he is not without mental resources; and he has now the prospect of being immediately employed by Sir Edward Barnes, as a superintendent of the Kandyan road-makers; and, in order that he may be able to act efficiently and usefully in that capacity, he is busily engaged in studying their language. At present, a narrow, and in many places, very wet foot-path, through extensive rice fields and thick jungle, is the only approach to his bungalow; and during the rainy seasons all communication with the head quarters of the district is frequently cut off by swamps, and a deep and rapid river. To this very country, however, many parts of which are so admirably adapted for agricultural purposes, I may hereafter call the attention of persons wishing to become settlers in Ceylon.

I have lately become acquainted with the Church of England Missionaries, the Rev. Messrs. Mayer and Ward, who reside with their families about twelve miles up the country, at a place called Baddagama. I understand that they went there at the request of some of the more respectable Singalese; and they are naturally expecting, under Providence, the best results from their personal exertions, and especially from their knowledge of the language of the natives. I find that in the year 1812, the number of nominal Christians in the Galle district, was estimated at 57,192; and of this number the village where these gentlemen reside contained 1,644; but the greater part of them were, I have no hesitation in saying, Christians in name only; for too many of them had become so with the view of securing their lands, and in compliance with an old Dutch law, by which they would have been forfeited, had they not professed Christianity. They have now, however, mixed up many of the ancient heathen religious rites of their ancestors along with such a proportion of their new religion as answers their purpose; but they, or at least most of them, continue to worship devoutly, or rather to fear, the host of devils they firmly believe in. Although the above numbers were, I understand, officially returned to Government, and although the country is populous, yet I have little hesitation in saying that, not one-tenth of them had more than a very slight idea of Christianity; and I must, therefore, from the information I have obtained from intelligent Headmen, consider the return to be altogether ridiculous. But the Singalese have in this instance shewn great readiness to assist these reverend gentlemen in building their houses; and Government has granted 2,000 rix-dollars towards a church. Mr. Mayer has, I hear, already established six schools for the instruction of boys, and Mrs. Mayer one for girls; yet, from what I have already seen and heard of the natives, I have no hope that these Missionaries, zealous as they are, will be able to make any serious impression upon the adult part of the population of the maritime provinces: indeed, I would look with far more confidence for success with the Kandyans, who have probably never heard the name of Christ, than to them. It is by judiciously established and well supported schools alone that we can hope to see any thing accomplished which can be relied upon, and that with the rising generation only. But how much and how loudly is every person in the United Kingdom called upon to aid the many excellent men who are now proclaiming the glad tidings of salvation to the benighted people of Her Majesty's vast Eastern dominions; and if we neglect this important and indispensable duty we shall undoubtedly, as a hitherto highly favoured nation, have much to answer for. I made these remarks at the time, and my apprehensions of the consequences of our neglect of this momentous duty have not by any means been removed, by the information contained in the annexed document, if it shews correctly all that had been done up to the year 1835—I shall, however, have again to revert to this subject.

For many miles on both sides of Galle, the cocoa-nut and other palm trees arrive at the highest state of perfection; but the usefulness of the cocoa-nut tree, in particular, is not I believe generally known, and therefore to this I must request attention. It affords food, drink, oil for light and other purposes, and when old enough, it is cut into planks adapted for house building, and for the construction of a class of vessels called doneys, which are used in these seas: the trunks are also made into canoes.

* See Appendix M.

The coarse fibrous stuff about the nut is spun into cordage of various kinds, and even cables, which float in water and are strong enough to hold the largest ships, are made of it, and found to be very durable. This stuff is also made into nets and lines by the fishermen; and the native ships and vessels have their rigging of the cordage, and their sails of a kind of coarse cloth, manufactured from it. It is likewise made into beds; and some of the inhabitants of the Maldive and other islands in the Indian Ocean are even clothed with it. The wood is also worked up into furniture for the houses of the more respectable classes of natives; and the various articles of this description are very cheap in Ceylon. The nut-shells are formed into cups and other domestic utensils. The houses in general are thatched with palm-leaves, which are neatly woven together for this purpose, and they are also wrought into mats, sacks, baskets, and brooms. If a branch is cut off near the top of a particular kind of palm, an aperture is thus made, out of which flows the sap, into a vessel placed for the purpose of receiving it: in this place it is called toddy, and is drunk by many persons early in the morning, before it is heated or caused to ferment by the powerful rays of the sun. It then, in some measure, resembles champagne in its effervescent qualities; and is considered by most people as an agreeable, useful beverage, for with some it acts as a gentle aperient. From toddy, sugar and vinegar are made, and when distilled, vast quantities of a kind of arrack are procured from it. Toddy, in a state of fermentation, serves for barm in making bread, &c. In short, there is no end to what may be said of the usefulness of these trees ; and the greatest injuries done to the Kandyans by our troops, during the late rebellion, were the destruction of the palm-trees (many of which were wantonly cut down), and laying waste their rice grounds, by breaking down the immense mounds or embankments constructed to retain the water, so essential in the cultivation of this grain, and which it must take years to repair or replace. The effects of this, and consequent starvation, are still so much felt, that I hear it is common for the people, in the Kandyan provinces which suffered most, to dispose of their cattle, many of which had become almost wild in the jungle, for rice, or money to enable them to purchase it ; so that some gentlemen, who speculated in this way, have become the owners of vast herds of cattle. A Captain of one of the Regiments told me, the other day, that he had thus acquired upwards of 500 head of cows and bullocks, besides many excellent working buffaloes, which animals are chiefly used in Ceylon for agricultural purposes.

The district of Matura has just been added to that of Galle; so that my command is thus made an extensive one ; and I have been informed, that it may probably be extended to Hambentotte, and that I am likely to be stationed here for some time to come ; but certainly not as an idler—such a character does not suit Sir Edward Barnes. To this I have no objection whatever; as the country is not only very healthy, but also agreeable; and, as I have at present various amusements in view, as well as objects of importance to attend to, I intend soon to visit many parts of it. I must, I find, reside occasionally at Matura, where there is a most comfortable and pleasantly situated Commandant's house. Matura stands upon the bank of a fine river, out of which, as I am informed by my Staff Officer, or Aide-de-camp, who was once stationed there, the alligators often came to steal the ducks or geese feeding on the lawn. But I am daily becoming anxious to see more of this really charming country; and now only wait to finish some business in which I am engaged, before I set out for Matura, as well as to visit a part of the district beyond it, if I can manage, at this season, to go so far. In the mean time, I think it right to remark that, judging from what I am told by several persons, upon whose veracity I can depend, the land wind in this part of the world, especially about Tangalle, has most surprising and even ridiculous effects; and it ought to be very carefully guarded against. For if a person sleeps exposed to its influence, it is more than probable that he will be attacked, if not with violent rheumatism, at least with severe pains in his bones, or all over him. I do not pretend to say that any instance of the kind, which I have had the power of inquiring into, has occurred since I have been here, but it is asserted, that some gentlemen have had their hair turned *quite grey by it in a single night;* and I certainly had mine most magnificently curled by it, to the great amusement of several persons who called upon me the following day. I asked one or two of them how it could have happened?—the usual reply was—"O, it was only the land wind." But they even venture to assert, that some persons have had their faces twisted by it in the most extraordinary and ridiculous manner; and that the distortions have been known to remain for weeks or months, and in some instances to have become permanent. But with the most perfect safety, we can sleep exposed to the delightfully refreshing sea breezes, almost without covering of any kind.

By incredulous and cautious persons the following may be thought a tough story; yet I cannot resist the temptation (and it is well the reader should be prepared for what he may expect to hear by and by) of mentioning, what has just been told me by a friend of mine, a civilian, holding a high official appointment, and who is now staying with me. He was once upon a time travelling through the jungle, somewhere between Batticaloa and Kattregam, when a wild boar suddenly attacked his palanquin; upon which the bearers instantly threw it down with him in it, and, along with a servant and some other attendants, fled in the greatest terror, leaving him on the narrow path to the mercy of his assailant. The side or sliding doors of the palanquin were at the moment nearly closed; yet, notwithstanding they were so, the furious brute contrived to bolt through both,and as he passed, he tore my friend's leg with his tusks in a most dreadful manner!—I suppose something approaching to incredulity must have been expressed in my countenance; for, in confirmation of what he asserted, he pulled up his trousers, and shewed me some deep scars in his leg, which were, certainly, not likely soon to be obliterated. This is undoubtedly, though true, a staggerer. But my friend Mr. Farrell has now a native servant on his establishment, who, in a hunting or shooting excursion, was actually tossed by a furious buffalo up into a tree, in which he stuck fast *unhurt*, fully thirty feet from the ground; and though, it may be well supposed that he was greatly astonished, he was delighted at having got off so cheaply!

Passing over the occurrences of about a month, and matters which need not be brought to the reader's notice, I find what follows among my memoranda. I now go frequently to Matura for amusement, and change of air and scene. My house there is good, but I have not as yet occupied it, having been induced to take up my abode with the Collector, who is a well-informed and most agreeable companion. The provincial Judge too, evinces as strong a desire to be both friendly and sociable, and this, the reader should be aware, is a matter of considerable importance here, where society is so limited.

Matura stands upon a low neck of land; the sea, at this season, dashing furiously on the beach, close to one side of it; and a noble and most beautiful river flows gently upon the other side. From a neat bridge, there is a fine view of the river, which has at its mouth (like most of the rivers I have already mentioned) very much the look of a lake. In front, and at the distance of about five hundred yards, an extensive wood of palm-trees appears to advantage ; and in the rear of the fort, there is a considerable town inhabited by Dutch, Portuguese, and Singalese ; but which is entirely concealed from the fort by a grove of old and fine trees of various kinds. The fort itself, which, like Galle, is ornamented and shaded by beautiful tulip trees, contains only the Commandant's, the Judge's, and the Collector's houses ; a Church and barracks for about a hundred soldiers, with good quarters for officers in proportion. In short, it is a charming place, situated in an enchanting country, always greatly liked by those stationed there ; and a settler may rely upon finding its neighbourhood a perfect paradise to reside in.

The road, I may say, the whole way from Galle to Matura, is good ; running close to the beach, and occasionally through really fine scenery ; it is also so well shaded by tall palm-trees, that the rays of the sun, even at noon, can seldom reach those who are travelling along it. Soon after passing a small village, called Kogal, situated upon the sea shore, and about nine miles from Galle, there is a large river, that likewise expands into a lake, which is crossed at its mouth in large ferry boats. At Balligam, more than half-way, there is to be seen a figure sculptured in a rock, of about ten or twelve feet in height, which is said to be that of a Rajah. The people tell me that it has stood there for many hundreds of years; and upon a well wooded hill near it is a finely situated temple of great antiquity. Both are well worthy of a visit, especially the latter, as from it there is one of the finest views imaginable, including Balligam's enchanting rocky bay, dotted with little wooded islands. There is also here a good rest-house, where I usually breakfast; for when travelling in Ceylon, we almost always take with us our cooks and other servants, in order that we may get along not only independently but also comfortably. From thence I send on my servants; and having allowed the heat of the day to pass, I perform the remainder of the journey in the cool of the evening, on horse-back, and so as to get to Matura in time for dinner. It may be very convenient, and to the taste of some people, to be carried in a palanquin, but I cannot endure it, as it invariably heats me exceedingly; so much so, that I intend never to submit to the annoyance it occasions, unless I am obliged to take a long and rapid journey.

About four miles from Matura, Dondra head presents itself—a bold promontory, almost entirely covered with trees of different kinds; it is a very fine and striking object, in a view which every one must admire. This is the point which ships generally make in approaching the island; and from whence they also take their departure. It is situated within a few miles of the 6th degree of north latitude. I never went to the low and seemingly rugged point, on which stands something like a pillar of considerable height; but the rocky substance of which the promontory is composed, being of a bright yellow and reddish colour, it contrasts strongly with the ever-green woods above it, and presents a kind of uncommon scenery, rarely to be found in any part of the world. On the highest point of the promontory, where I one day spent fully two hours, enjoying the fine views, and the cooling breeze from the ocean, is a small rude temple, and the grave, as the people say, of a god or devil, only twenty feet in length. They told me, with great gravity, that he often gets up in the night to regale himself with boiled rice, and a drink of pure water; and both are therefore always kept in readiness for him. His allowance is certainly liberal, in proportion to his supposed size, and the poor people's credulity; and it is therefore not at all surprising that his priests look fat and sleek. I could not resist the temptation of desiring the interpreter to say to the one in attendance at the temple that I hoped he believed in his god having a good appetite? He looked slyly at me, and in a way which made me fancy that, had we been alone, he would have laughed.

Lower down, on one side of the promontory, and amidst native houses and palm trees, are to be seen a great number of stone pillars, which may, at a remote period, have been part of a magnificent building of some kind or other, probably a temple. It is said, but upon what authority I know not, to have been erected by Hindoos, who, many centuries ago, under a warlike leader, conquered this island. These ruins are well deserving of a visit from a stranger; and should he have a turn for investigating antiquities, he will find much here to interest him and excite his curiosity; especially if he should be one of those enthusiasts, who attach importance to legends of Boodhoos, their achievements and incarnations. Those legends, however, ought at least by us to be looked upon as the vestiges of an early corruption of the true faith; and as belonging to a system of religion which had its origin, probably, in the traditions of the promise made in paradise of the Messiah; of which, no doubt, mention was made by Noah and his family after the flood; and conveyed to various parts of the earth by their descendants, at the period of the confounding of the one tongue or language, and consequent dispersion of mankind.

It has been well and justly remarked, by an elegant writer, that the district of Matura possesses many picturesque beauties. "Some times venerable and majestic trees formed a shade over our heads; sometimes we travelled amidst flowering shrubs; sometimes through cultivated meadows and fields of smiling corn. Nature breathes around an eternal spring; flower blossoms and fruits adorn the woods at all seasons. A vast wilderness of noble plants rises in ten thousand beautiful landscapes, displaying a majesty and richness of scenery and raising emotions of delight and admiration, which cannot easily be described." This certainly is a very vivid and fascinating description of a country, and in this instance it is a correct one. But how often have I felt afterwards, in passing through or residing in the forests of Ceylon, how awfully impressive is the stillness of noon! Every animal seeks the deepest shade. The fish conceal themselves at the bottom of rivers or lakes, except where the over-hanging foliage screens them from the rays of a too fervid sun. Not a bird is on the wing; and all nature seems as it were to be at rest, were it not that the almost appalling silence is broken only to be made the more impressive, by the continued low buzz or humming of thousands of insects. How powerfully have I felt, in the thickly-wooded neighbourhood of Matura, all this combination of the great and little of so much that is wonderful in nature! But as soon as the evening begins to be somewhat cool, the world seems again to start into new life. Every creature is in motion, and in search of its prey, or of the food it requires of some kind or other, which the Almighty has so bountifully provided for them all. The wild-fowl, of various kinds, fly in large flocks towards their haunts; the Pea and Jungle fowl call their respective broods around them for the night; even the Jackal begins to howl for its prey. Numbers of flowers, which had closed their leaves before the scorching beams of the sun, now gently unfold them, to remain open to receive the dew which usually falls so abundantly. Here also the pretty moon-flower among the rest, the leaves of which had been shut all the day, opens completely as if to behold the sun's grandeur, as he takes his leave of us in surprising brilliancy? I may be an enthusiast in fine scenery, and in my admiration of nature's perfections and loveliness; but I declare, that to behold them, as here displayed, would in my opinion amply make up for the inconveniences and annoyances attendant upon a long voyage; for the impressions they leave upon the mind can never be truly described, or if felt expressed.

It is generally believed, that birds within the tropics, though they have much more splendid plumage than those we find in Europe, cannot sing: this is not the case here; for several of them have the sweetest notes I ever listened to; and one in particular sings so delightfully as to have acquired the name of the Ceylon Nightingale, from its notes being heard for some time after sunset. But, even when the moon does not afford what may be here truly called her silvery light, we do not always remain in that profound darkness I have before spoken of; for no one, who has not beheld it, can form an idea of the effect produced at night by thousands and tens of thousands of Fireflies and other insects, which emit phosphoric light! I have taken one of them, and put it inside the glass of my watch, and have been able to see the hour distinctly by its flickering light.

I need here scarcely remark, that the districts of Galle and Matura, and the parts of the island to a considerable extent around them, (and I have yet to speak of the fine, interesting and sporting country inland from them), are those to which I particularly beg the attention of persons intending to settle in Ceylon. I would recommend them—if they do not arrive there—to lose no time in finding their way to Galle; where they can hire a house, at a moderate rent, for a few months; in which they can reside comfortably, respectably, and without incurring unnecessary expense; and they can thus have ample time to look about them, make all their arrangements, and decide as to the part of the island in which they may consider it most desirable, and consonant to the objects they have in view, to establish themselves permanently. This cannot be done so cheaply at Colombo. I trust, however, I may be pardoned for saying, that it would not only be humane but wise policy, on the part of Government, to afford such persons every assistance; and whatever their objects may be, to aid them in removing the obstacles which stand, or are designedly thrown, in the way of their being able to settle themselves as speedily and economically as possible; for their future prosperity, as well as their becoming desirable colonists, in a great measure, depend upon this.

CHAPTER VII.

> "God made the country, and man made the town.
> What wonder then, that health and virtue, gifts
> That can alone make sweet the bitter draught
> That life holds out to all, should most abound
> And least be threaten'd in the fields and groves?"—COWPER.

GOVERNMENT ESTABLISHMENT FOR BREEDING HORSES IN DELFT ISLAND—CUTCH HORSES—AN ACCIDENT—STRANGE OCCURRENCE—A BOY CARRIED OFF BY A TIGER—DIGNITARIES OF THE LAW IN CEYLON—REMARKS—EXCURSION UP THE GIUNDURA RIVER—SIR EDWARD BARNES'S EXTENDED VIEWS FOR PROMOTING THE WELFARE OF THE ISLAND—GALLE VINDICATED FROM LORD VALENTIA'S ASPERSIONS—EXCURSION TO, AND AMUSEMENTS AT, KOGAL LAKE—GREAT WANT OF FEMALE SOCIETY AT OUT STATIONS, &c.

WHEN I left Ceylon, there was, (and I believe it is still kept up), a Government establishment in Delft island, off the coast of Jaffnapatam, where a number of horses were bred; but, whether from want of due attention in procuring the proper blood or race of horses, from which the stock were originally propagated, or whatever else might have been the cause, they were not held in high estimation, and were considered not to be worth, (when any of them could be purchased), the prices usually demanded for them. Yet this expensive establishment consisted of a Superintendent, a Clerk and

Secretary, a Clerk of the Stud, Interpreter, and a Maniagar of Delft. When, therefore, country vessels occasionally brought cargoes of cheap and inferior horses to the island from Cutch, and other parts of the continent, they were soon bought up upon speculation, though it was known that few of them turned out well. As an instance of this, I beg to mention, that I was riding the other evening, on what is called the Circular road, with Captain L—— of the 73d Regiment; and when going at a hand gallop, his horse—one of these Cutch brutes lately imported—contrived to turn suddenly round, and to kick at me, (not at my horse), with surprising fury. He, however, fortunately missed his aim, as far as it was directed at me, but he completely ruined the handsome Arab I rode; for he literally broke his thigh bone to pieces high up. Such was the violence of the kick, that my poor animal had very nearly fallen under me, and, considering the rate at which we were at the time going, it is surprising that I was able to keep him up until I could dismount. When this occurred, we were about three miles from Galle; and it being at once evident that the beast could not be cured, I sent off for a musket, my blubbering horse-keeper, who had long and faithfully served Colonel MacDonald of the 19th Regiment;—horsekeepers always contrive to keep up with us, and are in general greatly attached to the horses of which they have the care. On the return of my messenger, the sufferings of my Arab were instantaneously terminated.

Captain L—— was, as it may be supposed, greatly distressed at what had so unluckily happened, but he was not to blame; for though he was aware that Cutch horses are almost always vicious, yet, judging from what he had seen of his, he imagined that he was not so. The Arab steeds, however, which we so much covet, are rarely vicious. I had lately paid about seventy guineas for this fine animal; and as I was convinced it would be difficult to procure another like him in the island, I decided that it would be best to send off at once my horse-keeper to Madras for another, (the grass-cutter went along with him), which will probably cost me from eighty to a hundred guineas, including expenses upon the road, the passage to Ceylon, &c. All this made good horses very dear at that time; but I am glad to find, from a return which I intend to introduce when I come to speak of agricultural produce, stock, &c., that horses have of late years greatly increased in numbers, and consequently are now much lowered in price.

I must here mention what I find among my memoranda. A few evenings ago, a friend of mine, Dr Evers, who has the charge of the medical department in this district, had, with some other officers, come to dine with me, and whilst waiting till dinner should be announced, we were all walking backwards and forwards in the long verandah in front of the house; when four large hanging lamps, which had been previously burning brightly, were suddenly and to our great surprise extinguished.

Candles were also burning in shades on the table at the time ; so that I was able to take one of them to aseertain the cause of this extraordinary occurrenee ; for the lamps being suspended inside glass shades also, the wind eould not possibly have blown them out. Our surprise was, therefore, great indeed, to find, that they had aetually been put out by a large floek of bats, which had flown into the shades ; and in which they lay so thiek, one over another, as to eover over the now scareely smoking burners !

I am well aware, indulgent reader, that I must never fail to keep thc worthy Baron Munchausen beforc my eyes, when giving accounts of the strange oceurrences which so commonly take place in this extraordinary and interesting part of the world ; nor must I ever forget the treatment thc celebrated travcller Bruce met with from the world in gcneral, but especially from the now proved to be unnecessarily ineredulous and bigoted reviewers of his works : but in spite of all this, I must mention what has just happened. A very fine Singalese boy, well known to me, has been earried off from his father's door, not above a mile from the fortress, by one of our troublesome neighbours—a tiger. Upon hearing the cries of the poor fellow, the whole family instantly set off in pursuit of the tiger, and were soon able to rescue the boy from his elutehes ; but before they eould aceomplish this, he was almost dcad, and so dreadfully laeeratcd that he breathed his last in a few minutes. This distressing event grieved me so much, (for I had frequently amused myself in trying to make the boy understand the very few words I have acquired of Singalese), that I vowed vengeance against the whole tiger race; and therefore offered as a reward for every one produced, dead or alive, whether caught in a trap or otherwise, a certain quantity of gunpowder, which the natives cannot purchase. In consequence of this, four have already been taken in traps, constructed much like our cage rat-traps, only, in place of iron, they are made of tough branches of trees, bent over, and fixed strongly into the ground. The baits, as I before mentioned, are pariah dogs. When my now powerful and promising dog Bran was shewn one of the largest tigers in a trap, I was delighted to find that he was both willing and ready to attack him; but, of course, I would not allow my intended companion to run the risk of such an unequal combat.

As I think it may amuse the reader, and give him some idea of how we managed such matters formerly in Ceylon, I must acquaint him (and in doing so I have, of course, to revert to my notes) that the Chief Justice of the island came to Galle a few days ago, upon an official tour, when, as in duty bound, I had to be particularly careful that he was received with all the honours due to his exalted rank and station; for here he is, indeed, a most important personage, with an income of some six or seven thousands per annum. There is likewise a Puisne Justice, in the receipt of a comfortable salary; the incomes of both have, however, since been greatly reduced. When they travel in the discharge of their duties, they are attended, wherever they go, by a band of natives, armed with lances, and are likewise surrounded by a host of tom-tom beaters, who drum away with all their might, and by a set of fellows blowing, as loudly and discordantly as possible, the most horridly squeaking pipes imaginable; thus altogether forming such a ridiculous group, that it is impossible to refrain from laughing at the kind of absurd stage effect produced: indeed, I often fancied that it even surpassed the scene delineated so admirably by Butler, when he tells, that

> "To this town people did repair,
> On days of market or of fair,
> And to crack'd fiddle and hoarse tabour
> In merriment did drudge and labour;
> But now a sport more formidable
> Had raked together village rabble:"

but no doubt all this parade and show (so highly prized here by civilians in general), were supposed to make a strong impression upon the minds of the natives, and to increase, in their eyes, the importance of the law dignitary.

As you approach Galle, the road for a short way, passes close to one of the principal batteries; and, to perform our part in the august ceremony, I had ordered that the usual salute of fifteen guns (18-pounders) should be fired; whether intentionally or not I cannot pretend to say, but it was fired a little too late, and precisely over the heads of the escort, palanquin bearers, and other attendants, including the collector, principal judge, &c., some on foot, and others in palanquins, or on horseback; and it acted rather powerfully upon the nervous systems of most of them. This I certainly would have prevented, could I have reached the battery in time; and had I been aware that there were two ladies in the cortege, who had accompanied the Chief Justice, in order to see this delightful part of the island. No notice could, of course, be taken of this too marked attention, nor of the uproar and disarray which had been caused, partly by the guns, but almost as much by my staff officer's horse—another Cutch brute—running away with him, nearly through the midst of the mass of followers, knocking down or trampling upon some of them. I was greatly vexed at what had happened; but my having a European Guard ' Honour drawn up in front of the King's house, which had been duly prepared and embellished after the Singalese fashion for the Chief Justice's reception, by people sent by the Collector for the purpose, and my waiting upon him and the ladies, attended by a number of the officers of the garrison, immediately after their arrival, removed, I trusted, all unpleasant feeling, if any such had existed.

They remained here a week, during which time I had the pleasure of pointing out to them the finest and most interesting parts of the neighbourhood, or other objects worthy of notice. They then went on to Matura, in the same splendid style as that in which they had arrived at Galle, where the Judges also held a Supreme Court. I took care to arrive at Matura before them, in order to see that proper attention was paid to them there, and to prevent such another farce from being performed as that which had afforded so much amusement and laughter, especially to the subs at Galle; and again I had the pleasure of pointing out to them some of the antiquities and many of the beauties of that lovely, but rather too densely wooded district, which I think they cannot soon forget.

Since that period, great and important changes have taken place in Ceylon, in its laws, regulations, and even modes of administering justice, &c.; and I suppose we are to look upon what has been done in these respects as great improvements, and as calculated to benefit and civilize the people. At all events, they have been taught, whether wisely or not I do not pretend to say, to consider themselves of importance in the state; and, from what I hear, notions of equality with Europeans have been instilled into them, of which many thought formerly they ought neither to be allowed to have an idea, nor was it thought politic that they should ever imagine that they could acquire such an equality. They have, however, I must say, been wisely freed from performing certain duties, such as attending upon and doing absurd honours to great civilians, &c.; and also,—though the wisdom of this may be doubtful—from going to battle, or labouring without payment, as their ancestors were accustomed to labour of old, when called upon to assist in any great national undertaking, either personally or by deputy, as an acknowledgment that they held their lands according to a kind of feudal system in force amongst them, under their sovereigns, from time immemorial. Whether these changes, for most of which neither their habits, customs, religious advancement, nor improved morals, had in any degree prepared them, will be for their future welfare, or tend to the security and advantage of the British empire in this part of the world, time alone can shew; but we are taught by experience, that all sudden and ill-digested political changes are, at least in too many instances, dangerous.

At the period I allude to, (I speak from experience, and it is not likely that any great improvements or changes have since been made), all Europeans in office were more or less in the habit, probably in order to save themselves trouble, of leaving a great deal too much to the discretion of Headmen, who happened to be about, or in some way attached to, them; such as Cutchery or other Modeliars, Mohandirams, Interpreters, Corals, Vidhaus, Shroffs, &c.; all of whom acted under the authority of Provincial Judges, Collectors, or Agents of Government in the provinces, and therefore, in most cases, could do just as they pleased. These high functionaries, who in general were unacquainted with the language of the people, could know little more than what was brought before them publicly or in Court; for the natives were too much in awe of these influential subordinates to venture to complain of their conduct; and no one will, I suppose, pretend to say, that they were insensible to bribes. Now it would never answer for respectable European settlers to be brought into contact with native Headmen, who, if not duly propitiated in some way or other, could easily contrive to throw obstacles in their way, which they would find it very difficult to overcome. This circumstance, ought, therefore, to be duly considered in all its bearings, and such arrangements should be made, in time, as would obviate the inconveniences and annoyances to which settlers might otherwise be subjected, especially in first coming to the island. Surely a great deal of this authority would be much better and more safely lodged in the hands of respectably educated Dutch or Portuguese residents, or in those of European settlers, who may have been some time in the country, and have acquired a knowledge of its laws, customs, and language.

On my return to Galle from Matura, I set out for the interior, but in a direction towards the Kandyan country, in which, I believe, few Europeans have ever been. I had provided for the occasion, (as I did when I went with two friends upon an excursion from Colombo, soon after our arrival in the island) two good and well thatched boats; one for myself, and a gentleman who accompanied me, and the other for my servants. We set off by the canal which connects Galle with the Giundura river, up which we were to ascend; having previously arranged with the Headman of that part of the province to meet us at a certain point, so as to be ready to afford us any assistance we might require in accomplishing what we had in view. This man was under considerable obligation to me, for it had been in my power to render his brother essential service; a circumstance which had its due weight throughout the journey, not only with him, but with the people in general, and was, I believe, the chief cause of my being received—independent of what I was entitled to as Commandant of the district—in so really flattering a manner. So constantly and assiduously was I followed or attended, that the good people's over anxiety to oblige, became at last irksome to me. Wherever I landed, crowds of them were in readiness, under their petty Headmen, to receive and welcome me; and the ground was invariably covered with white cotton cloth, even down to the water's edge, for me to walk upon to the house which had been built or fitted up for me.

At the places where we halted for the purpose, the whole country was turned out to attend us to hunt deer, elks, &c. Upon these occasions, numbers of men, who seemed to delight in and understand the sport, went into the jungle, and extending themselves for miles, drove every thing before them towards the places where we were stationed in readiness to fire at the game as they bolted out of the woods. The loud noises or uproar of tom-toms, pipes, shouting, &c. especially the last day, when we were joined by a number of Kandyans, was quite as animating as such sports can be rendered by any Highland chieftain. We had, moreover, to look pretty sharply about us, and to take care and have our guns in readiness, as it was impossible to say whether an elephant, a tiger, a wild boar, a deer, an elk, a hare, a pea or jungle-fowl, of which there were hundreds, would make their appearance, perhaps close to us. We were told that two or three elephants and several wild hogs were seen the last day of our really delightful field sports; but none of them were driven towards us. We, however, fired away as fast as we could, and killed between us three deer and an elk—of which, being our first, we were very proud—some hares, and a deer not much larger than one of them, and many pea-fowl, &c.: in short, until we were tired of firing. No accident whatever occurred, which is not usually the case upon such occasions.

I have already spoken in high terms of Ceylon scenery; but what I saw during this excursion, fully equalled, if it did not surpass, what I had before met with; and any description of it, which I might attempt, would fall far short of the reality. The soil in all directions seemed to be rich, and the country to a considerable extent was occupied and well cultivated. We were particularly struck with one spot, where the river runs rapidly round the base of a hill, which rises abruptly fully four hundred feet above its banks, clothed to its summit with noble trees of various kinds. Farther back, were mountains which rose in succession, and whose lofty tops were then hid in clouds, that rolled slowly along them; their sides, however, as high up as we could see, were also densely wooded. On the opposite bank of the river, we particularly admired an exceedingly bright green cultivated plain, of a circular form, fully half a mile in diameter, terminated, or rather surrounded, by some detached hills shaped like sugar loaves, and entirely covered and adorned with magnificent and lovely trees decked in foliage of various hues. Here was combined together, and fascinatingly displayed, as bold and fine scenery as I ever beheld—it was quite such a paradise as that in which we may suppose Adam and Eve to have been placed. It is, indeed, a wonder that the natives have not selected it as the traditionary abode of the first parents of mankind; as they have long claimed this honour for their certainly enchanting island, and desire us to behold what has been handed down to them in proof of its having been so—that is to say, Adam's Peak and Adam's Bridge. At all events, the former, all over the east, is looked upon to be a sacred mountain.

Amidst this beautiful and striking scenery, and whilst planning farther operations, we were obliged, by very wet weather setting in suddenly and sooner than we expected, to think of retracing our course down the stream. To give the reader an idea of what rain is in this part of the world, I have only to mention, that an arch, ornamented with flowers, erected for me to pass under on landing, and fully ten feet in height, was in a single night overtopped by the river, which had previously been flowing gently along some feet beneath; so that in the morning, to our surprise, we saw it rushing and foaming over the highest part of the arch; indeed, it was soon after carried away by the flood.

Thus our agreeable excursion and sports were put a stop to; for, observing that, in spite of the rain which continued at intervals to fall, the people were still putting themselves to great inconvenience in following me wherever I went, I thought it best to start at once for Galle, and such was the rapidity of the current that in about eight hours we reached home, having descended a distance, as I calculated, of about fifty miles in that time. In going at this rate, I passed the Missionaries' houses I before mentioned, which are very prettily situated on the high bank of the Giundura, about twelve miles above Galle, and where I intended, on returning, to have stopped for a few hours, had not the state of the weather prevented me.

In making this excursion, I had other objects in view, besides amusement. There is a kind of road or path that lies upon the left bank of the Giundura, through Gangeboddèpattoo, to a village called Nantoonpitty, where it crosses it, and from thence is supposed to run, through a very hilly and mountainous country, to Ratnapora, in the Saffragam district. I was required by Sir Edward Barnes, who had always important objects in view, to ascertain if the Giundura was fit for boats as high up as

Nantoonpitty, and also, what was the state of the roads from it to Ratnapora, or to any part of the road leading from the latter to Alutneura, on the way to Badúlla, in Upper Ouvah. I had not, however, any intention of examining the latter upon this occasion, and was, as I have shewn, turned back by the weather before I had reached Nantoonpitty; my attempt, therefore, for the present, has been fruitless. Indeed, from the information I was able to obtain, the undertaking must be a difficult one, and can be much better accomplished by descending from Ratnapora than in ascending from Galle. Upon my representing this to be the case, I believe the attempt was directed to be made from Ratnapora, but I never heard the result. Yet, a line of communication from Galle to Badulla, partly by water, and partly by a properly laid out road, running through a rich and beautifully wooded country, fit for many agricultural purposes, and which, if sufficiently cleared, would also be pasturable, though it is now greatly infested by wild beasts, would be of vast importance to Ceylon; for thus, I may say, would be established direct intercourse between Kandy (the road betwixt that city and Badulla being already complete), and Galle, the only good sea-port on the west coast of the island. But where are now the means to be found for carrying out such a wisely conceived plan?—They have, I fear, been sacrificed to that spirit of modern philanthropy or insatiable hankering on the part of well meaning but short-sighted men, who long to benefit the whole human race; and in which, often injudicious, attempts they have already occasioned the throwing away of millions upon speculative views and unattainable objects. But it was well for Ceylon, that Sir Edward Barnes availed himself, in time, of what he found at his disposal; and hastened to do so much, upon his own responsibility, towards its permanent security and prosperity; much, however, of the latter has been attributed to the measures of his successors in the government.

Whilst up the country, I found, after a long search, some of the, even here, highly prized Rajah plants, as they are called. They have most beautiful purple-coloured leaves, with fibres running through them, strongly marked, as it were, with gold; and, judging from the high situation in which they grew, I have little doubt of their being sufficiently hardy to bear the climate of the south of England. I have just sent off, by a lady going home, six of these splendid plants—three for herself, and three for a friend of mine, to whom she has promised to deliver them, if they stand the voyage.

I hope I may be pardoned for intruding upon the reader's attention the following remarks; but, really, travellers do at times take great liberties, and also often see countries and the various objects of interest they contain in very different lights, or rather according to the humour they happen to be in at the time. I am, at all events, led to think so, from having lately looked into Lord Valentia's

Travels in India; from which I find he landed at Galle, and that he has honoured it and the adjacent country with his notice.

Although nothing can be much finer, or more striking than Galle and its neighbourhood as you enter its picturesque bay and harbour, yet Lord Valentia appears to have seen the landing place only, and evidently considered nothing else worthy of his attention. The right side of the bay, in going in, is formed by a bold promontory, almost covered with trees. Upon the side of this promontory, and towards the bay, there is a handsome bungalow, which, from its being well situated, and built in a neat and even elegant style, tends greatly to improve the view. In front, there is a low sandy beach covered with groves of tall palm trees, which extend down to the water's edge. The Collector's and Mr. Gibson's houses (the latter gentleman well known for his benevolence and hospitality), appear to great advantage, embosomed in rich and variegated foliage. On the left, Galle, surrounded by high ramparts, stands prominently forward; the British colours displayed on its lofty flagstaff, and more elevated points, adorned with flowering tulip-trees.

One would be led to suppose, from what his Lordship says, that the fortifications of Galle are of little importance; but in this respect he is mistaken; for, though not altogether modern, they are of considerable strength. He tells us, that Colonel Madison, the Commandant, escorted him to his house through a steep and narrow street. It certainly cannot be called level, yet it is *only fifty feet* wide, with a row of beautiful tulip-trees on each side of it. This street, when I arrived at Galle, had been much neglected; but it has now been put into complete repair, and some of the trees, which from great age were nearly dead, have been replaced by others; so that the approach to my house, (then Colonel M.'s), is really handsome, and must always have been so. There is a great advantage in this part of the world, in planting tulip-trees in streets or elsewhere; for when any of them decay or die, they have only to be taken out, and replaced by large healthy branches, which quickly take root, and before long become as fine spreading and flowering trees as the others.

I suppose, by what Lord Valentia terms a bason he means the harbour. But he must have been under some strange delusion; for in this *bason* at least twenty Indiamen of the largest class, and numbers of smaller country vessels, can anchor safely and conveniently; the anchorage, however, is not good throughout the whole extent of the bay. He farther remarks, that the air is cooled by the sea breeze; and Colonel Madison represented the place to be tolerably healthy—but he adds, "that there must be a complete clearing of the belt between the mountains and the sea before we can either reside in, or conquer it, otherwise it will continue a grave to Europeans;" and he then proceeds to speak of the situations usually chosen by the Dutch for towns. In these remarks his Lordship is now quite incomprehensible; at least, none of them apply to Galle. For I take occasion here to mention, that it stands upon a peninsula, on a rocky foundation, and is a good height above the level of the sea. At the distance of about seven or eight (or more) hundred yards from the walls, there are, as I before stated, some hills of moderate elevation, partly covered with trees; and upon one of them is built a handsome Portuguese Chapel; and though there are, here and there, numbers of fine trees, as well as patches of jungle, yet much of the country is not only cleared but well cultivated, for many miles back; and therefore I know not what he means by a belt to be cleared, unless an earthquake, of which we have no account, has altogether changed its features. In this space to be cleared, I suppose he includes the broad and level glacis or esplanade of the fortress, which at all seasons is covered with the most verdant grass, and has a small pure stream running through it, carrying off the superabundant water from the canal; and there has just been formed, at the end of this esplanade, and near to the sea, a delightful walk, on both sides of which have been planted, all the way to the large bazaar, tulip and other trees, which will soon form an agreeable shade, at all hours of the day, for the benefit of those going to or returning from it. With Sir Edward Barnes's sanction, numbers of additional trees have been planted upon the ramparts, and in such of the streets as are wide enough to admit of them; and the houses upon both sides of these streets being well and substantially built, and in general considered comfortable, I wish particularly to call the attention of settlers, having commercial objects in view, to the conveniences which many of them possess for such purposes.

Lord Valentia also talks of a thunder-storm endangering the magazine,—which he asserts is built in an insecure place; now the fact is, that at the time Lord Valentia was in Galle, there were then no less than three as good magazines as are to be found in any fortress, built substantially, years before, by the Dutch in places of the greatest safety, and they are still as good as ever.

It is true, that we have heavy showers of rain from both monsoons, but they are looked upon as blessings vouchsafed to Galle, and its charming neighbourhood; as they are the cause of much agreeable coolness, fertility and salubrity, though his Lordship seems to have fancied the contrary was the case. Having made every inquiry from the oldest inhabitants, Dutch, Portuguese, and Singalese, I cannot find that Galle, its district, or the adjoining ones, were ever unhealthy; indeed they have always been so much the reverse, that the wonder is that more people do not come here from other parts of the island, and from the Continent of India, for recovery of health. I made these remarks at the time; but for such a purpose I have yet to speak of the cold, healthy, and renovating Horton Plains, Nuwara Ellia, and the other mountainous tracts in the interior. As a proof, however, of the purity of atmosphere which exists at Galle, I have only to observe, that we can generally keep butcher's meat, notwithstanding the great heat at noon, for two (or occasionally more) days after it is killed. This they can do in very few places on the Continent of India, and, I believe, never in the West Indies; and it is surprising how little we are plagued with flies.

I must now, in concluding these remarks, beg leave to say, that it appears to me, that my Lord Valentia, in his day, took very undue liberties with Ceylon and its climate; but if we could divest our minds of the idea of absurdity, would it not be entertaining to read the full and true accounts, which some modern travellers and tourists are kind enough to give us of the manners, customs, doings, dresses, &c. &c. of the people of the countries through which they so expeditiously pass, I may say in a box, (for what else is a palanquin?) or upon horse-back at full gallop, as some of our great travellers proceed, especially through Asia Minor, and other eastern countries. Most of them, from severely felt but unseen causes of inconvenience, are very unfit to follow their leader, a hardy Tartar, and quite unable to describe objects, of which, *en passant*, they have scarcely had a glimpse.

But, having mentioned the dresses of the people of countries thus delineated, allow me to ask, where are such splendidly apparelled fellows to be met with, as the different grades of Headmen in Ceylon? An official document, or government regulation, on this important head, which is inserted in the Appendix, will prove this to any one who may be curious in such matters.*

On the road to Matura, and about seven miles from Galle, there is a small village, as I before mentioned, called Kogal, and a comfortable rest-house near the sea shore; and, at a short distance from it, there is also a beautiful lake. Thither I frequently go for change of air and scene, and to amuse myself in shooting and fishing in the lake and sea, both of which are, as old Izaac Walton would have said, well stored with fish. When last I was there, I observed that a Headman, who resides in the neighbourhood, looked with great contempt at the fishing tackle I was using in the lake, which consisted of one of our fine but strong silk reel lines, to which I had attached a Limerick hook, a supply of which I had brought out with me from Ireland; and I often had cause to regret afterwards, that I had not come out better provided with both, as well as with good gut. I imagined that I was doing tolerably well, for I was taking good sized fish fast enough, but he thought otherwise; and very gravely proposed to teach me how to fish, if I would go next day to a retired part of the lake, which he pointed out, where it terminates in a long and narrow creek. I proceeded thither in a boat at the time appointed; when, to my surprise, I found, that in place of using lines, nets, or large cónical baskets, as the fishermen caste usually do, he intended to employ two men

* See Appendix N.

to catch the fish; and I also perceived, as the water was clear, that they had contrived to drive into a corner, and to keep in by a kind of basket work, a vast number of large ones. The Coral now set his men to work, and down under the water the two men went, in quick succession, and they every time brought up a fish in each hand, which they threw into baskets held by the Coral and others to receive them. By this expeditious process, we in a few minutes, had more fish than we knew what to do with; and as I saw it was expected from me, I was obliged, though an experienced angler, and a pupil of the said Izaac Walton's school, to confess at once, and much to the Coral's delight, that I knew nothing whatever about fishing. I was really much amused; but this piscatory feat reminded me of what happened in France, when I was there on the staff of the Army of Occupation. One day, when the hounds were in hot pursuit of a hare, which was running well, and affording excellent sport, out started from behind a bank, a rather respectable looking Frenchman, who very coolly shot the hare just before the hounds; and who, when the huntsman, &c. reached the spot, seemed greatly pleased with what he had done, and at having so dexterously—as he no doubt thought—made sure of the game! Several whips were up in a moment, and the astonished Frenchman got some cuts, before he could be rescued from the enraged sportsmen, by others who were more inclined to laugh than to be provoked, and ready to make due allowance for French ignorance of our rules of sporting. Now my friend the

Coral's only idea of the pleasure of fishing, (like the Frenchman's eagerness to get hold of the hare,) was the securing quantities of fish; and he could not possibly have imagined that *playing* a salmon or ten-pound trout, for half an hour, could possibly be looked upon as sport.

There are two or three small wooded islands in this fine lake, literally swarming with flying-foxes; which I consider as the most extraordinary creatures to be found in Ceylon. They are, in size and colour, nearly like foxes in England. They have wings attached to their hind legs, which, when extended, are about four feet from the tip of one wing to that of the other; their hind feet are armed with long, strong, semi-circular claws, with which they lay hold of the branches of trees; and thus suspended, with their heads hanging down, they sleep during the day. I am sure that I saw not less than fifty on one tree, and upon the islet there were hundreds. Being anxious to get hold of one of them, to examine it closely, I fired a barrel of my gun, loaded with heavy shot, amongst them, and brought down five, which were only wounded. Such irritable, furious tempered creatures I never beheld; they contrived to lay hold of long and thick sticks, which we had procured to kill them; these they in several instances bit through, and it took many blows, well laid on, before they could be put *hors de combat*. The report of the gun produced a general alarm among them; and they flew about us, and their wounded companions, in such numbers, that I could have fancied myself surrounded by harpies, whose screams were in the highest degree discordant, and almost alarming. The Singalese boatmen begged for those which were killed ; giving me to understand that they were good to eat ; and of this I have no doubt, for they chiefly feed upon nuts and fruits of various kinds, of which, in a single night, they have been known to consume vast quantities.

In a neighbouring island, I found myself in the midst of a number of most venerable looking monkeys, with black faces and long white beards. One of them which, on account of his great size, was shot by my staff officer, who, with Mrs. F—, had come with me on this occasion to Kogal, was so huge a fellow, that we made her believe for some time that he was a bear. This elderly gentleman was likewise given to some of the low caste people to be feasted upon.

I cannot refrain from here observing how much, in a country like this, the want of female society is often felt by those who are accustomed to it at home. Mrs. F— could seldom, consistently with her domestic duties, and the necessary care of her five children, accompany, on such occasions, her husband, to whom she was greatly attached. When she could manage to do so, she never failed to render them truly agreeable to us ; so much so, that we always heard with regret the usual announcement, "that she could not possibly be any longer absent from her family ;" who had been left at Galle, they being as yet too young to be brought with them. Monsieur de Chateaubriand has beautifully observed, "that the wife of a Christian is not a mere mortal; she is an extraordinary, a mysterious, an angelic being; she is flesh of her husband's flesh, and bone of his bone. By his union with her, the man only takes back a portion of his substance. His soul as well as his body is imperfect without his wife: he possesses strength, she beauty; he opposes the enemy in arms, he cultivates the soil of his country; but he enters not into domestic details. He encounters afflictions, and the partner of his nights is there to soothe them; his days are clouded by adversity, but on his couch he meets with a chaste embrace, and forgets all his sorrows. Without woman he would be rude, unpolished, solitary; he would be a stranger to grace, which is no other than the smile of love. Woman suspends around him the flowers of life like the honeysuckles of the forests which adorn the trunks of the oaks with their perfumed garlands. Finally, the Christian husband and his wife live and die together; together they rear the issue of their union; together they return to dust, and together they again meet beyond the confines of the tomb, to part no more." Among my notes I find also what follows, (and I trust I shall be pardoned for thus concluding this chapter). It is perhaps unwise to dwell too much upon such a picture of domestic happiness, as it can only cause unavailing regret; for I am well aware, that as long as I remain in this island my days must be spent at our stations, where there will seldom be much society, or at least such as can be considered desirable. I therefore have been already taught to value what we now possess. Ceylon is certainly one of the most beautiful, charming countries in the world to reside in; but what we so much want, amidst its enchanting scenery, is the being to whom we can say, that it really is so; and in whose absence

> "Then the lily no longer is white;
>   Then the rose is deprived of its bloom;
> Then the violets die with despite,
>   And the woodbines give up their perfume."

CHAPTER VIII.

"And over him, art striving to compaire
With Nature, did an arbour green disspred,
Framed with wanton ivie, flowering faine,
Through which the fragrant eglantine did spred
His pricking armes, entayl'd with roses red,
Which dainty odours round about him threw;
And all within with flowers was garnished,
That, when mild Zephyrus emongst them blew,
Did breathe out bounteous smells, and painted colours shew."

SPENSER.

ARRIVAL AT BOVEGODDÉ LAKE IN A THUNDER-STORM—SHOOTING, AND ALLIGATOR FISHING THERE—SINGALESE LADIES; THEIR FAST FADING BEAUTY—THE CEREMONY OF CLOTHING THE PRIESTS—WATER FIGHT BETWEEN TWO ASPIRANTS FOR THE LOVE OF A DARK-EYED MAID—ANNUAL ARRIVAL OF COUNTRY VESSELS AT GALLE — MOORMEN DESCRIBED—PEOPLE OF THE MALDIVE ISLANDS—AN EMBASSADOR SENT BY THE SULTAN TO GALLE—OBSERVATIONS—GALLE A FAVOURABLE POINT FROM WHENCE EFFICIENT MISSIONARIES MIGHT BE SENT TO SEVERAL PARTS OF THE EAST—REMARKS—MANNERS AND CUSTOMS OF THE MOORMEN—A GRAND PROCESSION—THE DRESS OF THE MOORS—ANOTHER VISIT TO BOVEGODDÉ LAKE — AMUSEMENTS, SPORTS, ETC.—A KEEN PORTUGUESE SPORTSMAN.

I HAD now contrived to make myself popular with several of the Headmen, by trifling acts of kindness, and by exerting myself in various ways for them, when I could do so with propriety; so that I had only to send to any part of the district, and, no matter what might be the object I had in view, my wishes were always willingly and readily complied with. The people were, besides, greatly pleased at my going so often among them, and my doing so offered me frequent opportunities of gaining useful information upon matters otherwise not easily obtained.

About a week ago, I had requested a Coral to have a hut built for me at a lake called Bovegoddé; and I had sent my servants forward in the morning, to have every thing ready for me when I should arrive, as I purposed remaining there for a few days. I set out from Galle on horseback about three o'clock in the afternoon, expecting to have an agreeable ride of about sixteen miles before dark. The sky, however, soon after I started, began to portend a thunder-storm; and being detained some time longer than I calculated upon in crossing the Giundura river, before I reached Hiccoddé night had almost closed in around me, the thunder-storm had commenced, and I had fully five miles farther to go through the woods; but I was aware that the path I had to travel was not infested by wild elephants, buffaloes, or boars, from which we have chiefly to apprehend danger in many parts of Ceylon. Although pretty well acquainted with the path, yet I thought it best, in such a night, to take a guide with me from Hiccoddé, and the horse-keeper, as usual, kept up with my horse, a noble animal which he had just brought from Madras, and which I was delighted to see was not afraid of thunder. The country through which we passed, was in some places hilly, and generally thickly wooded. We had not proceeded a quarter of a mile beyond Hiccoddé when the storm attained its utmost violence and sublimity, and a more magnificent scene cannot well be imagined, than what the hills, rocks, woods, and water presented, as they were every instant illumined by most vivid lightning, followed by the roar, or rather tremendous report of thunder, and pouring of rain, such as the good people at home have no idea of. Being very lightly attired, in white jacket, trowsers, &c. and a broad straw hat, I did not mind a wetting; and my horse-keeper and guide's garments being still more simple, only stripes of calico rolled round their waists, and not likely to be much injured by water—we continued our journey, though I believe that both my attendants thought me mad to encounter such weather for mere amusement. I expected, however, soon to reach my hut, where I knew I should find not only dry clothes, but also a comfortable dinner and a bottle of wine ready for me. But when I arrived on the shore of the lake, I was both surprised and delighted, to find that such excellent accommodation had been provided for me; for, in place of a hut, which I had asked for, there stood before me a neat bungalow with a verandah round it, which I found contained three small rooms and a kitchen; and there was besides a detached shed, for my horse, horse-keeper, and grass-cutter, all of whom live and sleep together. The walls of the bungalow were lined inside with very white calico; the ceilings also were of the same material, and the whole was ornamented with the so-much admired Ceylon mosses, and flowers of various kinds, such as Glorina superba, common and water lilies, roses, jasmine, &c.; in short, my arrival at this enchanting bungalow, which stood close to the water's edge, and upon a small, level, and very green lawn, amidst the commotion and sublimity of such an elementary warfare, far surpassed any scenic display I ever beheld: in truth, it was well calculated to impress the imagination of an enthusiast like me with feelings both of awe and delight. Although the rain continued to fall in torrents, yet my friend the Coral, with two inferior Headmen, and their followers, were in waiting to receive me; but, after thanking them for all they had done, indeed overdone, I begged that they would return as soon as possible to their homes. I hope I may, however, be pardoned for remarking, that Europeans may be in Ceylon for years, but unless they lay aside their too soon acquired habits of indolence, and foolish alarms about wild beasts, snakes, jungle fevers, and other diseases, which keep many in a constant state of unnecessary apprehension, and accompany, in excursions like this, a Provincial Judge, Collector, or other person in authority, they can have little chance of knowing much of the natives, their ways or doings. All that I have mentioned had, on this occasion, been obligingly prepared for me by tho Coral, without my being allowed to incur a farthing's expense.

Whilst I remained at Bovegoddé, I had excellent sport, and shot quantities of water-fowl of various kinds; such as wild ducks, teal or widgeon. The obliging Coral, who sometimes accompanied me, one day told me, that if I would allow him, he could conduct me to a place where I might rely upon having excellent sport. Of course, I consented to go with him, and just before sunset, he brought me to a spot where the lake becomes so narrow that its banks are connected by one of those strange, high, single plank bridges, which are to be met with in many parts of Ceylon; and I can assure the reader, that to cross rivers or lakes by means of one of them, especially if they happen to be deep and contain alligators, is very far indeed from being an agreeable undertaking. I there found a seat prepared for me, as the Coral had no idea of sport attended with any kind of fatigue. As soon as it began to darken, the numbers of birds, especially water-fowl, which passed through this narrow opening, to roost upon the trees on the banks of the lake, and which flew low and slowly along, were considerable; I therefore had little else to do, but to sit or stand, and fire away until darkness prevented me from any longer seeing the birds. This was mere slaughtering, and did not deserve the name of sport, as many of them were brought down almost at my feet; the Coral, however, was highly delighted, and I had to appear to be equally so. The peacocks I had killed in the course of the day were the finest I had ever seen; measuring nearly nine feet from their heads to the extremities of their splendid tails. Being desirous of obtaining for a lady, in Galle, a quantity of the fine feathers of a bird which I consider to be of the bittern or heron kind, part of the plumage of which is like horse-hair, and as white as snow, I shot several of them, and also two of those strange creatures, flying-foxes. I had the day before, after a long morning walk and much fatigue, contrived to shoot two very lean deer, an elk, and two wild hogs; one of which being only wounded, turned furiously upon us; but a ball from my second barrel put an end to her headlong career, when she was within ten yards of us.

I was told by the people, that in the long and narrow lakes, extending towards the north, there are many alligators; and having expressed a wish to see the Singalese mode of taking and destroying them, they readily agreed to gratify me; and this led to my having most excellent and extraordinary sport in hunting, or I should rather say fishing them! They were not long in finding in Bovegoddé lake, and wounding with large and heavy spears a large alligator, which managed to escape from them into deep water. After a short search, they found another; but as he was only about fourteen feet long, they soon dispatched him with their long spears. There was no risk or amusement whatever, in this way of slaughtering them; for, when once the barbed spears were driven into them, they could make no resistance.

I soon became tired of and disgusted with this butchering occupation; and requested that an intelligent blacksmith might be sent to me from Galle, to whom I explained, after a good deal of trouble, what I wanted; and by making a pattern in wood, I got him to fashion for me, for next day's sport, a small trident-shaped spear or harpoon, which had a socket to receive a long handle, made of tough and pliable wood, which could be easily disengaged when the alligator was struck. In this way I fully expected to have the fellow fairly caught and held fast by the barbs. I also hoped that, by means of a line fastened to the harpoon, I should be able to play him, as we do pike or salmon at home.

Though apparently little satisfied with my contrivance, and inclined to laugh at the idea of my thus catching alligators, the people assembled in considerable numbers, at one of the deepest and more distant lakes, where alligators were known to be numerous, in order to see how I was to proceed; but, they at the same time assured me, that their mode of dispatching them was by far the best and safest.

I took with me in the canoe a Singalese, whom I had remarked the day before to be dexterous in using the spear, and who seemed to know where to look for alligators. Encouraged by me, he had not been long poking about among some tall reeds, which grew in the tolerably deep and dark coloured water, before he drove the instrument well into a good sized one. The wounded animal instantly twitched the long and pliant handle out of his hands, and away he went, dragging along the canoe, with us in it, in fine style, causing the water as it were to boil around him. In a few minutes, however, he became sluggish: and at last lay like a log at the bottom. We then paddled to the shore, and giving the greatly astonished and amused people the end of the line, they hauled him out of his oozy bed, already almost dead; the harpoon having been forced, notwithstanding the hardness of his back, nearly through his body, in which it held fast, as I expected, by the long and strong barbs—he was nearly eighteen feet in length.

Not long after, we had another upon our hooks or barbs, which afforded still less sport, and contrived to get away from us. But a third, of even larger size than the first, and which we were some time in finding, went off when struck, in the most furious manner imaginable; and, in giving him line, my companion awkwardly became entangled in it, and was pulled out of the canoe into the lake! As he seemed unable to swim, I instantly seized him by the large roll of hair, which they all wear on the crown of their heads, but I could not venture to pull him in, lest he should upset the small canoe. I contrived, however, to cast off the line attached to the harpoon, and which still stuck fast in the alligator, and then made for the bank, paddling as well as I could with one hand, and holding up my ally by the hair with the other, and in such a position, as to prevent his laying hold of the side of the unsteady canoe. Having soon safely landed him, he without hesitation got once more into the canoe, and we set off to endeavour to recover the line and harpoon, and perhaps the alligator, which I concluded had been too much alarmed to venture to touch the poor fellow when in the water. Luckily, we soon perceived the line about a foot under water, got hold of it, and gave a tug, to ascertain if our customer was still at the end of it—upon which off he went in good style; but had scarcely gone ten yards, when, like the first, he came to a dead stand and would not move. He was therefore similarly hauled to land, amidst the shouting of our assistants; but he was still alive, and well able to give battle, which he did stoutly, by laying about him with his tail, at the same time gnashing his terrific teeth, and uttering a strange sort of noise or cry. The people, however, soon settled him with their long spears and clubs.

Before my return to Galle, I had another day's sport of this kind; and I fully intend to have many more: the Singalese, moreover, had now become satisfied that my contrivance was not a bad one, though they still preferred their own safer and more expeditious plan; and in this idea they were confirmed, by what they in one instance saw; for a large alligator, which I had struck with the harpoon, rose instantly to the surface, within a yard or two of the canoe, and looked so fiercely at me, that I thought it best to send a ball through his head; which settled him in a moment. I had thought it well to have my gun with me; but it was so fastened to the canoe, that, in case of an upset, it could not be lost in the lake. I must now beg to assure the reader, that I never in Scotland, Ireland, nor in any other part of the world, had half such amusing and interesting sport from salmon, pike, or trout, as on this occasion from alligators; and should he be an amateur, and ever have the good luck to come to Ceylon, or to be in a country where such sport can be enjoyed, I hope he will adopt my plan, and try his hand at Alligator-fishing.

During my stay at Bovegoddé, several presents were sent me by some of the high caste people. One Lady, in particular, sent eleven men, each carrying a different kind of fruit upon his head, in a tray or a large flat wooden dish. I could, of course, only express my thanks for her kindness; for waiting upon her was quite out of the question, and altogether contrary to etiquette. But, notwithstanding their precautions or shyness, I have occasionally contrived to see some of the high caste ladies, both young and old; the former, who are by no means very dark complexioned, were often pretty, neat, and clean in their dress and persons, and they wear a profusion of gold and silver ornaments, most of them very large. If I might venture to give an opinion, in a matter of such importance, I should be inclined to say, that Singalese Belles would be much to the taste of Turks; as they have almost all a tendency towards comfortable corpulency. A late Monarch's criterion of beauty —"fat, fair and forty"—would not, however, answer as a rule here; yet even he, fastidious as he seems to have been, might have approved of many of them under twenty; but at a very early age, they lose all their beauty; and, too often become ugly, old, withered-looking hags. They likewise become confirmed betel-chewers, which greatly and quickly impairs that loveliness which they almost all possess when young, as it renders their really fine teeth, gums and lips—at least, to us Europeans—of a disgusting reddish colour. This, to Singalese beaux, is unimportant; they are not given to kissing.

I witnessed here a ceremony which I had not before heard of, and which amused me greatly. It was that of the women clothing the Priests of one of the temples, eight in number; and this I find is done annually, Cotton, of which vast quantities grow, I may say, wild in Ceylon, (and to this I request the attention of settlers,) is prepared, dyed yellow, spun, and woven into cloth—all in one day; and, as "many hands make light work," these drones stood in the evening at the shrines of their gods in new garments, before hundreds of the people. The ceremony was performed in the temple, to the deafening and astounding noise of at least twenty tom-toms, and several loud squeaking and squalling pipes, beaten and blown with surprising zeal and devotion the entire day, and which were distinctly heard all over the country.

I likewise saw at Bovegoddé what the people called a *water fight*, between, as they told me, two competitors for a dark-eyed maid: one of the lovers, the challenger, being highly exasperated by the pangs which the green-eyed monster—jealousy, generated in his heart. They both stood up to their knees in the lake, opposite each other; and, with their hands, constantly dashed the water, in a curious and expert manner, into each other's faces. I saw the combatants thus—I can scarcely say, hotly engaged, about nine in the morning; and, at three in the afternoon, they were still hard at work, and the battle was then still doubtful; for, according to established rule, whichever of the two warriors, no matter what may be the pretence or cause, stops first, if it be only for a moment, dashing water at his adversary, is considered to be vanquished. Hundreds of people were looking on, apparently deeply interested in the result; as he who is thus overcome, as they assured me, is never known again to aspire to the hand of the lady who has caused the antifebrile combat. What a pity it is, that this cooling mode of settling disputes, is not introduced into the Green Isle, and made to supersede the sprig system, so prevalent there.

I confess that, when business at last compelled me to think of returning to Galle, I left Bovegoddé and my kind Singalese friends with regret. I, however, promised soon to return, and the Coral, in order to induce me to do so, undertook to have the bungalow, &c. taken care of; and requested that I would only let him know a day or two before I left Galle, so that he might have the shrubs and flowers replaced by even more beautiful kinds than those which were now beginning to fade, and which I had so much admired.

The season has now arrived, when we daily see vessels of a strange construction and rig come into Galle harbour, from some parts of the Continent, and from the islands in the Indian ocean. The traders and sailors on board of them are as singularly and differently dressed; their manners, customs, religions, modes of thinking and acting, are also as various as the languages they speak. To a person lately from Europe, this is a very striking and amusing scene. Some of them come to dispose of their native commodities or produce; but the greater part to purchase articles of English manufacture to take back with them. As a mart for the people of the East, Galle has, however, greatly fallen off; and the inhabitants tell me that not a quarter the number of vessels arrive now-a-days as formerly; and they, I believe truly, assign as a reason for this, that the articles those strangers require can now be bought cheaper elsewhere. By far the finest race of men amongst this heterogeneous assemblage are the Moors, who are almost all tall and well proportioned, with countenances both handsome and intelligent; and the noble white flowing beards of the venerable looking old men give them a very dignified appearance. These Moors, or Moormen, as they are usually called, are a trading, enterprising people, with a very martial look; even their gait is soldierlike. Numbers of them are settled in Ceylon; but they keep up constant intercourse with their own tribes, which are scattered all over the East.

The natives of the Maldive (or, as the people call them, Mahaledive) islands, are also a fine, intelligent looking people; and we have directions from Government, to treat them, on all occasions, with every possible attention, as a mark of our high approbation of their humanity, and as a return for their kindness and hospitality to Europeans, especially to such as have the misfortune to be shipwrecked upon their islands. Their King sends annually by an Ambassador, as he is called, trifling presents to the Governor-General of Ceylon, and also to the Commandant of Galle; and, as the one coming here is daily expected, I have already been furnished with the present I am to make the King in return for what he usually sends.

It surprises me, that the people who annually congregate here from so many countries, most of whom, at least almost all of the higher castes, can read and write, and who are far from being either ignorant or barbarous, should be still so little advanced in the knowledge of navigation; especially as they have, for so many years past, been in constant intercourse with us, and have had every day opportunities of seeing how boldly our ships stand out into the ocean. Notwithstanding these advantages, they continue to sail at stated seasons, and before the periodical winds; coming with the one and returning with the other monsoon. During their slow progress, in their badly constructed vessels, they as seldom as possible venture out of sight of land; thus they are a very long time in performing a voyage, which to us would only be the business of a few days; in short, they are no farther advanced in a knowledge of navigation than the world was when Paul was carried prisoner to Rome. They know little or nothing of taking an observation of the sun, to determine even their latitude, and the instrument they use for this purpose, (when they use any), is of the most rude construction; though not much more so than the old quadrants, some of which were shewn to me in Portugal as curiosities, from having belonged to the early navigators of that nation; and which were, most likely, superior in make to those used at that period by the English. At night, the natives of India still steer by the stars, or more frequently, when practicable, they anchor close to the land, and wait for morning.

But the assembling at Galle of so many people from different countries seems to point it out as a *centre* from whence Missionaries of the Church of England might, if sufficient pains were taken, set out even at the express desire of some of the more influential merchants, when they return to their homes. The authorities of Galle, by a little civility and attention to such visitors, could easily gain their good will and confidence ; which would naturally be extended to the Missionaries, with whom they might become intimate even before their departure, and which would insure for them afterwards, and in the course of their labours, at least, respect and attention from their countrymen. On the part of the Missionary a perfect knowledge of the language spoken, and capability of teaching in it, are most essential points, which ought never to be overlooked, in the selection of those who are desirous of devoting themselves to the conversion of the heathen, or who may have to contend with the followers of Mahommed, with many of whom they must expect to come into contact. Ignorance of the language of a people, and only acquiring it by slow degrees among them, and in the daily habits of intercourse, as is too often the case, is much against a Missionary being able, however great his zeal, to inspire those whom he wishes to instruct in a new religion, with that necessary respect for himself personally, or for it. Indeed, an imperfect acquaintance with the language spoken in the country he goes to, gives the would-be teacher an appearance of inferiority, even in intellect, and certainly in argument ; consequently, in place of gaining, he daily loses ground, and ultimately becomes an object of neglect and even ridicule.

Seeing this great difficulty in the way of our being able to return of ourselves, or by the aid of others, to the true God, I am lost in awe and wonder, when I consider the inscrutable dealings of Providence with men. The confounding their language at Babel—as some have presumed to imagine—and their consequent dispersion throughout the world, had, as some suppose, the effect of producing all the various systems of idolatry and absurdity, always and still so prevalent; but what are they all, but corruptions of the one true religion established in Paradise, of which they still retain some of the principles or emblems? These, by degrees, were further corrupted, and continued to be more and more so, by always erring mortals, until a knowledge of their Creator and Preserver was entirely lost on earth, except where He himself, who declares that, "My ways are not your ways, and My thoughts are not your thoughts," was graciously pleased to preserve it—that is to say, among the descendants of Abraham. But, in the fulness of time, the Messiah came into the world, to call mankind out of the darkness, or total ignorance into which they had fallen, when left to themselves and their own devices, and to restore to them a knowledge of the true God. Yet, the propagation of this great and essential truth, has always been, and is still, mysteriously retarded, for some wise purpose, by the diversity of language or tongue to be met with in every part of the world. Galle, however, appears to be a favourable point, from whence efficient Missionaries might proceed, with every prospect of accomplishing as much as is intended to be accomplished, until the "times of the Gentiles shall be fulfilled."

What I have just introduced, may, perhaps, by some, be considered an unnecessary digression; but, I have still,—in order to shew the modes of acting, and the feelings by which certain classes of the natives of the East are influenced,—I have still to mention one curious circumstance. A wealthy merchant, lately settled here, whose son and heir had attained an age when it is usual to perform some religious ceremonies, deemed it incumbent upon him to comply with the custom, and therefore,—to use his own expressions,— called together, from the countries round about, his relations and friends, to eat, drink, and be merry with him, for many days, upon the joyful occasion. The day for the commencement of the ceremonies had been fixed, and a great feast prepared, which did not cost the merchant less than 3000 dollars, when two priests, and some of the better class of Moormen, waited upon me, in due form, as Commandant, to represent that this upstart, as they styled him, though rich, was not by birth entitled to go with his friends, as they intended, through the streets, with tom-toms beating, pipes playing, colours flying, artificial representations of towers, temples, &c. illuminated and carried by men, attended by others, letting off magnificent fireworks;—in preparing which the Moormen are very ingenious.

As these are points of vast importance here in the eyes of the people, I thought it right to consult those who I supposed could set me right; and the result was, that I found myself reluctantly obliged to prohibit the procession, as I apprehended that riots, if not bloodshed, might be the consequence; for the parties were greatly exasperated against each other.

The much distressed merchant now waited upon me, accompanied by all his friends, and by several other priests, some of them resident in Ceylon, and others from the Continent, in order to prove to me, that by birth he was fully entitled to do all I have mentioned; but that the opposing party, his enemies, were offended, because he had not thought fit to invite them, and feast them also; and that they, besides, wished to take advantage of his being an unprotected stranger in Galle. I had, therefore, again to take the matter into consideration.

Both parties sent in memorials, (going to the expense of having them translated into English), containing arguments for and against the indulgence being in this instance granted. At last they completely puzzled me, and fearing there would be a battle between them, I thought it best to act for myself, and to permit the merchant to do as he pleased; and the more so as I saw clearly, that both jealousy and bad feeling actuated the hearts of his opponents; and in this view of the case I was confirmed, by three of the oldest and most respectable Moors, who declared, after long and due deliberation, "that he was entitled to celebrate the religious and other rites as he intended, and, if only sanctioned by the Commandant, he would be justified in humbling his adversaries, even unto the dust." Under such circumstances it was necessary to take precautions, so as to insure tranquillity; but Galle, I believe, never before witnessed a more brilliant display than on this occasion. "To do me honour, for having enabled him to maintain his just rights," the worthy merchant had the procession assembled about nine at night in front of the King's house, where most of the fireworks were let off. His son, literally dressed in cloth of gold, and almost covered with costly ornaments, was then brought into the room where I sat with some friends, personally to express his father's and his own thanks for my kindness; but this was done in such an abject and humiliating manner as to annoy me exceedingly. Before this, he had paraded the streets, surrounded by his relatives and friends, each carrying a large blazing torch, who sung or rather shouted with all their might, making the very houses shake again with their acclamations, the beating of tom-toms, squalling of pipes, and the loud reports of fireworks.

These Moors dress in a neat and becoming manner. Their robes, as I may call them, are made of fine white calico, of a very large size, and drawn in tight at the waist, round which they have a belt of worked calico. On their heads, they wear a small cap or turban ; and in their ears very large and long ear-rings, usually of gold or silver, inlaid with precious stones of various colours, which are often of great value.

Having for a few days nothing of importance, in the way of business, to attend to, I was again glad to escape from mere trifling concerns, as well as from the common routine of military matters, and to set off for Bovegoddé, accompanied by Mr. F—, the Staff Officer of the district. We found, as I expected, every thing prepared for us by the Coral, and our other friends, who were assembled, as usual, to receive us; and who obligingly offered to procure for us as many fowls and eggs, and as much milk, &c. as we might want, and to be also serviceable in any other way we chose to point out. I, however, found it necessary to tell them, that I could not possibly think of accepting as presents any articles of food, nor even fruits, but must be allowed to pay for them; and I begged that the Coral, in order to convince me that he was ready to oblige me, would now accept of a trifling present I had brought with me, of a couple of palampores, and also some powder and shot, which I knew they had difficulty in procuring. He readily and good-humouredly agreed to my terms, which pleased me the more, as I did not feel comfortable, at having, when last at Bovegoddé, been obliged to accept of presents, even though they were chiefly of fruit. But, worthy reader, I suppose, that you have now concluded, that I have altogether, unwisely, given over taking any care of, or precautions for, the preservation of my health, in a country such as Ceylon was of old represented to be. At all events, I confess that I now at all hours go about, in spite of the climate, shooting snipes even under a vertical sun, driving deer and other animals in the jungle; and, in short, doing just as I please, and as I did formerly as a sportsman in merry England, or in any other part of the world; and would not you, if similarly tempted, do the same?—especially if you could bag, without much trouble or difficulty, and without a dog to point the game for you, twenty or thirty couples of snipes in a few hours, although it might be about noon; and, in the mornings and evenings, some deer, elk, hogs, pea and jungle-fowl, and probably a few alligators. This can easily be done in this part of Ceylon; and I assure the reader, that a few days ago, and in a short space of time, I killed thirty-two couples of snipes—which I consider the best bird that we bring to our tables; and my companion, Mr. F—, brought down twenty-one. Snipe shooting in the heat of the day may, I admit, be unsafe for some people; but the wonder would be, how a real sportsman could possibly withstand the temptation of bagging, without firing into flocks, thirty or forty couples of snipes. But only imagine, that you see me walking quietly along, in an old and somewhat wet paddy-field, my huge dog Bran at my heels; and though he does not point, he has been trained, (and this is only one branch of his education), to go forward after I fire, to bring and lay at my feet the game killed, whatever it may be, but not until he is told to do so; and Bran is a sensible dog, though certainly not a beauty. A native also usually walks behind me, to carry the game, and holds up an umbrella, under which I stand when loading my gun. In some places, I have almost to kick up the snipes; and so numerous are they, that they occasionally fly out of a swampy place in a large flock. In truth, I could kill far more than I have stated, were I to fire into such a mass of birds, and were it not that I get tired of firing: but, I have besides to recollect, that fine powder, as well as Walker and Parker's patent shot, are rather expensive articles in this part of the world. I think, however, that I have now been sufficiently explicit, to enable a sporting reader to understand what snipe shooting in the sun is in Ceylon; and I shall only add, that I often bring home in the bag, two or three couples of the beautiful large painted snipe, which are so much admired, not only for their plumage, but also on account of their size and superior flavour.

We had brought with us a shark hook, which I had procured from a ship in Galle harbour, and with it we tried to catch the alligators; but we were greatly puzzled as to what sort of bait to use. We had no difficulty in floating the hook with a few pieces of the buoyant reeds, which grow, along with flags and sometimes bamboos, upon the shores of lakes; and amongst which alligators are usually to be found; but on this occasion, they seemed not to fancy either pieces of beef, or dead ducks or fowls; and as for cruelly attaching those birds alive to the hook, even if they could have been kept above water, we could not think of doing so. We, therefore found, at last, that, with all our contrivances, we were unable to entice these dangerous creatures to bite at our baits. In short, this mode of angling soon became tiresome, though it reminded us of what we had read of the giant's piscatory amusements:—

> "His angle rod made of a sturdy oak,
> His line a cable, which in storms ne'er broke,
> His hook he baited with a dragon's tail,
> And sat upon a rock, and bobb'd for whale."

As we had thus completely failed in our attempts to take alligators with bait, we had recourse to my plan of the harpoon; and, having gone to one of the more distant narrow lakes, to which we had the small canoe carried, we soon had sport enough. Mr. F—— and I went in the canoe; and he being an excellent hand at the paddle, and I having now become a tolerable adept with the harpoon, we managed so well, that we were never even in danger of being upset, nor did any accident whatever happen. An alligator killed on this occasion was fully, as we calculated, twenty-one feet in length; but he did not afford half so much sport, nor did he dash along in anything like the style, which those of about sixteen or eighteen had done. Very few of them shewed much spunk when they were once brought on shore; and after having given a few thumps with their hard tails, they were quickly settled by the people with their spears and clubs, who now seemed greatly to enjoy the sport. I was told, that some of the low castes were very deeply interested spectators; for they fully intended, as soon as we were gone, to have good slices of the alligator's flesh to take home with them, as a treat for themselves and their families. Not one of the alligators, after being landed, ever attempted to bite the natives, though they generally displayed their terrific rows of sharp teeth.

The following day, we went considerably farther into the country than I had done when here before, and in a direction where there are several lakes or long ponds, frequented by multitudes of water-fowl; of which we shot so many, that we were induced to send, to our friends at Galle, presents of ducks, teal, &c. to whom they were most acceptable; for gunpowder being very scarce and dear, the Singalese (if they could even shoot), cannot procure it, and are therefore, on this account, as well as from want of inclination, I may say, never sportsmen; wild fowl are, consequently, but seldom seen in the bazaars. The soil and features of the country, which we hurriedly passed through, seemed to be much the same as in the neighbourhood of Bovegoddé—that is, thickly wooded, but evidently capable of being much improved by cultivation; the first steps towards which are, of course, clearing, and in some places, partially draining.

In the evening, I was told, by one of the servants, that there was a great sportsman residing in the neighbourhood, who killed numbers of beasts and birds, whenever he could afford to purchase, or, by any means procure, powder and shot for the purpose. He was styled by the natives, Don Pedro, &c. &c., he being descended from the ancient Portuguese conquerors of the sea coast. I sent for him, intending to profit from his knowledge of the country, and also to make him, if I found him obliging, a present of some coarse gunpowder, which I had brought with me from Galle. To my surprise, I found that he was a person who had before particularly attracted my notice. He had a strongly marked Portuguese countenance; but his complexion was evidently not a little darkened, either by climate, or, by what was more likely, a dash of Singalese blood. He wore an amazingly broad-brimmed straw hat, with a green ribbon tied round its low crown; a blue and white striped and very short jacket; tight white cotton pantaloons; no shirt, neckcloth, nor stockings; but he had on a pair of old shoes or slippers, tied with brownish coloured tape—in short, he was one of the most perfect figures I had ever beheld.

He assured me, in English, which he spoke tolerably well, that he could take us to places where we should have the finest shooting in the world—especially snipes and waterfowl of all kinds; and certainly we were not disappointed, for we saw far too many of both, as they often got up in such flocks as quite astonished us. I had given Don Pedro a large supply of powder and shot; and he very soon convinced me, that he was as keen a shot, and as droll a fellow, as I had ever met with. He had, however, no idea of firing at single birds, but always into the most numerous flocks, bringing down with his very old, clumsy and heavy gun, at least half-a-dozen at each discharge; after which he invariably gave a hurra, or exclaimed as loudly as he could—Viva! I was really quite amused with the poor Don, who often came up to me, to express his delight, and to assure me that he had never before had so much powder to fire away, and to ask me, if in any part of the world I had ever had such sport!

When we returned in the afternoon to the bungalow, (for we had been out the whole day), the Don was informed of my alligator fishing, with which I was told that he was greatly delighted. He soon after came up to me, and requested that I would allow him to try what he could do with the shark-hook: and, as I had been altogether unsuccessful with it, I desired a servant to give it to him. In about half an hour, we were requested to go out, as he had completed his preparations. He had constructed, of reeds and flags, a small square raft, and, to my surprise, I saw fastened by a strong cord upon it, an unfortunate dog, which he had, before I arrived, set adrift on the lake, fully expecting that an alligator would seize him, before the raft was carried across the lake by the breeze, which at the time was blowing freshly from the sea.

To the cord, which went round the dog's neck, was hanging the shark-hook, indicating, too plainly, the fate that awaited him. The poor creature howled most piteously, as he was carried slowly along, the least movement he made all but upsetting the unsteady raft. I every moment expected that he must inevitably do so; indeed, the delighted Don now told me, with great glee, that he calculated this would happen, in which case he had no doubt, but an alligator would swallow both dog and hook, and that the floating raft would continue to point out to us where they were. I could bear this barbarity no longer; and, to his great surprise and disappointment, I sent off a servant in the canoe, to save the poor dog, which was brought on shore,—got as much as he could eat, and was then allowed to return to the jungle, from whence he had been brought to be used as a bait. At night, without my being aware of it, the shark-hook was again set, and I had afterwards reason to suspect, was baited with another pariah dog. In the morning, when the rope to which it was attached was pulled, it was ascertained that an alligator had swallowed the hook; he was soon dragged on shore, already more than half dead, and consequently afforded no sport whatever, for he had not only gorged the hook, but also the strong chain attached to it. I hope to be able to have Don Pedro with me in future excursions.

CHAPTER IX.

" 'Tis written on the earth's green breast,
In grass and smiling herbage drest,
And deck'd with many a gemmy flower,
And fruit tree rich, and greenwood bower,—
That God is love, who thus supplies
All living things' necessities,
And from his kind and liberal hanp
Profusion sheds on every land."

JOURNEY FROM GALLE, THROUGH GANGEBODDÉ-PATTOO, ETC. TO THE SAFFRAGAM DISTRICT—REMARKS—THE COUNTRY BRIEFLY DESCRIBED FROM BALANGODDÉ TO THE MOUNTAIN PASS BETWEEN SAFFRAGAM AND UPPER OUVAH—SOME NECESSARY OBSERVATIONS—RETURN FROM VELANGAHENA BY THE WAY OF RATNAPORA AND CALTURA TO GALLE—RECEPTION OF THE AMBASSADOR FROM THE MALDIVE ISLANDS—USEFUL REMARKS UPON THE SOILS OF CEYLON—THE CINNAMON TREE, ITS CULTURE, MANAGEMENT, AND PREPARATION FOR EXPORT—THE RUINOUS CONSEQUENCES ARISING FROM THE IMPOLICY OF LEVYING A HIGH DUTY UPON CEYLON CINNAMON—SALT, THE VAST QUANTITY FOUND IN THE LAKES ON THE SEA COAST OF THE MEGAM-PATTOO—LANDS WHICH MIGHT BE DISPOSED OF TO SETTLERS—THE VAST BENEFITS WHICH MAY BE DERIVED FROM A JUDICIOUS SYSTEM OF IRRIGATION—THE GREAT PROPORTION OF LAND NOW CLAIMED BY VEHARES, DEWARES, ETC.—CEYLON COFFEE EQUAL TO THAT GROWN IN THE NEIGHBOURHOOD OF MOCHA.

HAVING heard a great deal of the magnificent scenery, and healthy and fine country, which is situated between Ratnapora and the fort named after my friend Colonel Macdonald, of the 19th Regiment, I set off from Galle (much as I dislike that mode of travelling,) in my palanquin, in which I intended always to sleep; and took with me but one servant and a sufficient number of bearers and coolies, who carried light loads of supplies, which would be required by the whole party, including a corporal and three Malays, whom I found it necessary to take with me, as many parts of the roads were said to be infested with wild elephants, &c. I purposed, also, to perform the greater part of the journey on foot.

I took the road, or rather track, which I before alluded to, on the left bank of the Giundura river, which passes through the charming Gangeboddé-pattoo, and the wild country that lies betwixt Mantoonpitty and the Saffragam district; and at length, but with considerable difficulty, owing, I may say, to the total want of paths, through a very wild district, in which we had frequent alarms, and met with some trifling adventures, I got into the road from Ratnapora to Badulla, somewhere between a small village called Denewaka and Balangoddé, which cannot, as I conjectured, be much less than two thousand feet above the level of the sea. The latter, during the rebellion, was a military post of some importance, but is now of course neglected. I had for the last three days been working my way through a country in a very wild state, but capable of great improvement, if it had only roads fit for traffic carried through it. Until that is done no European should think of settling in it: indeed, the same may be said of all the country in this direction; for until roads are made, to connect certain well selected points with the Giundura, Kalloo, and other rivers, where they become navigable for paddy-boats, no agriculturist can hope to be successful in his pursuits, or to be able to effect any important object. The expense of sending his produce to a market, or to a port for shipment, would more than swallow up all the profits which might arise from it. The remarks which I now make particularly apply to that verdant, very hilly, and loftily situated tract beyond Velangahena, which I have yet to notice.

The scenery around Balangoddé, though wild, is very beautiful and picturesque, especially towards the northward, where there is a range of very striking mountains, which cannot fail to impress the mind with somewhat of surprise, and to excite the admiration of a person beholding them from the hill upon which the old fort is situated. After resting here for about two hours, we went on six or seven miles further towards Alutneura, passing through a country partially cultivated, and in many respects similar to that we had just left. I should observe, that soon after we left Balangoddé we had to cross what I believed to be a branch of the Welewy river, which from thence seemed to flow into a very rugged, thickly-wooded, and hilly territory, in which I was told that there were many wild animals. We halted for the night in some half-ruined houses, in what had once been a military post, situated about a mile from the temple of Alutneura; which edifice (after crossing what must be a furious torrent in the rainy seasons,) I visited in the evening; and though I was given to understand by the priests that it was fully a thousand years old, yet it was still in a good state of repair. I saw nothing worthy of notice in this Dewalé.

Next morning was so delightfully cool—indeed, the coolies were shivering with cold—that I could have fancied myself in England. The scenery, especially the immense mountainous range to the northward, continued to be most magnificent and striking. As we proceeded towards Kalapahané, about thirteen miles from Alutneura, the country became more and more wild, hilly, and rocky; some of the hills were bare, some wooded, and others covered only with a kind of long, coarse grass, of a deep green colour. Mists were, as usual, floating above and down the sides of these lofty mountains, occasionally passing over us, and then extending themselves so as to assume the appearance of fine lakes in many parts of the lower country to our right. In fact, the scenery the whole way to Kalapahané was of the most magnificent and imposing description; but I observed as I went along, that the country had here and there the marks of having been formerly inhabited and cultivated, though it now appeared, I may say, to be wholly deserted by man. We halted to breakfast at Kalapahané, which was once a military post, but had now for some time been abandoned. We then proceeded to cross the mountain of Idalgashena, which was really a laborious undertaking, as its summit is said to be upwards of 4,600 feet above the level of the sea. I shall not attempt to describe the splendid mountain scenery I beheld in ascending this pass, between Saffragam and Upper Ouvah; but when I got through it, I all at once saw an immense extent of hilly country, covered with exceedingly green grass, situated in the midst of lofty and bluish-coloured mountains. No jungle whatever was to be seen; and it was truly striking, and at the same time pleasing, to look from mountain to mountain, over a great extent of verdant and generally rounded hills, which were spread out, as it were, before me, like one of those fascinating and attractive paintings, which we cannot believe, from their overcolouring and transcendant loveliness, to have been copied from nature. But what an extent of pasture land, placed in a cool and favourable climate, is there for Europeans to settle in, had Sir Edward Barnes only had time to carry out his gigantic conceptions and plans, for making roads to it and through it; which is all it wants to render it available for many agricultural purposes! A road, in his time, was completed from Kandy to Badulla; and, in furtherance of his views, has of late years been carried on to Horton Plains, Nuwara, Ellia, &c.; but where are the roads by which the produce of this fertile country could be conveniently conveyed to a sea-port or market? I am aware that people can go in that direction to purchase cattle for the stations upon the sea-coast, and which are usually given in exchange for articles of English manufacture; these they can drive down the passes and through the jungle, but little else can be carried into, or out of it, except on the shoulders of coolies.

An European settler, to make his produce profitable to him, must be able to take it himself by carts or boats to a market; and surely, though the means employed by Sir Edward Barnes can no longer be spoken of, yet it ought to be a great national object, to throw open a fine and valuable territory to enterprising men, who are anxious to employ their capital in its cultivation; and who can do so advantageously, from being able, as I have already shewn, to procure native labourers at a moderate rate of wages. But want of roads is as insuperable a barrier to industry as want of labour. Yet look at North America, the Cape of Good Hope, New Holland, and Van Diemen's Land, except where convict labour has been made available, and I may now add, New Zealand, the few and thinly scattered natives of which cannot give much assistance to emigrants—at least, such as they can long afford to pay for, while Ceylon in all respects —even including roads—must stand pre-eminent and inviting.* I therefore trust that Sir Robert

* But to convince any one, however sceptical, that the better classes of settlers can no longer afford to pay for labour at the

Peel, and Lord Stanley as Colonial Secretary, will give this most important subject that consideration it so well merits. But the account (which the reader will find in the Appendix) of the proceedings of a public meeting lately held in London, (the wishes of the gentlemen present have, it seems, been submitted to Lord Stanley,) will shew whether I am right or not, as to the view I take of the ruinous consequences which must ensue to settlers possessing some capital, if they employ mechanics and labourers from Europe in our new colonies. No doubt it must be an object with landowners and speculators, by every means to induce and encourage emigrants of all classes to proceed to the parts of the world where their cheaply acquired territories

rates necessarily demanded for it, the following notice I should consider sufficient; for it must be evident, that it is not so much the redundancy of labour, as the want of means to pay for it, which causes the distress alluded to.

"EMIGRATION TO THE CANADAS.

"The government agent for emigration has caused a copy of the following notice to be posted at the Dublin Custom House, as a caution to persons about to emigrate:—

"Government Emigration Office,
Custom House, Dublin, Aug. 11, 1842.

"The latest advices from New Brunswick continue to describe the redundancy of labour which still exists; and that, consequently, great distress prevails there.

"Persons intending to proceed to that colony are hereby warned, that too many emigrants have arrived there already this season.

"J. E. Hodder, Government Agent."

are situated; but it must surely be evident, that it would be well if such persons were, before they went out, to make due inquiries, and then seriously consider, if they can afford to pay, or if the labouring classes can possibly long be paid, the amount of wages, &c. set forth at these meetings, as well as in numerous works lately published, extolling the advantages to be derived from emigration, no matter as to what part of the world it may be directed.*

But having made too long a digression, I must now bring to a conclusion the brief account of this very agreeable excursion. We had still a deep glen to cross before we could reach Velangahena, and in doing so, I observed, here and there, among patches of trees, some very beautiful wild flowers and shrubs; but I was particularly struck with a few fine rhododendrons, which I could scarcely have expected to find in so elevated and exposed a situation; at least, in such perfection. After spending a very cool and delightful evening, and a night much too cold for my almost naked followers, at the old military station of Velangahena, where, I had previously decided, that my journey in this direction was to terminate, I set off at sun rise the following morning, on my return to Galle; taking Alutneura, Denewaka, Ratnapora, (a most delightful military station, situated amidst rocky, wooded hills and deep valleys, and upon a branch of the fine Kalloo river,) and Idengoddé in my

* See Appendix O.

way to Caltura; thus passing leisurely and agreeably through one of the most beautiful and picturesque countries imaginable. I have already spoken of Caltura, and it is therefore unnecessary again to express my admiration of that truly delightful station. From thence I proceeded by the sea coast to Galle. Though during our progress we were sometimes very near coming in contact with elephants, &c. yet we had no adventures, nor did any accident happen of sufficient importance to be brought to the reader's notice.

On my return to Galle, I was told that the vessel having on board the Maldive Ambassador had just reached the harbour. On the following day, he in due form announced his arrival, and requested to know, when I would honour him with an audience; and as I found that, according to long established etiquette, it was necessary to make him wait my convenience—that is, for a short time,—I named a day at the end of the following week for the ceremony of his reception: until then, no notice was to be taken of him.

The day fixed upon having arrived, I requested the attendance, at the King's house, of all the officers of the garrison, in full uniform; and in the verandah a number of Headmen were in waiting, in grand costume, headed by the Guard Modliar, who presided on the occasion as master of ceremonies. The Government barge, covered with an awning, ornamented with flags, and the crew in their best apparel, had been ordered off to the vessel, to bring His Excellency and suite on shore. A guard of honour, of the 2nd Ceylon Regiment, (Sepoys) received him with presented arms, the moment he set his foot upon the wharf; and amidst the Singalese body guard, which attends the judges at circuit and upon other grand occasions, and all the tom-toms and pipes the Collector could muster, His Excellency was conducted to my presence, carrying the Sultan's letter upon his head, and followed by a number of coolies bearing the usual present; which consisted of some handsome mats for covering couches, made in the Maldive islands, and a quantity of fish variously prepared there, and considered by the natives of Ceylon as great delicacies, but at which an European stomach would revolt. There were likewise some other trifling articles.

The letter, which was carefully enclosed in a green silk bag, ornamented with silver stars, I opened in His Excellency's presence; had it translated into English, and read aloud to me. I give it as handed to me; and it will, I hope, be looked upon as a curiosity, as translated from the original by a Singalese, high in office, who was duly impressed with its great importance.*

"TRANSLATION,—As (Sultan Moohammedoo Moohadien Iskander Koolesoondere Kattiribowene Maha Radoon,) present ten thousand millions of compliments and respects to the Governor at Galle and beg leave to inform.

"We beg that the friendship existed between us from the ancient time may be continued, and your assistance granted to us for the protection of ourselves and our Island Mahaledive from enemies should you hear that any attack is made against us.

I then, according to custom, and through the medium of the interpreter, inquired after the health of His Highness the Sultan and his consort, and also after that of all His Highness's family—which I understood was very numerous—promised him, in the usual manner, our protection and succour, in case he was attacked by any enemies; and, in short, made a very fine speech, which was carefully and almost, as I was assured, verbatim translated and communicated to the Ambassador. He was then sprinkled with rose water, duly treated with betel, &c. and dismissed in the same imposing style as that in which he had come; being promised an answer, in writing, to the Sultan, and permission to depart in a fortnight. When that period, which etiquette required, had elapsed, the

"When the Dhonies or vessels of this island arrive at the ports of the British settlements upon trade, or whenever they meet with any accident owing to bad weather or other circumstances, they have always received every assistance from you till this time, which I beg to be continued.

"I have sent a trivial present herewith, and have to request that you will excuse this ambassador for any error that may be found of him, and to allow this his vessel to be returned without delay, and I present ten thousand millions of respects to you.

(On the top of the letter is marked with a stamp.)

Galle, 3rd January, 1821.

Translated according to the interpretation of Philippos Perera Rasappa, by me D. Ahabeyisekere, 2nd Modliar and assistant interpreter, Galle Cutcherry.

Interpreted by me."

same ceremonies were gone through; and my answer to His Maldive Majesty, translated into his language, and written and embellished in the first-rate style of the Singalese, was carried on board upon the Ambassador's head; and thus ended this annual ceremony, during the performance of which, I had to sit in state, and to do my best to maintain all becoming gravity, which I sometimes found it hard enough to do, when I happened to glance my eye at the more than half risible countenances of some of my European companions.

Time now stole imperceptibly away. I made other excursions in various directions, and always returned from them highly gratified, and more and more pleased with what I saw of this charming and valuable island. But, though intended from boyhood for the military profession, and educated accordingly, I have always had a turn, or I should rather say, a strong predilection, for agricultural pursuits; and as a rather extensive acquaintance with the nature and qualities of soils is essentially requisite to fit one to be a farmer, I had occasionally, and at various periods, made remarks upon some of those I met with in Ceylon. These I kept amongst my other memoranda; as I imagined they might afterwards be useful to myself, as well as amusing and interesting to some of my friends at home, if ever I should be permitted to return to Europe. But luckily, happening to see what Dr. Davy has so clearly and ably given under the head of soils, in his excellent account of the interior of the island, I lost all confidence in my own theories, and therefore I do not hesitate to make use of the materials thus presented to me; being well aware how judicious his remarks are, and how much they may benefit those who intend to settle in Ceylon. I must here, however, state, that I consider some of his observations to apply more particularly to the Kandyan than to the maritime provinces; for in both, but particularly in the latter, I have seen vegetable matter, (though I had not the means of testing and confirming what I venture to assert,) forming, to a considerable extent, an ingredient in the composition of soils; but this I must admit was more the case in spots where they were of a very dark brownish colour, and of a loamy nature. These are to be found chiefly amongst the hilly and also in the nearly flat country, extending from where the palm-trees cease to grow in great numbers on the sea coast; and occupying, I may say, a broad belt towards the mountains in the interior; in which space, (sometimes, ten, twenty, thirty or perhaps forty miles inland,) I have found every tree and plant thriving in a most vigorous and extraordinary manner. It must, however, be understood, that I here speak of parts only of the fine country, fit for so many agricultural purposes, that lie in the extent I have mentioned in the interior from the district of Caltura to that of Matura; and I am not aware that Dr. Davy had an opportunity of examining minutely the soils in that direction.

The soils of Ceylon have, certainly, points of general resemblance, as might be expected from considering the geological conformation of the island. With very few exceptions, they are almost all derived from the decomposition of gneiss, of granitic rock, or of clay iron-stone; of nearly all of them, the principal ingredients are quartz, in the form of sand or gravel, and decomposed felspar in the state of clay, with more or less oxide of iron. Carbonate of lime is rarely to be detected in the soil; and in no instance has phosphate of lime been discovered. Dr. Davy farther remarks, that it is commonly supposed, that, in tropical countries, in which vegetation is so luxuriant, and wood almost universal, the soil must abound in vegetable matter. This is not the case in Ceylon. With one exception, all the natural soils he examined, contained between three and one per cent only of vegetable matter. (I think it right to give this as his opinion, though I have been led not altogether to coincide in it.) The exception alluded to is that of soil from an elevation of between four and five thousand feet above the level of the sea, where the temperature is comparatively low, and the ground very damp. The small portion of vegetable matter that usually occurs, may rationally be referred to the high temperature of the climate, producing rapid decomposition, and to the heavy rains which will not allow vegetable matter to accumulate. To this latter cause, also, in all probability, may be assigned the great scarcity of calcareous matter.

The best and most productive soils of Ceylon are a brown loam, resulting from the decomposition of gneiss or granitic rock, abounding in felspar, or a reddish loam resulting from the decomposition of clay iron-stone, called in Ceylon, Kabookstone. The soil of the cinnamon garden, in the neighbourhood of Colombo, (as well as that near Galle and elsewhere, in which the cinnamon tree is grown; and in many places it is produced naturally,) is a remarkable instance of the silicious kind. The surface of the ground in many places, where the cinnamon plant flourishes, is white as snow this is pure quartz sand. Below the surface a few inches, where the roots penetrate, the sand is of a grey colour. A specimen of this, dried thoroughly, was found to consist of—

98 . 5	silicious sand
1 . 0	vegetable matter
0 . 5	water
100 . 0	

It may appear surprising that the cinnamon plant should succeed best in so poor a soil; but, other circumstances considered, it admits of explanation. The garden is nearly on a level with the lake of Colombo, its situation is sheltered, the climate is remarkably damp, showers are frequent, the temperature is high, and uncommonly equable. These are the principal peculiarities to which the excellence of the cinnamon, and the luxuriant growth of this valuable shrub, in a soil apparently so unpromising, may be justly attributed. These may appear to Dr. Davy and others, to be sufficient reasons of the superiority of the cinnamon tree in the neighbourhood of Colombo; but the soil, undoubtedly, best suited for it, is the loose white sand alluded to; yet around Negombo, Caltura, Matura and Galle, it is produced of, I believe, equal quality, though in very different situations. I must now, however, as this is the most valuable product of Ceylon, speak more fully respecting it; and in doing so, I shall not confine my remarks to what came under my own notice; but will freely make use of such information as may be afforded by others, who have taken pains to acquire a knowledge of its growth, and management, until it is shipped for Europe.

The interior is supposed not to be so well adapted for the growth of the cinnamon as the sea coast; at least, that hitherto brought from thence is coarser and thicker in appearance, and of too rich and pungent a taste. The best description, and that which grows in the gardens around Colombo, and at the other places mentioned, is obtained from what is termed the Laurus Cinnamomum. This is a tree of small size, from four to ten feet in height: the trunk is slender, with a number of branches shooting out from it on every side. The wood is light, soft, and porous, and in appearance resembles that of the common osier. A vast number of roots and fibres run out from the root of the tree, and shoot up rapidly into slender twigs, which form, as it were, a bush around it. The leaf, though not of so deep a green, resembles that of the laurel. When the leaf first appears, it is of a red or scarlet colour, but it afterwards changes gradually to green. The blossom is white, and when in full blow, seems, as it were, to cover the tree in a very beautiful and striking manner. This tree produces a species of fruit resembling an acorn, but not so large, which, when ripe, is gathered by the natives, in order to extract oil from it; this they use for perfuming their bodies and hair, and, when mixed with cocoa-nut oil, it also gives a very pleasant and good light.

When the tree is old and decays, it is usually burned down to the ground; the roots are then seen to shoot up again in long straight plants, much better formed than the preceding ones. The bark of these shoots is extremely valuable.

There are several different species of cinnamon trees to be found in various parts of the island; but only four sorts are barked, and all of these are of the Laurus cinnamomum kind. Till Ceylon was possessed by the Dutch, cinnamon trees grew entirely in the wild state; and it was supposed, both by Europeans and natives, that it was in that state alone it was to be found in perfection; and that upon being planted it always degenerated. Experience has since shewn, that the cultivated cinnamon is in every respect equal to the wild. The Dutch Governor, Falk, was the first who attempted to rear cinnamon trees, and soon succeeded in raising several thousands, which yielded cinnamon of the first quality. After this, he formed cinnamon gardens around Colombo. His successors, however, did not follow his example; but cut and collected cinnamon wherever they could find it. When we took possession of the island, the woods were therefore found by us in a neglected and greatly exhausted state. It was Governor North who so much improved, and enclosed with broad embankments, the present cinnamon gardens, and who made through them the pleasant circular road. The plantations, besides yielding cinnamon of an equal quality with that found in the wild state, were then rendered infinitely more convenient, and, from the trees being planted in rows, the people, in barking them, had not, as of old, to creep through intricate and pathless jungle in search of those fit for the purpose. There were formerly two seasons in which the cinnamon trees were barked. The greater quantity was collected during what was called the grand harvest, which lasted from April to August. The little harvest was between November and January. Each district, where the cinnamon grew, was bound to furnish yearly a certain quantity, in proportion to the number of villages and inhabitants it contained. For this service the people had a certain proportion of land allotted to them rent free: they also enjoyed other privileges in proportion to the quantity of cinnamon which they delivered.

Those who were employed to bark the trees were called Choliahs, and over them were placed officers, whose business it was to superintend the workmen, to take charge of the woods, and to prevent cattle or improper persons from trespassing. The cinnamon was prepared as follows for exportation. It was the duty of the Choliahs to find out trees of the best quality, which their experience enabled them to do. Such branches as were three years old, and appeared proper for the purpose, were then lopped off with a large crooked pruning knife. From these branches the outside thin coat of the bark was scraped off, with a knife of a peculiar shape, concave on the one side, and convex on the other. With the point of this knife the bark was ripped up lengthwise, and the convex side was then employed in gradually loosening it from the branch, till it could be entirely taken off. In this state the bark appeared in the form of tubes, open at one side; the smaller of which were inserted into the larger, and then spread out to dry. When it was sufficiently dried, the bark was made up into bundles of about thirty pounds weight each, and bound up with thin pieces of split bamboo twigs. These bundles were then carried to the Government stores. It was next sorted according to quality. The best cinnamon is rather pliable, and ought not much to exceed in thickness stout writing paper; it should be of a light yellowish colour; and possess a sweet taste, not so hot as to occasion pain, and not succeeded by any after taste. The inferior kind is distinguished by being thicker, of a darker and brown colour, hot and pungent when chewed, and followed by a disagreeable bitter taste.

After the quality had been carefully ascertained, it was made up into large bales, each about four feet long. The weight of each bale at the time of packing up was eighty-five pounds, yet it was marked and reckoned only eighty, five pounds being allowed for loss by drying during the voyage to Europe. These bales were all firmly bound and packed up in coarse cloth, made from coir, the filament which surrounds the cocoa-nut. In stowing the bales in the ship, black pepper was sprinkled among them, so as to fill up the interstices; and by this means not only was the cinnamon preserved, but both spices were improved.

I have no intention to speak of cinnamon oil, or of the process pursued for extracting it, in what I may call the Government laboratory at Colombo; which, when I was there, was under the able management of Dr. Farrell, Inspector-General of Hospitals. I have, however, said quite sufficient of the cultivation and collection of cinnamon to enable any settler, desirous of speculating in that valuable insular production, to see his way before him, and to arrange accordingly. I have now farther to remark, that, owing to the very high duty still charged upon cinnamon in Ceylon, and the rivalship we are beginning to experience in various quarters, but especially from the Dutch in Java, and their other Eastern possessions, it is high time that steps should be taken to prevent the supply of this valuable spice, which is daily more and more called for in many parts of the world, from falling into the hands of competitors, who are so strenuously exerting themselves, in the hope of altogether supplanting Great Britain in the cinnamon trade. If this should ever happen, the prosperity of Ceylon will be seriously affected and retarded. But surely, the vastly increased produce and the demand for it, which would certainly follow the lowering of the duty, would amply compensate the Colonial Treasury for any sacrifice thus imagined to be made of the public revenue.

We hear of Colonial grievances, but, of them all, there is none which appears so urgently to call for attention and correction by the competent authorities in England, as the fiscal rigour with which this important branch of trade, and until lately, in spite of every disadvantage, profitable agricultural produce of Ceylon, has for several years been visited; which has naturally led, I regret to say, to its decay; and, if persisted in, must ultimately prove most injurious to it. Cinnamon is an ancient, and was long the most valuable product, and exclusive Government monopoly of this colony; but if it continue to be treated as though still the monopoly it has for some time ceased to be, and subjected to fiscal exactions of an amount disproportionate to the first cost or ultimate value of the commodity, the cultivation of it bids fair to disappear rapidly. It must, at no distant period, cease to be numbered amongst Singalese productions, and will owe its fall to the unrestricted, unburdened competition of other colonial and foreign possessions; where, thanks to almost prohibitory duties on its export in Ceylon, the cinnamon tree has, we are told, become naturalized, and been extensively propagated. By memorials from the Merchants and Planters of London, interested in various associations connected with Indian affairs, these facts have been brought before the Treasury, the Colonial Office, and the Board of Trade, whether always judiciously or not, I do not pretend to say; but, as the Memorialists affirm, with little profit, and, indeed, with scarcely a hearing, until Sir Robert Peel himself was specially addressed by those bodies; the result of which was, the assurance of a partial mitigation of the grievance complained of; which affords encouragement to hope for its total disappearance when he shall become better acquainted with the real state of the case. But it must never be forgotten, that Ceylon has, perhaps unavoidably, large civil and military establishments to be provided for; which, if its affairs were wisely and prudently managed, could be easily met by a very moderate and at the same time judiciously imposed taxation; but not such as must continue, as at present, so seriously to affect the insular productions. I do not by any means intend to insinuate that either the Civil or Military in Ceylon are overpaid: on the contrary, I am convinced, (judging from what is set forth in Mr. Bennett's "Manual of Useful Information") that both insular pay and allowances have been too much reduced.

In 1833, the Cinnamon trade was thrown open to the public at large; but, in order to cover the failure in revenue resulting to the Colonial treasury, a duty of no less than 3*s.* per lb. was levied—a duty nearly equal, at that time, to one hundred per cent. upon the upset price of 3*s.* 6*d.* per lb. for the first quality of cinnamon, then fixed by the local authorities on the Government stock in hand; to a hundred per cent. upon the second quality, rated at 3*s.*; and to three hundred per cent. upon the third or worst quality, valued at 9*d.* per lb. It followed, necessarily, that little, if any, of the third quality was exported, but the first and second only. Eventually the prices of cinnamon declined in European and other markets, so that the third sort was only saleable on the spot at 1½*d.*, thus establishing, in a three shilling duty, an incredible taxation, at the rate of four thousand per cent. In 1840, the export duty on cinnamon was lowered from three shillings to two shillings per pound; and so far a beginning was made in the right direction, although then, as some persons assert, too late to be of any benefit to the planters and merchants. For in the mean time, the Dutch, with their usual perseverance, had introduced and successfully followed up, in the island of Java, the culture of cinnamon, the export of which was encouraged, by the article being subjected to only the very moderate duty of four per cent.

It is also interesting to learn, that this branch of agricultural industry, is extending to British Guiana, Jamaica, and other countries, with every prospect of a prosperous result. The export duty there is only 2½ per cent. By the produce of Java, the cinnamon of Ceylon is already to a considerable extent supplanted in the markets on the Continent; which need occasion no surprise, seeing that the quality of the former is already accounted equal to that of the latter island. The samples of Java cinnamon, reported upon by brokers connected with the trade, are represented to be of a quality little inferior, if not fully equal, to the produce of Ceylon; and that it only requires to be more generally known to render it appreciated as Ceylon cinnamon has hitherto been. Thus, in all probability, the limited demand for this article that now exists will ere long be supplied from those sources, to the total exclusion in the Continental markets (where 7-8ths of the consumption at present lies) of the produce of Ceylon. The effect of this rivalship, growing out of the interference in the European market in an article as cheaply produced, and of equal quality, but unburdened with the same ruinous fiscal and other charges, has naturally been a decline in the prices, and a decrease in the consumption, of Ceylon cinnamon.

But it is not Ceylon in its most gainful and peculiar branch of agriculture that has alone been injured by the heavy duties levied there on export, and in England, for a length of time on import.

What may be called the Metropolitan State has suffered by the same causes to a great extent; because, the price being so greatly enhanced by those excessive duties, the consumption of cinnamon was necessarily limited, and placed beyond the reach of most people even in domestic economy. But cinnamon is now largely used in the mines of Spain and America, on account of its sanitary properties in the prevention of diseases to which the miners are liable, in the pursuit of their unwholesome vocation in those insalubrious localities. Much more might be given, in detail, in elucidation of what has been asserted, but I trust sufficient has been said upon the subject to attract the attention of Government to a matter of such national importance; for, independent of what was sent to other parts of the world, there went in 1840 (according to an excellent article given in the "English Chronicle" of the 1st of September, 1842,) to

Spain, &c. . . .	144,291	lbs. of Cinnamon.
Mexico	36,990	Do.
Italy, &c. . . .	48,397	Do.
France	33,664	Do.
British West Indies	41,704	Do.

I must now proceed with the observations still required upon the soils of Ceylon. One of the best examples of a ferruginous clay soil, derived from the decomposition of clay iron-stone, occurs, according to Dr. Davy, about two miles and a-half from Colombo, in that beautiful part of the country through which the Negombo road passes, decorated and shaded by the finest foliage in the world. This soil is reddish-brown; a specimen of it, well dried, was found to consist of

83 . 5	ferruginous clay.
16 . 5	water, with traces of vegetable matter.
100 . 0	

The power this soil possesses of retaining water in an eminent degree, is an excellent quality in such a climate, and to it, probably, is owing its marked fertility. I have here, however, to observe, that even in Great Britain, when I saw that the soil I cultivated was from any cause unable to retain moisture, I have remedied the defect by applying certain quantities of common salt, of which I have yet to speak, before I conclude this chapter.

The most striking instance to be adduced, of soil destitute of calcareous matter, and incumbent on a bed of coral, is the common soil of the coral island Delft, which I have before mentioned, celebrated for its excellent pasturage. It is a dirty yellow, very fine sand, slightly cohering, which consists, in a dried state, of

95 . 0	silicious sand coloured by iron, with, perhaps, a very little alumine.
2 . 5	vegetable matter.
2 . 5	water.
100 . 0	

Nor hardly less remarkable are some of the soils of Jaffnapatam. Two instances may be mentioned,

—one of a soil of a tobacco field, which was manured by means of sheep, like turnip ground in England; the other of rice ground, which receives no manure, but is carefully irrigated. The tobacco soil, of a reddish brown colour, collected when perhaps partially exhausted, the crop not having been long taken off the ground, consisted of

95 . 5	silicious sand, coloured by iron, with a few particles of calcareous matter.
2 . 0	vegetable matter.
2 . 5	water.
100 . 0	

The rice-soil, of a light grey colour, containing a good deal of straw in a finely divided state, consisted of

95 . 5	silicious sand, with traces of iron, carbonate of lime, and alumine.
2 . 5	vegetable matter.
2 . 0	water.
100 . 0	

It seems extraordinary that in this island, the foundations of which are calcareous, there should be so little calcareous matter, and so large a proportion of silicious matter, in the soil. It is a subject deserving of minute inquiry on the spot: perhaps the fine silicious sand is drifted there by strong winds from a distance; and perhaps, as already hinted, the calcareous matter is washed out in process of time, by the action of the heavy periodical rains.

In relation to agricultural improvement, the subject of soils is, of course, highly important; and no where is it more deserving of attention and investigation than in Ceylon, where the ground is in its original state, and where, (unless Jaffnapatam be an exception), no attempt has been made by man, either to correct the faults or increase the productiveness of the soil, by the use of manure.

Dr. Davy, in speaking of salt, ably remarks, that "the importance of the subject is greater than may appear to a casual reader—the monopoly of the salt of the Megam-pattoo, yielding to the Government a revenue of at least £10,000 a year; the whole island being almost entirely dependent on this district for the supply of this necessary of life. It may be farther remarked, that the importance of these lakes has not reached its maximum, and that their value is yet but partially understood. Were they but scientifically managed, they might be made to yield, not only any quantity of salt, sufficient to supply all India, but almost any quantity of magnesia might be extracted from the residual brine. And in procuring wood-ash, which this preparation would require, it would be necessary to burn the jungle, with which great part of the country is overrun;—an operation that, in all probability, would be of infinite service, both in increasing the wholesomeness of the air, and in checking the increase of wild animals, so hostile to the agriculture of the country."

This is an object well deserving the notice of

those persons who may intend to proceed to Ceylon; for I believe, that salt is no longer a Government monopoly, and it does not appear that any duty is charged upon its export; but, for what reason I know not, when I made the following notes, there did not seem to be any intention of encouraging the people of the United Kingdom to become settlers in this, in many points of view, important and valuable island; which, in size, is little inferior to Ireland. Unless, however, this is done, and done wisely, it will never attain one-tenth the value to which it might be brought, if under the management of Europeans, who, in all human probability, would prosper, soon become wealthy, and, in a political point of view, be of vast importance in the Eastern world.

A great proportion of the land, which, I conclude, is now claimed by the Crown, (I find these remarks also among my memoranda taken at the time), could, with every advantage to the public, be sold at a fair price; and a considerable extent might likewise be obtained, upon reasonable terms, by purchase from the natives both of the Kandyan and maritime provinces. If this were done, the injurious jungle would quickly disappear; the destructive wild beasts would soon be either much reduced in numbers, or forced to retire into the thickly wooded and in many places almost inaccessible mountains, so as no longer to be an impediment to improvements in agriculture. The fine rivers and brooks of Ceylon, (as I hope to be able to shew hereafter), could at no very great expense be made to irrigate a vast extent of country, at present of no use whatever to man. By this means, also, the superabundant waters, being made to flow evenly over much of the surface, would either be carried off by powerful evaporation, or pass away into the ocean, without being allowed to stagnate and form pestilential and extensive swamps. The climate, as the low stunted jungle disappeared, would daily become more healthy; the quantity of rice and other grain, which the soil could then constantly produce, would be truly astonishing; and there could never be an apprehension of a failure of crops from the want of rain, which is often the case not only in some parts of the interior, but also on the continent of India. The generally well filled rivers—always so at certain seasons—would be sufficient to water a vast extent of country; and in effecting this great and essential object, we should only have to follow and improve upon the system of irrigation pursued of old by the natives, and in which they still—though on a limited scale—excel; and thus fertility would be given to immense tracts of land, now lying waste and of no value, but, on the contrary, detrimental, as they are allowed to harbour elephants and thousands of other animals, in the highest degree destructive to cultivation. How far it might be necessary to use manures, in order to prepare the soil for certain kinds of grain, especially those which do not require, like rice, to stand in water, time and experience would shew; yet water alone, with which Ceylon is so greatly blessed, could be made by European skill and industry to perform wonders. It appears to me, however, that there is little prospect of the natives being induced to extend their present cultivation, unless they are, by some extraordinary means, roused to exertion; yet many of them, I have no doubt, could be induced to labour in the fields belonging to Europeans, if duly encouraged, and that a prospect of a fair though moderate remuneration were held out to them.

There is one serious drawback, which I must not omit to mention, and which must always operate against extending the cultivation of the soil—viz. that such a vast quantity of the finest and best situated land has been made over to the various Veharès or temples, throughout the island, by the poor ignorant people being terrified, on their death beds, into doing so by their wily priests. These deceivers too often succeed in convincing them, when their minds are weakened by disease or suffering, that unless their patrimonial lands, or certain portions of them, are made over as propitiatory offerings,—often to devils,—their souls after death will have to undergo the most excruciating and lasting tortures. Being thus frightened out of his senses, the dying man at last gives into the views of the priests, who then most zealously and piously assemble a host of tom-tom beaters and pipers; and, by way of keeping off some of the malignant demons and propitiating others, away goes the land for ever from the unlucky family, and the poor tortured sufferer is literally drummed and piped out of the world, in the most terrific manner imaginable. This horrible and cruel practice had become so common, and was causing such serious injury, and actual ruin to many families, that the attention of Government was at length attracted to it, and a salutary law was enacted, which in a great measure has put a stop to the mischief. Far too much has, however, already been done; and which, I have no hesitation in saying, it would be wise to undo. Many will agree with me in this; but certainly such an idea as that of making heathen priests disgorge, would never for a moment be tolerated by those who think it right to continue the payment of £6,000. a year to the idol of Juggernaut!

If such a system of agriculture, as I have hinted at, were adopted and judiciously encouraged in Ceylon, grain would then become, most probably, its staple commodity, though at present it appears not to produce sufficient for its inhabitants. What vast quantities might be grown for exportation to the continent of India, and to the islands in the Indian Ocean, which often stand in need of a supply to prevent a threatened famine. But, besides this "staff of life," it might be made to yield almost every kind of tropical produce, as also a much larger quantity of cinnamon; and as for coffee, for the growth of which both its soil and climate are so admirably calculated, it is thought by many, that it can already rival Mocha in that article; which, like tea—in spite of the doctors—has become, throughout a great part of the world, a necessary of life. I beg, moreover, to add, that I was told by a well informed and intelligent person, a native of the island of Bourbon, once famous for its coffee, that it has now greatly fallen off in producing any of good quality ; and this he attributed to all the trees, of a particular kind, having either died or been destroyed, from their value being unknown. They had formerly grown in places where the coffee plants most flourished, and since the latter have lost the partial shade or shelter which those trees afforded, their produce has every year become more and more of an inferior description. The person who gave me this information, could not remember the name of the tree which is become extinct there, and I merely mention the circumstance, as it may, probably, be not unworthy the attention of coffee growers in any part of the world.

CHAPTER X.

"The purple Morning left her crimson bed,
And don'd her robes of pure vermilion hue,
Her amber locks she crown'd with roses red,
In Eden's flowery gardens gather'd new."
GODFREY OF BULLOIGNE.

MOST PEOPLE NEEDLESSLY ALARM AND ANNOY THEMSELVES BY CONSTANTLY THINKING OF DANGERS TO BE APPREHENDED FROM SNAKES, ETC.—SHARKS AND SEA BATHING—BATHS—A HINT TO TRAVELLERS AND TOURISTS—A CEYLON BAZAAR—ANOTHER VISIT TO KOGAL LAKE—AN ATTEMPT AT A STAG HUNT—A STRANGE, FLATTERING, AND UNEXPECTED OFFER—A KANDYAN BEAUTY DESCRIBED—ANOTHER EXCURSION UP THE GIUNDURA RIVER; FINE SCENERY NEAR ITS MOUTH—NATIVE SERVANTS—INJUDICIOUS MANNER OF BRINGING UP, AND EDUCATION OF, CHILDREN OF EUROPEANS IN CEYLON—A PLAN SUGGESTED—OBSERVATIONS—POPULATION OF THE ISLAND—REMARKS, ETC.

IT might be supposed, that in Ceylon we should be exposed to great annoyance, if not to danger, from snakes and reptiles of all kinds; but although I have now been here for some time, I have met with only a few of the former, which always endeavoured to escape from me, so that I had no opportunity of ascertaining whether they were venomous or not. A large centipede, about a month ago, contrived to get inside my stocking, but it did not bite me; and one morning, in putting on my coat, I, with my hand, forced a large black scorpion out of the right sleeve, yet it also did me no harm whatever. Yesterday evening, when at dinner with a party of friends, what the native servants called a *bad* snake quietly glided across the room, and out at the opposite door into the garden walk, where one of them killed it. Upon examining its teeth I found it was not venomous; but most people are inclined to fancy every snake to be so. As I before mentioned, we have here but few flies; and though I hear there are bugs, I have not as yet seen any. Fleas—my plague in every other part of the world where I have been—are in Ceylon only to be found on dogs. As long as I live I shall never forget the amazing quantities of these pests which assailed us in the fortified town of Peniche, in Portugal; many officers and soldiers were tormented by them to such a degree as to be wholly deprived of sleep; and in consequence were attacked with fevers, produced actually by want of rest. Muskitoes are not by any means so numerous nor troublesome here as in North America; but nowhere was I ever bitten by them. They, however, contrive to annoy us a good deal, and often all night long, by their constant and wearisome buzzing, especially if care be not taken by the servants to close our muskitoe curtains; which, if properly attended to, completely exclude them. It may be well here to mention, that some persons have imagined, that not only muskitoes, but also malaria, the supposed cause of fevers, may thus likewise be shut out. At all events, I would recommend those who are obliged to sleep in the jungle, or in the neighbourhood of swamps, to be, if possible, provided, as I have always been, with these very light and therefore portable curtains; they can be easily fitted into a palanquin, in which all experienced travellers invariably sleep at night in this part of the world. But some persons are constantly thinking of snakes, reptiles, &c. and the consequences of being bitten or stung by them; and, in proportion as they do so, they alarm and, I must say, needlessly annoy themselves; for people are very rarely injured by either. I should, however, mention, that the ocean around Ceylon so swarms with enormous sharks that it is very unsafe for Europeans to bathe in it, as these monsters greatly prefer their white skins to those of the darker complexioned natives; but as bathing is most conducive to health, sufficiently large spaces to swim in are enclosed with strong stakes driven into the sand, to protect the soldiers from their attacks.

Gentlemen, both of the civil and military services, in general bathe every morning as soon as they return from their usual exercise, and just before dressing for breakfast. The bath is always filled with water the evening before; and, as the night air is usually very cold, the water becomes equally so, and consequently refreshes and invigorates those who use it, and enables them to bear up against the heat of the day.

These remarks may very likely appear trifling; but I trust that a desire to afford information, and to gratify an untravelled reader, whilst I endeavour, at the same time, to give him some notion of the habits Europeans acquire in this country, and also of their modes of living, may induce the better informed to pardon me if I am sometimes tedious or prolix. I hope, however, as we proceed together hereafter, he will have less reason to complain of me in these respects. But I must here observe, that I know of no place to which one can go with so much advantage, in order to see something of the ways or doings of the mass of the population of any country, as to their markets or bazaars; but if a traveller attempts, as many do, to describe all he sees, and to repeat all he hears, he must write volumes, and, after all his pains, come far short of pourtraying the reality.

I more than once endeavoured, as I find by my notes, to describe the bazaar at Galle, where people from various countries are often to be met with; but I soon found that I could not hope to be able to effect my object; and therefore—I think wisely—gave up the idea; and, as the shortest and easiest way of accomplishing—though I had so far failed—the purpose which I had still in view, I determined to employ the pencil and paints of a native artist, and to make him sketch for me, in his own style, some of the groups usually to be seen in such places. In order that I should understand what he had tried to delineate, he wrote in each compart-

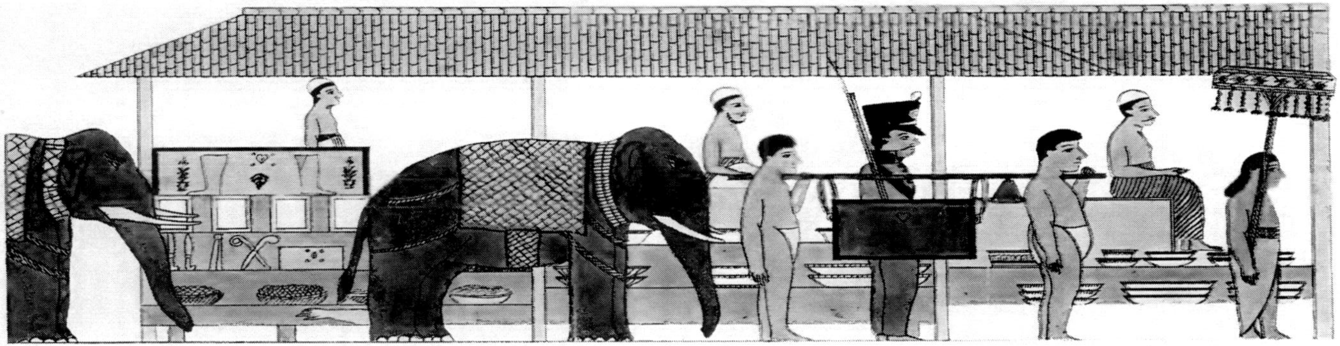

MOORMANS PHYSICAL MARKET — PLATE MARKET — PLATE SHOP

Published by T and W Boone London 1843 — P Gauci lith

RICE MARKET. — BEADS MARKET — MALABARMANS CLOTH MARKET

ment of the picture what it contained. These notices I had translated by a Headman into English, and, such as I received it at last, I beg to present it to the reader. But this hint will, I trust, be useful to many modern travellers and tourists, who often, through an over anxiety to become popular writers, and perhaps to shew off their learning and graphical powers, get into sad scrapes, such as, in this instance at least, I have prudently avoided.

However much Galle may have since changed for the worse, it had, at the time I now speak of, a numerous garrison, and was really a gay and very agreeable station. We had constantly quoit and cricket matches, hand and foot-ball, and other amusements, going forward, especially in the evenings. The officers, also, had frequent shooting parties in the neighbourhood, and gave now and then garrison balls and suppers; and, as Commandant, I, of course, took my turn; and so did some of the English residents, and one or two of the more respectable Dutch families.

We have here several kinds of beautiful beetles; but there is one in particular, called the Diamond beetle, which in splendour and brilliancy far surpasses all I have seen in any other part of the world. It is so seldom met with, that I had to beg several of the natives to be on the look out for one of them, which was at last found and brought to me by my horse-keeper; when I was really astonished at, I may say, the fiery flashes it emitted when placed in different lights. This fine specimen I sent as a present to a friend in Ireland. There is also here, as I am told, though I never met with one of them, the kind called the Queen beetle. This astonishing insect is said to be larger than the Diamond beetle, being about an inch and a half in length; and, what is truly wonderful, she carries just below her middle two bright lights, which do not flash and glimmer like that of the fire-fly, but give as steady a flame as gas, displaying two perfect, but exceedingly small globes, which afford light sufficient in the darkest night to enable one to read print by them. When carried into a dark room in the day-time, she immediately, as it were, lights her lamps; and instantly extinguishes them when brought again to the light. There is another sort, usually taken for the Diamond beetle, which are very numerous and beautiful, but very inferior to it.

At one of our balls, the young and handsome wife of an officer had been led—whether from whim, or from what motive I know not, though most likely her only object was to excite admiration—to adorn that part of her white dress which flowed gracefully around perhaps the prettiest feet and ancles in the world, with these beautiful but very common beetles, which had a most striking and exceedingly attractive effect; so much so, that she was envied by the other ladies, and admired by the gentlemen. The lovely Mrs. H——, however, as lovely women usually do, had set the fashion; at the next ball, therefore, the ladies' dresses were profusely besprinkled with shining beetles; but, alas! too many of them had not considered, or probably knew not, that it was far from judicious thus to attract notice to what are too common, indeed, rather prevalent in some parts of the United Kingdom, and are called *mullingars*. If, therefore, it should ever become the rage for ladies at home to deck their ball dresses with beetles, or any other sparkling and too enticing ornaments, let many of them beware of falling into the error committed by the belles of Galle. But the present trailing or draggling fashion seems to have rendered this caution unnecessary, as concealment is, perhaps wisely, the order of the day.

Again wishing for a change of scene, I had arranged with some of the Headmen, that they were to meet Mr. F——— and me at the head of the Kogal lake, with as many of their people as they could conveniently assemble; as I wished to try if I could manage to have a stag-hunt, something in the style which is considered so truly animating and delightful to sportsmen at Killarney in Ireland; and which, we are told, inspires as lively a pleasure as the imagination can conceive to arise from the chase. At Kogal we could not, I confess, make the shouting of men, and beating of tom-toms, loud as they were—be re-echoed from hill to hill, and from rock to rock, as is the case at that most picturesque of Irish lakes; yet our sport on this occasion was at least joyous and truly inspiriting.

The place I had selected was, the day before, in military phrase, carefully reconnoitred. It consisted of several finely wooded heights, divided from each other by lively green rice fields, and small meadows of a swampy nature, covered with a kind of coarse grass, into which, as I was informed by the people, the deer were often seen coming from the jungle and distant forests, to feed in the mornings and evenings. From the heights, the ground sloped gradually down towards the beautiful and generally unruffled lake; upon which I had a boat in readiness for the chase, if we could only contrive, by shouting and tom-tom beating, to drive any of the deer into the water.

As I had not much apprehension of danger from alligators, at least at this season, in the limpid lake, I had brought my noble dog Bran with me; being anxious to see how he would behave, when he should, for the first time, see such game. We were all at the point fixed upon, before there was even that slight but lovely tinge of red upon the eastern horizon, that here, usually, so beautifully precedes the dawn of day; and, what with the number of people assembled, and the strict silence preserved, the scene reminded me much of those to which I was formerly well accustomed in other parts of the world, when, as one of Picton's Brigade-Majors, I had to array troops intended to assail a redoubt, or an enemy's position before daylight; for the craft of war, and that of field-sports, such as these, in many respects strongly resemble each other.

We soon began to extend the insufficient number of people, so as to rest each flank of our long and too loosely formed line upon the lake; thus enclosing a considerable space of ground, including a partly wooded promontory in some degree projecting into it, and also some of the heights and meadows to which I have alluded. When all were ready to advance, I gave the signal from the left, by firing off both barrels of a gun, which was responded to by Mr. F—— on the right, and by the shouting of the people, and the loud pipes and tom-toms, all along the line, which in this order moved slowly towards the lake. Having now set the beaters fairly in motion, Mr. F—— and I, according to agreement, made at once for the boat, in which we had left Bran and our guns in charge of the boatmen, and of two Malays I had brought with me, who had for some time been my permanent orderlies.

As the sun rose in his usual splendour, the scene became every moment more and more animating and interesting. The shouting and beating of tom-toms increased, and gradually approached us. Some deer came suddenly out of the wood at a point where it nearly reached the shore of the lake; but, on looking round them, they, in evident alarm, again retired into it. Then a single deer, with fine antlers, followed by some fierce-looking hogs, and half-wild buffaloes, and preceded by a flock of pea and jungle fowl appeared and disappeared in a similar manner. We now began to see the people, in the open spaces, moving slowly towards us; so that in the utmost anxiety, we awaited the result of my experiment. Two deer and many peacocks came out of the jungle, not thirty yards from us; but we would not be tempted to fire; for we wished them, if possible, to be forced to take the water. A more than usually loud shout reached our ears; and in an instant I saw, that some deer, buffaloes, and hogs, had broken through the line of beaters; for away they went, at speed, towards the distant wooded hills. We hoped, however, that some might still remain enclosed in the quickly narrowing circle of beaters; and as they now approached closer to the lake, the shouting and drumming increased in proportion. The flock of pea and jungle fowl, being driven to the very edge of the cover, at last took wing, and flew back over the heads of their now rapidly closing pursuers, uttering their wild and melancholy calls, in order again to collect their widely scattered broods. At last, when the beaters had arrived within less than a hundred yards of the lake, two fine stags, with splendid antlers, and a doe, ran down to the water's edge, looked into it, pawed the ground for a moment, stared around them in evident terror, and then all three plunged at once into the lake, and swam stoutly for the opposite shore!

In an instant, we were after them, in full cry, which was duly answered by the people, who now crowded the lake shore—many of them, highly excited, paddling after us in their canoes. We soon began to gain upon the three deer, which were still swimming close together. Bran, whose eagerness could no longer be restrained, was allowed to spring into the lake, and very soon had one of the stags by the ear. As I feared the other, now some way a-head, would reach the shore before he was overtaken, I fired at him, and shot him seemingly dead; for he instantly sunk, and never rose to the surface. But, as we had now to return to Bran's assistance, the doe, though wounded by Mr. F——, was able to reach the bank and gain the jungle. When we approached the stag, still held by my powerful dog, we saw at once that he was quite exhausted, and more than half drowned; we therefore lost not a moment in fastening a rope to his antlers and round his neck; and thus keeping his head above water, we towed him, in triumph, towards the shore, where the people, still shouting loudly and wildly, awaited our arrival. Bran, however, bull-dog like, kept his hold, nor could he be disengaged until the stag was dragged by the people, almost dead, out of the lake; when he was put out of pain, and made fit, by the dexterous Malays with their kreeses, for the larder.

Thus ended this really interesting and animating stag hunt, which had far exceeded my expectations; for I scarcely hoped that the beaters, too few in number, would at one time have been able to force any of the deer into the lake. When it was over, I was sorry to hear that two Singalese had been knocked down, trampled upon, and seriously injured, by the deer and buffaloes—even though only half wild, when they so furiously broke through the line. I must here, however, say, that nothing could exceed the good humour and readiness with which these obliging people attended to all our directions, when explained to them, as to keeping at a certain distance from each other, whilst going through the cover: indeed, they all seemed to enter warmly into the spirit of the chase; and when we were about to take leave of them, they told us, that they hoped we intended to try our luck some other day; for, independent of the sport we had had, they were always thankful to those who destroyed deer, either by hunting or shooting them, as their crops were at night constantly and greatly injured, and even occasionally destroyed by them.

We now proceeded down the lake towards the village; and, as we were passing within, perhaps, a hundred yards of one of the banks, upon which numbers of tall reeds, and a kind of broad flags grew, and even extended some way out into the water, I was struck with the extraordinary and beautiful colours which their flowers, or as I rather supposed those of some of the water-lily kinds, so brilliantly displayed. Wishing to get nearer to them, I steered the boat more on that side of the lake, with the intention of taking some of them with us to the rest-house, as there were none there; and Mrs. F—— being expected by breakfast time, I wished to procure them for her, as she was fond of flowers. I observed, that when I proposed this, Mr. F—— smiled, but did not reply. He, however, immediately after, started up suddenly in the boat, and discharged his gun, apparently at some object which I did not perceive; when, to my amazement, away flew in all directions, fluttering among the reeds and flags, my beautiful water-lilies, which were, as if by enchantment, transformed into birds larger than wood-pigeons, and adorned with the most splendid red, blue, and greenish coloured plumage imaginable—all of them, as they rose and flew slowly along, dragging their thin and long legs after them. I concluded at once, though my companion called them flamingoes, that they were a species of coot or water-rail, but by far the largest I had ever seen. There were great numbers of them among the reeds and flags, which they would not quit even when fired at; Bran was therefore, allowed to half swim, half scramble amongst them, and when the birds got up before him, we knocked them easily over, and thus had good sport. Being soon tired of firing, we began, with Bran's help, to pick up the killed and wounded, all of which we could not find; but we took away with us in the boat, fully three dozen of them. Some of them were dressed for breakfast, some roasted, some made into pies, and others into curries; but, in whatever way they were cooked, we found them to be excellent and well flavoured.

Soon after breakfast the boats, which a Headman had obligingly sent out early in the morning, came in from sea, with a quantity of fine soles and other fish, which they had caught; and amongst them were two seer-fish, which in flavour are not unlike mackerel when just out of the water; but they are often taken of a very large size. I have seen one of them carried upon the shoulders of two men, the one walking before the other, yet the head and tail of the fish were hanging so low down, as now and then to touch the ground. I should, therefore, venture to say, that many of them must weigh, at least, forty or fifty pounds. It being easy to procure plenty of shrimps or prawns for sauce, I am inclined to think, that the reader, should he be at all of a piscivorous turn, would have had no objection to have been one of the party at dinner; especially as he would have had an opportunity of helping us to decide as to the qualities of some sparkling Champagne, which, (as we had not an experienced native to cool it with saltpetre), our servants contrived to bring in tolerably well cooled, in wet bags, hung up in the shade, and exposed to the refreshing breeze from the ocean.

Now, worthy reader, before we proceed farther together, I must take the liberty of mentioning, that an old friend of mine, who was what is called a good kind of a man, had fortunately a very excellent and prudent kind of a woman for his wife. He had, moreover, an unconquerable habit of what is termed "drawing a long bow;" but which he never did, except in the most harmless manner possible: indeed, his best stories were generally, whether he was sensible of it or not, I do not pretend to say, told at his own expense; for he was really a very good-natured fellow. Whenever his most useful wife, who was well aware of her husband's failing, perceived that he was on the point of uttering a "bouncer," without looking up from her work, (for she was a very notable, industrious lady), she would say, but in the gentlest tone imaginable, "Bill, my dear, mind your stops." Now, reader, as I may sometimes, as we travel together, tell what you may perhaps be inclined to consider a rather tough story, you may, therefore, like this good lady, feel disposed to remind me of my stops —be it so, but as my notes are before me, and as it is from them that I continue in a great measure to compile the account of some of my doings in Ceylon, I shall not, even though it may be thought that I take "traveller's liberty," shrink from proceeding in what I have undertaken.

I ought to have been much flattered by a high compliment which was now paid me, and which I should not venture to mention, were it not that it may tend to illustrate, in a very striking manner, the ideas entertained, at that period, upon certain points by the Singalese. It will also shew, in how different a light we ought to view their motives, feelings and actions, if we attempt (erroneously it is likely to be) to draw conclusions as to the state of morality amongst them; especially if we do so upon our received notions of it. But from all I hear, chastity, at least what we consider such, is not a a virtue in very high repute amongst the Singalese; for the women are only considered to have degraded themselves, when they become attached to a person of low caste; which, in their eyes, is an unpardonable offence or crime.

A few weeks ago, in one of my excursions up the country, I was unexpectedly caught in a thunderstorm, attended as usual, with heavy rain; which compelled me to take shelter, for about two hours, in a house belonging to, what was represented to me to be, a high caste family, which happened to be the nearest at the time. It being known who I was, I was admitted not only into the outer apartment, where the family usually assemble, but, to my surprise, there was no attempt whatever made to keep the ladies, of whom there were five or six, young and old, out of the way of a stranger; and they certainly did not seem to be debarred from staring at him. One of them, a very pretty girl, of sixteen or seventeen, alone appeared to be somewhat shy; yet even she continued, from time to time, and from behind her mother, to eye me, my large dog, and the gun which I held in my hand, very closely, as if afraid especially of me. I desired one of the people with me, who spoke English, which none of the family did, to assure her, that the dog was one of the best natured creatures in the world, that the gun was not loaded, and that I did not eat young and lovely girls. This seemed greatly to amuse them all, for they now crowded round me, and began, with more confidence, to look at me and my dress, and to ask me a number of questions, giving me to understand that they had seen very few white men. I was so pleased with the shrewdness of one of the young men, that I told him, if he would come to my house the next time he was in Galle, I would give him, as he had a gun, some powder and shot, with which he might shoot the deer and other animals, that so often trampled down and destroyed such quantities of their rice.

As soon as the rain ceased, I took my leave of them, not imagining I was ever to hear or see more of them, unless some of the men should think fit to come for the powder and shot I had promised. But a few days ago, my head servant laying aside, to my surprise, his usual gravity, came into the room, where I was writing after breakfast, to say that there were three Singalese men in the outer verandah, who wished very much to see me. I asked him if he knew what they wanted, as I was busy, and did not like being interrupted. He replied, rather mysteriously,—"I can't tell—men only tell master himself." "Desire them then to enter; and do you come along with them to interpret, as I suppose they do not speak English."

Upon their coming into the room, I at once recognised my country friends, who had so obligingly sheltered me from the rain, and I desired the servant to say to them, that I was glad to see them, and that, whilst I was getting the powder and shot ready for them, it would be well were they to go with him into the kitchen to eat rice, as they must be hungry and tired after so long a walk.—" The men much obliged to master; but that was not all they come for;—they thank master for powder and shot too." " What then do they want?" " The men want to do master much pleasure and honour—like master plenty—them Singalese people—father and two sons—(one of the latter my shrewd acquaintance)—want to know if master like to have their young sister, to live in house with master." " What!—the pretty girl, who was so much afraid of me?" " Yes, masten she want very much to come (said he smiling) to serve master, and take care of master?" " Tell them that this is a matter, which will require to be considered. But tell me also, Appoo, is it the custom in your country for people, especially those of high caste, to offer young ladies to serve gentlemen?" " Yes, master—when want to do great compliments and pleasure."

I saw at once, that a refusal, however kindly worded, would give great offence where, certainly, none was intended. " Say to them that I will speak to them again on the subject, after they have eaten rice." I thus sent them off; but I immediately after recalled Appoo. " How am I, Appoo, to get out of this scrape, and yet not offend the young lady, or her family?"—" Master send her and her mother some present, and bid the men say, ' master send another day—can't tell now—if master no like pretty girl.' " I accordingly sent the necessary presents, gave a larger supply of powder and shot to the brother than I had intended, and dismissed them, seemingly quite satisfied with the result of their embassy; and I have not heard any more of them.

I have since found, that Dr. Davy has most skilfully depicted the beauty and symmetry of the ladies of Ceylon; so correctly, indeed, that I must take the liberty of transcribing from the learned Doctor's admirable work; and the reader will then truly wonder, how it is possible for any one to withstand the effects of the charms of the Kandyan and Singalese beauty and perfections. But I am told, that such an occurrence, as that of a lady being offered, especially to civilians of a high rank, was of old by no means uncommon here; and I always suspected that my worthy Appoo, who had been up the country with me, had, with a view to his own advantage, a hand in the business just alluded to. I should suppose, however, that a better description than Dr. Davy's cannot possibly be given of a Cleopatra, who could for a time, even allure a Cæsar from his ambitious aspirations, and enslave the heart of a Mark Antony.

"The Singalese women are generally well made, and well looking, and often handsome. Their countrymen, who are great connoisseurs of the charms of the sex, and who have books on the subject, and rules to aid the judgment, would not allow a woman to be a perfect belle, unless of the following character, the particulars of which I shall give in detail as they were enumerated to me by a Kandyan courtier, well versed and deeply read in such matters :—' Her hair should be voluminous, like the tail of the peacock, long, reaching to the knees, and terminating in graceful curls ; her eye-brows should resemble the rainbow ; her eyes, the blue sapphire and the petals of the blue Manilla-flower. Her nose should be like the bill of the hawk ; her lips should be bright and red, like coral on the young leaf of the iron-tree. Her teeth should be small, regular, and closely set, and like jasmine buds. Her neck should be large and round, resembling the berrigodea. Her chest should be capacious ; her breasts, firm and conical, like the yellow cocoa-nut, and her waist small—almost small enough to be clasped by the hand. Her hips should be wide ; her limbs tapering ; the soles of her feet without any hollow, and the surface of her body in general, soft, delicate, smooth, and rounded, without the asperities of projecting bones and sinews.' "

The above ably drawn picture is admirably calculated to give a correct idea of a Kandyan beauty in every respect but one, and that is her nose ; for I must say, that much as the doctor, and his well versed and deeply-read friend the courtier, may incline towards the hawk-bill form, I must declare, in justice to these ladies, that such as I had an opportunity of seeing were in that point what these connoisseurs would no doubt have considered somewhat defective ; for in my estimation of what a belle ought to be—though I do not object to a slight degree of aquiline form—I by no means approve of her being hook-nosed; nor, I might add, should she have flat feet. It may, moreover, be here remarked, that, according to the conformation of both men and women, their persons, but especially those of the men, are more remarkable for what would indicate agility or flexibility, than strength of body or limb. As for the dress and ornaments of both sexes, I shall not presume to say a word more than I have already done; for Dr. Davy's description of both (and I refer the reader to his work) is perfect. But with regard to the ways or customs of countries, the ideas of their inhabitants as to what is right and wrong, however changeable they may be, must always produce or dictate their modes of thinking and acting for the time; and have we not heard of a worthy baronet who, in the simplicity of his heart, offered his daughter to an admired author. And have we not also been told, how a gentleman of great wealth, having offered either of his two daughters to a gentleman, to whom he took a fancy, with £30,000. as her fortune, the very conscientious and disinterested youth replied, that he could not possibly think of taking only £30,000. with *one;* but he had no objection to take *both daughters* with £60,000; and the same prudent spirit makes a Kandyan lady take four or five brothers as husbands; for thus she wisely concentrates her own and the whole of the brothers' property in the one family.

I must again beg the attention of those desirous

of settling in Ceylon to a part of the country well worthy of their notice. I find what follows, almost verbatim, in my notes taken at the time.

I have just returned from another delightful excursion up the Giundura river, and I am sorry to think, that the fine scenery of the very healthy and charming country through which it glides, in its bright course to the sea, should be so little known and appreciated. As yet not much has been seen by Europeans of the interior of this part of Ceylon; or I am convinced that many not only here, but also on the Continent of India, who have begun to feel the effects of a residence in debilitating stations, would be induced to visit a land in which nature exhibits herself often in grandeur, and always in endless and interesting variety; and where the naturalist would have spread out before him as wide and fine a field for research as any other part of the world can present. Here he would behold, in striking points of view, lofty mountains one half the year clad in light to a height of at least 8000 feet above the level of the sea; the other half enveloped in clouds, which often, to his astonishment, would dart forth from their black and generally moving masses, the most dazzling lightnings, which are instantly succeeded by such awe-inspiring thunders as surprise and intimidate even an accustomed beholder! Majestic trees, fine shrubs, and beautiful flowers, many of them—at least to me—quite new and unknown, display their gigantic proportions or their delicate tints and textures, in all those inimitable shades of colouring which painters in vain attempt to copy; many of the kinds propagating themselves—if I may so speak—without the aid of man to sow or plant their seeds or roots; and which have probably, since the flood, been "wasting their sweetness on the desert air." Here also the wonderfully generated, and as surprisingly fed or provided for, insect tribes are as numerous, as extraordinary in their conformation, as worthy of minute examination, as various and interesting in their instincts and habits, as can be met with in any part of the globe, where they most abound. In short, no inquirer into the wonders of nature need apprehend that his time will here be either uselessly or unprofitably spent. But I hope I may be pardoned for observing, that I have often had the misfortune to meet with persons, considered to be great travellers and tourists, evidently without souls: for I have had all the trouble of conducting them through the grand and impressive scenery of Scotland, North Wales, and parts of Ireland;—I have also acted as bear-leader to some of them, amidst the awe-inspiring cataracts and fearful rapids of North America, and even along the rugged banks of the terrific Chaudiere;—I have taken every possible pains to attract their attention to the roaring, thundering, torrents, and foaming whirlpools, whose very aspects and horrors make some men shrink, as it were, within themselves, and feel their littleness in the presence of Him who formed them; and whose arm alone can stay their progress;—and, how provoking it is, after all you have done, to hear, perhaps in an indifferent tone of voice—"*how pretty it is.*" Now I maintain, that such men and women are without souls; at all events, I do not wish for their presence here, where in the neighbourhood of cloud and tree-capped mountains* and precipices, on always verdant plains, and upon the banks of limpid rivers, flowing, in general, rapidly through a rich and picturesque country, a pure, salubrious atmosphere may be breathed; and where there are few malignant diseases to be seriously apprehended: in short, where there is "health in the gale, and freshness in the stream!"

These and many more attractions are to be found amidst the hills and round the bases of the mountains, which, in some places, rise and tower over the sources of my favourite Giundura, which has its rise in the wild tract to the southward of Adam's Peak, and flowing from thence past the fine object Hienadoew, or what we call the Haycock, and the beautifully situated villages, or rather hamlets, of Maplegammé, Oudavallevité, Badegammé, Gangegammé, and Wakewallé, at last empties itself into the sea about four miles to the northward of Galle. Though inferior in size to

* It is amidst these mountains (but approached in the opposite direction,) that the fine, healthy, and even cold plains before mentioned, where an English atmosphere may be breathed, and which are so well described by Major Forbes in his "Eleven years in Ceylon," have been since found.

many of the others in the south of Ceylon, this river is navigable for paddy-boats, as high up as the Haycock-hill; and it may be ascended still farther, (as I did in a smaller boat, which was towed, for the purpose, after the large ones which we had for our accommodation,) without any inconvenience whatever, unless the river should happen to be flooded, when this would become impracticable. Both banks are, in some places, extensively cultivated; but they never thereby lose that strikingly beautiful and picturesque appearance, by which an admirer of fine scenery is sure to be captivated. If restoration to health should be the traveller's object, he could erect a temporary and very comfortable bungalow, (which is here done by the natives for a mere trifle,) upon the spot he might select, in any elevated yet sufficiently shaded and sheltered situation, about Badegammé, or somewhere higher up the river. But, if he has a soul, the loveliness and attractive character of the scenery will most probably tempt him to fix himself either at Oudavallevité, or between that place and Maplegammé, (the climate higher up would be much cooler, but there are no roads,) where he will find a cleanly, healthy, and well disposed people, ready and willing to supply his wants, with such articles as they possess and can easily spare.

But some for amusement, change of air and scene, may wish to visit the always verdant banks of the Giundura, or those of some of the other fine rivers, which flow into the sea on the south and west coasts ; and they may be assured, that besides having the gratification of wandering amidst the most beautiful sylvan scenery imaginable, they will also have excellent field sports in almost every direction; but especially towards Tangalle, where elephants, buffaloes, deer, hogs, and other game, or what we consider such, are usually to be found in great abundance in the places they frequent, which are the wooded mountains or hills, or large patches of jungle, surrounded by plains, in general of limited extent, into which the animals, pea or jungle fowl, &c. can always be driven and shot or hunted; and so cool and delightful is the temperature, especially as you ascend towards the mountains, that such sports may be enjoyed, without risk to health, and without any serious inconvenience—at least, what a sportsman would consider such—from heat, until nine and sometimes ten in the morning; and the evenings also are very pleasant. But I must warn an invalid, that he should be cautious how he practises snipe-shooting, however much he may be tempted, during the oppressive heat of the day.

I had been informed, that a branch of the Giundura comes from the south-eastward, and that its course is more gentle than any of those I had before ascended, which were far too rapid in most places for pleasant fishing; and being told that in this branch there were abundance of fine fish, I decided upon exploring it, in order to ascertain if it were practicable for boats; and if so, I purposed to ascend it. I took with me my two trusty Malay orderlies, some of my servants, and a few coolies to carry light loads, in case we should land. I was likewise told—though I could seldom depend upon the information I got from the natives—that there were many deer, and birds of various kinds to be met with; and although there were tigers, hogs, and probably some wild, or nearly wild buffaloes, yet there was not much likelihood of our falling in with any other dangerous animals.

We went up the Giundura till we arrived at the branch I allude to, and which I expected to have found lower down; but we had only ascended it five or six miles, when our farther progress was arrested by the water becoming too shallow for even small boats. Making them, therefore, fast to some large trees, the wide spreading branches of which extended almost across the now narrow, and in some places, rocky river, affording a most agreeable shade; and it being then 3 P.M., I decided upon remaining where we were, at least for the night; as not only the spot we had reached, but the country in general, which was hilly, seemed to be both lovely and cheerful, and by no means too much wooded for sylvan sports; indeed, it appeared to be also admirably adapted for coffee plantations.

Here I spent two very pleasant days, in fishing, shooting, and in sporting excursions into the neighbouring country. The fishing was good, as far as the numbers caught may be considered so. I was, however, greatly disappointed, as none of the fish exceeded a pound in weight, and very few of them would even look at an artificial fly. The pea and jungle fowl shooting was, however, excellent; and I also shot several deer; and I did here, what I had never done before, nor have since,—I knocked over, at a distance of more than two hundred yards, with a single ball, a stag and a doe, which, by creeping cautiously through the jungle, I brought into a line; they both fell at once, so severely wounded, as to be unable to rise again.

We returned to Galle, without meeting with any adventure worthy of being mentioned; but from every excursion I make, in this and in other directions,—of many of which I have taken no notice, being apprehensive that I might tire the reader,—I came back more and more impressed with and convinced of the loveliness of the country, lovely even in its wildness and over-luxuriance of foliage, and of its being well adapted for many agricultural purposes.

To the point where the canal from Galle joins the Giundura river,—to which I wish again to guide the reader—and where there is good snipe-shooting, I often repair in the evenings. I have a boat covered with an awning, which is easily rowed by two Singalese, whom I have in waiting for me at a particular part of the canal; and in her I start for my evening's snipe-shooting, about 2 P. M. As the boatmen speak only a few words of English, the book I take with me constitutes my chief amusement till about 4 o'clock; by which hour I reach the snipe ground. The canal is carried, for about four miles, in nearly a straight line, through a pleasant valley. In some places it is narrow, and in others it opens out to the width of perhaps half a mile. Both its gradually sloping banks are for the most part covered with a fine smooth, bright green sward, and terminated, as it were, a little way above, by hills adorned with trees of various kinds; some of them bearing ripe and others unripe fruit, and their leaves being of many different shades of green, brown and purple. The whole mingling together, produce an agreeable variety of objects, which would otherwise be tiresome from their too great sameness; and such is here the power of vegetation, that this is kept up at all seasons; indeed, I may say, spring, summer, and autumn reign here throughout the year.

Where the canal terminates, we find the Giundura flowing through a plain of some extent, which during part of the year is of the most lively green, being almost an entire expanse of rice fields; when, however, the river periodically overflows its banks after the heavy rains, this flat, being then nearly covered with water, assumes the appearance of a spacious lake, surrounded by hills rich in foliage, on the gently sloping sides of which are to be indistinctly seen, in groves of palms, some hamlets; the neat looking houses being all well white-washed gives the country an appearance of greater cheerfulness than it would otherwise possess. I generally turn towards home a few minutes before sunset; and then, as the sun goes rapidly down, (for here we have little or no twilight,) the scenery becomes all at once diversified and truly enchanting—the hills on the one hand, I may say, glowing in all the fervour of his rays, and shining in striking contrast to those already in deep shade on the other, and all suddenly softening down into gloom, or at times becoming partially lit up by the moon, which here shines so brightly in the pure, clear atmosphere. All this makes a beholder, if not a Stoic, feel the strongest emotions of admiration and delight, and ought, surely, to call forth the praises of Him, who, in his goodness, has done so much for us, his unworthy, unthankful creatures. On such occasions I seldom reach home before eight o'clock, generally bringing with me a good supply of game; but no one is kept waiting for me, and, except it be my cook, scarcely any one else is inconvenienced. I always find that such excursions, especially those which are extensive, and even into the wilderness, do much towards promoting both health and cheerfulness. In a climate like this, occasional relaxation from business, and the tiresome routine of military parades, drills, &c. is always a treat; and do we not invariably find ourselves afterwards better prepared for the common occupations of life?—for in the world, whatever may be our station or calling, we all have certain duties or tasks to perform, which we cannot neglect without being lowered even in our own estimation.

I have already shewn the number of schools established in Ceylon for the education of the natives; but, before I conclude this chapter, I think it will be useful to say a few words respecting native servants, and the bringing up and educating of the children of Europeans. With regard to the former, as servants they are excellent. They cannot, in the usual acceptation of the word, be called dishonest, for they will not steal your clothes, plate, &c. or what is given into their charge; but they will plunder you unmercifully, if you are foolish enough—as almost all of us were of old—to allow them to provide articles of food, &c. usually required for family consumption; this is more particularly the province of your Appoo, or head servant, who will cheat you in the most barefaced manner himself, yet it is a point of honour with them not to allow any one else to do so. I knew intimately a Commandant of a district, who held also a civil appointment in the interior, who had a first-rate Appoo, (a high caste fellow,) who kept his table for him, as he never troubled himself with accounts, or in looking after his expenditure: indeed, his *trustworthy*, whenever he attempted to do so, brought him in such a list of trifling and other items, said to be paid for daily, as rendered it out of the question for him to form an opinion, whether they were really required in house-keeping or not. To save himself further trouble, he always gave Appoo two or three hundred dollars at a time, for which sum he was to account after it was spent.

Matters went on in this way for a long period; and, though every article furnished by this functionary was exceedingly cheap, yet the Commandant's expenditure was enormous. At last his lady came out to him from England, and then matters soon took a very different turn; for she was one of those sensible persons who look a little after their household affairs, and did not care whether asking the price of an article, in a store of *Europe goods*, was to be considered genteel or not. This lady had only assumed the reins of government a short time, when one morning Appoo made his appearance.—"Ma-am—long time no see wife—want go to Colombo see wife.—Ma-am, want much all this from Colombo—(producing a long list of articles)—Ma-am, give me thousand dollars—I bring up plenty good, all Ma-am wants." The lady looked at Appoo's list of wants, &c. and told him there was no necessity on that account to go to Colombo, as she could do very well without laying out a thousand dollars in the way he wished. He remonstrated, and said that the cook would not stay, (appoos and cooks generally understand each other,) as he could not dress dinner without they were got, and they could not be had at the station. But, in spite of all he could say, he was sent off with a "flea in his ear;" being told that she was the best judge as to what was required in the house. Appoo was wise enough to see that his profitable occupation was gone. He went and complained to the lady's European maid, that her mistress was no lady. "She look plenty sharp after everything—no great lady." He then told her, that other ladies whom he had lived with never looked at accounts; that it was not fit for a great lady to do so; that he easily made a hundred per cent. out of them; but with his new mistress he could not make fifty; and he was therefore determined not to remain, if "master left all to ma-am," and he was equally so to take the cook with him; and then they would soon see how they could get on in the interior without them. Next morning Appoo was sick, or pretended to be so; and he could only expect to recover under the care of his wife at Colombo. He was allowed to depart; but, to his surprise, the cook, who had become attached to the family, would not go with him. The second servant was raised to the dignity of Appoo; and before long, as he was not allowed, though well enough inclined, to make cent per cent, the Commandant found that it was necessary to begin to look out for Government debentures, as the best and safest way of remitting money to England; and, what surprised him greatly, his table was much better kept than when Mr. Appoo had the management of it, as well as of his purse. Now, all Europeans are thus more or less subject to this kind of imposition, and it would be well for them if they were to take a hint from what has been said of the Commandant's lady, and act as she judiciously did; for, as I before remarked, almost all the necessaries of life are very cheap at Ceylon, but the native servants will double their prices if allowed. This, however, is almost the only way in which, I may say, Europeans can be seriously imposed upon; for all native servants receive a certain moderate sum monthly as wages, they finding themselves in everything. I foolishly brought out with me a Portuguese servant, who had lived with me for some years, in the hope that he would be invaluable; but I was sadly disappointed in this respect, as he was useless, and only an expensive burthen to me all the time I was in Ceylon.

The Ayas, or native maid servants, invariably spoil the children of Europeans, by every kind of indulgence; for they are left, I may say, entirely in their charge (their parents, in general, being taken up with their own doings or dissipations,) until they begin to be amusing; when they are too often allowed to come to table, and to eat and drink everything injurious to them. I have seen a little, pale-looking fellow, of six or seven years of age, breakfast on very hot rice and curry, rendered more piquant by English pickles and grated ham; tiffin on the same, dine on the same, with the addition of English cheese, washed down with Hodgson's ale, or wine. The consequence is, that he has no appetite; he daily becomes more pallid and wretched in appearance, so much so, that at last his alarmed and injudicious parents decide upon sending him to England, unfairly attributing, in almost every instance, to the climate, what has been caused by their own apathetic conduct or imprudence. I should therefore suggest, that situations such as I have spoken of up the Giundura river, or even on the lofty Horton plains, Nuwara, Ellia, &c., should be selected by European teachers of children, male and female, for nurseries or schools, to which the children of Europeans, settled in Ceylon, might be sent at a very early period of life; indeed, the earlier the better. Let the ladies and gentlemen establishing these seminaries be satisfied with fair remuneration for the care and instruction of the children or youths committed to their charge; for they can have built, at a cheap rate, any extent of comfortable bungalows they may require, in the Singalese or Kandyan manner—the walls being usually of stones or clay, and the large ant-hills being pounded and used as mortar. But, as this would be an object of national importance, it might be advisable, that all buildings for schools, &c., should be, at least in the first instance, erected by Government. Let the children's diet in these seminaries be simple, and as much as possible like what is usually provided in respectable English boarding schools; but, above all, care should be taken that they are amply supplied with good (and here very cheap) buffalo's, cow's, or goat's milk. If this hint were attended to, even by European parents who might prefer keeping their children with them in cool and desirable situations, I am convinced that there would no longer be any necessity for their being sent, at an enormous expense, for health or education to Europe, or to any other part of the world.

It strikes me, however, that it would be most desirable, that every school in Ceylon, whether for European or native children, or youths, should be under the control and sole management of a Bishop and the Clergy of the Church of England as established there. Sectarianism of all kinds, if not discountenanced, should not be encouraged; and much more active measures than have hitherto been pursued might be taken for the conversion of all the native inhabitants to pure apostolical Christianity, as now taught and practised in that ancient Church, which was founded in Britain a few years before that of Rome. But I must here request the reader's attention to a document in the Appendix,* which will shew him, at one view, of what a mixed people the population of Ceylon was composed in the year 1835; since which period, it is however supposed to have considerably increased. In this return are included the Dutch and Portuguese natives; for an excellent account of whom—though the picture may be rather overdrawn—I must refer the reader to "Percival's Ceylon." It may, however, surprise him, that I have taken so little notice of these people; but the fact is, we have little or no intercourse with either, especially with the latter; for, although their ancestors were once of importance in the island,

* Appendix P.

A CEYLON PORTUGUESE.

Published by T and W Boone London, 1843

they have so completely degenerated, through reduced circumstances, want of education, and intermarriages with the Singalese, Moors, &c. that it may be truly said of them, "that the mighty have indeed fallen;" so much so, that I believe the Portuguese race in Ceylon will, before many years have elapsed, have become extinct, or be no longer distinguishable. My European Portuguese servant is quite ashamed of them; so much so, that when any one wishes to try his temper, they have only to say to him, that he may, probably, be able to procure something they name amongst his countrymen. On hearing this, he instantly fires up, and declares that they are not his countrymen; for they cannot even speak Portuguese; their language being more than half Singalese. Indeed, the figure of the Portuguese butcher, in the Bazaar picture, given in this chapter, is a good likeness of a Ceylon Portuguese. I must, nevertheless, beg leave to introduce another—that of a more respectable individual, who holds a petty situation in Galle, and who appears in the grand costume, in which he is delineated, upon great occasions.* But who, in

* Before the brilliant colours were rubbed off, by a servant who attempted to wash away the dust that had accumulated upon him, his little hat was of dark blue cloth, his coat the same, faced with red, and ornamented with silver buttons; the cloth rolled round his middle and hanging low down, had a black ground with a broad border like a rich India shawl; the handle of his sword was of gold, the belt white; the cord that from his left shoulder suspended his silver flask on his right side, was of scarlet and black silk alternately; the handle of

either of the sketches, (both by native artists), would recognize the race of men of whom it was said, when they first appeared upon the coasts of the island, " that a new people was arrived, white and beautifully made, who wore iron coats and iron caps, and drank blood and ate stones; who gave a gold coin for a fish, or even a line; and who had a kind of instrument that could produce thunder and lightning, and balls which, put into these instruments, would fly many miles, and breach ramparts, and destroy forts."

his lance was painted like the staff carried by one of the men escorting prisoners, along with Malay soldiers in the Bazaar picture. His slippers were of buff leather, his feet and legs bare and dark bronze-coloured, like his face and hands, &c. The above is mentioned in case any one may wish to clothe the figure in its original colours.

CHAPTER XI.

Whan shaws beene sheene, and shraddes full fayre,
And leaves both large and longe,
Itt's merrye walkyng in the fayre forrest
To heare the small birdes songe.

The woodweele sang, and wold not cease,
Sitting upon the spraye,
So lowde, he wakened Robbin Hood,
In the greenwood where he lay.

INVITATION TO AN EXTENSIVE HUNTING, SHOOTING AND FISHING EXCURSION—PREVENTED FROM GOING BY A VISIT FROM THE GOVERNOR, ETC.—SET OFF UPON AN EXCURSION INTO THE COUNTRY INLAND FROM MATURA AND TANGALLE—FIRST NIGHT IN THE JUNGLE—FIRST DAY'S FISHING——FALL INTO THE RIVER AMONGST ALLIGATORS—AN EVENING WALK—COME UNEXPECTEDLY UPON AN ELEPHANT IN THE JUNGLE—A REPAST IN THE JUNGLE, AND A SECOND NIGHT SPENT IN IT—THE DEVIL CRIES AND FRIGHTENS THE SINGALESE SERVANTS—A COMPARISON BETWEEN ELEPHANT SHOOTING IN CEYLON AND ON THE CONTINENT—A MORNING'S RIDE IN THE JUNGLE—UNEXPECTED RENCONTRE WITH BUFFALOES—SECOND DAY'S FISHING—ADVENTURES—AN INTERESTING DIGRESSION FOR THE BENEFIT OF ANGLERS—CHANGE OUR STATION IN THE JUNGLE—A BATTUE, ETC.

MR. FARRELL has just been good enough to invite me to accompany him in an extensive hunting, shooting and fishing excursion into the country to the northward of Kattregam, or even as far as Lower Ouvah, where he says we may have princely sport, and gallops for many miles over the brightest green sward which I have ever beheld. Some of his people have been out to reconnoitre, and they report that they have never seen so many animals of all kinds, such as elephants, buffaloes, deers, elks, hogs, &c.: in short, that there is every prospect of our having excellent sport.

Having mentioned to an intelligent Headman that I intended to accept of the invitation, provided I could get leave from Sir Edward Barnes—for which I had applied—to be absent for about three weeks or a month from the district, as it would require at least that time to get through all Mr. Farrell had been good enough to plan for me; he shook his head, and asked me, if I was acquainted with the part of the country into which Mr. Farrell purposed taking me?—I replied that I was not, except by report, but I believed that there were abundance of wild beasts to be met with in it; and that I had not forgotten what had happened to Colonel Hardy in the neighbourhood of Hambentotte.—"Very true," he gravely replied, "but I can tell you, that it is at times, owing to the great quantity of low jungle with which it is in many places covered, known to be sickly. Mr. Farrell, as I well know, from being formerly attached to the Cutchery of which he had the charge, never gives such matters a moment's consideration when hunting is in question; and it was only a short time ago, that a young gentleman, lately from England, who went with him, for sport, in that direction, was taken ill with fever, and died before he could have any medical assistance. I would therefore advise that you,—fond as you seem to be of hunting and shooting—should be satisfied with what sport the Galle and Matura districts afford; where, though there is now not so many elephants to be met with as formerly, the country is always healthy, and consequently sporting is there attended with little or no risk, unless you go too far inland from Matura, in which direction there are plenty of wild beasts. They, however, rarely approach the sea coast, except when driven down by the people, when it is intended to entrap a number of elephants for exportation to the continent; but this has not been done for many years."

This was certainly good and well meant advice; but the temptation was too great to be withstood, as I might, perhaps, never again have had an opportunity of joining Mr. Farrell in his splendid field sports, which I have before endeavoured to describe. But, most likely, all turned out for the best, for the Post or Tappal, a few days after, brought me, in place of the leave of absence I expected, a letter from Colonel Hamilton, the Military Secretary, and one from my friend Mr. M——; the former apprized me, that the Governor purposed passing through my district, on his way to Batticaloa, when it would be requisite that I should be at Galle to receive him; and the latter acquainted me, that he, Mrs. M—— and family, intended, about the same time, paying me a visit. Thus an end was put to my hopes of accompanying Mr. Farrell, and I never afterwards was able to visit him in that truly sporting country.

But my friends having left me, after, at least to me, a very delightful visit of about a month, and it having been intimated to me, that I may expect, before long, to be removed into the Kandyan provinces; and being anxious, previously to my going there, to see something of the country inland from Matura and Tangalle; I purpose starting to-morrow, as I have already sent forward most of my servants, my two Malay orderlies,* who are become greatly attached to me, and some coolies carrying light loads; and, as I expect that, during the whole time I am absent, I shall be obliged to take up my abode in temporary huts, run up by my own people in the forest or jungle, I have likewise despatched my palanquin and the usual number of bearers. Upon this occasion I was accompanied by Mr. F—, my staff officer.

Our people had gone off two days before us, with directions to wait our arrival at a small village called Morvoké, on the borders of the Kangeboddé-pattoo. At dawn, therefore, on the third morning, Mr. F— and I started on horseback, (Mrs. F—, little dreaming of where we were going), to over-

* A good likeness of Malay soldiers is given in the Bazaar picture.

take them. We proceeded by a kind of road or path, (we had a guide with us), leading to Morva, and from thence towards the Wellewey river, a branch of which I had seen in my excursion to Saffragam and Upper Ouvah, which was represented to me as flowing through a part of the country exceedingly well watered by streams tributary to it, in some of which I was told there were large alligators. I had therefore sent on the harpoon ; but how we are to manage without a canoe, I cannot as yet pretend to say. We have also sent forward fishing rods and tackle, as I am given to understand that there are abundance of fine fish to be caught, which I am in hopes will afford us some sport, especially if a particular species, mentioned to me by Mr. Farrell, have ascended the Wellewey from the sea ; and, as the rainy season is past, I expect that they will now have done so.

We rode slowly on, to enable our horse-keepers to keep up with us, and thus we had ample time and opportunity for seeing a good deal of the country upon both sides of the intricate path we had taken. The whole day it very much resembled, in point of scenery, what I had seen and admired so much upon the banks of the Giundura ; and I shall therefore not take up the reader's time in giving a minute, and probably tiresome, description of its sylvan and other beauties, rich spots of pasture, and green corn fields. We fed our horses, and breakfasted upon what we had brought with us, at a small hamlet called Parnekané; and about six in the evening reached Morvoké, a miserable village, where we found our people, who had every thing ready for us, as we were to stay there for the night.

Next morning, at dawn of day, we all set off together, and soon found ourselves in a very beautiful but somewhat wild country; here and there much wooded, and occasionally difficult to get through, in which one might begin to expect to fall in with beasts and birds of various kinds. Very soon, however, we could not perceive a single human habitation, and the country, every mile we went, became wilder and wilder. We halted to breakfast upon the bank of a small stream; and about noon we resumed our journey. As for the rivers, of which there were several coming from a hilly and rather mountainous tract, I suppose that neither an English rod, line, or hook, were ever used in them, in tempting the finny race. But fishing more than shooting had been my chief inducement in coming here; and a true-hearted brother of the angle can alone conceive the pleasure I anticipated, in practising our delightful art in streams, probably, never before touched—if I may so speak—by a European fisherman.

We halted about 4, P. M. and took up our abode, in rural simplicity, under the agreeable shade of some magnificent trees, close to the bank of a river, where we intended to remain for the night, and where the servants, with the help of the Malays, soon erected two huts—one for us, and the other for themselves. Mr. F— and I, taking our guns with us, and attended by the Malays, armed, went a short way up the river, In some places it was deep and very black looking, and in others, it glided rapidly over a gravelly bottom, where its waters were so clear as to enable us to see many of the fish with which it abounded. Not wishing, however, to be too long absent from our easily alarmed followers, we returned to the encampment before sunset, by which time they had prepared a sufficient quantity of wood to enable us to keep up large fires during the night. A comfortable dinner soon made its appearance, to which, having earned an appetite by exercise, we did ample justice, as well as to a bottle of old Madeira ; after which we thought it time to retire to rest, having previously arranged, that the Malays and servants were to keep a look out, in turn, during the night, and to give us notice if any wild beasts should approach the encampment.

We were twice or thrice disturbed in the course of the night, by our watchmen coming to tell us of the roaring or growling of animals ; but, as our fires burned brightly, the intruders were evidently deterred from approaching sufficiently near us to be seen. Our servants, however, already began to evince symptoms of terror, at being brought into what may be called the confines of the wilderness.

Next morning attended, as the evening before, by the two Malays, we again ascended the river. In most places its banks were so thickly wooded, and adorned with various kinds of fine shrubs, as to prevent us for some time from commencing our intended operations. In others, however, this was not the case; but in going up the stream, in order to find a more suitable spot for fishing, we observed the fresh footmarks of some elephants, and also those of deer, hogs, &c. which had evidently been there to drink in the course of the night. This induced us to be more on the alert; and, therefore, before we ventured to throw a line upon the water, we carefully examined our guns and rifles, and posted one of the Malays where he could best keep a look out, so as to give us notice of the approach of any animals.

We tried several kinds of bait; such as insects, which were very numerous; small pieces of dough, made of wheaten flour, and sweetened with sugar; boiled rice, &c.; but with very little success. In the mean time, the other Malay had brought some small fresh-water shrimps, which I had sent him to look for, and which are commonly to be found in most rivers in Ceylon; these the fish, which were something like gudgeons, took fast enough, but few of those we caught were larger than herrings. We therefore moved higher up, to a place where the river rushed foaming and fretting amongst some rugged rocks, before it fell into a large, deep, and black looking pool, which seemed to promise well for sport. Almost the first throw, I had hold of a fish very like a bream, fully a pound and a-half in weight; which, as I used a line of fine gut, brought from Ireland, afforded very fair sport. We soon—still using the small shrimps as bait—caught more of these fish, some of them fully two-pounders. But, tiring of this kind of fishing, I thought I would try what could be done with an Irish fly; as I recollected that my friend Mr. Farrell had told me, that in the rivers about Hambentotte, he had found the red-hackle, with a little gold upon it, to answer well, especially with the fish that come up from the sea. This I ascertained to be the case here also; but though fish of various kinds, and some of them very beautiful, took the red-hackle, still most of them preferred the shrimp to any thing else. I notwithstanding persevered with the fly, as those I caught with it were the largest, most lively, and afforded the best sport; yet I must say, inferior to what a burn-trout of the same size would have done. My companion, however, who was very little of a fisherman, stuck to the shrimp, and seemed to be sufficiently amused with that humbler mode of fishing.

But, whilst anxiously watching my opportunity to hook one of a number of considerably larger fish, of a different and more shining colour, than any of those hitherto taken, which rose at the fly rather lower down the stream, but without taking it, I slipped off the rock on which I stood, and down I went into the deep pool beneath! In an instant I rose to the surface; but, strange as it may seem, I did not recollect that there were, probably, alligators in it, until I felt myself dragged quickly and forcibly out of the water, by the collar of my jacket, by the Malay who luckily was standing near me at the time, and who had been greatly amused at my, to him, new mode of catching fish. When he had safely landed me, he, with a very serious and much alarmed countenance, said to me—" Sir, take care of alligator!"—and I certainly then felt, from a sort of shudder that ran through my frame, at the idea of being crunched by one of them, that indeed, it would have been no joke, had I been seized hold of whilst in the water.

This put an end to our fishing for the present, as I had to go back to the huts to change my wet clothes, and also to prepare for a walk in the evening into the neighbouring woods; as we had engaged a native, whom with difficulty we had been able to persuade to go along with us, to guide us to a place, where he said we should be sure to see deer, elks, &c.

After threading our way for, perhaps, two miles, through, in most places, a thick jungle, composed chiefly of the most beautiful creeping plants I had ever seen, our conductor, who led us with great caution, stopped suddenly; whispering to me, as I was next to him, Allia!—at the same time pointing across an opening to a large patch of lofty trees, interspersed with jungle. He then made signs to us to take off to the right, so as to avoid an elephant which he continued to point at; but which I, for my part, could not see, though one of the Malays assured me that he did distinctly, and that he was swinging backwards and forwards his long trunk, and flapping his ears, according to their custom when standing in the shade, in order to drive away the flies which so much plague them. This made us change the direction in which we had been moving, as neither Mr. F—— nor I had any intention, that evening, of encountering such an antagonist; especially as he seemed to be peaceably inclined. Our guide then led us through some other clumps of jungle, still cautioning us, by signs, to move with as little noise as possible, lest we should disturb the game, which he evidently expected to find, in an open space, upon the other side of the wood. On emerging from it, we saw before us, dozens of large pea and jungle fowl, which, on perceiving us, instantly ran off with great swiftness. But there were, after all, only two deer to be seen feeding on the far side of a rather extensive swampy plain, and at such a distance from us, that I scarcely hoped we could get near enough to be able to bring them down with buck-shot. Having, however, sent one of the Malays a little way round, so as to attract their attention, we both ran forward as fast as we could into the opening, in the hope of getting nearer to them before they could see us. My companion selected one of them, and I the other. We had moreover agreed, that should we fail with buck-shot, we were to try what could be done with the balls in our other barrels. We fired almost together. The deer I aimed at was apparently hit, yet he made off into the jungle: that which Mr. F—— had fixed upon, fell, but instantly rose again, and was also making its escape, when I fired, and sent my ball through his body; upon which he tumbled over, and before we got up to him he was quite dead. This was a large fat stag, with short antlers, when compared with those of the deer killed at the Kogal lake. The Malays with their kreeses soon cut off the parts we wanted; and, as darkness was now setting in rapidly, it was high time for us to be off. The remainder of the carcass was left for the jackals, wild dogs, and other animals, to devour, which they would be sure to do in the course of the night.

By the time that we got back to our huts, it was quite dark. We therefore lost as little time as we could in dressing for dinner, (a ceremony I never, if possible, neglected), to which we sat down soon after seven; and, worthy reader, I flatter myself that you would have had no objection to have joined us at our not to be despised repast; and though the cook had not, of course, had time to dress the venison, yet it will no doubt make its appearance, in the shape of a pasty to-morrow. Our dinner, however, (and I hope I may be pardoned for troubling the reader with an account of it), this day consisted of a pair of boiled fowls at the head, and two roasted ducks at the foot; on one side rice and fish curry, and on the other a ham, which would, we trusted, be seen at breakfast the following morning. We had also sweet potatoes and the vegetable called Brinjal, which is not altogether to be despised. I had desired Appoo, upon this occasion, to bring up with him a supply of Hodgson's pale ale, a sufficiency of old Madeira, and a few bottles of Champagne; and with one of the latter, tolerably cooled, we refreshed ourselves after a day of rather active operations, which we had now time to talk over. We then began to make arrangements as to what was next to be done, as the fishing was good, and the country, in a sporting point of view, was all we could wish. We ultimately decided upon remaining where we were for the following day; but we purposed to try another river, a little further to the eastward, in which the man who had acted as our guide had told us that there were larger fish than in the others; and up which there seemed to be a path leading towards the mountains, and through a hilly country very thinly if at all inhabited.

We had settled all this by the time our second course made its appearance;—it consisted of a shaddock tart—a favourite with most of us, as it is not inferior to an apple, and very superior to a Yankee pumpkin pie—and also of a guava dumpling; which was followed by a dessert of several kinds of fruit, nuts, almonds, &c. Thus, even a comfort-loving reader may perceive from this, a common bill of fare, that, whether upon an excursion or not, from having our cooks and other servants with us, we are always supplied with nearly as much as when stationary; and an Appoo was in those days looked upon as not worth his salt, who could not easily manage to produce what I have mentioned, and much more when necessary, without our troubling ourselves about it. Such matters some very wise persons may pretend to despise; but I can tell them, from experience, that no one has a better right to indulge in a substantial repast—with its usual accompaniments—than a soldier or sportsman in the field; and I know fishing to be a most appetite-giving occupation; and why, I pray, should they not, when they can command some of the good things of this world, partake of them in moderation, and with thankfulness to Him who enables them to furnish their tables, even in the wilderness, so plentifully, and at the same time with so little comparative expense?

Having thus settled our plans for the morrow, and made ourselves comfortably at home till about ten, we thought it high time to look to our fire-arms, and also at the watch-fires, which had been duly prepared before dark, in order that they might again burn for the night with sufficient brilliance to scare away any wild animals which might chance to be roaring around us. These necessary precautions being taken, we laid ourselves down to rest, having so arranged matters as to leave us little to apprehend any disturbance during the hours of darkness.

All remained tolerably quiet, considering where we were, during the night; but next morning, one of the servants most solemnly, and with much appearance of dread in his countenance, declared that he had heard, when sentinel, the devil cry several times in a terrible manner, and also in a strange and piteous tone of voice, which some of these superstitious people pretend to be acquainted with; and he therefore had begged of Appoo to inform me of what he had heard, as most assuredly—according to their ideas—an accident or mischief of some kind or other would happen to one or more of us, and that, too, before long; and they therefore hoped that I would take warning in time, and go back to Galle. Of course, I only laughed at them, and made light of their absurd fears. I told Appoo, that I thought they had known me better than to suppose that I was sò easily to be deterred from pursuing any object I had in view; and they might rely upon it, that I would go still further into the country, wild as it was, before I should think of returning. This seemed to alarm them all greatly, except the Malays, who joined us in the laugh at their superstitious terrors; which I was inclined to believe were in a great measure pretended, as I had reason to suspect that they were more afraid of wild beasts than of devils. The Malays, however, had told me, that the fellow who had so unwillingly acted as our guide, was constantly talking of devils; and had assured them, that the part of the country we were in swarmed with them, especially a little nearer to the mountains.

As I understood when I left Galle that there was a road, or rather path, which led from where we were towards the Wellewey river and the very wild country beyond it, I intended to try to reach its banks, although it was said to be there flowing amidst a complete wilderness, infested by wild beasts of many kinds; and as I concluded that certain points, to which my attention had been directed, could not be very far off, I had proposed to my companion, that we should mount our steeds at dawn of day, go some distance forward in order to reconnoitre the country, and return to the encampment in time for breakfast.

The morning being very fine and favourable we set out accordingly, followed by our horse-keepers, each carrying a gun loaded with brass balls, upon which alone we knew we could depend, should we fall in with elephants; though we had no intention of becoming assailants unless we were attacked by them. We had a very pleasant ride, mostly through an undulating and partially wooded country; yet at times the very narrow and intricate path, upon which the jungle was fast encroaching, was scarcely fit for a horse; and it often wound through thick, and in some places seemingly impassable jungle, where it would have been very awkward to have met either elephants or buffaloes, if we could not by some means or other contrive to make them go quietly out of our way. But we had much less uneasiness about falling in with a herd, than with a single elephant; for it is, in general, when we encounter a stray one, that real danger is to be apprehended. A herd almost always makes off, placing themselves, if they happen to have young ones with them, between you and them, as if instinctively afraid of your injuring or firing at them, and thus apparently preferring to expose themselves, rather than their young, to the danger which they apprehend from man. When we meet with a single elephant it is usually a male, which, probably, after a severe conflict with the others, has been beaten and driven out of the herd, and thereby rendered so desperate, that he will instantly attack, in the most furious manner imaginable, any opponent. In such a case there is no use whatever in firing at him, nor indeed at any elephant, if you are at a greater distance than fifteen or twenty yards, and then only with brass balls; as lead ones rarely penetrate his kind of Indian-rubber hide, and often flatten upon it or against a bone.

But the reader may probably have read an account given in the papers some years ago, of an unfortunate elephant, rendered outrageous by some means or other, in a menagerie in London, at which a most cruel firing was kept up for at least an hour before it could be killed with lead balls We also read of an elephant in India, for the murdering of which a large party started one morning, having mustered for the purpose thirty-one tame ones. The writer gives us a long and a detailed account of their proceedings; which were, in my opinion, truly barbarous. Whole vollies were fired by the courageous party, some of them discharging two, three, and four barrels at the unfortunate creature, which, after all, was only wounded and rendered more desperate, as the guns were discharged at a distance of a hundred, eighty, and sixty yards. It is therefore not surprising, that, being thus cruelly tormented, the highly enraged animal should have repeatedly charged the whole phalanx of mounted amateurs, who were firing volley after volley at him; and this he appears to have done, to their great alarm and dismay, very nearly effecting the destruction of some of them. But, after the valorous party had been rolling and tumbling about in howdahs upon elephants' backs, in a swamp, the writer tells us, that they "again advanced upon the elephant in the form of a crescent, in the full expectation of a desperate charge; nor were we mistaken. The animal now allowed us to come within forty yards of him, when we took a very deliberate aim at his head, and on receiving this fire he made a most furious charge; in the act of which, and when within ten yards of some of us, he received his mortal wound, and fell as dead as a stone. Mr. B——, a civilian, has the credit of giving him his death-wound, which, on examination, proved to be a small ball from a Joe Manton gun, over the left eye; for this was the only one, of thirty-one that he had received in the head, which was found to have entered the brain."

This was considered a grand day's sport; but it seems to me to have been only a most cruel and barbarous business, and forms an extraordinary and striking contrast to our mode of proceeding at Ceylon, even with the wildest and most desperate elephants. It is an established custom, with those who admire and delight in elephant-shooting, to walk deliberately up to the animal, which generally stands staring at the intrepid, or rather foolish being, who thus ventures to approach to within, probably, a dozen yards of his trunk! A small brass ball, which never flattens, aimed at the upper part of the head, and particularly at the space over either of the eyes, or at the eye itself, by being fired from beneath, instantly takes effect, when down drops the huge monster to rise no more! If one of the barrels fail, the other almost invariably, and the next moment, does the job. But, for my part, I cannot see anything deserving the name of sport in thus bagging such game, and at such imminent risk to the amateur; for if he misses his aim, or is in some instances unsupported by a steady companion, upon whom he can depend, his destruction is certain; he being much too near when he fires at the elephant, to have a chance of escaping from him, enraged as he must be by being, probably, only wounded. Yet this is considered here to be noble sport, perhaps because few Europeans have coolness or fool-hardiness enough to peril their lives in the forest against such a terrible antagonist. The people are, however, always obliged to us for destroying elephants, which do so much mischief to their crops, and are therefore ready enough to point out to us where we may find them; they were, besides, at the time I made these notes, increasing in numbers throughout the island, but particularly in the Kandyan provinces.*

After a rather slow ride for about two hours, during which we occasionally knew not which path,

* The reader is referred to Major Forbes' "Eleven Years in Ceylon," in which he will find a masterly account of Elephants and Elephant-shooting.

or what appeared to be such, we ought to take, we at length came into a very wildly picturesque country, the features of which were greatly changed from that in the neighbourhood of our encampment. Neither to the right nor left, nor any where before us, did we see the usual signs of its ever having been inhabited; at least, it must have been very thinly so at any time. In some of the openings we had glimpses, as it were, of deer and other animals, but they would not allow us to get near enough to have a shot at them, or even to say what many of them really were, though once or twice we thought we could make out some large black beasts, very like bears, which moved more slowly into the jungle. At one time, we came unexpectedly upon a kind of swampy meadow, here and there overgrown with flags, and near one end of it was a large pond, round which rose some reeds and tall bamboos. On approaching it, which we did cautiously, we suddenly heard the loud puffing and blowing of some large animals; and, through an opening, we could perceive the bluish backs, faces, standing out horns, and raised noses—all that was above the mud and water—of several buffaloes, which were enjoying themselves in it. Upon their discovering us, they all rushed out, bellowing and snorting dreadfully, but luckily they emerged at the opposite side of the pond to that upon which we stood, hardly well knowing what we should do. We had dismounted and taken the guns from our horse-keepers, and I confess I was not at all sorry when they all made off into the woods, unmolested by us. When we first saw what they were, we were both, I must say, desirous to have a shot at them, as we could easily have hit some of them, and we seized hold of our guns for the purpose; but, fortunately, we thought in time that it would be madness to do so, as in all probability the whole herd, (and there were at least a dozen of them), would have turned upon and attacked us, in which case, as our horses, owing to the badness and swampiness of the path, could scarcely have gone out of a walk, we, as well as our runaway horse-keepers, might have been at their mercy.

We saw here such vast numbers of pea and jungle fowl, wood pigeons, doves, &c. that we decided upon having, perhaps next morning, when we should all be upon the march, a regular battue, as the country seemed to be most admirably suited for the purpose.

In Ceylon, it is usually remarked, that wherever we fall in with great numbers of peafowl, we may make up our minds that either elephants or tigers, or probably both, are not far off, as they are almost always found together; yet we saw none, although, in two or three places, the deep prints of the feet of several of the former convinced us they had been there, and it was evident that a large herd had passed recently. Bringing back therefore our greatly frightened horse-keepers to their usual post, at the tails of the horses, and it being then later than we calculated upon, we thought it best to retrace our steps. We now, however, made up our minds, that should we find the path on our return obstructed by elephants, which was not improbable, we would try what effect brass balls would have upon their skulls, if we could not by any other means contrive to get them out of our way.

We now, therefore, kept a sharp look-out, so as not to be again taken by surprise; but this was scarcely necessary, as we knew that our horses would be sure to give us timely notice if we should come upon elephants: indeed, it then becomes very difficult to induce them to go forward; for the horse and elephant seem to have a natural mutual antipathy, and always shew, in a most marked manner, that they smell and have a dislike to each other. We, however, met with nothing but pea and jungle fowl, and of the former we shot three hens, which answer well enough for curries; but this we did not do until we saw by the smoke from the encampment, that, being near home, we might venture to take the balls out of the barrels of our guns, and substitute large shot for the purpose.

Just before we turned back, we had remarked, that about eight or perhaps ten miles farther on, there was every appearance of a river running amongst several thickly wooded hills; in consequence, we settled, that the following morning we should direct our march upon that point, and, as I hoped, be there able to erect our huts upon the bank of the Wellewey, or at least, upon that of one of its tributaries.

Whilst we were at breakfast Mr. C——, a young officer, who, notwithstanding the directions I had given, had lost his way several times in the woods whilst in search of us, arrived at the huts. In the hope of having a few days sport, he had volunteered to bring me some letters which I expected from Colombo. One of them informed me that a General Court-martial was to assemble at Galle, for the trial of an officer for neglect of duty, &c.; and, much to my annoyance, Sir Edward Barnes had directed, that, as Commandant of the district, I should act as prosecutor. This made it necessary for me to be back in Galle a few days sooner than I had intended; but I did not, in consequence, give up my purpose of reaching the Wellewey, though it became necessary to alter the day I had fixed upon for the inspection of the garrison of Matura.

Immediately after breakfast, accompanied by our new and highly delighted ally, we started for another bout of fishing up the river which I before alluded to; and had not proceeded two miles,—most of the way under the shade of some fine trees,—when we came to a place, which seemed to be admirably calculated for the purpose; for the river being rather low at the time, and running rapidly from one dark pool to another, over generally a rocky and gravelly bottom, and almost always clear of the trees, we had no reason to apprehend that our lines would, as was often the case the day before, become entangled in them. To my surprise, however, Mr. F—— showed to-day, I must say, a great want of taste, and but little or no inclination, for the noble piscatory art; and confessed to me—O shade of Isaac Walton!—that he would prefer trying his hand along with Mr. C—— upon the pea and jungle fowl, pigeons, doves, &c. which were, certainly, very numerous in all directions. I therefore sent one of the Malays along with them, keeping the other with me, to prevent my being surprised by any animals, which might approach the river whilst I was fishing.

The reports of their guns soon gave me to understand that they were busily engaged. I therefore thought that I would also see what I could do in the river with the red hackle, which had answered so well the previous day; but, after exerting my utmost skill for some time, I could only manage to get a few rises of certainly fine large fish; not one of which, however, seemed to be inclined to touch the artificial fly. I consequently had nothing for it, but to try once more the shrimp; and almost the very first throw really astonished me, for I soon had hold of a weighty and lively fish, which took the line to perfection—at times springing quite out of the water! He, however, soon exhausted his strength; when I had little difficulty in landing him handsomely upon a shelving rock, which enabled me to bring him easily out of the water. He appeared to me to be nearly four pounds in weight, with a dark greenish back, and silvery belly, with small dull yellow fins, and quite unlike any of those taken in the other river. I, of course, persevered with the shrimp; and before an hour and a half had elapsed, I had secured, in a hole full of water in the rock, altogether about a dozen of the same kind of fish, some of them larger and others about the same size as that first caught; and, I must say, I have seldom, in any part of the world, had better sport with bait—no, not even in the Richelieu, where it flows past St. John's in Lower Canada, and abounds in that excellent fish, black bass, many of which I caught with the worm when stationed there some years ago, and which afford the bait fisherman amusement almost equal to what he meets with from sea trout in some parts of Scotland and Ireland.

I beg here also to mention, that I sometimes caught fine pike in the Richelieu, when going by water from St. John's to Isle-aux-Noix; all I had to do, was to tow a long line after the boat, with the proper sized hook attached to it, dressed exactly like one of His Majesty's red and white regulation feathers, which the pike took greedily. I was taught this profitable mode of fishing, (and I would recommend those settled upon the banks of that fine river to adopt it) by that excellent and keen sportsman, Colonel Yates of the 49th, then stationed with his regiment in Isle-aux-Noix.

As the fish were not taking so fast as at first, I now thought that I would move to a pool a little way lower down the river; which, in appearance, promised quite as well as that I was leaving, and where I would once more try the red hackle. I therefore called to the Malay who kept watch, to come along with me ; and when he joined me, he was not a little surprised, at the display I had proudly made of my fine fish ; for I had laid them out, in order that they might be seen to advantage, side by side on the rock ; but I intended to put them back into the hole until my companions returned, which they had promised to do in about three hours. I still, however, heard them firing away, and, judging from the reports of their guns, which were loudly repeated by the echoes amongst the hills, they could not as yet have gone above a mile and a half from the river.

After a few rises from fish apparently larger than any I had yet caught, one of them at last fairly took the fly ; and went off in such style, as would have rejoiced the heart of any amateur. As the gut I used was fine, I believe I was at work little less than ten minutes, before I could venture to land him ; for I had neither cleek nor landing net ; but when he was close to my feet, and I was in the act of stooping down to lay hold of him, he made a sudden spring, and, being but slightly hooked, he got away from me. But, I had now become as keen, and was as much delighted with the sport, as the rural lover is said to have been with the riches and charms of his mistress, when his eyes glared,

> "Whilst Cupid's wing just gave a flutter,
> O'er the gay widow's crocks of butter !"

I now felt convinced that these fish had come up from the sea; as they completely answered the description given me by Mr. Farrell of those he supposed to have done so.

After a few minutes' rest, under the now agreeable shade of a magnificent tree, which spread out its branches over the rocks, and nearly extended them to the water's edge, I again set to work, and was not long in getting hold of another thumper, which likewise went off beautifully, so much so, that it required no little skill and ingenuity to manage him; for in spite of all I could do, he constantly sprung out of the water. He, however, by this so much the sooner exhausted his strength, that in about the same time as I had been engaged with the other, I laid him captive at my feet—he must have been almost a five-pounder.

Being thus agreeably and profitably occupied, time stole away imperceptibly; and, as my friends firing had a few minutes before ceased, I was in hopes of their soon re-joining me; for, in truth, what with the exertion of such fishing, and the heat, which had become excessive, as the breeze could not reach me in the bed of the river, I was by this time well inclined to go home. At this moment the Malay came to me, in all haste, to say that I ought to move, as he was sure the two gentlemen were coming this way, pursued by some large animals; for he had seen them running, as fast as they could, across an opening in the woods and towards the river. I instantly cut off my line and flies, and, to save time, put them inside my straw hat, wound up the line, unscrewed the fishing rod, and gave it to the Malay to carry; looked carefully at the flints and priming of my gun, and made the Malay do the same; and then mounting the bank I determined, at all risks, to stand my ground, and, if possible, to succour my friends in distress.

We had scarcely finished these preparations, when, closely followed by the Malay, the two gentlemen, made their appearance, almost breathless; but laughing immoderately. As soon as F—— was able to speak, he said that he had fired at a very large peacock, as he ran across a narrow opening in the jungle; upon which out of it rushed, crushing and breaking the smaller trees and shrubs around him, an enormous elephant. C——, whom I had cautioned to reserve one of the barrels of the gun always loaded with a brass ball, instantly took aim, and fired at the monster's head, when not twenty yards from him; but he did not fall, being only hit, some inches under the eye. F—— fired almost at the same instant, and as he said, with equal coolness; yet, still the animal fell not, though it staggered and seemed to be greatly stunned by the blow. Soon recovering, however, he continued his headlong course after them; and the Malay, firing in the hurry of the moment at random, called out to them to run for their lives. This they certainly all three then did in earnest. Many a fall they had; often did they stick fast among the long and tough creepers and prickly jungles, through which they had, sometimes, to force their way; not knowing all the while whether the elephant was still pursuing them or not; so that, by the time they reached me, they were—at least the two gentlemen—almost naked, the greater part of their clothes being left behind them, hanging in shreds upon the bushes and projecting spikes of the prickly-pear. Their laughter, when they were approaching the river, was caused by the figures they cut in each other's eyes, and of course they knew well they would in mine. Being convinced that the elephant had long ago given up the chase, and that we might now keep ourselves cool, I conducted them to the hole in the rock; and in triumph shewed them all my fine fish! requesting, at the same time, that they would produce their game. They had, they said, shot some pea and jungle fowl, a good many pigeons, &c. but that they were all, as I might well suppose, left behind in the woods; and as for the elephant, they were convinced that, had they not been in such a hurry, they might have bagged him; for they were quite certain that he must die, or probably had already died, of the wounds he had received.

We now took up the largest of the fish, and returned to the encampment; I, of course, vain enough of my success, and rather inclined to boast; and they by no means dejected or abashed at their defeat and flight; the blame for the latter they wished to throw upon the Malay, who had called out to them to run. When we reached the huts, and Appoo heard of their adventure with the elephant, he looked very grave, and said to me, "Sir, I told Master, bad come, when devil cry at night."—"Never mind, Appoo, he probably may treat us to another cry, in a night or two, at the Wellewey-ganga;—but, in the mean time, let us have at dinner to-day a good curry of some of the largest fish."

As soon as it had become sufficiently cool—that is to say, about four o'clock—we walked out, with our guns, into the jungle, to try if we could find the *certainly dead* elephant. He was nowhere to be seen; but the marks of his feet shewed plainly, that he had been able to go off into the woods to the eastward, as we could thereby trace, for some distance, the direction he had taken. We, however, picked up a few of the pea-hens, which had been slain and left behind; and returned with them in good time for dinner, after a very delightful walk, through a country fit not only for the abode of man, but also for many agricultural purposes.

The reader may well suppose, that, what with the admirably dressed venison pasty, a first rate fish curry, &c. our dinner in the jungle was this day not by any means to be despised; and we did not fail to do ample justice to the excellent fare placed before us, as well as to another bottle of cool Champagne. After the cloth was removed,—as was the fashion in those days—I contrived to mount my favourite hobby, that of recounting my fishing exploits, in various parts of the world; and

I told, much to my own satisfaction, if not to that of my friends, the following story.

Once upon a time, I spent a long leave of absence from my regiment, at a place I rented in Wales, situated in the neighbourhood of an ancient baronial castle; close to which was a pond, full of the largest and finest carp I had ever seen; which, day after day, in spring, summer, and the beginning of autumn, I had watched swimming about, sometimes almost touching the bank, and at others only shewing their broad backs, as they moved slowly along, almost on the surface of the water. Having permission from the wealthy proprietor to fish as often as I pleased in the pond, I had tried every kind of bait I could think of, or had ever heard of, such as red-worms, the cadis, grasshopper, &c. &c., but all to no purpose;—I could not catch one of them! I therefore gave up all hope of succeeding with such old and seemingly cunning fish; and consoled myself for my frequent disappointments, with the fine sport I had with trout, and sometimes salmon, with which the neighbouring brooks and rivers were supplied.

About the middle of August, it became necessary for me to go to Cheltenham; and when there I met, at the boarding house where I resided, a worthy clergyman, as great and as keen a fisherman as myself. It may therefore be supposed, that having become acquainted, we often spoke of our respective feats in the piscal line, upon various occasions, in which we imagined we had distinguished ourselves; but I must admit, that though I had more than once *doubled the Cape,* yet my brother of the angle invariably compelled me "to hide my diminished head;" even when I gave him, what I considered, would-be finishers.

One day, in the course of such conversation, I happened to mention what I considered my astonishing and complete failures in the attempts I had made to catch the large carp in the pond in Wales. "Will you, when you return home," said my new clerical ally, "proceed exactly as I am about to point out to you?"—I readily assured him that I would certainly follow whatever instructions he should give me. "Then," said he, "you must treat the carp with blue-ruin." "What do you mean?" "I mean, Sir, that you must treat the carp with their favourite beverage, *blue-ruin,* or in other words, with *gin,* or *hollands,* as blue ruin is vulgarly styled." "What, Sir, do you suppose that I am mad enough to ruin myself? Only think of my diluting a large pond with gin!" "By no means, Sir, you must use it in reasonable quantities; and also exactly as I was about to tell you, had you allowed me to edge in a word even sideways." "I am all silence." "Well, Sir, when you return home, take of fresh bread—the heart of a roll is the best—small pieces of the size of peas,—work them well between the finger and thumb, to make them more adhesive;—dip them, two or three times, in *blue-ruin,* with a sufficiency of white sugar dissolved in it:—put them, when properly prepared for use, into a small tin box, amongst some cotton saturated with the said *blue-ruin*, and which will prevent them from becoming too dry. Put one of these pellets upon your hook, which must not be too large, as carp have small mouths, and then see what you can do in the pond."

I confess, I was still somewhat incredulous, notwithstanding the high authority of such an experienced artist as the worthy parson represented himself to be, and the dogmatical style in which he was pleased to issue his instructions. I resolved, however, as he seemed to be greatly offended at my very evident unbelief, to make the attempt as soon as I got back to Wales. I did so, and the *blue-ruin* acted like magic! Nay, so wonderful was my success, (no one else being able to take a single carp,) that my repute as a skilful fisherman rose to the highest possible pitch; so much so, that, whenever the owner of the pond wanted carp to stew for company, he, or rather his lady, always requested, that I would be so good as to catch them; as her gamekeeper, who, when hired, pretended to understand fishing in all its branches, was found to be so deficient, that she began to think seriously of discharging him, on account of the ignorance he betrayed in not being able to take carp as I did, with only small bits of bread. Although matters never went to extremities with the gamekeeper, yet often did I hear of the poor fellow being soundly rated upon this account by his awful lady. I therefore fully intended to have acquainted him with the secret of the blue-ruin, but, being suddenly ordered off to my regiment, and before the fishing season had commenced, I forgot to do so; and I conclude, that the carp are as numerous now, and more weighty—some of them were fully sixteen pounders—than when I first treated them, according to the worthy parson's advice, with *blue-ruin.*

My two friends, during the recital of this interesting account of carp fishing, had, I must confess, more than once yawned, but I trust the reader has no inclination to follow their example; yet, as I am apprehensive that I may have tired his patience, I shall now go on to say, that the usual precautions having been taken, we passed the night without any serious disturbance from either beast or devil; and, about half an hour before dawn of day, we were all upon the line of march for the Wellewey river.

As we went along, we heard two or three times the trumpeting of elephants, and low growling of other wild beasts, to the right of the path; and, in one instance, some of the former seemed almost to have got upon the ground which we had just passed over. We thought it prudent, therefore, to shout as loudly as we could, and continued to do so, occasionally, for some minutes, which appeared to have the desired effect; for when the day dawned, or rather when the sun rose, in all his usual splendour, we neither saw nor heard any thing more of the animals, which had kept us upon the alert, from the time we left the huts. The rear was brought up by the Malays; my companions and I, prepared for events, riding in front. When we approached the swampy meadow, where the previous day we had surprised the herd of buffaloes, we pushed more rapidly forward, in order to dislodge them from the pond before our people should reach it; but there were none of them in it, nor were they to be seen in any direction. Having in consequence dismounted, and given our horses to their keepers, we at once commenced, as we had before arranged, the battue; the peacocks by their wild cries, as they sat perched in lofty trees, indicating where we might be sure to find their generally large broods, in company with numerous flocks of jungle-fowl.

In less than an hour several were slain: indeed, more than we, or a much more numerous band of carnivorous travellers, could possibly have wanted, had they solely depended upon their guns for food. We were moreover soon tired—at least I was—of this kind of sport; for having once set these birds running, and being seldom able to flush them, we had to set off as fast as we were able towards any openings in the jungle through which they were likely to pass, in order to get perhaps a shot or two each at them. In crossing some soft parts on the jungle, I observed distinctly the old foot marks of many elephants; and the fresh ones of what I thought must have been those of both tigers and bears; yet we saw none of them, nor did we meet with any adventure. But, being now greatly fatigued and heated by this mode of hunting, we were glad to rejoin our people, who had impatiently waited for us in considerable uneasiness in the open space where we had left them. We then resumed our march in the supposed direction of the Wellewey. As we went forward, we twice saw places, where there had been human habitations, but now only parts of their mud walls remained; all the cocoa-nut trees, which once had stood around them, had evidently been pulled down and broken by elephants: indeed, every thing indicated that they had been for many years deserted by man.

It was past 11 A.M. before we came to a river; but whether it was or not that we were in search of, we could only conjecture. It, however, flowed through a wild, hilly, and seemingly less thickly wooded country than that we had just left; but the scenery, and apparently rich soil upon its banks, were of a very superior kind, and particularly attracted my attention. Excepting, however, the kind of path, which looked more like what would have been made by animals than by men, we could find no other, either up or down the stream, which was fordable in several places; and at the fords, we saw abundant proofs of various kinds of beasts having either recently crossed, or that they had come down on both sides of the river to drink.

Having selected a suitable spot, clear of jungle, and shaded by some lofty trees, all hands set to work to construct our huts; and, as plenty of materials were at hand, they were soon finished, and even in time for a late breakfast, for which the morning's exercise had well prepared us. I must now, however, observe, that I was greatly struck with the enchanting beauty of the spot we had reached; and the following Singalese description of their charming country is most appropriate to it, and may be considered as by no means an over-drawn picture—" it is celebrated for the cold and lovely waters of its rivers, for its mountain torrents, and for its flowery groves, spreading in the air their sweet-scented pollen;—which is the crown of the Virgin Island, rich in mines of all kinds of precious stones, like a maid decked with jewels."

CHAPTER XII.

> ". . . . . . But who can paint
> Like Nature? Can Imagination boast,
> Amid its gay creation, hues like hers?
> Or can it mix them with that matchless skill,
> And lose them in each other, as appears
> In every bud that blows?"—THOMSON.

AN ELEPHANT DISCOVERED CLOSE TO THE ENCAMPMENT, AND SHOT — AN EVENING WALK IN THE FOREST — REFLECTIONS — ANOTHER NIGHT IN THE JUNGLE — THE DEVIL CRY — UPROAR AMONG THE ANIMALS DEVOURING THE CARCASES OF A BUFFALO, AND THE ELEPHANT SHOT —A MORNING WALK IN THE FOREST—EXCELLENT SHOOTING—SET OUT TO FISH—A SPLENDID THUNDER-STORM—INTERESTING FISHING—STARED AT BY A TIGER—ADVENTURE WITH A HERD OF BUFFALOES—EVENING WALK IN THE JUNGLE—SPORTS—LOSE OUR WAY IN RETURNING TO THE ENCAMPMENT—A NIGHT SCENE—A REPAST AFTER THE FATIGUES OF THE CHASE—ATTEMPT TO ASTONISH BEARS AND OTHER ANIMALS—ANOTHER NIGHT IN THE JUNGLE—OBSERVATIONS—A MORNING'S RIDE, AND A DEER SHOT—ALARM OF OUR SERVANTS AT BEING LEFT IN THE ENCAMPMENT—FISHING AND SHOOTING—REMARKS.

BEING a good deal tired and even exhausted, by the heat we had been exposed to during the morning's march, we decided that we would neither fish, shoot, nor do any thing in the way of sport, until evening. But, whilst I was reading out, for my companions' amusement, from Brantome's Lives

"Des Dames Illustres," that of the beautiful, but unfortunate "Marie Steuart, Reyne D'Escosse, et jadis Reyne de nostre France,"—all of us being, for coolness sake, in very light attire—one of the servants ran into our hut, in great alarm, exclaiming that he had just seen an elephant in a clump of trees, to which he pointed, not more than three hundred yards off. I, at least, had no wish whatever to encounter such an antagonist, if I could avoid doing so; but it was, in council, deemed advisable to dislodge him, as otherwise we might have to move our encampment; and to do so, none of us were inclined. It was therefore settled, that we should attack him—that is, if we could not by any other means induce him to retire, and that, too, without delay.

Having carefully loaded our guns with brass balls, we moved forward all three together; the Malays, who seemed greatly to enjoy the fun, forming a supporting column in our rear. It was also arranged, that if the elephant stood his ground, I was to have the first shot;—how then was it possible for me not to perform my part upon the occasion?

By entering at a projecting point of the jungle, and being led, much against his will, by the servant who said that he had seen the elephant, we were able to come within a short distance of him, before he could perceive us. When he did so, or rather when he heard the noise which we could not avoid making in approaching him, however cautiously, he suddenly turned round upon us, cracking and breaking the smaller trees and branches, as he shuffled forwards towards the edge of the clump of jungle, so as to face us. I think we were then not more than fifteen yards from his head. I fired, and my two companions did so likewise, and with the utmost coolness; when down fell the huge creature, quite dead, almost at our feet! But, to our astonishment, away went some other elephants and a buffalo, which we had no idea were in the middle of the cover, trumpeting loudly, and crashing every thing that obstructed their passage; and, most fortunately for us, they did not seem to have missed their unlucky companion, as we could hear them, for some time, continuing their impetuous course through the jungle, and towards the wooded hills to the eastward. As for the buffalo, in her hurried attempt to escape, she took to the right, and thus fully exposing herself, Mr. F—— fired his second barrel at her, which breaking one of her fore legs, she fell, with a great crash, not more than twelve yards from us; and whilst she was endeavouring to rise, Mr. C—— sent the ball from his other barrel through her body, which instantly ended her sufferings. I confess, however, I should have been glad had she escaped; as she seemed to be only half wild. We had in this instance managed admirably, and we were therefore not a little proud of ourselves; for upon examining the elephant, which though large, had very short tusks, we found that no less than two of the balls had entered the brain, and the third had penetrated the head from the root of the trunk. This feat was performed, and we were all back in the huts, talking the matter over, in less than half an hour from the time we had left them.

In the evening we took a walk, with our guns in our hands, as we wished to get a shot at a deer, should we be lucky enough to fall in with one; for we all admitted that a venison pasty, or even a fat haunch roasted, ought to satisfy us sportsmen, even if we had had more fastidious appetites than we possessed. I should here remark, however, that the venison of Ceylon is very inferior to that of Great Britain, being seldom fat, and too often tasteless or insipid food; yet several parts of a deer or elk make good pies and soup; and, when jugged like a hare, forms an excellent dish, although we have not here port wine to use as an ingredient.—As for buffalo beef, it is wretched coarse stuff, fit only, at best, for soup.

Besides shooting a deer or two, another of our objects was to reconnoitre the river, in order to find out where it would be best for me to fish the next day, whilst my companions made another attack upon the pea-fowl, or any thing else they might chance to fall in with: indeed, they both declared that they considered bagging pea and jungle-fowl quite as good sport as pheasant shooting in England, in which opinion, however, I by no means coincided. We therefore resolved upon ascending the river, or at all events to keep as near to its banks as we could; and, as we soon came upon some good sized openings in the woods, we found this far from being so difficult a task as we expected. We had not gone more than two miles when we came to what had formerly been rice fields, but which had evidently been long neglected; the mounds made to confine the water for irrigation having been entirely destroyed. This induced us to look for houses, and from the decaying stumps of some once fine cocoa-nut trees, either cut down, or broken by elephants, we soon found where they had stood; little else, however, remained, but their crumbling walls, which were nearly hidden by various kinds of fine shrubs and beautiful wild flowers, many of the latter, by the places they now occupied, plainly indicating that they had been long deserted by man; yet still

> " . . . . Nature did an arbour green disspred,
> Framed with wanton ivie, flowering faire
> Through which the fragrant eglantine did spred
> His pricking arms, entayled with roses red,
> Which dainty odours round about him threw;
> And all within with flowres was garnished,
> That, when mild Zephyrous emongst them blew,
> Did breathe out bounteous smells, and painted colours shew."

I was aware that we had now got into what was of old considered to be part of the Kandyan country, and that the path we had hitherto followed, would ultimately lead us into Lower Ouvah; and that during the rebellion, our troops had sometimes marched in this direction, when the people, alarmed for the consequences of falling into their hands, from knowing well that they had provoked their enmity, abandoned their dwellings, and had not since returned to them. Amongst the ruins, which here and there were to be seen,—some of them upon such a scale, and of such superior workmanship, as quite surprised us—we saw evident marks, that the wild beasts of the forest had resumed what had once been their ancient possessions ; and it would now, from their greatly increased numbers, be an undertaking far beyond the power or means of the almost disarmed Kandyans to expel them. Indeed, there is not a doubt, but that they were then daily more and more encroaching, even upon the inhabited parts of the maritime provinces. War, I grieve to say, every where, and under all circumstances, is nearly the same ; and the necessity for it is always deeply to be deplored, as it invariably brings in its train misery and desolation. For the time allotted by Divine Providence a warlike nation is in the ascendant, every thing seems to prosper with them, and they carry their conquests into other and even distant lands. Again, when the iniquity of such a nation is full, and rises up in judgment against them, and when their rulers, perhaps, are foolishly boasting, that they have made themselves or their position so strong that they cannot be moved, the fiat goes forth, and a mightier nation comes, in general suddenly, upon them, and their country, in its turn, is made desolate.

Who that witnessed the awful visitation of Portugal, can ever forget the sufferings of her people, when they were driven before the then triumphant French behind the lines of Torres Vedras? The old, the young, the high born dame, and the wife of the peasant, in short, the entire population of provinces, thronged the different roads leading to Lisbon. Many, whom I had before known living in affluence and retirement, had to endure, comparatively, greater wretchedness than the common beggar, and were exposed to equal starvation. To many of all classes the officers and soldiers of the British army gave all the food they could possibly spare, to enable, sometimes, even the members of a lately rich family to crawl slowly along upon roads strewed with the dying, or those who were already dead, from the effects of too great and unbearable fatigue, or who were unable to proceed from actual want of nourishment of any kind, for they had been obliged, in many instances, to fly before the enemy's rapidly advancing cavalry, leaving all they had collected behind them; and we were at the time informed,—and I believe correctly,—that a considerable number of ladies, old and young, who had for safety, and under the charge of some priests, taken the mountain road from Guarda to Leiria, and who had hoped that they would not be followed or known of in that out-of-the-way direction, fell into their hands, and were treated with every possible indignity. Let us, however, imagine if we can, the distracted feelings of so many unfortunates the night before they set out from their beloved homes,—what restlessness, discomfort and terror must have pervaded their minds, when thus awakened from a comparative state of peacefulness to the actual miseries of war. Great Britain has not for very many years been so scourged; and may she never again experience such calamities. But when the fugitives from the interior had even got out of the reach of the French, their miseries were not then by any means ended; for it was impossible to maintain and lodge, even in the most wretched manner, so vast a multitude, as were thrown almost destitute into so small a space, although the capital of the kingdom was included within it. All who witnessed what then took place, have only to endeavour to recall to their remembrance the scenes of want and woe they beheld, and they must readily admit that war is everywhere, and under all circumstances, nearly the same; and those who aided in expelling the French from that then ruined country had another opportunity of seeing its fearful effects, for the towns, villages, hamlets, convents and country houses, being nearly all reduced to ashes, the yet smoking ruins pointed out to us the roads taken by the French columns in their disastrous retreat into Spain. During that retreat they were closely pressed by our exasperated troops, many of whom had been kindly and hospitably treated by the Portuguese, and were indignant at beholding the calamities brought upon Portugal, by such a ruthless mode of warfare, which they were seldom able either to prevent or mitigate.

France, in her turn, became the theatre of war;

but it fell not then in all its horrors upon her, such as she had too often inflicted it on other countries. Her day, however, may yet come; and let her mark well the consequences which may arise from fortifying her capital. If her sons, eager to avenge their defeats, and feeling humiliated as well as indignant at the disgrace to their arms of having La Belle France occupied by the allies, cannot by a wise King be restrained from deeds of violence, and if, as is not unlikely, they should once more be vanquished, she may rely upon it, that she cannot always expect to fall into the hands of a merciful and influential conqueror, who can induce the chiefs of other nations to spare her; and when, the wall and fort-enclosed space being much too extensive to be successfully defended, it may one day become the grave of myriads, the victims of a mad and reckless ambition, and of an insatiable thirst for universal dominion.

I hope I may be pardoned for having thus digressed—but, I must now remark, that were it not for the destruction of the cocoa-nut, bread-fruit, and a few other trees, as well as the embankments, formed at great labour, to confine the waters required for irrigating the rice fields, no country can suffer less from the effects of war than Ceylon. Its climate is so mild or temperate, that, unless it be during the rainy seasons, the people have no need of substantial buildings. Their wants are few, and their clothing—at least that of the lower castes—consists merely of long strips of cotton cloth, rolled round their middles, and hanging down to their knees. If forced, from whatever cause, to abandon their dwellings, they have only to remove their few effects to a suitable situation, where materials are always at hand for building and thatching new ones. In both ancient and modern history, we read of vast cities, such as the mighty Babylon, &c. of which, excepting stones, or broken bricks, and mounds, or heaps of rubbish, no vestiges remain; and, generally, thus perish all the works of man—

> "But mighty Nature bounds as from her birth,
> The sun is in the heavens, and life on earth;
> Flowers in the valley, splendour in the beam,
> Health in the gale, and freshness in the stream."

Such great changes do not, however, surprise those who have travelled, especially in the East; for almost all the dwellings of the people there, as we may fairly conclude, having been constructed of mud, wood, and other perishable substances, time, a conflagration, floods, the white ants, and other destructive insects, soon obliterate or consume all such structures; the inhabitants, probably, perishing during a war, in the flames, or by pestilence and famine; or perhaps they removed to other settlements, out of the reach of their conquerors; and thus it is, that so little now remains for investigation, or to satisfy curiosity. Yet, in Ceylon, I have no doubt that an antiquary can have as ample a field for research or speculation, amidst its numerous and surprising ruins, and its remaining stupendous works, achieved by its ancient inhabitants, and he may hear as many legendary or traditional tales connected with them, as in any other part of the world.

Thoughts like these occupied my mind, whilst endeavouring to discover among the rapidly overgrowing shrubs, flowers and trees, more of the ruins of what probably had been temples, as well as of the simple, but generally snugly situated abodes of the Kandyans of former days; but at length, the train of them was broken by my observing, coiled up on the top of a crumbling wall, a large harmless house, or, as it is called, rat-snake, which performs the duties of a cat in this part of the world. As soon as it perceived me, it glided gently and quietly away, uninjured by me, into a corner occupied by some beautiful flowering creepers—chiefly wild jasmine—which had taken complete possession of the interior of the building. But we had now spent a good deal of time in exploring these ruins, and also in amusing ourselves by throwing sticks and stones at a number of small, green, cross-grained monkeys, which had taken up their abode in some tall trees overhanging a brook, that, among a profusion of foliage, stole unseen, but was distinctly heard murmuring, under two old and long-neglected orange trees, as it ran past the end of what had, seemingly, been once a large temple. It is really curious to see with what surprising agility and dexterity these little creatures spring from the branches of one tree to those of another, several of them with their young ones riding, legs astride, upon their projecting hips, their faces turned inwards, and their weight supported by a paw placed round their waists, precisely as the Singalese women, in general, carry their pretty, nicely oiled, and, as it were polished, little, quite naked children.

Having been thus tempted to stay too long, and the sun being about to set behind the finely wooded hills to the westward, we were obliged to hasten back to the encampment, without any additional provision having been made for our table, except a few turtle doves; thousands of which, as well as pigeons, were unceasingly cooing in the woods we passed through: indeed, I was well aware, that there could be no want in this respect; and moreover, I felt somewhat anxious to see, before it became quite dark, that our watch-fires were made sufficiently large to insure their burning brightly until morning; as it was evident that we were among neighbours likely to be both encroaching and troublesome. Our servants had, I conclude, been of the same opinion, for they had not only provided a larger supply than usual of both dry and green wood, but, of their own accord, they now also offered again to take it in turn, along with the Malays, to watch and to give us notice of any alarming appearances or noises during the night. I therefore stipulated with my two companions that we should, at stated hours, visit our sentinels, in order to ascertain that they were really upon the alert.

After doing that justice it merited to a good

dinner; and having nearly worn out the early part of the night in agreeable chat, over a bottle of excellent Madeira,—not having forgotten to introduce a bottle of Champagne during the repast—I proposed, before we should retire to rest, to read for my friends' amusement, and in the hope of inspiring them with a liking for my favourite pastime, in which I was sorry to see that they were both sadly deficient, some accounts or anecdotes of fishing; but with which I have no intention of occupying the reader's time, as, like them, he might probably feel inclined to yawn, during the recital of the most interesting parts of the story. But soon finding that they had no taste for "the gentle art," I begged to know whether they wished for more wine, or would prefer coffee being brought in, before going to bed. As both seemed inclined for the latter, I told them that I would only see that all was right before I lay down, as I could distinctly hear a vast deal of howling of jackals close to us.

On my going up to the sentinel, one of the Malays, he said he had never in the whole course of his life, much as he had been in the jungle, heard such a tearing and worrying as were going on in the wood where the dead elephant and the greater part of the buffalo lay; and he was certain that hundreds of animals, especially jackals and wild dogs, were closely engaged in fighting over and devouring the carcasses. Of this I was soon fully convinced, (for I was really astonished at the uproar kept up,) and I concluded it would be best to send some rounds of buck-shot among them, in order to disperse them; but this the sagacious and experienced Malay did not approve of; it would, he thought, be much wiser to let them alone, as they were evidently far too well occupied, to be likely to trouble or come near us for the night; and he was sure that the brightly blazing fires would deter all other animals from approaching our huts. But he now requested me to listen, and I would soon hear, what our foolish servants talked so much of—that is to say, the "devil cry," for he had just heard it. In less than a minute, I was certainly much surprised at the extraordinary dismal, or melancholy kind of sound I heard, seemingly about three or four hundred yards off; and I confess that I have not the most distant idea by what animal or bird it was uttered. I desired the Malay, however, to say nothing of it to the servants, as it would only uselessly alarm them, and tend to increase their absurd superstitious apprehensions of approaching calamities.

As my companions, on my return to the hut, were not in bed, I requested that they would come out, quietly, to hear "the devil cry;" but, although we listened attentively for some time, the strange sound was not repeated. The uproar in the wood had, however, considerably increased; and we thought we could hear, as it were, the growling of bears and other large animals; yet, having nothing but bright star light, we could not make out what was going forward, nor of what species the brutes were, which seemed to be so busily occupied.

Though the night had, certainly, not passed without noise, yet nothing else had happened to annoy or disturb us; and getting under arms at dawn of day, and having as usual taken a cup of hot coffee, (which I strongly recommend Europeans residing in Ceylon to do every morning,) we decided upon crossing the river at a ford a little lower down; for, as the country in that direction seemed to be more open, we hoped to fall in with a deer, hog, or some animal which would afford a substantial supply of food for the encampment, of which we now began to be in need, having all become tired of pea and jungle-fowl, whether roasted or in curries; and as for the cold venison pasty it had totally disappeared. The reader ought also to recollect, that meat of any kind, in this climate, will seldom keep above a day, especially in temporary huts like those which we now occupied Before setting out, I however thought it would be well, in case of our failing in procuring a deer, to take with me some small shot; being aware, that if we should come to a swamp, which was more than probable, I should be sure to find plenty of snipes, and perhaps water-fowl. As for the unlucky pea and jungle-fowl, we agreed that no more of them were to be slaughtered until after breakfast; and as I concluded that the heat would then prevent my companions from continuing the battue too long, so much the more powder and shot would thus be saved.

We were more fortunate, and had much better sport, than I calculated upon; for, having come upon some extensive marshy meadows, which seemed as if they had once been rice grounds, with here and there small ponds of muddy water, which had evidently been recently stirred up by buffaloes or elephants wallowing in them, we found a good many teal, ducks, &c. in or near them, as well as hundreds of beautiful white paddy-birds, considered, I know not why, unfit for food; which scarcely took any notice of us, or seemed to be alarmed at our approach. Of the former we shot several; and as for snipes, I, as the only tolerable snipe-shot of the party, was quite tired of firing at them; so that we were soon ready to return with an ample supply of provisions; and, what were looked upon as great prizes, we had killed three of those curious and almost black ducks, with long and surprisingly thin necks, the bill terminating in a very fine point, which are considerably larger in the body than the common duck in England. We saw some deer at a distance; but could not manage to get sufficiently nigh them to have a chance of bringing them down: indeed, our firing so much at snipes and other birds caused the deer to retire into the jungle.

The morning had been exceedingly cool and pleasant, so that we had not only enjoyed an agreeable walk through a finely-wooded country, in many places adorned with shrubs of various kinds, and lovely flowers; but we had also had excellent sport. We therefore returned to the huts, before nine o'clock, literally groaning under the weight of our game, though most of it was carried by our always ready and obliging Malays. It may probably be said, that I am no true sportsman, but I consider this very superior sport to bagging elephants or buffaloes.

Had it not been for the sake of the exercise, always invariably taken in shooting, and likewise that I was anxious to assist in procuring a supply of food, I would have preferred commencing at daylight an attack in this, I may suppose, untouched river, upon the fish; with which, judging from its appearance, I hoped that it abounded; for I fully agree with the angler-poet, who, in rehearsing the delights of fishing, says

> "Then soon as morn has chased the shades of night
> And streaked the purple east with rosy light,"

that a real fisherman ought to be up and doing; but as angling, at least in the way in which I intended upon this occasion to pursue the pastime, was much less fatiguing and heating than shooting, and as in some places I could do so under the grateful shade of lofty and widely spreading trees, I had to be content with setting out about eleven o'clock, to fish down the river; whilst my two allies, accompanied as before by one of the Malays, were to re-commence hostilities upon peacocks and all manner of birds, in the neighbouring woods and jungle. I had moreover desired Appoo to send something for tiffin, to a place I pointed out, about a mile and a half down the river, where they agreed to join me at two o'clock, by which hour they would, most likely, after their exertions, stand in need of refreshment.

I had scarcely reached the part of the river where I intended to fish, when I perceived towards the mountains that the horizon had assumed, and was every moment more and more assuming, an exceedingly dull lurid appearance, so that even the more level country around me soon became enveloped in the deepest gloom; which, contrasting strongly with a dark reddish colour in the sky to the westward, produced that extraordinary aspect of the heavens, which, in this country, usually portends the most awful thunder-storm.

Thus warned, I sought for shelter till it should pass away to the westward. A strange calm prevailed for a few minutes, during which not a leaf of a tree was seen to move; and even the birds had ceased to sing, and the numerous insect tribes to send forth their almost incessant humming, buzzing, or chirping sounds; next, large flocks of paddy and other birds were to be seen flying, in search of shelter, before the now rapidly approaching storm.

At first, slight gusts of wind were felt, that only raised and whirled about the fallen withered leaves from the ground, which, being mixed with sand and dust, almost suffocated, and annoyed us greatly;

but this lasted only a few minutes, for the storm now burst furiously over us. Flashes of lightning and loud peals of thunder seemed even to shake the ground, as well as the projecting rock under which we stood out of the reach of the dense body of water falling around us; and we could thus admire, quietly, the war carried on in the elements. This splendid natural phenomenon did not last above half an hour; for the sun broke suddenly through the last of the dark masses of clouds, and instantly restored to surrounding objects their usual or rather improved verdure, beauty and brilliancy! Such changes of weather are common in this part of Ceylon, and have always the effect of rendering the atmosphere, for at least a few hours, more cool and agreeable; at all events, I expected, that in this instance the rain which had fallen would improve my sport in the river, which was only very slightly discoloured by it.

I must not tire the reader, who, perhaps, has no soul for the music of the fishing-reel, with a minute account of my feats upon this occasion, for they were much the same as before, and the fish were fully as large as those basketed on the previous day; and as I did not tumble into the river, nor encounter an alligator, my adventures, except in one instance, were not much more interesting or worthy of being recorded. But, whilst I was busily playing a good sized fish, I am inclined to think that a tiger peeped out of a patch of jungle at me, from the opposite side of the stream: but instantly disappeared, upon my eyes, as I fancied, meeting his!—I might have been mistaken, but still I am convinced that I was not: nevertheless, I, in a moment, threw down my fishing-rod, snatched up my gun that lay on the ground near me, loaded with brass balls, and stood prepared for events. Whatever it might have been, it was now, however, gone; yet, I confess, that a curious kind of tremor or odd sensation, ran through me, which induced me to call out loudly to my Malay sentinel to come to my aid, which he immediately did. But though we, without delay, crossed the river a little higher up, in order to make out what animal it could have been, and, if prudent, fully determined to shoot him, yet, we found or saw none: but there were, though slightly imprinted, the marks of the feet of a large beast, which had, unquestionably, been at the very spot where I fancied that I had seen the face and glaring eyes of a tiger. This was, undoubtedly, most interesting fishing; but, under such circumstances, I suspect that even the keenest and coolest brother of the angle could scarcely, with composure, have continued his piscatory amusements.

Before the time appointed, my completely-exhausted and most thirsty companions made their appearance at the place fixed upon; and this day, also, without the produce of their labours. Most gladly and eagerly did they avail themselves of the refreshing and exhilarating draught presented to them, of a large and well-filled glass each, of that favourite beverage brewed in England, and so well known all over India, by the name of Hodgson's pale ale; some bottles of it having been well cooled in a spring issuing from a rock in the bank of the river. What a blessing it is to find in Ceylon, at least in the southern half of it, so many beautifully clear, pure, and where not exposed to the sun's rays, actually cold brooks and fountains! which, in such a climate, are invaluable: indeed, I believe that no country on earth is more favoured in this respect. Having thus refreshed themselves, (and what would not a worn out traveller in an African desert have given for such refreshment!) their appetites, which excessive heat and fatigue had taken away, returned, and they could do something like justice to the food set before them. They were then able to tell me, that while in eager pursuit of game, of which they had shot a considerable quantity, they all at once came upon a pond, in which, and wallowing in the mud, were a herd of buffaloes. Being surprised and unprepared, they had very imprudently taken to their heels, when instantly out rushed the whole of the buffaloes after them, in a compact body, and apparently with the intention of charging them! Fortunately, at the suggestion of the experienced Malay, they turned round, and boldly faced their pursuers, which then also halted, tearing up the ground with their horns and feet, and bellowing with all their might, as is their custom when about to attack. But, being now close to a patch of jungle, the sportsmen retreated slowly, but still facing their foes, into it,—

the terrific brutes closely following them! The moment, however, they were able to get out of their sight, they changed the direction of their retreat, and finding some openings amidst the jungle, through which they could pass, still concealed from the buffaloes, they, by hard running, were soon clear of them; yet they could distinctly hear them dashing straight a-head, not many yards to their right. Very wisely, they had not ventured to fire, though they had each a ball in one of the barrels of their guns, the other being charged with shot. Had they foolishly fired upon such a large herd, as they represented this to be, and thereby increased their rage, there is no saying what might have been the consequences; for I believe, and it is what I have often heard, that there is not so dangerous an animal in Ceylon to encounter, as the once infuriated buffalo. The reader may therefore easily imagine the completely exhausted state, after nearly a mile's run, in which my friends arrived at the river, and how much they stood in need of a restorative. As for my being peeped at by a tiger, if it really was one, across a narrow river, it was nothing to be compared with the danger they had been in. We now, however, laughed heartily at each other, and at the valour we all had evinced, (for I candidly confessed how much I had been frightened,) under the circumstances in which we were respectively placed. It is a very different thing to go up prepared to shoot an elephant, to what it is to be taken by surprise, and to be suddenly and unexpectedly charged by a furious herd of buffaloes, or pounced upon by a tiger, as a cat springs upon a mouse.

But, whilst we talked, and laughed at each other, we thought that we heard a sound like that of large animals rushing through the jungle; and, as it were, breaking off the branches of trees, probably, two or three hundred yards off, and in the direction we might now look for the victorious buffaloes, had they been able to trace the fugitives; and we were not long in ascertaining, that the noise we heard was occasioned by their actually coming towards the river, very likely as thirsty as my friends had been, not long before, when they arrived upon its banks. The servants and coolies, who had brought tiffin, at once crossed the stream, and ran off towards the encampment. But we determined to get up, valiantly, into two trees, which stood close to the bank of the river, and in them we all, including the Malays, resolved to await their approach; expecting that the result would be a supply, though not of the most acceptable description of food, for the encampment. We had scarcely made ourselves snug among the sufficiently high branches, before about a score of huge buffaloes were within a short distance of us. As they had not perceived us, the sudden and unlooked-for fire opened upon them, completely surprised and disconcerted them; for they all instantly turned round and fled in every direction: some of them being wounded, but only a terrific bull so badly as to be unable to follow the rest;—him I singled out, and the second ball from my gun brought him down.

Having achieved this easy victory, we immediately made preparations for returning to the huts, which we did loaded with fish, and with a few of the best parts of the buffalo, which were soon cut off by the Malays with their sharp kreeses; and taking also with us the plates, knives, forks, &c. which had been used at tiffin, and abandoned in their terror by our run-away servants.

A fine and rather cool evening induced us to take another walk in the woods; partly with the intention of looking for some of the dead birds, which my friends, in their hurry to escape from the buffaloes, had left behind them; but more particularly, with the view of being amused by a number of large bearded monkeys, which we had seen, high up in some trees, as we came along. But, to our delight, we met with more birds of many kinds than we had expected, and consequently had such good sport, that we were tempted to proceed farther into the jungle than we were aware of; for, on looking to the westward, I saw that it was high time to return; and well might we have said with the ancient bard,—"hast thou left thy blue course in the heaven, golden-haired son of the sky?"—he had indeed; and it therefore became necessary for us instantly to wend our way towards the huts, or we might not probably be able to find them by the pale light of a moon only a few days old, and which, if we did not step out, would be hidden behind some finely wooded hills to our left, that still served as objects to guide us to our temporary home.

Thus warned of the lateness of the hour, (for, as I before remarked, we have here only a few minutes twilight) we loaded ourselves with as many of the birds, which we had just shot amongst some rushy ponds of muddy water, as were worth carrying; these we tied at the ends of long and light pieces of bamboo, balanced upon our shoulders, as coolies here carry their loads. We now proceeded homeward; but we had a much longer walk before us than we calculated upon; and did not reach the encampment till we were completely tired and exhausted. Our servants had been long expecting us back; and were become very uneasy at being left alone in the so much dreaded jungle, and at our being out at so late an hour in so wild and dangerous a country, "where the boars in the woods are many."

Several times we went astray in the labyrinths of the forest; and I was often uncertain whether we should that night reach the huts; as the moon had set, and darkness had hidden from our sight such objects as might have enabled us to find them. Indeed, we should have crossed the river at a wrong ford, and thus have passed them altogether, had I not, by chance, recognized some remarkably fine trees—by that time covered with fire-flies—hanging in an extraordinary manner over the rocky bed of the river, where I had been in the forenoon when fishing; for until then I really did not know where we were; and to have lost our way in the dark, in such a "howling wilderness," would have been by no means an agreeable predicament. I then, however, as guide, went forward confidently, though every moment expecting to fall in with some of the animals, of which, the night before, we had heard so much. But the uncommon and exciting situation, in which I thus found myself placed, brought vividly to my recollection the following beautiful lines of Ossian.—"The chase is over. No noise on Ardven but the torrent's roar.—Night comes apace, thou blue-eyed maid! Grey night grows dim along the plain. I saw a deer at Crona's stream: a mossy bank he seemed through the gloom, but soon he bounded away. A meteor played round his branching horns! The awful faces of other times looked from the clouds of Crona." We soon, however, arrived at the encampment; but I cannot say, that we had heard no noises but the torrent's roar; for, in approaching it, the howling of dogs and jackals, and growling of animals prowling around our already lit watchfires, were loud enough to make us feel far from comfortable.

Before we had time to dress for dinner, a most plentiful repast was displayed upon the board; and as the events of the day had been interesting, and afforded ample subjects for agreeable and mirthful conversation, I do not remember, upon any occasion in the jungle, having spent a more pleasant evening; or that I ever so much enjoyed my share of a bottle of Champagne,—of which we had still a few left—as well as a fair proportion of fine old Madeira; for I do not pretend to be one of those squeamish or over-refined sportsmen, who cannot play their part in an attack upon their own game; or who refuse to wash down the greater part of a wild duck with a glass of generous wine. But I must at the same time beg, that the good-natured reader will not for a moment imagine, though I occasionally, and with the intention of shewing how we fared in the jungle, speak of good cheer, that I am either a bon-vivant or a toper; and I must assure him, that though I here do my best to merit the blessing of a good appetite, that I am neither the one nor the other; but, how can any one, unless he eats and drinks as a man ought to do, bear up against fatigue and violent exercise in any country, but especially in a hot and naturally debilitating climate like this.

The usual arrangements for the security of the encampment during the night having been duly attended to; and we having made up our minds to remain where we were for another day, (how much I regretted that I had not time to penetrate further into this fine sporting country, in which, no doubt, may be found soils well suited for various agricultural purposes); we directed the sentinel to call us at the very first appearance of the dawn of day. As we had here no village cock "to crow salutation to the morn," although the shrill harsh cry of the jungle-cock in some degree answers the same purpose, we thought it best that he should rouse us out of our slumbers; upon receiving which signal we purposed mounting our horses, to take advantage of the many openings we had observed in the jungle, and to ride considerably farther than we had yet gone, in the hope of getting a shot at deer or elks; of which, judging from the marks of their feet that we had seen, there ought to be many in the direction we intended to take.

But, in order to see if it were not possible to disperse the assemblage of brutes, which came nightly to devour the carcasses of the elephant and buffalo, and thereby to insure something like tranquillity in our neighbourhood, we had, before we left the encampment for the evening's shooting, determined to try the effects of fastening our two spare guns in such a manner to trees, as would insure that the balls fired from them would strike the parts of the prey which seemed to be esteemed the greatest delicacies. Not having with us sufficiently long cords to attach to the triggers, we had to use, as substitutes, the long thin and tough stems of creepers, of which there were abundance growing in all directions. These we drew rather tight, making them fast to the buffalo, and to one of the fore legs of the elephant, which, by his having fallen upon his side, was raised nearly three feet from the ground; so that any large animals, going to play their parts at supper, would be sure to run against them, pull the triggers, and probably receive the contents of the barrels in their bodies. About nine o'clock we heard one of the guns go off, which was followed by the most extraordinary uproar, growling, &c. which can well be imagined; for it had, apparently, seriously discomposed such keen guests as had given the preference to the beginning of the feast to the end of the fray. This was followed by quietness for perhaps a quarter of an hour, when we heard the jackals, especially, as busily at work as ever; and soon after, off went the other gun, which seemed to have the same effects as the first. But, as we considered the better part of valour to be discretion, we did not deem it advisable to go before morning to see the result of our stratagem. When the servants ventured to do so, nothing whatever was to be found to shew whether any injury had been sustained by the gourmands or not; and though some of them might have received severe, or even mortal wounds, yet they had been able to go off into the jungle.

How exciting, and how similar to the life of a soldier in the field, is that of the sportsman in a country like this; where, night and day, we must be constantly upon the alert, and ready to turn out armed, at a moment's notice. Indeed, if precautions, such as we here adopted, are neglected, it would be unsafe to pass even a night, in such a forest as we were now in, surrounded by hosts of brutal foes. Large fires will, I am convinced, always keep them at a respectful distance; but although this had been attended to, and that they were blazing brightly, yet about two o'clock in the morning, a servant, who had just relieved, as sentinel, one of the Malays, came to our hut to acquaint us that he had seen two large beasts, which he thought were bears, among some trees, not thirty yards off. Upon this announcement, we instantly got up, and accompanied the poor frightened fellow back to his post; when pointing to the spot, where he thought he had seen them, we anxiously watched it, in the hope that something would move; and it was not long before we were in this respect satisfied; as, certainly, two or three huge black objects were to be perceived, distinctly enough, moving slowly along between the trees and us. We therefore drew one of the brass balls out of our guns, (which being covered with well greased leather to prevent their injuring the barrels, we could at all times easily do), and loading them with large buck-shot, we resolved to treat our visitors with a volley. Taking deliberate aim, therefore, we fired nearly together, and I suspect that none of them could have escaped untouched; for they instantly set up a horrible growling, and seemingly made off into the jungle; and had it not been for the uproar and fighting of the animals, which still continued around the carcasses, we had no reason to complain of being otherwise disturbed for the remainder of the night. But our remaining so near the dead elephant and buffalo was very imprudent; as we might have been certain, that they would attract into our neighbourhood the numerous carnivorous prowlers for food.

How strikingly beautiful, and at the same time inspiring with devotional feelings, is the dawn of day in a tropical region! I regret, however, to say, that it is of very short duration; for the sun is soon above the horizon, and the fervour of his all-penetrating beams is felt every minute to become more and more overpowering; but, how gloriously are they reflected in the clear, pure waters of rivers like the Wellewey and its tributaries, as they flow through a splendidly wooded and wildly picturesque country. In most directions, the finely foliage-decked hills, rose gradually to some height; but in others, rocky banks, almost gaudily adorned with lovely shrubs and flowers, most enchantingly presented themselves; amongst which, many beautiful birds, "in loud acclaim," seemed to express their gratitude to Him who preserves and feeds them so bountifully.

Amidst all this enchantment, and about a mile and a half lower down, we crossed the river, and went forward in an easterly direction. We had only gone a few miles when we came into a more open country, in which we saw grazing, buffaloes, hogs, deer, and even, to our surprise, a small breed of cattle; that is, bulls and cows, such as we have in some parts of Scotland and Ireland, which seemed to be quite as wild, and as difficult to be approached, as the other animals. I had now, I must confess, some doubts, if the buffaloes by which my friends had been attacked the previous day, and which were afterwards fired upon by us all, were altogether wild, though they had every appearance of having been so. We could also perceive smoke issuing out of the jungle at the far end of the plain, which we concluded might have been from the fires made by the people to whom the cattle belonged. We, therefore, set off, at a canter, towards the spot; but we had no sooner entered the plain, than the animals feeding in it made off in all directions; and when we had advanced about a quarter of a mile, our farther progress was arrested by a considerable extent of very wet, marshy ground, in many parts of which the water appeared to be deep. This we did not attempt to ascertain, as, most probably, it was well stocked with alligators; I was, therefore, satisfied that I had acted rightly in leaving my faithful dog, Bran, behind me at Galle. Quantities of reeds, flags, and bamboos, were, I may say, growing out of the water; from amongst which there rose, and flew slowly away, such immense flocks of wild-fowl of various kinds, as made us regret that we had not pushed forward, and established our encampment somewhere on the borders of these extensive meadows, in which there must be such excellent sport; and we felt, on this account, the more disappointed, as we were aware that we had no alternative, but to start the following morning on our return to Galle. Yet, very likely, all was for the best; for, judging from the appearance of this part of the country, I should be inclined to suspect, from its wild and undrained state, that the miasma, which is supposed to occasion fevers, may probably prevail, at certain seasons, in it; and must, it may be concluded, continue to do so, until it is rendered fit for cultivation; when, very likely, it would be most productive of rice, and, perhaps, sugar; for both of which it seemed to me to be admirably adapted.

As the heat began to be oppressive, especially in the open plain, we were glad to seek the shade which many parts of the adjoining woods afforded. We, however, purposed, in returning, to move silently and cautiously along, and to keep a good look out; as we had every reason to expect, from having carefully watched the direction a few of the deer which had escaped from the plain had taken, that they must still be near us, and probably in some of the open spaces we had passed through; and in this we were not disappointed; for we had not gone two miles, when we perceived, though they did not see us, a buck, a doe, and a young one along with them, grazing in a meadow, thickly covered with a coarse kind of grass. I held my companions' horses, so as to allow them to steal up close to them. They both fired at the buck, which seemed to be a fine fat one, with large antlers. Being not more than thirty yards from him, he fell the moment the guns went off, and was quite dead when they came to the spot where he lay. We now regretted that we had not the Malays along with us, with their sharp kreeses; and as for our horse-keepers, as they were of no use, but rather an incumbrance, we had left them at the huts. We had, therefore, nothing for it, but to leave the carcass where it was; and my companions proposing to have another battue after breakfast, whilst I amused myself at the river, it was settled that they should return to the meadow, of which they carefully took the bearings, with one of the Malays and some of the coolies, to cut off and carry home the best parts of the buck.

Our servants, it seemed, had last night been again greatly alarmed by one of them, when sentinel, having heard the *devil cry*; so much so that they appeared to be afraid to remain in the encampment without us, or the Malays. Some of them, indeed, and the coolies, (the most timid creatures in the world), who were not to accompany my friends to the place where the fat buck was slain, were, or pretended to be, desirous of going with me to see how I managed to catch such fine fish. This I positively refused to listen to, or comply with; as Appoo, the cook, his assistant, the horse-keepers, grass-cutters, &c. must, to their great terror, have remained behind. I therefore loaded, in their presence, one of the spare double-barrelled guns, and proposed to leave it with them, to shoot the devil, or any thing else that might molest them during our absence. Yet, not one of them, but my old horse-keeper, would even touch a loaded gun, and it was not until after a good deal of persuasion that I at last prevailed upon him to fire it, *if I would take out the balls*, as a signal of distress;

when I promised, upon hearing it, to return immediately to the rescue.

This weighty point being settled, apparently to their satisfaction, we at last set out; but before we did so, I tried to convince them, that this *crying devil* was only a species of owl, or Scotch nightingale! I know not whether the reader may have heard the story before; but a countryman of mine, hearing a thorough-bred John Bull tauntingly assert, that there were no nightingales in Scotland, boldly contradicted him, declaring that there were plenty of them in that part of it from whence he came. The Englishman, in derision, insinuated that he *doubted the fact*, and called upon the irritated Scot to describe them. "Describe them, ye gowk,—that I can soon do; they have lugs like a cat, and a neb like a hawk, and at night they gang whoo, whoo, whoo!" Now I assured them, that I had no doubt, but that their whooing or *crying devil* was certainly a Scotch nightingale. This did not, however, by any means seem to satisfy them; but I find that Major Forbes, in his "Eleven Years in Ceylon," is inclined to be of the same opinion.

We had excellent sport; and no glaring-eyed tiger, huge elephant, furious buffalo, or growling bear, in any way interfered with our amusements. I, for my part, never remember having performed better with rod and line, since I first threw a fly on a river or loch. The flies, bait-hooks and gut, which I had brought with me, were nearly all expended, and I had, at last, actually to desist, from want of means: indeed, I never imagined that in these almost unknown, and I think I may say, untried streams, I should have had such sport; and as I now daily expect to be ordered to proceed into the Kandyan country, I may never have it again, at least, in this part of Ceylon.

My companions returned, escorting the coolies, loaded with venison, and several birds, which they had shot in the woods; in some parts of which, they had been, as they informed me, highly amused in pelting, with sticks and stones, the large bearded monkeys that I have before alluded to; whilst they, grinning hideously at them, frequently caught the sticks, and threw them back at the insolent invaders of their probably hitherto peaceful sylvan retreats. I was, however, assured that none of them were fired at; as nothing can be more distressing than to see how like human beings these poor creatures apply their hand-like paws to the wound, and look at their assailant with so much sorrowful intelligence and great suffering pictured in their countenances, that he must have a hard heart, who, witnessing their misery and pain so strongly portrayed, can fire at them a second time.

The remainder of the day, and the following night, were spent much in the same way as those preceding had been. Some elephants had again approached rather too near to the huts; but, finding that they had got into a suspicious neighbourhood, they passed on, as soon as they perceived us, and we saw no more of them. The carcass of the one shot upon our first arrival here, as well as what little remained of the buffalo, had now, however, become so offensive, as to taint the air even as far as our encampment, so that it was high time to leave the place. This we did at dawn the following day, and after a pleasant ride, through a country I have before spoken of as beautiful, rich in soil, and fit for the abode of man, we reached by breakfast time the huts we had formerly occupied; which had, seemingly, not been visited by man or beast, during our absence from them.

Having repaired, as well as I could, some of my nearly worn out tackle, I went after breakfast to the black looking pools, in which I had before had such good fishing, and again enjoyed excellent sport, until all my gut was carried away; when necessity and the oppressive heat compelled me to desist. My companions, I suspect, though they would not acknowledge it, being quite tired of shooting, they were good enough to accompany me to the river, in order, as they were pleased to say, to witness my dexterity in the "gentle art." I therefore felt called upon to exert myself so as to astonish them; but when I could fish no longer, I endeavoured to beguile the few hours, which must intervene till dinner-time, in reading to them the old ballad of "Chevy Chase," as we all lay enjoying ourselves under the agreeable shade of an immense tree. This poem I found in a volume of "Elegant Extracts," which I usually took with me in such excursions, and with which I could amuse myself or others, (for here we have no circulating libraries to resort to,) in case of a wet day, or if we should chance not to be otherwise or better engaged. The scenery of the green wood around us, though far more magnificent than any thing of the kind Scotland could of old have been supposed to possess, was sufficiently appropriate; but here we had no chance of a Douglas coming to interrupt our sylvan sports, with whom we could break a spear; nor was it necessary, unless a tiger or bear assailed us, and contrived to lop off a limb, to fight "in doleful dumps upon our stumps," as Witherington is said to have done. He, however, is not the only one who fought in this heroic style, as we find recorded in the year 1546, at Lilliard Edge, the following lines:—

> "Fair maiden Lilliard lies under this stane,
> Little was her stature, but great was her fame;
> On the English lads she laid many thumps,
> And when her legs were off, she fought upon her stumps."

I hope it may not be thought that I have given too long an account of this, to me, the most delightful excursion which I had as yet made in this lovely and truly interesting island; and I must, therefore, in bringing this chapter to a close, beg that it may be supposed, that we all at last found ourselves, safe and sound, within the walls of Galle, where orders awaited me, that, as soon as the General Court-martial, which I before mentioned, had finished its proceedings, I was to give up the command of the district to a field officer, appointed to succeed me; and then proceed to assume that of the Seven Korles and its dependencies.

APPENDIX.

A.

STATE OF THE THERMOMETER, &c.

ON THE OUTWARD VOYAGE.

ON APPROACHING MADEIRA.

Date.	Wind.	Thermometer.		Weather, &c.
		Shade.	Sea.	
Mar. 1	W.	54°	53°	Stormy.
2	W.N.W.	56	54	Clear., with strong breeze.
3	N. W.	60	58	do. do.
4	N. W.	61	60	Clear. Made the Island.

FROM MADEIRA TO THE CAPE OF GOOD HOPE.

Date.	Wind.	Thermometer.		Latitude.	Longitude.	Weather, &c.
		Shade.	Sea.	NORTH.	WEST.	
Mar. 6	N. by W.	63°	62½°	30° 58′	17° 35′	Fine, clear.
7	N.	62	64	28. 33	18. 57	do.
8	N.	64	68	26. 35	19. 57	do.
9	W.	67	68	25. 20	20. 26	do. wind variable.
10	W.N.W.	70	68	25. 10	21. 2	do. do.
11	W.N.W.	70	70	22. 43	22. 2	Cloudy.
12	N.N.E.	70	70	22. 44	22. 2	Clear, and almost calm.
13	E.	70	71	22. 2	22. 47	Very fine.
14	E. by N.	70	69	20. 43	24. 21	do.
15	E. by N.	71	68	18. 40	25. 48	do. with some clouds.
16	E. by N.	72	70	16. 36	26. 21	Very fine.
17	N.E.	74	70	14. 50	26. 10	do.
18	N.N.E.	76	74	13. 15	24. 43	do.
19	E.N.E.	78	74	11. 42	23. 26	do. but hazy.
20	E.N.E.	78	76	10. 41	22. 40	Fine, but almost calm.
21	E.N.E.	78	76	9. 3	21. 15	Very fine, and good breeze.
22	N.	78	78	7. 52	20. 20	do. do.
23	N. by E.	81	81	6. 21	19. 26	do. do.
24	N.N.W.	82	83	4. 36	19. 28	do. ther. in sun 92°.
25	N.E.	84	84	3. 18	19. 32	Clear, and light winds.
26	N.N.E.	86	84	2. 12	19. 32	do. ther. in sun 104°.
27	Variable.	84	82	1. 11	19. 22	Clouds, much lightning, thunder, and rain.
				SOUTH.		
28	E. by S.	84	86	0. 25	19. 20	Bright and fine.
29	Variable.	84	82	1. 2	19. 32	Clouds, thunder, and rain.

FROM MADEIRA TO THE CAPE OF GOOD HOPE—*continued.*

Date.	Wind.	Thermometer. Shade.	Thermometer. Sea.	Latitude.	Longitude.	Weather, &c.
				SOUTH.	WEST.	
Mar. 30	Variable.	84°	83°	1° 24′	17° 45	Clouds, thunder, and rain.
31	S. & Var.	85	84	1. 45	16. 54	do. do.
April 1	Variable.	83	84	2. 46	17. 1	Clouds, lightning, thunder, & rain.
2	do.	84	84	3. 24	16. 40	do. do. and very sultry.
3	do.	80½	83	4. 14	16. 35	do. do. do.
4	S.S.E.	84	83	5. 13	17. 20	Very fine.
5	S. by E.	83	83	6. 48	18. 50	do. and strong breeze.
6	S.S.E.	82	82	8. 44	20. 33	do. do.
7	S.E. by E.	80	80	10. 56	21. 42	do. do.
8	S.E.	82	80	13. 16	22. 20	do. do.
9	S.S.E.	79	78	15. 24	23. 14	do. do
10	S.E.	79	78	17. 49	23. 32	do. do.
11	S.E.	78	77	20. 0	23. 57	do. do.
12	S.E. by E.	80	77	21. 52	24. 11	Cloudy and very squally.
13	E.N.E.	78	78	23. 51	23. 54	Fine and clear.
14	E.	81	78	24. 27	23. 24	do. do.
15	N.	79	78	25. 5	22. 50	do. do.
16	S.E.	78	78	25. 48	21. 14	A gale.
17	S.E.	77	77	25. 15	20. 10	do. very severe.
18	S.E.	75	76	26. 38	21. 15	do. do.
19	E. by S.	74	74	28. 8	20. 47	do. do.
20	E.	74	73	30. 13	20. 0	Strong breeze.
21	N.E.	74	71	31. 44	18. 19	do.
22	N.E.	71	68	33. 13	16. 42	Fine weather.
23	N.W.	71	68	33. 30	14. 48	do.
24	N.W.	73	68	33. 30	12. 4	do.
25	N.W.	73	68	33. 20	8. 11	do.
26	N.W.	73	68	33. 14	4. 49	do. but fresh breeze.
27	N.W.	71	68	33. 19	1. 8	do. do.
					EAST.	
28	N.W.	71	67	33. 34	2. 57	do. do.
29	S.S.W.	68	66½	33. 34	6. 37	do. do.
30	E. by N.	65	67	33. 34	8. 32	Light winds and variable.
May 1	W.	68	68	33. 46	9. 40	do. but fine.
2	S.E.	67	65½	33. 2	11. 49	Strong breeze.
3	S.E.	68	66	31. 34	13. 19	Very do.
4	S.E.	70	64	33. 36	12. 25	do. do.
5	S.E.	72	66	34. 38	11. 43	Moderate.
6	S.	68	67	36. 26	12. 6	Fine breeze.
7	S. by E.	69	66	35. 46	13. 29	Cloudy, and light winds.
8	E.	70	67	35. 0	14. 23	Almost calm.
9	W.	68	66	34. 47	14. 45	do.
10	W.S.W.	68	64	34. 47	15. 58	Fine breeze.
11	S.E.	68	63	33. 47	Standing off and on.	A gale.
12	S.E.	61	53	33. 58		Almost calm.
13	do.	63	52	34. 2		Calm.
14	S. by E.	63	53	34. 4		Light breezes.
15	S. by E.	62	56	34. 19		do.
16	S.E.	62	57	34. 30		Almost calm.
17	S.E.	64	58	Off the Cape.		do.
18	N.	66	60			do.
19	N.	65	61			do.

N.B.—In May, the thermometer at the Cape ranged from 62 to 65 degrees. The weather cool and agreeable. There were sometimes strong winds from the S.E. but they did not last long, and were usually followed by calms.

FROM THE CAPE OF GOOD HOPE TO CEYLON.

Date.	Wind.	Thermometer. Shade.	Thermometer. Sea.	Latitude.	Longitude.	Weather, &c.
				SOUTH.	EAST.	
May 29	N.W.	60°	62°	36° 21′	21° 5′	Strong breeze and rain.
30	N.W.	56	57	36. 9	24. 26	A gale, with heavy rain and hazy.
31	N.W.	55	56	36. 2	29. 20	do. do.
June 1	N.W.	68	70	35. 34	31. 0	Almost calm, but hazy.
2	N.E.	70	71	35. 47	33. 23	Strong breeze and rain.
3	N.	70	70	36. 14	36. 11	do. do.
4	N.W.	70	66	36. 10	39. 34	do. do.
5	W.	66	66	35. 12	43. 15	do do.
6	W.S.W.	67	66	34. 16	45. 54	Fine breeze and fine weather.
7	W.	70	68	33. 12	48. 59	do. do.
8	S.W.	70	68	31. 37	51. 17	Light wind and fine.
9	E. by S.	69	70	30. 14	51. 59	Very fine.
10	E.	72	70	28. 6	51. 54	do.
11	E.	74	72	27. 0	51. 47	do. but almost calm.
12	N.E.	80	77	26. 32	51. 45	Light breeze.
13	N.N.E.	78	77	26. 18	52. 31	do.
14	N.	76	74	26. 12	53. 51	Squalls, with rain.
15	S.	74	73	25. 44	54. 16	Fine breeze.
16	E.	76	76	23. 38	54. 14	do.
17	E.	78	78	21. 40	53. 49	Light breeze.
18	E.	79	77	20. 46	53. 26	do.
19	E.	80	77	19. 0	52. 50	Strong breeze.
20	E. by S.	80	78	16. 24	52. 9	do.
21	S.S.E.	78	78	13. 38	51. 13	do.
22	S.E.	80	78	10. 16	48. 48	do.
23	S.E.	80	79	7. 13	49. 44	do.
24	E.S.E.	81	80	4. 44	50. 44	Moderate.
25	S.E.	83	81	2. 44	51. 53	Fine.
26	S.E.	83	81	1. 13	53. 46	do.
				NORTH.		
27	S.E.	83	84	0. 4	55. 54	do. ther. in the sun, 90°.
28	S. by E.	84	84	0. 58	58. 5	do.
29	S.	84	84	1. 8	60. 53	do. ther. in the sun 100°.
30	S. by W.	84	84	1. 13	60. 53	Fine breeze, ther. in the sun 101°.
July 1	S. by W.	84	83	1. 19	66. 62	do.
2	W.	85	85	1. 24	68. 14	do. ther. in sun 102°.
3	W.	86	84	1. 9	70. 39	do.
4	W.	85	84	1. 4	73. 10	do.
5	S.W.	85	84	—	—	Light breeze.
6	S.W.	85	84	—	—	do.
7	S.W.	85	84	—	—	do.
8	S.W.	87	82	—	—	Made the land.

Apppendix B.

GOVERNMENT ADVERTISEMENT.

His Excellency the Governor is pleased to publish the following particulars for the information and guidance of persons travelling from one station to another in this island, and officers of Government, civil and military to whom the same may relate, are required to govern themselves accordingly.

1st.—After the 1st of April next the Collectors of Dictricts are authorized, from time to time, to grant reasonable advances and assistance to postholders or persons in charge of rest-houses, for enabling them to purchase articles required by travellers, such as rice, eggs, and milk; and such supplies may accordingly be had at all places where such persons are stationed.

2ndly.—A quarterly tariff of prices will be fixed by the Collec or and other principal servants of Government in each District, for the several articles of supply according to instructions, which will be published for general information, and the postholder or keeper of the rest-house will be allowed to charge 25 per cent. on these prices.

3rd.—All complaints of travellers against those persons are to be addressed to the Collector of the District, who will inquire into the circumstance, and, if necessary, report the same to Government, that the postholder or rest-house keeper may be removed if any instance of misbehaviour is substantiated against him.

4th.—All gentlemen of his Majesty's service, civil and military, Dutch inhabitants, strangers and others, travelling with conveyance and attendants, are required to subscribe their names in a book to be kept by the postholder, or rest-house keeper, and also to specify the payment of any articles with which they may have been furnished, it being found that the abuses hitherto complained of have principally arisen from referring the payment of such accounts to servants.

5th.—The postholder or rest-house keeper is to report to the Collector, any instance in which violence may have been used, the established charges not paid, or any other impropriety committed by travellers or their attendants, and in addition to such redress as the law affords, his Excellency hereby declares that such conduct will be marked with severe animadversion through the proper official channels of each service. Collectors of Districts are to report all complaints of that nature to the Chief Secretary for his Excellency's information.

6th.—Complaints against persons not in the service or employ of Government, are to be inquired into by the Collector, in his capacity of Justice of the Peace, or referred to any other Magistrate having local jurisdiction, and it is particularly recommended, and expected by his Excellency, that abuses committed by servants, being of greater frequency and more complained of than any other, be in all cases prosecuted according to the existing laws.

7th.—The Commandants of corps and stations from which military detachments may be made, the officers in charge of such parties, and all other officers under whose command they may come, or who may in any manner be employed or concerned in conducting such service, are to consider it their particular and imperative duty to prevent and redress all attempts at violence, fraud or impropriety by those under their command, and to report the occurrence of any material causes of complaint to proper authority.

8th.—The places undermentioned are those, at which postholders or rest-house keepers are stationed at present, and where supplies of rice, fowls, eggs and milk, may be procured.

North.	*North.*	*South.*
Jayelle	Palverynkatto	Pantura
Maravely	Poonereen	Bentotte
Andipany	Claly	Cosgodde
Putlam	Elephant Pass	Amblangodde
Pomparippo	Condicolom	Hickode
Marchitottah	Matele	Belligam
Arippo	Alambiel	Dickwelle
Mantotte	Kokelay	Rannie
Werteltivoe	Cutchavily	Platoopane
Ilpecarve		

9th.—At any station not above specified or hereafter notified as a station of supply, travellers are not to expect or require supplies to be provided for them; but are expected at the principal towns to procure their necessaries without the assistance of Government, and for intermediate places, not having an establishment, they must bring with them whatever may be necessary; any attempt to obtain articles of supply from the neighbouring villages by compulsion will be rigorously prosecuted.

10th.—It having been represented to Government, that very considerable hardship is frequently imposed on the inhabitants residing in the neighbourhood of the rest-houses on the northern and other roads, where the population is extremely scanty, by the practice of pressing them to serve as chule-bearers without any sort of remuneration, the following restrictions are hereby established—

1. The postholder, or headman of any rest-house, or station, shall provide chules and chule-bearers for his Excellency the Governor, the Hon. the Chief and Puisne Justices, the Chief Secretary to Government, Members of Council, the Hon. and Venerable the Archdeacon, and his Majesty's Advocate Fiscal, in such numbers as they may require, subject to the rate of pay, hereinafter specified.

2. No other gentleman of H. M. service, civil or military, or any other person, shall be entitled to demand chules or chule-bearers, without producing an ola or road order to that effect, from the Chief Secretary to Government, or the Collector of the District.

3. The Collector of each District, shall on application grant such order, only to the Commandant, Collector, Provincial Judge, and sitting Magistrate, of his own, or any district; also to any European or Native Officer proceeding in charge of troops, and to any foreigner, or stranger, of such rank as in his discretion may entitle him to this distinction—and to no other person on any occasion whatsoever; but this prohibition is not meant to deter the postmaster from engaging the voluntary services of chule-bearers to any traveller, European, or native, who may think proper to pay.

4. On receipt of the Chief Secretary's or Collector's order, the postholder or headman shall provide chules and chule-bearers, allowing two men for each palanquin, or horse, and two to accompany a party of baggage coolies—receiving in advance for each man half his pay—at the rate payable to any other coolies—these chule-bearers shall not be compelled to proceed further than the next rest-house or station, when they shall receive the remainder of their pay—and an entry of their names, and the payment, shall be made in the postmaster's minute book.

By his Excellency's command,

(Signed) JOHN RODNEY,
Chief Sec. to Government.

Chief Secretary's Office,
Colombo, 2d March, 1815.

APPENDIX C.

REGULATION FOR CARTS AND COOLIES.

The Head Cooly will be obliged to procure Coolies according to the following Regulations.

	Rds.	Fs.
One Cooly per day	,,	4
,, half day	,,	2
,, Working on the sea or sea beach	,,	6
,, to the Great Pass or to an equal distance	,,	4
From Colombo to Pantura	,,	9
,, Caltura	1	,,
,, Bentotte	1	4
,, Galle	3	,,
,, Matura	4	,,
From Colombo to Negombo	1	,,
,, Chilaw	2	,,
,, Putlam	3	,,
,, Calpentyn	3	6
From Colombo to Manar	6	,,
,, Jaffnapatam	9	,,
,, Trincomale	12	,,
,, Batticaloa	16	,,

CARTS

	Rds.	Fs.
The hire of a cart from the Great Pass to the Fort	,,	7
From the Great Pass to the Pettah .	,,	5
,, Little Pass to the Fort .	,,	5
From the Little Pass to the Pettah .	,,	3
,, Sea beach or Waterport Gate to the Pettah	,,	3
,, ,, or Fort .	,,	2½
For every turn in the Fort or Pettah .	,,	1

No. 1. The head cooly who is obliged to procure coolies for a journey, is responsible for them when he receives the money.

No. 2. All coolies travelling, to receive 1 fanam per day during the time they are detained at any place on the road.

No. 3. No cooly is obliged to carry more than 40 lbs. to any distance farther than three English miles.

No. 4. All coolies who work at day labour are to begin their work at seven in the morning, and leave off at half-past five, two hours to be allowed them for their dinner.

No. 5. Two places will be fixed, one in the Fort, and another in the Pettah, where coolies are to be found at all hours.

No. 6. At the fish bazaar will be a servant of the police to procure carts at all hours.

No. 7. Every cart to be numbered.

No. 8. Those who hire a cart to pay the taxes for the cart 1500 lbs.

No. 9. The carts will be permitted to pass in the Main-street of the Pettah for the benefit of merchants and the proprietors of carts.

No. 10. When this regulation shall be published, every cooly or person letting carts shall be liable to punishment on any grounded complaint, or it being proved that he asked more than the stipulated prices.

By his Excellency's command,

(Signed) WM. BOYD,
Act. Sec. to Govt.

Colombo, 2nd January, 1800.

Appendix D.

A STATEMENT of the QUANTITY and VALUE of VARIOUS ARTICLES of MERCHANDIZE IMPORTED into CEYLON in 1835.

The Right Hon. Sir Robert Wilmot Horton being then Governor and Commander-in-Chief.

DUTY PAID.	ESTIMATED VALUE IN STERLING.								Total
	From Great Britain.		British Colonies.		United States of America.		Foreign States.		
	Quantity.	Value.	Quantity.	Value.	Quantity.	Value.	Quantity.	Value.	
		£. s.		£. s.		£. s.		£. s.	£. s.
Apples	.. ..	..	.. ..	..	280 lbs.	7 5	.. ..	..	7 5
Almonds	83 lbs.	1 6	12 cwts. 69 lbs.	19 2	..	..	.. ..	..	20 8
Ammunition	1,620 lbs.; 64¾ bgs.	254 0	330 lbs., 83 bxs, 52 bgs., 500 pcs	34 17	..	..	20 lbs.	1 10	290 7
Arms	169 pieces; 3 pairs	285 15	5 pieces, 1 pair	16 19	..	..	9 pieces	7 9	310 3
Biscuit	15 cwts. 2 lbs.	167 14	40 cwts. 1 lb.	109 7	90 lbs.	2 5	224 lbs.	4 4	283 10
Butter	1,217 lbs.	66 9	955 lbs.	23 15	..	..	.. ..	..	90 4
Barley	1,119 lbs.; 1 parcel	20 15	.. ..	..	..	..	.. ..	..	20 15
Beer	240 hogsheads, 1,990¾ dozs.	2,460 19	10½ hgshds., 230 dozens	183 18	..	..	.. ..	..	2,644 17
Blacking	39 pints; 18 cakes	1 0	17½ dozen pints	15 13	..	..	.. ..	..	16 13
Bottles (empty)	5,190 dozs.	260 0	53 gross, 6¾ dozs.	38 10	..	..	29½ gross	22 12	321 2
Baize	.. ..	..	.. ..	..	..	..	.. ..	..	..
Baskets	.. ..	..	298 number	4 1	..	..	.. ..	..	4 1
Beads	.. ..	..	5 bdls., 605 lbs., 73 strings	20 1	..	..	5 strings, 112 papers	4 12	24 13
Bricks and Tiles	.. ..	..	108,150 pieces	38 3	..	..	491,400 pieces	155 6	193 9
Chalk	.. ..	..	.. ..	..	..	..	.. ..	..	..
Cloth, Linen	40,233 pcs. 5,477 yds.; 3,917 doz.	24,376 18	464,611 pieces, 1,280 yds., 844 dozs.	90,558 6	..	..	7,677 pcs. 101 doz.	1,323 17	116,259 1
	Carried forward ..	27,894 16	.. ..	91,062 12	..	9 10	.. ..	1,519 10	120,486 8

A STATEMENT OF THE QUANTITY AND VALUE OF VARIOUS ARTICLES OF MERCHANDIZE IMPORTED INTO CEYLON IN 1835—(*contd.*)

DUTY PAID.	ESTIMATED VALUE IN STERLING.								Total.
	From Great Britain.		British Colonies.		United States of America.		Foreign States.		
	Quantity.	Value.	Quantity.	Value.	Quantity.	Value.	Quantity.	Value.	
		£. s.		£. s.		£. s.		£. s.	£. s.
	Brought forward..	27,894 16	.. ..	91,062 12	..	9 10	.. ..	1,519 10	120,486 8
Cloth Woollen .	650 yards . .	487 10	228 yards . .	35 18	..	..	160 yards .	36 0	559 8
Cheese . .	114 cwts. 66 lbs. .	653 5	1,161 lbs. . .	64 13	654 lbs.	41 4	.. ..	..	759 2
Cutlery . .	190 pcs.; 689 doz. 262 cases; 192 cards; 387 sets; 51 pairs; 7½ gross .	946 17	1,353 pcs. 11 pairs	16 18	..	..	.. ..	..	963 15
Confectionary & Preserves .	72 cwts. 34 lbs.; 6 pints; 163 doz. quarts .	658 17	51 bdls., 798 cwt. 62 lbs., 103 bottles, 43 jars .	535 17	..	..	12 btls., 58 jars, 14 boxes, 817 baskets, &c. .	95 15	1,290 9
Casks (empty) .	112 number .	43 15	.. ..	..	..	..	.. ..	..	43 15
Chocolate .	460 lbs. . .	46 0	28 lbs. . .	3 10	..	..	.. ..	..	49 10
Calogambo and Caypoe .	.. ..	..	405 cwts. 74 lbs. .	731 3	..	..	1,463 lbs. . .	23 15	754 18
Cotton, Loose .	.. ..	..	74 cwts. 39 lbs. .	55 4	..	..	.. ..	..	55 4
Candles . .	.. ..	..	64 lbs. . .	4 8	..	..	.. ..	..	4 8
Cardamoms .	.. ..	..	.. ..	..	..	..	.. ..	..	..
Clocks, Wooden	.. ..	..	.. ..	..	6 number	12 0	.. ..	..	12 0
Copper . .	49¾ cwts. . .	278 10	29 cwts. 17 lbs. .	248 16	..	..	20 lbs. . .	1 18	529 4
——— Caps .	.. ..	..	.. ..	..	..	..	.. ..	..	..
Coloured Paper	.. ..	..	13 lbs. . .	1 19	..	..	.. ..	..	1 19
China Roots .	.. ..	..	66 cwts. 66 lbs. .	125 17	..	..	177 cwts. 70 lbs. .	351 8	477 5
Cotton and Silk Thread . .	212 dozs.; 300 lbs.; 6 gross; 12 boxes .	61 4	322 cwt. 98 lbs. 54 dozs., 7 bxs. 11 bundles .	1,974 14	..	..	795 lbs. 5 catties, 12 bundles .	48 2	2,084 0
Corks . .	.. ..	..	.. ..	..	..	..	61 gross .	18 0	18 0

Canvas	174½ bolts	174 10	32½ bolts	34 15	..	..	..	..	209 5
Chain Cable	..	..	..	..	..	..	1 number	45 0	45 0
Canoes or Boats	2 number	11 15	32	141 3	1	25 0	..	..	177 18
Camphor	..	..	..	..	..	..	..	..	..
Corondo Stones	..	..	..	..	..	..	..	..	..
Coffee	..	..	1 cwt.	2 16	..	..	..	..	2 16
Crape	..	..	..	..	..	..	..	..	..
Crackers	..	..	3 boxes, 900 packs	33 12	..	..	55 boxes	65 9	99 1
Curiosities	..	..	..	..	..	..	..	..	..
Curry Stuffs	..	..	2,314 cwts. 71 lbs.	2,261 6	..	..	106 cwts. 4 lbs.	88 17	2,350 *3
Chariot	1 number	100 0	..	..	..	..	..	..	100 0
Chess-Boards	..	..	7 boxes	1 15	..	..	..	..	1 15
Drawings Paints	..	..	..	..	..	..	..	..	..
Dammer	..	..	..	..	..	..	186 lbs.	2 7	2 7
Earthenware	208 sets; 7,319 dozs.; 465 pcs.; 1,870½ pairs	1,207 0	6 casks, 1 set, 85,230 pieces	672 18	..	..	204 boxes & bdls. 153,284 pieces	860 16	2,740 14
Flour	..	..	20 kegs, 1 barrel	27 0	1 barrel	1 10	..	..	28 10
Flannel	417 yards	43 15	78 pieces, [illegible]0 yds.	88 11	..	..	..	..	132 6
Fishing-Lines & Hooks	..	..	2 dozens, 4 lbs.	3 9	..	..	..	..	3 9
Fruits and Vegetables	..	..	3 bags, 8 pots, 123,000 nuts, 875 lbs.	10 7	..	..	..	..	10 7
Furniture	..	..	31 pieces	21 7	..	..	30 pieces, 1 set	12 6	33 13
Flints	..	..	980 dozens	24 2	..	..	..	..	24 2
Glass Wares	1,306 dozens	780 15	15,921 pieces, 16 pairs, 32 bdls., 22 boxes	218 16	..	..	1,387 pieces	14 15	1,014 6
	Carried forward..	33,388 9	..	98,403 6		89 4	..	3,183 18	135,064 17

A STATEMENT OF THE QUANTITY AND VALUE OF VARIOUS ARTICLES OF MERCHANDIZE IMPORTED INTO CEYLON IN 1835.—(*contd.*)

DUTY PAID.	ESTIMATED VALUE IN STERLING.								Total.
	From Great Britain.		British Colonies.		United States of America.		Foreign States.		
	Quantity.	Value.	Quantity.	Value.	Quantity.	Value.	Quantity.	Value.	
		£. s.		£. s.		£. s.		£. s.	£. s.
	Brought forward ..	33,389 9	.. ..	98,403 5	..	89 4	.. ..	3,183 18	136,064 17
Ghee	.. ..	..	385½ gallons	42 0	..	..	.. ..	..	42 0
Glue	.. ..	..	.. ..	..	..	..	.. ..	..	..
Grain	.. ..	..	.. ..	..	..	..	.. ..	..	..
—— Rice	.. ..	..	816,929½ parrahs	101,188 16	..	..	115,944 parrahs	14,416 0	115,604 16
—— Paddy	.. ..	..	372,255¾ ,,	20,418 7	..	..	60,905 ,,	3,518 10	23,936 17
—— Wheat	.. ..	..	43,102½ ,,	7,053 8	..	..	667 ,,	148 11	7,201 19
—— Other sorts	.. ..	..	18,164 ,,	1,887 12	..	..	38 packages	4 17	1,892 9
Grinding-Stones	.. ..	..	53 number	4 8	..	..	52 number, 2 pairs	2 4	6 12
Gunny Bags	.. ..	..	50 bls., 47,203 pcs.	714 18	..	..	.. ..	..	714 18
Gold and Silver	.. ..	..	9¾ lbs.	18 10	..	..	.. ..	..	18 10
Hats & Bonnets	932 number	475 10	244 number	99 9	..	..	.. ..	..	574 19
Hams	90 cwts. 88 lbs.	540 0	565 lbs.	29 19	..	..	51 lbs.	2 10	572 9
Haberdashery	Quantity too numerous to be specified	2,220 8	.. ..	1,089 19	..	..	.. ..	404 18	3,715 5
Hardwares	Ditto ditto	1,527 15	2,676 pieces, 12 gross, 121 cwts. 69 lbs.	824 7	..	..	95 pieces	5 0	2,357 2
Hookah Tobacco	.. ..	..	1,021 lbs.	12 15	..	..	.. ..	..	12 15
—— Snakes and Bottles	.. ..	..	.. ..	..	..	..	.. ..	..	..
Iron	6,366 cwts. 97 lbs.	3,248 1	815 cwts. 20 lbs.	1,025 7	..	..	.. ..	..	4,273 8
Jaggery	..	..	79 cwts. 57 lbs.	126 19	..	..	.. ..	..	126 19
Jars (empty)	.. ..	..	.. ..	..	..	..	.. ..	..	..

Jewellery . .	303 pieces; 11 sets; 16½ dozs.	165 5	.. ..	..	..	..	10 pairs . .	62 8	227 13
Images . .	.. ..	..	.. ..	..	..	..	.. ..	..	..
Lead . .	63 cwts. 73 lbs. .	99 15	438 lbs. . .	6 0	..	..	924 lbs. . .	12 5	118 0
Liquors . .	2 doz. qts.; 92¾ doz. pints .	181 5	26 dozens . .	28 12	..	..	49 bottles . .	10 10	220 7
Leather & Skins	.. ..	..	1,137 corges .	281 15	..	..	.. ..	..	281 15
Medicines, Country	.. ..	..	639 cwts. 89 lbs. .	1,159 2	..	..	936 lbs. . .	32 9	1,191 11
——— Europe .	37 doz.; 13 cases; 1 jar; 1 bottle .	185 18	8,714 lbs., 42 boxes, 12 bdls. 15 bottles, &c.	290 2	..	..	126 lbs. . .	1 12	477 12
Maccaroni and Vermicelli .	6 boxes . .	3 0	.. ..	..	..	..	.. ..	..	3 0
Millinery . .	Too numerous to be specified .	3,286 8	.. ..	682 5	..	..	1 box, 71 rolls, 10 yds. 276 pcs.	212 1	4,180 14
Musical Instruments . .	138 pcs, 2 cases, 84 strings	546 5	17 pcs. 60 strings	50 8	..	..	.. .	..	596 13
Metal Wares .	6 doz. 203 pieces	59 15	24 cwts. 105 lbs. 1,476 pieces	211 1	..	..	3,531 lbs. . .	176 11	447 7
Marine Stores .	68 pcs. 1 set, 2 lots	408 15	6 cwts. 44 lbs 183 bdls. 34 pcs.	125 10	..	..	.. ..	..	534 5
Mats . .	.. ..	..	1,950 yards . .	63 13	..	..	305 yards . .	8 2	71 15
Nankeen . .	.. ..	..	189¾ corges . .	379 14	..	..	.. ..	..	379 14
Oilmen's Stores	To numerous to be specified	788 15	.. ..	533 13	..	..	.. ..	48 17	1,371 5
Oils of all sorts	1,631 galls. 98 doz. pints.	454 16	11 doz. 76½ galls. .	29 19	..	..	2 dozens, 8½ galls.	5 1	419 16
,, Salad .	.. ..	..	.. ..	..	..	..	.. ..	..	
	Carried forward . .	47,581 0	.. ..	236,781 13	..	89 4	.. ..	22,256 4	306,708 1

A STATEMENT OF THE QUANTITY AND VALUE OF VARIOUS ARTICLES OF MERCHANDIZE IMPORTED INTO CEYLON IN 1835.—(*contd.*)

DUTY PAID.	ESTIMATED VALUE IN STERLING.								Total.
	From Great Britain.		British Colonies.		United States of America.		Foreign States.		
	Quantity.	Value.	Quantity.	Value.	Quantity.	Value.	Quantity.	Value.	
	Brought forward	£. s. 47,581 0		£. s. 236,781 13		£. s. 89 4		£. s. 22,256 4	£. s. 306,708 1
Oil—Linseed	.. ..	..	.. ..	..	..	..		..	
„ Turpentine	.. ..	..	.. ..	..	..	..	.. ..	..	
„ Gingelie	.. ..	..	.. ..	..	..	..	.. ..	..	
Opium	.. ..	..	1,049¼ lbs.	1,165 7	..	..	188¼ lbs.	150 8	1,315 15
Pepper	.. ..	..	427 cwts. 16 lbs.	463 16	..	..	3,505 lbs.	52 1	515 17
Perfumery	10 bxs. 338 doz. 63 lbs. 57 phials	305 11	Too numerous to be specified	216 12	..	..	196 phials, 6 doz.	8 9	530 12
Paints of all sorts	51 cwts. 11½ lbs.	122 7	4 bxs. 1 bag, 15½ galls. 3,196 lbs.	164 1	..	..	24 lbs.	1 16	288 4
Plated Wares	.. ..	..	7 sets	4 13	..	..	.. ..	..	4 13
Playing Cards	120 dozen packs	120 0	15½ dozen packs	15 19	..	..	.. ..	..	135 19
Pins and Needles	295,375 lbs.	263 16	101,600 number, 9 lbs. 2 books	43 11	..	..	.. ..	.	307 7
Prints & Drawings	553 pieces	46 15	95 packs, 2 books	7 6	..	..	42 packs, 4 books	4 12	58 13
Pipeclay	.. ..	..	.. ..	..	..	..	.. ..	..	
Palanquins	.. ..	..	2 number	9 8	..	..	3 number	7 8	16 16
Pots and Pans	.. ..	..	416,842 pieces	820 10	..	..	42,276 pcs. 14 bags	89 12	910 2
Precious Stones	.. ..	..	488 lbs.	12 5	..	..	.. ..	..	12 5
Quicksilver	.. ..	..	155¾ lbs.	63 2	..	..	.. ..	..	63 2
Rattans	.. ..	..	12¾ cwts.	10 19	..	..	.. ..	..	10 19
Rose Water	.. ..	..	2 jars	3 0	..	..	.. ..	..	3 0
Rosin	.. ..	..	222 lbs.	1 0	..	..	.. ..	..	1 0

Seeds . .	.. ..	.	11 cwts. 10 lbs. .	16 12	..	..	.. ..	..	16 12
Snuff and Cigars	121½ lbs. . .	48 0	447 lbs. . .	163 10	27¾ lbs.	14 1	53 lbs. . .	5 11	231 2
Sago . .	.. ..	..	54 cwts. 41 lbs. .	54 15	..	..	.. ..	..	54 15
Salted and other Provisions	Too numerous to be specified	1,271 14	.. ..	569 3	..	..	.. ..	..	1,840 17
" " Fish	Ditto .	57 9	.. ..	175 13	..	..	.. ..	2,074 14	2,307 16
Spirits . .	7,129 gallons .	1,509 19	1,035½ gallons .	374 8	..	..	1,096½ gallons .	270 3	2,154 10
Stationery .	Too numerous to be specified	825 15	.. ..	1,129 12	..	..	61 boxes . .	433 16	2,339 3
Saddlery .	74 pkgs. 30 pairs, 84 sets, 6 doz. 7 cases .	792 5	4 cases, 83 packages, 7 pairs	44 4	..	..	2 sets . .	4 13	841 2
Soap . .	10 cwts. 2 lbs. 2 jars 21½ doz.	55 10	180 cwts. 101½ dozens, ½ box	515 15	..	..	12 cwts. 86 lbs.	30 15	602 0
Silk, &c. .	.. ..	..	144 pces, 4 rolls, 368 yards .	114 12	..	..	16 pieces, 19 rolls	93 13	208 5
Soft Sugar .	214 lbs. . .	7 2	2,113 cwts. 10 lbs. 2 boxes	3,035 19	..	..	263 cwts. 75 lbs.	383 12	3,426 13
Scales, Beams, and Weights	.. ..	..	1 set . .	2 0	..	..	.. ..	..	2 0
Saltpetre .	.. ..	..	230¼ cwts. . .	367 5	..	..	16 bags, 182 lbs.	55 16	423 1
Sandal Wood .	.. ..	..	982 lbs. . .	34 19	..	..	52 lbs. . .	2 11	37 10
Screens . .	.. ..	..	.. ..	..	..	..	.. ..	..	
Silver Wares .	299 pkgs. 2 pcs. 1 set .	390 15	.. ..	..	..	..	5 dozens . .	42 1	432 16
Shells & Couries	.. ..	..	1,180 number, 7 baskets .	4 5	..	..	.. ..	..	4 5
Slates & Slate Pencils .	.. ..	..	60¾ dozens .	5 9	..	..	.. ..	..	5 9
Spices . .	.. ..	..	45 cwts. 108 lbs. .	217 15	..	..	175 lbs. .	6 8	224 3
Strings for Violins	.. ..	..	.. ..	..	..	..	.. ..	..	
Staves . .	.. ..	..	1,512 packages .	371 0	..	..	.. ..	..	371 0
Steel . .	.. ..	..	5¼ cwts. . .	12 5	..	..	.. ..	..	12 5
	Carried forward	53,397 18	.. ..	246,982 3	..	103 5	.. ..	25,974 3	326,467 9

A STATEMENT OF THE QUANTITY AND VALUE OF VARIOUS ARTICLES OF MERCHANDIZE IMPORTED INTO CEYLON IN 1835.—(*contd.*)

DUTY PAID.	ESTIMATED VALUE IN STERLING.								Total.
	From Great Britain.		British Colonies.		United States of America.		Foreign States.		
	Quantity.	Value.	Quantity.	Value.	Quantity.	Value.	Quantity.	Value.	
		£. s.		£. s.		£. s.		£. s.	£. s.
	Brought forward	53,397 18		246,982 3		103 5		25,974 3	326,467 9
Sulphur	.. ..	..	62 cwts. 65½ lbs.	266 14	..	..	4 cwts, 98 lbs.	20 10	287 4
Sugar Candy	.. ..	..	106 cwts. 89 lbs.	465 14	..	..	162 cwts. 53 lbs.	643 17	1,109 11
Smoking Pipes	134 gross	67 0	.. ..	..	..	..	.. ..	..	67 0
Sattin Wood	.. ..	..	13 pieces	2 10	..	..	.. ..	..	2 10
Supan Wood	.. ..	..	2,960 lbs.	8 10	..	..	.. ..	..	8 10
Tin	8 cwts. 9,000 sheets	61 0	756 sheets, 89 cwts. 51 lbs.	30 4	..	..	.. ..	..	91 4
Tar	265 barrels	397 10	2 barrels	10 0	..	..	.. ..	..	407 10
Toys	7 cases, 18 pieces	51 15	19 boxes, 1,300 bdls. 22 bags, 27,958 pieces	63 5	..	..	137 boxes, 3,700 pcs. 36 pairs.	24 3	139 3
Tapes	.. ..	..	27 bdls. 108 yards	5 19	..	..	.. ..	..	5 19
Tea	.. ..	..	3,607¼ lbs.	585 3	..	..	5,336 lbs.	886 5	1,471 8
Tinsel	.. ..	..	4,406 sheets, 50 rolls	22 13	..	..	.. ..	..	22 13
Timbers & Planks	.. ..	..	842 pieces	135 1	..	..	.. ..	..	135 1
Tom John	.. ..	..	.. ..	..	..	..	.. ..	..	
Tools	.. ..	..	.. ..	..	..	..	.. ..	..	
Tortoiseshell	.. ..	..	105¼ lbs.	229 15	..	..	243 lbs.	525 15	755 10
Turpentine	.. ..	..	.. ..	..	..	..	.. ..	..	
Twine	.. ..	..	29 cwts. 79 lbs. 8 bales	83 9	..	.	.. ..	..	83 9
Tanks, Iron	46 number	312 0	6 number	45 0	..	..	.. ..	..	357 0
Tutenague	.. ..	..	894 lbs.	11 6	..	..	.. ..	..	11 6
Tombstone	.. ..	..	1 number	12 0	..	..	.. ..	..	12 0

Umbrellas	618¼ dozens	605 5	965 number, 58 chests	381 13	..	..	5,259 number, 180 boxes	593 17	1,580 15
Washing or Bleaching Sand	.. ..	..	45 bags, 360 pkgs.	29 5	..	..	.. ..	..	29 5
Watches and Clocks	.. ..	..	.. ..	..	.	.	.. ..	..	
Wines	85¼ pipes, 2,365¼ doz. 2,026 galls.	7,171 2	2 pipes, 16 hhds. 981½ dozens	1,308 15	..	..	26 pipes, 327 doz.	1,333 12	9,813 9
Wearing Apparel	263 doz. pieces, 1,046 doz. pairs	1,482 17	179 doz. pgks. 434 doz. pairs	391 7	..	..	5 pkgs. 2 boxes, 476 pairs, 2 doz.	76 0	1,950 4
Walnuts	.. ..	..	.. ..	..	..	..	.. ..	..	
Wires	1,280 strings	25 5	.. ..	..	..	..	.. ..	..	25 5
Woollen Stuffs	660 pieces, 13 doz.	319 15	70 pieces, 5 yards	7 5	..	..	.. ..	..	327 0
Total	.. ..	63,890 7	.. ..	251,087 12	..	103 5		30,078 12	345,159 16
DUTY FREE.									
Books	82 boxes	2,050 0	20 cases, 4 parcels	202 16	..	..	.. ..	..	2,252 16
Hoop Iron	2,048 bundles	512 0	42 bundles	10 10	..	..	.. ..	..	522 10
Machinery	491 packages	2,500 0	Bookbinders' tools, & printing press	33 2	..	..	.. ..	..	2,533 2
Seeds	3 boxes, 24 baskets	15 0	.. ..	..	..	..	.. ..	..	15 0
Wearing Apparel	103 cases	1,030 0	4 cases	54 10	..	..	.. ..	..	1,084 10
Asses	.. ..	..	12 number	4 10	..	..	.. ..	..	4 10
Horses	.. ..	..	39 number	311 5	..	..	.. ..	..	311 5
Live Stock	.. ..	..	894 number	162 18	..	..	18 number	3 8	166 6
Potatos	.. ..	..	85 bkts. 3 cwts. 64 lbs.	26 17	..	..	.. ..	..	26 17
Total Duty Free	.. ..	6,107 0	.. ..	806 8	..	..	.. ..	3 8	6,916 16
„ Paid	.. ..	63,890 7	.. ..	251,087 12	..	103 5	.. ..	30,078 12	345,159 16
Grand Total	.. ..	69,997 7	.. ..	251,894 0	..	103 5	.. ..	30,082 0	352,076 12

A STATEMENT OF THE QUANTITY AND VALUE OF VARIOUS ARTICLES OF MERCHANDIZE EXPORTED FROM CEYLON IN 1835.

DUTY PAID.	ESTIMATED VALUE IN STERLING.								Total.
	To Great Britain.		To British Colonies.		To the United States of America.		To Foreign States.		
	Quantity.	Value.	Quantity.	Value.	Quantity.	Value.	Quantity.	Value.	
		£. s.		£. s.		£. s.		£. s.	£. s.
Arrack	1,362¾ gallons	54 10	1,479 leaguers; 110½ gallons	7,162 7	..	..	.. ..	..	7,216 17
Arrecca Nuts	.. ..	..	49,666 cwts. 33 lbs.	10,308 16	..	..	726 cwts. 31 lbs.	188 2	10,496 18
Becho-de-Mar	.. ..	..	.. ..	..	..	..	407 cwts. 74 lbs.	203 17	203 17
Bees' Wax	.. ..	..	.. ..	..	..	..	.. ..	..	
Chanks	.. ..	..	630,192 number	1,398 4	..	..	41,063 number	110 4	1,508 8
Cinnamon —									
1st sort	11,717¾ lbs.	2,050 15	5 lbs.	0 18	..	..	900 lbs.	157 10	2,209 3
„ 2nd „	102,373¼ lbs	10,238 5	1,493¾ lbs.	149 10	4,000lbs.	400 0	14,423 lbs.	1,442 10	12,230 5
„ 3rd „	175,177 lbs.	6,569 5	.. ..	..	..	..	17,453 lbs.	654 10	7,223 15
„ Chips	6,725½ lbs.	14 0	.. ..	..	..	..	50 lbs.	1 15	15 15
„ Oil	1,295¾ oz.	129 10	.. ..	..	..	..	.. ..	..	129 10
Clove Oil	.. ..	..	.. ..	..	..	..	.. ..	..	..
Cocoa Nuts	7,000 number	4 5	7,381,802 number.	6,700 5	..	..	5,685 number	5 17	6,710 7
„ Oil	104 gallons	4 5	33,394 gallons	1,669 14	..	..	3,337 gallons	145 13	1,819 12
Coffee	.. ..	..	.. ..	..	..	..	13,080 parrahs	6,540 0	6,540 0
Confectionary and Preserves	.. ..	..	.. ..	..	..	..	.. ..	..	
Copperas	.. ..	..	10,950 cwts. 16 lbs.	3,276 19	..	..	.. ..	..	3,276 19
Cotton Thread	.. ..	..	.. ..	..	..	..	.. ..	..	
Dammer and Rosin	.. ..	..	1,430 cwts. 50 lbs.	453 12	..	..	.. ..	..	453 12
Ivory	414½ lbs.	31 0	234¾ lbs.	15 15	..	..	.. ..	..	46 15

Loose Coir	.. ..	..	5,395 cwts. 72 lbs.	1,256 4	..	..	142 cwts. 42 lbs.	23 14	1,279 18
Palmeira Leaves	.. ..	..	553 bundles; 108,000 pieces	6 17	..	..	.. ..	..	6 17
,, Rafters	.. ..	..	552,504 pieces	5,354 11	..	..	7,701 number .	81 9	5,436 0
,, Ropes	.. ..	..	.. ..	..	..	..	.. ..	..	..
Plants . .	.. ..	..	605 number	1 10	..	..	.. ..	..	1 10
Ponato (Palmeira Nuts prepared)	.. ..	..	125 cwts. 10 lbs.	32 17	..	..	.. ..	..	32 17
Sapan Wood .	.. ..	..	.. ..	..	..	..	13,324 lbs. . .	33 5	33 5
Seeds . .	.. ..	..	1,098 cwts. 109 lbs.	450 17	..	..	79¾ cwts. . .	37 4	488 1
Shells . .	.. ..	..	.. ..	..	..	..	.. ..	..	..
Sea Moss .	.. ..	..	90 lbs. . . .	1 10	..	..	.. ..	..	1 10
Tortoiseshell .	.. ..	..	21 lbs. . . .	21 0	..	..	.. ..	..	21 0
Tobacco . .	.. ..	..	9,866 cwts. 8 lbs.	8,386 12	..	..	554 lbs. . .	4 15	8,391 7
Tamarind Stones	.. ..	..	2 cwts. 31 lbs.	1 0	..	..	.. ..	..	1 0
Tinsel . .	.. ..	..	.. ..	..	..	..	.. ..	..	
Total Duty paid	.. ..	19,095 15	.. ..	46,648 18	..	400 0	.. ..	9,630 5	75,774 18
DUTY FREE.									
Arriopo . .	.. ..	..	266 cwts. 106 lbs.	10 0	..	..	.. ..	..	10 0
Arrow Root .	2 boxes .	1 0	.. ..	..	..	..	.. ..	..	1 0
Asses . .	.. ..	..	.. ..	..	..	..	.. ..	..	
Birds' Nests .	.. ..	..	.. ..	..	..	..	1 box . .	5 0	5 0
Bark, for Tanning . .	.. ..	..	240 bags; 99 cwts. 95 lbs. .	132 14	..	..	.. ..	..	132 14
Baskets, Mats, &c. . .	.. ..	..	79 bundles, 32,853 pieces	72 17	..	..	200 pieces; 23 bundles . .	2 16	75 3
	Carried forward ..	1 0	.. ..	215 11	..	..	.. ..	7 16	224 7

A STATEMENT OF THE QUANTITY AND VALUE OF VARIOUS ARTICLES OF MERCHANDIZE EXPORTED FROM CEYLON IN 1835.—(*contd.*)

DUTY FREE.	ESTIMATED VALUE IN STERLING. To Great Britain. Quantity.	To Great Britain. Value.	To British Colonies. Quantity.	To British Colonies. Value.	To the United States of America. Quantity.	To the United States of America. Value.	To Foreign States. Quantity.	To Foreign States. Value.	Total.
		£. s.		£. s.		£. s.		£. s.	£. s.
	Brought forward	1 0		215 11	..	..		7 16	224 7
Beetle Leaves	.. ..	..	.. ..	..	..	..	.. ..	..	
Bees' Wax	20 cwts. 23 lbs.	84 15	.. ..	..	..	..	.. ..	..	84 15
Becho-de-Mar	.. ..	..	128 bags, 1,076 cwts. 34 lbs.	604 4	..	..	.. ..	..	604 4
Buckets	.. ..	..	109 number	5 10	..	..	.. ..	..	5 10
Bricks and Tiles	.. ..	..	5,400 pieces	4 15	..	..	.. ..	..	4 15
Beer	.. ..	..	114 dozens	42 15	..	..	.. ..	..	42 15
Cardamoms	126 cwts. 53 lbs.	337 14	.. ..	..	..	..	2 bags	5 0	342 14
Chaoga, or Dyeing	.. ..	..	498¾ cwts.	266 3	..	..	.. ..	..	266 3
Chunamb	.. ..	..	1,537 parrahs	7 16	..	..	.. ..	..	7 16
Cocoa Nut Shells	.. ..	..	120,400 number	74 8	..	..	.. ..	..	74 8
„ Oil	205,596 gallons	10,279 16	.. ..	..	..	..	.. ..	..	10,279 16
Coir, Rope, &c.	421 coils, 220 pieces, 3,275 cwts.	1,211 10	7,664 cwts. 101 lbs.	2,582 15	..	..	25,000 lbs. 365 coils	257 10	4,051 15
Coffee	914 bags, 22,071 cwts. 20 lbs.	45,970 0	2,802 parrahs, 235 cwts. 26 lbs.	1,870 0	..	..	9,651½ parrahs, 521 cwts.	4,667 15	52,507 15
Cinnamon	.. ..	..	.. ..	..	..	..	.. ..	..	
„ Wood	3 logs	1 0	.. ..	..	..	..	.. ..	..	1 0
Confectionary and Preserves	.. ..	..	2 jars, 5 pots, 164 lbs.	5 0	..	..	.. ..	..	5 0
Cloth, Linen	.. ..	..	3,220 pieces, 5 cases	1,660 12	..	..	810 pieces	92 5	1,752 17
„ Wares	.. ..	..	.. ..	..	..	..	.. ..	..	
Cotton, Loose	.. ..	..	19 bags, 150 lbs.	2 5	..	..	.. ..	..	2 5

Curiosities	16 boxes	80 0	4 boxes	15 0	..	..	.. ..	..	95 0
Curry Stuffs	.. ..	..	515 cwts. 48 lbs.	138 16	..	..	.. ..	..	138 16
Copper	.. ..	..	2 cases, 2,100 lbs.	105 0	..	..	.. ..	..	105 0
Carsingoes	.. ..	..	870 number	2 14	..	..	.. ..	..	2 14
Chain Cable	.. ..	..	1 number	45 0	..	..	.. ..	..	45 0
Chocolate	.. ..	..	150 lbs.	15 0	..	..	.. ..	..	15 0
Ebony Wood	1,272 cwts. 46 lbs.	190 15	3,769 logs, 657 cwts. 49 lbs.	1,455 5	..	..	742 logs, 256 cwts. 23 lbs.	371 7	2,017 7
Elephants	.. ..	..	7 number	82 10	..	..	.. ..	..	82 10
,, Teeth	.. ..	..	.. ..	..	..	..	.. ..	..	
Earthen Wares	.. ..	..	2 crates, 3 casks, 47 dozens	130 15	..	..	.. ..	..	130 15
Fruits and Vegetables	.. ..	..	121,379 packages	127 6	..	..	2,830 packages	1 6	128 12
Firewood	.. ..	..	2,000 pieces, 8,500 billets	7 18	..	..	.. ..	..	7 18
Furniture	3 pieces, 13 boxes	134 10	147 packages	50 8	..	..	.. ..	..	184 18
Ghee	.. ..	..	3,042 measures, 10,905 lbs. 150 jars	370 6	..	..	10 jars, 100 measures	17 10	387 16
Gunny Bags	.. ..	..	4 bales, 230 pieces	95 18	..	..	.. ..	..	95 18
Grinding-Stones	.. ..	..	80 pairs	4 0	..	..	.. ..	..	4 0
Grain	.. ..	..	717½ parrahs	29 2	..	..	100 parrahs	7 10	36 12
,, Paddy	.. ..	..	.. ..	..	..	..	.. ..	..	
Gorkas	.. ..	..	329 cwts. 6 bags	22 15	..	..	.. ..	..	22 15
Glass Wares	.. ..	..	28 cases	413 0	..	..	.. ..	..	413 0
Grease	.. ..	..	.. ..	..	..	..	.. ..	..	
Gingelie Oil	1,248 gallons	156 0	.. ..	..	..	..	.. ..	..	156 0
Horses	.. ..	..	12 number	73 10	..	..	.. ..	..	73 10
	Carried forward	58,447 0	.. ..	10,525 17	..	..	.. ..	5,427 19	74,400 16

A STATEMENT OF THE QUANTITY AND VALUE OF VARIOUS ARTICLES OF MERCHANDIZE EXPORTED FROM CEYLON IN 1835.—(*contd.*)

DUTY FREE.	ESTIMATED VALUE IN STERLING.								Total.
	To Great Britain.		To British Colonies.		To the United States of America.		To Foreign States.		
	Quantity.	Value.	Quantity.	Value.	Quantity.	Value.	Quantity.	Value.	
		£. s.		£. s.		£. s.		£. s.	£. s.
	Brought forward	58,447 0	.. ..	10,525 17	..	..	.. ..	5,427 19	74,400 16
Honey	.. ..	..	360 gallons, 1,734 measures	51 5	..	..	.. ..	..	51 5
Horns	206 cwts. 106 lbs.	107 15	59 cwts. 21 lbs.	19 13			.. ..	..	127 8
Hides and Skins	200 number	40 0	387 pieces, 2885 lbs.	98 15	..	..	.. ..	..	138 15
Haberdashery	.. ..	..	1 case	35 10			.. ..	..	35 10
Iron	.. ..	..	806 cwts. 103 lbs.	70 10	..	..	.. ..	..	70 10
Jaggery	.. ..	..	6,382 cwts. 14 lbs. 25 bskts. 889 bundles.	950 17	..	..	12 baskets	2 1	952 18
Live Stock	.. ..	..	56 number	28 11	..	..	2 number	1 6	29 17
Metal Wares	.. ..	..	15 lbs.	1 3	..	..	.. ..	..	1 3
Millinery	.. ..	..	1 case 2,200 pieces	209 5			.. ..	..	209 5
Marmel Water	..	..	64 bottles	2 10	..	..	.. ..	..	2 10
Medicines	..	..	1 case	19 15	..	..	.. ..	..	19 15
Nails	.. ..	..	9 casks	87 5	..	..	.. ..	..	87 5
Oils	.. ..	..	979 galls. 3 csks. 36 doz. 37 measures	204 14	..	..	.. ..	..	204 14
Oilman's Stores.	.. ..	..	29 pots, 31 jars, 17 cases, 36 doz. 108 lbs. 66 btls.	73 8	..	..	22 pots, 2 bottles	1 13	75 1

Precious Stones.	.. ..	..	1 parcel	5 0	..	..	.. ..	..	5 0
Pepper	78 cwts. 92 lbs. 294 parrahs, 74 bags.	379 6	180¾ parrahs, 74 cwts. 76 lbs.	188 15	..	..	4 bags	7 5	575 6
Plumbago	1,822 bxs. 4,952¾ cwts.	1,108 5	100 boxes, 470 cwts, 60 lbs.	99 15	..	..	.. ..	..	1,208 0
Staves	.. ..	..	100 packages	42 1	..	..	.. ..	..	42 10
Spirits	.. ..	..	877$\frac{7}{10}$ gallons	175 15	..	..	.. ..	..	175 15
Shark Fins	.. ..	..	77 cwts. 7 bags	158 16	..	..	.. ..	..	158 15
Salt Fish, &c.	.. ..	..	525 cwts. 7 lbs.	122 10	..	..	.. ..	..	122 10
Salt	.. ..	..	54,892 parrahs	687 6	..	..	.. ..	..	687 6
Shells	22 boxes	110 0	28 boxes, 4 bskts.	115 0	..	..	3 boxes	13 0	238 0
Seeds	.. ..	..	31½ parrabs, 5 cwts. 40 lbs.	6 5	..	..	15 bgs. 100 parrahs	26 3	32 8
Sattin Wood	.. ..	..	1666 logs, 2,081 pieces	591 9	..	..	634 logs	131 8	722 17
Sapan Wood	1,034 cwts. 47 lbs.	296 8	128 cwts. 16 lbs.	35 15	..	..	2,960 lbs.	6 10	338 13
Salt Provisions	.. ..	..	1 tierce	6 0	..	..	.. ..	..	6 0
Stationery	.. ..	..	13 cases	608 15	..	..	.. ..	..	608 15
Sponge	.. ..	..	89 lbs	5 11	..	..	.. ..	..	5 11
Soft Sugar	.. ..	..	7 cwts. 61 lbs.	7 10	..	..	.. ..	..	7 10
Timber	.. ..	..	14,961 pcs, 7635 sticks, 194 bdls. 31,836 laths.	911 10	..	..	392 parrahs, 325 sticks	25 2	936 12
Toys	.. ..	..	3 cases	30 15	..	..	.. ..	..	30 15
Tools	.. ..	..	75 pieces	5 13	..	..	.. ..	..	5 13
Twine	.. ..	..	1 cwt. 38 lbs.	1 18	..	..	.. ..	..	1 18
Tallow	6 casks	11 5	.. ..	..	..	..	.. ..	..	11 5
Vinegar	.. ..	..	970 gallons	15 9	..	..	.. ..	..	15 9
Winnows	.. ..	..	8,037	9 13	..	..	.. ..	..	9 13
	Carried forward	60,499 19	.. ..	16,210 17	..	..	.. ..	5,641 7	82,352 13

A STATEMENT OF THE QUANTITY AND VALUE OF VARIOUS ARTICLES OF MERCHANDIZE EXPORTED FROM CEYLON IN 1835.—(*contd.*)

DUTY FREE.	ESTIMATED VALUE IN STERLING.								Total.
	To Great Britain.		To British Colonies.		To the United States of America.		To Foreign States.		
	Quantity.	Value.	Quantity.	Value.	Quantity.	Value.	Quantity.	Value.	
		£. s.		£. s.		£. s.		£. s.	£. s.
	Brought forward ..	60,499 19	.. ..	16,210 17	..	..	.. ..	5,641 7	82,352 13
Wearing Apparel	.. ..		213 dozens . .	127 10	..	..	.. ..	..	127 10
Wines . . .	.. ..	..	{ 6 pipes, 263 galls 194 10/12 doz. . }	559 0	..	..	.. ..	..	559 0
Wrecks . .	.. ..	..	2 lots . .	87 0	..	..	.. ..	..	87 0
Total Duty Free .	.. ..	60,499 19	.. ..	16,984 7	..	..	.. ..	5,641 7	83,126 3
,, Paid	.. ..	19,095 15	.. ..	46,648 18	..	400 0	.. ..	9,630 5	75,774 18
Grand Total .	.. ..	79,595 14	.. ..	63,633 5	..	400 0	.. ..	15,271 12	158,901 1

Mr. Bennett, in his "Manual of Useful Information," acquaints us that

the total value of Imports in 1840—1841, amounted to	£530,473 14 3	
Ditto 1839—1840 ditto	483,627 16 5	
Increase	46,845 17 10	
The total value of Exports in 1840—1841, amounted to	£310,360 10 4	
Ditto 1839—1840 ditto	275,592 10 1	
Increase	34,778 0 3	

These Documents shew the growing importance of Ceylon, and that no fear should be entertained that too much land (not above a quarter of it yet under cultivation) may be appropriated for agricultural purposes; and which must be still more evident, when it is considered, that one-fifth of the value of the Imports had been paid to Foreign Countries for food only.

The following additional Documents will also be interesting to many persons.

APPENDIX E.

SHIPPING, MANUFACTURES, MINES, AND FISHERIES, CEYLON, 1835.

SHIPPING, 1835.

PLACES.	INWARDS.			OUTWARDS.		
	Ships.	Tons.	Men	Ships.	Tons.	Men.
Great Britain . .	16	4,959	—	18	5,462	—
British Colonies . .	1,200	55,336	—	1,208	62,431	—
United States . .	2	454	—	1	274	—
Foreign States . .	186	12,377	—	54	3,889	—
Total . . .	1,404	73,126	17,612	1,281	72,056	13,563

APPENDIX F.

MANUFACTURES, MINES, AND FISHERIES, 1835.

MANUFACTURES.	SHIPS BUILT.		MINES AND QUARRIES.			FISHERIES.		
Number, Name, Situation, and Description of Manufactories, Mills, Works, &c.	No.	Tons.	Number, Name, Situation, and Description of the Mines and Quarries.	Name of the Mineral Substance.	Quantity Produced, and Value.	Number of Ships and Boats employed. Ships.	Boats	Value of Fish taken.
WESTERN PROVINCE.								£. s. d.
1,433 Looms. — The descriptions of cloth manufactured are handkerchiefs, table-cloths, napkins, towels, sail-cloths, white course cloths, and cloths used for dress by the natives . . .. . 84 Oil-Mills.—The oils expressed are cocoa-nut, gingelie, and mee . . . . . 2 Steam-Engines	None		12 Quarries.	Ruby, cattaye, topaz, blue sapphire, crystals, and plumbago.	Tons. Cwts. 543 7 2154 Pieces.	..	2,672	17,501 7 6¼
SOUTHERN PROVINCE.								
371 Looms. — Table-cloths, towels, sheets, handkerchiefs, and cloths used for dress by the natives . . . . . 1 Oil-Mill	None		14 Gem Quarries	Cattaye, topaz, tormalin, sapphire, and cinnamon stone, Iron, 6,000 lbs.	£. s. d. 46 17 6d Tons. Cwts. lbs. 2 13 64	..	2,050 boats	5,360 4 8¼
EASTERN PROVINCE.								
536 Looms . . . . . 12 Oil Mills	2	..	None . .	..	..	..	250 boats . .	691 13 8½
NORTHERN PROVINCE.								
945 Looms . . . . . 3 Oil-Mills	None		None . .	..	..	..	634 boats . 240 rafts .	34,347 11 8½ including value of pearl oysters. 21,975 6 3½
							Total Value	79,876 3 11

Appendix G.

ORDINANCE enacted by the Governor of *Ceylon*, with the Advice and Consent of the Legislative Council thereof, for establishing a new Tariff of Duties on Goods Exported and Imported.

Ordinance establishing a New Tariff of Duties.

Whereas it is expedient to establish a new tariff of duties, to be charged on goods exported from and imported into this colony,

Preamble.

1. It is hereby enacted by the Governor of Ceylon, with the advice and consent of the Legislative Council thereof, that from and after the 1st day of January, 1837, the 33d clause of the Regulation No. IX. of 1825, the Regulation No. IV. of 1829, intitled, "For promoting the growth of certain Articles of Agricultural Produce in the Island of Ceylon, and for the encouragement of Agricultural Speculation," and the Regulation No. VII. of 1830, intitled, "For amending the Tariffs of Duties imported and exported, and for encouraging the Warehousing of Cotton," except in so far as respects any offences then already committed, or any fines, penalties, dues, or liabilities then accrued, or the repeal of any previous Regulations, be, and the same are hereby repealed.

Former regulations repealed.

2. And it is further enacted, that from and after the said 1st day of January, 1837, all goods exported from any port of this colony, whether coastwise or otherwise, or imported into this colony from parts beyond the same, except such as are declared free, shall be liable to and charged with duty according to the rates specified in the tariff to this ordinance annexed.

Goods subject to duty according to tariff.

3. And it is further enacted, that the value of all goods to be exported or imported, and chargeable with duty *ad valorem*, shall be declared by the exporter or importer thereof; and if upon examination, it shall appear to the collector or comptroller of customs, or their assistants, that any such goods are

Where duty chargeable *ad valorem*, importer or exporter to declare value.

If value untrue. not declared according to the true value thereof, it shall be lawful for such collector, comptroller, or their assistants, within two days from the day of such declaration, to seize and take such goods for the use of the Crown, any law or usage to the contrary notwithstanding. And the collector, or comptroller, or their assistants, shall thereupon, in the case of goods entered for exportation, cause the amount of such valuation, and of the duties, if any shall have been paid upon entry, to be paid to the exporter or proprietor of such goods in full satisfaction for the same; and in the case of goods entered for importation, shall cause the amount of such valuation and duties, if any shall have been paid upon entry, together with an addition of 10 per cent. upon such valuation, to be paid to the importer or proprietor of such goods in full satisfaction for the same, and shall dispose of all such goods by public auction for the benefit of the Crown.

Restoration on condition. 4. And it is further enacted, that in case any goods shall be taken as undervalued as aforesaid, it shall be lawful for Government, or for the collector or comptroller of customs, to order the same to be restored, in such manner and on such terms and conditions as they shall think fit to prescribe. And if the proprietor of the same shall accept the terms and conditions so prescribed, he shall not have or maintain any action for recompense or damage on account of such seizure and taking; and the person making such seizure shall not proceed in any manner for condemnation.

If proprietor unable to estimate value. 5. And it is further enacted, that in any case in which the importer or exporter, or proprietor of any such goods shall declare himself unable to estimate the proper value thereof, the collector or comptroller of customs, or their assistants, shall set a value thereon, and the valuation so set shall be binding and conclusive upon the exporter, importer, or proprietor thereof, and the duties shall be charged and paid upon such valuation, any law or usage to the contrary notwithstanding.

Wearing apparel and baggage duty free. 6. And it is further enacted, that all wearing apparel and personal baggage of whatever description, accompanying the owner, shall be admitted to importation duty free, except such portion thereof as shall, on examination, appear to the collector or comptroller of customs to be imported for the purpose of sale.

Goods warehoused for re-exportation free.

7. And it is further enacted, that all goods (except cinnamon, cassia, and cassia buds) which shall be entered and warehoused for re-exportation at the ports of Colombo, Galle, Jaffna, Trincomalee, shall be exempt from duty of customs.

Goods carried coastwise.

8. And it is further enacted, that whenever goods shall have been exported coastwise from any one port to any other port of this colony, the full amount of custom duty paid on the export thereof shall be repaid to the shipper, or his agent, on production of a certificate, signed by the collector or comptroller of customs, or their assistants, at the place of relanding, (and which such collector or comptroller is hereby required to give without delay,) that such goods have been relanded in the same packages unopened, provided such shipper or agent shall on so exporting the same, have entered such goods to be carried coastwise, and shall have specified the place or places of relanding, and provided such certificate shall be produced within the period of three months from the date of exportation.

Goods imported or exported without payment of duty.

9. And it is further enacted, that every person who shall export or import any goods on which the duties shall not have been paid, with intent to evade payment thereof, and every person who shall ship or land, or assist in shipping or landing, or shall receive on board or on shore any goods on which the duties shall not have been paid, with intent to defraud Government of such duties, shall for each offence be liable to a fine not exceeding ten times the amount of the duties payable on such goods, or when that cannot be ascertained, to a discretionary fine, and in default of payment of such fine, to imprisonment, with or without hard labour, not exceeding six calendar months, and such goods shall be forfeited for the use of the Crown.

Tariff of Import Duties.

	£.	s.	d.
Ale, porter, and all other malt liquors in hogsheads, each hogshead - - -	0	10	0
Ditto, per dozen quarts, in bottles	0	0	6
Books, printed, free.			
Bullion, free.			
Cattle, free.			
Coin, free.			
Garden seeds, free.			
Goods, not otherwise enumerated, and not discharged of duty, being of the growth, produce, or manufacture of Great Britain and Ireland, or any other part of Europe, for every 100*l.* of the value thereof in this market .	4	0	0
Goods, being of the growth, produce, or manufacture of any other place, for every 100*l.* of the value thereof in this market .	10	0	0
Horses, free.			
Implements and tools for agriculture, and for any kind of manufacture, free.			
Instruments, scientific, free.			
Liqueurs, viz :—			
French, per quart bottle . .	0	0	9
British { Cherry Brandy . . . Ditto Ratafia . . . Raspberry Brandy . . Ditto Ratafia . . Rum shrub, and all other British liqueurs . . } per doz. pints	0	4	6
Machinery for agriculture or any kind of manufacture, free.			
Maps, free.			
Opium, per lb. . .	0	1	0
Paddy, per bushel . . .	0	0	3
Pearls, free.			

	£.	s.	d.
Precious stones, free.			
Regimental clothing, free.			
Rice, per bushel	0	0	7
Spirits, per gallon	0	4	6
Stock (live), free.			
Timber, free.			
Wines, viz :—			
Madeira, per pipe	3	0	0
Ditto, per dozen quarts	0	1	9
Teneriffe, per pipe	1	10	0
Ditto, per dozen quarts	0	1	0
English Claret, per ditto	0	4	0
Port, per gallon	0	0	6
Ditto, per dozen quarts	0	1	9
Lisbon, White and Red, per pipe	2	0	0
Ditto, per dozen quarts	0	1	3
Sherry, per gallon	0	0	6
Ditto, per dozen quarts	0	1	9
French Claret, per hogshead	2	0	0
Ditto, per dozen quarts	0	2	3
Champagne, per ditto	0	5	0
Burgundy, per ditto	0	5	0
Stein Wine, per ditto	0	1	9
Ditto, in cask, per gallon	0	0	6
Constantia, per dozen quarts	0	4	0
Ditto in cask, per gallon	0	1	7
Cape Wine, per gallon	0	0	1
Ditto, per dozen quarts	0	0	3½
Barsac, Sauterne, Vin de Grave, and all wines not otherwise enumerated, per dozen quarts	0	1	9
Malmsey Madeira, per pipe	5	0	0
Ditto, per dozen quarts	0	2	6
Sercial, per pipe	5	0	0
Ditto, per dozen quarts	0	2	6
Tinto, per pipe	5	0	0
Ditto, per dozen quarts	0	2	6

Tariff of Export Duties.

	£	s.	d.
Apparel (wearing) and personal baggage, free.			
Bullion, free.			
Cattle, free.			
Cinnamon, per lb. .	0	2	6
Ditto, if assorted as the third sort by the Government assorters, per lb. .	0	2	0
Cinnamon oil, per ounce . .	0	1	0
Goods, not otherwise enumerated or discharged of duty, at the rate of, for every 100*l.* value thereof . . .	2	10	0
Horses, free.			
Pearls, free.			
Precious stones, free.			

Given at Colombo, this 23d of December, 1836,

By his Excellency's command,

P. Anstruther, Colonial Secretary.

Appendix H.

STEAM-VESSEL ESTIMATE.

DETAIL OF WAGES.

		£.
Captain		400
First mate		150
Second mate		100
Surgeon		100
Carpenter		80
Gunner		50
Steward		50
Serang		30
Eight Lascars		96
Six Lascars		48
		1,104
First engineer	£.300	
Second engineer	200	
Third engineer	100	
		600
Twelve stokers, at £2. per mensem per man		288
		£.1,992 × 4 = £.7,968

VICTUALLING.

Captain, table allowance to provide table furniture of all kinds, and to mess mates, surgeon, chief engineer, and steward	600
Carpenter, gunner, two engineers	238
1 Serang, 14 Lascars, 12 Stokers	162
27	£.1,000 × 4 = £.4,000

Captain to be allowed 5 rupees per mensem.

	£.
Coals	20,000
Depôts and contingencies	3,072
	35,040
15 per cent on £100,000 for wear and tear, and to keep up the boats	15,000
	£.50,040

I estimate the income as follows:—

	£.
Passage money to be taken:	
£50. 10 passengers to and from Calcutta, monthly, 240	9,600
£40. 10 passengers to Madras coast, 240 .	8,160
£30. 5 passengers to Ceylon, including the Straits, 120	3,000
10 native passengers, 400 . .	4,000
£20. from Socotra to Suez, 600 passengers annually, thus drawn into the main trunk, to Suez from Socotra	8,400
	£.33,160

Profit on passengers, allowing the captain 10*s* for victualling per diem . . .	33,160
20,000 additional letters (if this route be adopted) at 2*s* 6*d*	2,500
50,000 periodicals, &c. at 1*s*	2,500
100,000 newspapers, at 6*d* . . .	2,500
200,000 letters, additional postage, at 1*s* .	10,000
Government despatches to Ceylon, Madras, and Calcutta, from England and intermediate places .	5,000
Law-deeds, parcels, invoices, samples, jewellery, treasures, &c.	5,000
	£.60,660

If steam communication is with Bombay only, there will be a greater number of passengers than otherwise from thence. The annual number of passengers that at present pass to and from Bombay are, arrivals, 287; departures, 316; total, 603.

	£.
Say 400 passengers at £40. profit	16,000
For deck and steerage passengers . . .	4,000
For newspapers, periodicals, invoices, law papers, parcels, samples, bullion, &c.	10,000
200,000 letters at 2*s* 6*d* each	25,000
Receipts to Bombay . . .	55,000
Add £.30 profit on the above number of passengers in the maintenance, 400 × 30	12,000
Profits between England and Bombay .	£.67,000

COALS REQUIRED EACH YEAR.

	Tons	Each Voyage between	Tons.
At Suez	1,250	Suez and Camaran	104
Camaran	2,256	Camaran and Socotra	85
Socotra	4,584	Socotra and Bombay	136
Bombay	1,632	Socotra and Galle	160
Galle	3,672	Galle and Calcutta	136
Calcutta	1,740		
TOTAL	15,134 tons a year, of which about 14,000 will go by the Cape of Good Hope		

APPENDIX I.

REPORT ON THE PAUMBUN PASSAGE.

THE distance between Point Rameen or Tonnetory, in the Ramnad province, and the opposite coast of Ceylon, is about sixty-two miles. In the intervening space are situated the islands of Ramisseram and Manar, separated from each other by Adam's Bridge, and from the coasts of Ramnad and Ceylon, by the narrow channel or straits of Paumbun and Manar.

The Manar channel is about a mile in breadth, and separates the island of Manar from Ceylon. It is navigable for small dhonies only and country boats. The island of Manar, which is a dependency of Ceylon, extends about twenty miles across the straits in a north-west direction. At its west end commences the bank called Adam's Bridge, which runs about thirty miles also in a north-west direction to the island of Ramisseram. This island is about ten miles in length, and is separated from the coast of Ramnad by the channel of Paumbun one mile and a quarter in width,

The Manar channel was surveyed under instructions from the Ceylon government, by the late Captain Dawson of the Royal Engineers, and Mr. Stewart, the master attendant of Colombo, who described it as a long, narrow, and very winding channel, having about six feet of water in the the shallowest parts, with the exception of a bar opposite to its south end, on which there is not more than three or four feet of water. This channel, from the account given of it by the officers who surveyed it, does not appear to be capable of any material improvement.

The sand bank, called Adam's Bridge, is a very extraordinary formation. It is only about a quarter of a mile in breadth, and consists entirely of sand, partly above and partly below water, collected apparently by the surf and currents, and unsupported, as far as could be ascertained, by rock. The east end of it was pierced by the Ceylon officers to the depth of thirty feet, and nothing found but sand; on each side of the bank, at the distance of two and a half or three miles, the sea is six fathoms deep, and quite free from obstructions of every kind.

There are three principal openings or channels across the bank, one near the island of Manar, called the Tal Manar passage; the second eight miles further to the west, and the third about eleven miles from the island of Ramisseram, termed the Tannycoody passage. This last was examined and surveyed on the present occasion. It is narrow in the centre, and thirty feet deep, with broad curved bars opposite to its two ends, on which there is not more than five or six feet of water. The bank between it and Ramisseram is entire, and several feet above water. The Tal Manar passage was examined by the Ceylon officers, and resembles exactly that of Tannycoody, but it is not so deep, there being only about three feet of water on its north bar.

The intermediate opening was not examined, but from its appearance, as well as from the description given of it by the fishermen who frequent the place, there can be no doubt of its corresponding very nearly with the other two. It is said to be rather deeper than the Tal Manar passage, but not so deep as that of Tannycoody.

In the vicinity of the Tal Manar and Tannycoody openings, the bank is visible above water for several miles, intersected by only a few narrow openings, but towards its centre it is chiefly covered with water, and very little sand is to be seen, though from the surf breaking exactly on the line of the bank, the depth of water cannot exceed two or three feet.

During both monsoons, on the lee side of the bank, to the distance of from half a mile to a mile, there are great numbers of irregular shifting sand banks scattered about, on which there is from two to four feet of water, with passages between them eight or nine feet deep. The weather side, on the contrary, particularly towards the end of the monsoon, is in a great measure clear of such banks, and the surf breaks on its shore nearly in a straight continued line. When the monsoon changes, the strength and prevailing direction of the current change too, and the loose sand of which the shifting banks are composed, on what was the lee side being stirred up by the surf and sea, is swept by the current through the channels, and deposited on the opposite side, partly on the bars and partly in loose detached heaps along the bank. These deposits appear to be further increased by the sand thrown upon the weather shore by the surf, which, as soon as it becomes dry, is carried by the wind across the bank into the sea on the other side. It was observed, when the wind was tolerably strong, that a continued stream of sand was swept across the bank into the sea on the lee side. The beach of Adam's Bridge, therefore, to the distance of about a mile on both sides, is continually changing and shifting; on the weather side it is generally clear, except immediately opposite to the channels where there are always projecting bars, while on the opposite side there are many loose banks scattered about, and constantly changing and varying in position and extent as the monsoon advances, and according to the state of the sea and weather.

During both monsoons rather a high surf breaks on the weather side of the bank, but the south-west monsoon produces much the highest surf, accompanied by a long heavy swell. During part of the north-east monsoon the surf breaks on both sides of the bank.

Dhonies in ballast and fishing boats occasionally pass through the openings in fine weather, but the passage is attended with some difficulty and danger, and is not common.

There is an account, I was informed, given in the records of the Dutch government of Ceylon, of a Dutch fleet having on one occasion escaped from a Danish fleet by passing through the channels of Adam's Bridge : if this be authentic, either some of the channels must have been deeper in former days, or the ships must have been of a small size. It is probable, indeed, that the depth and extent of openings are constantly changing, from the effect of a current and surf, and the quantity of loose sand floating about the bank, and that they will not be found of the same size for any length of time ; they appear to be affected by every change in the weather, the currents and surf, and most likely vary considerably in depth in different seasons.

If it be possible to obtain anywhere through the straits a channel sufficiently deep for all classes of ships, it must, I think, be sought for in some part of this bank, and even here the practicability of opening such a channel, and of keeping it open, is very doubtful. A strong double bulwark of stones across the bank, extending into deep water on both sides, with a narrow opening of 100 or 200 feet, might I think with reason, be expected to accomplish the object. The velocity of the current would probably keep a narrow fixed channel of that description always sufficiently deep, and sweep off any sand that might be carried into it either by the sea or by the wind, and as the bulwark would extend into deep water beyond the shifting sands and the influence of the surf, there would be little risk, I think, of its ends being filled or choked with sand. The danger to be chiefly apprehended is the formation of bars opposite to the ends of the channel, similar to what are now found in front of the natural openings, particularly on the south side, where, from the superior strength of the south-west monsoon and heavy swell, sand banks are always the largest and most numerous ; but of this, I think, there would not be much danger ; the quantity of sand carried through the channel, from its being beyond the influence of the surf, would probably not be very great ; and as the current would be rapid and extend into deep water, it is likely that what did pass through it would be dissipated and disappear.

The cost of such a work would, however, be very great indeed, and could only be justified by its being considered an object of high national importance to have a passage sufficiently deep in time of war for the largest vessels. In the event of a struggle for the superiority at sea with an European enemy, the advantages of such a channel would be invaluable; but it is doubtful whether the benefits which commerce would derive from it, great as they undoubtedly would be, would warrant an undertaking, the expense of which, under the most favourable circumstances, must be very large, and the success, from a variety of causes which neither can be foreseen nor guarded against, uncertain.

There remains to be considered the Paumbun channel, or strait between Ramisseram and the Ramnad coast, which affords, perhaps, the only prospect of a moderately deep channel such as would benefit commerce generally, and the coasting trade of India in particular, without the necessity of incurring a very large or disproportionate expenditure.

The examination of the Paumbun passage has accordingly, and in conformity with the instructions of Government, occupied the whole of the attention and time of the officers deputed for the purpose of surveying the straits, with the exception of a few days devoted to the inspection of Adam's Bridge.

The obstacles to be overcome at Paumbun are a dam or ledge of rock, extending from the island of Ramisseram to Point Ramen or Tonnetory, on the opposite coast of Ramnad, and an irregular sand bank a little to the south of it.

The dam is 2,250 yards in length, and runs east and west; it is bounded by two parallel ridges of rock about 140 yards apart; the north ridge is considerably the highest, and is termed the first or great dam; it is in most places visible at low water, though nowhere sufficiently connected to prevent entirely at any time the passage of the water. The line of the south ridge or dam can also be distinctly traced at low water, but only a few detached rocks on it even then appear above water; the whole or greater part of the space between these two ridges is filled up by large irregular masses of rocks in various positions, but generally in directions nearly parallel to the principal ridges, and usually several feet lower than them.

The continuation of the rock or dam can be readily traced on the main land and island of Ramisseram, in its natural position, and in uniform layers."

Major Sims, in continuation of his long report, proceeds to point out how these immense obstacles may be removed or overcome; but the labour and expense would be so enormous, as to deter a wise government from making the attempt: indeed, the finances of our Eastern empire are not in such a flourishing state, as to admit of Major Sims's proposal, if practicable, being entertained.

Appendix J.

PROCLAMATION.

At a Convention held on the second day of March, in the year of Christ 1815, and the Cingalese year 1736, at the Palace in the City of Kandy, between his Excellency Lieutenant-General ROBERT BROWNRIGG, *Governor and Commander-in-Chief in and over the British Settlements and Territories in the Island of Ceylon, acting in the name and on behalf of his Majesty George the Third King, and his Royal Highness George Prince of Wales, Regent of the United Kingdom of Great Britain and Ireland, on the one part, and the Adigars, Dessaves and other principal Chiefs of the Kandyan Provinces, on behalf of the Inhabitants, and in presence of the Mohattales, Corals, Vidhaans and other subordinate Headmen, from the several Provinces, and of the people then and there as-*

sembled on the other part, it is agreed and established as follows :—

1st. That the cruelties and oppressions of the Malabar Ruler in the arbitrary and unjust infliction of bodily tortures and the pains of death without trial, and sometimes without an accusation or the possibility of a crime, and in the general contempt and contravention of all civil rights, have become flagrant, enormous and intolerable, the acts and maxims of his Government being equally and entirely devoid of that justice, which should secure the safety of his subjects, and of that good faith which might obtain a beneficial intercourse with the neighbouring settlements.

2d. That the Rajah Sri Wikreme Rajah Sinha, by the habitual violation of the chief and most sacred duties of a Sovereign, has forfeited all claims to that title or the powers annexed to the same, and is declared fallen and deposed from the office of King—his family and relatives, whether in the ascending, descending or collateral line, and whether by affinity or blood, are also for ever excluded from the throne—and all claim and title of the Malabar race to the dominion of the Kandyan Provinces, is abolished and extinguished.

3d. That all male persons being or pretending to be relations of the late Rajah Sri Wikreme Rajah Sinha, either by affinity or blood, and whether in the ascending, descending, or collateral line, are hereby declared enemies to the Government of the Kandyan Provinces, and excluded and prohibited from entering those Provinces on any pretence whatever, without a written permission for that purpose by the authority of the British Government, under the pains and penalties of Martial Law, which is hereby declared to be in force for that purpose—and all male persons of the Malabar caste now expelled from the said Provinces are, under the same penalties, prohibited from returning, except with the permission before mentioned.

4th. The dominion of the Kandyan Provinces is vested in the Sovereign of the British Empire, and to be exercised through the Governors or Lieut.-Governors of Ceylon for the time being;

and their accredited agents, saving to the Adigars, Dessaves, Mohattales, Corals, Vidhaans, and all other chief and subordinate native Headmen, lawfully appointed by authority of the British Government, the rights, privileges, and powers of their respective offices, and to all classes of the people the safety of their persons and property, with their civil rights and immunities, according to the laws, institutions, and customs established and in force amongst them.

5th. The religion of Boodhoo, professed by the chiefs and inhabitants of these Provinces, is declared inviolable, and its rights, ministers, and places of worship, are to be maintained and protected.

6th. Every species of bodily torture, and all mutilation of limb, member, or organ, are prohibited and abolished.

7th. No sentence of death can be carried into execution against any inhabitant, except by the written warrant of the British Governor or Lieut.-Governor for the time being, founded on a report of the case made to him through the accredited agent or agents of the Government resident in the interior, in whose presence all trials for capital offences are to take place.

8th. Subject to these conditions, the administration of Civil and Criminal Justice and Police over the Kandyan inhabitants of the said Provinces is to be exercised according to established forms and by the ordinary authorities, saving always the inherent right of Government to redress grievances and reform abuses in all instances whatever, whether particular or general, where such interposition shall become necessary.

9th. Over all other persons civil or military residing in or resorting to these Provinces not being Kandyans, civil and criminal Justice, together with Policy, shall, until the pleasure of his Majesty's Government in England may be otherwise deelared, be administered in the manner following.

1st. All persons not being commissioned or non-commissioned military officers, soldiers, or followers of the army usually held liable to military discipline, shall be subject to the magistracy of the accredited agent or agents of the British Government in all cases, except charges of murder, which shall be tried by special commissions to be issued from time to time by the Governor for that purpose. Provided always, as to such charges of murder wherein any British subject may be defendant, who might be tried for the same by the laws of the United Kingdom of Great Britain and Ireland in force for the trial of offences committed by British subjects in foreign parts, no such British subject shall be tried on any charge of murder alleged to have been perpetrated in the Kandyan Provinces, otherwise than by virtue of such laws of the United Kingdom.

2nd. Commissioned or non-commissioned military officers, soldiers, or followers of the army usually held amenable to military discipline, shall, in all civil and criminal cases wherein they may be defendants, be liable to the laws, regulations and customs of war, reserving to the Governor and Commander-in-Chief, in all cases falling under this ninth article, an unlimited right of review over every proceeding, civil or military, had by virtue thereof, and reserving also full power to make such particular provisions conformably to the general spirit of the said article as may be found necessary to carry its principles into full effect.

10th. Provided always, that the op[illegible]ion of the several preceding clauses shall not be contravened by the provisions of any temporary or partial proclamation published during the advance of the army; which provisions, in so far as incompatible with the said preceding articles, are hereby repealed.

11th. The royal dues and revenues of the Kandyan Provinces are to be managed and collected for his Majesty's use and the support of the Provincial establishment according to lawful custom, and under the direction and superintendance of the accredited agent or agents of the British Government.

12th. His Excellency the Governor will adopt provisionally, and recommend to the confirmation of his Royal Highness the Prince Regent in the name and on behalf of his Majesty, such dispositions in favour of the trade of these Provinces, as may facilitate the export of their products, and improve the returns, whether in money, or in salt, cloths, or other commodities useful and desirable to the inhabitants of the Kandyan country.

GOD SAVE THE KING.

(Signed) ROBERT BROWNRIGG, *Governor.*
EYHELEPOLA,
MOLLIGODDA, *1st Adikar and Dissave of the Seven Korles,*
PELIME TALAWE, *2nd Adikar and Dissave of Saffragam,*
PELIME TALAWE, *Dissave of the Four Korles,*
MONARAWILA, *Dissave of Ouwa,*
RATWATTE, *Dissave of Matele,*
MOLLIGODDA, *Dissave of the Three Korles,*
DULLEYWE, *Dissave of Walapane,*
MILLAWA, *Dissave of Welasse and Bintenne,*
GALAGAMA, *Dissave of Tamankada,*
GALAGODA, *Dissave of Nuwara Kalawiya.*

In presence of J. D'OYLY, *Chief Translator to Govt.*
JAMES SUTHERLAND, *Dep. Sec. to Govt.*

APPENDIX K.

PROCLAMATION.

By His Excellency Lieut.-General SIR ROBERT BROWNRIGG, *Knight Grand Cross of the Most Honourable Military Order of the Bath, Governor and Commander-in-Chief in and over the British Settlements and Territories in the Island of Ceylon, with the Dependencies thereof.*

A Dispatch, of which the following is a copy, having been received from the Right Honorable Lord BATHURST, one of His Majesty's Principal Secretaries of State, respecting the Convention concluded in Kandy on the 2nd of March, 1815, the said Dispatch is published for general information.

No. 37.

Downing Street, 13*th October*, 1815.

SIR,—In my Dispatch of the 30th of August, I informed you that I had referred to the consideration of His Majesty's Law Servants, those articles of the Convention for the settlement of the Kandyan country, which had been the subject of discussion.

I have now the honour of transmitting to you a copy of their opinion—which is so full upon all the points submitted to he ir consideration, as to render it unnecessary for me to furnish you with instruction, beyond that of adhering to the principles which they have laid down. And in order to prevent any uncertainty, as to the liability of military persons in the Kandyan country to remain subject to martial law, I am to acquaint you, that although His Royal Highness the Prince Regent has generally approved the Convention by which that territory has become annexed to His Majesty's dominions, His Royal Highness has declined adopting the pre-existing laws and courts of Kandy, as forms of the King's civil judicature, until more detailed information shall have been obtained as to the nature of the laws, and the changes which it may be expedient to introduce in their administration.

I have the honour to be, &c. &c.

(Signed) BATHURST.

Governor Sir ROBT. BROWNRIGG, K.G.C.B. &c. &c.

In conformity with the principles laid down in the opinion of the Law Officers of His Majesty's Government in England, (to which principles the Governor is instructed to adhere), it is hereby declared and notified as follows: to wit.

1st. That the Provision contained in the 1st Section of the 9th or provisional article of the Convention, respecting Commissions to be issued by the Governor for the trial of charges of murder in certain specified cases, will cease to be in force from henceforth.

" 2ndly. That the ancient laws of Kandy are to be administered till His Majesty's pleasure shall be known, as to their adoption *in toto* as to all persons within those provinces, or "their partial adoption as to the natives, and the substitution "of new laws and tribunals for the trial and punishment of His "Majesty's European subjects, for offences committed therein."

"3dly. That persons committing those offences cannot be "tried by the Supreme Court, as at present established for "Ceylon, till the Kandyan Provinces are annexed to or made "Dependencies of that Settlement or Government. But that "British subjects may be proceeded against in England under "the 33rd Henry VIII. chap. 23rd."

4thly. Concerning the second section of the said ninth or provisional article, that the same being, in substance, conformable to the provisions of the Mutiny Act and Articles of War as applicable to the present state and condition of the Kandyan country, will, until His Majesty shall otherwise provide, remain in force, and extend to "all persons who are Commissioned, or "in the pay of His Majesty as Officers, or who are listed or in "pay as soldiers."

GOD SAVE THE KING.

Given at Colombo the 31st day of May, 1816. By Command of His Excellency the Governor,

JOHN RODNEY, *Chief Sec. to Govt.*

To be published in the Kandyan Provinces. By Order of His Excellency the Governor,

JAMES SUTHERLAND, *Secretary, Kandyan Provinces.*

APPENDIX L.

PROCLAMATION.

By His Excellency Lieutenant-General SIR ROBERT BROWNRIGG, *Baronet and Knight Grand Cross of the Most Honourable Military Order of the Bath, Governor and Commander-in-Chief in and over the British Settlements and Territories in the Island of Ceylon with the Dependencies thereof.*

ROBT. BROWNRIGG.

Preamble. Recital of Cession of Kandyan Provinces to Great Britain.

1. THE Chiefs and People of the Kandyan nation, no longer able to endure the cruelties and oppressions which the late king Sri Wikreme Rajah Singha tyrannically practised towards them, prayed the assistance of the British Government for their relief, and by a solemn Act declared the late King deposed, and himself and all persons descending from or in any manner related to his family incapable of claiming or exercising royal authority within the Kandyan provinces, which were by the same solemn act ceded to the dominion of the British sovereign.

Moderate exercise of power by the British Government.

2. The exercise of power by the representatives of his Britannic Majesty, from the date of that Convention, the 2nd March, 1815, till the hour that insurrection broke out in the month of October, 1817, was marked with the greatest mildness and forbearance towards all classes; the strictest attention to the protection and maintenance of the rites, ministers, and places of worship, of the religion of Boodhoo; and a general deference to the opinions of the chiefs, who were considered as the persons best able, from their rank and knowledge, to aid the Government in ensuring the happiness of the mass of its new subjects. In exacting either taxes or services for the State, an extraordinary and unprecedented laxity was allowed to take place in order that the country might with more ease recover from any evil effects sustained by the contrary practices of the late King. In assessing punishments for offences, even where a plot to sub-

vert the Government was proved, the spirit which always characterizes the British rule was strongly to be contrasted with the ancient and frequent recurrence of capital executions, preceded by the most cruel and barbarous tortures.

Flourishing state of the country.

3. Under this mild administration on the part of the British Government, the country appeared to rest in peace. Cultivation was increased, and Divine Providence blessed the exertions of the labourers, and rewarded them by plenteous crops; yet all this time there were factious and intriguing spirits at work seeking for an opportunity to subvert the Government, for no purpose but to assume to themselves absolute power over the lives and properties of the general mass of subjects, which, by the equal justice of British authority, were protected from their avarice, or malicious cruelty.

Notwithstanding these benefits plots have been formed against the State.

Motives of the factious.

Time and manner of executing the plot.

4. These plotters against the State were found among the very persons who have been restored to honours and security by the sole intervention of British power, and the opportunity of raising disturbance was chosen when relying on the merited gratitude of all orders of the Kandyan nation. The Government had diminished the number of troops, and the insurgent leaders, unconscious or forgetful of the extensive resources of the British empire, thought, in setting up the standard of rebellion, as easily to effect their purpose of expelling the English from the country, as the people had been deluded to prostrate themselves before the phantom whose pretensions they espoused, merely to cover their own ambitious views of subjecting the nation to their arbitrary will.

Manifestation of the power of the British Government.

5. After more than a year of conflict, which has created misery, and brought destruction on many, the efforts of the British Government, and the bravery of his Majesty's troops, have made manifest to the Kandyans the folly of resistance; and that in the Government alone resides the power of protecting them in the enjoyment of happiness. The flimsy veil which the rebel chiefs threw over their ambitious designs was torn aside by themselves, and the pageant, whom the people was called to recognize as the descendant of the gods, exposed as the offspring of a poor Cingalese empiric.

Detection of the imposition practised in the person of the Pretender.

Reasonable to expect delusion in future would be more difficult.

6. After such a display to the public of depraved artifice and injurious and unfeeling deception, the Government might reasonably hope that a sense of the misery brought on them by delusion would prevent the great body of the people from listening to any one who should attempt in future to seduce them to rebellion against its beneficent rule. But it is also incumbent on it from a consideration of the circumstances which have past, and the evil consequences which have ensued on the blind obedience which the people have thought due to their chiefs instead of to the sovereign of the country, to perform, by its inherent right, such parts of the practice of Administration, as by occasioning the subject to lose sight of the majesty of the Royal Government, made him feel wholly dependent on the power of the various chiefs, which, to be legal, could only be derived to them by delegation from the sovereign authority of the country.

Expedient to guard against a recurrence of the evil consequences, and to demonstrate to the people that the Government is entitled to their obedience in superiority to the chiefs.

Declaration of the supremacy of the British Crown exercised through the Governor and his agents.

7. His Excellency the Governor, therefore, now calls to the mind of every person, and of every class within these settlements, that the sovereign majesty of the King of Great Britain and Ireland, exercised by his representative the Governor of Ceylon, and his agents in the Kandyan provinces, is the source alone from which all power emanates, and to which obedience is due. That no chief who is not vested with authority or rank from this sovereign source is entitled to obedience or respect; and that, without powers derived from Government, no one can exercise jurisdiction of any kind, or inflict the slightest punishment. And finally, that every Kandyan, be he of the highest or lowest class, is secured in his life, liberty, and property, from encroachment of any kind, or by any person, and is only subject to the laws which will be administered according to the ancient and established usages of the country, and in such manner and by such authorities and persons as in the name and on behalf of his Majesty is herein declared.

No chief entitled to obedience or respect but when vested with authority by Government.

Equal rights of every Kandyan subject.

Delegation of the Governor's authority to the

8. The general executive and judicial authority in the Kandyan provinces is delegated by his Excellency to the Board

Board of Commissioners, and to Resident Agents in certain Dessavonies.

of Commissioners, and under their general superintendence, to Resident Agents of Government in such Dessavonies of the said provinces in which it may please his Excellency to place such Agents, with more or less authority or jurisdiction, as by their several instructions may be vested in them, and of which the present disposition and arrangement is hereinafter contained.

All chiefs to perform duty under the orders of the Board or other British agents.

9. The Adigars, Dessaves, and all other chiefs and inferior headmen shall perform duty to Government under the orders of the said Board of Commissioners and British Agents, and not otherwise.

No person to execute office but under written appointments. Signed by the Governor for superior chiefs, and by the resident for inferior headmen, or provisionally by agents in the Dessavonies. except in villages allotted to personal service of Dessaves.

10. No person shall be considered entitled to execute the office either of the higher or lower class of Headmen unless thereto appointed by a written instrument, signed, in respect to superior chiefs, by his Excellency the Governor, and for inferior Headmen by the Honourable the Resident, or provisionally, by any Agent of Government thereto duly authorized, excepting in certain villages or departments which will be allotted for personal services to the Dessave, in which the Dessave shall, as before, have the sole privilege of making appointments.

Honours to be paid to chiefs as before, except as under. Prostrations abolished.

11. Honours shall be paid to all classes of chiefs entitled to the same under the former Government, in so far as the same is consistent with the abolition which the British Government is resolved to effect of all degrading forms whereto both chiefs and people were subjected under the ancient tyranny, and which a liberal administration abhors. All prostrations therefore, from, or to any person, including the Governor, are henceforth positively, as they were before, virtually and in fact abolished, and the necessity which existed, that chiefs, or others, coming into the presence of the Sovereign Authority should remain on their knees, is also abrogated. But all chiefs and other persons coming before, meeting, or passing any British officer, civil, or military, of rank and authority in the island of Ceylon, shall give up the middle of the road, and if sitting, rise, and make a suitable obeisance, which will be always duly acknowledged and returned.

Kneeling in presence of the sovereign authority abrogated. Respect to be paid to British officers of rank by chiefs and others.

12. It is also in this respect directed, that on entering the hall of audience, every person shall make obeisance to the portrait of his Majesty there suspended; and as well there, as in any other court of justice, to the presiding authority. And it is further enacted, that when his Excellency the Governor, as his Britannic Majesty's representative, travels, he shall be attended by all the persons in office belonging to each province in manner as they attended the former kings of Kandy, except that the Dessaves may always use palanqueens beyond the river Mahavillaganga, within which limit the Adigars only have this privilege, and that when any of the Members of his Majesty's Council, or the Commissioners for the Kandyan provinces, or the Commanding Officers of the troops in the Kandyan provinces, travel into any province on duty, they be met and attended in such province as the great Dessaves were, and are to be attended; in their provinces, likewise, the Resident Agents, and the officers commanding the troops in each province are in their provinces to be similarly attended, and receive like honours.

Respect to his Majesty's portrait in the hall of audience. And to authority presiding in Courts of Justice.

Attendance on the Governor in travelling.

Attendance on other officers of Government travelling on duty.

13. The chiefs holding the high offices of 1st and 2nd Adigar will be received by all sentries whom they pass in the day with carried arms, and by all soldiers off duty, or other Europeans, or persons of European extraction, by touching their caps, or taking off their hats; and by all natives, whether Kandyans or not, by rising from their seats, leaving the middle of the street clear, and bowing to the Adigars as they pass. And to all other Dessaves and other chiefs, all natives coming into their presence, meeting or passing them, are to make a proper inclination of the body, in acknowledgment of their rank.

Salute by sentries to 1st and 2nd Adigars.

Respect by Europeans.

By natives.

Respect to other chiefs.

14. The Adigars, Dessaves, and other chiefs, shall further be entitled to proper attendance of persons of the different departments in such numbers as shall be determined by his Excellency on the Report of the Board of Commissioners, provided that where such persons are not belonging to the villages or departments allotted to the Adigar, or Dessaves, the application for their attendance, when required, must be made

Attendance on Adigars, &c.

Persons entitled to sit in hall of audience, or in presence of British agents.

to the Resident in Kandy, or to the agents of Government in the provinces in which such agents may be stationed.

15. The persons entitled to sit in the hall of audience, or in the presence of the agents of Government, are those chiefs only who bear commissions signed by the Governor, or to whom special license may, by the same authority, be given to that effect. Of these only the two Adigars, or persons having the Governor's letter of license, can sit on chairs, the others on benches covered with mats, of different heights, according to their relative ranks. In the Courts hereinafter mentioned of the Agents of Government, when the assessors are Mohattales, or Corales, they may sit on mats on the ground.

Respect to priests and processions of Budhoo religion. General protection of all other religions. Erection of places of worship under the Governor's license.

16. As well the priests as all the ceremonies and processions of the Budhoo religion, shall receive the respect which in former times was shewn them, at the same it is in nowise to be understood that the protection of Government is to be denied to the peaceable exercise, by all other persons, of the religion which they respectively profess, or to the erection, under due license from his Excellency, of places of worship in proper situations.

Fees on appointments abolished. Except in temple villages. All taxes and duties abolished. Except a general tax on paddy land of a portion of the produce.

17. The Governor abolishes all fees payable for appointments either to Government, or to any chiefs, excepting for appointment in the temple villages, which will be made by the resident on the recommendation of the Dewe Nileme, or Basnaik Nilemes, appointed by the Governor; the Dewe Nileme, or the Basnaike Nileme, receiving the usual fee; also, all duties payable heretofore to the Gabbedawas, Aramudale, Awudege, and all other duties or taxes whatsoever, are abolished, save and except that now declared and enacted, being a tax on all paddy lands of a portion of the annual produce, under the following modifications and exceptions, and according to the following rates.

General rate of tax fixed at 1-10th of the annual produce.

18. The general assessment of tax on the entire paddy lands of the Kandyan provinces is fixed at one tenth of the annual produce, to be delivered by the proprietor, or cultivator, at such convenient storehouse, in every province, or sub-

division of a province, as shall be, with due regard to the interests of the subjects, appointed by, or under the instructions of the revenue agent.

In certain districts which have stood firm in loyalty the tax reduced to 1-14th.

19. To mark the just sense which his Excellency has of the loyalty and good conduct of the chiefs and people of Oodanoora, the Four Korles, the Three Korles, and the following Korles of Saffragam to wit: Kooroowitti Korle, Nawadoon Korle, Colonna Korle, Kukula Korle; Atakalan Korle, the Uduwak Gampaha of Kadewatte Korle, the Medde Korle except the villages Udagamme, Gonilande, Kolutotte, Golettetotte, Mollemore Piengiria, and Mulgamma, and the following Korles of the Seven Korles, viz. Tirigandahaye excepting the villages Hewapolla, Katoopittiye, and Torrewatere, Oodapola Korle, Kattugampaha Korle Oodookaha, Kattugampola Korle Medapattoo, Petigal Korle, Yagame Korle, Rakawah Patto Korle, Angamme Korle, Yatekuha Korle, and of the villages Pubilia, Kongahawelle and Nikawelle, lying in the Oodoogodde Korle of Matele. The Governor declares that the rate of taxation in these provinces, or Korles, shall only be one fourteenth part of the annual produce.

All lands forfeited in rebellion, and which may be restored to the former owners, to pay 1-5th.

20. But, on the contrary, that it may be known that persons who are leaders in revolt or disobedience shall meet punishment, all lands which may have been declared forfeited by the misconduct of the proprietor, shall, if by the mercy of Government, be restored to the former owners, pay a tax of one-fifth of the annual produce.

Temple lands exempted from taxation. Reservation of gratuitous service from certain inhabitants of temple villages.

21. The Governor, desirous of shewing the adherence of Government to its stipulations in favour of the religion of the people, exempts all lands which now are the property of temples from all taxation whatever; but as certain inhabitants of those villages are liable to perform fixed gratuitous services also to the Crown, this obligation is to continue unaffected.

Lands belonging to certain loyal chiefs exempted from tax.

22. All lands also now belonging to the following chiefs, whose loyalty and adherence to the lawful Government merit favour, viz.

Mollegodde Maha Nileme,	Ratwatta Nileme,
Mollegodde Nileme,	Kadoogamoone Nileme,

Dehigamme Nileme,
Mulligamme Nileme, lately Dessave of Welasse.
Eknillegodde Nileme,
Mahawallatene Nileme,
Doloswalle Nileme,
Eheyleyagodde Nileme,
Katugaha the elder,
Katugaha the younger,
Damboolane Nileme,
Godeagedere Nileme,
Gonegodde Nileeme, formerly Adikaram of Buintenne,

shall be free of duty during their lives, and that their heirs shall enjoy the same free of duty, excepting with regard to such as paid Pingo duty, which shall now and hereafter pay one-tenth to the Government of the annual produce, unless when exempted under the next clause.

Lands of chiefs holding offices exempted during their continuance in office.

23. All lands belonging to chiefs holding offices, either of the superior or inferior class, and of inferior headmen, shall, during the time they are in office, be free of duty.

Lands of cinnamon peelers exempted from taxation. Also of cultivators of Royal lands. And of attendants allotted to Dessaves, Katepurule, and Attepattoo people.

24. All lands belonging to persons of the castes or departments allotted to the cutting of cinnamon shall be free of duty, also lands held by persons, for which they are bound to cultivate, or aid in the culture, of royal lands ; and also the lands of such persons who may be allotted to the performance of personal service to the Dessaves, by the Board of Commissioners, and of those who perform Katepurule or Attepattoo service gratuitously, it being well understood that the persons last mentioned have no right or authority whatever to exact or receive fees or fines of any kind when sent on public duty, which they are required to perform expeditiously and impartially.

Veddas to continue tribute of wax.

25. The Veddas who possess no paddy lands shall continue to deliver to Government the usual tribute in wax.

All presents prohibited. Provisions to British officers, chiefs, troops, or other servants of Government travelling, to be furnished for payment.

26. All presents to the Governor, or other British authorities, are strictly prohibited. In travelling, every officer, civil, or military, chiefs, detachments of troops, or other servants of Government, on notice being given of their intended march, or movement, are to be supplied with the provisions of the country in reasonable quantity, and on payment being made for the same at the current price.

27. All fees, on hearing of cases, to Dessaves, or others,

except as hereafter mentioned, which are for the benefit of Government, shall be, and are abolished. Fees on hearing cases abolished.

28. The services of the Adigars, Dessaves, and other superior chiefs, to Government, shall be compensated by fixed monthly salaries in addition to the exemption of their lands from taxation. Remuneration for service of superior chiefs.

29. The services of the inferior chiefs shall be compensated as above by exemption from taxation, and that they also receive one twentieth part of the revenue paddy, which they shall collect from the people under them to be allotted in such portion as the Board of Commissioners shall, under the authority of Government, regulate. Remuneration to inferior chiefs.

30 All persons shall be liable to service for Government, on the requisition of the Board of Commissioners, and agents of Government, according to their former customs and families, or tenures of their lands, on payment being made for their labour, it being well understood, that the Board of Commissioners, under his Excellency's authority, may commute such description of service, as, under present circumstances, is not usefully applicable to the public good, to such other as may be beneficial. And provided, further, that the holding of lands duty free shall be considered the payment for the service of the Katepurule and Attepattoo departments, and persons allotted to the Dessaves' service, and also for the service to Government of certain persons of the temple villages, and in part for those which cut cinnamon; and also that the duty for clearing and making roads, and putting up and repairing bridges, be considered a general gratuitous service falling on the districts through which the roads pass, or wherein the bridges lie, and that the attendance on the great feast, which certain persons were bound to give, be continued to be given punctually and gratuitously. The washermen also shall continue to put up white cloths in the temples, and for the chiefs, gratuitously. All persons liable to general service for payment.

31. All Kadawettes and ancient barriers throughout the country shall be from henceforward discontinued and removed, and the establishments belonging to them for their maintenance and defence abolished, the services of the persons Kadawettes and services attendant abolished.

usually employed therein being applied to such other more beneficial purpose as the Board of Commissioners shall determine.

Rules for service of Kunamaduwe, Talpatwaduna, Kareas, and PandanKareas.

32. And it being necessary to provide rules for the service of certain persons who were to perform duty to the person of the King of Kandy. viz. the Kunamaduwe, or palanquin bearers, the Talepatawedunakaria, or talpat bearers, and Pandankareas, or torch bearers; it is ordered by the Governor, that such persons being paid for the same, shall be bound to serve in their respective duties, the Governor, the Members of His Majesty's Council, any General Officer on the Staff of this army, the Commissioners for Kandyan affairs, the Secretary for the Kandyan provinces, and the officer commanding the troops in the interior.

Powers of agent of Government to punish neglect of duty.

33. And for ensuring the due execution of all the above ordinances relative to the collection of the revenue, and performance of public duty by all chiefs and others; his Excellency empowers and directs that the Board of Commissioners in Kandy collectively, or in their several departments, and the agents of Government in the provinces, shall punish all disobedience and neglect by suspension or dismissal from office, fine, or imprisonment, as particular cases may require and deserve, provided that no persons holding the Governor's commission may be absolutely dismissed, but by the same authority; and no other chiefs, but by the authority of the Honourable the Resident, but as well the Commissioners as other agent, duly authorized by instructions from the Governor, may suspend chiefs of the superior or inferior order on their responsibility, for the disobedience or neglect of the order or interest of Government, reporting immediately as the case may require, to the Governor, or the Resident, their proceedings for approval or reversal.

Details of Judicial administration in cases wherein Kandyans are defendants.

34. And in order that justice may be duly, promptly, and impartially administered throughout the Kandyan Provinces to all classes, his Excellency the Governor is pleased to declare his pleasure to be touching the same, and to delegate and assign the following jurisdiction to the public

officers of Government for hearing and determining cases wherein Kandyans are concerned as defendants, either civil or criminal.

35. Every Agent of Government shall have power and jurisdiction to hear and determine alone civil cases, wherein the object of dispute shall not be land, and shall not exceed in value fifty rix-dollars; and also criminal cases of inferior description, such as common assaults, petty thefts, and breaches of the peace, with power of awarding punishment, not exceeding a fine of rix-dollars twenty-five, corporal punishment with a cat and nine tails or rattan not exceeding thirty lashes, and imprisonment, with or without labour, not exceeding two months, in which terms of imprisonment and fine, such agents are also limited in punishing neglects or disobedience of orders according to the provisions above detailed. Powers of Agents of Government sitting alone. In civil cases. In criminal cases.

36. The Second, or Judicial Commissioner, shall, sitting alone, have power to hear and determine civil cases, wherein the object in dispute shall not exceed rix-dollars one hundred in value, and also criminal cases of inferior description, with powers of punishment as in the last clause conferred on Agents of Government. Powers of Judicial Commissioner sitting alone.

37. The Second or Judicial Commissioner, and such Agents of Government in the Provinces to whom the Governor shall delegate the same by his instructions, shall hold at Kandy, and in the Provinces, a court for the trial of all other civil cases, and of criminal cases, excepting treason, murder, or homicide, with powers in criminal matters to assess any punishment short of death, or mutilation of limbs or member, which court shall consist, in Kandy, of the Second Commissioner and two more chiefs; and in the Provinces of the agent of Government, and one or more Dessaves of the Province, and one or more Mohattales or principal Korales, so as there shall be at least two Kandyan assessors, or of two Mohattales or Korales where no Dessave can attend. Courts to be held by Judicial Commissioner and Agents authorised, to consist of themselves and two Kandyan assessors, to try all civil cases, and all criminal cases except treason, murder, and homicide.

38. The decisions of the courts in the Provinces shall be by the agent of Government, the Kandyan assessors giving their advice, and where the opinion of the majority of such assessors Mode of decision in courts of Agents of Government.

Reference in certain cases to court of Judicial Commissioner.

differs from the opinion of the agent of Government there shall be no immediate decision, but the proceedings shall be transferred to the court of the Second Commissioner, who may either decide on the proceedings had in the original court, or send for the parties and witnesses and rehear the case, or order the Agent to take further evidence, and shall decide the same.

Appeals to Judicial Commissioner.

39. Appeals also shall lie from the decisions of such Agents to the Court aforesaid of the Second Commissioner in civil cases, if the appeal is entered before the Agent in ten days from his decree, and the object in dispute be either land or personal property, exceeding rix-dollars one hundred and fifty in value; in which case execution shall stay, and the proceeding be transmitted to the said Commissioner's Court, which shall and may proceed in the same as in the cases mentioned in the former article. Appeals also may be allowed upon order of the Governor, or the Board of Commissioners, although not entered in ten days, if application is made in a year.

Mode of decision in Court of Judicial Commisioner.

Reference in certain cases through the Board of Commissioners to the Governor.

Appeals to the Governor.

40. The decisions in the Court of the Second Commissioner shall be by the said Commissioner, the Kandyan assessors giving their advice; and if the opinion of the majority of such assessors shall be different from that of the Second Commissioner, the case whether originally instituted, or in appeal, or reference from the Agent of Government, shall be transferred to the Collective Board, and by them reported on to his Excellency the Governor, whose decision thereon shall be conclusive and without appeal; but in civil cases decided by the Second Commissioner, either in original, or brought before him by appeal or reference, appeal shall lie to the Governor if entered before the Second Commissioner in ten days from his decree, and if the object in dispute be either land or personal property exceeding in value one hundred and fifty rix-dollars, in which case execution of the decree shall be stayed, and the proceedings be transmitted to the Governor. But appeal may be allowed by order of the Governor on application within one year from the date of the decree.

41. Appeals to the Governor will be disposed of by his Excellency, in correspondence with the Board of Commissioners, according to justice.

Disposal of Appeals by the Governor.

42. In criminal cases no sentence either by the Second Commissioner, or the Agents of Government shall be carried into effect, if it awards corporal punishment exceeding one hundred lashes; imprisonment with or without chains or labour, exceeding four months; or fine exceeding fifty rixdollars; unless after reference to the Governor through the Board of Commissioners, which will report on the case and sentence; and after his Excellency's confirmation of such sentence.

Limitation as to execution of sentences in criminal cases.

43. The Honorable the Resident may, when he thinks needful, assist and preside in the Court of the Judicial Commissioner, and that the Resident may also hold a Court for hearing cases, to consist of himself and two Kandyan chiefs or assessors, under the provisions respecting references and appeals, and limitation of execution of sentences in criminal cases prescribed to the Judicial Commissioner, and to preserve regularity, the records of such the Resident's judicial proceedings in each case shall be deposited with the Judicial Commissioner on the conclusion of the same.

The Resident may preside in Court of Judicial Commissioner, or hold a separate Court.

44. In all cases of treason, murder, homicide, the trial shall be before the Courts of the Resident, or of the Second Commissioner and his Kandyan Assessors, whose opinion as to the guilt of the defendant, and the sentence to be passed on any one convicted, is to be reported through the Board of Commissions with their opinion also to his Excellency the Governor for his determination.

Mode of proceeding in cases of treason, murder or homicide.

45. All cases, criminal or civil, in which a superior chief is defendant, shall be originally instituted and heard before the Resident or the Second Commissioner; all other cases shall be instituted before the jurisdiction in which the defendant resides. Provided, that in civil cases the plaintiff may appoint an attorney to prosecute in his behalf, as may the defendant to defend his case.

Jurisdiction where superior chiefs are defendants reserved to Second Commissioner. Jurisdiction in other cases.

46. In civil cases the losing party may be by the Second

Assessment of

fines in civil suits. Commissioner, or Agent of Government, discretionally ordered to pay a sum to Government of one-twentieth part of the value of the object in dispute, not exceeding in any case rix-dollars fifty.

Civil jurisdiction of first and second Adigars. 47. The first and second Adigar shall and may execute civil jurisdiction over all Katepurules and their property, subject to appeal to the Second Commissioner, and also over such other persons and property as the Governor may by special warrant assign to the jurisdiction of either of these two great officers, subject to appeal as aforementioned. And the Second Commissioner, or any agent of Government may refer cases for hearing and report to him in his court to the Adigar, Dessaves, or Mohattales.

Criminal jurisdiction of Adigars. 48. The Adigars shall have jurisdiction to punish disobedience of their orders and petty offences, by inflicting corporal punishment, not exceeding fifty strokes with the open hand, or twenty-five with the rattan on the back, or by awarding imprisonment for a term not exceeding fourteen days.

Of Dessaves. 49. The Dessaves, or chiefs holding the Governor's Commission, may also punish offences by corporal punishment not exceeding twenty-five strokes with the open hand, and of imprisonment for a term not exceeding seven days, and similarly the principal Mohattales, Liennerales, and Korales being in office, may inflict corporal punishment for offences on persons over whom they might have exercised such jurisdiction under the former Government, not exceeding ten strokes with the open hand, and may imprison such persons for a term not exceeding three days. Provided that the several persons on whom the above power is exercised, shall be duly and lawfully subject to the orders of such Adigar, Dessave, Chief, Mohattale, Liennerale or Korale, and that no such power shall be exercised on persons holding office, or on persons of the low-country, foreigners, or on Moormen of the Kandyan provinces; and provided, that in all cases where imprisonment is awarded for a term exceeding three days, the prisoner be sent with a note of the sentence to the Second Commissioner, or the nearest Agent of Government to be confined.

Of Mohattales and Korales.

50. To ensure a due and uniform administration of justice. It is declared and enacted by his Excellency, that all evidence before the Resident, the Second Commissioner or other agent of Government, in a civil or criminal case shall be taken on oath; which oath in the case of Kandyan or Hindoo witnesses shall be administered after the evidence is taken (the witness being previously warned that such will be the case) at the nearest Dewale before a Commissioner or Commissioners ordered by the Court, to see that the witness declares solemnly that the evidence he has given is the truth, the whole truth, and nothing but the truth; that no exemption can lie to this mode of giving evidence, except where Budhist priests are examined, and that every person, except a priest, giving evidence must stand while he delivers it.

Mode of receiving evidence and administering oath to Pagans.

51. The people of the low country and foreigners coming into the Kandyan provinces, shall continue subject to the civil and criminal jurisdiction of the agents of Government alone, with such extension as his Excellency may by special additional instructions vest in such Agents, and under the limitation as to execution of sentences in criminal cases herein before provided as to Kandyans in the 42nd clause, until reference to the Governor through the Board of Commissioners, except in cases of treason, murder, and homicide, in which such persons shall be subject to the same jurisdiction now provided for Kandyans, and that the same line shall be pursued in cases wherein a Kandyan Moorman shall be defendant

Jurisdiction over foreigners, and over Kandyan Moormen.

52. And his Excellency the Governor takes this occasion to confirm the provisions of his Proclamation of the 2nd March, 1818, respecting the Moormen; but to explain that they are nevertheless, when living in the villages wherein also Kandyans reside, to obey the orders of the Kandyan chief, or headman of the village, on pain of punishment by the Agent of Government for disobedience, notwithstanding anything in the said Proclamation contained.

Confirmation of privileges of Moormen.

53. According to such known rules justice will be accessible to every man, high or low, rich or poor, with all practi-

Exclusive local jurisdiction of

Board of Commissioners.

cable convenience, and the confident knowledge of impartiality of decision. And to give effect to this plan for the administration of justice, and to collect the public revenue, and ensure the execution of public duties; his Excellency is pleased to assign to the immediate control and exercise of jurisdiction of the Board of Commissioners the following provinces: the Four Korles, Matele, Oodapalata, including Upper Bulatgame, Oodanoora, Yatenoora, Tumpanne, Harrissiapattoo, Doombera, Hewahette, Kotmale, the part of Walapala lying west of the Kuda and Ooma Oya and the Hooroole, Tamirawane Maminiya and Ollagalla Pattoos of Nuwera Kalawiye, in which all the higher judicial duties and the

Agents of Government to hear minor cases in Four Korles and Matele.

collection of revenues will be made by the Commissioners of the Board, but in those limits there will be besides two Agents of Government to hear minor cases at Attapittia, in the Four Korles, and at Nalendin Matele.

Powers of Agent of Government in Ouva.

54. There will be an agent of Government resident in Ouva, to whose immediate jurisdiction are assigned the provinces of Ouva, Welasse, Bintenne, Weyeloowa, and royal village of Madulla; all civil and criminal cases will be heard by him, with the exceptions mentioned, and under the rules detailed above; he will give orders to collect revenue, perform public service, suspend and punish headmen for disobedience, and exercise general powers of government in those limits subject to the superintendence of the Board of Commissioners.

Similar in the Seven Korles.

55. Similarly an agent of Government in the Seven Korles will exercise jurisdiction over that province, and the northern part of Nuwere Kalawiye. An agent of Government in

In Saffragam.

Saffragam will perform like duties in that province. An

Three Korles.

agent of Government will reside in the Three Korles with like powers; and the Collector of Trincomalee will hear all cases,

Of Collector of Trincomalee in Tamankadewe.

and collect the revenue, and cause public service to be performed in the same manner at Tamankadewe.

Reservation of powers of making further provisions and alterations.

56. In all matters not provided for by this Proclamation, or other Proclamations heretofore promulgated by the authority of the British Government; his Excellency reserves to himself and his successors the power of reforming abuses,

and making such provision as is necessary, beneficial, or desirable. He also reserves full power to alter the present provisions, as may appear hereafter necessary and expedient, and he requires in his Majesty's name, all officers, civil and military, all Adigars, Dessaves, and other chiefs, and all other his Majesty's subjects to be obedient, aiding and assisting in the execution of these or other his orders, as they shall answer the contrary at their peril. Enjoining general obedience.

Given at Kandy, in the said island of Ceylon, this Twenty-first day of November, One Thousand Eight Hundred and Eighteen.

By his Excellency's command,

(Signed) GEO. LUSIGNAN, *Sec. for Kandyan Provinces.*

GOD SAVE THE KING!

I have no intention of writing a history of Ceylon; but the foregoing official documents must interest, if they do not greatly amuse many readers. They, at all events, afford much insight into the state of the country at the period when these memoranda were taken; and the great changes which such decisive measures have wrought in Ceylon, have undoubtedly led to its present state; for without the entire subjugation of the island, no great or beneficial step could ever have been taken. As we proceed, however, the effects of Sir Edward Barnes's wise and energetic measures will be evident; indeed, when he assumed the government, it was essential in order to insure public tranquillity at the moment, and that ultimate prosperity which he had in view, that they should be both wise and energetic.

Appendix M.—EDUCATION, CEYLON, 1835.

Schools, &c. 1835.

Name of the Parish, and in what County or District.	Public or Free School, and where situated.	Number of Scholars. Males.	Females	Total.	Mode of Instruction.	Mode of Support. Government. £. s. d.	Voluntary Contributions. £. s. d.	Expenses of each School. £. s. d.
PUBLIC SCHOOLS.								
Western Province.								
	School at Halftsdorp	50	..	50	Spelling, reading, writing, arithmetic, grammar, and catechism	71 0 0	..	71 0 0
	" in the Fort	100	5	105	Ditto	110 0 0	..	110 0 0
	" St. Thomas's Church	50	..	50	Ditto	48 0 0	..	48 0 0
	" St. Thomas's Church	..	32	32	Ditto	30 0 0	..	30 0 0
	" at Galkissc	22	..	22	Ditto	24 0 0	..	24 0 0
	" Morottoo	40	..	40	Ditto	42 0 0	..	42 0 0
	" Morottoo	..	..	..	Ditto	24 0 0	..	24 0 0
	" Pantura	54	..	54	Ditto	36 0 0	..	36 0 0
	Orphan School at Colpetty	24	42	66	Ditto	677 9 5½	..	677 9 5½
	Wolfendahl School in the Pettah	90	24	114	On the improved plan; English, reading, writing, and the principles of religion and morals; arithmetic, grammar, geography and history	52 0 0	..	52 0 0
Chilaw and Puttlam	School at Chilaw	13	..	13	Ditto	62 0 0	..	62 0 0
	" Calpentyn	47	..	47	Ditto	34 10 0	..	34 10 0
	" Calpentyn	28	..	28	Ditto	30 0 0	..	30 0 0
Southern Province.								
Galle	School at Galle	46	..	46	Ditto	48 0 0	..	48 0 0
	" Galle	40	..	40	Ditto	48 0 0	..	48 0 0

	Eastern Province.							
Trincomalee . .	School at Trincomalee	40	..	40	Ditto	60 0 0	..	60 0 0
Batticaloa . .	„ Batticaloa	39	..	39	Ditto	30 0 0	..	30 0 0
	Northern Province.							
Jaffna . . .	School at Jaffna	55	12	67	Ditto	60 0 0	..	60 0 0
Manar . . .	„ Manar	56	..	56	Ditto	48 0 0	..	48 0 0
	Central Province.							
Kandy . . .	School at Kandy	43	..	43	Ditto	178 16 0	..	178 16 0
Badulla . . .	„ Badulla	32	..	32	Ditto	18 0 0	..	18 0 0
Matelle . . .	„ Matelle	26	..	26	Ditto	36 0 0	..	36 0 0
							Total . .	1,767 15 5½
	REGIMENTAL SCHOOLS.							
	Western Province.							
Colombo . .	58th regiment school at Colombo	18	19	37	Reading, writing, &c.	10 0 0	..	10 0 0
	97th regiment school at Colombo	41	30	71	Dr. Bell's system .	10 0 0	..	10 0 0
	Ceylon rifle regiment at Colombo	185	1	186	Reading, writing, arithmetic, English, and Malay's arithmetic .	18 0 0	..	18 0 0
	Gun Lascar school at Slave Island	22	..	22	Common	..	18 6 0	18 6 0
	Eastern Province.							
Trincomalee . .	61st regiment school at Trincomalee	14	21	35	Dr. Bell's system .	10 0 0	..	10 0 0
	Central Province.							
Kandy . . .	78th regiment school at Kandy	40	19	59	Ditto	10 0 0	5 0 0	15 0 0

EDUCATION, CEYLON, 1835.—SCHOOLS, & —(*continued.*)

Name of the Parish, and in what County or District.	Public or Free School, and where situated.	Number of Schools.			Mode of Instruction.	Mode of Support.		Expenses of each School.
		Males.	Females	Total.		Government.	Voluntary Contributions.	
	FREE SCHOOLS, CHURCH MISSIONARY SOCIETY.							
	Western Province.							
Colombo	Christian institution at Cotta	24	..	24	By classes	..	By the Church Missionary Society in England, and voluntary contributions in Ceylon.	214 2 $10\frac{11}{16}$
	English school at Cotta	35	..	35	Ditto	..	Ditto	210 10 $1\frac{1}{2}$
	Girls' school at Cotta	..	53	53	Ditto	..		
	Cingalese school at Cotta, at 14 stations	354	46	389	Ditto	..		
	Southern Province.							
Galle	Seminary at Baddagama	13	..	13	.. ..	..	Ditto	35 13 $7\frac{1}{8}$
	Girls' school at Baddagama	..	98	98	.. ..	..	Ditto	22 4 $8\frac{1}{4}$
	Boys' school at Baddagama	42	..	42	Ditto	..	Ditto	97 16 $4\frac{1}{2}$
	8 Cingalese schools at 8 stations	354	..	354	Ditto			
	Northern Province.							
Galle	Seminary at Nellore	30	.	30	A modification of the common native mode	..	Ditto	121 10 $1\frac{1}{8}$
	English school at Nellore	25	..	25	Ditto	..	Ditto	61 13 $8\frac{1}{4}$
	17 Tamul schools at 16 stations	386	37	423	Ditto	..	Ditto	
	Central Province.							
Kandy	English school at Kandy	45	2	47	By classes	..	Ditto	26 0 0
	Tamul school at Kandy	42	..	42	Ditto	..	Ditto	21 0 0
	6 Cingalese schools at 4 stations	122	21	143	Ditto	..	Ditto	81 0 0
							Total	891 11 $5\frac{7}{16}$

WESLEYAN MISSIONARY SOCIETY.

Station	Schools							£. s. d.
Western Province.								
Colombo . .	3 Schools at Colombo, at 3 stations	153	11	164	English . . .	..	..	87 0 0
	3 Schools at 3 stations . .	160	3	163	English and Cingalese	..	..	29 2 6
	41 Schools at 41 stations . .	1,576	199	1,775	Cingalese . . .	..	..	279 18 7¼
Southern Province.								
Galle . .	2 Schools at Galle . . .	165	65	230	English . . .	..	..	36 0 0
	12 Schools at 12 stations . .	507	67	574	Cingalese . . .	..	..	77 16 9
Matura . .	2 Schools at Matura, at 2 stations	40	7	47	English . . .	..	..	40 10 0
	14 Schools at 13 stations . .	573	164	737	Cingalese . . .	..	..	97 3 0
								647 10 10¼
					Salaries, &c.			262 13 0
					Expended in Schools in 1834-35 . .			35 10 0
					School repairs, &c.			6 18 5
								952 12 3¼
Eastern Province.								
Trincomalee .	4 Schools at 4 stations . .	124	24	143	..	..	..	..
Batticaloa .	1 English school at Poeliantivoe .	20	..	20	..	..	..	..
	6 Tamul schools at 6 stations .	277	..	277	..	..	..	..
Northern Province.								
Jaffna . .	1 English school at Jaffna . .	200	60	260	..	..	..	..
	5 Tamul schools at 5 stations .	344	10	354	..	..	..	..
Waddemoratchie .	7 Tamul schools at 7 stations .	388	..	388	..	..	..	..

EDUCATION, CEYLON, 1835.—SCHOOLS, &c.—(*continued.*)

Name of the Parish, and in what County or District.	Public, or Free School, and where situated.	Number of Schools.			Mode of Instruction.	Mode of Support.		Expenses of each School.
		Males.	Females	Total.		Govern-ment.	Voluntary Contributions.	
AMERICAN MISSIONARY SOCIETY.								
Northern Province.								
Jaffna	Seminary at Batticotta	177	..	177	..	..	..	500 0 0
	Central boarding-school for girls at Oodooville	..	75	75	..	..	..	220 0 0
	4 Central English schools at 4 stations	217	..	217	..	..	..	24 10 2
	147 Native schools at 94 stations	4,745	1,062	5,807	..	..	..	700 0 0
								1,444 10 2
					Total Annual Expenditure of the Free Schools £			3,283 13 $10\frac{11}{16}$

PRIVATE SCHOOLS.

Western Province	501	Under the superintendence of the Vicar-General of the Roman Catholic congregation.
Southern "	5	
Eastern "	70	
Northern "	247	

APPENDIX N.

DESCRIPTION OF THE DRESS OF THE NATIVE HEADMEN.

Rank, Description, or Caste of Headmen.	Coat.	Trimming.	Sword.	Belt.
WELLALE CASTE.				
Maha Modeliars.	Velvet, Silk or Cloth	Gold or Silver Lace, Loops and Buttons	Hilt and Scabbard of pure massive or wrought Gold or Silver inlaid with Gold.	Of Gold or Silver Lace or Silk, embroidered or spangled with Gold or Silver.
Modeliars of the Gate or Guard.	Silk or Cloth	Ditto	Hilt and Scabbard of Silver inlaid with Gold.	Ditto
Modeliars of the Attepattoe, Modeliars of the Corles, Mohotiars of the Guard and Attepattoe, and Mohandirams of the Guard.	Ditto	Ditto	Hilt and Scabbard of Silver : Hilt inlaid with Gold.	Ditto
Mohandirams of the Attepattoe, the Basnaike, and Padicarre Mohandirams, and the Mohandirams employed as Interpreters in the Courts of the several Provincial Judges.	Ditto	Ditto	Hilt and Scabbard of Silver, and the Eyes and Tongue of the Lion's head of Gold.	Of Gold or Silver Lace, but not spangled.
The Corals, Mohandirams, and Mohandirams employed as Interpreters in the Courts of the Sitting Magistrates.	Silk or Cloth	Gold or Silver Lace & Buttons	Hilt and Scabbard of Silver, and in the middle of the Scabbard a plain Silver Plate.	Of Gold or Silver Lace, but not spangled.

DESCRIPTION OF THE DRESS OF THE NATIVE HEADMEN—(*continued.*)

Rank, Description, or Caste of Headmen.	Coat.	Trimming.	Sword.	Delt.
WELLALE CASTE—(*contd*)				
Arrachies.	Cloth or Linen	Silver Buttons and Loops	Hilt and Scabbard of Silver with two plain plates of Tortoise-shell on the Scabbard.	Of coloured Ribbon, embroidered with Flowers of Silver Thread.
Canganies.	Ditto	Ditto	Hilt of Horn inlaid with Silver, the Scabbard of Horn or Wood, with eight Silver Bands.	Of coloured Ribbon without embroidery.
FISHERMEN AND CHANDOO CASTE.				
Modeliars and Mahavidahn Modeliars.	Silk or Cloth	Ditto	Hilt and Scabbard of Silver, and the Eyes and Tongue of the Lion's Head of Gold.	Of Gold or Silver Lace, but not spangled.
Mahavidahns, Mahavidahn Mohandiram, Pattengatyn Mohandiram, and all other Mohandirams of the same Caste.	Cloth or Linen	Ditto	Hilt and Scabbard of Silver, in the middle of the Scabbard a plain plate of Tortoise-shell.	Of Gold or Silver Lace.
Arrachies.	Ditto	Silver Buttons & Silk Loops	Hilt of Horn, embellished with Silver, with three Tortoise-shell plates.	Of coloured Ribbon embroidered with Silk.
Canganies.	Linen	Ditto	Hilt of Horn embellished with Silver, the Scabbard of Horn or Wood with two Silver plates.	Of plain coloured Ribbon.

Blacksmiths and Washermen Caste.				
Mahavidahns Mahavidahn Mohandirams.	Cloth or Linen	Silver Buttons and Loops	Hilt and Scabbard of Silver with one plate of Tortoise-shell on the Scabbard; and two plates of Tortoise-shell on the Scabbard worn by the Washermen.	Of Ribbon embroidered with Flowers of Gold or or Silver thread.
Arrachies.	Linen	Silver Buttons & Silk Loops	Hilt, Horn, embellished with Silver, the Scabbard of Horn or Wood, with three Silver Bands.	Of plain coloured Ribbon.
Canganies.	Linen	Horn or covered Linen Buttons	Hilt of Horn, the Scabbard of Horn or Wood, with three Copper bands.	Of plain Ribbon.
Barber's Caste.				
Vidahn Mohandiram.	Cloth or Linen	Silver Buttons and Loops	Hilt and Scabbard of Silver, but on the Scabbard there must be two plates of Tortoise-shell.	Of coloured Ribbon, embroidered with flowers of Silver Thread.

The Titular Headmen of each Rank are to be dressed in every respect as the Headmen of the Rank and Caste to which they belong, but as a distinguishing mark the word "TITULAR" is to be engraved on the Hilt of the Sword.

APPENDIX O.

COLONIZATION OF THE CAPE OF GOOD HOPE AND NEW ZEALAND.

LAST week a meeting of merchants, landowners, and others interested in the prosperity of the Cape of Good Hope, took place at the London Tavern, Bishopsgate-street, for the purpose of adopting measures to prevent it from being overlooked in any Government scheme of emigration, in consequence of a despatch from the Governor, Sir G. Napier, dated March 15, 1841, and addressed to Lord John Russell, wherein his Excellency disputes the fact mentioned in the memorial of 1000 of the principal inhabitants, which points out the advantages likely to accrue to the colony by the Government setting apart £12,000. annually from quit-rents on the Government lands, in order to provide free passage for mechanics and labourers from Europe. The meeting was numerously attended, and Mr. D. C. Guthrie was called to the chair. Mr. Bagshaw entered into the various objections of the despatch, and concluded by moving—"That the Cape colony labours under great disadvantages from the want of a sufficient number of steady and industrious labourers, for the profitable employment of whom, as well as for additional capital, there is a wide field in the colony." Mr. Maynard, in seconding the motion, said he knew a property in Albany, only twenty years ago a wilderness, which was bought for £3,600. He also mentioned that in public tenders carpenters were put down at 10*s.* 6*d.* a day, and that shepherds' assistants were receiving from £15. to £30. per annum, with food and lodging. Mr. Venning moved the second resolution—"That it was the opinion of the meeting, that the state of the colony was truly set forth in the statement of the memorialists." Mr.

Borradaile read a long memorial to Lord John Russell, signed by 250 landowners and merchants resident in this country, to which his Lordship returned an answer,—"That he did not consider the Cape an unfit place for emigration, but only objected to making the Government bankrupt for the purpose." The meeting was also addressed by several gentlemen, and a deputation appointed to wait on the Right Hon. Lord Stanley, Secretary for the Colonies, in support of the statements of the two memorials. One of the speakers said, that in his estate of 5,000 acres, only 360 were under plough, for want of labourers, and that there were 7,500,000 acres of good land uncultivated. Mr. Burnie, in moving a vote of thanks to the chairman, commented on the absurdity of sending emigrants seventeen thousand miles, when the Cape was so near, and its climate so suitable to the English constitution.

But what a truly admirable scheme of Colonization would not the following be, could only the point of *paying for, and being paid for labour*, &c. be got over. Till this can be done, it were well that the British public would look upon such schemes as Utopian. In proof of the necessity for this, they need only be referred to what has been stated in the concluding chapter, as to the expense of house-rent, board, food, &c., &c., in our new colonies.

MR. RENNIE TO THE NEW ZEALAND COMPANY.

London, 28*th July*, 1842.

Gentlemen,—The public expect that the Directors of the New Zealand Company, while seeking to secure the interests of their shareholders by realizing an adequate return upon the capital employed, will not limit their operations to trafficking in land, but will act in the capacity of national agents for promoting the colonization of New Zealand, and for applying upon an extended scale, and under the improved arrangements which experience may now suggest, the saving principle of defraying the cost of emigration by means of the value which the peopling of a new country confers upon its land.

Participating in this expectation, I address myself to your

court, with the twofold object of stating the grounds of our conviction that there exists at the present moment an urgent necessity for making immediate preparations for conducting an extensive emigration from this country to the colonies, and of submitting for your consideration the outline of a plan in which a body of persons whom I represent on this occasion are desirous of engaging, for founding, under the auspices of the company, another settlement in New Zealand.

After calmly surveying the various remedial measures which have been either adopted or proposed for removing the causes of this distress, we have arrived at the conclusion that extended colonization affords the only means by which the causes of the distress which has overspread the country can be permanently abated. To remove without transferring distress, to preserve the peace of the country, to save the institutions of England from being swept away in an uncontrollable rebellion of the stomach, it is necessary that we should resort to some immediately effectual means of providing for the unemployed and destitute masses. But in what way can immediate relief be afforded? To this momentous question, in our opinion, only one answer can be given: convey the unemployed labour of the United Kingdom to the unoccupied lands of the colonies; adopt an extensive scheme of systematic colonisation.

The adoption of an extensive plan of colonisation would afford instantaneous relief; it would occasion an immediate increase in the demand for shipping, and for all the various materials required for the equipment and maintenance of the emigrants; and while it thus enlarged the field of employment, it would diminish the number of hands seeking to be employed.

But though the conveyance of a portion of our unemployed population to the unoccupied lands of the colonies affords, we think, the only effectual means by which markets can be opened and the causes of distress removed, yet it does not appear that the executive government is prepared to originate any extensive plan of emigration. It may even be questioned whether, in a movement of this character, Government should take the initiative. An extensive scheme of emigration, if adopted in the first instance as a ministerial measure, might be rendered unpopular by being represented as compulsory, and might be cried down by the ignorant and prejudiced as a species of transportation; while, were it undertaken by a public company, it would be less open to such unfounded objections, and would be presented more in the character of a voluntary and spontaneous movement on the part of the people themselves.

Having thus endeavoured to explain the grounds of our conviction that it has become indispensably necessary, as regards the mitigation of distress, the preservation of the public peace, and the security of life and property, that immediate arrangements should be made for the adoption of an extended scheme of emigration, and being of opinion that, in the present state of public feeling, it is expedient such arrangements should originate with an incorporated company rather than with the executive government, we now proceed to lay before the court of directors the outline of the plan in which we are ourselves desirous to embark for founding, under the auspices of the Company, another settlement in New Zealand.

The new act of systematic colonisation consists in defraying the expense of conveying the unemployed labour of the mother-country to the unoccupied land of the colonies, by means of the marketable value which the approach of an industrious population confers on the previously valueless wastes of a new country. The results of the experiments which have hitherto been made in the practice of this art are encouraging and instructive,—encouraging, as affording a practical demonstration of the principle that the cost of emigration may be defrayed by means of the value it creates; instructive, as suggesting precautions for avoiding the causes of difficulty and retaliation which have occurred in the earlier experimental settlements. Some allusion to these causes may be usefnl.

The provisions introduced into the act of Parliament erecting South Australia into a British province rendered the commission of practicable errors unavoidable. The act prescribed the limits of the province before the character of the country included within those limits could be adequately known; it forced preliminary land-sales to absentee proprietors; and it precluded the colonisation commissioners from commencing their operations by advancing the surveys, and by adopting precautions for the accommodation of the settlers on landing, and for placing them on their locations without delay and expense.

These impediments to early progress would be avoided under the arrangements now contemplated. It is proposed that the new settlement should be founded on some eligible site on the eastern coast of the Middle Island of New Zealand. This part of the coast has been selected because it presents the very important advantage of having been already examined, and found to comprise an ample extent of fertile land, and to contain several safe and commodious harbours.

An advantageous site for the new settlement being in the first instance secured, we propose that the company commence their operations by sending out a preliminary expedition, consisting of surveyors, civil engineers, mechanics, and a few agricultural labourers. On the arrival of the preliminary expedition at its destination, the surveyors should proceed to lay out the town, and the engineers to construct a landing-place, a wharf, and a road from the wharf to the centre of the town. At the same time a portion of the mechanics should be engaged in erecting, in the immediate vicinity of the wharf, an extensive range of sheds for the reception of goods, and a spacious building, comprising a large dormitory, for the immediate accommodation of the first body of colonists on their landing. These objects being effected, a portion of the mechanics might perhaps be employed in erecting a church and a school-house. And while these several operations are in progress, the agricultural labourers should be employed in clearing and cropping an extensive suburban farm, which the company might judiciously cause to be stocked with the best breeds of cattle and sheep from the Australian colonies. After sufficient time has elapsed for the proximate completion of these important operations, or some of them, the first body of colonists, consisting of a due proportion of capitalists and labourers, should be despatched from this country.

Under these arrangements, the new settlement will present

a field for the immediate commencement of productive industry. The impediments to early progress which occurred in the first experimental colonies will be removed; the labour and cost of landing and conveying the goods of the settlers will be abridged; the settlers on their arrival will not be exposed to hardship and privation; they will be placed at once upon their locations, and will be enabled to purchase at moderate prices the seed and stock previously provided by the company. The capital which ought to be devoted to immediate cultivation will not be exported for the purchase of provisions. The settlement will be made from the first an appropriate residence for a civilised community.

MODE OF PROCEEDING.

I. It is proposed that the company shall select 100,600 acres of land for the settlement.

II. Of the 100,600 acres thus selected, 600 acres may be divided into 1,600 town sections of a quarter of an acre each; 20,000 acres may be divided into 1,000 suburban sections of 20 acres each; and 80,000 acres into 1,000 rural sections of 80 acres each.

N. B. The area of the town is proposed to be reduced from 1,000 acres to 600, because in the first settlement the larger area has been found to occasion inconvenient expansion and distance. Of the 600 acres, 200 will be reserved for streets, roads, wharfs, squares, and public buildings and works. The remaining 400 acres will be divided into 1,600 sections, of a quarter of an acre each. A section of a quarter of an acre in a town of 600 acres may not be less valuable than a town section of one acre in a town of equal population extended over 1,000 acres. Suburban sections are suggested as affording the prospect of a rapid increase in value from proximity to the town.

III. The lands of the settlement may be distributed into 1,600 allotments — namely, into 1,000 allotments, consisting each of one town section, one suburban section, and one rural section; and into 600 allotments, consisting each of one town section.

IV. The company should offer for sale in this country, at the price of 125*l* each, the 1,000 allotments, consisting each of a town, a suburban, and a rural section.

V. In awarding the first-named 1,000 allotments to purchasers, the priority of choice should be determined by lot. The remaining 600 allotments, consisting each of one town section, should be offered for sale at the price of 25*l* each. Provision should be made to enable purchasers to choose consecutive numbers, so as to hold two or more adjoining sections if they desire them.

VI. The sum of 140,000*l* to be received by the company for the 1,600 allotments offered for sale may be appropriated as follows :—

First. The company might retain, for defraying expenses not otherwise chargeable, for guarding against unforeseen difficulties, and for its commission upon the transaction.	£40,000
Secondly. The remaining 100,000*l* should be primarily charged with the expenses of surveys and management ; after defraying which the residue to be thus applied, viz. One-half to emigration ; one-half to public works, such as roads, wharfs, bridges, and buildings for the reception of the first emigrants.	100,000
Total.	£140,000

By this arrangement, after setting aside an adequate sum for the company's expenses and remuneration, the large fund of 100,000*l* will be employed in defraying the expense of the surveys and management, in sending out labour to the colony, and in effecting those improvements by which labour is abridged. This arrangement will be found more beneficial to the capitalist who employs labour, than that of devoting a larger portion of the proceeds of the land-sales to emigration, as was done in the former settlements founded by the company. The quantity of work performed by two labourers, in a settlement provided with wharfs, roads, and bridges, will be greater than that which could be performed by those labourers on a settlement not provided with these important facilities for rendering industry effective. Immediate labour, when not aided by the results of previous labour, can accomplish little. When the means of communication are imperfect, a great portion of the available labour of the community must be devoted not to immediate production, but to overcoming the difficulty of transport. Estimated not by the number of hands, but by the quantity of work, the actual supply of labour will be increased by diverting a portion of the proceeds of the land sales from emigration to the execution of works by which labour is abridged.

On behalf of a body of persons who contemplate the formation, under the auspices of the company, and on the plan herein sketched out, of a settlement in New Zealand, to be situated on the eastern coast of the Middle Island, I have the honour to be, gentlemen, your most obedient servant,

(Signed) GEORGE RENNIE, junior.

REPLY OF THE NEW ZEALAND COMPANY.

New Zealand House, Broad-street-buildings,
August 12th, 1842.

Sir,—I am instructed by the Court of Directors of the New Zealand Company to acknowledge the receipt of your letter, dated the 28th ult., on behalf of a body of persons contemplating emigration to New Zealand, in which you suggest the formation by the company, on the plan pointed out in your letter, of a new settlement to be planted on some eligible site on the eastern coast of the Middle Island. The court has given this proposal its serious consideration, and I am now directed to communicate to you its views on the subject.

The directors of the New Zealand Company feel it incumbent upon them at all times to do the utmost in their power to further the views of persons desirous of emigrating, and to prove to them that the company is ever ready to perform its functions as a national instrument of colonisation. The directors deem this duty to be the more imperative upon them in times like the present, when general distress pervades this country, for which, extensive colonisation appears to offer the best if not the only prospect of substantial relief. I have therefore to inform you, that the court is willing to entertain the proposal of a new settlement on the eastern coast of the Middle Island of New Zealand, *provided that Her Majesty's Government will consent thereto upon such terms as shall afford the company a reasonable remuneration for the responsibility and risk of the undertaking,* and provided no insuperable difficulties shall be found to arise out of circumstances now unforeseen. With respect to the plan which you have submitted, the court sees no objections to its outline: but desires to be understood as reserving its final judgment as to the details until the enterprise shall be somewhat more matured.*

The intention of the company to establish at proper opportunities a succession of distinct settlements upon the coasts of New Zealand has been for some time before the public, and the motives of that intention will be sufficiently understood by reference to the directors' third report. It is only requisite, therefore, to add, that you are at liberty to make generally known the readiness of the company in the present instance to entertain the principle of your proposal; and when you shall have obtained an assurance of the approbation of Her Majesty's Government, the directors will be prepared to enter into further communications with you, and with the parties whom you represent, in order that your wishes may be carried into practical operation.—I have the honour to be, Sir, your most obedient servant,

(Signed) JOHN WARD, Secretary.

George Rennie, jun., Esq.,
1, Chesham-place, Belgrave-square.

* The question of the price of the land is thus left entirely open.

Appendix P.

POPULATION, BIRTHS, MARRIAGES, AND DEATHS IN CEYLON, IN 1835.

COUNTY or DISTRICT.	WHITES.		FREE BLACKS.		SLAVES.		TOTAL.		Aliens and Resident Strangers.	Population to the Square Mile.	Persons employed in			Births.	Marriages.	Deaths.
	Males.	Females	Males.	Females.	Males.	Females.	Males.	Females.			Agriculture.	Manufactures.	Commerce.			
Western Province	1,275	1,273	257,144	235,461	373	332	258,792	237,066	1,829	111·78	111,601*	13,391*	11,456*	10,377	4,960	6,887
Southern ,,	559	599	142,810	121,780	431	342	143,800	122,721	573	44·27	71,694	11,366	9,040	11,292	1,787	5,087
Eastern ,,	415†	395†	25,844†	23,536†	12†	11†	26,271†	23,942†	3,143‡	10·90	8,930†	3,017†	1,427†	1,546†	465†	1,165
Northern ,,	478	518	112,223	112,928	12,605	11,910	125,306	125,356	1,446‡	41·65	67,662‡	18,992‡	12,454‡	4,323‡	1,174‡	2,491
Central ,,	185	144	84,821	71,541	687	694	85,693	72,379	3,834	53·68	84,727	3,931	8,531	2,431	1,816	1,570
Total, exclusive of the Military	2,912	2,929	622,842	565,246	14,108	13,289	639,862	581,464	10,825	50·39	344,614	50,697	42,908	29,969	10,202	17,200
Military and Civil Ordnance Officers, with their Families.																
Western Province	1,145	292	1,482	1,183	—	—	2,627	1,475	—	·92	—	—	—	88	36	121
Southern ,,	209	79	522	496	—	—	731	575	—	·21	—	—	—	28	9	36
Eastern ,,	521	124	352	253	—	—	873	377	—	·25	—	—	—	25	6	89
Northern ,,	14	21	266	210	—	—	280	231	—	·08	—	—	—	13	6	12
Central ,,	715	160	1,001	629	—	—	1,716	789	—	·83	—	—	—	77	25	28
Total Military	2,604	676	3,623	2,771	—	—	6,227	3,447	—	·39	—	—	—	231	82	286
Grand Total	5,516	3,605	626,465	568,017	14,108	13,289	646,089	584,911	10,825	50·79	344,614	50,697	42,908	30,200	10,284	17,486

* Excepting the Seven Korles Division, where no Returns have been kept. † Excepting the Bintenne Division, ditto. ‡ Excepting the Neuwerakalaniye Division, ditto.

Appendix Q.

Official Statistical Account of the Sickness and Mortality at Galle, during a period of seventeen years.*

The fortified town of Galle lies on the sea-coast, about 72 miles to the south of Colombo. The country between the two stations is almost uniformly level, and covered to the water's edge with plantations of the cocoa-nut; but towards Galle the mountains approach nearer the coast, and the surface becomes more undulating and varied.

This fort, like Colombo, stands on a low rocky peninsula, commanding the entrance to an extensive bay. It is rather more than a mile in circuit; and, except at one point, where it is joined to the main-land by a narrow isthmus, is entirely surrounded by the sea. The rocky nature of the surface, and the gentle slope in every direction, prevent water from lodging, and most of the soil in the vicinity is of too light a nature to admit of the formation of marshes. There is a considerable extent of cultivation, and the country is not over-run with that dense jungle, which is supposed at several of the other stations to favour the production of febrile and other diseases.

Though further to the south, yet being more equally exposed to the influence of both monsoons, the temperature of Galle is not quite so high as that of Colombo, and during the cold season it sometimes falls several degrees lower; the annual range of the thermometer is from 71° to 87°, and the mean daily variation throughout the year has been estimated at 4 degrees.

On referring to the conformation of the island to the north-east of Galle, it will be found to admit of the monsoon winds even from that quarter reaching the station without passing over any considerable extent of land; and as those from the south-west blow direct from the ocean, there is nothing to interrupt the

* I have inserted this account, that those who are disposed to become settlers in Ceylon, may have indisputable evidence of the healthiness of a part of the island which I have so largely described and recommended.

course of either, except the wind draws to the northward, which it sometimes does during December, January, and February a considerable degree of chilliness is then experienced, particularly in the evenings and mornings, though the days continue hot.

As the winds of both monsoons, in their passage across a vast expanse of ocean, become saturated with moisture, which is rapidly condensed into the form of rain on reaching the coast, the annual fall at this station is supposed to be greater than at any other in the island, but no measurement of the exact quantity has been obtained.

The barracks of the White Troops are situated in different parts of the fortification, and consist of seven buildings of one story each, of stone or coral, with tiled roofs and brick floors. They are surrounded by verandahs, and described as being well ventilated, and in every respect adapted for the healthy accommodation of the troops. Each soldier has upwards of 600 cubic feet of space, which might be increased, if necessary, as the buildings are more numerous than is required for the present strength of the garrison. The hospital stands upon one of the bastions, which is elevated about twenty feet above the level of the sea, and washed by the tide. It is surrounded by a verandah, and contains two wards, affording ample accommodation for the small number of sick usually under treatment.

A company of the Malay Regiment is also quartered in huts recently erected for the purpose, and there is a small hospital adjacent for their sick. Abundance of water is supplied to the garrison from an excellent well within the fort.

The mortality among the Black Troops will hereafter be adverted to. The following Table shews that which occurred among the White Troops composing the garrison during a period of 17 years:—

Years	1820	1821	1822	1823	1824	1825	1826	1827	1828	1829	1830	1831	1832	1833	1834	1835	1836	Total.	Average.
Strength	178	119	89	91	94	84	170	326	323	165	175	255	256	263	213	145	144	3090	182
Deaths	2	9	1	2	5	3	2	6	7	..	4	6	5	4	6	5	4	71	4
Ratio per 1000 of Mean Strength	11	76	11	22	53	36	21	18	22	..	23	24	20	15	28	34	28	..	23

Thus the mortality has averaged only 23 per thousand of the strength, being exactly the same as at Gibraltar during the same period, and even this has not in every instance originated in disease contracted at the station; all the deaths in 1832, for instance, are said to have taken place among soldiers of the 78th regiment, sent from Colombo in such a state that their recovery could not be expected; and in 1836, also, the mortality was increased in consequence of several soldiers in bad health being sent from Trincomalee. It is possible, also, that similar circumstances, of which we have no note, may have added to the deaths in other years; so that on the whole, the mortality cannot materially have exceeded that which is usual among soldiers even in the healthiest of climates, though the situation lies nearer the equator than any of the possessions of the British Crown.

Table shewing the principal Fatal Diseases among the White Troops at Galle.

	Total Deaths in 17 Years	Ratio of Deaths annually per 1000 of Mean Strength.
By Fevers	6	1·9
Diseases of the Lungs	8	2·6
,, Liver	12	3·9
,, Stomach & Bowels	24	7·8
,, Brain	7	2·3
Dropsies	5	1·6
All other Diseases	6	1·9
Accidental and Violent Deaths	3	1·0
Total	71	23·

The comparative exemption enjoyed by the troops at Galle, even at a period when all the other stations in the island were suffering severely from fever, has often been the subject of remark, and is amply borne out by these results; for on reference to the abstract from which they are framed, it will be seen that only two deaths from remittent fever took place in the course of 17 years. Almost all the cases which came under treatment were of the common continued form, and of these the proportion which proved fatal was not greater than is usual in the healthiest climates.

Nothing can afford a more convincing proof that the influence of this class of diseases by no means depends either on elevation of temperature, or proximity to the equator, than the circumstance that at this station, within six degrees of the line, and where the thermometer is never below 71°, the mortality from fever, even on the long average of 17 years, has been only $1\frac{9}{10}$ per thousand annually, while in Canada, from 45° to 52° remote from the line, and where the temperature during a considerable part of the year is below zero, the mortality by the same class of diseases, in a similar period, averaged $2\frac{4}{10}$ per thousand.

The deaths from diseases of the lungs have also been very few; indeed this is the only station at which there appears to be any considerable exemption from them. Diseases of the liver are comparatively rare, and those of the bowels, which prove so fatal in other parts of the island, are very considerably modified here, the proportion of deaths from them being scarcely one-third of the general average. This arises from their assuming in most cases the milder form of diarrhœa, which rarely proves fatal. Dysentery seldom makes its appearance except among old soldiers who have suffered under it before their arrival.

Cholera has not prevailed here in an epidemic form since 1819, when about 4 per cent. of the white troops died by it. Indeed this station has been remarkably free from epidemics of any kind, during the 17 years under review, and it would be difficult to point out any place within the tropics equally healthy for so long a period.

END OF VOL. I.

Map of the Island of CEYLON.
BRITISH MILES
SEVEN KORLES
NEURA KALAVA
Longitude East of Greenwich

EXCURSIONS, ADVENTURES AND FIELD-SPORTS IN

CEYLON

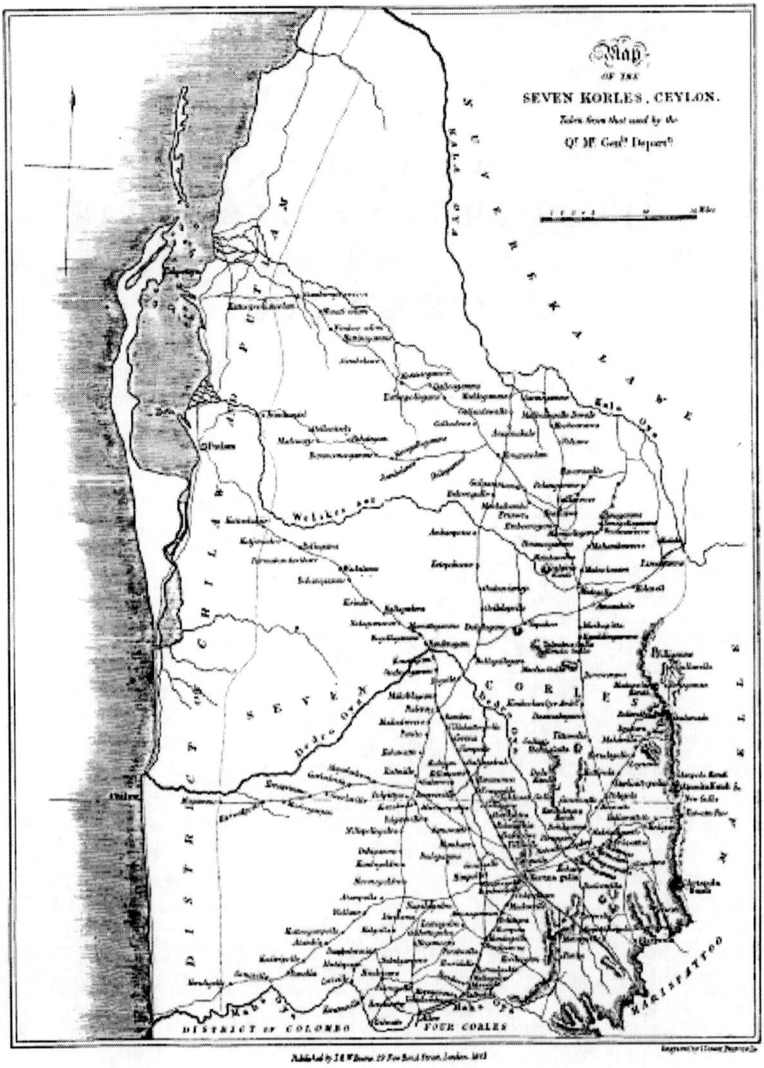
Map
of the
SEVEN KORLES, CEYLON.
Taken from that used by the
Qr Mr Genl Departt
DISTRICT OF COLOMBO
FOUR CORLES
MARISPATTOO

EXCURSIONS, ADVENTURES AND FIELD-SPORTS IN CEYLON

ITS COMMERCIAL AND MILITARY IMPORTANCE

JAMES CAMPBELL

IN TWO VOLUMES

VOL. II

WITH B/W AND COLOUR ILLUSTRATIONS

Published by

Facsimile Publisher
12 Pragati Market
Ashok Vihar, Ph-2
Delhi-110052
facsimilepublisher.com

Distribution Network
gyanbooks.com
India, USA, Canada, UK, Australia, France

ISBN : 978-93-5324-467-5 (Set)
ISBN : 978-93-5324-469-9 Vol. 2 (HB)
First Published, London, 1843

2nd Impression 2020

Printed at: Gyan Press, Delhi.

Excursions, Adventures and Field-Sports
In
Ceylon
Author: James Campbell

EXCURSIONS,

ADVENTURES, AND FIELD-SPORTS

IN

CEYLON;

Its Commercial and Military Importance,

AND

NUMEROUS ADVANTAGES TO THE BRITISH EMIGRANT.

BY

LIEUT.-COLONEL JAMES CAMPBELL,

FORMERLY OF THE 48TH AND 50TH REGIMENTS,

AND FOR SEVERAL YEARS COMMANDANT OF THE DISTRICTS OF GALLE AND THE SEVEN KORLES, AND JUDICIAL AGENT OF GOVERNMENT.

"There is continual spring, and harvest there
Continual, both meeting at one time."

IN TWO VOLUMES.

VOL. II.

LONDON:

T. AND W. BOONE, 29, NEW BOND STREET.

MDCCCXLIII.

CONTENTS OF VOLUME II.

CHAPTER I.

PAGE

CHAPTER II.

CHAPTER III.

PAGE

CHAPTER VII.

CHAPTER VIII.

CHAPTER IX.

CHAPTER X.

CHAPTER XI.

CHAPTER XII.

CHAPTER XIII.

APPENDIX.

CEYLON.

CHAPTER I.

"High cliffs and rocks are pleasing objects now,
And nature smiles upon the mountain's brow;
The joyful birds salute the sun's approach;
The sun too laughs, and mounts his gaudy coach,
While from his car the dropping gems distill,
And all the earth, and all the heavens do smile."—Lee.

SET OFF FROM GALLE FOR THE SEVEN KORLES—JOURNEY FROM COLOMBO TO KURUNAGALLA—KURUNAGALLA DESCRIBED, AND ITS IMPORTANCE AS A CENTRAL STATION POINTED OUT—REMARKS—KANDYAN MEN AND WOMEN—NUMBER OF STRANGERS CONSTANTLY PASSING THROUGH KURUNAGALLA—PRINCELY ELEPHANT SHOOTING IN THE SEVEN KORLES—MODE OF LIVING IN THE INTERIOR—PADENNY, OFTEN AN UNHEALTHY STATION—A COBRA-COY AND ITS EGGS—AN EVENING SCENE AT A LAKE—THE SHORES OF THE LAKE SUPPOSED TO BE INFESTED BY DEVILS—A TOUGH STORY—ANOTHER EQUALLY SO—REMARKS—HOUSE OR BUNGALOW BUILDING IN THE INTERIOR—BRITISH SOLDIERS' OPINION OF BLACK-FELLOWS IN GENERAL—A BRITISH GRENADIER DRESSES AS A NATIVE AND WALKS THROUGH THE BAZAAR—OBSERVATIONS—KANDYAN TILLAGE, ETC.

In the Galle and Matura districts I had passed nearly two of the pleasantest years of my life; and

I confess, although I now had the prospect of increased emolument, as Commandant in the Kandyan provinces, that I would, at the time I was removed, have greatly preferred remaining where I was. I liked the people, and I had no reason to imagine that I had in any way rendered myself unpopular with them. I must also say,—and I do so with feelings of gratitude to Him to whom I was indebted for it—that in no other part of the world had I ever, under any circumstances, enjoyed such excellent health as in this the nearest to the equinoctial line, but by far the coolest part, if I except the lofty mountainous regions, of Ceylon. It is upon this account, and from its being likewise well known to be very healthy, that I have been so anxious to draw the attention of settlers to it.

It is unnecessary to say any thing of the country between Galle and Colombo, as I travelled through it, and made some remarks upon its beautiful though rather too uniform appearance, when I first arrived in Ceylon. Having sent forward my servants and incumbrances of all kinds, I was carried in two nights to Colombo in my palanquin, having rested the intermediate day at Bentotte, and enjoyed a delightful row on the lake. To my great annoyance, I was detained a whole month at Colombo, as a member of a General Court-martial, assembled for the trial of that strange and well known character, Major O'Shaughnessy, late of the 45th regiment. Having at length got through that most disagreeable and disgusting business, which had however, afforded me ample time to renew my intimacy with my friends there, I set off for Kurunagalla, the head quarters of the district of the Seven Korles.

I travelled the fifty-four miles to that place on horseback, and by easy stages; in order, as I went along, that I might have time to look about me, and to see the country; and I also wished to spend a day or two with some of the officers employed in superintending the making of the new road to Kandy, which passes through Kurunagalla. The officers thus employed are often changing their places of abode. They build, (as I recommend settlers to do when they first go into the interior,) their own temporary bungalows; generally selecting the most beautiful and convenient situations, amidst wild but usually fine scenery. The country, (and I beg the reader will remember that I am still chiefly guided by my memoranda, made at the time,) is in a great measure covered with thick jungle; but in many places there are openings of no great extent, surrounded and adorned with fine trees of many kinds. On the whole, indeed, it resembled, though it was by no means equal to, that which extends inland from Matura; into which I had lately made such an agreeable and interesting excursion. It may, however, be fairly spoken of as a valuable tract of country, especially for a considerable extent around Allow, on the Maha-oya, or great river; yet still too much of that wearisome uniformity prevails, of which I before complained, as being the characteristic of the flat, or commencement of the hilly country. The soil seems every where good and capable of great improvement by cultivation; when it would, no doubt, produce most kinds of fruit, herbs, or grain, peculiar to a tropical climate. Elephants in considerable numbers range through it, especially to the northward of the Maha-oya, and even where it seems to be rather thickly inhabited; but, although, during my journey, I frequently saw the prints of their large feet, yet I met with none of them: indeed, in the day time, they always remain in the most retired parts of the forest or jungle. An often rugged, narrow and intricate path, rendering it necessary to have a guide with us, winds through the country in which the new road is now making. The road is almost a straight line from Colombo to Kurunagalla, and greatly shortens the distance betwixt these places.

I had heard much of the beauty of the scenery around Kurunagalla, and it has quite come up to my expectations. The cantonment for the troops is built nearly in the form of a square. In outward appearance, the houses or bungalows are very like neat, comfortable thatched cottages, and afford much better accommodation than I had looked for. The Commandant's house and offices occupy one side of the square, and have gardens behind them, laid out with great neatness and regularity by my predecessor in the command of the district. There are several good sized rooms in the house, all upon the ground floor; that style of building being not only the simplest, but also found to be the coolest. It would likewise be the most agreeable, were it not that reptiles of all kinds can too easily get into our rooms at night, which they do in great numbers during the rainy seasons. The other three sides of the square are occupied by the houses of the officers and troops, guard house, &c. At a short distance from the cantonment, there is a bazaar, where the natives are allowed to reside, which is already of considerable extent, and contains a numerous population, although little more than a year ago scarcely a hut stood upon the spot; and we can now procure in it, at reasonable prices, many articles we want.

Kurunagalla, is situated to the westward of some rocky mountains, which, being only about half a mile distant, shelter it from the disagreeable influences, often experienced in the interior, from land wind, which prevails during the north-east monsoon; but the country, from thence to the ocean on the west-coast, being almost flat, it has all the benefit of the salubrious and refreshing south-west winds. This (March) is the hottest season here, as well as at Colombo and Galle; and I imagine, that there is not much difference in the temperature of the three places; the thermometer at noon in the shade being, generally, at 82 to 85 degrees; but the night air here, though rather cooler than upon the sea coast, is by no means so safe to be exposed to. The rocky mountains rising abruptly, and close to the cantonment, (one of them is about 1000 feet in height, and another 500, called the Elephant rock, from its, in some measure, resembling that animal in form,) are very fine and most striking objects; being in some places quite bare, and in others covered, even to their summits, by a mass of most verdant foliage.

The principal roads, which meet at Kurunagalla, as a centre, are those from Colombo, Kandy, Trincomalie and Manar, by the way of Putlam; and the town being situated in what is considered the greatest agricultural country in Ceylon, it will, very likely, soon become a place of some importance. The quantities of rice and other grain, peculiar to this part of the world, that this province produces; are considerable, and might be rendered ten times greater, if such an object suited the views of Government, and if sufficient encouragement and support were given even to the native tillers of the soil; for, from what I hear, and have already seen, I am convinced that the Kandyans are, beyond comparison, superior in agricultural knowledge and practice to the people in the maritime provinces; and are far from being, as many are apt to suppose, either ignorant or barbarous. There is also another old, but level road, that could easily be straightened and improved, which connects Kurunagalla and the small port of Negombo, only thirty miles distant, to which, taking advantage of the great river, for a considerable part of the way, could easily be sent the produce of the province, and from thence be shipped for Colombo, or for any other part of the island; and when there was a surplus, it might also from thence be forwarded to the continent of Asia, where grain is often required, in addition to what is grown in the country. I beg, however, here to observe, that the value of Ceylon, as a rising colony of Great Britain, in which both European and native industry ought to be encouraged, is by no means sufficiently understood or appreciated; and how greatly would this value be increased, if the Kandyans were able to profit from the science of, and example which might be set them by, British settlers. But this is a part of the island to which I would, as yet, beg the attention of those only who are desirous of growing grain, as I intend more particularly to point out hereafter.

My predecessor here, Major Martin, of the forty-fifth regiment, now returned to Badulla, deserves very great credit for all he has accomplished, (and it would be well if those who, in new colonies, have labour at their command, would follow his example,) especially in making and cultivating gardens, &c.; for so abundantly are those here stocked with several kinds of (chiefly) common vegetables, that officers, soldiers, and indeed every one in any way connected with us, has as much, free of expense, as they can use. He likewise did much to make the cantonment comfortable; and, with considerable ingenuity, brought excellent water from the rocks into it, and into the gardens, where, in a climate like this, it is almost always so much wanted. These gardens are thus not only made really useful, but also highly ornamental to the place, they being well laid out, and tastefully enclosed with evergreen and flowering hedges. In short, this station owes everything, in the way of improvements, to him, and it only now becomes my province to see that they are properly kept up. Mrs. Martin had also her flower garden; but there are still to be seen the marks of the large feet of a wild elephant, which one night walked through it, crushing a part of the hedge and destroying many a beautiful flower, several of them new to us, and which had been collected in various parts of the district. As soon as the gigantic visitor was aware that he had been trespassing, and that he had got, unexpectedly, amongst a number of houses, he instantly took to flight, at the same time trumpeting so loudly as to disturb the slumbers of the whole garrison.

I feel that our society here is rather limited, consisting only of two ladies, and eight officers; but I trust we are all inclined to be sociable and obliging to each other. There are, besides, several out-posts, dependencies of Kurunagalla, with which we keep up constant intercourse.

I reached this place, as I hoped I should, only in time to escape the periodical rains, which commenced soon after my arrival—and how it does thunder and rain at this moment!—the *water* I ought to say—for rain, in our acceptation of the word, does not by any means express the immense deluge which is falling. It usually begins to come down in earnest about four, P. M., and often continues till midnight. The mornings are, in consequence, delightfully cool; and so charming is all around us, and at the same time so different from the sea-coast, that I am really enchanted with the, to me, new and beautiful scenery; and what is here a great advantage, and duly appreciated by some of us, our rides and walks are not only numerous, but in many respects agreeable.

My command is rather extensive, being, at least, a hundred miles in length, by about sixty in breadth, occupying the greater part of the central provinces, which are situated to the northward of the Kandy District; and from the Maha-oya to an undefined distance into Nuverekalawé, a wild country beyond the Kalla-oya; and from the Chilaw and Putlam Districts, to the mountainous border of Natelé. To watch, and keep in subjection the people of this newly-conquered country, it may be thought that the force at my disposal is very inadequate; it being only three companies of European Infantry, about two hundred Malays, (I had my two orderlies transferred to a company here), of the 1st Ceylon Regiment, and a company of the 2nd, (Caffres) one hundred strong, who are fine, hardy, stout, good-humoured fellows, and excellent road-makers. This number of troops is, however, sufficient, as the people, though numerous, are, from all I hear, well disposed, and only want to know our ways, and what is required of them, in order to try to please us; but I hope, though they do not as yet appear to have done so, that they will soon be able to understand and appreciate our mild and equitable mode of managing them. The only serious annoyance they are obliged to submit to, is in being compelled to make the new roads, without payment of any kind; but this cannot last long; and as they, and their forefathers, have been for ages accustomed to a kind of feudal system, and have, from one generation to another, held their lands under their king upon condition of serving him as soldiers, or as labourers in accomplishing any great undertaking, however extravagant it might be, (some of which I shall hereafter notice,) few of them have, as yet, been heard to murmur, or even express the slightest discontent. What they find going on is new to them, and their astonishment is daily excited, when they see rocks, and every natural obstruction in the way of our carrying roads over stupendous mountains, and across deep and rapid rivers, flying, as it were, before us, by the application of the power of gunpowder, scientifically directed. Even those who are not employed upon the roads, come from a great distance, to behold the wonders performing; none of them, probably, aware that the removal of these impediments, which hitherto prevented the rapid movement of troops and their supplies, constituted their safety and protracted their subjugation.

Sir Edward Barnes's views, (and these remarks were made at the time), and his present undertakings, are certainly enlightened, and upon a grand

and comprehensive scale; and if he is not thwarted or checked by the injudicious interference of those in power, he must soon go far towards calling forth the resources of this valuable appendage of the Crown, as he is not only doing much, in many respects, to benefit the island generally, but is also carrying excellent roads through a very mountainous and difficult country, thus throwing it open for future agricultural and other improvements; and this great work is likely to be accomplished at a trifling expense, by his wisely availing himself (although it will probably be looked upon by the good people at home as a harsh measure,) of the labour which the laws and customs of the country have placed at his disposal.

I can perceive but little difference in the looks of the Kandyans from the people upon the sea-coast, unless it be, that the former are more robust or powerful men, who allow their beards to grow long, which give them a more respectable and commanding appearance than the former have. As for the Kandyan women, I have not, as yet, seen many of them; for they seem, or rather pretend to be, as wild as deer, and as we ride along they fly from us, into the woods or jungle, into which we seldom can, or wish to, follow them; though we sometimes, for amusement, give chase after them; and when we do so, whatever it may be that they are carrying, they are sure to throw it away, in order to facilitate their escape. But when they think themselves safe and out of our reach, we can hear them laughing merrily, evidently at our fruitless attempts to catch them. These pretty coquettes, however, know well enough that we will neither take nor injure what they leave behind them; and, as soon as they are certain that we are gone, they always return to re-possess themselves of it. But even the birds and beasts seem to partake of this fear of white men, for none of them will allow us to approach them, unless we steal along with the greatest care and caution; whereas, they take but little notice of the natives.

It was not long before I ascertained that Kurunagalla was a great and troublesome thoroughfare; and that I was not likely to be often without visitors, as it is a very convenient halting place between Trincomalie, Kandy, and Colombo; and consequently I have rather too many opportunities of exercising the rites of hospitality; and that towards persons I never before, perhaps, heard of or had seen. The country around us being also known to be greatly infested by elephants, many of my friends—and these I shall be delighted to see—talk of visiting me, in order to have the glorious opportunity of running the risk of being crushed under the feet of these enormous creatures, should their shot fail to prove instantaneously fatal, at a distance not exceeding fifteen yards. This, however, is looked upon here as a princely sport; *mais, chacun à son gout.*

The rainy season being now I may say over, I daily venture to extend my rides and walks into the really beautiful country around us. In some directions, we might fancy that we see laid out before us handsome parks, like those that in England surround the gentlemen's seats, which are finely wooded, but by no means too much so. To the westward we can easily get through the country; as there are here and there large open spaces, covered with the most beautiful green grass, in which, in the mornings and evenings, may be seen deer, elk, half wild and tame buffaloes, &c.; but it is always difficult to get near enough to either deer or elk to have a shot at them, with any hope of killing.

The roads, moreover, are already so good, that in riding we seldom wish to leave them, except for the purposes of the chase or shooting; and in this enticing amusement many fancy that I am too often engaged. The sport here may, indeed, be truly said to be interesting; for we cannot tell, especially after wet weather, whether we are most likely to fall in with a snipe or an elephant; but the latter can in most instances, and with a little prudent management, be avoided; for they are equally as anxious to keep out of our way as we are to steer clear of them. I am, besides, almost always, when shooting, attended by one or both of my orderly Malays, who keep a good look out as we go along. I find, upon every occasion, that these men possess a surprising degree of sagacity in knowing where to look for the particular kind of wild animals or birds I may be in search of; and as they are brave and faithful, I have scarcely ever any reason to apprehend danger; and, if I do get occasionally into a scrape, I know that they will stand by me. Yet I never go into the forests or jungle, without having in my waistcoat pocket, in case they should be wanted, half a dozen brass balls, covered with leather, ready to be slipped into the barrels of my gun.

I did not expect to have heard so much as I have done of alligators in this part of Ceylon; but I find that they are frequently to be met with in the numerous ponds or tanks, especially in the lower parts of the province; but Knox, in his "Historical Relation" of this island, tells us, that "in these ponds are alligators, which, when the water is dried up, depart into the woods, and down to the rivers, and in the time of rain come up again into the ponds." About a mile and a half from Kurunagalla, there is what I look upon to be an artificial lake of some extent, in which I suspect that there must be alligators; for the other evening I shot there one of those long taper-necked ducks, &c. I have before mentioned, which fell, seemingly dead, into the water, and which, I have little doubt, was instantly taken down by one of them. Having got a canoe upon this lake, I intend, before long, to try if I cannot drive the harpoon I brought with me from Galle through the hard backs of some of them. Yet, even the idea of there being alligators in the lake, makes me very uneasy about my fine, sagacious dog Bran, which is becoming daily a more daring and useful companion to me. Unluckily, he is too fond of the water, always bringing out for me such birds as are shot, and fall into it.

We have just been able to establish at Kurunagalla a public bakery, which was very much wanted; for we had previously to get our bread all the way from Negombo by coolies, a distance of fifty miles. We must, however, contrive to do as well as we can without sea-fish at our tables; but in other respects, they are quite as well supplied as those of our friends at Colombo, and in other parts of the island. We have plenty of fresh water fish, when we wish for them, and even in a pond in my garden, made and stocked by my predecessor, there are some fine large ones; but they are not much liked. I may also mention, in order to shew a settler how he may get on here, that I have already great numbers of geese, ducks, and fowls; and I have likewise two fine buffaloes, that supply me amply with milk, which, I may say, costs me nothing, as the Kandyans, obligingly, furnish me with the buffaloes, and leave them with me, for their feeding, as long as they give milk; but when they become dry, they take them away for agricultural purposes, replacing them by others. I may, perhaps, be excused too, for mentioning that to keep pace, in some measure, with the rest of the world in literary information, I have sent to me regularly from England, two of the best Reviews, besides English weekly papers, and have also the Madras and

Colombo papers: a friend likewise forwards to me, occasionally, an interesting new work or two; so that I hope I may thus, and with the help of the few books I have always with me, be able to spend, in tolerable comfort, the kind of Robinson Crusoe life I must expect to lead in this, as yet, but little known country.

I may say, that at this moment we have not a sick man in the district; and this part of it, in particular, has hitherto been considered as healthy. I have, however, just returned from visiting the garrison at Padenny, which has too often shewn itself to be a sickly station. Captain L— of the 73d Regiment now commands there, and receives, as agent of Government, an allowance of about £200 per annum. Padenny is situated in the fiat division of the island, and is about fifteen or sixteen miles north from Kurunagalla. The soil in its neighbourhood is very rich, and produces great crops of rice, and other grain. An old Boodhoo temple, built upon an insulated rock, from whence there is an extensive view over a seemingly agreeable, though rather thickly wooded, country, has been fixed upon, it may be supposed, on account of its strength, as a military post, for the abode of both officers and soldiers. This rock is surrounded by low marshy jungle and fine paddy fields, with here and there pools of stagnant water, which are often entirely dried up; and from such a country may be expected to arise that malaria which is thought to produce fevers and other diseases; from an attack of one of which, a young friend of mine—perhaps too fond of field sports—fell a victim a short time ago. I have pointed out to Sir Edward Barnes what I consider to be the cause of the unhealthiness of this station; and have requested to be allowed to remove the troops to a place I have fixed upon in another direction, which I hope will prove to be more salubrious. But we cannot altogether abandon this part of the district, as it is said, though I suspect erroneously, to contain a population of about 80,000 souls. That of the whole Seven Korles is also, I imagine, greatly overrated; as is the case with the Kandyan provinces in general; but it suited the views of a few of the first Commandants of districts, to magnify the importance of, and to represent as very populous, their respective commands.

I staid only one night at Padenny; and, soon after sunrise, the following morning, I arrived at Eregoddé; where there is a good rest-house, on the bank of the Didroo-oya, a fine clear river, of which more particular mention will be made hereafter. I breakfasted there, and then returned to Kurunagalla, through a very beautiful and not too much wooded country. In every direction around Eregoddé, are to be seen numbers of fine ebony trees, though many of them have been cut down to make bridges. There is one of these bridges near the rest-house, constructed entirely of the centre parts of these valuable trees, which are found to resist the attacks of white ants better than any substance that we can find for making them, excepting stone, which is scarce.

There has just been brought to me one of those large and extraordinary creatures called by the natives Cobra-coys. Three grenadiers, who were walking on the shore of the lake, which I have before noticed as being near Kurunagalla, came suddenly upon her, whilst in the act of covering up an egg in the sand and gravel. As soon as she seemed to be aware that what she had done was discovered, she, to their surprise, turned towards them, as if intending to defend her egg, brandishing her tongue in that furious threatening manner which I before mentioned that they do when provoked. But the soldiers, arming themselves with long sticks, decided upon attacking her; as they knew that I had expressed a wish to see some of the eggs of these curious creatures. Being very strong, and easily excited, she defended herself and eggs much more determinedly than they expected, striking at them, as they assured me, with her hard and powerful tail. The soldiers, however, soon killed her, and good-naturedly carried her, attached to a long pole, to the cantonment, together with seven of her eggs, which they found buried in the sand, a little way below the surface. They are about the size of that of a goose, the shell pure, white, and very hard, and, no doubt, they are hatched by the heat produced by the action of the sun upon the sand. I suppose this strange creature is classed with the lizard. That brought to me by the grenadiers was eight feet and a half long, and fully two round the body: she had four very short legs, which she uses as fins when in the water, and with which she manages to get along awkwardly but quickly on land. I hear that they are considered delicious food by some castes of the natives. Indeed, they must be very like the so highly prized guanas of the West Indies and South America, which are made into a soup, said to be superior to that of the turtle. I would not, however, allow my cook, who expressed his readiness to evince his skill, to treat me, or my friends who were that day to dine with me, with cobra-coy soup.

The more I see of this fine province the more highly I am inclined to estimate its value; not only in an agricultural point of view, but also on account of its central position, and capabilities of improvement. But, to my great surprise, the officers, in general, some of whom have been here for a considerable period, seem to know as little of it as when they first arrived; habits of indolence, and seeming want of curiosity, preventing most of them from extending their rides or walks beyond a few miles from the cantonment, and then, perhaps, they only jog or crawl along upon the new roads, in order to see what is going forward. I am still endeavouring to amuse myself in every possible way; and am not willing to allow either climate or wild beasts to give me uneasiness; for, if I did, I might as well stay at home, like other people. It is probable, therefore, that I have already seen more of the country, its intricate paths, and magnificent scenery, than any of them; for, in a cursory way, I have visited even some rather distant parts of the province, and, during the several hurried trips I have made, have paid a good deal of attention to the features of the country, and to such parts of it as I fancy are likely hereafter to suit my views in hunting or shooting excursions. The reader may also suppose, that, as a true and experienced fisherman, I have not been unmindful of the rivers. I have also been to Kandy; and have seen all that is thought worthy of notice in its neighbourhood; but as they have been already fully described by others, I have no wish to occupy the reader's time with what I find in my memoranda respecting them. I have likewise been to Fort King; and there I saw a splendid country, fit for many agricultural purposes; but for the same reason I shall not, at least for the present, say more of the fine, wild, and truly enchanting scenery in that direction, than that I was not disappointed in it.

A few evenings ago, I persuaded an officer stationed here, who is by every one looked upon as a strange, flighty, poetical genius, with some odd notions of the sublime and beautiful floating in his brain, to accompany me to a part of the country, where, I assured him, that he should see something worthy of his notice. We proceeded, by a wild and solitary path, to the upper end of a lake, where I knew that the very striking and extraordinary scenery would be sure to call forth his most rapturous expressions of delight and astonishment, and with which I hoped to be not a little amused; especially when we should emerge from a wood, through which I intended to lead him, when there would be presented before him, perhaps, one of the most surprising scenes to be beheld in any country. But, at one time, I was apprehensive that we must have returned without effecting my object; for after threading our way through thick jungle, scrambling over rocks, and other obstacles, (for I did not then know the right path), he on horseback, and I walking, I found it almost impossible to get him forward; his stubborn steed would not be led, and he, therefore, had no alternative but to ride, at the imminent risk of breaking his neck. In spite, however, of all difficulties, we at last reached some high ground, commanding a full view of the lake, which is from thence seen spreading itself out to a considerable breadth, its waters being usually quite unruffled; for the wooded hills, which here, in a great measure, surround it, almost always prevent the breezes from disturbing its mirror-like surface.

Upon beholding the beauties and wonders suddenly displayed before him, my companion instantly exclaimed, that if ever a paradise was to be found on earth it was now before him! The bridle fell upon his horse's neck; and, with uplifted hands, there he sat, in mute amazement and admiration; his looks far surpassing my utmost expectations. It was then, in order to stir up the wild spirit within him, that I exclaimed, now is the time to "break the bands of sleep asunder, and rouse him with a rattling peal of thunder;" and, suiting the action to the word, I fired off both the barrels of my gun, as did also the two Malays, whom I had previously told to do so. The reports were again and again, as I expected, loudly reverberated by the echoes, from rock to rock, and hill to hill, and the effect of them called forth a mixture of poetical effusions, both appropriate and absurd, in such a strain as quite surprised and amused me. In fact, I had some difficulty to recall him from the clouds to earth, and to all that lay so enchantingly around him!

Let an enthusiastic reader fancy that there is spread out before him a lake of some length, and of moderate but unequal width; and let him imagine it to be, as it really is, a very beautiful lake; extending itself from beneath his feet, as he stands upon a rather lofty point projecting into it. Rocky precipices rear their wooded crests to his right and left, and behind him; some of them adorned with such trees as the teak, talipot, &c.; beautiful little patches of bright green meadow appear, here and there, as if in contrast to the profusion of variegated jungle foliage, that extends down to the water's edge. On both sides, he must also suppose the country to be intersected by ravines of some depth, clothed with trees, (many of them in blossom), and decked with shrubs and flowers. Here and there in the lake are islets, covered with a few tall trees and low growing jungle. But what was most surprising, until they were alarmed and put to flight by the discharging of the guns, scarcely a spot, either on the shores of the lake or in the islets, was to be seen, upon which large birds, many of them as white as snow, had not perched themselves, whilst hundreds of others were flying in all directions, across and around the lake, in search of places upon which to roost; as it is here that such vast numbers assemble nightly for that purpose. The sun was just setting; for it had taken us longer than I calculated upon to get to the point on which we stood, and his rays, which still reached parts of the distant mountains, as well as the nearer hilly country, could no longer penetrate to us. Most of the lake was therefore already in gloom; yet the opposite rocky banks were still brightly lit up, and their wooded forms, with even the birds upon them, being beautifully reflected in the clear, smooth water, added much to the strangeness and splendour of the scene. It is therefore no wonder that my enthusiastic companion should have fancied himself in paradise.

It was lucky that I had, as usual, my dog and the two Malays with me, or I believe I could not have got the wonder-struck poet, or rather his steed, out of the labyrinths and difficulties into which I had led him. He was certainly, at times, in considerable danger, chiefly owing to the stubbornness of his horse, the extent of which the uncertain light of a new moon only enabled us partially to estimate, as most of our way lay through a rocky and thickly-wooded country, infested by elephants, tigers, and other animals; we, however, met with none of them, and reached Kurunagalla in safety.

I cannot imagine why the fine country in the immediate neighbourhood of this lake is not inhabited; but it is not improbable, that it may be looked upon by the Kandyans—as the banks of lakes and large rivers in general are by them—to be at all times unhealthy. I have, notwithstanding, been for some time past thinking of building a bungalow near the spot where the views of the country and lake are so splendid and extraordinary; for, if no good reason can be assigned against my doing so, there could be no difficulty in having one erected. The water-fowl shooting there is excellent, and it would be a delightful spot to retire to occasionally for a few days; but what surprises me greatly, and makes me hesitate, is that the people whom I have asked about the shores of this lake, and why there are no houses there, invariably give me evasive answers, or pretend to know nothing about them. Having, they say, no object for going in that direction, they never do so; and it is true, that by no chance have I ever met one of them there—at least at the upper end of the lake. I shall, however, not be surprised, before long, to hear, that its banks are looked upon as the favourite resort of devils; and were the worthy Robert Knox to be believed in this, as he deserves to be in every thing else he has touched upon in his Account of Ceylon, we must consider the whole country to be full of them; for he even tells us, that he has himself often heard them calling at night.—That I have got into a part of the world in which I may daily, if so inclined, hear wonderful stories of devils, sorcerers or charmers, is most true; yet, I must allow the probably incredulous reader to believe as much or as little as he pleases, of what I am about to relate, upon the authority of two gentlemen, who could not have been easily deceived.

Captain L—, now commanding at Padenny, went lately out elephant shooting, and when not more than twelve yards from a large tusked one, he coolly took aim and fired at him, intending to send the ball through his head; but, in place of doing so, he only wounded him in the neck; which so enraged the enormous animal, that in the most furious manner possible he instantly charged Captain L—, who, having gone up so very near, as to be almost, I may say, within the reach of his trunk, had no hope whatever of being able to escape. While the Captain was in this critical situation, a Kandyan, who had for some time kept close to his heels, threw himself between him and the elephant, pronounced rapidly, but distinctly, a few words, and stopped the enraged animal coming on in full career; he then held forward his arms, and uttering some other words, in a very loud tone of voice, the elephant turned round, and fled, trumpeting most harshly and frightfully, breaking and crashing trees, and every thing before him! Let the reader only imagine the few yards of ground covered with brushwood, that separated Captain L— from an animal, which, in his progress through the jungle, prostrates the smaller trees and bushes as easily as I would standing corn; the brief space of time allowed — say a couple of seconds; and the whole that took place; and he must be lost in amazement!

Upon Captain L—'s inquiring what had become of the man who had in so wonderful a manner saved his life, he was told that he had gone off into the jungle the moment after he had driven away the elephant; and upon his insisting upon knowing who he was, as he was anxious to do something for him, he was then informed that he was one of their most powerful charmers, and that it was very uncertain whether he, Captain L—, would ever be able to find him, or to induce him, whatever might be the recompense held out, to come to him.

There dined with me, amongst other gentlemen, the evening that Captain L— gave the foregoing account of his marvellous adventure with the elephant, Mr. T— of the Royal Engineers; who observed that Captain L—'s escape was certainly not easily to be accounted for, but that he was the less surprised at it, after what he had himself witnessed about a month before. A Kandyan woman, who now resides about two miles from Kurunagalla, had become so outrageously frantic, or actually mad, or, as the people supposed, possessed by a devil, and her strength had increased so wonderfully, that six men were required to hold her, so as to prevent her from injuring herself or others.

Mr. T—, with some difficulty, contrived to be allowed to remain in the house, which he was anxious to do, in order to witness the proceedings of a charmer, as he understood that one of them had been sent for, who was every moment expected. He soon after arrived, bringing with him only three very small twigs, or ends of branches of a tree. He commenced his operations by commanding in a loud voice all present to be silent at their peril. He then approached the woman, and gave her some slight taps with the twigs on her head, body, arms, legs and feet; and continued doing so, at intervals of about three minutes, for perhaps half-an-hour; when he ordered the men who held her, to let her go. She then lay, seemingly, sound asleep; but when she awoke about two hours after, she got up, apparently quite unconscious of what had occurred, and went about her usual occupations in the house, in a perfectly quiet and sane state of mind.

I give the above stories, I believe correctly, and as they were told by both gentlemen; who were well informed, and highly educated, and not in the slightest degree inclined to be superstitious. But, may I ask,—if the latter charmer could by any means have acquired a knowledge of animal magnetism, of which we see and hear so much in the present day, and during the influences of which it is pretended that the nature of many diseases may be ascertained, and certain remedies pointed out, and even the most severe surgical operations be performed upon an unconscious patient. I am aware that the beloved child of a lady of high rank, and of a pious turn of mind, was given over in Paris by her physicians. She was therefore induced, —and what will not a mother do under such circumstances?—as a last resource, to go herself to consult the magnetizers, who were then beginning to be famous for cures performed by them in France, and who, she was assured, could prescribe a certain remedy for her child. After going through their usual formula, they mentioned what would cure the child;—and it recovered! She has, however, ever since deeply deplored her weakness and infatuation; and imagines that she might just as well have gone to the Witch of Endor to consult her, as to these somnambulists. But all over the Kandyan country the same notions prevail as in Knox's time, that in every unlucky transaction of life the devils are concerned; and when such occur, or when they are afraid of their happening, these charmers or necromancers are consulted, and generally well paid; for which they order certain ceremonies to be gone through, or dances to be performed, in honour of some devil or devils, who are declared by their priests to be the authors of all the ills or misfortunes which befal the human race, and that it is alone through their influence with them that they can be prevented.

I saw the other day in a wood, about two miles from this, a most extraordinary picture, of a set of devils, (almost a copy of which is given here as I found it in Dr. Davy's Ceylon), and before this large daub, there were hung up three red cocks, which had just been killed and offered up as propitiatory sacrifices. On my approaching the spot, in order to see what the people assembled were doing, and pretending that I would ride over the hideous figures as well as the offering, they all fled in the greatest terror; for they fancy—but for what reason I know not—that evil spirits have no power whatever over us: and before the charmer commenced his operations upon the mad woman, as I have just mentioned, he appeared to be very anxious that Mr. T— should leave the house; but was induced, by some means or other, not to take any notice of his being present.

All the troops at Kurunagalla are now busy constructing a temporary place of worship for Europeans, which will answer until a more permanent chapel is finished; also a good rest-house, with offices attached to it, for travellers, and new houses for themselves; the old ones, having been built of mud and wood only, and thatched with cocoa-nut tree leaves, or thin reeds, are fast decaying, and would soon, under the active operations of the white ants, altogether disappear. The Kandyans bring in the materials from the forest or jungle, and the work is carried on, under my own superintendence, by the British and Malay soldiers. The latter are a most useful and ingenious people, and possess so many good qualities, that I am every day becoming more attached to them; and I can perceive that, though our soldiers despise all *black fellows,* yet they look upon Malays as not to be classed with others, and seem tacitly to admit that they are a race of men from whom something useful may be learned. Malays in general are low in stature, but strong and muscular, with certainly unprepossessing countenances, though expressive of intelligence and great daring. They have usually been described as fierce, revengeful, and cruel, especially when roused to madness by jealousy—a passion to which they are said to be most prone—so much so, that it has always been deemed prudent to take measures to prevent our soldiers from exciting it; yet I have not heard of an instance, since I have been in this part of the world, of a Malay having "run a muck," as it is called; to excite themselves into which fury, when they are said to be truly ferocious and bloodthirsty, they swallow a large quantity of opium, which intoxicates them, or rather produces a degree of madness.

The British soldiers, the other day, probably with the view of having something to laugh at, dressed out a grenadier in every respect as a native, and sent him into the bazaar at a time when it was crowded with Kandyans, Moormen, and other people from the maritime provinces, whose astonishment was great at beholding a white man, looking like a giant, stalking slowly and solemnly along—it was like what Saul may be supposed to have been among the people; for the effect which this change of dress produced was as great and striking as it is to see a man, six feet in height, dressed out in woman's apparel; and nothing could possibly have more completely shewn what immense fellows Englishmen in general are, when compared with the people of this part of the East, who nevertheless are not, as far as I can judge, inferior in size to the natives of India.

But, having thus alluded to the native costume, I hope I may be excused for adding, that a dress, approaching to that worn by Asiatics, would not only be more becoming than that we now use, but would also be exceedingly conducive to health (no matter what might be the nature of the climate we might be exposed to), were it adopted by Europeans in general. Suppose the head to be protected by something like a turban, it would be secured from the sword, as well as from the powerful rays of the sun in tropical and other hot countries, and we should then be less subject to fevers. Were it not from habit, the neck requires almost as little covering as the face; and habit alone makes it necessary for us to have such quantities of clothing upon our shoulders, legs, arms, and chest. The Asiatic mode of wrapping long pieces of cloth round the loins, which are, in general, made to hang down as low as the middle of the leg, *girds up the loins*, whilst it protects the stomach and bowels from cold and sudden changes of weather, and thereby prevents dysentery, and other bowel complaints, to which Europeans (it may be concluded, from want of this protection) are so liable, in most parts of the world. The ample trowsers and drawers of the Turks, and other people of Northern Asia, from their being drawn in at the waist, and allowed to flow loosely around their limbs, approac h the nearest to this; even our tight boots and shoes tend to chill the feet, in place of causing the warmth expected from them. When I have reflected upon this—especially in a tropical climate—and have consulted medical men, with the view of obtaining their opinions upon the subject of dress, I have been led to conclude, that it is to be regretted, that it has not long ago been more attended to; at least, so far as our soldiers and sailors are concerned; and it will, I think, be admitted, that the soldier-like appearance, as well as the comforts of our troops, would be vastly improved and increased, were they to be clothed a good deal more in the Asiatic fashion. To this, I would, however, beg to call the attention of persons intending to settle in Ceylon.

But, in a military work—the proper place for such subjects—I, not long ago, presumed to speak of arming our athletic soldiers with short swords, of the old Roman shape, with which, if properly instructed, they would do terrible execution; and which, when required, might be fixed quite as well to the musket as the bayonet. Did not our troops at Aden lately see and feel what Arabs can do, when fighting at close quarters with their kreeses? and Malays are fully equal to Arabs in daring and dexterity with their deadly weapons.

The British soldiers being here almost entirely debarred from the use of ardent spirits, beyond what is daily issued to them, they conduct themselves with so much propriety, and are in such a high state of discipline, that they are allowed, when they please, to be absent from evening parades, or roll-calls, and have only to ask for leave from the captain or officer, commanding their company, when they wish to be so. Many of them having in their walks become acquainted with the Kandyans, they appear to be on the best possible terms with each other; yet, I am sometimes uneasy, lest the ladies may occasion misunderstandings; for the soldiers are very obliging, both to them and the men; even assisting them—as many of the latter are absent road-making—in the cultivation of their fields. It amuses me greatly, as it does the Kandyans, to see how admirably some of the men work the buffaloes or oxen, in the rice fields, and also, afterwards, in treading out the grain; and here, as of old in Judea, the cattle so employed are never muzzled. But so correctly are the Kandyan modes of proceeding, in some of their agricultural pursuits, shewn by Knox, in his "Historical Relation," that I copy, for the benefit of those intending to become settlers in Ceylon, what he has given in his most useful work.

CHAPTER II.

"Great is our Lord, and great is his power: yea, and his wisdom is infinite. But the Lord's delight is in them that fear him: and that put their trust in his mercy. Who covereth the heaven with clouds, and prepareth rain for the earth: and maketh the grass to grow upon the mountains, and herb for the use of man. Who giveth fodder unto the cattle: and feedeth the young ravens that call upon him."

KANDYAN TILLAGE—DIFFERENT KINDS OF RICE GROWN IN WATER—KANDYAN MODE OF WATERING FIELDS—A SPECIES OF RICE THAT NEED NOT BE GROWN IN WATER—PERIODS OF SOWING AND REAPING RICE—PROCESSES PURSUED IN PREPARING THE GROUND, AND IN SOWING RICE, &C.—REAPING, &C.—TREADING OUT THE CORN, AND CEREMONIES OBSERVED—USEFUL OBSERVATIONS—CERTAIN KINDS OF GRAIN THAT ANSWER IN DRY SOILS, WHEN WATERED ONLY BY THE PERIODICAL RAINS—A RETURN GIVEN OF CEYLON PRODUCE AND STOCK, &C. IN THE YEAR 1835—REMARKS.

EVER since I had been in Ceylon, I had taken, as I before observed in speaking of its soils, a lively interest in its welfare, in its productions, in its commerce, and in investigating its capabilities of improvement; and had therefore endeavoured to make myself acquainted with the modes of cultivation pursued by the natives for the various kinds of grain grown by them; and being in the Seven Korles, which is the principal agricultural province of the island, I had taken more than ordinary pains to acquire information upon the subject. Having however, by chance, cast my eye over the very correct account of Kandyan tillage, given by the excellent and observant Robert Knox, I find it to be so superior to any thing of the kind yet attempted, that, for the benefit of those intending to become settlers in Ceylon, and also with a view to amuse our home agriculturists, I shall not hesitate, as I proceed in my remarks, to avail myself of his assistance, when I find that it suits my purpose to do so.

The Kandyans cultivate various kinds of grain; but all of them are different from those grown in England. The most important is rice, or as it is there called paddy, and, as Knox quaintly observes, it is "the choice and flower of all their corn, as being the staff of their country."

They have several kinds of rice, which are named according to the different periods they require for their ripening; but in taste they are nearly all alike. Some of them require seven months before they come to maturity, called *mauvi;* some six, *hautaal;* others will ripen in five, *honorowal;* others in four, *henit;* and others in three, *aulfancol:* these are all the same price. That which is soonest ripe is most agreeable to the taste, but yields the least increase. All these kinds of rice

In using the water for irrigating their fields, they cut a gap at one end of the bank, and allow it to run off gradually, and as it is wanted. To this great attention is paid.

There is another kind of rice, which grows and ripens, though it does not always stand in water; and answers in those places or situations where the people cannot contrive to overflow the ground with water. The rains which fall are generally sufficient for its growth; but it is inferior in value, and differs both in smell and taste from the sorts cultivated in the watered fields. I am, however, of opinion that this inferiority is in a great measure owing to want of attention on the part of the natives in the cultivation of this grain; for, if more pains were taken in working or stirring up the soil in which it is grown, so as to admit of the heavy periodical rains penetrating sufficiently deep into it, the quality of the corn would be much improved, and it is not unlikely that the quantity would be increased. Manuring, also, which is never practised, would probably have a beneficial effect.*

A considerable expense is incurred in the East Indies, in manuring and working the ground in which the sugar canes are grown, and without which the cultivators could not expect a remunerating crop.

The usual seed-time, (though this varies according to situation, whether to the eastward or westward of the mountains,) is the months of July and August, and the harvest is about February; but, in cultivat-

* See Appendix A.

Drawn on Stone by [illegible] Published by T and W. Boone, London, 1843 9, North Cres[illegible] Bedf[illegible] Sq.

PLOUGHING.

ing land that is well and certainly watered by rivers, the people possessing it pay no attention to seasons; for they sow at any suitable time of the year. The paper in the Appendix, marked B, will be found a most useful document, as connected with the maritime provinces.

The Kandyan plough, as has already been shewn, is only what may be called a crooked piece of wood, something like an elbow; it merely tears up the ground as unevenly as if it were done by hogs. They then overflow the field with water. They plough twice before they sow; but before they give the first ploughing, they let in water upon the land, in order to make it soft and the easier to be worked. After it is once ploughed, they usually make up the banks; for if they were to put off doing so till after the second ploughing, the soil would have become mere mud, totally unfit for banking. These banks are indispensable, not only as paths for the people to walk upon through the fields, who otherwise must go in the mud, but also to keep in and contain the water overflowing the ground. They make these banks as smooth and level as a bricklayer would a wall with his trowel; for in this respect they pay great attention to neatness. These banks, at the top, are not above a foot in width. But after the land is ploughed, and the banks are finished, it is again laid under water, and remains so till the time for the second ploughing, when it becomes exceedingly muddy, as much from the trampling of the cattle as from the plough; for the more it is stirred up the better. Sometimes they use no plough the second time, but only drive their cattle through and through the field, until the soil is made sufficiently muddy.

The land being thus prepared, it is still kept overflown with water, in order that the weeds and grass may be destroyed. They then soak in water for a night the corn which they intend for seed. The next day it is taken out and laid in a heap, covered over with green leaves; and thus it remains for five or six days, so as to make it sprout. They then wet it again, and lay it in a heap covered over, as before, with green leaves; and thus it is caused to shoot out its blades and roots: whilst this process is going forward, they have prepared the ground for sowing, —which is thus done: they have a board, as before shewn, about four feet long, which they drag over the land by a pair of buffaloes or oxen; not flat-ways, but upon its edge, which is so done, that the earth and weeds may be well mixed together; and it also levels and makes the ground so smooth and even, that the water afterwards stands equally over it. It still remains covered with water whilst the seed is growing, and until it is become fit for sowing, which is in about eight days after it was put into water to soak. The seed being ready, they let off the water, and with boards of about a foot in length, fastened to long poles, they dress the land over again; laying it very smooth, and making small furrows in it, that in case rain or other water should come in, it may drain away; for more water now would very likely

Drawn on Stone by P. Gauci. Published by T and W. Boone, London, 1843. 3, North Cres.t Bedf.d Sq.e

SMOOTHING FIELDS.

rot the seed. They then sow, which they do with great evenness, strewing the seed carefully with their hands.

The ground now remains without any water, until the grain has grown three or four inches above it. There had been gaps made before in the banks, to let out the water; these are now stopped up to keep it in; which is not only to nourish the corn, but to kill the weeds; for they always keep their fields as clean and neat as a garden. When the grain has grown about nine inches high, the women are employed to weed it, and to pull it up where it has grown too thick, so as to transplant it to places where it may be wanted. It then stands overflown, till the grain is ripe; when they let the water off, in order that it may become dry, and fit for reaping. They never, as I before remarked, use manure of any kind; but their mode of ploughing, trampling, and soaking the ground, apparently obviates the necessity for it.

The Kandyans are excellent reapers, and as they had assisted each other in tilling the ground, they do so likewise at harvest. They first reap one man's field, and then go to the next, and so on, until the whole of the grain is cut; and their custom is, that every man, during the time his corn is reaping, has to find all the rest with food. The women's work is to gather up the corn after the reapers, and to carry it all to one place.

When the corn is to be trodden out, (half a dozen

buffaloes will tread out fifty bushels in a day), they select a place convenient to their dwellings, where they lay it out around a space, about twenty or thirty feet in diameter; from which they cut away the whole of the turf or surface, whatever it may be. They then perform, as Knox tells us, and as I have seen, certain ceremonies. "First, they adorn the place with ashes, made into flowers and branches, and round circles. They then take divers strange shells, and pieces of iron, and some sorts of wood, and a bunch of betel nuts, (which are reserved for the purpose), and lay all these in the very middle of the part, and a large stone upon them. Then the women, whose work it is, bring each their burthen of reaped corn upon their heads, and go round the pit three times, and then fling it down. After this, without any more ado, they bring in the rest of the corn as fast as they can. For this labour, and that of weeding, the women have a fee due to them; that is, as much corn as shall cover the stone, and the other conjuration instruments, at the bottom of the pit."

I trust, in being thus minute, that I have not worn out the reader's patience; at all events, even if I have done so, I shall make no apology to any one intending to become a settler in Ceylon; as all I have said, must, I hope, be useful to him. But, I beg here to observe, that in considering, and describing as I have done, the cultivation of rice in this island, it must have struck many, that

Drawn on Stone by P Gauci.

Published by T and W Boone, London, 1843

9, North Cres.t Bedf.d Sq.e

the process pursued by the Kandyans seems to aim at bringing the soil, in some degree, into a state resembling that of many parts of Egypt, so beneficially flooded by the Nile; and it ought to be a useful hint to our home agriculturists, and convince them of the vast importance of water, when employed scientifically, and for the purposes of irrigation, either for some kinds of grain, or for herbage. This is decidedly an object deserving, in a national point of view, the most serious attention of influential men, as it might, perhaps, tend, along with the aid which chemistry is now affording the agriculturist, to render the United Kingdom so much the more independent of supplies of grain and cattle from foreign lands.

I must now, in continuing the subject, further remark, that the usual mode of separating the rice from the husk is by pounding it in a large mortar, made of hard wood. But, besides this grain, which is indeed the staff of life all over the East, there are other inferior kinds cultivated in Ceylon, as has been already shewn; but I now more particularly allude to the Kandyan provinces. In them is often grown a sort of grain called by Knox *Coracan*, which the people usually grind into meal between two stones, and make cakes of it. This grain answers both on the hills and in the plains; and when sown in good ground, yields very great increase. *Tanna*, which, like the above, is a small grain, not larger than mustard-seed, is a good deal grown in some parts of the interior, as well as on the sea-coast, and yields an astonishing increase, when sown in a soil suited to it; and what would it not do if the ground were properly manured? It usually throws up several stalks, and on each stalk one ear, containing thousands of grains. The people parch the tanna in an earthen pan, and then it is beaten in a mortar to unhusk it. It is boiled like rice, but swells much more; it then becomes of a bright yellow colour;—it is considered very wholesome and nourishing food. I have asked the Kandyans, why they did not cultivate tanna, and other grain that grows on dry ground, more extensively; but, their usual answer was, that their forefathers never grew more of them than they now do. This may be one reason; but I believe the fact is, that grain grown on the high ground, or in places to which water cannot be conveyed, demands much more labour than these people are inclined to bestow upon them; for, in general, the tall trees and jungle must be cut down and cleared away; and the managing a large, heavy, awkward machine, something like a plough, which they use in tearing up a tough and matted surface, is not at all to their taste; especially when to all this trouble must be added that of enclosing the space to be tilled, with posts driven into the ground, and bound together with strong runners, to keep out deer and other animals. In short, few of them are willing to undertake such a job, however great may be the produce which might be looked for, as the reward of their labour.

Indian corn or *maize*, is not so much cultivated here as might be expected; and the people do not seem to use it often as food. *Gram* might be easily produced in Ceylon, in great quantities; and as it is the grain found to answer best for feeding horses, fattening sheep, &c. it is surprising, that a sufficient quantity of it is not grown, to obviate the necessity of importing it from other countries; for gram, with the roots of a kind of coarse couch grass, dug out of the ground and carefully washed by the grass-cutters, constitute, I may say, the only food given to horses; and the strongest proof of their nutritive qualities, is, that in no part of the world are horses to be seen in finer condition.

A kind of *pea* or *vetch* is a good deal cultivated; and, in preparing it for food, it is managed nearly in the same way as tanna. There are also several other kinds of grain occasionally grown, which succeed perfectly well on dry ground, though only watered by the periodical rains; but, in general, they are not much esteemed. I believe, however, that I have now been sufficiently explicit upon these interesting heads, to satisfy any settler, or the most inquisitive agriculturist; and I am convinced, that by what has been brought to their notice, this beautiful and valuable island has been considerably raised in their estimation, yet not more than it deserves to be.

I have already spoken of cinnamon; but the culture of coffee has for some time past been greatly upon the increase; so much so, that I should suppose, if sufficient attention be paid by those employed to manage the trees or plants, it may soon be brought to as great perfection as in any part of the world. The trees being raised from seed, are afterwards transplanted into moist and shady situations, commonly found at the base of hills or mountains. To the roots of the plants small streams of water are conducted; for at certain seasons they require to have a constant supply of moisture; it is therefore impossible that any where such admirable situations for the cultivation of this now necessary and valuable article of daily consumption can be found, as in the interior of this well-watered island: indeed, many are of opinion, that the coffee already produced is quite equal to that procured at Mocha. The many wet and moist parts of the country, which I have already pointed out, are also admirably adapted for the growth of mulberry trees. The attention of the natives may therefore be wisely and profitably directed to the silk-worm: in short, Ceylon only requires to be better known, to be duly valued as a colony; and, in further proof of this, I give a return of its produce and stock, &c. in the year 1835, which will shew how greatly these have been increased since I made this remark. *

Although Knox's account of Ceylon was given to the world so far back as the year 1681, yet no one,

* See Appendix C.

I am convinced, can point out any material change which has taken place in the manners, ideas, or customs of the Kandyans since that period; and those who have opportunities of obtaining the best information, or of estimating their character, must admire the astonishing correctness with which he has described every thing that came under his notice: indeed, so great is his accuracy, that even those who can peruse his work upon the spot, will, I have no doubt, readily admit, that a more faithful account of an unchangeable people, (if I may use the expression, when considering the bar which castes present to changes and improvements,) and of their wonderful country, cannot possibly be given by the most able and accomplished writer. Such a writer, if not altogether deterred from entering upon subjects almost exhausted, may probably adopt a style of composition more suited to the taste of the present day; but he must not hope to be able so perfectly to carry a reader—if I may so express myself—along with him, as Knox has done; and any one attempting to describe the ancient Kandyan kingdom, or to write its history, would evince his discretion and good sense, in previously consulting his "Historical Relation." At all events, whatever may be considered as wanting, has been amply and ably supplied by an author who styles himself "Philalethes;" since his time by Dr. Davy; and lastly, by Major Forbes; and any attempt to go beyond them, or farther back, must, I suspect, be a failure, or end in the fabulous.

In concluding this chapter, it may be well to remark, that it is not improbable, but that the idea of a system of mutual aid in agricultural matters, which has been practised for hundreds, I may say thousands, of years in the Kandyan kingdom, was adopted by that unhappy man, Mr. Owen, from the hints given by Knox in his "Historical Relation;" which induced the former to plan the establishments he did in Scotland and America; and which his evil genius is now leading him to attempt in England. The system, at first sight, seems to be really good; and it certainly works well amongst the primitive Kandyans; but Mr. Owen most incautiously, and seemingly in ignorance of human nature, altogether omitted in his wild theories what is so essential towards enabling men to live together, in any thing like harmony,—that is to say, *religion;* and though that professed by the Kandyans is both heathenish and grossly superstitious, still it was found to be sufficient to bind people together by certain indispensable obligations, without which it is impossible to look for permanence in human institutions.

CHAPTER III.

> "As one who spies a serpent in his way,
> Glistening and basking in the summer ray,
> Disorder'd stops to shun the danger near,
> Then walks with faintness on, and looks with fear."

A SOLDIER LOSES HIS WAY IN THE FOREST, AND GIVES AN ACCOUNT OF HIS EXTRAORDINARY ADVENTURES — HE CHASES A PEACOCK, AND FALLS IN WITH AN ELEPHANT —UNSUCCESSFUL ATTEMPTS TO GET CLEAR OF THE FOREST—A NIGHT SPENT UP IN A TREE — FINDS HIMSELF AMONG SNAKES—ARRIVES UPON THE BANK OF A RIVER —WHAT OCCURS TO HIM IN FOLLOWING ITS COURSE— A TOUGH STORY; BEING A STRANGE ADVENTURE WITH A YOUNG ELEPHANT—WHAT FARTHER OCCURRED TO HIM IN FOLLOWING THE COURSE OF THE RIVER—ARRIVES AT A DESERTED HOUSE IN THE FOREST, AND WHAT HE SAW THERE—HIS ILLNESS INCREASES—CARRIED BY KANDYANS INTO KURUNAGALLA, AFTER WANDERING FOR ABOUT SEVEN DAYS IN THE FOREST—REMARKS.

For a considerable period, a great deal is given in my note-book, which it is unnecessary to bring into this work. But a soldier, named Thomas Jones, was one morning reported to have been absent all night; and, though every inquiry was made, and the woods searched in all directions, he could not be found:—no one had seen or heard of him.

The second day, as he was still absent, caused some uneasiness to be felt about him; and soldiers, under the non-commissioned officers, were sent to make farther inquiries, especially amongst the Kandyans; as, on the evening upon which he was missed, they probably might, by chance, have seen him going along the roads, or through their grounds; but, they all returned unsuccessful. Having no apprehension, in a country like this, of his having deserted, I now became afraid, as he was known to be fond of evening walks, lest he might have lost his way in the intricacies of the neighbouring forest, and either been starved to death, or killed by wild beasts. I, therefore, had Kandyans sent in search of him; and a reward was offered to any one, who would bring him to Kurunagalla, or to any of the out-posts. In short, every thing possible was done to find him, dead or alive, but all in vain: we could get no tidings whatever of him. Seven or eight days had elapsed since he disappeared, and we at last had given him up as lost, or rather as killed by elephants, buffaloes, or tigers, when he was, to our delight, brought into the cantonment by a number of Kandyans, who had found him asleep, in a distant part of the extensive forest, through which the road to Trincomalie passes. The poor fellow was emaciated in person, and looked so like an idiot, that I knew not, at first, what to think of him;—he seemed scarcely to know me, or any one else; and could only laugh in a strange hysterical manner when spoken to. He appeared indeed to be in such an extraordinary state of debility and fatuity, that I was apprehensive he had altogether lost his reason; which, I was aware, is not unfrequently the case with men who lose themselves in the dreary and extensive woods of North America. He was therefore taken to the hospital, where the surgeon gave him some composing medicine, which soon produced a most sound sleep; from which he did not awake till the following morning, when he had quite recovered his senses; and in the course of a few days he was able to acquaint us with what had happened to him during his absence. The account which he gave—and I had no reason whatever to question its veracity—was so extraordinary and interesting, that I was induced to make a note of it; and I am the more desirous of introducing it here, as it will, along with what I have said of the country inland from Matura, give the reader a tolerably correct notion of Ceylon forest and jungle scenery. Many did not believe the strange story he told; but I was disposed to consider as truth what he related so minutely and circumstantially; which was nearly as follows:—

The evening of his disappearance from Kurunagalla being unusually fine and cool, he had been induced to walk out alone upon the Trincomalie road. Seeing, as he went along, a very large peacock run across it, within a few yards of him, he was tempted to give chase; picking up, as he did so, some stones, which he continued, as he ran, to throw at the bird. But in a short time, to his surprise and alarm, and when he had run himself out of breath in the fruitless and often circuitous pursuit, he began to doubt of being able to find his way back into the road. He tried to do so in two or three directions, but could see nothing of it; and therefore thought, that the best thing he could do, was to climb up into a tall tree, in order to see the sun, which the height of the surrounding woods prevented him from doing. He hoped that he should then have no great difficulty in directing his course towards the cantonment. After fixing upon certain objects to guide him, he descended from the tree, expecting soon to get clear of the forest, and into the road. But, unfortunately, and before he had gone many yards, he, to his great terror, espied through the jungle, and in the direction he intended to take, an elephant standing under the wide spreading branches of some trees, flapping his large ears, and swinging from side to side his long trunk, which they usually do when stationary. He therefore was afraid to proceed, and thought that he had no alternative, but either to stand still, or take off to the right, where the jungle seemed not to be quite so thick and impassable as to his left.

But, whilst he was attempting this, the shades of night closed gradually around him, and he soon became quite at a loss what to do, or which way to turn; and fancying that he heard another animal, which he concluded must also be an elephant, moving through the jungle close to him, his alarm so much increased, that he took to his heels, and ran for some time as fast as he could, and the thickness of the prickly brushwood would admit of. The farther he ran, the more he became frightened and bewildered; and, in place of getting clear of the forest, he was only penetrating deeper into it.

As it had now become dark, he thought that his best plan would be to climb up into a tree, then close to him, which he was able to ascend, from its branches hanging lower down than the others, and to remain in it till morning. To his great joy, however, it soon became a fine bright moonlight night; which led him to hope, that, if he were to exert himself, he might yet be able to get clear of the jungle; especially as from the tree he had seen what he supposed to be the rocks near Kurunagalla. Having, therefore, carefully considered the direction he was to take, he descended from the tree, and set off once more, at as quick a pace as the thickness of the underwood would allow; but, after going at this rate for about an hour, and not getting into an open country, his fears rapidly increased, and to such a degree, that he again determined to get up into a tree, and to remain in it till daylight. He now however took up with him a branch of a tree, so as to be able to defend himself should he be attacked by bears, of which he had heard there were many in the forest.

After spending a most miserable night, during

which he durst not close his eyes, he saw some elephants, and other large and small animals, pass near the tree, at the top of which he sat in great terror; but they seemed not to have perceived him. At sun-rise, having fixed upon objects which he hoped would point out the direction he was to take, he again descended, and started in full expectation of soon getting clear of the woods; but, he had only gone a few hundred yards, when the great height, even of the underwood, which was intermixed with the branches of the taller trees, put it out of his power to determine, whether he was steering a straight course or not. He, however, now resolved to go on; as he hoped that he must at least reach the border of the forest, which he knew extended to within two miles of Kurunagalla.

But after several hours walking, and at times running, he became more and more frightened and bewildered; and, being now completely worn out by over-exertion, he was obliged to sit down in utter hopelessness upon a large fallen tree, in order to consider what he could possibly do to extricate himself from the labyrinth in which he saw that he had got entangled. But he had scarcely sat down two minutes, ruminating upon his unhappy plight, when he had again to start. A large snake, with a curious mark, something like a pair of spectacles, on the back of its broad neck, came out at one end of the hollow tree on which he sat, and raised itself up, as he thought, in a most terrific and threatening manner. Having before seen that kind of snake, he knew it to be a Cobra de capello, and consequently he thought it best to make off as fast as he could; and he thus became more and more at a loss what to do, or how to direct his course.

Having at length reached a more open part of the forest, where numbers of fallen and decaying trees lay, as it were, tossed and rolled over each other, as if by the violent effects of a hurricane, and where there were numbers of young trees and shrubs growing in great luxuriance, he again, to his great terror, saw gliding amongst them numbers of snakes of various sizes and beautiful colours, which his disturbed imagination made him fancy were all poisonous. One of them, in particular, which lay coiled up, and did not move at his approaching it, stared, as he thought, keenly at him! This snake, he had no doubt, was upwards of twenty feet long; it was of a yellowish and brown colour, with large blotches, as it were, of a darker hue all over it; which marks made him conclude, that it was one of the terrible rock-snakes, of which he had heard so much, which are said to swallow buffaloes, deer, &c. and which could easily have made a meal of his poor carcase. This immense snake did not, however, stir; but all the others made off as fast as they could, and seemed anxious to get out of his way, as he now moved slowly along and with great circumspection over the fallen trees, which often crumbled to pieces under his feet as he trod upon them, and thus he was kept in constant dread, lest he might, by accident, put his foot upon the snakes inside of them! This, which was but too just a cause for alarm, together with the apprehension, which constantly haunted his mind, of falling in with elephants, tigers, bears, or wild buffaloes, kept him in such a state of uneasiness, that he verily believed he should lose his senses.

To his great comfort, and when he was completely spent from fatigue and anxiety of mind, he came unexpectedly upon the bank of a fine clear river, (it no doubt was the Didroo-oya), with the water of which he eagerly quenched his now almost unbearable thirst.

Having thus greatly refreshed himself, he made up his mind to follow the course of the river; hoping that it would soon lead him to some of the habitations of the natives, who, no doubt, would readily shew him the way home. But he had only gone a short distance, when, to his surprise, he heard a loud chattering over his head; and looking up, he saw that he was surrounded by a host of large bearded monkeys, which continued, as he went along, to grin and chatter most gruffly at him. Knowing well how to manage them, he began to throw stones at them; but he was vexed to find that this sent most of them off. A few of the largest of them, however, remained, which, in revenge for the stones cast at them, threw down fine cocoanuts, from the few trees of that kind which grew upon a spot, where, seemingly, a house had once stood. Two of these he broke to pieces by throwing them against trees, and with their contents considerably recruited his strength; he then, carrying the remaining nuts with him to serve for his next meal, proceeded slowly and cautiously down the river.

He thus went on for some hours; but could observe no change whatever in the appearance of the country, which would indicate that he was approaching an inhabited part of it; but, on the contrary, it became wilder and wilder. He durst not think of quitting the bank of the river, lest he might again become entangled in the so much dreaded mazes of the forest. The gloom, that now gradually increased, gave him notice that he ought to lose no time in looking for a tree, in which, he saw there was no alternative but to spend another long and dreary night; probably in watching and in constant terror. Having soon found one fit for the purpose, he sat down at its root to sup upon his remaining cocoa-nuts. He now became uneasy with respect to another supply of food; for during his progress by the side of the river,—indeed, to be able to proceed he was often in its bed—he had not seen a single cocoa-nut tree, since those which he had left in possession of the monkeys. Having armed himself with a long pole, so as to be prepared for the attacks of the so much dreaded bears, (there are none in that part of Ceylon,) he went up, for the night, with a heavy heart, into the highest branches of the tree; betwixt two of which he contrived to jam himself, in the hope of getting some sleep. He, however, could not place himself so as to remove from his mind the apprehension of falling; consequently his prospects of rest, or even tranquillity, were truly disheartening; for, very soon after the night set in, his clothes became quite damp with the most chilling dew imaginable, and this he felt the more unbearable, as he had to sit in a very awkward position, holding on with one or both of his benumbed hands, whilst he distinctly heard elephants and other animals moving about on all sides of him. Some of them he even saw, by the light of the moon, go down into the river to drink, and then return into the forest; in the depths of which he often heard the cries of whole packs of jackals and wild dogs, as if in hot pursuit of some animal which they had evidently selected for their prey. It may, therefore, be well supposed that during this wearisome night he never once was able to close his eyes.

Hungry, exhausted, and depressed in spirits, he once more, and as soon as it was light, pursued his course down the right bank of the river; as on that the trees seemed to be less lofty, and the jungle more open, than on the left, upon which he had hitherto travelled. He could perceive that there were, here and there, openings in the woods, in which deer and other animals were feeding; but he was afraid to quit the river, lest he might again lose himself in the woods; and so great was his apprehension of this again occurring, that he determined to move on, still taking the stream as his guide. Very soon, however, both its banks became so completely covered with jungle, intermixed with prickly-pear, and other low growing shrubs and runners, that he saw his only chance of getting forward was by proceeding constantly in its bed; the water in which was luckily low at the time. But, from want of proper nourishment and sleep, he began to find that his strength and spirits were fast giving way; and, coming to a more open and rocky part of the bed of the river, he had not the power to resist the inclination he felt to lie down upon it. In spite of the great and even oppressive heat of the sun, he instantly sunk into a most profound sleep, from which he did not awake for several hours; for he saw by some of what are called the "four o'clock flowers," a few of which happened to grow under the tall trees that finely ornamented the bank of the river, that it was past that hour of the day. But, let even the strongest nerved reader only imagine, how greatly his fears must have been augmented, when, before he had moved ten yards from where he had slept, he observed in a hollow part of the rock, in which had been lodged some sand and soft mud, during the floods in the river, the recent marks of the feet of some large animals, probably of tigers!—and as he was convinced they were not there when he arrived at the spot, they must, he concluded, have been made whilst he had slept so soundly, and was entirely at their mercy!

Being deeply impressed with the conviction of the almost hopelessness of the situation in which he had been so recently placed, he was first led to thank God for his wonderful preservation; and he then prayed, most fervently, that He, who was, indeed, able to protect him, though surrounded by such numbers of terrible animals, snakes, and reptiles of all kinds, would be graciously pleased to continue to do so. The very idea, however, of becoming their prey, or even the object of their attack, made his blood, as he remarked, run cold.

His object was now to find something to eat; and perceiving, as he went forward (every moment disturbing pea and jungle-fowl, as well as many other beautiful birds) a kind of reddish berries, which he had often before met with in the woods, and had heard that the Kandyans used occasionally as food, he thought he would venture to try them; but, as they had a sour and rather disagreeable taste, he did not consider it prudent to eat many of them, though they were apparently quite ripe. He now again set off, in the hope that, before dark, he would fall in with some cocoa-nut trees; but, unless there happened to be monkeys in them, and he could contrive to make them throw down some nuts, he had no chance of a supper; for he could not possibly get up to them, as these trees have no lower branches to lay hold of, by which a person may be assisted in climbing. He had not, however, gone much farther, when he found himself among a good many of these valuable trees, growing close to the river, and in the kind of grove that they formed were the ruins of what seemed to have been only a temporary hut. Some of the trees had, he saw, been recently broken down, evidently by elephants, in order to get at their tops, all of which had been eaten; but several of the nuts lay scattered about upon the ground. He then perceived, high up in the other trees that had been left standing, a number of the small greenish monkeys which were hopping about, as if unconscious of danger; yet sometimes looking, grinning, and chattering at him. There were also, flying amongst these and other trees, some toucans with immense bills, and hundreds of small parrots, with bright green, yellow, and red plumage, which kept up such a noisy and harsh screaming as almost drove him distracted; for his head now ached violently, doubtless from his having imprudently slept so long exposed to the powerful rays of the sun. He therefore lost no time in collecting as many of the nuts as he could carry; after which he recommenced his laborious task of forcing his way through the jungle, or scrambling along in the sometimes very rugged and often winding bed of the river.

Having bathed his aching temples in a cold clear spring, which he soon after found issuing from a rock, he derived some relief from it; yet he still felt himself far from well; and having, though little inclined to eat, supped upon a few of his lately acquired cocoa-nuts, he determined, that this night he would fasten himself in the tree he had selected for his sleeping place, with some of the long and strong runners that are almost every where to be found in the jungle. Having done so carefully, he would gladly have slept; but, what with the alarming noises around him, made as on the night before by various kinds of wild beasts, his constant apprehension of being attacked by bears, the piercing night air, and the heavy dew which again chilled him, he was scarcely able to close his eyes. Besides the numerous causes of his depressed state of mind, he had also to regret that he had nothing to cover him, but the usual undress worn at that period by soldiers in Ceylon; viz.—a light and scanty forage cap, rather tight white cotton jacket, shirt, trowsers, stockings, and shoes; all of which were now much torn or worn, in the unusual exertions he had been obliged to make to force his way through the jungle. When day dawned, he slowly and heartlessly descended from his roosting place, shivering with cold, but delighted to find that the violent headache had left him; and when the rays of the sun were able to penetrate to where he sat for a few minutes considering what he should do, he felt much revived, and even strengthened by this genial warmth.

In order to prepare for the day's journey, he thought it best to dash to pieces the rest of the cocoa-nuts which he had brought with him; and, after eating all that he could find in two of them, he took the kernels out of the others, and rolled them up in his jacket, which he took off, for the purpose of carrying in it his supply of provisions more conveniently than he could otherwise have done. He was desirous of saving the milky or watery substance inside of them; but, not having even a pocket-knife with him, he had no other way of getting at the kernels but by breaking the nuts to pieces, and was therefore seldom able to procure any of the fluid.

Being now furnished with at least a day's provisions, he once more went forward, in rather better spirits, and renewed hopes of this day falling in either with houses or some of the Kandyans. At one time, he was certain, that he heard the shouting of men some distance to his right; and instantly making towards the place from whence the sounds seemed to have come, he went on briskly, overjoyed at the idea that his pains and perils were drawing to a close. Before, however, he had gone a mile into the forest, the rapidly thickening jungle and deepening shade again alarmed him, and made him apprehensive that he might become involved in its labyrinths. He was moreover afraid that he might get once more amongst elephants and snakes; indeed, he began to see some of the latter gliding off to their retreats, the moment they even heard him approaching. Therefore, though disheartened at not hearing repeated the sounds which had so much gladdened him, he considered that it would be best and safest to go back to the river, and to continue following its windings. But while he was returning towards it, he saw through some tall trees, with but little brushwood growing under them, in the direction he was about to take, three elephants, quietly feeding, one of them very much smaller than the others. The latter quickly perceiving him, though he tried to conceal himself, first went towards the two old ones, and then turning suddenly round, ran, as if in play, after him. He therefore made off as fast as he could, looking on every side, in hopes of seeing some tree which he could ascend, but not one presented itself fit for his purpose, none of their branches being low enough for him to grasp. Thus running, and not being, in his haste to escape, sufficiently cautious, down he fell, just before his young and frolicsome pursuer; which stopped short, upon seeing him lying on the ground,—stared at him for a moment—then approached nearer;—touched him with its trunk;—turned him gently over and over before him;—and felt and smelt him again and again! All this time the terrified wight's greatest fear was, that the inquisitive beast would put his large and seemingly heavy foot upon him, (for he was more than half grown,) and thus finish him at once, as a kitten would put a mouse out of pain, when tired of playing with it. Neither of the old ones having, however, as yet come up, or taken any notice of their hopeful's amusement, but, on the contrary, continued feeding, about two hundred yards off, upon the leaves of a tree, it struck the poor fellow, who had in some measure recovered his senses, that the best thing he could do, was to spring up suddenly, and shout as loudly as he possibly could; and then endeavour to make off. His doing so completely startled the young elephant, and sent it back, bellowing, towards the others; when all of them rushed after him, breaking or bending the smaller trees and brushwood, as well as every thing else that obstructed their course. Fear lending him speed, he was soon able to leave them behind; and after a long run, arriving completely exhausted and out of breath, at the place where the evening before he had procured the cocoa-nuts, he there, without loss of time, and still impressed with the terror which his rencontre with the elephants had occasioned, got up into a tree, and remained in it for some minutes, until he felt that he was again able to continue his laborious journey. But, in addition to his other mishaps, he had been obliged, when the young elephant was amusing itself in turning him over, and in order to be better able to run, to leave behind him his jacket, containing his supply of cocoa-nut. There were, however, a few, that he had before rejected, still lying on the ground, and, having broken them, he filled his forage-cap with the best of their kernels, and once more went forward, but determined, if possible, not again to quit the river.

He had not gone a mile and a half, when he again saw abundance of the kind of berries which he had eaten the day before; but, suspecting that they had caused his illness, he would not venture to touch them. Arriving, however, at a place where the woods were not so thick as elsewhere, and where the ground, in one or two spots, had the appearance of having been cultivated, and as if houses or large buildings had once stood upon it, he saw to his great joy not only two fine jack-trees, but also several others called by the Kandyans jombo-trees; all of them loaded with fruit. He gathered some of the latter, which resemble apples; only their white and red colours are brighter, which give them a more beautiful and inviting appearance. These he found to be quite ripe and well-flavoured. After several fruitless attempts, he at last contrived to climb up into the jack-tree, and to throw down more of its large fruit than he had any occasion for. A single one of them contains, perhaps, two or three hundred nuts or kernels, which are not unlike chesnuts. He was aware, that these nuts may be safely eaten raw; but he regretted that he had no means to make a fire to roast them, when they are not only much better tasted, but also more wholesome. He had heard of fires being kindled by rubbing for some time two pieces of dry wood together: this he tried to do; but after rubbing until he was tired, he found that he could not succeed; and he regretted this the more, for could he have lit a fire, as there was plenty of dry wood at hand, he could easily have kept it blazing all night, and thus have deterred wild beasts from approaching him; and moreover, he might then have ventured to have slept upon the ground. But it was high time to proceed, for the sun had already passed over his head; and he still hoped that before night he might fall in with houses, or else get into a more open country. Loading himself, therefore, as well as he could, with jacknuts and jombos, he recommenced his journey in rather better spirits.

He had only scrambled along about half a mile, (for the jungle had again become as thick and many of the trees as lofty as ever,) when he arrived at what he thought was a footpath; for it evidently came down to the river, and appeared to be continued upon the opposite bank; yet he could not be certain whether it was really a path, or only an opening through which the wild beasts came at night to the river to drink: indeed, there were sufficient marks to convince him that many of them frequented it for that purpose. In consequence, he made up his mind not to be on any account tempted again into the woods, but still to follow the course of the stream. All at once, however, its banks became rocky, steep, and almost entirely covered with various kinds of shrubs or low growing jungle; and the water looked, in most places, to be so dark and deep, that he was alarmed lest there might be alligators in it. Under these circumstances, he found it necessary to diverge a little to the left and into the forest, in order to be able to get forward. But, he had scarcely gone a hundred yards, when he suddenly heard, before him and to his left, a loud noise like the grunting of hogs; and, to his dismay, he saw that he had got almost into the midst of a drove of these dreaded animals! He therefore instantly turned round and fled; and most happy was he to find that they did not take notice of or pursue him.

When he came again to what he had considered to be a path or road, he crossed the river, as he thought it would be best to pass upon the opposite bank the wild boars, which had so frightened him. Having reached it, he again endeavoured, as much as possible, to follow the stream, ruminating upon the many wonderful and providential escapes, which he had had during the course of this eventful day; yet deriving, as he expressed himself, much comfort and support from those beautiful lines of the Psalmist, which a pious parent had made him, when a boy, commit to memory; and which were, under such circumstances, brought so vividly to his remembrance. "Whither shall I go then from thy Spirit, or whither shall I go then from thy presence? If I climb up into Heaven, thou art there: if I go down to Hell, thou art there also: if I take the wings of the morning; and remain in the uttermost parts of the sea; even there also shall thy hand lead me: and thy right hand shall hold me. If I say, Peradventure the darkness shall cover me: then shall my night be turned to day. Yea, the darkness is no darkness with thee, but the night is as clear as the day: the darkness and light to thee are both alike." Thus being taught to rely upon an Almighty arm, and upon Him that heareth prayer, he felt, indeed, comforted and supported, and again went forward, as fast as he could, for two or three hours; but he could not perceive any appearance whatever of a human habitation, nor even a single cocoa-nut tree;

the same endless jungle or forest still surrounded him. He therefore, and very naturally, became once more alarmed and depressed in spirits; especially when he looked at the worn and tattered state of his clothes, and felt that he had no alternative, but to pass another dreary and probably piercing cold night in a tree; for he still considered that he could not possibly be safe from the attacks of wild beasts or snakes any where else. The very idea of the sufferings he must again undergo, brought on a sort of shivering all over him; indeed, he began to fear that he was attacked with ague, or some other fever; and if this were the case, he must, he thought, give up all hopes of escaping out of the terrible "howling wilderness," in which he thus found himself inextricably involved. Being now, moreover, completely tired, and the rapidly increasing gloominess of the forest warning him that the day was near its close, he began to look around him for a suitable tree for another night's lodging.

This he soon found, and having supped upon some of the cocoa-nut stuff, and a few of the jack-nuts, he ascended amongst its branches until he thought he was sufficiently high to be out of danger. He then fastened himself, as he had done the night before; and, to his great delight, soon perceived, that the very large leaves of the tree which he had selected, covered and sheltered him so well, that he felt himself much better off and warmer than he hoped to have been; and he now even trusted, as there did not appear to be any dew, in being able to spend a more bearable night than he had anticipated. Being greatly fatigued, he soon fell into a sound sleep, from which he did not awake until the sun was actually risen, and he had begun to feel the warming and reviving effects of his beams upon his much emaciated frame; yet he thought himself better in health, though considerably weaker, than the day before. He was, however, as he expressed himself, strangely confused in his head, his temples throbbed violently, and he began to suspect that his memory was impaired: indeed, this is not at all surprising, when all the sufferings that he had gone through are considered.

Ascending to the very top of the lofty tree, in which he had slept, he looked around him, in the hope that some known object would present itself. He saw distinctly some mountains in the direction in which he thought Kurunagalla lay; but they appeared to be a considerable distance off; and he was now quite aware, that by going down the stream he was leaving them still farther behind him, yet he durst not think of retracing his steps, nor of quitting the banks of the river; and therefore concluded, that he had now no alternative but to follow its course as long as he was able. To his right some mountains could be seen; but they were even farther off than those which he supposed lay near Kurunagalla. In every other direction, except where a few rounded hills or rocks presented themselves, the country was quite flat, and almost entirely covered with woods; yet some small spots in it were here and there to be seen, with remarkably green grass growing upon them. Having descended, he felt himself very little inclined to undergo fatigue, or to encounter new dangers with wild beasts or snakes, his dread of which had, in fact, greatly increased;—he therefore thought he would, for that day, only take short walks into the surrounding country, always moving with the utmost circumspection, whilst he endeavoured to find either houses or some of the people. But in case of his being unsuccessful, he purposed returning to the tree, in which he had been so much better accommodated than in any of the others he had fixed upon for his night's abode; and he had the less reluctance to adopt this plan, as he had some of the jombos and most of the jacknuts left: indeed, sufficient of the latter for, perhaps, two days' consumption.

Having breakfasted, more with the intention of recruiting his strength than because he was inclined to eat, he had nearly made up his mind that he would leave his supply of food behind him, concealed amongst the branches of the tree to which he intended to return; but, as he might again lose his way in the woods, he thought it best not to do so. Therefore, taking the whole of it with him, he, in the first instance tried the left bank of the river, as he had observed an opening amongst the trees in that direction. Soon falling in with a flock of peafowl, he had become so nervously apprehensive of danger in every shape, that even their loud and wild cries, as they ran off or took to wing, startled and alarmed him, and made him almost think of returning; he, however—always moving very cautiously—at length came to the opening he had seen from the tree; but, before he entered it, he saw through the foliage that there were some deer feeding upon the luxuriant grass with which it was covered; and just beyond them stood a large buffalo; but whether it was wild or tame he could not tell. In consequence, and as he thought it would be most prudent to return to the river, he moved off so quietly, that neither the deer nor the buffalo perceived him. It should here be remarked, that this very natural but over-sensitive apprehension of danger must have been the principal cause of his not getting clear of the forest; for, I have no doubt, from what I know of the country, that had he only left the river in the morning, and gone boldly forward in the direction in which he supposed that Kurunagalla lay, he could not have walked many miles—though certainly through a country in which he might have met elephants—without falling in with either houses or people. I admit, however, that it is easy to say how a person, so circumstanced, should have acted; but, to judge fairly and rightly, we ought to consider ourselves in a similar situation; when it is more than probable that we should be equally timid and perplexed.

On his return to the tree, he lay down at its root to rest himself, and in the hope of recovering from a strange kind of confusion with which his brain felt as if oppressed; and which increased his anxiety to proceed down the river. Yet he thought that, before he would do so, he ought to make another attempt to penetrate a short way into the woods on the opposite bank of the stream. In about an hour feeling himself rather better, he crossed the water, which was there easily forded; but he had gone only a short way, when seeing the prints of elephants' feet, he again almost decided upon going back; but on looking more closely at them, he became satisfied that they had not been recently made, and in consequence thought that he would again venture to proceed. In doing so, he took care to make marks upon the ground, and to break, as he went along, parts of the lower branches of trees, as by doing this, he hoped the more easily to find his way back to the river and to his tree.

When he had gone about a mile into the forest, still moving slowly and with great circumspection, to his great joy he saw before him some tall cocoa-nut trees; in fact so many, that he felt certain that a house must, as usual, be amongst them. This proved to be the case—but, alas! only its ruinous mud walls remained; and these were overgrown with shrubs, runners, &c., which indicated that the place had long been deserted. Why it had ever been selected as the abode of man, unless it were as a hunting station, or for the purpose of looking after cattle feeding in the jungle, amongst which there were, here and there, patches of excellent pasture, he could not imagine; as there were no appearances whatever of there ever having been in the neighbourhood either paddy or any other fields. There were, as is usually the case in such situations, numbers of parrots, and small monkeys, hopping about amongst the branches of the trees; and along with them, some of that curious kind of the latter, which he had not before seen, which are pure white in colour, and have long white beards. Some of the cocoa-nut trees had been broken or pulled down, apparently by elephants; but he could find no nuts, nor could he, by any means, cause the monkeys to throw down any of them; nor was there any kind of fruit to be seen. He now observed, among and about the ruins, great numbers of large and small lizards, and some beautiful snakes; but all of the latter made off the moment that they saw or heard him approaching.

He then perceived what might have been a footpath, leading seemingly further into the forest, but he was afraid to follow it; and, as he was about to return to the river, he was struck with horror to behold, as if reclining upon the large root of a jack-tree, a human skeleton. This, very naturally, much alarmed him; as he at once concluded that the person, whoever he might have been, might have there met the fate, which probably awaited himself, from an elephant or some other animal; but, he also at the same time remembered to have heard, that when the Kandyans were severely visited with small-pox, or even with the worst kinds of jungle fever, especially with the former, and when some of the members of the family had died of the prevailing malady, it was not uncommon for them to abandon not only their dwellings, but also such of the sick as were unable to go along with them. He therefore quieted his fears in some degree, by concluding that it was not unlikely the almost bleached bones before him were the remains of one of these unfortunates, who had probably laid himself down there and died, either from the effects of disease, thirst, or starvation. Close to the skeleton, and partially covering it, was a large piece of a talipot-leaf, which he was glad to take along with him, as it was light and very easily carried, and would shelter him greatly at night from cold, rain, or dew. Taking it hurriedly up, as if robbing the dead, and quitting the spot, he made all the haste he could towards the river; to which, and to his tree, he was the more anxious to get back, as the sky had suddenly assumed that appearance which indicates an approaching thunder-storm. He had scarcely reached the tree before the thunder began to roll tremendously over his head, and the rain to fall in torrents; but the talipot-leaf, so opportunely found, as well as the leaves of the tree, kept it out so well, that when it cleared up, which it did just before sun-set — though he felt much chilled, and very unwell—his person, as well as the few rags which he had left, were still quite dry.

How the following nights and days were got over, he could not tell; for his illness increased, his intellects became more confused, and his head again ached violently; but he believed, that he was chiefly kept alive, and enabled to proceed still further down the river, by the jacknuts which he carried with him, and by a few other cocoa-nuts, that he, providentially, found upon the ground; the trees upon which they had grown having been pulled down by elephants; with some of which, as well as with other animals and snakes, he thought that he recollected having had other rencontres and adventures. The circumstances attending them, or how he had escaped, he could not, however, even pretend to be able to describe; for being, at last, completely worn out with fatigue, suffering, and disease, and supposing death to be at hand, he resigned himself to his fate. The last thing he remembered was his sinking down from exhaustion, upon the root of a large tree, which he had no longer sufficient strength to ascend. There he was found, apparently asleep, by some Kandyans, who, according to their usual habits, had, at a very early hour, left their homes, to go into the jungle in search of some of their buffaloes and cattle, which had strayed into it. He being no longer able to walk, they, with great kindness, carried him to the cantonment; where they received the thanks and reward, which their humanity and attention had so well merited.

In finishing this chapter, I beg to be allowed to remark, that if the reader wishes to form a tolerably correct idea of the vast tract of flat country that extends to the north of the island, he has only, in imagination, to accompany the unlucky wight, whose adventures have been given in it, during his most perilous wanderings in the forest or jungle. That tract may be spoken of, as almost a complete wilderness, infested by wild beasts; and although the various kinds of trees, shrubs, flowers, or herbage, which he met with, have not been pointed out or described, (for they were unknown, or nearly so, to the wanderer), yet, if the reader is curious in such matters, he has only to refer to Mr. Bennett's "Manual," to obtain all the information he may require upon these heads.

CHAPTER IV.

"There is continual Spring, and harvest there
Continual, both meeting at one time :
For both the boughs do laughing blossoms bear,
And with fresh colours deck the wanton prime,
And eke at once the heavy trees they climb,
Which seem to labour under their fruit's load."—SPENSER.

THE ANCIENT KINGS OF KURUNAGALLA—THE RUINS OF THEIR PALACES, &c.—A NEW MODE OF MAKING A FIRST-RATE COOK—REMARKS—A HORSE-KEEPER DESCRIBED—EXCELLENT WATER-FOWL SHOOTING—ADVENTURE WITH A TIGER—RIDICULOUS ATTACHMENT OF A CAT TO A DOG, AND ITS EFFECTS, &c.—A COMPARISON BETWEEN CEYLON SPORTS, AND THOSE SO HIGHLY EXTOLLED IN THE "FAR WEST" OF AMERICA — A NIGHT AND A DAY RENCOUNTER WITH ELEPHANTS — SCENERY IN THE NEIGHBOURHOOD OF KURUNAGALLA DESCRIBED—TWO TIGERS FIRED UPON AND WOUNDED—PEA AND JUNGLE-FOWL SHOOTING, WHEN A PROPERLY TRAINED DOG IS USED, LITTLE INFERIOR TO THAT OF PHEASANTS IN ENGLAND — AN ADVENTURE — FURTHER REMARKS UPON CEYLON SPORTS, &C.

I HAVE here as a neighbour, and associate in authority, Mr. ——, the Civil Agent of Government, who seems to be an intelligent and well informed young man ; but I do not, as yet, know much of him. He is now busily occupied in building a splendid mansion for himself, within half a mile of the cantonment, on the very spot where, of

Published by T and W. Boone, London, 1843. P. Gauci, lith.

old, stood the palace of the Kings of Kurunagalla; for this extensive province, according to native historical documents, which are said to have been carefully preserved, had once a Rajah or Monarch of its own; but, this was before the country came under the Kings of Kandy. Of one of the former, the following tale is told by Knox; and it will shew in how far Kandyan traditions may be relied upon as historical facts. But we may suppose, if ever such a man existed, that he might have taken delight in the truly princely pastimes set forth in the annexed painting, by a native artist.

" The country of Neurecalava (to the northward of the Seven Korles) formerly brought forth great plenty of corn, occasioned by reason of its large waterings. A neighbouring kingdom, the kingdom of Cournegal, which lies in Hotcourley, in those times was brought to great dearth, at which the King sends to the people of Neurecalava, that they would bring a supply of corn to his country, which they did in great store upon beasts in sacks, and arrived at the King's city: and there, for the more expeditious measuring out every householder his proportion of corn, they made a hole in the sacks, and let it run out, still driving on the beasts before them; and all that was shed before every man's house was to be his share. This exceedingly gratified the King. Afterwards, the King, to requite them, asked " what they most needed in this country?" They answered, " They had plenty of all things, only they wanted Caba Mirris;" that is, turmeric and pepper. The King, to gratify them, sent them such a quantity of each as his country could afford. As soon as this was brought to the people of Neurecalava, they went to measure it out to every man his portion, but, finding it of so small a quantity, they resolved to grind it, as they do when they use it with their victuals, and put it into the river to give a seasoning to the water, and every man was to take up his dish of water thus seasoned. From whence Neurecalava had its denomination, viz. from Neur, signifying a city, and Cahah that signifies turmeric; and lava, as if it were lalla, put into the river.

"The king hearing of this action of theirs was offended, in that they so contemned his gift, but concealed his displeasure. Some time after, he took a journey to them, and being there, desired to know how their country became so very fruitful. They told him, it was the water of the river pent up for their use in a very vast pond; out of which they made trenches to convey the water down into their corn grounds. This pond they had made with great art and labour, with great stones and earth thrown up of a vast length and thickness, in the fashion of a half moon. The king afterwards took his leave of them, and went home, and by the help of his magicians brake down this vast dam that kept in the water, and so destroyed the pond. And by this means this fruitful country, wanting her water, is become as ordinary land as the rest, having only what falls out of the sky."

There are many such legends of or connected with Kurunagalla, and of the Attagalla or Elephant rock; which, as I have before remarked, rises upwards of five hundred feet in height, close to it. A kind of path and steps, cut here and there, in the face of the, in some places, bare rock, leads to the top; but to reach it is rather a nerve-trying undertaking. As you ascend, you pass a temple, where they shew you an imitation of the celebrated foot-mark of Boodhoo, on the summit of Adam's Peak. You then come to a ruinous wall, built across a kind of cavity, which seems to have been intended to bar all approach in that direction. Near to this are some stone pillars and a tank, with steps cut in the rock, to enable the priests to get to the water. There are also the ruins of buildings on the exposed face of the rock; but for what purpose they were designed, I cannot pretend to say. On the highest part of the rock, there are, besides, the ruins of what evidently has been a temple. I go occasionally up to this point, as from it, during the north-east monsoon, Adam's Peak and the adjacent mountains can be seen towering in the clouds; and also to enjoy the extensive and splendid views which the country presents in all directions, as well as to be refreshed by the cool morning air. But, by eight o'clock, the heat arising from the exposed parts of the rock, acted upon by the powerful rays of the sun, becomes so intense and unbearable, that I am always glad to descend before that hour. I conclude that these ruins must, in former days, have not only been intended for religious purposes, but, we may likewise suppose that they might, in times of trouble or danger, have been converted into a place of defence and security.

Many large stones, some of which are carved, and parts of pillars, which have been almost or entirely covered with heaps of rubbish and rank vegetation, were nearly all that remained of the ancient palace of the kings of Kurunagalla, and which having been dug out, are now using as materials in the construction of the Government Agent's mansion and offices; we may therefore well say, "Sic transit gloria mundi."—A vast mound of earth and stones is still, however, to be seen, marking what may have been the limits of the royal park, in which are standing some remarkably fine old trees, which may probably have flourished hundreds of years ago. When this mansion is finished, and the ground laid out as the Agent of Government intends, there will be few abodes superior, or perhaps equal to it, in Ceylon.

Not this gentleman, but another civilian, with whom I afterwards became acquainted, had adopted a most excellent plan for improving the practical knowledge of his head cook; but I am not quite sure, that the system would answer in England.—Whenever this artist over or under-did, or spoiled a dish, or his master fancied that he had done so, whether it were a goose, a turkey, a peacock, a ragout, a curry, or whatever it might be, he had his choice, whether he would eat the whole, or as much of it as went out from table, or receive a certain number of blows, well laid on, with the pliant cane of one of his lascareens, or body-guard! Young men, who have never been taught to obey, being thus entrusted with power in distant lands, where there is but little control exercised over them, are, it is to be feared, very naturally inclined to become petty tyrants; and we cannot be surprised at this, when we recollect, that they come from school, to be placed perhaps for a few months in the office of the Secretary of Government; in which having acquired—chiefly in copying letters—a very slight knowledge of business, they are sent off to some of the least important or out-of-the-way stations, as collectors, &c. at a salary of probably five or six hundred a-year, with the prospect before them of soon being in the receipt of a thousand or more annually; and thus they are, at once, entrusted with almost absolute power over thousands of the natives. The effects of this upon such young men may be easily foreseen. It is to be hoped, however, that the great and important political agents, who, in the East India Company's territories, are authorised to over-rule our experienced military commanders, are differently initiated into business, as well as into a knowledge of political economy.

It appears by my notes, that the reader narrowly escaped being still further wearied by a dissertation upon the advantages which our colonies derive from having very young men employed as civilians in them. He owes his escape to the appearance in front of the house, of my apparition of a horse-keeper, leading backwards and forwards a noble Arab steed. I must, however, before I mount for my evening's ride, beg leave to describe this strange appendage of mine;—a real curiosity of his kind; nearly six feet in height; skin, muscle, and bone, without an ounce of fat upon his whole gaunt carcass. Let the reader only fancy, that there moves before him such a long stalking figure, with a very large red turban (he is a Malabar), on his head; a white cotton cloth wrapped several times round his loins; with a sky-blue jacket—which he rarely puts on—thrown gracefully over one shoulder, and a double-barrelled gun upon the other, and in his hand a sort of long brush, with which he occasionally flaps off the flies, which annoy the impatient and spirited horse. If the reader does this, he has before his eyes a perfect creature of this genus. The being I describe is most obliging, and always punctual to the time he is ordered to bring out his charge, to which he is greatly attached;—but, unfortunately, like Baron Munchausen's greyhound, he has run so long and so fast, (for he always, if possible, keeps up with me), that he has nearly run himself off his legs; and, I suppose that I shall, one of these days, have nothing for it,—as I should be sorry to part with him,—but to convert him into a turnspit, and attach him to the cook; yet, I greatly fear, that he is too proud to submit to such degradation.

But I must now invite the reader to accompany me, in one of my evening rides, to a neighbouring lake; for I wish him to understand and duly appreciate the wild fowl and other shooting which I can constantly enjoy there. I have already spoken of the thousands of birds of various kinds, that come to roost for the night on the shores of lakes; but there are hundreds besides, which are constantly to be seen swimming on their usually tranquil surfaces. Those which I chiefly make war upon, are curlews, ducks, teal, &c.; for just as the sun is going down, and until it becomes quite dark, the former arrive in surprising numbers. In this part of the world, these birds, though the same in shape and nearly in colour, are of a much larger size than those to be met with in the United Kingdom; they are also well-flavoured, have no fishy taste whatever, and are therefore always considered a good dish at our tables, whether roasted or in a curry.

There is a very pleasant ride upon the new Kandy road, which is carried from Kurunagalla through a fine and picturesque country, having the Elephant rock for some way upon the left. I proceed along it, until I get within half a mile of the lake, or large tank, which I have before mentioned; where I leave my horse in charge of his keeper, who walks him about until my return, so that after the evening's sport is over, I can, when so inclined, ride home in good time for dinner. I, however, when the evenings are cool, prefer walking back to the cantonment. But, taking my gun from the horse-keeper, attended by my two Malays and Bran, I proceed through the jungle to the lake, and then along its beautiful shore, firing at ducks, &c.; and when they fall into the water, Bran always brings them out to me; and this I allow him to do, as I believe I have no reason to be afraid of alligators, there being few or none of them, at least at the lower end of the lake. Having arrived at a spot over which the curlews always fly in vast numbers, and generally within reach of my gun, I there station myself, to await their coming; but, as twilight here lasts only a few minutes, I fire away as fast as I can, almost every shot bringing down, one, two, or more curlews; and it amuses me greatly, to watch the expressions of astonishment pictured in the countenances of the gentlemen I bring with me, when they see and hear the large birds falling around them, and sometimes nearly upon their heads; for I very often have two double-barrelled guns with me.

Occasionally, I take a canoe and paddle out to the islands; and as there are always in them plenty of those birds which we call water-rails or flamingoes, between them and teal I have excellent sport until the curlews arrive, which they do every evening; so that we usually go home loaded with birds of one kind or another. With part of this spoil I am happy to be able to supply not only my own but also my neighbours' tables; none of whom have any turn for field or water sports such as these; which I, at all events, greatly prefer to bagging elephants, tigers, or buffaloes.

One evening, about a week ago, when waiting at the lake for the arrival of the curlews, and having sent the Malays to secure the canoe, as well as to look after some fish that I had caught, I happened to go round a small patch of jungle, to see what had become of my faithful Bran; when I perceived him busy at work, tearing and enlarging a hole in the ground, as if anxious to get at a rat, or some animal he smelt in it; and, fearing it might be a snake, I thought it best to call him to me. But on looking, by chance, to the right, to my horror, I saw a tiger couched among some bushes and reeds, with his eyes intently fixed upon my poor, unsuspecting dog! Having only large duck-shot in both the barrels of my gun, I instantly slipped a brass ball into one of them; and then called as loudly as I could to the Malays to come to my assistance, in the hope that the noise I made might scare away the tiger. Fortunately, Bran was not aware of the vicinity of, nor did he see, the tiger, or I fear, that he would, without hesitation, have attacked him, for now he is not afraid of any animal; when, in all probability, he would have been torn to pieces. My shouting had, I was rejoiced to see, the desired effect; for the tiger, giving a kind of low growl, fixed his greenish glaring eyes upon me, and in such a way as made me feel, I confess, rather uncomfortable. To my great delight, however, he began to back slowly into the jungle; and I did the same, in the most polite manner possible, towards the lake, with my gun pointed at him, and my eyes steadily fixed upon his. I, nevertheless, had no intention whatever of firing, unless obliged to do so; and the reader may imagine how rejoiced I was, when he totally disappeared behind some trees to my right, and just at the moment that I was joined by the almost breathless Malays, who had come, in all haste, to my aid. They very justly remarked, that it was most fortunate I did not fire; for had I missed, or only wounded the tiger, he most certainly would have sprung upon me. By this time my noble dog, which had thus been saved, had got his head and neck into the hole that he had enlarged; so that he had neither seen nor had any suspicion of what had been going forward. I candidly confess, that the fright I had felt, quite took away any fancy I might have had for sport that evening; but, in returning home, seeing some teal swimming about in the lake, I thought I would have a shot or two at them. As they rose from the water, I pulled the trigger, but the gun did not go off; and the reader may imagine what my sensations were, when I saw that it was the very barrel which I had kept levelled at the tiger, and upon which, had he sprung at me, my life depended!—It was rather an old gun, with the maker's name upon it; but I now resolved, that in future, I would trust only to my "*Joe Manton*," which had been made on purpose for field sports in

India. Let me, however recommend, that every one intending to go out to Ceylon as a settler should be careful, whether he may wish to be a sportsman or not, to take out with him a double-barrelled gun, upon which he can depend; and he will be acting wisely if he ascertains that the barrels are sufficiently strong, not to be injured by firing brass balls out of them. I am not an advocate for rifles.

A most ridiculous and tender friendship subsists between Bran and a cat named Goody, brought all the way from Galle. And both of them are so much attached to me, that their fondness often both inconveniences and annoys me; as I find it difficult to prevent them from following me, wherever I go. I lately went for a few days to Colombo; but before I left Kurunagalla, my Portuguese servant, the only one Bran will condescend to obey, had to shut him up, and also confine him for some time after my departure; but, no sooner was he liberated than he set off in search of me, followed by the cat. Where they went no one could tell; but it was long after dark before they returned. Food was offered to them, of which the cat partook readily enough, but Bran would not even look at it, and kept constantly howling the whole night. As soon as the doors were opened in the morning, away he again went into the woods, apparently in search of me. Towards night the cat also disappeared; but on the following morning they came back together. The cat had marks of blood all over her, and had evidently been fighting; and as for Bran, he was dreadfully torn and mangled, especially about the throat; and his long ears were hanging down in shreds upon his cheeks; making him, though never a beauty, ten times more hideous in appearance than ever. I have no doubt, but that he had been engaged, (not unlikely in the defence of his friend Goody), with either the large wild dogs or the jackals, of which there are hundreds roaming about nightly in the neighbouring woods. He had now, therefore, to be again tied up; but the cat sat generally beside him, seemingly partaking of his grief; so that, when I returned from Colombo, the greatly attached dog was actually reduced to skin and bone. It is unnecessary to mention their extravagant joy at seeing their so long absent master. Often, to my surprise, when out shooting, or even riding, and having Bran with me, and when three or more miles from Kurunagalla, I have heard a cat mew near me, and on looking around, I was sure to find that it was Goody up in a tree, perhaps, over my head. She then readily, when called, came to me to be petted; but would again disappear after rubbing herself up two or three times against Bran, and occasionally leaving at his feet a bird that she had caught in the woods. Thus she would come and go, but always contrived to be home first, and ready to receive us in the verandah. I must beg that the good-natured reader will pardon me for having introduced this canine and feline—may I call it?—episode; which, had I any thing of the bard in my composition, should not have appeared in the lowly garb of prose. My object, however, in thus seemingly trifling with the reader's patience, is more particularly to introduce my faithful companion Bran to him, as he is to hear more of him hereafter.

I have now been long enough in this province to have seen and become acquainted with most of it. I am often absent from Kurunagalla for a week or ten days at a time, upon shooting or fishing excursions. Upon such occasions, acting as I did at Galle, I usually take with me all my servants but the Portuguese, who remains behind in charge of the house, &c. The Kandyan Headmen are equally as ready and obliging as those in the Galle district, to build for me temporary bungalows, wherever I require them. There is one gentleman here, Captain R—, who is something of a sportsman, and ready enough to accompany me, when I ask him; but, he cares as little for fishing, and fine or picturesque scenery, indeed, for scenery of any kind, as the horse he sometimes rides. I do not, therefore, often request the pleasure of his company in such rural excursions, although I must say, that he is very good-natured and easily pleased.

Having such facilities of going wherever I fancy, I again often avail myself of the delightful field-sports of the forest and jungle; not like the wanderers and trappers of the "far west" of America, in every kind of what I at least consider wretchedness and filth; (yet, whose dreary mode of life, is envied by some adventurous spirits;) but, on the contrary, surrounded with more than the necessaries of life; that is to say, if the produce of the chase in the wilderness, as well as the fish caught in the rivers, well cooked, can satisfy the ordinary wants and good appetites of sportsmen; the nights being spent, till bed time, in perhaps talking over the feats performed during the day; and such conversation being enlivened by a sufficiency of excellent Madeira, and, occasionally, by even a bottle of well-cooled Champagne or claret. I do not, however, thus again speak of our usual mode of living in the woods in order to make a parade or boast of it, or that I care for such things; but, I do so, with the view of shewing, that even the most comfort-loving being, might go along with me, without having any anxiety as to what he is to eat or drink, or any apprehension of being obliged to endure "far west" dirt, vermin bites, and every sort of discomfort. I cannot, however, undertake to guarantee him against his having to encounter wild beasts; or that his rest shall not be broken at night, by elephants coming too near, or even, sometimes, into the encampment. As for seeing plenty of game of various kinds, or what we here consider such, he may, in almost every direction, be certain that there will be no disappointment in that respect. Yet all I can pretend to do, "in my humble way," for those who may be good enough to accompany me in my excursions, is nothing when compared with what that prince of sportsmen, my friend Mr. Farrell of Hambentotte, can treat those to, who have the pleasure of going with him to his hunting grounds. There, every hundred yards they go, they may probably have opportunities of evincing their coolness and dexterity, and I may add, their courage also; if the elephant, buffalo, or wild boar shooting or hunting be their object.

How delightful and enticing it is in a country like this, to start before dawn of day, so as to be able to reach, in proper time, the verdant meadows and openings in the jungle, usually encompassed by the most splendid blossoming and other trees and shrubs, wherein deer and various animals are often to be met with; but from whence, as soon as the sun is above the horizon, they retire to the most secluded parts of the forest or jungle, in which they remain till evening; and where, owing to the thickness and often impenetrable nature of the latter, they can seldom be got at. Wild boars, or hogs, invariably thus disappear, and this is the reason why they are so rarely met with in the day time; and such are also the habits of the wild buffaloes, and those huge animals, elephants. Those amateurs, therefore, who are desirous of encountering them, and of bearing off their tails, (or brush, as it is styled,) as trophies of their victory, must look for them in such out-of-the-way parts of the country.

I now find in my notes, an interesting account given me by an officer, who was for some time attached to the district, as Assistant Commissary, of an adventure which he had in the jungle, as he was leading an advanced guard during a night march, in the time of the Kandyan rebellion. He was moving cautiously along, followed by a corporal and four privates, when, at a sharp turn in the very narrow path, he came suddenly upon two elephants, one of which, while the officer was in the act of firing his gun, instantly raised his trunk, and struck him a terrible blow with it, which knocked him down under his belly. He then put one of his immense feet upon the officer's *cap*, which had fallen off in the scuffle, pressing it several inches into the ground! At the same moment, the party Mr. E—— had with him also fired upon the elephants, of course with common lead balls; and, though so close to them, without much effect; for they were both able to make off into the jungle. Mr. E—— was then taken up, senseless, from the blow which he had received from the elephant's trunk; and although a considerable period had elapsed when he told me this story, he had not then by any means recovered from its effects. His life was, however, undoubtedly saved by his cap having providentially fallen off; and as it lay on the ground, only a few inches from his head, the greatly enraged, and probably stupified elephant, had evidently intended to crush the latter to atoms under his foot!

My gardener, a tall handsome grenadier, who had along with several of his comrades followed my predecessor in command here, being one morning in pursuit of a herd of elephants, which had unceremoniously walked into the cantonment, was, as he thought, singled out and chased by one of them, and was unfortunately overtaken before he could ascend into a tree he had just reached; when the powerful creature, seemingly only desirous to get him out of his way, pushed him against a tree with his trunk, in shuffling along; but with such violence as almost to cause his instant death. Even now he suffers much from the effects of this *slight squeeze*, from which I do not think he will ever perfectly recover; for he is still subject to a spitting of blood.

Besides the benefit always derived from regular exercise, the pleasures of the chase, and the refreshing influences of the morning air, how truly striking and beautiful is the scenery in many parts of this fine province; especially at the moment when the rays of the sun first gild the summits of the neighbouring rocks, and generally well wooded hills and mountains; whilst the deep valleys are still filled with dense volumes of mist, as is usually the case here at dawn of day; and which gives them the appearance of being beautiful lakes, the waters of which are seemingly unruffled by the slightest breath of wind. To enjoy such scenery in perfection, (and it almost daily varies,) I start at a gallop, to the great delight of my fleet and playful Arab, perhaps half an hour before dawn of day; and soon find myself six or nine miles from Kurunagalla, on the new road to Kandy, as it passes through deep ravines and over rugged mountains. But, I usually turned round, at a spot from whence I can command one of the grandest and most striking views imaginable; for not only have the valleys, to the right and left, still retained all the appearance of being the most enchanting lakes, whose shores are clothed with trees of various shades of the greenest foliage, but the whole of the flat country, below and before me, and towards the northward, looks as if it were the ocean tranquilly spread out, as far as the eye can reach; the wooded summits of hills or rocks, which here and there rise above the plain, appearing on it like small and very beautiful islands. This mist, which, during the night, had been generated in the valleys and low lands, is often gradually drawn up, like a curtain, as the sun mounts majestically and in tropical brilliancy, above the lofty range of mountains to the eastward.

I sometimes invite the gentlemen staying with me, as well as those resident at Kurunagalla, who like a gallop at that early hour, to accompany me to this enchanting spot; when they invariably acknowledge, that they never before beheld any thing so surprisingly beautiful as this—as I may call it—watery deception. Some years ago, when marching one night in Ireland, from Ballyshannon to Enniskillen, I remember that, towards sunrise, as we moved slowly along the road, which at the time lay considerably above the shores of Lough Earn, I greatly admired delusive scenery, something similar to that I have, in vain, attempted to describe. It certainly presented itself in great loveliness, especially to our left; but, although it was really fine and striking, it yet wanted the high colouring, the variety of shades of green, brown, purple, and blue, and likewise the sufficiently towering mountains, which this part of Ceylon possesses, and displays to such astonishing advantage.

Another of my favourite morning rides is along the road to Padenny, where scenery of a different kind presents itself. A rocky ridge, generally well wooded, and here and there decorated with fine acacias, lies to the right; but which in few places rises sufficiently high to deserve the name of mountains, at least, in a country like this. To the left there is a good deal of cultivation; and also a considerable extent of that park-like scenery to which I have often alluded. Occasionally, these deceptive mists extend themselves all over this country, and even as far as the Matelé mountains, on the other side of the ridge. When this is the case, I am sometimes tempted to leave my horse with his keeper on the road about five miles from Kurunagalla; and ascending on foot, with my gun in my hand, to the highest point of the rocks, called Yakdessa Galla, by a very rugged and intricate path, I there look around me, as from thence is to be seen, perhaps, as splendid scenery, though of a softer character, as that which I admire so much from the mountains on the Kandy side. There I stand as if in an island surrounded by others, which are the wooded hills and rocky points appearing above the morning mist; the mountainous country, towards Kandy and Matelé, looking like a bold, distant continent, from which I seem, as it were, separated by a most transparent sea, dotted with small and lovely islands. This is, however, I must confess, a somewhat dangerous pursuit of beautiful and delusive scenery; for this range of wooded rocks is much frequented by elephants and wild hogs, but particularly by tigers; which are often seen, even close to the cantonment, especially in the patches of acacia trees, which are so much admired. Not long ago, while looking for deer, to the eastward of the ridge, and when about a mile or two from the Didroo-oya, and perhaps not far from the part of the country through which the soldier must have passed who was lost in the forest, I by chance fell in with two of them. They did not perceive me, nor the two Malays with me, as they were busy feasting upon the carcass of some animal they had killed; therefore, by instantly securing Bran, and taking advantage of a patch of jungle, we were able to approach near enough to take a deliberate and certain aim at them. One of them, that at which both the Malays fired, appeared to be severely wounded, as it made a sudden and high spring from the ground the moment their rifles were discharged. The one I aimed at, was also evidently struck; yet, though we followed them for some time, they were both able to reach some rugged and thickly wooded rocks, into which it would have been both highly imprudent and useless to have pursued them. When we went up to the spot where the tigers were when we fired at them, we found that they had been devouring a buffalo calf, seemingly but a few days old; which it is probable they had carried off from some house in the cultivated country, to the westward of the rocky ridge, where they are constantly committing such depredations.

It may, however, be imagined, that I give much too favourable, glowing, and perhaps fanciful a description of Ceylon scenery; but, to shew whether I do so or not, I must request the reader's attention to what that accurate observer, and able delineator, Dr. Davy, says in the account of his travels in the interior of this wonderful and interesting country. "It is of consequence to know, that by ascending the mountains of the interior, according to the degree of elevation, (and I beg the attention of those intending to settle in Ceylon to this), you may find the average temperature of every latitude between Ceylon and England; and enjoy, amongst the finest scenery of nature, the purest and most refreshing atmosphere. * It is too sanguine, perhaps, but I cannot help anticipating it, that a time will arrive, when the mountain-tracts of Ceylon, many of them of surpassing beauty in their wildness, now merely charming deserts, will be inhabited and cultivated by Europeans, and made the nurseries not only of our plants, but, which is infinitely more important, of our religion and virtues, our arts and sciences."

* This opinion is also fully confirmed by Major Forbes, when he speaks, in his "Eleven Years in Ceylon," of Nuwara-Ellia Horton Plains, &c.

"Mists, like dews, are much more common in the interior, than on the coast of the island; and in the deep moist valleys amongst the mountains, than in other situations. Very often, in such situations, they form of astonishing density, and resemble an expanse of water so much, that, to a spectator, in the clear cool air on a mountain above, were he ignorant of the features of the country, they would appear to be genuine lakes. The beauty which these mists give to mountain scenery, is greater than can be well imagined. Occasionally, after sunrise, the mists, that have formed in the higher mountain-hollows, are displaced by the wind, and poured in immense volumes down into the warmer valleys, producing a sudden chillness and extreme humidity of the air, that is very disagreeable, and a sudden reduction of several degrees of temperature."—"Mountains are always the regions of clouds;—nor are the Kandyan mountains an exception. Hardly a day together, are the loftier mountains free from clouds; and during the whole of the south-west monsoon, Adam's Peak, and the adjacent mountainous regions, are concealed by them."

Always at dawn of day, pea and jungle-fowl are calling wildly and crowing in all directions; but I seldom think it worth my while to look after them, though I have my daring and sagacious dog Bran now so well trained, that I can make him go round to the far side of the trees or clump of jungle, in which a flock of the former may have roosted for the night, and have not yet come down to feed; and on my making signs to him, or whistling in a particular way, he always does his best to drive them towards me; when I can easily contrive to bag some of them. But, often, when only slightly wounded or winged, they make off through the jungle at such a rate, that were it not for Bran, who is perfectly up to his business, I should seldom have a chance of getting one of them. I manage to shoot the jungle-fowl much in the same way, especially the cocks, which, when fighting, are both ireful and regardless of danger; so that the sport I have with them and peacocks, as I now practise it, may be considered as not very inferior to pheasant shooting in England. Still, I must admit, that it is too laborious to be continued long after sun-rise. In the wild state, neither the pea nor jungle fowl can be considered worth as much as game; being usually tasteless or insipid, and not even making good curries. When we can, however, get hold of the young ones, (Bran has often caught half a dozen of them for me in a morning,) and feed them for some time upon grain, but particularly upon gram, they then become excellent and well-flavoured. (I beg the attention of settlers to this.) Yet, to shew what may occasionally happen here in shooting such game, I must mention, that a few days ago, I came suddenly, in a retired part of the jungle, upon one of the largest and most splendidly-tailed peacocks I had ever seen. He was perched upon the highest branch of a tall tree, which rose above a thick clump of brushwood. I fired at and brought him down, fluttering, into it; when out rushed, right at me, one of the finest elks that I had met with in Ceylon; one of his horns, in his furious charge, just grazing my shoulder! My companion, Captain K—, instantly fired; but being in far too great a hurry, he missed his aim. Recovering, however, from my surprise, I lodged a charge of heavy duck shot in the flank of the elk, which staggered him completely. But, in spite of this, he was able to make off, followed closely by Bran, the Malays, Captain K—, and myself, in full chase. After a short run, we found that Bran had got hold of him in the midst of a thick patch of very prickly jungle, into which I was afraid we could not get to his assistance; until I saw my experienced Malays, kreese in hand, cutting their way through every thing, who very soon exposed to our eager gaze my gallant dog holding the elk by the throat! In all my adventures, since I had been in Ceylon, I never before was in such imminent danger as I was from the large antlers of this fine elk upon this occasion; and I was now taught—if I before wanted such a lesson—that a stag or elk at bay is an antagonist not to be trifled with or despised.

I must here mention another good shot, which I one evening made at a deer. I was shooting snipe in an old swampy paddy field, and had fired at one; when, suddenly, and to my great surprise, a fine doe fled, in great alarm, out of a patch of jungle close to me. Having but one barrel remaining loaded, and that with only *No. 9 shot,* I had no expectation whatever of being able to bag her: and yet I thought at the moment that I ought not—cruel as it certainly was—to allow her to go off without, at least, a salute. Taking aim, therefore, at her ear, I fired; when, to my astonishment, down she fell! and in an instant Bran had hold of her. Upon this occasion, I had no person with me, and had consequently to walk some distance to my horse-keeper, who was holding the horse upon the road. Then mounting, I rode back to the cantonment, and brought from thence some soldiers, who carried home my prize; all of them wondering at a deer having been killed with snipe shot! I ought not, however, to omit mentioning, what I find recorded in my notes, that the doe was young, and not more than ten or twelve yards from me when I fired, and that I used upon the occasion my first-rate "Joe Manton."

I must again admit, that snipe-shooting is always, and rightly, considered here a dangerous amusement; and I would not advise any one to persevere too much in it, especially during the heat of the day, when the greatest numbers are invariably to be met with, and when they lie best; for it is, certainly, imprudent to be wading through mud and water, exposed to the powerful rays of a noon-day sun, at so short a distance from the equator. A dog is, I may say, altogether unnecessary, unless employed as I do mine; for, the snipe sometimes get up, as I walk along, in dozens; which always confuses a young sportsman, who is naturally in too great a hurry to fire, and consequently misses his aim, if he even gives himself time to take any. Indeed, I have seen my friends empty their powder-flasks and shot-belts, without being able to have themselves accounted sportsmen, according to the notions of an old friend of mine, who, in my boyish days, when I enthusiastically spoke of the numbers of grouse which I had seen during the course of the day, would say to me, in his dry way :—"Give me the sportsman who brings home the game."

Snipe in Ceylon, as in most parts of the world, are migratory; leaving the island in October and returning in March. They are of the same size as those we meet with in such numbers in Ireland, and weigh about four ounces; but I very often have killed what in Ceylon are called painted snipes, which are much larger, and adorned with the most beautiful plumage imaginable. Some persons, however, consider that the Ceylon snipes are inferior in flavour to those at home; but, I could never discover any difference in this respect, and always thought them, and wild fowl in general, the very best birds which were brought to our tables. But, with such excellent sport all around me, it may surprise the reader, that I should have thought of going any distance in search of more; especially as vast numbers of water-fowl remain at the neighbouring lake the whole day, and can always be found in their usual haunts, close to the roots of trees, that extend their long fibres, in many places, into the water; or amongst the reeds or flags which grow in it, and upon the banks. To make these birds take wing, I have only to send Bran to flounder about in the cover, so as to start them; and when they fall into the water, he brings them out to me. This, to him, seems to be the greatest possible enjoyment. Novelty and variety are, however, always longed for and sought after by most people; especially when, as in this country, the interest excited by them is heightened by the adventures, which are almost always attendant upon the chase in the wilderness; and, besides, to have any thing like good fishing, I must, I find, go low down the Didroo-oya, or even into the wild province of Neurecalava; which, though once both fertile and thickly peopled, is now a vast and almost uninhabited desert.

CHAPTER V.

"Emongst wide waves, set like a little nest,
As if it had by Nature's cunning hand
Been choicely picked out from all the rest,
And laid forth for ensample of the best:
No dainty flowre or herb that grows on ground,
No arboret with painted blossoms drest,
And smelling sweet, but there it might be found
To bud out fair, and her sweet smells throw all around."

SPENSER.

FARTHER REMARKS UPON CEYLON SPORTS—AN ADVENTURE WITH A WILD BOAR—A FEMALE ELEPHANT CRUELLY AND UNNECESSARILY WOUNDED — BEAUTIFUL FLOWER-DECKED RECESSES IN THE DEEP BED OF THE DIDROO-OYA—FISHING AND BATHING IN ITS POOLS—KANDYAN BRIDGES—A CURIOUS AND BEAUTIFUL FOUNTAIN—REMARKS—HOW SOME OFFICERS MANAGE TO GET ON PROFITABLY IN THE KANDYAN PROVINCES; GIVEN AS A HINT TO SETTLERS—MAD JACKALS—OBSERVATIONS UPON SITUATIONS SELECTED FOR THE RESIDENCE OF EUROPEANS, ETC.—VISIT TO THE TEMPLES AT OLLEGAMMÉ, WHICH ARE HEWN OUT OF THE SOLID ROCK—THE FINE COUNTRY AROUND THEM; FIT FOR AGRICULTURAL PURPOSES—REMARKS.

WE have sometimes here, as I had in the Galle district, most delightful and animating sports; and such as, if they were described as they ought to be, would, it may well be supposed, induce some stout-hearted sportsmen, now that steam navigation is so much improved and extended, to set out from England, for a season's hunting and shooting in the green-woods of Ceylon; and why may not even an emigrant look forward to occasionally joining in and enjoying the pleasures of the chase; especially, when he thereby may be assisting in driving back into the wilderness the wild beasts that may have intruded from it, so as to be enabled more safely to extend his improvements and cultivation?

At the time I speak of, as the Kandyans had been disarmed since the rebellion, elephants and other animals had, in consequence, been allowed greatly to increase in numbers; and they had also become much more daring, troublesome, and destructive than of old. All over the country, there had been constructed, high up in the largest and tallest trees, what I may call nests; in which the people stationed themselves, for the night, to watch their crops, and to scare away from them the elephants, deer, hogs, &c. which came to eat and tread them down. From these nests, and in perfect safety, they formerly fired upon the invaders; but now, in order to drive them off, having no guns, they are obliged to depend upon very inefficient bows and arrows, shouting, and setting fire to quantities of prepared and easily ignited dry brush-wood. It is, therefore, always to the great delight of the whole country, that I announce my intention of having a battue in any of the Korles; when numbers of people, notwithstanding the hundreds employed upon the roads, readily turn out with tom-tom beaters and pipers, to assist in driving the game towards the places where we have stationed ourselves, (my visitors are now pretty numerous), to fire upon the elephants,—always the chief objects of pursuit on these occasions,—buffaloes,—when the people assure us that they are wild,—deer, hogs, hares, wild dogs, jackals, pea and jungle-fowl, as they, in terror, rush or fly past us—when numbers are usually slain. This is a kind of sport, or rather slaughtering of beasts and birds, most delightful and animating to some, but not much to my taste. The elephant shooters are, however, highly ,gratified, and in most instances satisfied, if, amongst the animals bagged, they can reckon a brace of elephants, a male buffalo or two, and a few wild boars; but many of the wounded invariably escape into the jungle, there, probably, to pine and die.

In a late excursion of this kind, I had a bungalow, &c. constructed for four friends and myself, at a place I had selected, on account of its agreeable situation, on the bank of the Didroo-oya. The battue had taken place in the morning some miles off; but the game had been, when routed and dispersed, driven somewhat in the direction of our temporary abode. We were aware that some elephants and other animals must be prowling about; but having, before dark, taken the usual precautions, and large fires being lighted, we had no apprehension that any of them would venture to approach us. In spite, however, of all that we had done to prevent our being disturbed, we were alarmed towards morning, by the cries of the servants and coolies; some of whom rushed into our bungalow, exclaiming that elephants, buffaloes and wild boars, had got in amongst their huts, and were, according to their account, actually treading them down. Of course, in a moment, we all ran out nearly naked, but well armed; when, firing upon the gigantic intruders, we soon sent them off, several of them being wounded. But, what with the trumpeting of elephants, grunting or rather growling of hogs, howling of jackals, our rapid firing and shouting, and the darkness of the night, (the coolies directed to keep up the fires having fallen asleep and allowed them to burn out,) the scene was to some of us animating enough, but to others rather alarming. In short, when we talked the matter over next morning at breakfast, we were most fully justified in laughing heartily at each other, and at the ridiculous parts which we had respectively performed.

We had just finished that meal, when one of the servants, who had been sent for some cold water from a spring, informed us, that he had seen a very large and certainly wounded boar, in a clump of jungle, a short way down the river. We, therefore, immediately decided upon going in pursuit of him, taking with us the two Malays and Bran.

The boar was soon found and dislodged;—upon which he made right at me, or the gentleman who stood next to me!--I instantly fired, and hit him, as did also my companion; but he was still able to continue his terrific and furious rush towards us. Being apprehensive of the consequences, I halloo'd Bran at him; and in an instant, he was, to my horror and dismay, borne along on the brute's back, holding fast by one of his ears. This gallant attack having, in some measure, diverted him from his evident object, undoubtedly saved me from his assault; but he passed, in the utmost fury, only a few yards to my right. Though well prepared, I was afraid to fire, lest I should kill my noble dog; which, in the way I have described, was carried off by the boar into the jungle, closely followed by us all, but especially by one of the Malays, who, soon overtaking him, severely wounded and quite exhausted, finished him with his rifle, Bran, as usual, still holding on by his ear!—He was an enormous brute, with dreadful tusks;—and, I candidly confess, that I felt somewhat *queerish*, when I looked at him as he lay extended on the grass, and thought, what a terrific rent his really fearful tusks might have made in my precious person, had it not been for Bran. We all however agreed, that this was most interesting sport; and that the occurrences I have mentioned were worthy of being recorded. It was also decided that my faithful dog's likeness should be taken by one of the gentlemen present, who had a turn for figure drawing; and, as I find the picture amongst my notes, I am induced to give it here; though I must say, that justice has not, by any means, been done to him.

Our servants, but the Kandyan coolies in particular, who had ventured cautiously to follow us, thought us a set of madmen, when they saw us going off after the ferocious wounded boar, which they all declared would certainly turn upon us; but, finding that we only laughed at them and their fears, and that we were resolved to attack him, they with much gravity shook their heads, and shrugged up their shoulders, very much as a Frenchman would have done; for the Kandyans make valour to consist in three things: viz.—"one is to fight against the enemy; another to hunt the elephant; and the third to catch hogs."

About a week ago, when again at the Didroo-oya, I one morning saw a herd of nine elephants, in a small open space, close to the bungalow and huts; but the poor animals, evidently, had no intention whatever of doing us or our abode the least injury.

Indeed, they seemed, as is usually the case when in herds, to be almost tame. One of my companions, however, a novice in elephant shooting, and before I was aware of his intention, fired at a large female elephant, and cruelly wounded her. She had a young one with her, about three feet in height, which, while they were going off into the jungle, she appeared to be most anxious to cover and protect, at whatever risk to herself. They are, as I before remarked, always known, but especially in the wild state, to be greatly attached to their young; and this was only another proof, of what has been often asserted, that there seems to be a kind of law implanted by nature in all animals, or rather they appear to be indued with an instinct, which, as it were, warns them to shun or fly from the face of man; and they will therefore rarely attack him, except when famished or provoked, or when they find that they cannot escape.

Occasionally, I had tolerably good fishing (though the fish caught were mostly small) in the Didroo-river, the waters of which are generally very clear and pure. Its bed is here and there rocky, and in some places the branches of the larger and more spreading trees, interwoven with beautiful flowering creepers of various kinds, and of agreeable perfume, form fine and lofty arches quite across its bed; so that, in these really splendid and shady retreats, it is usually as cool and pleasant, even at noon-day, as can be desired. As there are seldom any alligators so high up the river, the bathing in its deep pools, in which every thing can be distinctly seen, is excellent and truly refreshing; so much so, that we are often induced to remain in the water and swim about, longer than might be thought prudent; but, in a climate like this, and in such enchanting situations, who would not be equally tempted to run risks? And how much an enthusiastic admirer of fine sylvan scenery,—though it is mostly upon a diminutive scale—would be charmed with these wild recesses! In no part of the world, much of it as I have visited, have I ever beheld any thing so lovely as these fragrant and flower-decked dells! Taking advantage of such overhanging trees, the Kandyans have very ingeniously contrived, by means of the strong cable-like runner, almost everywhere to be found in the jungle, to suspend most curious and nerve-trying bridges across this and most other rivers; which, when flooded at the changes of the monsoons, become impetuous and otherwise impassable torrents. I have at such times crossed this roaring, foaming, and rapid river, by one of these truly frightful bridges, but I confess that I felt far from comfortable in doing so; yet the Kandyans—such is habit—both male and female, even with loads upon their heads or shoulder, trip along upon them, as they swing to and fro, as if perfectly unconcerned.

Sometimes, when fishing in the river, I have had my sport spoiled by the Malay sentinel, whom I always took care to post on such occasions in a situation from whence he could keep a good look-out, announcing to me the approach of elephants coming to drink, or that he had reason to suspect that a tiger or some other dangerous animal was rather too close to me. In such cases, I generally thought that "the better part of valour would be discretion"—yet, I must say, that these incidents rendered such fishing "interesting!"—My friend Mr. Farrell, from whom I borrow the expression, tells me, that his recreations of this kind are often rendered truly so, at the almost unknown streams in this part of the country; but he has not so much forbearance as I boast of, and, in most instances, likes to have a shot at the intruder upon his piscal amusements.

Upon an occasion of this kind, when I had been tolerably successful in fishing, I was informed by my sentinel, that a very ferocious looking buffalo was approaching. I therefore thought that I would give over fishing for that day, and take a walk down the generally shaded bank of the river, and endeavour to find a fountain, which I had been told was well worth seeing.

After nearly an hour spent in search of it, I at last came to an open space of fine green sward, close to the bank of the river, which was there delightfully shaded by some tall trees; in the midst of which was a circle, of about seven or eight feet in diameter, entirely covered with a brightly shining foliated substance, of a red and yellowish hue; and in the very middle of it, to my surprise and delight, I saw a beautiful diminutive jet d'eau, throwing up water of the same bright shining colour, fully three of four inches above the surface, and which fell, as it were, in a circle of little sparkling drops! I stood for some minutes really enchanted with the beauty of this extraordinary *fairy-well;* the water of which seemed full of gold particles. I therefore set to work, and strained out a small quantity of them, by pouring the water through my handkerchief; when to my increased delight, they looked "for all the world" like real gold-dust! Having made this discovery, I sent off one of the Malays to the bungalow for a quart bottle, intending to fill it with some of the *golden water;* and, in the mean time, having posted the other to look out, I continued, by the straining process, to collect more of the dust. When I was almost tired of waiting for him, the Malay returned, and having filled and carefully corked the bottle, we made the best of our way, as the sun was setting, towards the encampment.

The next day, I dispatched, by some coolies whom I was sending to Colombo for supplies, my precious bottle and a very small quantity of the dust, to a friend of mine, Dr. F——, who was skilled in mineralogy, as I knew but little of it myself, requesting that he would tell me what the beautiful substance, thrown up in the water, really was. His answer would have demolished all my castles, had I been building any;—it was "only the very finest specimen of *mica* he had ever met with."—I suspected this; but what I had seen before was either of a silvery white, or greenish colour. The fountain is, however, a very curious one, and its continuing to eject this beautiful foliated substance in its cold and otherwise limpid water is truly surprising; and had it been found in Ireland, or in any other country in which Romanism prevails, some saint would, no doubt, have long ago endowed it with many healing and purifying virtues.

Thus amused and variously occupied, time stole agreeably and imperceptibly away; but I ought now to mention, that such vast deluges of rain have for some time past fallen upon this side of the island, that the roads have thereby been so much injured, that Sir Edward Barnes is obliged to defer driving his curricle from Colombo, through Kurunagalla, to Kandy—the first vehicle of the kind which is to be allowed to run upon them—and the same cause has prevented all the new roads from being thrown open to the public. We are in hopes, however, that most of them will be ready in about another month. The labour upon them has been unavoidably great and compulsory.—No where in the East, and, perhaps, seldom in Europe, have undertakings of greater magnitude been accomplished at less expense, or in a shorter space of time. Modern philanthropists, and men ignorant of what was indispensably necessary, in the eyes of a superior genius, to promote the permanent welfare of Ceylon, and of its native population, as well as the interests of the British Empire at large, may think themselves justified in blaming Sir Edward Barnes, for taking advantage of ancient customs, in order ultimately to accomplish great national objects; but, I beg to ask such cavillers,—how could this valuable and important island ever otherwise, than by the plan adopted, have been open to improvements in agriculture, or to commercial advantages; and, may I not add, to the proffered blessings of Christianity?—For, we may be assured, that so long as the Kandyans remained independent within their strong-holds, or saw themselves so situated as at any time to be able to rebel with impunity; and were allowed to be still subject to the injurious restrictions imposed by religious prejudices and those of castes; nothing useful or beneficial could be effected among them. But when the importance of Ceylon will be better known—that is to say, when its position in the Eastern Ocean is fully undersstood, it will be evident, that it must be connected, by steam navigation, not only with Egypt, but also with that immense part of Asia to the eastward and northward, and with all the countries—which will be thereby greatly benefited—around the Persian Gulf, and those situated upon the now ascertained to be navigable river Euphrates, until it almost reaches the Mediterranean, with which a railway of fifty or sixty miles would connect it, probably below Antioch on the river Orontes; and it may be said, that it will also be connected with Africa and Europe. Then, indeed, its important position, and the advantages to be derived from its improved agriculture and commerce by European settlers, will be seen and duly valued;—and not till then will the enlarged views of a man like Sir Edward Barnes be properly comprehended and appreciated.

I do not come forward as the defender of either his plans or memory—I have no right or wish to be so: indeed, they require no defender; nor do I pretend that, at the time when I made these remarks, I foresaw what would be the result of the policy he so determinedly and wisely pursued. My sole object in venturing to make them, is to have the honour assigned to whomsoever it is due; (and Sir Edward Paget has much to lay claim to;) for, in truth, some of the panegyrists of those who have since governed Ceylon, are ready enough to attribute to them the now fast becoming evidently beneficial results of Sir Robert Brownrigg's, Sir Edward Barnes's, and Sir Edward Paget's measures. I may have already spoken in nearly the same high terms of Sir Edward Barnes's extraordinary exertions, because I felt impressed, at the time, with the conviction that he was doing every thing possible, in order to improve and benefit the whole island; and since I arrived in the Seven Korles, I have been better able, from what I saw going forward, (and in which I had to perform a part,) to draw conclusions that have been justified by results.

Our society here is, certainly, very limited; but a friend of mine, who commands in an exceedingly out-of-the-way and mountainous district, tells me, (and I give the information he affords for the benefit of those inclined to become settlers in the interior,) that, though still worse off, in this respect, than we are at Kurunagalla, he has many advantages over me in a pecuniary point of view.

He is, however, obliged almost entirely to devote himself to farming pursuits ; as upon his exertions in this way his family's daily food and comforts, in a great measure, depend ; for, as he remarks, "but little can be had in his part of the country from the people, for love or money." He has already from fifty to sixty cows, and thirty calves ; dozens of pigs and goats ; and numbers of geese, ducks, turkies, fowls, &c. He labours in his fields and garden, and he is an excellent gardener. His lady is there with him, and attends to the dairy and poultry, makes butter and even cheese, and *has an eye* to the eggs. She has likewise become experienced in rearing pigs. Their potatoes and cabbages are excellent, yet, in spite of all they can do, their sheep will neither thrive nor fatten ; but I am inclined to think, that they are all of the Jaffna breed, and that gram must be scarce. This is a strange life for a Military Chief and his lady to lead, but it cannot possibly, in such situations, be avoided for some time to come ; and it is more likely to make genuine *rurals* and keen sportsmen of most of us, than accomplished or experienced soldiers.

In going up to Kandy, Sir Edward Barnes stayed three days with us here, when he looked closely into every thing that we had done and were doing, but particularly at the roads ; and was pleased to approve of our exertions to meet his views and wishes. I find by my notes, made during his visit, that a very strange occurrence took place. An immense number of what were, by every one, supposed to be *mad jackals*, broke suddenly and furiously into the cantonment, and even dared to enter into some of the soldiers' houses, and also into my stables, in which, at the time, were Sir Edward Barnes's, and my horse-keepers, grass-cutters, and several coolies, some of whom were bitten most severely, before the animals could be killed or driven away by the soldiers, who, on hearing the cries of the servants, ran to their assistance. The medical gentlemen, who had accompanied the Governor on his tour of inspection, being providentially at hand, they instantly applied gunpowder to the wounds which the jackals had inflicted, which being ignited immediately gave them the appearance of having been seared with a hot iron. I never afterwards heard of any of the sufferers having been attacked with hydrophobia; so that this must either have been good surgical practice, or else the jackals, which had thus assailed these men, in such an extraordinary manner, and in the day time, were not under the influence of that terrible malady. A few days afterwards, having taken out his horse to exercise, my greyhound-like horse-keeper returned home in great haste, and in much alarm, to tell me, that a mad jackal had bitten the horse in the pastern. Upon examining it, I found that it had all the appearance of having been recently severely bitten, and, according to the plan I had seen pursued, I applied gunpowder to the part, and ignited it; and no symptoms of hydrophobia were ever perceived in my noble Arab. The terror throughout the country was, however, for the next three weeks or a month very great, for the jackals actually swarmed at the time in the neighbourhood; so much so, that no one liked to venture any distance either along the roads or into the woods, and all our doors and windows were most carefully closed, night and day, as long as the jackal panic lasted.

Badly as the troops in Ceylon are usually off in point of food, bedding, and what are looked upon as comforts, still, both officers and men, I may fairly say, are much better accommodated and supplied in the Seven Korles, than in any other part of the interior that I have visited, not even excepting Kandy. But, Lieutenant-Colonel Hook, who, I believe, was the first Commandant of the District, contrived to do much serious injury to this place, (and to what I am going to remark, I request the attention of settlers in Ceylon in general), by cutting down, under a mistaken notion of adding to its salubrity, many very fine and ornamental trees, that grew in great numbers and luxuriance, where the cantonment now stands, and which cannot be replaced for many years to come.

It may appear strange, that, in a land like this, of ever-green woods, we should regret the loss of trees; but many are of opinion—and whether they may prove to be right or not, time alone can shew—that they have found out the best way to keep the stations in the interior healthy; and their plan is, to preserve natural screens or defences of trees, so as to exclude certain winds, which are known to be occasionally noxious. It is now also supposed, that the unhealthiness of some posts was caused by their being placed on high grounds, where not a tree or a patch of jungle was left standing, to afford either shelter or shade. It is well known, that the changes of temperature, in such situations, even in a single night, are often very considerable, and very trying to the constitutions of many; so that to this ill-judged exposure we are inclined to attribute much of the sickness, which at times has shewn itself not only amongst the British, but also amongst what may be considered the native troops. We now, therefore, fix upon situations for cantonments, more after the manner in which the Kandyans choose the sites of their dwellings, than had been formerly the practice; that is to say, the most wooded parts of the country, where we clear away the low growing jungle immediately on the spot, leaving almost all the tall and spreading trees; so that, even at noon, the sun can have but little effect upon the ground, and the injurious suddenly chilling winds, which check perspiration, are likewise thus excluded. The reader may easily imagine, where any pains are taken to preserve ornamental trees, and attention is paid to simple sylvan embellishment, with the fine shrubs and flowers that are almost every where to be found, how delightful such retreats may be rendered in a country like this, where all natural productions thrive so luxuriantly. That excellent plan—(and let settlers also mark this,)—of making soldiers build their own houses or temporary barracks, ought never to be lost sight of, in any case where it is practicable. The Kandyans invariably, whenever fever, small-pox, or other diseases shew themselves among them, and when deaths have occurred, consider the part of the country they are residing in to be sickly, and therefore desert it *for the time*, and build new houses at some distance off, either in the mountains, or in a situation separated from their former abodes by hilly or rising grounds, when they usually find, that the disease, whatever it may be, disappears;—thus shewing, that it was confined to the spot which they had abandoned.

I have uniformly observed, that the natives, from what reason I do not pretend to be able to explain, always suffer from what are called jungle fevers, before Europeans are attacked by them. If this were more attended to, and the latter instantly removed to a distance, even in the same district, I have no doubt but that we should hear less of the effects of these formidable diseases. It is of little consequence deserting a parcel of, perhaps, old houses or huts, which had cost little or nothing in building, and the whole wood work of which had, very likely, been eaten through and through by white ants, and therefore might be supposed to require to be renewed every three or four years, and sometimes oftener; and I have always found, that soldiers considered their work upon such occasions as only an amusing employment, in a country where, unfortunately, they had too little to do that was useful, or calculated to break in agreeably upon the usual monotony of their lives.

I only waited until Sir Edward Barnes had left the district, in order to proceed, according to his wishes, upon a tour of inspection towards the north-east parts of the province; and I must say, that, much as I had heard of it, I found the country in that direction very beautiful, and in many respects superior to what I had been led to expect. During my progress, I was at one time not far from Fort Macdowall, where a friend of mine, Lieut.-Colonel S—— then resided, and had charge of the district of Matelé. According to the map, given at the commencement of this volume, which was furnished by an officer of the quarter-master-general's department, that district is divided from the Seven Korles by a range of seemingly thickly wooded mountains. As the roads, or rather paths, across them, were represented to be bad and rocky, I did not like, (chiefly on account of my horses' shoes, which could not have been replaced if worn out or lost so far from home,) to proceed to pay him a visit in his solitude; which otherwise I would have done, in order to see how he managed the Government elephant-catching establishment, of which he had there also the superintendence.

Ollegammé, one of the last villages of the Seven Korles in that direction, is really a charming place;

very delightfully situated at the foot of the mountain, in a fine hilly, and I should imagine if a little more cleared, healthy country, fit for many agricultural purposes, but especially for coffee plantations. About two miles from it, the side of a vast rock, partly covered and adorned with fine old trees, has been excavated and formed into temples; dedicated, I believe, to all the gods or demons worshipped or feared in Ceylon. I happened to arrive there at the time of a great annual festival; when a vast concourse of Kandyans of all castes, male and female, and of all ages, had assembled. I saw hundreds of them prostrate before their huge idols and strange paintings; and, I confess that, at the moment, I should have had no objection to set to work, and to have knocked to pieces the whole of the absurd objects of this worship. But, after all, this would have done no good; and these extraordinary temples may, perhaps, before many years have elapsed, be dedicated to the worship of the true God.

To arrive at the temples, we had to ascend a very steep stair—I may almost say a perpendicular one—cut out upon the face of the rock, of about two hundred feet in height; but, when we reached them, we were amply repaid, by the splendour of the views in all directions, for the labour we had had in climbing up to them. The Veharés pointed out to us, as those of Boodhoo, were the largest which I had, as yet, seen in Ceylon, and the images, as well as some of the curious paintings in them, were numerous; the former were, however, only rudely executed, but the colouring of the latter, though we were told that they were more than a thousand years old, was as brilliant as if only recently finished. I beg leave to give specimens here of some historical paintings of this description, by native artists.

These temples, being hewn out of the solid rock, are really well worthy of a visit from a traveller; for they must have been rendered what they are by the continued labour of thousands of men for many years. Upon two of them are inscriptions, in characters of which I had no knowledge, and I was told that even the priests themselves were unacquainted with them. They, as well as the people assembled, seemed to be very uneasy at our presence, especially at such a time; and some of the higher castes, who came out to me, were greatly alarmed, lest my large and fierce-looking dog Bran should be allowed to follow me into the temples, as they assured me he would pollute them. But, as I had no intention whatever of hurting their feelings, or of giving offence, I left him outside in charge of the Malays, by a party of whom I was attended upon this delightful journey.

The Kandyan ladies assembled upon this occasion, were, at first, and on our unexpected arrival, very much inclined to take to their heels; but, by degrees, their alarm seemed to subside; and some compliments which we contrived, through the person who acted as interpreter, to pay to the sable beauties, were soon well enough received. Curiosity

THE KING, ABOUT TO DIE, TELLS THE PEOPLE HIS LAST WISHES.

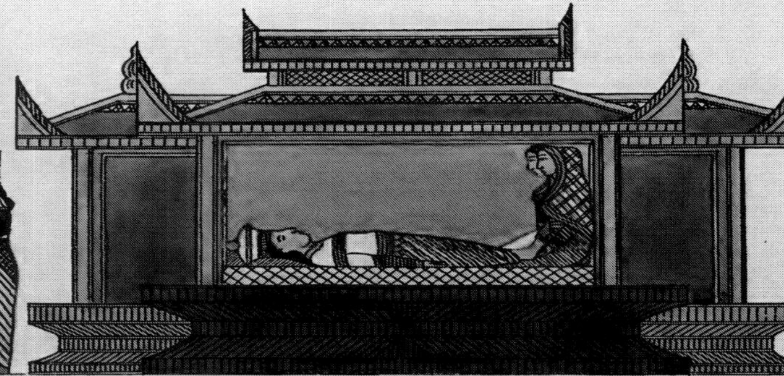

THE KING DEAD

Published by T and W Boone London 1843

P. Gauci, lith

THE KING'S TWO SONS MEET TO FIGHT FOR THE CROWN.

THE QUEEN & HER TWO CHILDREN. THE KING HEARING THE CASE OF A POOR MAN THE K

VING ALMS TO A POOR MAN

THE KING GIVING ALMS TO A POOR FAMILY.

(most of them having never before seen an European), at last quite overcame their terrors; especially when they saw, that we were not, by any means, such dreadful, cruel-looking animals, as they had been taught to suppose us. But, I am sorry to be obliged to acknowledge, that the conduct of some detachments of our troops, during the rebellion, had entitled them to much and deserved censure. The people of Ollegammé and its neighbourhood had, however, very inconsiderately fired upon some of our soldiers, on their march from Trincomalie, and they were severely punished for their temerity; but our troops had not then forgotten the massacre of their unfortunate comrades, who had been made, by Major Davie, so unwisely and with so much weakness of mind, to lay down their arms; which cruel and diabolical outrage was too long remembered and direfully avenged.

We were delighted with the views from these very ancient Rock-temples; and how truly impressive must all in and around them be upon the imaginations of such superstitious people as the Kandyans; for the priests of Ollegammé, like those in other parts of the world, evidently knew well how to select the most striking and awe-inspiring sites for their religious rites or incantations, as also for their abodes; taking care that they were surrounded, as in Portugal and other countries, by the finest and most fertile tracts of land. But the fertility of the soil, and its productive powers in fruits and vegetables of all kinds peculiar to Ceylon, and also in grain—there being abundance of water for irrigation—are truly surprising.

We remained one night at Ollegammé, and next morning, before dawn, we set off to cross a mountain ridge, of considerable height, in order to visit Eheylapola's large and delightful property and country residence; and from thence, after resting there the next night, we proceeded in a northerly direction, through, at first, a charming hilly country; but afterwards through what had many years ago been a fine and fertile plain, but was now become a desert, infested by elephants and other wild animals. This desolation had been, as the people wished me to believe, increased of late; for they pretend, that a good many of the natives of that part of the province, in order to avoid labouring without payment, had abandoned their dwellings, and gone off into the dreary country of Neurecalava, which lies to the northward, and is in many places an arid and almost trackless wilderness, extending towards Manar, and the Marre Waddie, on the north-east coast, and is most correctly described by Knox, as "full of wild elephants, tigers, and bears;" which, in times of extreme drought, that are frequent there, are forced to enter the more favoured parts of the country, where they commit great depredations in the cultivated lands; in some instances, totally destroying the crops. In this wilderness, these fugitives—they told me—suffered much from poverty and destitution, and were exposed to constant alarms and attacks from the wild animals; yet, they preferred enduring these annoyances to returning to their former abodes; for there they were not required to labour for their oppressors, as those who had remained were compelled to do. This is what I was told; but I suspect, that the Headmen are again playing their old game with the poor people, and are extorting from them whatever little substance or money they may possess, under the pretext of having them exempted from labouring upon the roads; so that those who could not pay, had no alternative but to do more than their proper share of the work, or to fly into the desert. They have thus not only been rendering us odious in the eyes of the Kandyans in general, but have also been keeping us, to suit their own views, entirely in the dark, as to the extent of the discontent produced by this, certainly, not unusual measure. I have thought it right to mention this to Sir Edward Barnes, who will, no doubt, have the circumstance inquired into; for if the amount of labour required for the roads was fairly distributed among the people, it would not by any means fall so heavy on this part of the province, as to produce such evils as those I have just alluded to, and which were brought secretly and cautiously to my notice; for the Kandyans are in great awe of their Headmen, and will rarely venture to come forward to complain openly of their injustice or extortions.

I find the foregoing as well as the following remarks among my notes, and I continue to give them almost verbatim.—The good people at home will no doubt be told of all the blessings which we are conferring upon the happy Kandyans, and how much they will be ultimately benefited, in being brought under our mild and paternal rule ; and that such are our intentions, there cannot be a doubt. At present, however, few or none of the natives understand or can appreciate our motives ; as their natural and confirmed habits, deep cunning and delight in deception, and their carelessness about religion of any kind, except where their worldly interests are concerned, render them quite unfit for and incapable of valuing the advantages of free institutions. How, indeed, can we look for this in such a people, when we have seen that neither the French, nor Spaniards, nor any other nations who have attempted to copy us, have been successful ;—but, on the contrary, have rather proved, that, like the Kandyans, they can only be managed by an absolute monarch or ruler. The United States of America are no exceptions ; as they are not yet blessed with a king or kings, possessing a wisely limited authority, but where is there to be found such absolute tyranny as that of the mob, which there, when it pleases, and in the name of freedom, supersedes the laws or annuls them ; indicating clearly, that a strong hand is required to restrain, and must sooner or later restrain, the people's unbridled licentiousness, or the most fearful results may be looked for. The arbitrary Kings of Kandy had for hundreds of years, and at their pleasure, called forth all the males for war, or for any great national undertaking; and they certainly often cut off the heads of the great men, whose ambitious views attached them to the court; but, according to the ideas of the people, these *trifling* severities appeared natural, or as only acts of retributive justice, and consequently were but little cared for; until so many, before unheard of, atrocities, committed by their last Rajah, particularly in destroying the family of one of the principal and most influential chiefs, roused and alarmed even the most apathetic. Such cruelties, in some degree, rendered him detestable in the eyes of his subjects; at all events, in those of many of the Headmen, who, it was believed, aimed at supplanting him; but he filled to the brim the measure of his folly and cruelty, when he dared to mutilate and treat in the barbarous manner he did persons under our protection. All these enormities, were considered good and sufficient reasons for our dethroning him, and for taking possession of the Kingdom of Kandy; but, if we do not perform what should, undoubtedly, be considered an imperative duty required of us, as a great and powerful nation, entrusted, for wise purposes, by Divine Providence, with the government of these people;—that is to say, if we do not endeavour, to the utmost of our power, to disseminate amongst them the pure and apostolical religion of the Church of England, we may yet have much to answer for. If this be neglected, the Kandyans, it may be supposed, would have been far happier, had they never seen the faces of Europeans. But, I lately heard a popular and influential preacher declare from the pulpit, that in no part of Scripture did it appear that any one was borne out in supposing that heathens could be saved, even though they had never heard the name of Christ. I was much struck at hearing such an assertion come from a Clergyman of the Church of England; and therefore began to consider if he was justified in making it, and in thus endeavouring to stir up a congregation to greater exertions in promoting the views of those who are so zealously engaged in sending Missionaries to all parts of the world. After much serious thought upon the subject, it appeared to me to be an undue limiting of the mercy and goodness of God; especially, when our Saviour himself had said, in speaking of the Pharisees, who would not believe in him;—"if ye were blind, you would have no sin: but now ye say, We see; therefore your sin remaineth." Now, whatever may be the will or intention of God as to the heathens, as he has not thought fit to divulge it, we should judge—if we may venture to judge—more charitably of their situation, knowing as we do, how gracious and merciful Our Heavenly Father is, and try to perform what is our undoubted and bounden duty;—that is to say, to do our utmost to have proclaimed to all men the glad-tidings of Salvation; "for the gifts and calling of God are without repentance. For as ye (the

Gentiles) in times past have not believed God, yet have now obtained mercy through their (the Jews') unbelief; even so have these also now not believed, that through your mercy they also may obtain mercy. For God has concluded them all in unbelief, that he might have mercy upon all. O the depth of the riches both of the wisdom and knowledge of God. How unsearchable are his judgments, and his ways past finding out."

CHAPTER VI.

"When sweet and blushing, like a virgin bride,
The radiant morn resum'd her orient pride;
When wanton gales along the vallies play,
Breathe on each flower, and bear their sweets away."

COLLINS.

AN UNUSUAL AND DANGEROUS ENCOUNTER WITH ELEPHANTS—DEER-SHOOTING; AND A SUDDEN AND AWFUL THUNDER STORM—CEYLON GARDENING—CULTURE OF TREES, SHRUBS, AND FLOWERS—FAILURE IN AN ATTEMPT TO PRODUCE GRAPES—CURIOUS AIR-PLANTS AND BEAUTIFUL FLOWERS—THE TALIPOT-TREE IN BLOSSOM—HINTS—A VISIT TO THE VILLAGE OF NAGAHAGEDRA—SPORTS IN ITS NEIGHBOURHOOD—A WASHERMAN CARRIED OFF BY AN ALLIGATOR—DEATH OF LIEUT. A—.—KOSPETA, AND THE MOUNTAINOUS COUNTRY AROUND IT, ETC.—THE NEW ROADS TO KANDY AND BADULLA—THE BEST MONUMENTS THAT COULD BE ERECTED TO THE MEMORY OF SIR EDWARD BARNES AND CAPTAIN DAWSON, ROYAL ENGINEERS—OBSERVATIONS—BUNGALOWS IN THE JUNGLE, ETC.—BEAUTIFUL BIRDS TO BE SEEN IN THE WOODS AROUND THEM—AN ADVENTURE WITH, AND A NARROW ESCAPE FROM, BUFFALOES—JOURNEY FROM KURUNAGALLA TO MANAR, IN ORDER TO BE PRESENT AT THE PEARL FISHING—DISAPPOINTMENT AS TO WHAT WAS TO BE SEEN—THE COUNTRY BETWEEN KURUNAGALLA AND PUTLAM SPOKEN OF AS FIT FOR AGRICULTURAL PURPOSES, ETC.

A FEW days after my return from the pleasant tour, of which I have spoken at the end of the last chapter, I had sent forward the two Malays to have the canoe ready for me, in a creek which I had pointed out to them. Leaving my horse with his keeper, at the usual place upon the road, I proceeded, with my gun in my hand, towards the lake, of which I have so often spoken; but I had only gone a short way, when I heard him calling loudly to me, evidently in great alarm, to come back. I instantly turned round, and began to run, in the hope of being in time to afford him assistance, if he stood in need of it; when, to my surprise, I heard a loud noise, which seemed to me to be occasioned by a drove of large animals rushing through the woods; and, before I could make out what they were, or decide as to what I ought to do, the great heads and trunks of three or four elephants appeared through the trees, coming along at a quick shuffling pace towards me!—I saw in a moment that I had no chance of being able to avoid them, as some others were at the moment passing both to right and left. I therefore had nothing for it, but to place myself as closely as I possibly could with my back against a large tree, and in such a position that the elephants could not see me till they were past or just passing. So, putting, in all haste, a brass ball into each of the barrels of my gun, there I stood, resolved to be passive, if the elephants did not mind me; but if they did, I certainly would endeavour to save my life, by firing into the brain of any assailant. I candidly confess, however, that I was much inclined to give up all hope of escaping, and consequently felt far from comfortable as to what might be the result. On they came, breaking or treading down the jungle that stood in the way. I think I reckoned sixteen or seventeen of them, young and old; I therefore wonder how I could have maintained the presence of mind I did under such circumstances!—I must however say, that seeing in the herd two young ones gave me some hopes that they would not be inclined for hostilities. I am quite certain, that two or three of the huge creatures saw me; yet, forward they all shuffled, and, apparently, did not consider it worth their while to harm me. But, when they had all passed, I felt more strongly than can, perhaps, be imagined, what a narrow escape I had had!—I first thanked God for my deliverance; and then, without well knowing what I was doing, took to my heels, and in a few minutes got into the road, where I found that my horse-keeper could scarcely manage to hold the horse, so much had he been terrified (for horses and elephants, as I before remarked, have a natural antipathy to each other), at the sudden appearance of such a large herd which had crossed the road within thirty yards of them. Seeing that they were proceeding through the jungle, in the very direction which I had taken, the horse-keeper thought the best thing he could do was to call me back, and thus, in his confusion, he caused me to run into the midst of them.

Finding that they had now taken a direction away from the lake, I desired the horse-keeper, who was greatly frightened, to go home with his charge, and I again set off to join the Malays; who, though they had seen none of the elephants, had become very uneasy at my having been so long in coming to them. But, as the curlews had just begun to arrive at the lake, I set to work, and soon brought down more of them than we could well manage to carry home with us. I must here remark, that had my safety in this instance, (as it did before in the case of the tiger) depended upon my gun's going off, I should not have been disappointed: indeed, I never now go any where without my "*Joe Manton.*"

One most enchanting evening, my sporting ally, Captain K— and I set off in search of some deer, which we had heard were then in an open space in the woods, considerably to the right of the Trincomalie road. Before we had penetrated very far, we saw at a distance, through a kind of vista, three or four animals, which, from their appearance, we supposed to be elks. This encouraged us to push on through the jungle; but, knowing how cautious they usually are, we took care to keep in Bran, lest he should alarm them before we could get sufficiently near to have a shot at them. In our eagerness and anxiety to effect our object, and having to go a long way round, we had not paid attention to a great change that had taken place in the appearance of the sky; and, just at sunset, it suddenly, and to our astonishment, became almost as dark as night! We had scarcely observed this change, before vivid flashes of lightning lit up the forest for a moment in the most brilliant manner imaginable, and then tremendous peals of thunder —tropical thunder—were heard above and around us, followed by darkness that, indeed, might be felt! Rain came down in torrents, so that water and fire seemed, as it were, amidst the most awful reports of thunder, fearfully mixed or jumbled together.—Even my usually daring dog was terrified, and began to howl.

We scarcely knew where we were, or how to steer, so as to find our way home;—all we could be certain of was, that we were about four miles from Kurunagalla; but how to get back into the road was the difficulty. Suddenly, a most splendid flash of lightning displayed to our view the rocky mountains which are close to the cantonment. This most dazzling flash, which was quickly followed by others, in some measure enabled us to direct our course towards our home; but we were aware that we had fully two miles of jungle to pass through, and it was not unlikely but that there might be elephants and other animals between us and the cantonment. Our hope, however, was, that the awful night, which, no doubt, had forced every bird, beast, or insect, to seek for shelter, would have compelled them to remain in the depths of the forest.

Becoming at last uncertain whether we were moving in the right direction or not, it struck me, that it would be well to try to induce my dog to take the lead, having before seen him evince great instinct, when I had lost my way in the jungle. This a little encouragement made him do. To my great delight, he seemed to guide us admirably and confidently; never going more than three or four yards in advance, and constantly looking back, as if to see that we were following him. We had some time before put brass balls into our guns; but though we had done every thing we could think of, in order to keep the water from the locks, we were soon convinced, that we could place no confidence whatever in them.

The storm increased, and we were now often up to our middles in the streams that were rushing along in the usually dry water-courses, which we had frequently to cross; yet not being by any means disheartened, we were able to bear up against the deluges of water, which continued to fall and flow in torrents around us. But, "the war of elements" ceased almost as suddenly as it had commenced. The moon forced herself through the vanishing clouds, and we had no longer any difficulty in finding our way, except what the greatly increased floods in the new water-courses presented; as they ran rapidly across or along our path, often with so much strength as almost to deter us from attempting to proceed. Bran had, however, been an excellent guide, and had led us in a most direct line towards the cantonment; where we at last arrived, in a most doleful plight, at about half-past seven. This was a short, but by far the most awful thunder-storm that I had ever been exposed to, in any part of the world; and I assure the reader, that such a terrific scene as I that night beheld cannot be soon or easily forgotten.

I am now become, (and I wish those intending to settle in Ceylon to attend to what I am going to mention), more an enterprising than a plodding or pains-taking gardener; and, although I sometimes make mistakes, and even blunder in so strange a way as, perhaps, to astonish wiser and more experienced amateurs, yet I contrive to pass my time pleasantly enough, and in a way rather useful than injurious to my neighbours.

I now manage to have in abundance tolerably good vegetables; such as cabbages, (though they seldom heart well), peas, beans, lettuces, endive, onions, leeks, and some others; but, if I expect that any of them are to come to perfection, I must have constantly fresh supplies of seed from England, and especially from the Cape of Good Hope. I also grow other vegetables peculiar to the country and climate, especially the brinjal, of which there are several kinds; and in these I never fail. It is, besides, a great source of amusement to watch how rapidly even a cabbage comes to maturity in this part of the world. I often try experiments, though I know that I am sometimes laughed at for so doing. I transplant, I prune, and propagate, many a beautiful tree, shrub, and flower, by means of layers, suckers, and seeds; most of them gathered even in the wilderness; and I am now thinking of attempting budding and grafting. I often practise taking off large branches from some kinds of trees, so as to form new ones, according to the Eastern plan, by causing water continually to drop upon matting bound round the part of a branch, into which a sufficient incision has been made, and where, in a short time, a good root is formed. The branch is then entirely sawed off, and, being planted in the place intended for it, we have, at once, a handsome tree of the same kind, producing the same fruit or blossoms as that from which it was taken. I likewise lop off large branches, particularly from the tulip-tree, which bears such beautiful yellow, tulip-shaped flowers, and grows to the height of seventy or eighty feet. They take root immediately, especially if planted during the wet seasons, and flower like the parent tree; so that the reader may imagine how easy it is to ornament or shade, as fancy dictates, a favourite spot, which we may select, in this land of ever-green trees, shrubs, and lovely flowers; where we can so soon create what the poet probably only imagined, when he tells us that

> "I know a bank whereon the wild thyme blows,
> Where ox-lip and the nodding violet grows,
> Quite over-canopy'd with lush woodbine,
> With sweet musk-roses and with eglantine."

But, the flowering tulip-trees, when intermixed with the darker leaved jacks, paler acacias, tall palms and tapering bamboos, as well as with those beautiful trees, usually covered with white, scarlet, and other coloured blossoms, so common in Ceylon forests, produce, where their foliage can be tastefully combined, a most striking and delightful contrast.

I frequently go with coolies into the forest or jungle, to look for and bring home various kinds of shrubs, lovely flowers, and runners; particularly those, with which they abound, that smell and look so like jasmine; but I regret, as I am neither a scientific botanist nor florist, that I cannot venture to describe, or even attempt to give the reader an idea of, the size, splendour, and beauty of many of these shrubs and flowers; especially of the varieties of the water-lily kinds, which are here magnificent! I also collect bulbs and seeds, (some of them were sent, by a friend of mine to the Botanical Gardens, in Dublin, where, I heard, they grew and promised to do well), and I have now people employed enclosing some ground, extending from the Commandant's house to a small brook that runs through a sort of meadow behind it, which I intend for a shrubbery and nursery. I am, however, badly off for books upon gardening, &c.; but, if I even went to the expense of getting them from England, they might be of little use here, where the growth of every thing is so surprisingly rapid, and the nature of the soil, in most places, is so different from those at home, that it requires, though seemingly not rich, little or no manure. This being the case, I might very likely be more puzzled than benefited by the hints or directions of European horticulturists and florists. I, at this moment, pride myself upon some splendid rhododendrons, brought from the mountains close to this; and also on a few very fine Egyptian gold-melons, the first of the kind introduced into the interior; and, I have not heard of their having been cultivated upon the coast. The seed I used came from the Isle of France; which it may, perhaps, surprise the reader to hear, is considerably hotter than Ceylon, although so much farther from the equator, and such high encomiums have been passed upon its delightful climate by St. Pierre and other writers.

As for pine-apples, I had almost omitted mentioning them; for they are now, I may say, as "common here as blackberries" are at home, so much so, that I have my pigs fed upon them; as I fancied, that they gave that particularly fine flavour to their flesh, usually remarked by my visitors. In growing them, we have only to screw out the tops of the finest brought to table, and plant them in any part of the garden, where, in a short time, they become as large and as fine pine-apples, as are to be found in any part of the world.

I find by Mr. Bennett's "Manual," to which I have several times referred, that he had been successful in introducing vines into Ceylon, which produce grapes in almost any part of it; but, at the time I made these memoranda, it was believed that the vine would only bear grapes in the province of Jaffna; and, having had some good plants sent to me from thence, I thought I would try what could be done here. After due deliberation, I set to work, (the plants had been some months in the ground,) as taught in a book, that I had read some time before, written by Mrs. Graham; who has taken a good deal of pains to shew how an artificial winter may be produced in a tropical country. I began, as directed, by leaving the roots of the vines during the cold or rather rainy season exposed to its influence, and attached to the ground by only the slightest fibres of the roots. At the proper time, I covered them up; previously manuring, as directed, with bullock's blood. But, let the reader only conceive my astonishment, when I saw that my vines, the most luxuriant in growth I ever beheld, were, to speak figuratively, inclined to run away from me; so amazingly rapid were the powers of vegetation thus strongly excited or produced! The shoots spread themselves out quickly in every direction; and having, apparently, overgrown themselves, the whole of them died down to the very roots, one after another, in a few days. Not being, however, easily deterred from any object I have in view, and notwithstanding this complete failure, I intend to make another attempt before I give up the point as hopeless, but I shall not again use manure of any kind; for, I should greatly like to enjoy the cooling breezes under the shade of a grape-producing vine, as well as under that of my own fig-trees; the fruit of which I have also in the greatest profusion and perfection, which, if gathered early in the morning, will be found to be both agreeable and wholesome, especially at breakfast.

I have found in the woods many pretty and curious air-plants; also both red and white roses, scented like those of England; and I believe I have likewise found what Knox calls hop-mauls; which are flowers produced by trees that have no leaves, and bear nothing else but flowers. They are very sweet-scented, much sought after, and highly valued by the young Kandyans, who adorn themselves with them upon particular occasions. These beautiful and extraordinary trees grow in situations such as are described by Shakspeare—

> "Where honey-suckles, ripened by the sun,
> Forbid the sun to enter; like to favourites,
> Made proud by princes, that advance their pride
> Against the power that bred it."

This season, a great and very unusual number of these magnificent and valuable trees called talipot have blossomed; most of them so splendidly, that I have been induced to ride miles to examine and admire them. The leaves of these fine trees, of which I have several that I use in excursions, are very light and fold up like a fan into a small compass; but being opened out to their full extent, they form almost a complete circle; when some of the largest will, I have no doubt, cover at least twenty-five men, if standing close together under them. I beg here to remark, that these leaves are usually cut into pieces of a certain size, and are carried by the people to protect them from both the sun and rain; and in the times of the Kandyan kings their soldiers always used them, not only for the above purposes, but also to sleep under at night. Many parts of Ceylon, and the continent of Asia, produce great numbers of these trees. As it is of the utmost importance, that troops upon a march, and especially at night when in the field, should be properly protected from the powerful heat of the sun, and also from the heavy dews and the rain which falls periodically, and in Ceylon sometimes suddenly and in seasons when it is not looked for, what I have just remarked ought to serve as a hint to our rulers in both countries, who ought, surely, to be anxious to preserve the health of the troops placed at their disposal. To find means for the conveyance of tents, for even a single regiment, is often, in the East, found to be no easy task; and, after all, they are of no use whatever to the soldier upon the march. I am aware, that officers are laughed at for using umbrellas; but, notwithstanding this is thought such an unmilitary practice, most of them do so when they are not under the eye of an absurd Martinet. I know, too, that of old it would have been imagined that a corps was totally ruined, if one of its officers had dared to set such an unsoldierlike example, as that of protecting himself, by any means, from the sun or rain. But the time for these absurd prejudices is pretty well gone by. At all events, if it were only for convenience as to conveyance, and in an economical point of view, it would be well to ascertain, how many entire talipot leaves would balance a tent, especially when it is wet with rain or dew, upon a camel's or bullock's back.

Like those we see in different kinds of palms, these immense leaves grow only at the tops of the tall talipot-trees, which are said not to bear fruit until they are about a hundred years old, when the tops, as it were, expand and elevate themselves to a considerable height, decked in a quantity of large and very pale yellow blossoms, like branches upon the stem of a fir-tree, and thus form the largest and most magnificent flowers imaginable, but which have an exceedingly heavy and disagreeable smell; perceptible for a considerable distance around the place where they grow. The fruit, or rather seeds, which are about the size of small plums, are next produced in vast quantities; and as soon as they arrive at maturity, the tree begins, gradually, to decay, and soon after dies. I have had a considerable number of the ripe seeds of the talipot-tree brought to me, and have planted them, in various parts of the jungle, in the hope that they will grow. In concluding these remarks, I must assure the reader, that, if ever he has the opportunity, it would be well worth his while to walk even twenty miles, to see one of these magnificent trees towering in full blossom over the forest!

In the direction of Negombo, and about fourteen miles from Kurunagalla, there is a miserable village called Nagahagedra, around which, for some distance, the country is looked upon as unhealthy, as its inhabitants are occasionally subject to severe attacks of jungle fever; and it is, therefore, rarely visited by Europeans. Having, however, been told that in its neighbourhood I should certainly have excellent sport, especially snipe and water-fowl shooting; and as in a tour of inspection, which I was about to make, it would be necessary for me to stay for a night or two somewhere in that direction; I had a bungalow built there for my accommodation, as well as for that of any friends who might be inclined to accompany me. Captain K— and a Lieutenant A—, of the 83d Regiment volunteered to be of the party; but the character of the country being pretty well known, and the latter having his wife, a very ladylike person, then at Kurunagalla with him, I was surprised, yet pleased, at his offering to accompany me; for he was both an intelligent and an agreeable companion. At this season, however, it was thought, by the natives, that we had nothing to apprehend from sickness, and we had, besides, every right to look forward to having fine weather.

The sport around Nagahagedra was so good, that we were tempted to prolong our stay there; for I might fairly talk of the snipes we killed, not in numbers but in bag-fulls. The reader may therefore easily imagine, what quantities of powder and shot were blazed away; as we all three, and often without being able to avoid doing so, fired into dense flocks of them. In short, in no part of Ceylon had I ever seen so many snipes; and as for water-fowl, there were a good many of them also, though they were by no means so numerous as at the lake near Kurunagalla; but where, I hear, they are now by no means so plenty: indeed, I did my best to kill and drive away too many of them.

After breakfast, one of the servants came into the room where we were sitting, to ask if I would see a native, who had something "plenty bad," as he said, to tell me. Upon his being admitted, he informed me, through the servant who interpreted, that he and all the males of his family were washermen;—that one of his brothers, only two days before, when busily employed in his calling, by the side of a deep pond, close to the village, and in the act of beating the clothes he was washing, as is their custom, against a large stone upon which he stood, had been suddenly seized by an enormous alligator, within five yards of where my informant was similarly occupied, and dragged, in a moment, down to the bottom!—He and his family would, therefore, be greatly obliged to us, if we would shoot this dangerous and terrible creature; which, in the heat of the day, usually lay basking in the sun near the edge of the pond, into which it always plunged the instant it heard the least noise. He added, that he was sure the alligator must now be there, and I should certainly see it, if I would only go to the spot; for there was a patch of jungle close to the pond, from whence he could point it out to me, without its being able to see us.

Of course, in order to make sure of the fellow, my "Manton" was instantly loaded with my best powder and brass balls. My two companions readily accompanied me to the spot which the washerman had mentioned; but, lest we should alarm the cautious alligator, he only went with me to the point from whence I was to see him. Sure enough, there lay the huge creature, not a dozen yards from me!—At first, I thought that what he pointed at was only the large trunk of a tree, thrown down and still retaining its rough brownish bark; it was, certainly, by far the largest alligator that I had seen. I now rested my gun against a tree, took deliberate aim at his head, and fired; then, as he tumbled over, in the act of rolling off the bank into the water, (which he did with a great splash,) I sent the other ball through his body. He instantly sunk to the bottom; but the change in the colour of the water, which was too dark to admit of our seeing to any depth, plainly indicated that it was tinged with blood. My two friends, and a number of people who had followed us, now ran up to us; but, great was their disappointment, when I could only assure them, that the alligator would certainly be found dead at the bottom of the pond. Long poles, &c. were, therefore, sent for; but, though we poked about for some time, it was all in vain,—we could not find him; and, as the heat at the time was excessive, we thought it best to return to the bungalow. The natives, however, persevered in the search, and at last got him out; but when he was opened, no vestige whatever, not even a bone of the unlucky washerman, was to be found in his stomach. It is more than probable, however, that there were other alligators in the pond; and although this fellow, from apparent age, size, and habits, was believed to have been the culprit, yet he, like many an honest creatúre, may have suffered for the guilty. Be this as it may, I intend, the next time I go to Nagahagedra, to take the small alligator spear or harpoon with me, which I brought from Galle; and to construct some sort of a raft, if I cannot procure a canoe, to go upon the pond in search of the game, and I have no doubt of having good sport.

I need scarcely mention, that this is not a part of Ceylon to which I wish to direct the attention of settlers; unless, as a great national undertaking, the Didroo river was to be led (as I mean to point out hereafter), through it; when, no doubt, as much of the country would, I conclude, be cleared of jungle, and the noxious stagnant water, in the numerous ponds, be swept away by it in its course to the sea, this part of the province would then be not only rendered healthy, but also surprisingly fertile.

On our way back to Kurunagalla, Mr. A—— told me, that the report of his gun, when he fired, shook and annoyed him a good deal; for his head-ached, and he did not feel himself well. I therefore strongly urged upon him the necessity of his procuring, as soon as possible, medical advice. This I conclude he did; for, a few days after, the Surgeon called upon me to report, that he considered Mr. A——, to be in great danger; as the fever, with which he had been attacked, could not be subdued. He therefore thought, as a last resource, that he ought immediately to be removed to the sea coast. He was consequently sent off, accompanied by his greatly alarmed and sorrowing wife; (both in palanquins) attended by their servants, and also by the Surgeon, as far as I could permit him to go with them. But, alas! poor A——'s days were numbered; for he died soon after reaching Colombo. This is, I grieve to say, too often the melancholy termination of what are called jungle fevers; which, I am convinced, can only be avoided by not going into, or instantly leaving, the part of the country where they prevail.

The district of the Seven Korles, towards Kandy, terminates at the Kospeta-oya; which is a furious torrent during the wet seasons. We have there built a good rest-house, with convenient offices attached to it, for travellers. I before observed, that Kurunagalla stands near the commencement of the Kandyan mountains; and as the road is judiciously laid out, and gradual in ascent the whole way to Kospeta, nothing can be more delightful than the ride to it. This post is situated on a rising ground, encompassed by lofty wooded mountains, the appearance of which often reminded me of many parts of the Pyrenees. It is really difficult to conceive, what a difference of climate there is, between the neighbourhood of Kospeta and the low level country beyond Kurunagalla. Colombo and the latter are not much unlike in this respect, but Kospeta is by many degrees cooler than either of them; so much so, that at times, I could almost have fancied, especially when standing on some of the elevated ridges, that I was in England. I, therefore, the reader may well suppose, go occasionally thither to be refreshed and invigorated by the bracing and cooling breezes, as well as to ramble, without restraint, amidst the beautiful, wild and imposing scenery, which very traveller must admire; especially as he proceeds towards and beyond Madawellatenné, and how strikingly grand, rugged, and finely wooded, are the precipitous rocks, mountains and ravines, down which in the rainy seasons vast bodies of water dash and roar in all directions, forming in many points of view cascades of the most picturesque description! This fine and wild scenery extends, I may say, almost the whole way to Kandy; but though the climate is cool and excellent, yet any attempts at bringing the country under cultivation, except for coffee, for which there are here and there favourable spots, would be far too expensive for any settlers to attempt. This, indeed, as I have before remarked, is the case with a vast proportion of the extensive mountainous regions in the interior; where the want of good roads (there are, I may say, none but the great ones) must, I fear, ever be an insuperable barrier to agricultural pursuits amongst them. The natives, certainly, in some places, grow small patches of rice, on the kind of terraces I have already spoken of, to which they contrive to convey the numerous brooks, the waters of which are all they require to be certain of having good crops. But all these tributary rivulets precipitate themselves into the Kospeta, which, after flowing rapidly through a very wild country, unites its waters with the Didroo-oya at Beddegammé, a very finely situated and delightful village; around which and indeed all through the hilly and almost impassable tracts I have alluded to, there is much excellent land, fit, if there were only roads, for many agricultural purposes. But the laying out and making such a noble high-way as that from Kospeta to Kandy, must, I conceive, be readily acknowledged, by those who have travelled along it, to have been an undertaking worthy of the enterprising and lofty genius of a Napoleon; and will, I trust, endure for ages, as the best and most appropriate monument, which could possibly have been erected, to the memory of Sir Edward Barnes and Captain Dawson of the Engineers, whose daring and energetic minds, robust frames, and manly habits, were so admirably calculated for carrying on, amidst innumerable difficulties, such a gigantic undertaking. But the road that has been carried from Kandy to Badulla, in Upper Ouvah (and from thence since extended to Horton plains and Neuwara Ellia), was attended in its formation with even greater difficulties. The whole of these stupendous works, do, at the same time, infinite credit to all the engineers and other officers employed upon them; many of whom were severe sufferers from the effects of exposure to all weathers, in situations far from congenial to men whose constitutions were not then inured to the trying vicissitudes of climates, not only in the lower flat, but also in the mountainous countries, in which, in quick succession, the scenes of their operations lay. It may be said, that, with the exception of the engineers, all the officers so employed were volunteers—no doubt, that was the case; but, what will not British officers undertake, when an example is set them by an energetic and admired commander?

The great objects in view, at whatever sacrifice of health to those employed, have at last been accomplished; and all attempts at rebellion, on the part of the Kandyans, must hereafter be as hopeless as fruitless. Neither their numbers nor their courage were ever by any means formidable;—the inaccessible nature of their country, and in some places its climate, were their only defence and security; and I believe, I may now confidently say, that thus a charming and most valuable island, almost equal in size to Ireland, has been permanently added to Her Majesty's dominions.

Imagining that nothing is so conducive to health, in every part of the world, as frequent changes of air and scene, I have had constructed, besides the bungalow that I have often mentioned, one on the Mongra-oya, about nine miles from Kurunagalla, to the left of the old Putlam road; and another upon the lower Didroo; but, although there is, sometimes, tolerably good fishing and excellent shooting in the neighbourhood of both; yet, they have been built in much too hot situations, to be either agreeable or, perhaps, healthy, though they are very lovely abodes. We, however, did our best to preserve as much shade as possible, by only very sparingly thinning the trees, most of which grew there to a great height; and amongst them, there are generally to be seen many most beautiful birds, which I occasionally shoot for the sake of their feathers. But, being ignorant of the art of preserving and stuffing them, except by using camphor, or by keeping them in camphor-wood trunks, which we get from China, I have not hitherto thought it worth my while to add much to my collections, which I intend hereafter sending as presents to England.

At these bungalows, birds of various kinds are exceedingly numerous, as is always the case in the neighbourhood of rivers and lakes; and also in places where the country is or has been cultivated. In the more retired parts of forests or jungle, they are scarce and usually very wild. I sometimes shoot the curious and exceedingly noisy toucan, which has such an enormous bill when compared with its diminutive body; both of which are finely striped with yellow, red, and sky-blue; also a bird in some degree resembling our black-bird, only it is considerably larger, and its plumage is like the most soft and glossy velvet. I am not acquainted with its name, nor did I ever hear it utter any kind of note. Another very beautiful bird often attracts my attention; it is about the size of the jay, with a black and white head, its throat is of a light blue, its breast greyish, its back and wings are of a beautiful purple, and about half an inch of the end of its tail is white. There is another bird, nearly of the same size, which utters a strange shrill sound as it sits on the loftiest branches of trees, particularly the ebony tree; its head, back and breast, are of a very bright green; its tail of different shades of very deep and bright green, with a broad black stripe across it, and it is tipped with white; its belly is of a kind of vermilion colour, and separated from its greenish breast by a white and black stripe.

In my notes, taken at the last-mentioned bungalow, I see that I attempted to describe—but, I may say, it was a complete failure—that extraordinary creature the flying-squirrel; as well as several fine birds, the beautiful and striking plumage of which had also attracted my notice; but, I find that those destructive pests, the white ants, have eaten through, and otherwise so much injured the paper, that I cannot make out the writing; all that is now legible, are some remarks respecting the Ceylon bird of Paradise, with its beautiful plumage and long white tail; the extremely loud noises caused by the numerous wood-peckers striking the trees; and the unceasing screaming of gorgeously adorned parrots and paroquets; and I add, what may be a useful hint, that my cook was in the constant habit of making excellent pies of the latter, as well as of the pretty grey and pinkish coloured turtle-doves. There were also vast numbers of bitterns of various kinds; and I am inclined to think, that what we call paddy-birds, with such pure white and horsehair-like plumage, ought to be classed with bitterns.

During a visit I lately made to the bungalow on the lower Didroo, one of my Malay orderlies was very nearly killed by a herd of buffaloes. Indeed, I, as well as the other Malay, had a most narrow escape from them. Early in the morning, we had gone down the river, and had passed through some fine park-like scenery, looking for deer; when we suddenly and unexpectedly came upon six or seven of these dangerous animals, which instantly charged us in the most furious way possible! We, for a moment, stood facing them; shouting loudly, and holding our guns pointed at them; but, as that did not stop their headlong career, I saw nothing for it but to fire; which I did, and knocked over one of them. Even this did not check the others; so that we had then no alternative but to take to our heels, and endeavour to get up into trees. This one of the Malays and I effected; but the other, missing the branch he sprung up to lay hold of, was, as I greatly feared, left completely at the mercy of two terrific male buffaloes, which tried to gore him. He, however, the next moment, made a second violent spring towards our tree; when we, fortunately, caught his arm and just saved him, by pulling him up into the branches, amongst which we were safely seated, and out of their reach. Two more of them were severely wounded before they could be beaten off, and before we could venture down to secure the one which I, at the first fire, had knocked over. This, I confess, was too perilous, to be considered either "interesting" or agreeable shooting.

I have another bungalow, built by the Malays and my servants, which is also rather hotly, yet beautifully, situated in the green-wood, in a very retired part of the country, close to the Didroo, and a very little way above where it is joined by the Mongra-oya. To reach it, I have to go by the way of Eregoddé, in order to get round the wooded rocks that extend from Kurunagalla towards the northward; and from thence turning to the right, and passing through patches of jungle, and amongst many fine trees, some of them bearing fruits of different kinds, whilst others are only in blossom, we arrive at the river, in which I have, at times, very good fishing. But the surrounding country is so very wild, and much infested by elephants and other animals, that I never go there without a guard of Malays, who are always ready and delighted to join in sylvan sports of any kind. But, though due attention is paid to have large fires prepared there, rarely a night passes, without our being roused and obliged to stand to our arms.

There is a good rest-house at Hondellé, about eight miles from this, on the new Colombo road, at the entrance of an extensive forest, where I occasionally go for a day's amusement; but my command extends nine miles farther on, to the Maha-oya, upon the left bank of which stands Allow, admitted to be one of the most beautiful stations in this charming island. A house of a superior description has lately been built there, in a well selected situation, commanding extensive and delightful views over a truly enchanting and fertile country. It is intended that the Governor shall reside occasionally there. But formerly, it was thought by many to be almost certain death, for any one to spend even a single night upon the splendidly-wooded banks of the Maha-oya, especially about fifteen miles lower down than Allow, where the old road, or rather path, crosses it; so prevalent was jungle fever said to be there. I cannot undertake to say that this may not still be the case; for the place is now carefully avoided by travellers; but Allow is looked upon, as yet, to be a perfectly healthy station.

We are, however, told, that some years ago, a company of light infantry, upon its march to Colombo, from a post in the interior, halted for the night on the bank of this river, at the place to which the old road leads; but, almost every one of them who slept there was immediately after taken ill, and, with the exception of a few who partially recovered, but had to be sent to England, the rest fell a sacrifice to the fearful effects of jungle fever. There are other places which are considered to be equally sickly, through which I have occasionally to direct the march of troops, who are proceeding to the east side of the island; but in the routes, with which they are furnished at Kurunagalla, I always take care to mention distinctly, that the men are upon no account to be allowed to halt at any of them, but to go on five or six miles farther; and though this precaution lengthens the day's march, yet it cannot, according to the prevailing opinion, be safely or prudently neglected. That most enchanting country which surrounds the large artificial lake of Minery is one of them; I however intend, before long, visiting that part of Neurecalava. Lower Ouvah, and also the greater part of the province of Wellassey, are also said to be, at times, unhealthy; I have therefore already spoken of them as parts of the island which settlers should avoid going into, at least, until they are, to some extent, cleared of the low-growing jungle.

The detachments of troops, to which I have alluded, as marching from this province towards the east side of the island, rarely get through the country without meeting with alarming and untoward adventures. Not long ago, a non-commissioned officer and fifteen men were attacked by elephants, close to Minery lake, and were so completely dispersed, that they could not be again assembled till the following day; one soldier was killed on the spot, and two others severely hurt. Such accidents, however, more frequently occur in unlooked-for rencounters with buffaloes, which not only use their horns, but also their strong fore-feet, with which they deal terrible blows.

Being thus, perhaps, too much engaged in amusing and interesting occupations, excursions, and sylvan sports of all kinds, many months now stole imperceptibly away. I went to Manar at the season of the pearl fishing, which takes place in the bay of Candachy; but of this I shall only remark, (so much having already been said by several writers upon the subject,) that I was greatly disappointed in what I saw, in the number of people assembled, and also in the produce of the fishery. In this journey, I was accompanied only by my own people; and, travelling by short and easy stages, I reached the sea-coast, skirted as usual by cocoa-nut trees, at Putlam, and kept the road by the sea-shore the remainder of the way to Manar; from whence I intended to have returned by the very ancient city of Anarajahpoora, in the hope of being able to visit its ruins, as well as those said to be scattered all over the country in its neighbourhood. But I was dissuaded from proceeding by that route, in consequence of Neurecalava being represented as then very sickly; and I was also assured, that, during the arduous journey I wished to undertake, we might expect constantly to fall in with wild beasts of all kinds. This so alarmed and disheartened my servants, that I had reluctantly to give up the idea of proceeding in that direction.

I performed the greater part of this, on the whole, pleasant journey on horseback, often shooting and otherwise amusing myself, as my people went quietly along the road or path; but especially as we passed through, I may say, the fine country that lies between Kurunagalla and Putlam, (a distance of sixty-two miles,) and particularly about a small village called Bogallegammé, near to which we crossed two sluggish rivers; which, after uniting their waters with that of the Didroo-oya, flow into the sea at Chilaw. A great deal of this country consists of the park-like scenery I have often alluded to, skirted or surrounded by large and dense masses of jungle, in which, no doubt, there were many wild animals, though we saw very few of them. It is, however, in many places, capable of being greatly improved by cultivation, if the waters of the rivers passing through it, in place of being allowed to run almost uselessly into the sea, were judiciously distributed for the purposes of irrigation; but this could only be done at the public expense, with the view of extending agriculture, and thereby increasing the insular revenue derived from it.

In crossing the two rivers I have above spoken of, as uniting their waters with those of the Didroo, I regretted not having brought fishing-tackle with me, for they both looked as if they contained large fish; indeed, we saw a few good sized ones, and perhaps I might have found in them some of those spoken of by Knox, who says, that "the people, who are very ignorant of the art of fishing with nets or lines, frequently caught them of the size of salmon," particularly in what he calls the Mavelaganga. The quantities of fish, however, in all the rivers, and even in the most insignificant brooks, are prodigious; but, in general, they are very small, seldom exceeding a pound in weight, and they therefore do not afford good sport.

CHAPTER VII.

"But wild beasts of the desert shall lie there; and their houses shall be full of doleful creatures; and owls shall dwell there, and satyrs shall dance there. And the wild beasts of the islands shall cry in their desolate houses, and dragons in their pleasant palaces; and her time is near to come, and her days shall not be prolonged."—ISAIAH, CH. XIII.

APPOINTED JUDICIAL AGENT OF GOVERNMENT IN THE SEVEN KORLES, AND THE PARTS OF NEURECALAVA ATTACHED TO IT—FARTHER REMARKS UPON CEYLON GARDENING, ETC.—A STRANGE ADVENTURE; BEING AN ACCOUNT OF A TRIP TAKEN BY A DOCTOR UPON AN ALLIGATOR'S BACK—ARRANGEMENTS FOR AN EXCURSION THROUGH A PART OF NEURECALAVA—MAGNIFICENT ROCK TEMPLES OF DAMBOOL—THESE TEMPLES, AND WHAT THEY CONTAIN, DESCRIBED—JOURNEY TO MINERY LAKE—ITS SHORES, ETC. DESCRIBED—KANDELLÉ LAKE DESCRIBED—REMARKS UPON CEYLON TANKS IN GENERAL—THEIR SURPRISING SIZE; AND THE VAST EXTENT OF GROUND SAID TO HAVE BEEN COVERED BY THE ANCIENT CITY OF ANARAJAHPOORA—THE POPULATION OF THE COUNTRY—USEFUL OBSERVATIONS.

SIR EDWARD BARNES (of whom I have spoken as I considered I ought to do, but to whom I was in no ways indebted for any thing he had done for me) having left the island, Sir Edward Paget assumed the government; when I was appointed Judicial Agent in the Seven Korles, and in the parts of Neurecalava attached to it. In a few weeks after, I received additional instructions, increasing the Civil and Criminal Jurisdiction, with which I had at first been entrusted, beyond what is expressed in the Proclamation of the 21st November, 1818, and that of the 22nd November, 1821. This appointment added considerably to my income, and conferred upon me, besides military authority, the same powers as are exercised by Civil Agents of Government in the Kandyan provinces. It brought a host of natives about me; such as Interpreters, Headmen of various ranks and castes, Lascareens, &c.; and, I very soon found that I was likely to have ample employment as a Judge. In fact, it had been ascertained, that the Civil Agent of the province was so overwhelmed with judicial business, that he could not possibly attend to the collection of the revenue, which alone gave him quite enough to look after. I still, however, managed to have occasionally time for a little amusement and relaxation; and was even able to enjoy my fishing and shooting pastimes and excursions. But, from holding my courts regularly, I am now also brought into daily intercourse with Kandyans of all castes, in whose eyes I am become a much greater personage than when I was a mere military commander. I have often to hear and decide cases of considerable importance, especially those connected with landed property; in which I am assisted by a certain number of the most respectable Headmen, who act as assessors, and who inform me what is the Kandyan law in particular cases, but only when I require them to do so. In criminal cases, I have also, assisted by them, to adjudge punishments, &c. according to the nature of the crimes or offences brought before me; when I trust I do my best to act not only as a just, but also as a merciful, judge; neither of which, drawing my conclusions from what I have already ascertained, my predecessors, the Kandyan Chiefs, who were entrusted by their King with the same power in the provinces as I now am, ever were. The native judges seem to have invariably decided in favour of the litigant who could bribe highest; and I am convinced—so long have they been accustomed to bribery and roguery—that the people cannot, as yet, imagine how it is possible for a judge to act impartially or uprightly.

I find from my notes, that I then received, regularly, supplies of garden seeds from various parts of the world; and consequently derived much more amusement than I did formerly from my horticultural occupations. I have now reason to be proud of my different and excellent kinds of melons, and also of some very large and fine cucumbers; but, I have again failed in my attempts to produce grapes, and have been almost equally unsuccessful in growing potatoes; for I get nothing but long stalks and leaves, and at the roots, things not larger than peas. I have, however, in abundance, white and red solid celery, large York and other cabbages (still great luxuries here); common and French beans, scarlet runners; three different kinds of peas, as many of onions; turnips, carrots, radishes, lettuces, (particularly the Malta),) leeks, &c.; and, though last mentioned, certainly the most valued--remarkably fine asparagus.

The few sheep I have being house-fed, they are doing tolerably well. As for geese, ducks, and fowls, I have more of them than I, and my friends, can use. It was only a few minutes ago, that I had the curiosity to ask Duckling—the name we have given the little squat Singalese who tends our flocks —how many ducks he was then driving out before him to feed upon the grass that grows so luxuriantly by the side of the brook I have already mentioned; "Only ninety-two—for, sir order plenty dead by him *co*key." I must however remark, that the ducks brought to table are always for some time well fed with grain, before they come into the hands of the cook. But, worthy reader, did you ever eat a boiled goose or duck, with onion sauce? Both, I am aware, are favourite dishes in Ireland; but I never met with them so dressed in England; nor would I recommend any young lady, who may have a design upon the heart of a gentleman, particularly if he should not be advanced in years, to partake of such dainties, at least in his presence, before the knot is tied. I had, however, invited Mr. O'Hara, of the 16th regiment, (a great favourite of mine,) and our Doctor to assist me, at dinner, in demolishing a boiled goose with the said onion sauce; and, as they were both usually very punctual men upon such occasions, I was much surprised at their not making their appearance at seven o'clock, my usual hour. Half-past seven came, but neither of my expected guests turned up: and there could be no mistake, for they had left me in the morning, after I had given them directions, as to a part of the lake where they might be certain of falling in with plenty of water-fowl; and they had promised, on their return, to join me at dinner.

At half-past eight the two long-looked-for gentlemen walked in; (of course, I had given up, for some time, the idea of having the pleasure of their company for that day;) they were very tired, and exceedingly hungry. They had soon found the part of the lake which I had pointed out to them; they had had excellent sport; and being loaded with teal, wild ducks, &c. they had proceeded to cross the lake at a place where it somewhat narrows, not far from its head, and where in the dry season, as I had told them, it was easily forded. The place, moreover, that I alluded to, could not be mistaken, for there were several large trunks of trees lying there in the water, which had fallen from age, and were slowly decaying. In fording the lake, the Doctor took the lead, closely followed by O'Hara. In order to get through it the more easily, they had to step upon some of the fallen trees, which I have just mentioned; in doing so, and upon a very large one, it suddenly slipped away from under the astonished Doctor, when down he fell upon his back into the water, with ducks, gun, and every thing else he carried. Reader, will you believe it?—he had mounted upon the back of an enormous alligator!—

O'Hara, in all haste, dragged out the terrified and half choked Doctor; and, having made good their retreat to the bank, they prudently decided that "the better part of valour would be discretion;" and in place of again attempting to wade through the lake, and to take another trip on an alligator's back, that it would be much wiser and better to retrace their steps, though it would take them, at the least, an hour and a half longer to do so, than if they had crossed to the opposite shore.

We were afterwards often much amused by the account which the Doctor gave of his marvellous trip upon the alligator's back; and the story, certainly, lost nothing of its interest in being retold. But the Doctor's adventure by no means surpasses what lately happened to a certain civilian, who had gone out by himself snipe-shooting. He was attacked, and in single combat disarmed, by a large bearded *monkey;* but whether he ever afterwards managed to get back his gun from the victor I did not hear; nor did I ever learn whether the venerable-looking monkey took a cool shot at his discomfited adversary.

Having been for a considerable time past much too closely engaged in judicial business, which frequently occupied me from 10 A. M. till 5 P. M., and becoming anxious for a little relaxation from such drudgery in a crowded and often much heated courthouse, I determined to start upon rather an extensive excursion into a new and not much known country. Going by the way of Dambool, I purposed to extend my journey, if I could manage it, to the beautiful but much dreaded neighbourhood of Minery Lake; from whence I hoped to be able to make my way across Neurecalava, so as to reach the Kalla-oya; and to return to Kurunagalla by Padenny, or by any path I might find leading homewards.

With these objects in view, as well as shooting and fishing, I took care to be well provided with supplies and even comforts; and amongst the latter I included my palanquin, as I had on former occasions experienced the advantage of having it to sleep in at night. I likewise took with me an escort of a corporal and eight Malays, in addition to my two permanent orderlies; leaving it to the latter to select such men to compose it as they knew to have a fancy for field sports, and who, if we should be attacked by wild beasts, would stand by us. I had, moreover, received a hint, that in the wilds of Neurecalava, there had lately been meetings held of a suspicious nature, by some of the discontented Headmen; but what their object might be, I could neither find out nor imagine. At all events, I thought it well, in case of necessity, to have a few brave and resolute men with me. My companions upon this occasion were my obliging and agreeable friend O'Hara, and the now more experienced and ardent sportsman, Captain K——, who was always ready for shooting or hunting excursions, but had no turn for fishing; indeed, O'Hara had just as little fancy for that gentle art as the Captain had.

With what delight, when we are in the enjoyment of health, strength, and spirits, do we set off in a country like Ceylon, before the dawn of day, upon a journey of this kind; knowing that our road lies through a dangerous yet interesting wilderness.—That wilderness is indeed highly interesting, not merely on account of its magnificent sylvan scenery, but also because there are many surprising heaps of ruins of great edifices scattered over its surface; all that a race now long extinct, or removed to other lands, have left behind them to indicate that here of old a potentate reigned and probably tyrannized over his subjects; that here fields were once cultivated and cities built by an industrious people; and that here the arts and sciences, at least to a certain extent, had flourished. Yet, in proof of this, so little is to be seen by a superficial observer, excepting the remaining embankments of vast tanks and canals, that it might almost be denied by a timid and inactive traveller that they had ever stood there. By the character of the country, as to its unhealthiness, and being greatly infested with wild animals, such a traveller is deterred from passing through it; or if he even ventures to pass, he scarcely allows himself time to examine the fragments of sculptured monuments and other objects which may by chance, and amidst an overwhelming and almost impassable mass of jungle, present themselves, very indistinctly, to his view.

I had before, with Mr. L—, a friend of mine, paid a short visit to Dambool, and was now anxious to shew its wonders to my companions. As it is a long and fatiguing journey to the temples, I had, on the previous day, sent on our people, with an excellent interpreter, about half-way; and now my companions and I set off on horseback to overtake them, expecting to do so about noon. The path, for a considerable part of the way, after passing the Didroo-oya, runs through patches of jungle, almost entirely composed of acacias, that thrive even in the most arid and seemingly unpropitious soil, which is there chiefly of a very white colour; being, as I was led to conclude, composed, in a great measure, of silicious sand; and might, there is little doubt, be found fit for the growth of cinnamon trees. It, however, renders the path, that in many places winds through the jungle, both exceedingly hot and laborious to travel; as, for several miles, not a drop of water is to be found. But I must here observe, that if one of the mountain rivers or brooks, to the eastward, were turned in this direction, and carried towards the northward, what a wonderful change would soon be produced in these now unproductive and desolate regions. When I before passed over this dreary plain, my dog had almost died of thirst, and from the effects of the excessive heat that there prevailed; and I only saved his life by carrying him occasionally—large as he is—before me upon my horse; for he had fallen down upon the burning sand, and could to all appearance go no farther; and what added greatly to my uneasiness on his account was that no water could be procured until we reached the rocks, out of which the temples of Dambool, or as the natives call them, Damboolloo Galla, have been excavated.

As Dambool is situated in such a dangerous and uninviting country to travel through, it has been visited, as yet, by very few Europeans; but, in the opinion of those who have been there, it is by far the greatest wonder in this wonderful island. The ascent to the temples is fatiguing; for, in order to reach the entrance to them, we have to proceed over the greatly heated face of the rock; which, except where the path has been carried through a narrow patch of jungle, is exposed to the powerful rays of the sun for an extent of not less than three hundred feet; and, I should say, that to the summit of the rock, it is fully two hundred feet more. The reader may, therefore, conceive the grandeur and imposing effect of objects, on such a scale, so situated; but, I must request of him, to go along with me, whilst I venture to give him even a very imperfect idea of the splendour and magnitude of these temples, and of what they contain. There are four temples, and they have all the appearance of having been hewn, at vast labour, out of the side of this insulated rock. A lofty arch, of an inferior style of architecture, first attracted my notice; at each side of which stands a large stone figure, as if placed there to guard the entrance. To our astonishment, we soon found ourselves in an immense excavation, painted and embellished in the most brilliant colours, at least two hundred feet in length, and one hundred in width, well lighted by numerous large windows and doors, divided from each other by masses of solid masonry, supporting, as it were, the immense weight of the over-hanging rock. In this temple there are many idols of a great size and of respectable workmanship, particularly four of them, seated on coiled up snakes, resembling cobra de capellos, which are made to expand their broad necks and heads over them.

I had transcribed these few remarks from my notes, when I recollected that Dr. Davy had visited these temples; and, on referring to his work, in order to compare his descriptions of them, with what it took me so long to write upon the spot, I find his account of what is there to be seen, so minute and superior to any thing of the kind which I could attempt to give, that I shall not hesitate to use the materials with which he has so ably and abundantly supplied me; at the same time begging that he will pardon me for having done so.*

"The temples which give this place celebrity, are parts of a vast cavern in the south side of the rock, at the height of about three hundred and fifty feet above the plain. The approach to them is up the eastern shelving extremity of the rock, through an archway of masonry, and along a narrow platform of solid rock open to the south, enclosed by a low wall, shaded by trees, and containing in its

* Major Forbes in his "Eleven years in Ceylon," also speaks of these celebrated temples, and has given a beautiful drawing of that of Maha Rajah.

area a cistern holding rain water, a very small temple and a bogah. This approach, platform and front raised our expectations very little, and did not at all prepare us for what we discovered on entering the temples.

"The Wiharé we first explored is the last in order from the entrance. It is about fifty-four feet long, and twenty-seven wide; and its shelving roof, which dips gradually inwards, where most lofty, is about twenty-seven feet high. It contains ten figures of Boodhoo, and a neat dagobah about twelve feet high. The figures are well executed and brilliantly painted, and most of them are as large or larger than the ordinary size of man. The roof and sides of the rock and the front wall are painted of the brightest colours, and illuminated with a number of figures chiefly of Boodhoo. The general effect of the whole is exceedingly striking and pretty.

"The next Wiharé, called the Alut Wiharé, is separated from the preceding, partly by an abutting rock, and partly by a wall of masonry, in which there is a door of communication. Its principal entrance is by a door in front. We were taken by surprise on entering this temple; we were astonished by its great size, the brilliant effect of an immense surface of rock painted of the richest colours, and by numerous figures of Boodhoo, which it contains in different attitudes and groups, all coloured in the most lively manner. It is about ninety feet long, eighty-one wide, and its shelving roof where highest, is about thirty-six feet high.

The figures which it contains are fifty in number. One statue of Boodhoo, in the recumbent posture, its head on a pillow resting on its right hand, is of gigantic size, about thirty feet long and well proportioned; its face is handsome, and its expression of countenance remarkably placid and benignant. Seven other statues of Boodhoo, in the standing attitude, are about ten feet high, and all the rest are as large as life, or very little less. Most of them are coloured bright yellow; two of them have red robes, and reminded me of the two classes of Lamas in Tibet, described by Captain Turner, who are distinguished from each other, by one wearing red and the other yellow garments. Towards the western end of the temple there is a well executed figure of King Kirtissiré, the last great benefactor of Dambool, in his robes of state, which very much resemble those worn by the last King of Kandy."

Between this temple and the next there is no direct communication. They are separated—according to my notes—from each other by a part of the rock that has not been hewn away. The portal by which we entered is in front; it is a lofty archway, as I before remarked, guarded on each side by figures in stone, intended to represent Janitors. "This temple, called the Maha-rajah Wiharé, almost as much surpasses in size and effect the last, as that does the first described. It is about two hundred feet long and one hundred wide, and appeared to me to be about fifty feet high where highest; nor does obscurity add to its grandeur; for it is perfectly well lighted through numerous windows, and several doors in front. It contains altogether fifty-three images, and a handsome dagobah, about eighteen feet high, the broad circular pedestal of which is ornamented with four figures of Boodhoo, each facing a different quarter, each seated on a cobra-de-capello, and shaded by its head and neck, as if by a hood. As in the two preceding temples, so in this the images are arranged in a row at a little distance from the sides of the excavations, but they are not grouped; and as in the last, none are placed near the outer wall, with the exception of the statues of two kings: at the western end of the temple the figures are arranged in a double row. The majority of the statues are Boodhoos of different dimensions, and in different attitudes; many of them larger, but none of them much, if at all, smaller than life. Besides forty-six figures of Boodhoo, there is, in company with them, one of Mitré Deo-rajooroowo, who, it is imagined, will be the next Boodhoo, the successor of Goutama; and one of each of the three gods,—Visnu, Samen, and Nata; the first in blue robes, the second in yellow, and the third in robes of white. The statues of the two kings alluded to above, as standing apart near the outer wall, are those of Wallagam-bahoo and Nisankai, at opposite ends of the temple: the first, representing the earliest benefactor of Dambool, is the rudest figure in every respect, and its dress is the simplest and least ornamented; the ears are long, and drawn down in the Malabar fashion;

there is a double-headed snake about the neck, the body of which serves as a necklace, and the heads as ear-pendants. At the eastern extremity of the temple, there is a little recess formed by a high projecting rock, the walls of which are covered with paintings illustrating the history of Ceylon, beginning with the earliest and most fabulous period, and continued down to the introduction of the bo-tree and the sacred relic.* The exploits of Wijeya, the first king, make a conspicuous figure, and cover a great deal of space; more particularly the voyage of this hero, which is represented by a boat surrounded by sea-monsters. The dedication of the island to Boodhoo after the arrival of the relic, is figured by a king guiding a plough drawn by a pair of elephants, attended by priests, &c.

"Towards the eastern end of the temple, there is a perpetual dripping of water that filters through the roof from hollows in the top of the rock, which are supplied by rain. The water as it drops is caught in a chatty, placed for the purpose of receiving it, in a small square inclosure sunk in the floor. Though the water is particularly good, no native, through superstitious dread, which restrains them, ventures to use it; and, when," says Dr. Davy, "I told a priest that I had tasted it, he replied that, though we might drink it, perhaps, with impunity, it would certainly prove fatal to them were they to indulge in it."

Before quitting this temple, in which there was

* For historical account of Ceylon, see Major Forbes's work.

a pleasure in remaining on account of its cool and fresh air, so different from the close and hot atmosphere of small Wiharés in general, Dr. Davy had an opportunity to witness the manner in which Boodhists worship their divinity. "The service was performed at the Governor's (Sir Robert Brownrigg's) desire, and without the least hesitation, under the direction of the chief priest, who intimated the wish to the people, and supplied them with flowers. Each person, on receiving his flowers, went and laid them before an image of Boodhoo, and accompanied the offering with a pious exclamation. The offerings being all made, and all the people arranged in a line before the images, and kneeling, the priest stood in the middle, and with a clear voice, sentence by sentence, recited the common obligations of their religion, the congregation repeating each sentence after him. The united voices of at least one hundred men in the highest key of recitative, or rather of the loudest exclamation, made the cavern resound, and had a fine awful effect, producing a thrill through the system, and a feeling and sentiment not to be described."

"The next and last temple, called the Dewaarajah Wiharé, because the god Visnu is supposed to have aided in the construction of its principal image, is very inferior, in every espect, to either of the preceding, especially the two last. It is about seventy-five feet long, twenty-one wide, and twenty-seven high; and so dark, that only a very imperfect view of it could be obtained, even with the aid of a lamp. It contains six images of Boodhoo, and one of Visnu, all of them of ordinary size, with the exception of that just alluded to as the principal figure, which is a gigantic recumbent Boodhoo, about thirty feet long."

Whether the cavern in which these temples have been formed, is natural, or partly natural and partly artificial, it is now, I suspect, difficult to determine; but, I am inclined to consider them, from what I saw and was told by the shrewd and odd looking priest, who most obligingly pointed out to us every thing worthy of notice, and who perfectly recollected Sir Robert Brownrigg's visit to the Wiharés, to be almost if not entirely artificial; and this, he observed, was the opinion of the priests in general. He likewise confirmed, and even went beyond, what Dr. Davy has said, as to the antiquity of the temple called Maha-rajah; as he assured me that it had been formed upwards of two thousand years ago; and that they possessed writings that would prove this, as well as their indisputable right to a great extent of country around Dambool. That it had been repaired and embellished, (the colouring was just as fresh as if it had only been finished the day before,) at least two hundred and thirty years ago, by one of their kings, who was highly extolled by the priest, for having laid out, in thus ornamenting and repairing the temples, the large sum (six hundred thousand pieces of gold) which is stated by Dr. Davy. This priest, like the generality of his grasping brethren, was, though crafty, evidently very superstitious, and in such awe of the demons worshipped, or rather feared and propitiated, all over Ceylon, as to make him cautious how he even ventured to speak of them; and yet he could not resist the temptation of being communicative. Indeed, the grave and mysterious manner in which he related to us, as historical facts, what had occurred in these temples, which was, of course, firmly believed by some of his countrymen who were present, has more than once been recalled to my mind by the hoary-headed keeper of Peel Castle, in the Isle of Man, who, a good many years since, had a legend composed expressly for his use and profit, as well as for the amusement and benefit of many credulous persons, by a joke-loving friend of mine. It was taken partly from Scott's "Peveril of the Peak," and partly from equally authentic documents, not omitting the *true* story of the Black-dog seen so often in the guard-room, by many a terrified soldier, besides other supernatural appearances and wonderful occurrences in many parts of that very ancient fortress or strong-hold; all of which the keeper has now told so often, and to the astonishment of so many visitors, that though, in some essential points, he widely deviates from the original, he himself at length firmly believes all he has so long been in the habit of declaring to be unquestionable *facts*. But, worthy reader, have not many good stories, much that has been admitted, even by learned men, to be authentic and historical, and still more that is only traditional, very little more to recommend them to our credence, than this legend of Peel castle?

I had ample time to visit not only all the temples of Dambool, but also the comfortable dwellings of the priests, in a pleasantly situated and cool room of which we dined and spent the evening—but not at their expense, wealthy as they might be supposed, were we to draw conclusions from the vast extent of territory which they pretend to claim, as belonging to the temples; which territory, however, is now almost without inhabitants, and covered with jungle. We likewise spent the night, very comfortably, in some of the dormitories, which were both clean and cool.

I ought, however, to mention, that before sunset we ascended to the top of the immense rock, out of which these temples are excavated; which, I believe, is nearly six hundred feet in height; and from thence—I can hardly add—*enjoyed* the extensive views over the surrounding country; for, I must say, that I felt, as it were, depressed in spirits, when I cast my eyes over such an uniform and dreary looking wilderness of foliage; rendered the more cheerless by the desolate appearance of some large and almost jungle-covered rocks that, here and there, rise abruptly to a considerable height above the plain. A priest who accompanied us, particularly called my attention to one of them; as upon and around it had been situated an ancient capital of the country, which had been built there, as he informed us, by one of their kings, long before Kurunagalla was made a royal residence, or had risen into importance. I had before drank of the pure and exceedingly cold water that filters through the rock, though warned by a priest, as Dr. Davy also was, as to what might be the fatal consequences; and, when we were on its summit, we saw the hollows, mentioned by Dr. Davy, and which contained at the time a considerable quantity of rain water. My companions had also partaken of the excellent beverage.

After we had dined, I desired the interpreter to bring in one of the most intelligent priests, as I wished to question him about his religion, the history of the temples, and what he knew of the country to the northward. Two of them came with him; the one who had pointed out the objects of interest in the temples, and a young man of very prepossessing appearance and manners; but, as they were now aware of my being an agent of government, they were, as I soon perceived, exceedingly cautious as to what they told me, unless it were connected with their rights—of which they seemed to be very jealous—and their religion.

Some of the stories they told me were mere fables, and reminded me of what I have already related of an ancient king of Kurunagalla, who, by the aid of a magician, destroyed the embankments thrown up, at vast labour, to collect water to be afterwards used for agricultural purposes, and who thus ruined the then fine country of Neurecalava. They, of course, spoke highly of the Boodhoo religion, and in admiration of its mild and excellent precepts. They admitted that there are devils, whom they teach the people to worship, or rather to dread and propitiate; but that there is one Supreme God, who formed the earth and the sky—perhaps, a triune God, whom I was inclined to think they adore in Visnu, Samen, and Nata. They alluded to transmigration of souls; but by this time I had become quite puzzled or lost, betwixt gods and the souls of good and bad men; the devils being, if I understood rightly what they asserted, those of the wicked who occasion misfortunes and sickness; whilst the good spirits continue, as they were on earth, to be friendly towards mankind. But as Boodhoo saves the souls of men, it is to him that the chief worship or honour is to be paid. In short, both priests seemed very willing to afford me ample information upon all points connected with their religion; and they also readily acquainted me with the situation of several extensive ruins, of great antiquity, scattered in various directions throughout the now almost pathless and overwhelming jungle; but whether they had been the work of their Kandyan ancestors,—as their priests asserted they were—or that of another, more ancient and more enlightened people, as I am inclined to suspect, I had no means of ascertaining. Indeed, they said that the Kandyans in general believed that the devils had had much to do with their construction, as well as destruction; especially those which are to be seen at and for many miles around Anarajahpoora.*

My interpreter, who writes the Singalese language correctly, examined some of the old docu-

* See Forbes's "Eleven Years in Ceylon," for an excellent account of them.

ments—writings neatly executed with a steel pen upon talipot-leaves—which the priests produced at my request; a few of which, (they asserted that they had others far more ancient), he assured me, were considerably more than a thousand years old. But those shewn on this occasion, almost entirely related to grants of land or money from various kings to the Wiharés, for certain reasons and purposes; and the antiquity of these deeds did not at all surprise me, as there had been laid before me, in court, deeds similarly written, which proved the claims of individuals or families to lands, of almost as old a date, and which were in as perfect a state of preservation, and the characters as legible, as if only just written.

Both the priests strongly recommended us to follow the usual path—bad as it was—in going to Minery; the country around which, they assured me, was at that season, considered to be by no means unhealthy. This greatly comforted the interpreter, our servants, and the coolies, who were beginning to be a good deal alarmed, both on account of the reputed sickliness of the country I intended to pass through, and likewise about the wild beasts which we were to expect to fall in with in the jungle. The priests also pointed out to us the necessity of taking guides with us, many parts of the road being both intricate and swampy; especially as far as a place they called Kaleodewé; but, above all they advised us, upon no account, to venture across the plains from Minery to the Kalla-oya, in which water was scarce and bad, without having persons with us, furnished by responsible Headmen, to point out where it was to be had, and in what directions the jungle was most open and passable. In place of steering by compass, as was our intention, we resolved to follow this advice, as it was, seemingly, kindly given; and their accounts of the country, I was glad to find, agreed with that I had received of it, from Mr. Auber, of the Quarter-Master General's department, who had obligingly furnished me with a map of that part of the island, which I afterwards found to be correct; and which, had it not been almost destroyed by the white ants, might have been advantageously added to that placed at the commencement of this volume, as it was upon the same scale. But, before closing my remarks upon Dambool, I must beg the reader's attention to some historical paintings, by a native artist, which will give him an idea of those to be seen there. I must also add, that any one who leaves Ceylon, without having seen these temples, will have lost an opportunity, which he may be afterwards sorry for :—that is to say, of examining and admiring what are, by every one who has visited them, admitted to be so worthy of being classed amongst the wonders of this wonderful island.

I have no intention of troubling the reader with a description of the dreary country through which we travelled to Minery, which we found to be much as we had anticipated; it was anything but agreeable. To convince him of this I need only say that we were several times obliged to cross swamps and to quit the

No. 1.

No. 2.

No. 3

No. 4

Published by T and W Boone, London, 1843

P Gauci, lith

N° 1.
N° 2
N° 3.
N° 4
N° 5
P. Gauci, lith.

path in order to avoid elephants, and as often to drive them out of it. We shot numbers of snipes and other birds, and also two deer; indeed, had we at this time been anxious for sport, we might have had enough of it; but we hoped to have much superior pastime in the green woods, as we passed through them after leaving Minery lake, which was the principal object that we had in view when we set out upon this journey.

We left Dambool with a guide, recommended to us by the priests, whom I promised to reward liberally if he was faithful, and soon got into a kind of path which led us to a place (the name of which is obliterated) a few miles beyond an ancient canal or aqueduct, still in good repair, where we halted for the night. The next day we passed through Pecollam, which is about fourteen miles from the village of Minery, situated at the farther end of the lake. The country we thus had an opportunity of cursorily examining may probably have been of old in a high state of cultivation; but it cannot be again rendered fit for the abode of man until some of the great tanks are repaired, and the waters are made to flow from them evenly over the entire face of the country. When that is done there cannot be a doubt but that its salubrity and fertility may be restored; but, unfortunately, to accomplish this it must be re-peopled; there being very few inhabitants, and those scattered thinly over a great extent of country.

We did not intend to take the servants or coolies far beyond Pecollam, but to leave them in huts which we meant to build in the woods, the talipot leaves we had brought with us serving for thatch. Captain K——, who cared nothing whatever for fine scenery, or the beauties of a country, was to remain with them. It had also been previously settled that O'Hara and I should, the following day, go on to visit and examine the lake shores; especially the immense mound constructed in olden times, for the purpose of collecting the water and forming the lake. Before dawn of day, therefore, without taking even the horse-keepers with us, but carrying our guns ourselves—loaded with brass balls—we set off upon horse-back for Minery; and in a short time getting clear of the thick and seemingly endless woods, through which we had chiefly travelled since leaving Dambool, we arrived at the upper end of the lake just as the sun rose above the trees, giving to its smooth waters and verdant shores the most splendid and strikingly beautiful appearance which can possibly be conceived. To our surprise, there was nothing of that dull uniformity that might be looked for in what had been formed by art; on the contrary, numerous finely wooded points projected irregularly into the lake, which, I conclude, must be fully twenty miles in circumference. I at once felt that I had never beheld such enchanting and diversified scenery as was here suddenly spread out before us!—We really wanted words to express our admiration of it! After gazing upon its matchless softness and loveliness for a few minutes, we continued our ride along the south-eastern shore; and as we came upon the several little bays or inlets, we were almost startled, yet greatly amused, at seeing the immense flocks of various kinds of birds, such as bitterns and paddy birds—the latter with plumage as white as snow—as well as many of those clothed in scarlet and green, which we call flamingoes; besides ducks, teal, &c. taking wing as we approached them. There were also alligators of great size, which waddled off as fast as they could into the lake, so that we had no doubt of its swarming with them; I was therefore glad that I had left my faithful dog Bran behind at the huts. We also occasionally saw, but some way off, a few large buffaloes, several deer, and what appeared to be hogs, feeding upon the verdant but coarse grass, which in some places grew to a considerable height; but they also on seeing us made off into the woods that every where skirt the narrow plains that surround the lake. We, however, had no intention of injuring or molesting them, as we carried guns for our own defence alone; having been told that we should, in all probability, meet with elephants, buffaloes, tigers, or bears, in the course of the day, which are said to be numerous in the neighbourhood of the lake.

During our ride, we had often to pass through old paddy-fields, out of which flew flocks of snipes; and we had also to cross what seemed to have been the beds of canals, or I should rather say aqueducts; but we did not meet a human being until we arrived at Minery, which is so miserable a place as scarcely to deserve the name of a village. There we found a few men, who were seated, or rather listlessly reclined, under the shade of their narrow verandahs, or under that of a large bread-fruit-tree; the only one I saw there, and which stood near to a temple, which I was surprised to find in such a miserable place. Having brought gram in nose-bags with us, we put up our horses to feed in a kind of rest-house, to which, owing to the badness and muddiness of the path, we had some difficulty in making our way. We then breakfasted upon what we had carried in our pockets; and, whilst we were so occupied, we contrived to make a Headman understand that we wanted a guide to conduct us to the great embankment.

We had not gone far from the village, when we got amongst a number of very tall trees, with a mass of almost impenetrable jungle under them, through which we had to force our way; but, whilst thus proceeding, we were not aware that we had got upon the mound; for, as we spoke only a very few words of Singalese, our most timid guide was of little or no use to us. In spite, however, of the impediments we had to contend with, we were at last, after pretty hard and hot work, in some measure able to ascertain, certainly to our disappointment, that the embankment, that kept in the water of this fine lake, was of considerably smaller dimensions than we expected to have found it; it being not more than five or six hundred feet long, and not above thirty in breadth, composed, as far as I could judge, of stones of various sizes, seemingly intermixed with earth and clay. It was not until our clothes had been a good deal torn, and after much exertion, that we got to the far end of it; and, from thence, to a spot from which, in consequence of the thickness of the jungle, we with difficulty could see the water issuing from the lake, out of two openings, formed of rudely cut stones of an immense size, which could not have been placed there without much labour and difficulty; unless the people who put them there had been acquainted with mechanical powers of which the present race of Kandyans are totally ignorant.

No attention being now paid by man to turn this great body of water to useful purposes, it flows over a vast extent of thickly wooded country, rendering it swampy, and consequently very unhealthy. This might, no doubt, be remedied by wise and energetic Government measures, and the soil rendered once more, as it is said to have been of old, exceedingly fertile and fit for the abode of man. Though this could now be accomplished only at much expense, and probably at a considerable waste of human life, yet it strikes me that it ought not to be altogether lost sight of; if ever this fine part of Ceylon is again to be improved and cultivated, as I firmly believe it will at a future period.

We were both too much fatigued and heated to attempt the farther investigation of such matters in an almost impenetrable jungle; which was as hot as a furnace, and seemingly swarming with wild beasts; and I must therefore leave it to a more enthusiastic and enterprising antiquary, than I can pretend to be, to find out what may be concealed amongst the tangled mass of underwood and runners, under which may probably long have been hidden some valuable and curious remains of remote antiquity.

Delighted to get away from such an uninviting place as Minery, we, on our return to it from the embankment, mounted our refreshed horses, intending to ride quietly back to the huts; but, the heat of the noonday-sun, the brightness of which was strongly reflected from the water, rendered it necessary for us to travel slowly, and as much under the grateful shade of the trees as possible. About one in the afternoon, the heat had become so overpowering, as there was not a breath of wind stirring, sufficient to move even the leaf of a tree, or to cause the slightest ripple on the surface of the lake, that we were forced to look out for something to screen us from the sun's unbearable rays. On reaching a projecting point that rose a little above the generally flat country, and across which our path lay, we were therefore glad to take shelter under the wide spreading branches of a teak-tree, from which there was a remarkably fine view of the whole lake, its shores, and the surrounding thickly wooded country; the back ground to which, especially towards the eastward, was formed by a range of lofty blue-coloured mountains; while to the westward the view was, I may say, only terminated by a continued horizon of woods. It was, in fact, a seemingly endless level surface of variegated foliage, except that, at considerable intervals, and at some distance off, there rose abruptly, wooded hills or rocks, some of them of vast size and imposing appearance, similar to that of which I have spoken as to be seen from Dambool, and upon and around which a capital of the country had been once situated. Many of the beautiful white paddy-birds were standing on the verdant bank, or had waded a few yards into the lake, in order to catch the small fish with which it abounds; and which they seemed to lay hold of, with their long sharp bills, with as much ease as they swallowed them. Among them here and there, lay stretched out at their full length some large alligators, apparently basking in the sun, whilst near them were feeding a few wild hogs, evidently unapprehensive of danger.

I thought at the moment, how much more peaceful and happy was the life of these feathered fishers, than that of the unlucky booby, which, at sea, is quite as dexterous in his calling as they are in theirs in a lake or river; but, no sooner has he completely gorged himself with fish, than he is forced by the unmerciful man-of-war-birds, as they are commonly called, to take wing from the surface of the sea, upon which he had been swimming about and enjoying himself for hours; and, as he rises, these warriors set to work and thresh him with their powerful wings, till they cause him to disgorge all the fish he has swallowed, which they invariably contrive to catch before they reach the water.

Minery lake and its shores were, at the moment I have alluded to, a perfect scene of brilliancy and almost tranquillity; and though so lovely, yet we doubted if the feelings—strange to say—which predominated in our minds, whilst gazing upon them, were not those of melancholy. This, as I may call it, fanciful mood, was however suddenly dispelled by the loud trumpeting of elephants, which greatly startled us; for they could not have been many hundred yards off, in the woods to our left. We therefore clapped spurs to our horses, and proceeded on our way for some time, and when the state of the path admitted of it, at a canter; the numerous flocks of birds flying away, and the alligators, as before, floundering into the lake as we approached them; for the road chiefly lay close to the water's edge. But, as we saw neither elephants nor animals of any kind likely to arrest our progress, we before long relaxed our pace; and having got back in safety to the huts, I found that, during our absence, a Kandyan had brought letters, forwarded by the District Staff Officer from Kurunagalla to Dambool; whence they had been sent on to this place by the priests. They informed me that, in about a fortnight, I might look for a visit from the Governor, who was soon to leave Colombo for the Kandyan provinces. This made it necessary for me not only to change my plans, but also to curtail the limits of my intended excursion; and to give up, at least for the present, my hitherto concealed intention of visiting Anarajahpoora. I must say, that this was a great disappointment to me, as from all I had been told, I was led to believe that there are to be seen, in many places in that direction, the ruins or remains of what must have once been tanks of vast magnitude, aqueducts, and temples, and of other large edifices; and, judging from the fragments of pillars and hewn stones, still forming parts of ruinous buildings, which here and there shew themselves above masses of jungle and runners, which we fell in with in crossing the country on our way to Minery, it was our opinion, as well as that of some persons who have seen them, that the people by whom they were constructed must have possessed a much greater knowledge of the arts than any of the present inhabitants of Ceylon, or probably their more enlightened ancestors, had an idea of. I am moreover aware, that Anarajahpoora was for many years the capital of the whole country, and that it was destroyed at the period of the final expulsion of the Malabars, who have so often proved such dangerous enemies to the Singalese. The country is now, I may say, one vast forest, almost without inhabitants; and may be said to have become, like ancient Babylon, the possession of the bittern and of wild beasts; but no fiat, at least that we know of, has gone forth, that it shall never again be inhabited. To make up, however, for the disappointment of not being able to go to Anarajahpoora, O'Hara and I settled that we would leave Captain K— and most of the people at the encampment, and, taking half the Malays and a few coolies with us to carry light loads, we would the next day proceed to Kandellé, which is about forty miles farther on towards Trincomalie, where there is another, and from what we had heard, a very fine lake, formed in the same way as that of Minery.

Having got back to the huts earlier in the day than we had calculated upon, and Captain K— having heard our accounts of the beauties of Minery lake, and especially of the excellent sport to be met with upon its shores, and having expressed a wish to see it, we very readily offered to return with him in the evening, as it would only be a short and an agreeable ride before dinner; and we might, besides, as Captain K— hinted, have a chance of getting a shot at the deer; which, probably about sunset, would leave the woods to feed upon the bright green grass that grows so luxuriantly in the narrow plains upon its banks. I therefore sent on at once my orderly Malays, armed, with four of the escort, who volunteered to go with them, and who good-naturedly proposed to carry back the game which might be shot.

I desired them to wait for us at the head of the lake, where the path first reaches the meadows, and from which point a traveller has the first complete view of it. Before four P. M. we mounted our well fed steeds, and easily overtook the Malays just as they arrived at the place I had described to them. There, leaving our horses and their keepers with an armed Malay to protect them, as they were too much afraid of wild beasts to remain alone, we set off to our left, along the western shore, when we soon found that the country, with the exception of where a kind of belt or stripe of sward extends all along at an unequal distance from the water's edge, was fully as heavy and tiresome to travel in, as that we had passed through in the morning. Here and there, however, it rose gently behind these meadows, and was covered, chiefly, with fine ebony-trees; which have a dark-coloured bark, with leaves something like those of the plum-tree, and therefore contrast strongly with those around them. We had only gone about half a mile along the very verdant and now more cool shore of the still glowing lake, when we saw a single deer, which made off the moment it perceived us, and without our having had an opportunity of firing at it. Proceeding onward, we observed what seemed to be an alligator, lying quietly in the midst of a number of white paddy-birds, which were very busily engaged in catching fish, without apparently apprehending danger from the huge creature, around which they hopped with the utmost unconcern. As Captain K— became most eager to send a ball or two through him, it was agreed that he and I were to steal as close up to him as we could; and for enabling us to do so, a small patch of jungle was favourably situated. We were to fire together;—

Captain K— aiming at his head, and I at his side, which presented itself well to me, and from which I was not thirty yards distant. Resting our guns against trees, we let fly at him; when he made a sudden bound from the ground, rolled over upon his back, and lay kicking with his short legs, and lashing with his strong muscular tail. We all instantly ran up to him; but, upon our reaching the spot, he was only able to grind his immense teeth, and fix his glaring eyes upon us, and uttering a kind of harsh sound and a deep moan, he became motionless. Captain K—'s ball had gone right through his head;—mine, from having been aimed a little too high, had only severely torn the upper part of his back, and seriously injured the bone. This alligator was about seventeen feet in length. Though we knew that his carcase would be of no use to us, yet, sportsmen-like, we had felt it impossible to resist the impulse or temptation of taking a shot at him. Soon after, Captain K— slightly wounded a hog, and shot a doe, which was the only head of game we got that evening.

The sun had just then set; and the twilight was rapidly fading into a serene and beautiful moonlight night, which we knew would, with the aid of hundreds of thousands of fire-flies, enable us easily to find our way home. The lake at the moment had its surface slightly influenced by a delightfully refreshing breeze, which barely stirred and rippled its otherwise tranquil waters; in which many objects were now unsteadily reflected. The distant mountains of Matelé were still distinctly to be seen to the south-eastward, and the jungle upon one of them seemed to have been set on fire. There were yet some fishermen out upon the lake in their canoes, which looked like black spots on the surface of the pale blue waters, over which they seemed to skim so lightly, as scarcely to leave a track behind them: in short, it was a glorious expanse of wood and water, such as an admirer of fine lake scenery delights to gaze upon, especially by moonlight; and perhaps, even with greater interest, than when he can behold objects more splendidly and gorgeously decked in the bright beams of a rising tropical sun; and truly, it was such a night, as that which we may suppose inspired the poet to deify and thus address fair Cynthia:—

> "Lay thy bow of pearl apart,
> And thy crystal shining quiver,
> Give unto the flying hart
> Space to breathe, how short soever;
> Thou that mak'st a day of night,
> Goddess excellently bright!"

My imagination now, however, readily suggested the idea, that hundreds of years ago, this very moon had shone with equal brightness upon almost the same objects; when these lovely lake shores, and the surrounding country, were the busy haunts of men, whose glory had now long departed, and whose race had almost become extinct, amidst the darkness of heathenism:—such, I felt, are the inscrutable ways of Providence!—but, what heavenly assurances of peace rejoice the heart of the Christian, who can realize to himself the following beautiful and consolatory lines:—

"Take comfort, Christians, when your friends
In Jesus fall asleep;
Their better being never ends,
Why then dejected weep?

Why inconsolable as those
To whom no hope is given?
Death is the messenger of peace,
And calls the soul to heaven.

A few short years of evil past,
We reach the happy shore,
Where death-divided friends at last
Shall meet to part no more."

Mr. O'Hara and I, on horseback, followed by our horse-keepers, grass-cutters, my two orderlies, and two other Malays, one servant, and half a dozen active coolies, set off, as he had settled, before dawn of day; and in due time, and without interruption from animals of any kind, reached Minery; which we only passed through, and proceeded on to an intermediate rest-house, (where I direct detachments to halt on their way to Trincomalie) between that place and Puliankadawetté. Here we halted to breakfast, so as to give time to our people to refresh themselves, and that our horses might be well fed; as, from the swampiness of the path we had all the morning been travelling in, they required a few hours' rest. The country which we had passed through was really fine and strikingly picturesque, as, for nearly the whole way, it had presented that succession of woods and open spaces, which I have already spoken of as forming splendid park-like scenery. We observed, however, about half a mile off the path, and to our left, a number of large wild buffaloes, feeding in a swampy plain, along with what seemed to be some deer and hogs ;—they took no notice of us ; and it was, certainly, not our intention to molest them.

In the afternoon, we pushed on, amidst scenery very similar to that we had travelled through in the morning, to Puliankadawetté ; a village quite as miserable as Minery, and exceedingly hot ; the only thing tolerable in it was the rest-house, in which we purposed to remain for the night ; as our attendants had had quite enough of marching for that day. But, when the evening had become somewhat cool, my companion and I took a walk for a short distance into the neighbouring woods, where we unexpectedly came upon what seemed to be an old aqueduct, the banks of which had in many places fallen in ; but, if it were again wanted for the conveyance of water to irrigate the country, it could be soon repaired and rendered serviceable. Soon after we had passed it, we came upon the prints of the feet of elephants, and other large animals ; but we saw only two wild hogs, at one of which I fired ; but I believe I missed my aim ; at least, they both made off, apparently untouched, into the jungle.

After spending a sleepless and very uncomfortable night from swarms of buzzing muskitoes, and particularly from the endless noises made by numbers of rat-snakes pursuing their prey amongst the thatch on the roof of the rest-house, we started at an early hour next morning, for a village called Permamadua, where, as we purposed to return to it in order to spend the night, we left the horse-keepers, grass-cutters and coolies, and went forward, with the Malays only, to Kandellé, another wretched village, in the rest-house of which we breakfasted, and gave time to the Malays to refresh themselves before we went, in a body, to the tank or lake, which is close to the village.

It was during the heat of the day, that we were obliged to set out to examine the shores of this beautiful wooded lake; which, like that of Minery, is encompassed or skirted by a narrow open space, covered with very green but coarse grass. After enjoying, for some time, the fine and diversified views, which the lake and country presented, we proceeded to a great mound constructed to confine the water, which I consider to be fully a mile and a half in length; and here, contrary to what was the usual custom of the people of old, it is formed in a straight line, from one mass of partly wooded and partly bare rocks to another. The height of the mound may be twenty-five feet; but, at the base of the sloping faces, it seemed to be about one hundred and seventy feet wide: it is, in short, an enormous mass of stones and earth, which must have been formed by the continued labour of thousands of men for many years; and, from the rounded and worn appearance of the nearly square or oblong stones upon its surface, I should conclude that its antiquity is very great. There is, however, another embankment, of almost equal solidity, about five or six hundred yards from that I have been describing. It was also required to keep in the water of the river that flows into the lake or tank, which, though it is not a quarter the size of that of Minery, seems to have been, in former times, of great importance, as it watered a large tract of land towards Trincomalie; which, no doubt, was rendered exceedingly fertile by it, but has now become an unwholesome wilderness, extending its pestilential influence, not only throughout this extensive country, but also over the finest harbour in the Indian ocean. I ought to observe, that the immense body of water flowing rapidly out of the lake, at two large and well constructed stone openings, and dashing amongst the rocks below, has a very grand and imposing effect; which is rendered the more impressive by the exceedingly deep gloom produced by the great mass of interwoven foliage that forms, as it were, a canopy over the rushing torrent.

I find the foregoing remarks upon this beautiful lake amongst my notes; but Dr. Davy so minutely and admirably describes it, in his work upon Ceylon, that I consider it would be unjust to him, if I withheld from the reader what he has said respecting it: he has also given some very accurate sketches of parts of its scenery.

"Kandellé contains about sixteen families, who

subsist on the produce of one large paddy-field. The lake or tank of Kandellé, which is close by, is a great work, and the best example of the kind of work, that I have ever seen. The lake is about three or four miles in circumference, and, like that of Minery, skirted with green plains. The embankment by which the water is confined is a mile and one-third long. It extends nearly in a straight line, from a rocky hillock at one extremity, to a high ledge of rocks at the other. Its perpendicular height may be about twenty feet; at its base, it may be a hundred and fifty or two hundred feet wide. Its face towards the lake is naked, sloped at an angle of about 45°, and composed of stones that rise one above the other like steps. The stones are of the same size nearly; from two to three feet long, about two high, and from one to two wide. They are of the same kind as the adjoining rock. It is, perhaps, worth remarking, that they have no sharp angles or asperities of surface; they have the appearance of quarried stones, rendered thus smooth by the action of the elements in long process of time. On the land side the slope is very gentle, and the embankment is of gravel and earth. The stone face of the embankment is shaded by trees of great size; the other side is covered with large forest-trees and thick underwood, in most places impenetrable. Besides the great embankment, there is a small one detached from it about a quarter of a mile, and nearly at right angles to it, similarly constructed. The lake has two outlets; the principal one about a hundred yards from the rocky ledge, through which a river is constantly flowing; and another near the opposite extremity of the embankment, which is commonly dry, and carries off water only when the lake is unusually high.

"The great outlet or sluice is constructed with much art and of vast strength; the channel is beneath a platform of masonry that projects into the lake about six feet beyond the line of the embankment, and is about twenty-four feet long. It is built of oblong stones from five to seven feet long, well wrought and nicely adapted to each other without cement. The top of the platform is flat; it contains a small cylindrical well, communicating directly with the channel below, and in which the water, in passing, rises of course to the level of the lake. The water passing through the embankment, appears on the other side gushing out in a noble stream through two apertures, formed by a transverse mass of rock, supported by three perpendicular masses. The transverse mass, which is now cracked in two, is about twelve or fourteen feet long, and four or five thick; and the other masses are of proportional size. The water rushing out in a considerable volume with great force, dashing amongst rocks beneath, in a deep gloomy shade, produced by overhanging trees, makes altogether a very striking scene. The work itself has a simple grandeur about it which is seldom associated with art; it looks more like a natural phenomenon than the design of man.

"The other outlet being dry, afforded an opportunity of seeing the entrance of the channel. At the foot of the embankment there was a circular pit, almost filled with leaves and branches; and a little anterior to it another small pit, the mouth of which was almost entirely covered and defended by a large long mass of hewn stone. The Kandellé river flows into the bay of Tamblegam. At Tamblegam a good deal of rich paddy ground is still irrigated by its stream; but with this exception, and the solitary field at Kandellé, instead of conveying fertility through its whole course, it runs entirely waste.

"The occurrence of these great tanks, in a country now almost entirely desert, makes a forcible impression on the mind of a traveller, and excites greatly his curiosity to know the causes of that change which has evidently taken place. The works themselves indicate that, at some former period, this part of the island must have been inhabited by a numerous people under a regular and probably an absolute form of government, and who had made considerable progress in the arts; and this is confirmed by the history of the country.* What the causes were that produced the change, are not all of them very obvious; one cause pointed out by history seems certain; and that may have been the cardinal one on which all the others hinged: I allude to the wars which the history of Ceylon, vague as it is, decidedly shews were carried on for a long series of years in the northern part of the island. During this disturbed period, reasoning from too certain

* See Forbes's Ceylon.

analogy, it may be taken for granted, that industry was checked, that disease and famine were the consequences, that the tanks were neglected, that morasses were formed and the jungle encroached on the cultivated land, that the climate became permanently deteriorated, and the population diminished; and thus, probably, by a progressive increase of destructive causes, the change in question was produced."

Dr. Davy again observes, that, about six or seven miles from the extremity of Minery lake on the road to Puliankadawetté, he crossed a pretty extensive plain; that on the right, this plain is bounded by jungle, in which he accidentally discovered a great embankment, exceeding in magnitude that of Minery. The mouth of the outlet of the old tank is a massive work, and still nearly in perfect preservation. It is a square well, with walls formed of large stones, some of which are twelve féet by four, neatly cut, and most nicely adapted to each other,—to use the technical phrase, "rabbitted together." It appears that he was unable to cross the embankment and examine the vent of the outlet on the opposite side. At a very little distance, and nearer Minery, he saw in the jungle an immense hollow, like the bed of a great river, intersected by pretty steep ridges of quartz-rock. Its bed was composed of fine sand, and was full of deep pools of clear water. How far it extended he could not say; the rocks, water, jungle, and want of time, prevented him from prosecuting the examination. Now, I confess, that all these interesting objects entirely escaped my notice; I had no idea of having passed so close to them.

Whilst slightly touching upon the subject of the wonderful tanks in the northern parts of Ceylon, I must here mention that Major Forbes, in his "Eleven years in Ceylon," informs us that about twelve miles from Dambool and near the village of Mahaellegamma, there is the embankment of a large tank, which is in good preservation, and contains a supply of water sufficient to irrigate a great extent of rice land. From this place to the sluice of the Kaláwa tank is seven miles; and in that direction, as well as towards the rising grounds of Dambool and Kandepallé on the one side, and Nikini seventeen miles from Dambool on the other side, the country bears the appearance of being occasionally overflowed; and probably this tract of country was all included within the limits of the immense reservoir. Major Forbes found the double sluice of the Kaláwa tank in perfect preservation, built of very large blocks of hewn stone, extremely well joined; and, as is the case with all tanks intended for the purposes of irrigation, the outlets for the water were on a level with the lowest part of the interior excavation. He adds, that the spill-water, as he terms it, is a great mass of solid masonry, and the length of the principal embankment, according to the accounts of it he received, was about five miles; at one of the places where it had burst, he ascertained the sides of the chasm to be *seventy* feet in height. Other lateral embankments, of still greater length, but of less height, completed this stupendous work, which, in a much more contracted form, had existed for many centuries before it was improved and enlarged by the king D'asenkelleya, a short time before he was murdered, A. D. 477. (Let the reader compare this date with that assigned to a great Chinese work, which I have to mention.) The remains of this tank alone, constructed under a very disturbed reign, and immediately after long-continued wars with the Malabars, who had only been expelled from the capital a few years before, shews that then a great population existed under the control of a despot who could direct their labours. A canal, called Jayaganga, was cut from the Kaláwa tank to Anarajahpoora, a distance of upwards of sixty miles. And Major Forbes adds, that the great extent of Anarajahpoora, covering within its walls a space of *two hundred and fifty-six* square miles, will not give any just grounds on which to estimate the extent of its population; as tanks, fields, and even forests are mentioned as being within its limits. Let those, however, who doubt that an immense population formerly existed in Ceylon, compare the prodigious bulk of the ancient monuments of Anarajahpoora, Magam and Polannarrua, with those erected by later kings of the island; then let them compare singly the remains of the Kaláwa tank, the Kandellé tank, which—as Major Forbes states—is now an extensive plain between Minery and Kandellé, or many others, with any or all the public works accomplished in Ceylon for the last five hundred years, and they may then be enabled to come to a right conclusion. In constructing the immense embankments of these artificial lakes, Major Forbes is of opinion, that labour has been profusely, and, often from want of science, uselessly expended; for he believes, that many of these great tanks, which are now in ruins, would, if repaired, be found inapplicable to the purposes of irrigation, for which they were designed. In this opinion I almost concur; but still, by going to work scientifically, and by taking advantage of the tanks that require no repairs,—such as Minery and Kandellé,—and by judiciously turning the course of some of the fine rivers, at present flowing uselessly into the ocean, much might be done, and at no great expense, towards restoring fertility as well as salubrity, to many parts of the island.

The accounts which we have of what Ceylon once was, are indeed surprising; and they would be beyond belief, were it not for the remains of the stupendous works, which have been spoken of. But how the inhabitants of a country of such limited extent, (for we ought to remember that Ceylon is scarcely equal in size to Ireland,) could possibly have effected so much as they, to our astonishment, appear to have done, is quite marvellous. Let us, however, for a moment turn our thoughts to that vast and extraordinary country, China; with which, there is no doubt, that Ceylon, in olden times, was intimately connected by commercial considerations as well as friendly intercourse; and in which such wonders have been accomplished by a numerous and industrious population, who, like the Singalese, were compelled, by despotic rulers, to *labour* when they thought fit, especially in deriving every possible advantage from the *water*, with which Providence had so highly blessed both countries; and let us remember, in proof of the close connection of the two countries I have spoken of, that the prevailing religion of China as well as of Ceylon, is that of Boodhoo. But the very valuable portion of the Chinese territory which has now been opened to connections with British commerce, and the magnificent "Grand Canal," are subjects well deserving attentive consideration.

The great plain forming that north-eastern portion of China, extends in length 700 miles from the great wall, north of Pekin, to the confluence of the rivers Yang-tse-Kiang and Kan-Kiang, 30 deg. N. lat. The former may be assumed to be its southern boundary as far down as Ngan-King. Towards the sea a line drawn from Ngan-King to Tcheou-foo will continue it; and on the west we must trace on the map a line from King-tcheou-foo (a town on the Yang-tse-Kiang) to Hoai-King-foo (on the Hoang-ho); and from thence to the great wall, about 50 miles N.W. of Pekin. Of this plain the breadth is unequal; thus to the north of 35 deg. N. lat., where it extends to the shores of the

Hoang-hai, and partly touches upon the mountain range of Chang-Tung, its width varies from 150 to 250 miles. Let the average breadth be assumed at 200 miles, and this portion of the area must be computed at 70,000 square miles. But the plain enlarges between 35 deg. and 34 deg. N. lat., so as to expand in the parallel of Hoang-ho to more than 300 miles east and west. Still more southerly, in the same parallel in which we find the embouchure of the Yang-tse-Kiang, it widens, inland, to a breadth of nearly 500 miles. On this estimate, the contents of the whole plain may be taken at upwards of 210,000 square miles. Its eastern portion is traversed by the Grand or "Imperial Canal." This majestic work, beginning to the south of the town of Hang-tcheou-foo, extends to the town of Lin-tchin-cheou, where it falls into the Eu-ho river, measuring, in a straight direction, from point to point, 500 miles, but in the line of its whole length perhaps 700 miles. And its design appears to have comprehended other objects besides those of internal navigation and carriage, namely, the draining and irrigation of the land; its features and execution are on a scale of vastness to which as applied to similar works we are strangers in Europe. Thus its depth, its breadth, the dimensions of its banks, &c. are such as would have been impracticable in any country not having a swarming population and the means of applying compulsory, or very slightly paid, labour, (allow me again to ask,—where has ever any great national object, or even that of a private individual, in a new country, been effected without cheap labour?) Its flood-gates and massive sluices are of extraordinary solidity, and exhibit evidence of a high degree of mechanical skill, if they cannot boast of much familiarity with the modern improvements of mechanical application. Throughout almost the whole of the line a perceptible current agitates its waters, as might be expected both from the enormous body restrained within artificial limits, and from the nature of the cuttings which have been opened for them. It is made to traverse lakes, sometimes of considerable extent; it is conducted through channels cut in many places out of the solid rock; it is carried over aqueducts of substantial masonry, in many instances from three to four fathoms above the level of the adjacent country. Streams and rivers are tributaries to it; its banks are lined with towns and villages; and native craft, of all kinds, are constantly navigating its broad surface.—Thus, by this great canal, and the rivers Yang-tse-Kiang and Kan-Kiang on the south, and the Eu-ho and Pei-ho, on the north, goods are transported from the base of the mountain-pass of Mei-king to the town of Tong-tcheou-fou, and the immediate vicinity of the imperial metropolis,—Pekin. Of this prodigious water communication, that portion which is to the south of the Hoang-ho was constructed about the seventh century; but it was not until six centuries afterwards, when the imperial residence was removed from Nankin by the victorious Tatars, that the more northern part was completed.

This noble plain is probably more thickly peopled than any spot of similar dimensions on the face of the globe. By the census of 1813, taken under the Emperor Kea-king, the provinces embraced in it comprised a population of no less than 177,000,000. Let the reader consider this; and let him not doubt, but that the "times of the Gentiles" are nearly completed; at the close of which the utmost parts of the earth shall become the possession of Him, for whom they have always been intended.

It is unnecessary to make any remarks as to what occurred during our journey back to the encampment, where we found that Captain K— had been enjoying himself, much to his satisfaction, whilst we were absent; for he had contrived to stock our larder amply with deer and hog's flesh, besides water-fowl and pea-fowl innumerable.

I must here state, that I find in my notes, taken at this period, farther observations and reflections upon the melancholy situation of this part of Ceylon; constantly subjecting, as it does, its few inhabitants to attacks of not well understood and dangerous fevers; but, I do not intend to trouble the reader with them, as I consider them to be rendered unnecessary, by my having seen, in a number of the "Athenæum," a very astounding account of the probable cause of malaria existing upon the Niger.

A certain quantity of the water of that river was sent by the Admiralty to Professor Daniels, of King's

College, in order to be analyzed; it having been found to be most destructive to the copper sheathing of ships. The Professor, it appears, has shewn that sulphuretted hydrogen, in combination with the sea and river waters, is the cause of this phenomenon; and it is more than likely that it is the miasma thus produced which occasions the destruction of so much human life in that part of the world; as this miasma prevails not only upon the Niger, but also upon many of the other rivers of Africa. The breathing even of diluted sulphuretted hydrogen is known to be most injurious to the lungs; but, if inhaled in a pure state, it causes instant death. Would it not therefore be well to inquire, if the waters of many parts of Ceylon may not likewise contain, though in a much less degree than those of Africa, this destructive gas; as it has been found that the neighbourhood of lakes, ponds, and rivers, even though not covered with jungle, often affords indications that malaria exists in the immediate vicinity. Would it not be desirable, therefore, that the medical officers in Ceylon should pay particular attention to this circumstance. Let any one only look at a Ceylon fresh-water fisherman, (an exact likeness of one of them, by a native artist, is given here), and say, if there must not be some unknown malignant agent at work, which can render him, and nearly all his caste, equally diminutive, and so often sickly and squalid-looking; and may not sulphuretted hydrogen, combined with the water in which he is constantly wading, be this injurious agent? I consider it, however, desirable to give the reader the purport of a paper read by professor Daniels at the Royal Institution, which fully bears me out in the opinion that I had formed, upon first hearing of his investigations, that this destructive gas is to be met with in other parts of the world besides Africa.*

* See Appendix D.

CHAPTER VIII.

"Forth from the thicket rush'd another boar,
So large he seem'd the tyrant of the woods;
With all his dreadful bristles rais'd up high,
They seem'd a grove of spears upon his back:
Foaming he came at me, where I was posted,
Whetting his huge long tusks, and gaping wide,
As he already had me for his prey."—OTWAY.

SET OFF FOR THE KALLA-OYA—A FURIOUS WILD BOAR SHOT —AN INSTANCE GIVEN OF THE PRESENTIMENT FELT BY SOME MEN OF EXTRAORDINARY COMING EVENTS, ETC.—A NIGHT IN THE FOREST, AND NEXT MORNING'S PROGRESS THROUGH IT—APPROACH AN OLD KANDYAN HUNTING STATION, AND THE FLIGHT OF A NUMBER OF PEOPLE FROM IT—THIS ACCOUNTED FOR AFTERWARDS—A RIDICULOUS AND MOST UNTOWARD MISHAP—EXCELLENT FIELD SPORT—A FEMALE ELEPHANT MOST BARBAROUSLY SLAIN, AND AN ELEPHANT CHASE—BEAUTIFUL BIRDS AND SNAKES —PROCEED THROUGH THE FOREST, AND ARRIVE UPON THE RIGHT BANK OF THE KALLA-OYA—A DELIGHTFUL ENCAMPMENT THERE—VERY INDIFFERENT FISHING—SURPRISING CEYLON SNAKE CHARMERS, ETC.—OBSERVATIONS— A GRAND BATTUE—REMARKS.

AT daylight, the morning after our return from Kandellé, we set off, in a body, to make the best of our way through the jungle and forest, towards the Kalla-oya; on the left bank of which we should be again in the Seven Korles, and near to a point where we expected to find a path that leads to Kurunagalla, through Padenny. We very soon saw that, without a guide to conduct us from opening to opening, and through parts of the country where there was less jungle than in others, and sometimes amongst noble trees, under which there was no brushwood whatever, we should have some difficulty in getting forward, especially with the palanquins and horses; and that, owing to the occasional swampiness of the ground, it was much pleasanter walking than riding. We therefore left our horses with their keepers, to be got on as well as they could, with the assistance of the always ready and obliging Malays.

We saw both deer and hogs, but, owing to the noise which we unavoidably made in passing through the woods, we had not a chance of being able to approach sufficiently near to get a shot at them. With Bran's assistance, however, we contrived to bring down a few pea-fowl—chiefly hens—as we wanted them for curries. About eight, A. M. when I calculated that we had thus proceeded about ten or twelve miles, and having reached a larger opening than we had hitherto come upon, I proposed that we should take up our abode for the remainder of the day and the following night, close to the edge of an ancient canal or aqueduct, the dry bed of which we had just crossed, and under the delightful shade of some widely spreading trees. I was the more inclined to halt at this spot, as the guide had previously informed me, that we should find water there, which would answer well enough for the horses; but, for ourselves, we should have to use that which we brought with us.

This plan being adopted, we set to work, and soon erected huts sufficient for our accommodation; and having breakfasted in the forest, as sportsmen ought to do,—that is to say, most plentifully upon substantials,—it was settled that we should take advantage of the agreeable shade which the tall and spreading trees in the neighbourhood seemed to afford, and endeavour to get a shot at deer or hogs, which we now hoped to be able to steal upon, by cautiously approaching the openings which we were aware could not be far off, and in which they were still likely to be feeding.

Accompanied by six Malays, (two of them, my orderlies, armed,) we proceeded slowly and quietly along; when seeing a drove of hogs feeding upon a kind of nuts, which at that season were falling from the trees, O'Hara and I managed to get a tolerably fair shot each at two of them, with lead balls. Only one of them seemed to be wounded; and, he had run but a few yards towards us in the utmost fury, when he was again hit by Captain K—, and so hard, that he rolled over and over. Bran in a moment had hold of him, and when the Malays got up to them, they found the boar was quite dead, and that the good dog still held him by the ear. I believe that O'Hara and I had fired at the same hog; at all events, three balls had gone through his body. He was soon cut up, and the best and fattest parts selected, to be taken back with us, on our return to the huts.

We again went on in the same cautious manner; but, in spite of our utmost care to avoid doing so, disturbing pea and jungle-fowl, as well as vast flocks of wood-pigeons and doves, at which we did not consider it worth our while to fire. But, as I expected, we now saw the prints of the feet of numbers of large animals, some of them those of elephants; yet, we met with none of them; until we came suddenly upon a kind of pond, the banks of which were very swampy, gaudily covered with large and beautiful water-lilies, and immensely tall-growing bamboos and reeds; amongst which, upon seeing us, instantly started up, in menacing attitudes, a large drove of as terrific looking buffaloes as I had ever beheld! We were all well aware, that it was much the safest and most prudent plan not to fire; for, if we even succeeded in killing or wounding some of them, the remainder would, to a certainty, charge us. We therefore secured Bran, and commenced retiring slowly, but always facing our furious foes, which were rendered the more hideous by being besmeared all over with mud. They followed us out of the swamp in which they had been wallowing, and on they came, pawing and tearing up the ground with their horns, and snorting most fearfully at us.

I believe that some of us now felt very much inclined to take to our heels; but, fortunately, we acted more firmly and judiciously. It was, however, high time to think of some mode of defending ourselves, or of getting, if possible, away from them; for, they seemed, every moment, more and more inclined to close with us. Accordingly, having managed so as to reach a tree, which could be easily ascended, with the help of the Malays, we all, except Captain K—, contrived to get up into it; he, being nearest the buffaloes, was unluckily too late, and had therefore no alternative left, but to run for it, which he did with more agility than I thought he possessed, and was consequently soon out of sight. There we were, however, safe and sound, up among the branches of the tree; and entirely out of the reach of the ferocious buffaloes; now not ten yards from us.

It was now our turn; and we, therefore, instantly singled out two of the most furious and leading males; one of which was in a moment knocked over, and the other, being severely wounded, was seized by Bran; but, he was soon obliged to let go his hold, as nearly the whole drove rushed headlong at him, and some of them even recklessly at the good tree which afforded us such complete protection. Their rage and ferocity was now quite astounding! But, another shot from my left barrel, and one from a Malay's rifle, having taken effect in two more of them, we all, at once, shouted as loudly as we possibly could; which at last set the rest of the drove off, with Bran hanging gallantly upon their rear, and doing his best to increase their speed. I must say, however, that they retreated bravely, and like experienced soldiers, some of them, occasionally, turning round and charging the annoying dog; which they did, by making a strange—if I may so speak—semi-circular rush with one of their horns pointed at him; but this he more easily avoided, than the blows they made at him with their powerful fore-feet, to escape which required his utmost agility and sagacity.

We now abandoned our impregnable position; which we had so hastily yet prudently taken up and maintained; and, having despatched the wounded buffaloes, we marched back in triumph to the camp, very well satisfied with a victory, achieved without loss or damage being sustained by any of us, in such a perilous, and, to a true sportsman, so exciting a rencontre. But Captain K— having, as it was supposed by our servants and the coolies, alone escaped to give an account of our disasters, his arrival at the huts, in such a doleful plight, and completely out of breath, threw them all into the utmost consternation; for they every moment dreaded and expected to hear the noise of the enraged buffaloes rushing through the forest, and coming on, flushed with victory, to assail them. It was only when they saw Captain K— mustering the two Malays, who had been left for their protection, and when they recollected that they did not know where to run to, that they were prevented from taking to flight. They had, certainly, heard our firing; but this only confirmed them in the idea of our being placed in a situation of great danger; and as Captain K— had made good his retreat, before he was aware whether we had all got up into the tree or not, he could not tell what might have happened. Our arrival in camp, loaded with spoil, such as it was, was therefore most joyfully hailed by them all; but especially by the interpreter, who had with much difficulty been able to induce the guide to remain with him; as it seemed that, having a turn for jungle sports, he was anxious to have accompanied us, or to have afterwards gone in search of us.

An excellent repast, and a sufficient quantity of good old wine, enabled us to spend a most agreeable evening. We talked over our adventures upon this and other occasions; and perhaps at times endeavoured to describe, in too glowing language or colours, scenes in which we had personally been engaged; but O'Hara and I soon perceived that Captain K— appeared to be very uneasy, lest we had formed an opinion derogatory to his courage, from what had occurred in our rencounter with the buffaloes. We at once assured him, that we entertained no idea of the kind; and, on the contrary, we both readily admitted that he had admirably covered our retreat to the tree, by being, as he well knew, the last to fall back; and, that when a drove of devils,—of which there were, at least, a score—made such a rush, chiefly at him and Bran, and which made it impossible for him to reach the tree, he had no alternative but to act as he did. This well-timed and only fair explanation, and my laughingly spouting the following absurd parody, set all to rights, as far, at all events, as we were concerned :—

He who ascends into a tree,
May next day climb again with me;
But he by buffalo that's gor'd,
May own, at once, that he is floor'd.

I still suspected, nevertheless, that he did not altogether admire the figure which he apprehended that he must have cut in the eyes of the cool and collected Malays; and I therefore felt convinced that he was foolishly inclined to attempt something ridiculous, in order to wipe off any stigma, which they might, I must say erroneously, attach to his reputation for valour. He, however, told us, with great gravity, that, from what he had dreamt the previous night, he had been led to anticipate, that something was about to happen to him; for, in his dream, he had had frequent encounters with, and most narrow escapes from, wild beasts; and he imagined that, at one time, he was knocked down by an enormous elephant; and awoke in the greatest terror, fancying that the huge creature stood over him, and had even raised his trunk in order to give him the finishing blow! He assured us too, that during the whole day he had not been able to get rid of the impression which the scene had made upon his mind. I saw at once that it would answer no good purpose to laugh at him; I therefore endeavoured to convince him that all he had stated could only be the effects of nightmare, under which he must have laboured, probably from having slept upon his back or with his head too low. In short, I did all I could, but in vain, to persuade him of the absurdity of allowing dreams or presentiments of any kind to make such an impression upon his mind; but he now retorted upon me, by asking if I had forgotten the tragical story of poor B. H——, and what had occurred at the storming of Ciudad Rodrigo?—and begged that I would now relate the circumstances, in order to convince O'Hara that there is something in the presentiments which men have been known to feel of extraordinary coming events. The story which Captain K—— had before heard, and now alluded to, is as follows:—Captain H——, of the — regiment, had just been promoted from a lieutenancy of grenadiers to a company in the second battalion; but being then in the field, he was, as usual, and when second battalions were at home, ordered to take command of a company in the first, the captain of which was absent. This fine corps was formed in the trenches, impatiently waiting for orders, from Sir Thomas Picton, to move on to the assault of the main breach; when Captain H—— came to the head of the column, and requested that he might, as a particular favour, be allowed to give up the command of the battalion company, to the subaltern who had so long had charge of it, and be permitted to rejoin the grenadiers, as they were to lead into the breach. This, of course, could not be complied with, and he was directed to return to his post, which was near the rear of the column. But as he was going off, and as the order for the advance of the regiment was given, he turned round and followed me for a few yards, and to my surprise, said that he hoped I would be good enough at least to comply with another request of his; which was, that I would the next day write to his brother in Ireland, and tell him how he, Captain H——, conducted himself that night; as he felt convinced he should not *outlive it.* I smiled at the absurdity of the request; but, as he seemed really serious, I hurriedly promised that, if I myself should escape, I would attend to it. It appeared, however, that he had scarcely returned to his post, when he again, and seemingly under some strong impulse, left it, and ran forward along the reverse flank of the column, till he found himself in the midst of the grenadiers, who were in the act of mounting the rugged breach; on the top of which he and Lieutenant P—— of the grenadiers were killed, and their gallant captain most severely wounded. The next day I fulfilled my promise, and wrote to Dr. H—— at L——, who, I conclude, must have received my letter. This is a strange story, yet nevertheless a true one.

It was now time for me to see that the three large fires, which had been duly prepared, were burning brightly; and that our sentinels were alert upon their posts, before I retired to rest for the night. I was also anxious to ascertain what was going on in the neighbouring woods; but especially in the direction in which by far the greater part of the carcases of the buffaloes, slain the previous afternoon, had been left to become the prey of the numerous wild beasts.

Upon my going out for these purposes, I found the fires in every respect as they should be, and our watchmen attentive to their duty; and I was not disappointed in my expectations, as to what was likely to be going on in the jungle; for the growling, snarling, howling, and barking, even exceeded what I had listened to, with such surprise, inland from Matura. The ferocious animals seemed to be hotly engaged in deadly conflict, and as if tearing each other to pieces; and, although this strange commotion was going forward nearly a mile off, the uproar occasioned could be distinctly heard in our camp. But what a wild forest scene was this, and how animating to an amateur of field-sports; who, no doubt, would have anticipated the delights of bagging some of the actors in it, as soon as the day should dawn! — The stars then, however, shone brightly; myriads of fire-flies flitted from bush to bush; it was a dead calm; and the otherwise perfect stillness of the night was only broken by the noisy and terrific conflict which I have mentioned.

Having had almost every thing packed up the night before, and in readiness in case of necessity to start, we were able before sunrise to set off in a body, to work our way through the wilderness; in which we every moment expected to meet with adventures of one kind or another. Our guide, who, (as the interpreter now informed me, was a first-rate sportsman,) had often been, for weeks together, in this part of the forest, killing in the Kandyan manner deer and hogs, and he assured us that if, by and by, we would only move along with as little noise as possible, (we were then, as usual, shouting with all our might to drive away the wild beasts,) he would soon bring us into the neighbourhood of some houses, annually frequented by hunters, and where, he had no doubt we would find plenty of both. He at the same time told us that, if we had no objection, he would take us a little way out of the direct line to the place he wished to reach on the Kalla-oya; but, that this would not signify, as he hoped that the number of animals we should fall in with would fully compensate for his having thus, in a slight degree, lengthened the day's journey. This was just what we wanted; as we did not know what was the best direction in which to proceed, in order to find game; and all of us now becoming most eager for opportunities of evincing our skill and dexterity, we again assured the guide that he should be well rewarded, especially with gunpowder, if he fulfilled his engagement. We now, therefore, continued our interesting and exciting march for about eight miles, in the same cautious way as we had done the previous day; chiefly through a magnificent forest, with occasionally a large extent of thick and tangled jungle amongst it; and in doing so, we saw, a short way to our right, two elephants, up to which, as I expected, Captain K— wished to go, with the intention of bagging one or both of them. I was glad, however, to see, that they were not inclined to afford him an opportunity of evincing either his perfect coolness or expertness; as they made off before he could get near enough to fire at them.

We now also had frequent glimpses of deer and hogs; but, as before, and owing to the noise we were, unavoidably, obliged to make in getting along through the jungle, we became fully convinced that it was impossible to approach sufficiently near to have a shot at them. The experienced guide, moreover, at last told me, that we should never do any good, if we continued to move in such a large body, with a palanquin and horses along with us; and, as the part of the country he had alluded to was at hand, he did not know how to advise us to proceed. He knew, as well as I did, that the servants and coolies would be frightened out of their wits, were we, sportsmen, to leave them behind us; it was therefore arranged that we should all go together to the hunting station he had spoken of, and leaving the servants, &c. there to prepare breakfast, we should, with most of the Malays, proceed a little way farther to the northward in quest of game, which the guide made sure of finding either in the openings or in the clumps of jungle, with which, in most places, the country in that direction was covered. This, we all agreed, was the best plan that we could adopt, so we went on accordingly.

But we now entered a totally different description of country, from that through which we had hitherto travelled, and which, in some respects resembled that in the neighbourhood of Kurunagalla, especially in the direction of Negombo; as it consisted of clumps of trees, with thick brushwood under them, encompassed by small but bright green grassy plains, in which, to our delight, we soon began to see herds of deer, buffaloes and hogs, quietly feeding; some of them not very far from us, and others at a considerable distance.

In consequence, we now took off to the right, in order to reach the houses, without shewing ourselves in the more open country; and soon seeing a few palm-trees, about a quarter of a mile off, which, as usual, indicated where they were situated, O'Hara and I mounted our horses and rode forward towards what seemed to be some miserable huts; but, to our surprise, a number of people fled from them, apparently, in the greatest alarm, upon seeing us approaching. My first impulse was to gallop after them, in order to assure them that they had nothing to fear from us; but, the next moment recollecting that I could not tell them so, and might only add to their fright, I thought it best to let them go off. Upon entering the kind of hamlet, we found fires burning, chatties upon them, and quantities of food cooking; but not a soul had remained behind, from whom we might have ascertained the cause of their alarm, or who might have assigned a reason for their sudden departure.

Our people having come up, I mentioned to the interpreter and guide what had occurred; when they both seemed to be equally as much surprised as we had been, and could not in any way account for the extraordinary number of people we had seen, nor for their having run away in so strange and incomprehensible a manner. It was only from what took place afterwards, that I was in some measure enabled to do so; at least I was convinced of my being correct in the conclusion I came to.

Not many weeks had elapsed, after my return to the Seven Korles, when I again heard of meetings of numbers of Kandyans in Neurecalava, but for what purpose I could not ascertain. Government, it however appeared, had obtained better information; and having learned that another Pretender to the Kandyan throne had set himself up in that wilderness, and had collected some people about him, who appeared resolved to support his pretensions, Major Frazer, of the Quarter-Master General's department, was sent off with a body of troops, with orders to proceed by forced marches, so as to lay hold of him and his abettors before they could be aware of our having heard of their doings or intentions. Whilst Major Frazer was thus proceeding by a road nearer to the sea-coast than that direct from the Seven Korles, I also heard of this Pretender and his followers; and I was correctly informed that they were then not far from Anarajahpoora. Without waiting for orders from Colombo, I therefore considered it to be my duty to march against him immediately; and I had made the necessary Commissariat and other arrangements, so as to be able to start that very night by torch-light, with all the Malays, and some companies of Europeans, for which purpose they were actually assembled; when I received intelligence, upon which I could depend, that Major Frazer had caught the Pretender, and some of his ill-advised adherents. This foolish aspirant to royalty was soon after honoured, as I understood, with the appointment of scavenger at Kandy!—So contemptible had such attempts at rebellion now become in the eyes of Government: but, I had then no doubt, that it was upon this ambitious youth, and a number of his infatuated followers, that I had come so suddenly and unexpectedly.

I must apologise for this digression, and beg of the reader to imagine that he now sees us stealing cautiously along through a considerable clump of trees intermixed with jungle, which effectually conceals us from a large herd of deer, feeding quietly just beyond it. During our stealthy progress through the clump, we were kept in constant apprehension, lest the number of pea and jungle-fowl, which every instant ran off or took wing, should alarm them before we could reach its outer edge; from whence we, and some of the eager Malays, were to fire upon them, not only with balls, but also with large buck-shot. Whilst I was thus cautiously pushing my way through the woods, and not paying that attention I ought to have done to the tangled masses of runners and branches overhead, or to impediments of any kind, which occasionally almost completely obstructed our passage, I unluckily struck my hat with great force against one of those curiously rounded nests, so ingeniously constructed and suspended from the slightest twigs or branches of trees, by the large red or brownish ants, which bite so dreadfully. Most certainly I had given it a *knock;* for I had even driven in parts of its sides and bottom ; and, in an instant, there fell down upon me, a shower of thousands of them, which, without a moment's delay, attacked me most furiously, inflicting exceedingly painful bites, much like burns. My companions, naturally enough, could not help laughing outright at the sudden exclamation which I had involuntarily uttered, and at seeing me throw down my gun, and in the greatest haste, with the aid of one of my orderly Malays, commence stripping myself without ceremony, stark naked. This I knew was the only way, (such an accident having happened to me once before), to dislodge my unmerciful assailants, which had already got within my shirt, trowsers, &c. I however begged of them to go on without minding me, otherwise they might rely upon it, all the game would be off. In little more than a second, I had pulled off and tossed from me all my clothes, as well as my broad-brimmed straw hat, which, from being so large and a good deal slouched, had prevented me from seeing this devil's-nest, and had caused the untoward disaster. But, assisted by the Malay, I had now to turn my shirt, jacket, trowsers, stockings, &c. inside out, and to shake and beat them against the ground and the trees, before we could entirely get rid of my obstinate tormentors; and, by this time, many large and very painful bumps had risen all over me from their bites. Before we had got through this rather tedious operation, my two allies and four of the Malays had discharged eight well loaded barrels at the deer; and, when I had again dressed myself and rejoined them, I found that they had bagged two fat bucks; and that Bran had gone off in pursuit of two others, which were wounded; one of them seemingly so severely, that they had little doubt, but that he would manage to hold him, until the Malays, who were running with all their might, could come up to his assistance. All had been admirably done, and I congratulated my friends upon their success; though I could not but, at the same time, express how strongly I felt my disappointment at having been, in such a ridiculous way, prevented from performing my part upon so exciting and interesting an occasion. Feeling, however, very uncomfortable, and still fancying that many of the ants were yet biting me, I reluctantly quitted the field, to return to the houses, in order to rub myself all over, as the Malays recommended, with some oil and lime-juice, which, they assured me, would soon assuage the pain I continued to suffer. Leaving, therefore, my companions and their attendants to finish what they had so well begun, I undertook to have breakfast ready for them, when they should return with the game; but, above all, I begged of them, that they would be sure to look after my gallant and faithful dog, which had gone on after the wounded deer.

As soon as I reached the houses, I sent back along with the Malay who had accompanied me, some of the coolies, to assist in bringing in the choicest parts of the venison, of which we had now, I trusted, got such a supply, as would enable my cook to display, as he usually did, his powers as a first-rate artist. But it was past 10 A. M., and the day had become exceedingly hot, before my friends and their followers made their appearance, literally loaded with spoil; for they had not only got the stag that Bran had pursued, but likewise a wounded doe, which had fallen from loss of blood and consequent weakness, at the moment she was entering a patch of jungle, where they saw her lying upon the ground, or they would not have thought of following her farther.

The day continuing to be very hot, and there not being a breath of air stirring, I thought that my companions would have been satisfied to remain quiet, at least, until evening; but they had observed, before their return from the morning's operations, some elephants enter a large clump of trees, about a mile off; and as Captain K—, in spite of my reminding him of his dream, was determined to have a shot at one of them, O'Hara, rather than allow him to go alone, volunteered to accompany and back him. As for me, I never had any fancy for elephant-shooting; and I was besides still suffering too severely from the effects of the now greatly inflamed and painful ant-bites, to think of sport of any kind, for that day. We had now, however, decided upon spending the night in the houses from which the Kandyans had fled, though I certainly would have preferred doing so in huts constructed by ourselves in the forest; but, there was water here, and the guide informed us that we should not find any—bad as we thought it—so good, until we reached the Kalla-oya, which we intended to do the following day.

The two sportsmen, attended by four most ready and willing Malays, set off before noon upon their expedition; but, in order to insure their greater safety, I made one of the latter, upon whom I knew I could depend, carry my trusty "Manton," carefully loaded with brass balls, to be kept in readiness as a reserve, or to be used by either of the gentlemen, in case they might prefer it to their own very inferior guns.

Although they thought that they had marked in several head of game, yet, they had been out fully three hours before they discovered an unlucky female elephant standing, unconscious of danger, in the coolest part of a thick and almost impenetrable clump of tall trees and jungle. With considerable difficulty, the two gentlemen contrived to creep up to within the usual distance of her, without her having the slightest suspicion of their proximity. Captain K—, with my Manton, then took deliberate aim at her eye, and fired, when down she fell. But, in an instant, the wood resounded with the trumpeting of elephants, the cracking and crashing of branches and brushwood, and the loud uproar caused by a host of enraged elephants rushing on to the charge!—Not a moment was to be lost by the startled sportsmen in making off. They were soon clear of the clump of trees, in which the elephant had been so barbarously murdered; but, in order to reach the next, they had now to run across an opening, for fully a hundred yards. In doing so, they were seen and pursued by three or four elephants; but, when about half way through it, they were enabled, though with much difficulty, to give their pursuers the slip, and at last to get clear of them. This chase might have been highly exciting *field sport* to the furious and greatly exasperated elephants, but was very far from being so to the fugitives, who undoubtedly had a very narrow escape; as their keen pursuers were, at one time, within a few yards of them, and it was only by doubling and squatting that they were ultimately able to steal away.

Upon their return, I at once saw the doleful plight in which both my friends were; but especially O'Hara, who was not accustomed to such violent exertion or exercise; and taking compassion upon them, (whilst I now enjoyed my laugh at their expense), I had tiffin and some well cooled Hodgson's ale brought in; to which, when they had changed their greatly disordered and torn garments, they were able to do something like justice. But Captain K— was now more confirmed than ever in the notion of the importance which ought to be attached to dreams; though he had to admit, that it is very difficult to interpret them; for, even this day's sought-for adventures had not terminated in his receiving a *coup de grace*, which of course he had calculated upon.

During the absence of my companions, notwithstanding the pain which I continued to suffer from the ant-bites, I was tempted by the numbers of beautiful birds which were flying about, or sitting quietly and practising their wild cries and notes amidst the branches of the trees, that grew around and close to the houses, to stroll out under their delightful shade. I was also anxious to shoot one of a large flock of the most gorgeously arrayed parrots, which I had as yet met with in any part of the island: indeed, I had not before seen any of the kind. I soon brought down one of them; and I find it thus described in my notes. It is considerably above the usual size of parrots; has a bright scarlet body, and wings of a dark blue, red, green, and yellow colours, curiously intermixed; a very long scarlet and light blue tail; and it is, I believe, altogether the most splendid bird, in point of plumage, to be seen in Ceylon. I really thought that I should never tire of admiring them, as they sat or hopped about from branch to branch, displaying to the greatest advantage their fine feathers, seemingly little disturbed by my presence, though I had just slain one of their companions. Most of the trees were covered with small reddish berries, upon which many of them were feeding, and at the same time uttering the loudest and most disagreeable screaming imaginable. There were amongst them some pretty birds, which I had not before heard of; and which had, as it struck me, selected very unsuitable associates; their feathers were of a yellow and bluish colour, curiously arranged and intermixed. They uttered, occasionally, some very sweet, low, melodious notes, which I was anxious to have heard more distinctly, but the loud screaming of the parrots rendered this almost impossible.

I saw here, likewise, some very beautiful snakes, lying as if basking in the sun, and near to their holes or places of concealment, which were situated, in most instances, at the roots of old or decayed trees, or under those high conical-shaped mounds, which are thrown up by the ants, but, being abandoned by them, are taken possession of by snakes, particularly by the cobra de capellos. None of those, however, which I saw, appeared to be venomous; at all events, they all glided off to their holes, the moment that they either saw or heard me approaching. In short, I find from my notes, that I had a very interesting noon-day walk in a Ceylon forest or jungle.

Finding myself—though certainly better—in the evening still unable to walk far, or fit for any kind of field sports, and my companions being as little inclined as I was to encounter dangers; as soon as it had become cooler, we walked out under the now truly agreeable shade of the lofty trees; and falling in with a number of both small and large monkeys, (the latter were of a greyish colour, with flowing white beards), we spent half an hour in throwing up sticks and stones at them ; an amusement which, as may well be supposed, greatly provoked their ire, and caused them to grin and gibber at us, in the most ridiculous manner possible. They even, sometimes, caught the sticks thrown at them, and threw them back at us, with considerable force ; yet, I must say, they were very bad marksmen, often hitting their companions instead of us, and thereby increasing their rage. In short, we maintained the unequal combat, until we were quite out of breath, and exhausted by throwing missiles of all kinds at them, and by laughing at their absurd and ireful grimaces.

On our return to the houses, we, of course, found a most comfortable repast ready for us, as well as a fair proportion of well-cooled old wine ; so that it would have been our own faults, had we not spent an agreeable and truly comfortable evening. But, during the night, owing to the unceasing noises kept up by the rushing backwards and forwards, and just over our heads, of some large rat-snakes, which had taken up their abode in the low thatched roof of the house we occupied, and the endless buzzing of muskitoes, we spent not only an uncomfortable, but also an almost sleepless night ; and consequently, the moment day dawned, we were all, once more, ready to recommence our journey. We now had several hours of pretty hard work, in occasionally forcing our way through some parts of the jungle, amidst which there rose, at long intervals, a few of those insulated rocks or hills I have before mentioned, as a distinguishing feature of this part of the country, which were covered with finely variegated foliage; and, in some instances, parts of them seemingly by ruins, of which the guide said he knew nothing whatever, except that the people, in general, believe that they were of old, and are still, the habitations of devils; who, surrounded by wild beasts, snakes and reptiles of all kinds, are constantly devising how they can do most mischief to mankind. We were, however, at last, not sorry to find ourselves out of the "howling wilderness," and upon the finely wooded right bank of the Kalla-oya, not far from the point for which we had steered, and where it was winding its slow course over a sandy and muddy bottom, which led me at once to fear that I was not likely to be able to display to advantage my dexterity as an angler. Indeed, we now all regretted, upon seeing its—at that season—rather diminutive stream, that we had not remained another day where we had spent the former, and where there was such an abundance of game of all kinds. But, at the recommendation of our excellent guide, we then proceeded lower down the river; in which direction he said that the country was more open, and where we should be nearer to the entrance of a path leading towards Padenny. As we went along, the river as well as the country changed considerably their appearance and character; for the bed of the stream became more rocky and gravelly; and at times, it flowed with some degree of rapidity, into more dark and apparently deeper pools, which gave me still some hopes of amusement in the piscatory line; and the woods seemed as if better suited to be the haunts of deer and other animals, which were more the objects of my pursuit than elephants or buffaloes.

At length, coming to a verdant spot, about fifty yards from the bank of the river, where the ground rose a little above the generally flat country, and where some fine teak and talipot trees afforded an agreeable shade, we resolved to go no farther, but there to erect our sylvan abodes; moreover, it was high time to do so, as it was past 10 A. M., the heat had become excessive, and we all wanted our breakfast.

Our servants having ample assistance from the Malays and coolies, they were soon able to lay out before us a most substantial repast; but, whilst seated at it, and conversing with my well-pleased and cheerful friends; I was struck with the similarity of our situation to that of Gil Blas and his knavish companions, in the forest between Villardésa and Almondabar, who had halted there after a fatiguing night's journey; of which such an admirable picture has been drawn by Le Sage.—"Nous nous enfonçames dans le plus épais du bois, et nous nous arrétâmes dans un endroit fort agréable, sur un gazon entouré de plusieurs gros chênes, dont les branches entremêlées formoient une voute que la chaleur du jour ne pouvoit percer.—Nous nous assimes. Nous tirames de la besace du frere Antoine quelque grosses piece de pain avec plusieurs morçeaux de viande rotis, et nous nous mimes á nous en escrimer á l'envi l'un de l'autre. Neanmoins, quelque appetit que nous eussions, nous cessions souvent de manger pour donner des accolades à l'outre, qui ne faisoit que passer des bras de l'un entre les bras de l'autre."—This I hope will give the reader a tolerably correct idea of the delightful situations which we usually selected as our resting places in the Ceylon forests; as well as a just notion of our morning repasts;—only he must for wine substitute tea or coffee;—and I must declare, (and I think that all experienced campaigners will agree with me), that after a long and hot march, there is nothing so refreshing and exhilarating as *green-tea.* How often, in Spain and Portugal, after a long and fatiguing march, have I enjoyed the refreshment of such a noon-day repast, amidst almost similar scenery; as well as the agreeable and friendly intercourse of my military associates! On one occasion, in particular, in the arid forest which extends for a considerable distance around Estremos, when I was travelling to Lisbon, in company with an officer of the 7th Fusiliers, just after the battle of Talavera, attended by my servant only, but all of us tolerably well armed, though very indifferently mounted. The road, at the time I speak of, had become very unsafe to travel, on account of a number of banditti, or rather smugglers who had become such, and who then frequented it. About nine in the morning,—

(when those who have travelled in that part of Portugal know how hot it becomes in August), we fell in with seven very suspicious-looking persons, who were much better armed than we were, and rode horses very superior to our starved and jaded animals. Whilst we, at once, rightly concluded what their calling was, they seemed to be equally aware of ours. We saluted each other most politely; we were glad to see that they made no demonstrations whatever of hostilities; and the reader may suppose that we were equally inclined for peace. They addressed us in Spanish, and I answered in Portuguese, which I spoke and understood best. The person who seemed to be their leader then good-humouredly asked us, if we had breakfasted? I replied that we had not, but that we intended soon to halt for that purpose.—"If," said he, "the English gentlemen will accompany us a little way off the road, they may join us at that meal;—and I believe, (looking knowingly at us) that we are better provided with the where-withal than they appear to be." We readily accepted the invitation; and I assure the reader, that I never enjoyed a breakfast more than I did that, under such strange circumstances, and with such associates, in the midst of a forest, chiefly composed of large cork and fir trees, that afforded complete protection from the powerful rays of a scorching sun. They soon produced an *outre*, or pig-skin, of excellent red wine, cold roasted fowls and eggs, and several large loaves of good white wheaten bread. We had with us, (and we were half ashamed to produce them), only some lumps of Commissary's lean boiled beef, three sea biscuits, and a small flask of *aquadente*, as the soldiers called a villanous kind of spirit. The whole being deposited on the grass, we set to work as if we had been old cronies; eating, drinking, and laughing immoderately, but chiefly at the oddity of our respective situations; for they had not even pretended to deny who they were, but seemed to be, on the contrary, proud of the new profession which they had adopted, as they said, from want of a better.

Having done ample justice to our repast, we embraced each other most lovingly, and parted the best friends in the world; the leader remarking, laughingly, that we were not the game whom they were on the look-out for; that they knew well we had little or nothing with us of any value in their eyes; and, they were besides aware that, even for that little, we would fight like devils. One of his people, he said, would shew us a path through the woods into the great road, upon which we should, in about half an hour, meet with a strong party of Portuguese cavalry, who were in search of them; but, he had no fear whatever that we would tell them where we had partaken of their hospitality, and where we had all been so happy together.

We were accordingly met by an officer at the head of about thirty dragoons. He asked us, in Portuguese, if we had seen or heard of the Spanish Ladrones, who were laying every traveller under contribution, but particularly those carrying merchandise up the country; some of whom had been killed and others severely beaten, but especially those who had resisted and shewn most courage. We shook our heads,—we did not understand him:—and, after all, though no one can pretend to justify it, a smuggler's life must be interesting, and also have something attractive or fascinating in its unlawful allurements, to those who are led away by the hopes of the immense profits to be thereby acquired, which can only be reaped in scenes of danger.

I had promised some of the respectable, venerable looking, and finely bearded Headmen, who, from time to time, had been summoned from the posts of the Seven Korles bordering upon Neurecalava, to attend my courts at Kurunagalla as assessors, that I would, before long, have a battue in their neighbourhood; in which, they had assured me that there were not only many elephants, but also abundance of all kinds of game; and, as I anticipated having both amusement and uncommon gratification upon the occasion; and, above all, that I should thus be able to surprise and astonish my companions, I had not, as yet, mentioned to them my intention of having—if I could accomplish it—such great doings during this excursion. As soon, therefore, as we reached the place where our huts were to be built, and where we purposed to remain the following day, I sent off the interpreter and guide, with directions to call upon some of the most influential Headmen, and to request them to have their people in readiness to beat the covers at dawn the next morning;

and also to desire that they would send persons sufficiently early, to conduct us to the part of the country, which their knowledge of it would enable them to select as the scene of operations. Of course, I cautioned them not to say to any one in the camp, on their return to it, a word of what they had done.

This being arranged, I proposed to my friends to shoot, fish, or do whatever they pleased, for their evening's amusement. As for me, I intended about one, P.M. to try what I could do with the fishing rod in the river. Captain K— decided upon ranging the neighbouring woods with his gun, attended by some of the Malays; but O'Hara preferred accompanying me, as I had no intention of going far from the huts; being still, in some degree, a sufferer from the effects of the ant-bites.

What the fishing in the Kalla-oya may be, when it is swollen by the periodical rains, and when, (judging from the appearance of its banks), it could be made to overflow and irrigate a great extent of country, I cannot pretend to say; but at the season I visited it, it was very far from being good. The largest fish I caught with the river shrimp was not a pound in weight; and as for the fly, the fish would scarcely deign to look at it; though they took, fast enough, even grains of boiled rice. In short, though I speedily caught a good many fish of various kinds, yet the sport was so inferior that I soon got tired of it; and therefore returned some time before sunset to the huts, a good deal disappointed; as, from what I had been told, I expected to have had much better.

On arriving at them, I found that some of the Headmen had, very obligingly, sent a party of jugglers to exhibit for our amusement, and also a supply of excellent fruit; but what we valued most was a large chatty-full of good milk; with which we had been wholly unprovided for tea or coffee for several days past. I suspected that the interpreter had given them a hint that such supplies would be acceptable to us; and that they were the only presents which I would receive.

One of these jugglers, or charmers, was by far the most expert and daring fellow I had seen perform with snakes; and he completely astonished us by the manner in which he pulled about, and treated with the greatest indifference and coolness, a very fine Cobra de capello, or Noya, as the Kandyans call it, about three feet and a half long, which he had brought with him. He handled it with great roughness, yet perfect confidence; he also struck and threatened it in so daring a way, that at last I suspected its poison fangs had been broken or extracted; but this I found was not the case; for, after he had taken much pains in order to irritate it, and soothe it when enraged, and had even put it into his bosom, I told one of the servants to desire him to open its mouth—not expecting that he would do so—and shew me whether the poison-fangs were extracted or not. He did so without the least hesitation; and there they certainly were, and in the most perfect state! Indeed, I confess that, in even going up to examine them, a strange sort of thrilling sensation ran through my whole frame, at the idea of being bitten by such a terrible yet beautiful creature. I then desired the servant to ask him, if the snake would bite me if I touched it?—He instantly replied, that it certainly would do so; and, seemingly afraid lest I should venture too near it, he, in great haste, put it back into the bag in which he had brought it. I inquired, also, if he would take the same liberties with a hooded snake just caught?—He replied, that he would not at first; but that he would do whatever I pleased with it, after he had had it in his possession for a day or two; and added, that he had caught the one just put into his bag, only four days before, and that it had not been offered any thing to eat, since it was dug out of the ground.

I wished to have given money to this surprising fellow and his companions, who, to amuse us, had performed so many wonderful feats in the usual dexterous Eastern style; but they would not accept of any remuneration whatever. I was assured by a high caste Kandyan,—one of the Headmen's brothers—who had brought them to the encampment, that the man who had taken such astonishing liberties with the Noya, was considered to be the most powerful charmer in the country; and it was upon that account that he had been sent to me, I having often expressed a wish to see the Kandyan, who had, as I before mentioned, saved Captain L— from the elephant at Padenny, and who could not, for some reason or other, be induced to come to him or me. How they contrive to acquire such power or command over animals and reptiles, I had, of course, no means of ascertaining: but, I am of opinion, that their art chiefly consists in daring to act confidently with them. This evening's exhibition, however, brought strongly to my remembrance what occurred between Moses and Aaron, and the wise men and the sorcerers; and the account given in holy writ puts it beyond all doubt, that the Egyptians possessed great and surprising powers in this respect; for, we read,—"and Aaron cast down his rod before Pharaoh, and before his servants, and it became a serpent. Then Pharaoh also called the wise men and the sorcerers: Now the magicians of Egypt, they also did in like manner with their enchantments: for they cast down every man his rod, and they became serpents: but Aaron's rod swallowed up their rods."

The reader may, probably, be surprised that I have so seldom spoken of snakes and reptiles of any kind, which are supposed to be so numerous in Ceylon; and that I have not given accounts either of my own adventures, or of those of others with them. The fact is, that much as I have wandered, as a sportsman, and an admirer of fine scenery, or in search of what is wonderful and surprising in so many parts of this extraordinary country, it was very seldom that I met with snakes in considerable numbers; and whether they were venomous or not I could not tell; as they invariably made off to their places of concealment, the moment that they either heard or saw me approaching. In one instance, in returning from the lake near Kurunagalla, I observed by far the longest and thickest snake, (I believe it was of the rock species,) I had met with, gliding across the narrow path, just before, and within a few yards of me. Wishing, if possible, to secure such an enormous creature for a friend in Colombo, to whom I had promised one, I fired one barrel of my gun, loaded with large shot, at its head, which it carried about a foot and a half above the ground; and the other, loaded with a ball, at its body, as it slid past me. Both shots took such effect, that I thought I must have killed it; yet, it was able to make off—certainly, most strangely and violently convulsed—into thick jungle that grew in masses around and over some rocks, amidst which I lost sight of it. Were I to venture to guess at its length, I should say, that it must have been fully twenty-five feet. I returned to the spot next morning, with a number of European and Malay soldiers, in hopes of finding it dead amongst the jungle-covered rocks; but, after a long and careful search, in all directions, we could see nothing whatever of it, and I cannot imagine what could possibly have become of it; for, we were even unable to discover any hole or place into which it might have glided and hid itself.

Another reason why I have made so few extracts, from what I find in my notes respecting snakes, is that Dr. Davy in his very superior and instructive work, upon the interior of this interesting island, has so ably treated the subject, and given such a clear and excellent account of the experiments he made, as to the effects of their poisons, that I should consider it both absurd and presumptuous, were I to venture to say more than I have done; and I, therefore, must refer any reader, curious in such matters, to his book, which cannot fail, in both deeply interesting and amusing him. I had the pleasure of once meeting Dr. Davy at the King's House in Colombo, and we were there introduced, by Lady Brownrigg, to each other; but, I regret to say, that I have never since met him in any other part of the world.

Having dined, as the reader may suppose, chiefly upon venison, dressed in various ways; and having like true-hearted sportsmen done ample justice to some excellent claret, which is so well prepared in England for the Indian market; and the usual precautions having been taken as to fires and sentinels; we spent a quiet and comfortable night in our pleasant and even, considering the situation, cool encampment. But, I must here again remind the reader, that my mentioning, in the way I do, such delicacies as venison, followed by first-rate claret, is by no means with the intention of making him fancy that I care for the good things of this world; I only do so in order to convince him of the superior style of comfort, in which Ceylon field sports may be enjoyed, in comparison with the deprivations and annoyances which must be endured in the "far west," and in most parts of America, where the hunter meets with too much of savage life to suit my ideas of gentlemanly field sports; much as the author of "Statistical Sketches of Upper Canada," or a "Backwoodsman," as well as a few others have said of them, and in their praise.

I had arranged with my companions that we were to start upon a shooting excursion into the neighbouring country, before dawn the following morning, with all the Malays but two, who were to remain for the protection of our servants, &c. at the huts. When, therefore, the persons I had sent for to conduct us to the scene of the day's operations arrived in camp, at the time fixed upon for our setting out, they had no suspicion of what was going forward. We had scarcely gone two miles down the river, when we found ourselves in the midst of Kandyans, who had been assembled in much greater numbers than I had expected; and the reader may easily imagine, how greatly surprised and pleased my friends were, when I told them, that all these people—most of them with long thin poles in their hands—had been brought there, in order that we might have, as I hoped, such a day's hunting, or rather driving of elephants and other animals, as, perhaps, had never before been seen in that part of Ceylon. I soon saw that they were all eager and ready to begin the battue, and delighted at the idea of the number of elephants, which, as they calculated, would that day be slain; for, they had of late been doing incalculable mischief to their crops; and a better place could not have been selected for the purpose; as the wild beasts, owing to the drought which had for some time prevailed, could find water almost nowhere else but in the Kalla-oya.

It was, from supposing this to be the case, arranged by the Headmen, who seemed to understand how to act, that the people, who had tom-tom beaters and pipers along with them, should first surround a considerable extent of country, including in it the path which leads to the south, and should gradually close in towards a given point, where we sportsmen and the Malays were to take post near to, or up in, some tall trees that stood on both sides of the path, and upon the left bank of the river; as it was intended to force the animals, found within the circle, across it and out of the Seven Korles, into the wilderness of Neurecalava.

Fully three hours had elapsed before a Headman, who had remained with us, recommended, as the beaters could now be distinctly heard coming towards us, that we should think of taking our stations, so as to be prepared for the approaching game. This we readily did with all our guns and rifles carefully loaded.

At length, the shouting of the people, and the increasing loudness of the drumming and piping announced to us that we ought to be on the alert; and a few minutes only had elapsed, when a messenger, who had been despatched by the leader of the beaters, arrived in great haste, to inform us, that they had enclosed a number of elephants, buffaloes, and other animals; and, that in an attempt made by the former to break through the line, but in which they had failed, some men had been knocked down, and it was feared that at least two of them were most seriously hurt; and, unfortunately, one of them was our faithful guide, who had so admirably led us through the wilderness.

As usual upon such occasions, immense numbers of pea and jungle-fowl began to run past us, and to fly over our heads across the river; the former uttering their loud and wild cries. Soon after, some deer, elks, &c. dashed along at a great rate. They were before long followed by buffaloes—wild and tame—hogs, dogs, jackals, and hares; but, at none of these had we any intention of firing.—"My eyes!" exclaimed O'Hara, who was close to me up in a large teak-tree, and who could no longer be silent; "don't you see that tiger?—May I not fire at him?" "Be quiet;—not a word;—none of these animals must be prevented from crossing the river." At this moment, our whole attention was directed to where the shouting had much increased, and to where the branches of the trees and masses of jungle were cracking, bending and crashing in such a way, as to convince us that the elephants were now coming towards us, and even into the open space through which the path runs, upon both sides of which we were all so safely and judiciously posted. In an instant after, a large herd of elephants, buffaloes, and hogs, intermixed, rushed into the space I have mentioned, and in which we expected them; all of them, I may say, within proper distance. As they were passing, each of us singled out the elephant or animal we wished to bring down. The firing did not last long; for, the moment it began, the drove of animals—the largest that any of us had ever seen—rushed, in the utmost terror, hustling and jostling each other, into the river, causing the most astounding uproar imaginable; the Kandyans, now in a body, and with their long dishevelled hair flowing loosely around their necks and shoulders, following closely at their heels, hallooing, drumming, and piping with all their might: in short, it was one of the most exciting, extraordinary, and truly imposing scenes that I had ever beheld!

Five elephants lay dead, or were dying before us, two on the left bank and three in the bed of the river; and several others, besides some terrific male buffaloes, had made off, severely wounded. Having two double-barrelled guns with me, I had fired four brass balls into the dense drove whilst they were passing close to me; and, I have no idea of having, in any instance, missed my aim. I must say, that this was by far the best managed and most murderous battue I had seen; and not only the Headmen, but their followers, were greatly pleased and satisfied, when they saw that we had chiefly confined our fire to the elephants; many of which, they had no doubt, would yet be found dead in the woods.

This was the first act of a truly princely battue.

But most of the animals, in place of crossing the river, as we had expected they would, having been forced by the beaters down its left bank, and the leaders being of opinion, that a considerable number might yet be driven up to our present station, it was settled that the Kandyans should be allowed time to rest and to eat their rice; and that we should go back to the huts to breakfast, and then return to our well-chosen post; by which time the beaters would have again extended themselves and recommenced operations.

The next act "came off" much in the same way as the first; but the animals this time driven towards us, were not near so numerous as before; for many of those which were at first enclosed had contrived, after knocking down and running over the people, yet without killing any of them, to break through the line of beaters, and to cross the river a short way lower down, than where we so anxiously waited for them, and thus to get off into the jungle. Notwithstanding this mischance, two more elephants, three wild buffaloes, a tiger, and two deer, were killed, and several others wounded; so that, upon the whole, the people were much pleased with the result of the battue; and as this was a useful and indeed necessary attack upon those very destructive animals, we were not a little proud of our having in one day actually bagged seven elephants, besides wounding several others; and in thus expelling so many wild beasts from a country through which they had been for some time roaming, to the no small terror and serious injury of its inhabitants.

The place where the great number of animals broke through the line being only a short distance from where we were stationed, I was able to see how they had managed to do so. Some elephants, headed by a few furious buffaloes, rushed suddenly upon the beaters, who were between them and a deep and dark-looking part of the river, which, no doubt, contained numbers of alligators. Many of the Kandyans, with their tom-tom beaters and pipers, being thus hemmed in, they had no alternative but either to submit to being crushed to death by the huge animals, or to take their chance among the alligators. In a moment, the water boiled, as it were, and foamed, from the commotion caused by men, elephants, hogs, buffaloes, &c. throwing themselves headlong into it, and swimming with all their might in order to get clear of each other. I conclude, therefore, that this unusual disturbance, terrified even its amphibious occupants, and made them look out for their own safety at the bottom of the river ; at all events, none of them were visible ; but, the terrific scene, the uproar and dreadful confusion in the water, and other attendant circumstances, had altogether a most nerve-trying effect even upon us who, in safety, witnessed it.

Now, friendly reader, as I do not wish to trouble you further with what I find in my notes, respecting the remainder of this pleasant and interesting excursion, I shall only remind you that, during its progress, we have travelled together over a good deal of country, with which I wished you to become acquainted; especially, as it had of old been not only exceedingly fertile, but also thickly inhabited. It may, undoubtedly, be rendered so again, but not by the efforts of European emigrants or settlers—it must be left, at least for some years, to the natives; who, encouraged and aided by a wise and paternal Government, may do much towards restoring it to its former opulence and importance. I hope, however, that I may not be thought presumptuous, if I say that one thing is most certain—if we are to enjoy tranquillity and repose in the United Kingdom, if our industrial population is not to become more and more demoralized, the condition of the great body of the people must be, by some means or other, improved; at least the same wages as are at present paid to agricultural labourers must be maintained; more constant and regular employment and sufficient food must be found for the working classes in general; not the unnecessary diet, and, I may almost say, luxuries, with which mechanism, or a practical acquaintance with the art of fabricating cotton into stuffs of various kinds, or metals, &c. into implements, fit for the markets of every part of the earth, have for many years past enabled an artisan, unsuitably, it is to be feared, to supply himself and family; but with an ample yet becoming sufficiency of daily food. Encourage judicious emigration by all fair means to our colonies; but as emigration cannot, in these countries, be converted into transportation, and as people will not, we may rely upon it, emigrate in such numbers as to affect, to any extent, the labour market at home, it is idle, until a new and greatly improved system—*a Government system*—is adopted, to look upon emigration as a means of immediately bettering the condition of those whom it, in too many instances, leaves behind, as a burden upon the country. But, it may be asked—why do not the young unmarried men, in place of remaining so, more readily enter our army?—I suspect the reason is that most of them have been brought up surrounded by too many *comforts*, for them to fancy living upon what a soldier, after paying for a considerable part of his dress, can spare for food, out of a shilling a day.

CHAPTER IX.

"I would express him simple, grave, sincere,
In doctrine uncorrupt; in language plain;
And plain in manner. Decent, solemn, chaste,
And natural in gesture. Much impress'd
Himself, as conscious of his awful charge,
And anxious mainly that the flock he feeds
May feel it too. Affectionate in look,
And tender in address, as well becomes
A Messenger of grace to guilty men."—COWPER.

HIS EXCELLENCY THE GOVERNOR VISITS THE SEVEN KORLES—A MISSIONARY, AND HIS LABOURS—MISSIONS IN GENERAL, AND REMARKS UPON THE ATTEMPTS MAKING TO EXTEND THE BLESSINGS OF CHRISTIANITY THROUGHOUT THE WORLD—EDUCATION OF THE CHILDREN OF HEATHENS—THE FOLLOWERS OF MAHOMMED LOOKING FOR THE COMING ON EARTH OF THE MESSIAH, ETC.—STATE OF THE KANDYAN PROVINCES FOR SOME YEARS AFTER THE SUPPRESSION OF THE REBELLION—THIS EXEMPLIFIED BY CAUSES BROUGHT INTO THE COURTS OF JUDICIAL AGENTS OF GOVERNMENT—OBSERVATIONS.

A FEW days after our return to Kurunagalla, our very popular and highly respected Governor, Sir Edward Paget, arrived there; and having made the usual inspections, and carefully inquired into every thing going forward in the Province, he was pleased to express his approbation of what had been done in order to promote the comfort of the troops, as well as the welfare of the natives; and, at the same time, to encourage us to persevere in the course we had been pursuing.

About ten o'clock on Sunday morning, on observing the European troops paraded before my house at such, in this climate, an unusual hour; he asked me the reason of their being exposed to the heat of the sun?—I replied that they were going, as usual, to church; when he at once proposed, that we should accompany them there. I was delighted at this; as he would have an opportunity of seeing and, perhaps, becoming acquainted with our pious and laborious minister; who, though a Wesleyan, always read for us the usual morning service of the Church of England, and invariably preached most excellent and instructive though extempore sermons.

I very soon saw that the Governor was not only pleased, but also deeply interested; and when the service was over, he asked me, if the gentleman, who had preached so well, and had read the service of the Church of England, was not a Wesleyan Missionary? I replied, that Mr. Newstead was so; but I believed that he highly approved of the doctrines and services of the Church of England, though separated from it, as many were, on account of what appeared to them unnecessary forms and observances; and I begged to assure him that I believed a more devoted, able and zealous missionary had not gone forth to convert the heathen. I then, as I saw that his interest increased, told him of much that Mr. Newstead had done and was still doing, in order to induce the people, not only in this but also in the adjoining districts, to listen to his instructions, and to embrace Christianity. Upon this, he desired me to bring Mr. Newstead along with me to the Commandant's house, in order that he might be introduced to him. His reception was far beyond what I had hoped or expected; and, after a long and interesting conversation, the Governor was pleased to direct, that I should afford Mr. Newstead every assistance in my power, so as to enable him to build school-houses, &c.; and, if neither the Collector nor I could command sufficient means for the purpose, I was to be sure to acquaint him with Mr. Newstead's wants of any kind,—adding, "they must be supplied; and, I am likewise most anxious to do every thing I possibly can to promote the religious and beneficent views which he obviously has so much at heart."

I hope I may be pardoned for saying, that had Ceylon been blessed with a few such Missionaries, as my valued friend Mr. Newstead, I should not have altogether despaired—degraded and unpromising as the state of the natives then was—of Christianity, in its mildest and best form, being established amongst them. I have seen a good deal of missionaries, and have witnessed their exertions, both judicious and injudicious, in various parts of the world; but, Mr. Newstead was the only perfect model of one I had met with. I believe I am correct in saying, that his private means considerably exceeded his very few wants; that his piety, learning, and charity, were great and unostentatious; his zeal in the cause of his Redeemer had probably rarely been equalled; for, his sole object and delight seemed to be, to spend and be spent in his service. A man of his penetration very soon saw, that but little could be gained by alone endeavouring to awaken to a sense of true religion the minds of the adult part of the population, who evidently cared very little about religion of any kind, unless when their selfish views or interests happened to be concerned—that is to say, in times of difficulty, danger, sickness, or when misfortunes befel them; such as losses of cattle, failure of crops, &c.; when nothing could convince them, but that they were all attributable to the malevolence of some devil. It was, therefore, I repeat, evident to Mr. Newstead, that it was only upon the rising generation that he could hope to make lasting religious impressions.

He usually resided at Kurunagalla, where he had built a neat and roomy chapel, a school-house, and a bungalow for himself;—the chapel was more for the use and benefit of the British troops, who sadly wanted religious instruction, than for those of the Kandyans. Having acquired, by great and unwearied assiduity, a sufficient knowledge of their language, he preached to the people in the simplest, yet most impressive manner, and proclaimed to them the glad-tidings of salvation, through the atonement made for the sins of the whole world, by the Son of God. Thus, and by the kindness and impressiveness of his address, he endeavoured to bring them, as John the Baptist did of old the crowds that followed him into the wilderness, to repent of their sins, to shew the fruits of their repentance, and to be baptized; believing, as those who have well-grounded hopes of being saved believe, that there is but one Mediator between God and man; and that deserting their idols, they should turn to the only true God, and lead, through the aid of His Holy Spirit, a new and righteous life. But, I fear he rarely found that even his great zeal and labours of love produced either the so much desired, or any permanent results. Always active and energetic, he had been able to build several school-houses in this and in the neighbouring Provinces; in which all who wished for instruction, but in particular children, who were the chief objects of his solicitude, were taught, without payment of any kind, to read and write; together with what I may call the rudiments of Christianity. He was also indefatigable in superintending in his schools the labours of the persons, whom he had brought sufficiently forward to be able to teach others. He was equally unwearied in his endeavours to promote the spiritual and everlasting welfare of us Europeans, who, in foreign lands, too often totally neglect religion; and, thus he did all he possibly could, to instruct and enlighten every one who would listen to his impressive and judiciously urged persuasions. I often feared that his rather delicate frame would have sunk under the weight of such over-exertion, in a climate like that of the level, or low parts of the Seven Korles and Neurecalava; but, I was well aware that, whatever might happen to him, he looked forward to his reward in another and a better world.

Soon after Sir Edward Paget's departure from the Province, Mr. Newstead seemed to set more zealously than ever to work, in order to increase the number of his schools; which, from its being now publicly known that the Governor took such a lively interest in them, were very well attended by both young people and children; but, I have reason to believe that he daily became more and more convinced, that it was with the rising generation alone that he could hope for success:—that is, upon whom lasting religious impressions could be made. I, however, find from my notes that I had, about this period, an amusing conversation with a petty Headman, whose son had become one of Mr. Newstead's pupils. He knew, he said, that we wished the Kandyan children to attend our schools, and he, therefore, had no objection to his son's doing so; but neither he, nor the boy's mother, liked his being punished.—"I did not," said I, "know that the teachers punished the children; but has your son been guilty of any crime?"—"No, none that I know of;—and yet," continued he, "after all, I believe that he deserved to be punished, for having allowed it to be found out that he had told a lie."—"Then it was not for telling the lie that you blame your hopeful son; but because he had not been cunning enough to conceal that he had done so.—Is this the morality, or are these the ideas, that you wish to have instilled into your son's mind?—If so, it would be better for you not to allow him to attend school; as he will there be taught that telling a lie, upon any occasion, or upon whatever pretence, is a crime detestable not only in the eyes of God, but also in those of every good man:—and, what is more, if you continue to pursue the line of conduct which you seem to have pointed out to your son, as that by which he is most likely to thrive in the world, you may, one day, be obliged to hold down your head in his presence; for, if he continues to receive instruction in Mr. Newstead's schools, he will certainly make you ashamed of telling an untruth, whatever may be your object in doing so."

The pious Christian reader, may lament to see, from what has been above stated, how next to impossible it is, to expect that any good or useful impressions can be produced in the minds of a people like the Kandyans, many of whom are by no means ignorant or barbarous; but who from childhood are, it is to be feared, trained to dissemble, to fawn upon those in power, and by every subterfuge to endeavour to deceive them; and even to laugh at their credulity. Such men, it appears to me, are in a far more hopeless state, than the ignorant savages, amongst whom a zealous Missionary is in constant danger, and subjected to innumerable vexations and annoyances.

Mr. Ellis, in his Polynesian Researches, tells us that, for many years, the first Missionaries were variously annoyed in all their attempts to preach the gospel to the South-sea islanders. "Sometimes, when they had gone to every house in the village, and the people promising to attend had left their houses, they then found, on reaching the appointed place, that only two or three had arrived there; at other times, they either talked all the while about their dress, complexion, or features, and endeavoured to irritate the foreigners by false insinuations as to the objects of their visit, or to excite the mirth of their own companions by ludicrous gestures, or low witticisms on the statements that were made. Brainerd remarks, that while he was preaching, the Indians sometimes played with his dog: but the first teachers in Tahiti were often disturbed by a number of natives bringing their dogs, and setting them to fight on the outside of the circle they were addressing; or they would bring their fighting cocks, and set them at each other, so as completely to divert the audience, who would at once turn with avidity from the Missionary, to the birds or dogs. On some occasions, while they were preaching, a number of Areois, or strolling players, passing by, have commenced their pantomimes or their dances, and drawn away every one of the hearers. At such times, those who had stood round the Missionary only to insult him by their insinuations, ridicule him by their vulgar wit, or afflict his mind by their death-like indifference to the important truths he had declared, have instantly formed a ring around the Areois, and gazed on their exhibitions of folly and of vice with interest and pleasure. In addition to these sources of disturbance, they were sometimes charged with being the authors of all the disasters and sufferings of the people, in consequence of praying to their God, whom the natives called a bad God when compared with Oro."

We find also, in these admirable Researches, that in the year 1809, Mr. Nott alone remained with the King in the island of Eimeo; the other Missionaries, with the exception of Mr. Hayward, having gone off to Port Jackson, in, I fear, utter hopelessness of being able to bring to a knowledge and belief of the Gospel, a people engaged in war, and betraying on all occasions so much indifference for Christianity. Things were then in such a state of dangerous uncertainty in these islands, that even the zealous and persevering Missionaries had been obliged, in sorrow more than in anger, or from feelings arising from disappointment, to fly: man had, indeed, done much, but in vain, to induce the *adult* natives to listen to and believe the gladtidings of salvation; when He, who alone can influence the hearts of men, first prepared King Pomaré for what was about to take place, by misfortunes; and then stirred up an irresistible spirit of inquiry within him. And thus, when all human means seemed to have failed, the Holy Spirit began, in His own time and way to act, and commanded light to shine out of darkness upon these, I may now say, Christian islands. It is, however, most interesting and useful to follow Mr. Ellis a little farther.—"When the Missionaries who returned from Port Jackson landed at Eimeo, the King received them with the warmest demonstrations of joy. Mr. and Mrs. Bicknell, the first who arrived, resided some time in the same house with him. He spent much of his time in reading and writing, in conversation, and in earnest inquiry about God, and the way of acceptance with him, through Jesus Christ,—and sometimes spoke in terms astonishing even the Missionaries themselves;" who, at this period, were subjected, by an all-wise Providence, to great domestic distress; but, their sorrows were much alleviated, in remarking the most encouraging appearances of the Divine favour, vouchsafed to the natives around them; so that we soon after find them establishing public worship, opening a school, and Pomaré, the king of Tahiti, publicly professing his belief in Jehovah the true God; and his determination to serve him. "He had for some time past shewn his contempt for the idols of his ancestors, and his desire to be taught a more excellent way, that he might obtain the favour of the true God. The natives had watched the change in his mind with the most fearful apprehensions. They were powerfully affected on one occasion, when a present was brought him of a turtle, which had always been held sacred, and dressed with sacred fire within the precincts of the temple, part of it being invariably offered to the idol. The attendants were proceeding with the turtle to the Morai, when Pomaré called them back, and told them to prepare an oven, to bake it in his own kitchen, and serve it up, without offering it to the idol. The people around were astonished, and could hardly believe the king was in a state of sanity, or was really in earnest. The king repeated his directions; a fire was made, the turtle baked, and served up at the next repast. The people of the king's household stood, in mute expectation of some fearful visitation of the god's anger, as soon as he should touch a morsel of the fish. The king cut up the turtle, and began to eat it, inviting some that sat at meat with him to do the same; but, no one could be induced to touch it, as they expected every moment to see him either expire, or writhe in strong convulsions. The king endeavoured to convince his companions that their idea of the power of the gods was altogether imaginary, and that they had been the subjects of complete delusion! but the people would not believe him: and although the meal was finished without any evil result, they carried away the dishes with many expressions of astonishment, confidently expecting some judgment would overtake him before the morrow, for they could not believe that an act of sacrilege, such as he had been guilty of, could be committed with impunity." The conduct and conversation of Pomaré in reference to the gods, on this and similar occasions, must necessarily have weakened the influence of idolatry in the minds of those by whom he was attended; and, if it produced no immediate and salutary effect upon them, it doubtless confirmed his own belief in the vanity of idols, and the folly of indulging either hopes or fears respecting them. But the history of this conversion of Pomaré, as well as the subsequent results of the labours of the Missionaries, are so extraordinary and interesting, that I must, in concluding the subject, refer the reader to Mr. Ellis's valuable work; assuring him, that he cannot rise from the perusal of it, without being both instructed and highly gratified. But I must, at the same time, beg that he will reflect upon the almost hopeless state of the adult population of Ceylon, too truly exemplified in the anecdote of the Kandyan and his son.

Interested and anxious as I am about such matters, it is so far gratifying to me to see, that some advances are now making in a country about which I was and am still so deeply interested; and, it is also, I must say, satisfactory to find, that I was not mistaken, in the opinions I formed some years ago, as to the results to be looked for, if the attention of Missionaries and others was more particularly directed to the education of the rising generation. I find, by the following extracts from the Thirteenth Report of the British and Foreign Bible Society, that the system of instruction, so successfully pursued by the Rev. Robert Newstead in Ceylon, is now extending its blessings over that beautiful and valuable island, and, with the blessing of God, is likely to continue to do so. I do not, however, pretend to say, but that a good deal had been done, before my time, on the sea coast of Ceylon, to give the people there a certain knowledge of Christianity; yet, it always struck me, that not much had been accomplished, beyond the outward professions first caused by the Dutch law, which I before alluded to; and which was afterwards kept up, as the people, but especially the Headmen, thought it wise to evince much sanctity, in order the more effectually to please their British rulers.

"The Committee in Colombo are proceeding with care in the translations, and choose rather to incur delay, than to endanger the fidelity of the work by unduly hastening it; hence it appears that the printing of the Pali has not yet been completed, and that a revision of the Indo-Portuguese New Testament has been determined upon. The translation of the Old Testament is advancing; and the Rev. B. Clough is engaged in the Book of Psalms, with a view to printing the edition of 2,500 copiés, noticed in last year's Report. The Committee of Colombo are continuing, at their own expense, the printing from Joshua to the end of 2nd Samuel; while the greater part of the proposed edition of the Pentateuch has been struck off at press. The issues of the Colombo Society have amounted to 2,158 copies."

The Rev. J. Knight transmitted some interesting information as to the operations of the Bible Society, and the course of instruction pursued in the schools. The Rev. D. Poor writes—"The number of students is 150; of whom fifty-three have been admitted to the Church, on a credible profession of faith of Christ. Of these Church-members, twelve are attending a course of theological studies. We have at present but one public service at the station on the Sabbath, which the students are required to attend; the remaining part of the day is spent by the several classes in the regular study of the Bible, varying the method so as to give variety to their studies. During the week, select portions of the Scriptures, both in Tamul and English, are used by different classes as books to be construed, and critically studied. This is done with reference to ancient history, sacred geography, and to some more obvious and important prophecies, the fulfilment of which is recorded, either in the Bible itself, or in class-books used in the summary."

The Rev. L. Spalding writes—"To keep up the interest of masters and helpers, I ask them every week, at our weekly meeting, if they have called on those to whom they have lent the books, to converse with them about their contents, &c. In this way I have a hundred or a hundred and fifty portions of the Bible constantly in the hands of the most respectable people in the villages about me. I am happy to add, that the plan excites more interest in those who borrow, as well as in those who lend, than I had anticipated. I have an opportunity to see once a month that the white ant has not destroyed them, and to hear the various remarks and questions of those who read them."

This is so far satisfactory: but, I cannot bring

myself to be otherwise than disappointed. when I refer to the return, which I have already given, of the number of schools, as well as the scholars who attend them throughout the whole island, that more has not been accomplished for some years past. We must, however, rejoice to see, that even so much has been done, in order to disseminate the truths of the Christian religion to the uttermost parts of the earth; and may we not say, that even China is gradually becoming open to their reception through the means of the late events.* Nothing should, however, more strongly convince the world at large, that Mahommed was not only the False Prophet, alluded to in Scripture, and that he was also an exceedingly talented and devilishly inspired man, than the able manner in which, to establish and perpetuate his erroneous and mischievous doctrines, he availed himself of what he found recorded in both the Old and New Testaments; and he even seems to have

* One of the reverend gentlemen, from whose Report I have just been quoting, speaks of portions of Scriptures, both in Tamul and English, being used as class-books to be construed and critically studied, including even some of the more obvious and important prophecies, the fulfilment of which is recorded in the Bible itself, or in class-books used in the seminary. I should like to see these elementary curiosities, which would, no doubt, be much to the taste of the members of the Irish Education Board; as they would, I must conclude, afford them a great deal of useful information about Romanism, as well as the religion of Mahommed; for, it is well known that, the latter,—as we ought to expect—is still that of a considerable portion of mankind throughout the East.

been endued, by the same inspiring power, in a surprising degree, with a certain comprehension of prophecy, and to have also had, as it were, a hint given him of the manner in which he was to calculate, so as to find the periods when certain great and important events to mankind were to take place.

We are told that a nameless person, who proclaimed himself to be the Imaum, or priest of the Mehdi, promised by Mahommed, has lately appeared in Yemen, and has drawn a crowd of 1,500 disciples after him. He announced no new doctrine, but preached the Koran in its purity, and enforced its precepts with strictness. He declared himself but the precursor of the Mehdi, who was already come on earth, and was now at Mecca; whence he would set forth, and appear before all true believers, in the fulness of time.

The number of his disciples or followers soon increased to 35,000. Meantime this Imaum was said to be "working miracles" in Mahommed Mehdi's name,—some of which are mentioned. Good Mussulmans are all alive to the importance of the announcement, and familiar with the prophecies relating to the Mehdi and his coming in the latter days, to fulfil the law and prepare for the millennium. El Hadisci Scheriff (the inspired writings of Mahommed's apostles) speak largely of this personage. The Gife, written by Ali, the son-in-law of Mahommed, specially contains prophetic announcements of his advent and proceedings. In short, the several sects of Mahommedans, however they may quarrel about doctrines, all seem to unite in the belief of this Arabian Messiah, of whose appearance I had previously been informed by a letter from a friend of mine stationed at Aden.

It is also said, that the Mehdi is to appear at Mecca in the fortieth year of his age; he is to call the true believers to his standard, and march at once to Jerusalem; where he is to reign with power and glory, dispensing justice throughout the earth, for seven or nine years. After this period, Dejail (the Arabian Anti-Christ) will rise up, march against him with a great army, and having proceeded as far as Elouadi, (a village adjacent to Bethlehem), an army of 70,000 angels, commanded by Jesus, will descend from heaven to earth at Damascus, and come to the rescue. The angelic forces will immediately march to Elouadi, attack Dejail's army, and utterly destroy both it and him. Then shall all the nations of the earth acknowledge the divine authority of the Mehdi; Jews, Christians, and Pagans, shall be converted, and the millennium shall commence. The letter from which I have been quoting (and which was given in the *Times*) goes on to say —"Your readers will naturally think this all very absurd, and possibly wonder how 35,000 men could be found to believe it: those, however, who have been educated to receive it as revelation, are equally ready to exclaim against the infidels, and to cut their throats besides, as one of the works of merit. The Scheriff of Mecca, (who is a greater authority than the Sultan in religious matters), does not attempt to speak of the Mehdi irreverently in his report of this second advent, or to make light of the consequences which have resulted from the credulity and enthusiasm of the Arabs of Yemen. He knows that the Ottoman Empire was based on a similar attempt, sustained by similar appeals to Jewish and Christian prophecies, and, in short, he knows that 35,000 Arab fanatics are capable of effecting any thing that can be accomplished by hands, lances, swords, and matchlocks."

Though all this may, indeed, appear to us to be very absurd, and the Christian reader will at once see where Mahommed and his apostles found the materials which enabled them to fabricate this delusion, yet it often surprises me to hear and see what may well be called strange doctrines, preached and published respecting the looked-for advent of the true Messiah, by those who, evidently, can never have sufficiently studied Scripture, nor can have read such elucidating works as "Faber's Sacred Calendar of Prophecy;" and it must surely be felt as a severe reproach by Christians, when they hear of the followers of the "False Prophet" seriously attending to such matters, whilst they—I must say foolishly—look upon prophecy as a *sealed book.* But, this is not to be wondered at, when many of our divines teach them to consider it as almost impious to inquire, or enter too deeply, into these matters; though they are presented to them in both the Old and New Testaments for their guidance: indeed, many say, that these prophecies are only so far useful, as they tend to confirm the truth, and explain the meaning, of the prediction after fulfilment;—but, are we not told to watch; and did not our Saviour reproach the Jews with knowing what conclusions were to be drawn from the aspect of the sky, while they were unable to discover the signs of the times?

Some may say, that this is altogether irrelevant matter, and more suited for a religious work, than for one, which many will, perhaps, imagine, borders upon fiction. I, however, have still to mention, as connected with the subject, that, on one occasion, when I was conversing with Mr. Newstead upon the state of the Syrian churches, he expressed his surprise at having, in an out-of-the-way part of the province, (somewhere, if I mistake not, beyond Olegammé) fallen in with a few small villages, inhabited by a number of persons, whom we might call Christians; and who did not appear to have become so through any connection or intercourse which they could have had with either Roman Catholics or Protestants. When or how they, or rather their ancestors, could have acquired the limited knowledge they possessed of Christianity, which was much darkened by the superstitions of heathenism, they could not tell; nor did they appear to have amongst them any writings upon the subject. They could only say, that the religion they professed, had been handed down to them, for many generations, from father to son. In appearance, they were like their Kandyan neighbours;

and they had never heard that their forefathers had, at any former period, come to Ceylon from the Continent. But, how strange, yet truly gratifying, it would have been to the Christian world, could Mr. Newstead (who as I before mentioned, is well acquainted with the language of the country), have been able to connect these interesting people with the Syrian churches discovered in Malabar by the excellent Buchanan, or with those recently found in central Asia, called Nestorian!

I must here observe, in farther elucidation of the native character, that I have often very extraordinary causes brought before me; for litigation has of late much increased, in consequence of some of the Judicial Agents of Government having been rendered competent to entertain any cases or suits whatever, concerning the right and title to land; and a retrospect being allowed, even so far back as when causes were in general decided unjustly, and in consideration of bribes given to native local judges, during the latter period of the reign of the last king. Thus, in spite of all I can do, I find that business rapidly accumulates; and that it occupies far too much of my time, as it is always exceedingly difficult to find out, whether the former judgment had been rightly given or not. The title-deeds produced in court on such occasions—always beautifully and distinctly written, or rather cut with a sharp instrument, upon talipot leaves—are, in most instances, of very ancient date. I had one before me a few days ago, which the assessors and interpreters made out to be upwards of nine hundred years old; and of the land, held upon the strength of it, a high caste family had been most unjustly deprived, through the aggression, and as it then appeared, unprovoked violence and villany, of a more powerful and influential neighbour; who had forcibly taken and kept possession of it, and had, moreover, so puffed himself up with the idea of his own importance, and the consequence which he derived from the number of his adherents and followers, that he at last seemed to have made up his mind to set the laws, or at least the civil authorities of the provinee, at defiance.

One day, whilst the rain was falling in torrents, and the state of the weather was altogether sueh that it might have been thought that no one who could have stayed at home would have left it, a very well-looking young man arrived, in great haste, at my house. His appearance denoted extreme terror; yet, it could not be supposed that a Kandyan, aeeustomed to it from his birth, eould have been in sueh an evident state of alarm on account of the "war of elements" then going forward. It was soon ascertained, that he was aeeompanied by an elderly woman, a younger brother, and two sisters, all of them remarkably handsome, and highly respectable looking people. My interpreter was sent for, and as soon as he arrived I was told that their being even seen in Kurunagalla, was considered as mueh as their lives were worth; and, if it had been discovered that they purposed escaping from the borders of Neurecalava, (where they had been closely watched,) with the intention of coming to complain to me of the conduct of a powerful neighbour, who had most unjustly taken possession of their lands, and now held them by force, he would most certainly have had them all murdered. The young man had seen me at the great elephant hunt, and had also heard, that if I were applied to, I would readily afford them protection and redress, and they had now come to petition for both.

Of course, I listened patiently to their long and truly melancholy tale, and, as usual, made notes of the principal points, to which I might afterwards have to refer; and, as it may interest some readers, I shall give a rather minute account of our mode of proceeding, in those days, in such cases—I first cited the aggressor to appear before me upon a certain day, to answer the complaint; and sent two Lascareens (or police-men) along with the bearer of the summons, which he would otherwise have been afraid to deliver. It was also, at the same time, signified to some of the neighbouring Headmen, that I held them responsible that the complainant and his family were duly protected from violence or ill-treatment of any kind; as I was aware, that without these precautions were taken, the poor people would not have dared to return home; and in order to shew that I was determined to protect them, I sent them back under an escort of a corporal and four Malays.

On the day fixed, the plaintiff attended with his

witnesses, and brought with him the old deeds I have just mentioned; but, the defendant did not think fit to appear; and I was informed that he had only laughed at the person who had delivered the summons. Upon this, as customary in such cases, I issued a warrant of attachment in the following form, written in Singalese, upon a long stripe of talipot leaf.

By the Judicial Agent of Government.

To ——— Lascareen. Kurunagalla ———

You are hereby ordered to seize the person of ——— and to bring him before this court forthwith, because he failed to appear according to the order given that he should attend to answer the complaint of ———.

The Lascareen, who carried this warrant, went under an escort of Malays, as I had reason to apprehend that violence would otherwise have been offered to his person; but, before they arrived at his house, the defendant had decamped, and could not be found. In consequence, I ordered the land in dispute to be sequestered, according to the following form.

By the Judicial Agent of Government.

To —— Lujeneralle of the District of —— Kurunagalla ——

You are hereby ordered to place in sequestration the —— because —— claims the same from —— who is reported by —— Lascareen, not be found so as to be brought to answer the claim, and you will forthwith report into whose charge you have delivered the said land.

So lawless, at this period, were the people represented to be in the part of the country in which the defendant resided, and where his influence was considerable, that it was deemed requisite that the order for sequestration should also be sent under an escort. After having ordered the sequestration of the land, and having received a report of its having been done, which created a great sensation among the Kandyans, who now began to see that I was in earnest and determined to enforce the laws, I had the usual notice affixed at the court-house, and at the place of abode of the defendant, for him to appear within a given time, viz:—

Court of Judicial Agent of Government.

By the Judicial Agent of Government. Kurunagalla ——

Notice is hereby given, that unless —— does appear before this court within three months from this date to answer the claim of —— the case will be heard and decided in his absence.

About eight weeks after the above notice had been given, the defendant, as I was informed, became alarmed; and thought that it would be best for him to come to Kurunagalla, with a few attendants only, in order to submit himself to my pleasure; for the decided manner in which I had found it necessary also to proceed in some other cases, as well as in this, had convinced the people that the laws, as well as the persons empowered to enforce them, must be respected. As I wished to proceed as leniently as possible, upon his making a most ample apology for his conduct—which, however, he did with a very bad grace,—I fixed a certain day for hearing the cause, upon which the parties and their respective witnesses were summoned to attend. But, on the day appointed, the effects of the intimidation exercised on the part of the defendant being now removed, the plaintiff, (many of whose relations and friends now began to stand up for him,) appeared, accompanied by his family and a few followers; but, the ruffianly looking defendant came numerously attended, in a good deal of state, as well as with pretensions to importance. I, however, understood afterwards, that his purpose was to have offered me secretly as a bribe—not supposing it would be rejected—some valuable gold ornaments, and he would have done so, had he not been prevented by a Headman, well known to me, and who told him, that if he ventured to do so, I would, most certainly, order him to be instantly tied up and well flogged.

According to the custom of the country, both litigants presented me with some of the finest fruits they could procure; which I received from them, in proof of my intention to act fairly and impartially.

I then proceeded, accompanied by some officers of the garrison, and attended by my orderlies, Lascareens, and a number of Headmen, to the court house, where three of the most respectable and intelligent of the latter, whose white beards gave them a most venerable and patriarchal appearance, had already taken their places as assessors, according to their rank.

The trial was long, and to me, fatiguing; but, towards its close, and when the defendant found that every thing had gone against him, and that, by his unjustifiable and illegal conduct, he had subjected himself to severe punishment, he became as mean and abject as he had before been presumptuous; and when I, justly, decided the case against him, and in the usual form required the assessors to say what punishment, according to ancient Kandyan, as well as a lately enacted law, he merited for such unjustifiable usurpation and unprovoked violence, as he had been clearly proved to be guilty of, they, in their grave and solemn manner, thus expressed themselves—"It would be good law, if the judge were to command that his head should be struck off; but, as that is not now the custom, the judge can act as he pleases. But, three years of hard labour, in chains, would be a merciful sentence." This was severe, yet I had no alternative but to be guided by it; all I could do, was to recommend that it might be considerably mitigated.

Nothing could now be more contemptible than the prisoner's demeanour; he even attempted to prostrate himself before me, using, at the same time, the most abject language that can be conceived. This, in our eyes, seems so degrading to human nature, as to create in us feelings of scorn rather than pity for the being who could do so. Every allowance ought, however, to be made for people like the Kandyans, whose feelings, habits and customs, differ so widely from ours, as altogether to prevent us, I may say, from having ideas in common, and must, it is to be feared, disqualify them, until great changes take place in their religion, in their notions of morality, and, I may add, propriety, from being placed, consistently, on an equality with British subjects; at least, with such as have hitherto settled in Ceylon.

Before, however, I conclude my remarks upon this curious state in which the Kandyans were at the time I made these memoranda, I must mention a very strange cause that now came before me. It may startle English ears—but a Kandyan lady had married five brothers! The eldest of them, for what reason was not stated, had seceded from the joint-stock concern, and married another woman; and having afterwards, by great economy and industry, contrived to accumulate some money, he had been able to purchase a few acres of land. He then died; upon which, very naturally, all he possessed was taken possession of by his (second) wife, for herself and two children. The lady, however, with her four remaining husbands and children, came into court, to claim any money or land which might have been in any way acquired or left by the elder brother. I was about to dismiss the case; but, on referring to the assessors, I was informed, that, according to ancient Kandyan law and custom, the deceased having, along with his four brothers, voluntarily married the lady, all he possessed at his death must go to the joint-stock company. I was, therefore, much against my will, obliged to decide accordingly. All I could do, was to refer the case to the Judicial Commissioner at Kandy, trusting that he would call the attention of Government to what appeared to me to be such an unjust law, that it could only be tolerated or submitted to by a people labouring under the always degrading yoke of heathenism, and that of castes, which have always thrown impediments in the way of changes or improvements of any kind.

Finding these remarks among my notes, I introduce them here, for the consideration of such readers as take an interest in the advancement of knowledge, and in the extension of free institutions throughout the world. But, from the strange state, in which I have, in various parts of this work, described the natives of Ceylon to have been, they were suddenly. yet, we are told, not *rashly reformed.* Direct taxes on cultivated land were — certainly most wisely—first moderated, then arranged, fairly levied, and finally redeemed; and, by an order of His Majesty in Council, compulsory labour, which had done so much towards securing the conquest of Ceylon, and in promoting public improvements, was abolished; and thus a whole nation passed at once from a state of degradation and habitual subserviency to that of freedom, which, it may be supposed, they could not possibly have comprehended. But this, we are are informed, has been done with perfect safety to the Government, and incalculable benefit to the subject. A rapid improvement in the face of the country, an increased revenue, (but does this agree with the accounts given of the state of the exports, and of the cinnamon trade?) an improved climate, and a most beneficial change in the native character, are represented as having been the fruits of this great change. We may, however, now inquire, if castes—that insuperable barrier to a people's improvement—have been by this important measure abolished? Have these people's religious prejudices been modified or overturned? Until these essential objects are effected, and until the natives of Ceylon are awakened to a real (not merely an apparent) sense, of pure Christianity, as inculcated by the Church of England, and of that morality which ought to flow from it, I must doubt the wisdom of placing them completely, and unprepared for so great a reform, upon a level with British subjects.

I am well aware that the views I take of this subject do not coincide with those of men looked upon as high authorities in such matters, and who are often quoted as such: that is to say, with the expressed opinions of Sir Thomas Munroe, Sir John Malcolm, and others; who, in considering the state of the vast population of our Indian possessions, do so as philosophers and politicians, and not in the way such men as the late Mr. Haldane did, who was willing to have devoted a large fortune towards endeavouring to bring to a knowledge of Christianity the millions of heathens, her Majesty's subjects there. In his most anxious and disinterested views in this (all-important) respect, he was frustrated by those in power; as it was (surely unwisely) supposed, that such religious notions as he intended to inculcate, would tend to cause a revolution, or to overturn the Honourable Company's Government in that part of the world. But, would not the ideas expressed and plans proposed by both the enlightened men I have mentioned, as well as by Colonel Walker, have fully as great, if not a greater, tendency to do so?

Sir Thomas Munroe, on this interesting subject observes—"The main evil of our system is the degraded state in which we hold the natives. We exclude them from every situation of trust and emolument; we confine them to the lowest offices, with scarcely a bare subsistence; and even these are left in their hands from necessity, because Europeans are utterly incapable of filling them. We treat them as an inferior race of beings. Men who, under a native government, might have held the first dignities of the state, who, but for us, might have been governors of provinces, are regarded as little better than menial servants—are often no better paid, and scarcely permitted to sit in our presence. We reduce them to this abject state, and then we look down upon them with disdain, as men unworthy of high station. Under most of the Mahomedan princes of India, the Hindoos were eligible to all the civil offices of government; and they frequently possessed a more important share in them than their conquerors."

And Sir J. Malcolm observes:—

"Our administration is cold and rigid. If it creates no alarm, it inspires little if any emulation. The people are protected, but not animated or attached. It is rare that any native of India, living under it can suffer injury or wrong; but still more rare that he can be encouraged or elevated by favour or distinction.

"I do not know the example of any great population, in similar circumstances, preserving through such a period of changes and tyrannical rule, so much of virtue, and so many good qualities, as are to be found in a great proportion of the inhabitants of this country.

"It is not to be expected," Sir J. Malcolm further states, "that we can ever completely succeed in establishing any cordial or social union with the natives of India. We are as foreigners, differing in manners, language, religion, and feelings, too much opposed to them to admit of our ever realising such hopes; but our efforts should nevertheless be continually directed to the object of reconciling them to their condition. Nothing can tend so much to this as their employment. The character of our Government debars us from entrusting them with military or political power; but this is the strongest of all reasons for bringing them forward in every manner that is unattended with danger. The acquisition of knowledge under a system which almost excludes the higher classes of our native subjects from any participation in the government of their own country must either rouse them to efforts against our authority, or sink them into a state of abject submission, and leave them with few objects of life beyond indolence and sensual indulgence."

And Colonel Walker remarks:—

"The most prominent feature in the civil government of the Company is the almost entire exclusion of native agency. The offices held by natives are only those of the lowest description, such as could not be the object of ambition to the European. To natives of rank and education no temptation is held out which can induce them to engage in the service of the Company. A very little consideration will be sufficient to shew that no circumstance tends more strongly than this to impair the efficiency of our Indian administration, and even to render its duration precarious.

"The admission of natives to offices of power and profit is the only mode by which they can be effectually conciliated. It is in vain to expect that men will ever be satisfied with merely having their property secured, while all the paths of honourable ambition are shut against them.

"This mortifying exclusion stifles talents, humbles family pride, and depresses all but the weak and the worthless. By the higher classes of society it is considered as a severe injustice; but these are the men of influence and consideration in the country—the men by whom the public opinion is formed;—so long as this source of hostility remains, the British administration will always be considered as imposing a yoke.

"The Romans, whose business was conquest, and who extended their yoke over the greatest part of the civilized world, may be safely taken as guides in the art of holding natives in subjection; that wise people always left a great share of the administration of the countries they subdued in the hands of the natives. The admission of natives to a moderate share in the administration of their country would present the most effectual means of deterring them from forming hostile designs, and of checking them if formed by others. The natives might be expected to become more attached to a Government from which they received not only protection, but the more envied boons of confidence and distinction."

Such ideas are quite to the taste of modern theorists; and what these accomplished and able men have so well put forth seems to be most plausible; but, can any statesman for a moment suppose, that men who can never in any way assimilate with us, on account of religious prejudices and castes, would, if entrusted with power and influence in their own country,—I do not speak of supreme power—be contented to remain subservient to those who must ever be looked upon as foreigners and intruders? Let us first endeavour to Christianize and educate the natives of India; and then, and not till then, can they be safely entrusted with power, or be employed in the manner proposed, without risking the permanence of British rule or sway in their country.

There are, however, in Ceylon, a class of men, who do not, by any means, receive sufficient encouragement; and who from education, knowledge of the country, and of the languages spoken in it, could render very essential services to the Government, at a far less expense, than must be incurred in employing European gentlemen in civil situations;—I mean the descendants of the Dutch and Portuguese; these often intelligent men, who have no home but Ceylon, seldom attain higher stations in it than those of clerks in the public offices; yet they are men who ought to be more worthily employed, and even in most of the situations now so inefficiently filled by Singalese. They would certainly require to be somewhat better paid than the latter; yet, this need not occasion any additional expense, as fewer European civilians would be wanted in the various departments of Government; and if the Singalese were thus to see that education and merit led to preferment, a stimulus would be given them to exert themselves, in order to become competent to fill, throughout the whole island, these so much coveted situations (which will one day be also, I trust, objects of ambition to European settlers and their children;) and, it will no doubt readily be admitted, that education must naturally produce a spirit of inquiry amongst them, before which there could be little doubt but that heathenism in Ceylon would soon disappear. This could be done there with perfect safety; but, to extend such a principle to our great Eastern Empire is quite another matter; for, in the former, religious prejudices of any kind have not that hold upon the minds of the natives that they have in the latter; and castes could not be long maintained in a country become Christian. It is through the opinion alone of our *invincibility*, that we are enabled to remain rulers of India. In Ceylon, public opinion is comparatively of little importance; and as long as Great Britain is mistress of the ocean, it must continue to be one of her Majesty's most valuable colonies.

Our modern reformers have free constitutions "cut and dry," or ready prepared, for every people and for every part of the world; but until it can be shewn that these liberty and equality systems are working well in the countries where they have been tried, we ought to remain sceptical as to the benefits they confer, at all events, upon men whose former ideas and habits have wholly unfitted them for their reception. Even those who extol what has been done by late Governors in Ceylon, express their doubts as to such legislation being applicable to our Indian empire. In deciding that question, let them look at what a free press is doing in that part of the world; let them weigh well the inconvenience and mischief it is constantly occasioning, by its giving the ill-timed strictures of men (and, strange to say, men employed both in civil and military capacities by the Government, they too often traduce) upon measures, the present motives or ultimate bearings of which they can neither know nor understand.

In, however, concluding these remarks, I beg leave to say, that I am not, by any means, one of those who wish to see public liberty abridged where it is understood and appreciated, as in England; it is only when I find it mischievous, and verging into licentiousness and popular tyranny, that I consider it high time to endeavour to keep it within reasonable bounds.

CHAPTER X.

> "Here, wafted o'ér by mild Etesian air,
> Thou country goddess, beauteous Health, repair;
> Here let my breast through quivering trees inhale
> Thy rosy blessings with the morning gale.
> What are the fields, or flowers, or all I see?
> Ah! tasteless all, if not enjoyed with thee."
>
> PARNELL.

A DESCRIPTION OF THE FLAT OR LOW LANDS OF CEYLON DURING A SEASON OF DROUGHT—A PLAN SUGGESTED, BY WHICH NOT ONLY CEYLON BUT, PROBABLY, A CONSIDERABLE PART OF THE EAST, MAY, IN TIMES OF SCARCITY, OR WHEN CROPS HAVE FAILED FROM WANT OF RAIN, BE SUPPLIED WITH RICE—FURTHER REMARKS UPON CEYLON SCENERY, ETC.—ADVENTURES AND ABSURD MISCHANCES—THE NORTHERN LOW LANDS VISITED WITH JUNGLE FEVER—ARRIVE AT COLOMBO—PROCEED TO GALLE IN ORDER TO PROCURE A PASSAGE TO BOMBAY—REMARKS—RETURN TO COLOMBO—DIFFICULTY IN GETTING RID OF AGUE, AFTER AN ATTACK OF JUNGLE FEVER.

I NOW regret to be obliged to draw a very different picture of this province, and of those to the northward of it, to that I have hitherto been doing; but, I must observe that I have never pointed them out as the parts of Ceylon to which I wished to direct the attention of those desirous of settling in it; at least, until much has been done to restore their fertility and salubrity. But, how distressing and disheartening it is, when the dry season in this part of the world is protracted, as was the case lately, beyond the usual periods when the rains are expected to fall!

Day after day, large black and dense clouds rolled over the tops of the neighbouring mountains; and to each we looked, but in vain, for water to refresh the parched, or I should rather say, burnt up earth; yet, for many weeks, only an occasional large drop fell. As there was, consequently, nothing left to be exhaled from the ground, we had no dew, nor moisture of any kind. The rivers and brooks, with the exception of my favourite Didroo, which, having its many sources in the mountains, is always, and even at such times, well supplied with water, were all but dried up; and at Kurunagalla, we were at length reduced to a single spring of water; but, it is, certainly, one of the finest in the country; and to it flocked hundreds of people, especially from the northward, where not a drop, fit to drink, was to be found. The trees and grass, usually so verdant, had assumed—if I may so speak—a most melancholy and sickly appearance; many of the former were almost entirely stripped of their leaves; and nearly all of them seemed drooping or dead. This, in Ceylon, unusually sad aspect of nature, had a strangely depressing effect upon our spirits; because, from our being so long accustomed daily to admire the most beautiful and lively shades of green, &c. as well as such a profusion of lovely evergreen shrubs and flowers, we felt so much the more the want of them; most of the latter were now nearly destroyed by the heat, and shrivelled up from being deprived of moisture: in short, the efforts of nature seemed as if suspended or exhausted.

At last, the gloomy clouds, which had been so long passing over us, burst, I may say, from their own overwhelming weight or fulness, and the floods of water descended in such surprising quantities from them, as vastly to exceed what I had ever before witnessed in any tropical country; both sheet and forked lightning shone and glanced around and over us far too brightly to be endured or gazed upon; and the peals of thunder, that instantly followed, were truly sublime!

The sun having been so much obscured during the greater part of this period of excessive drought, we ourselves suffered, comparatively, but little from heat, unless it were when a disagreeably hot and scorching wind occasionally blew; which we did our best to exclude, by carefully closing the doors and windows of our houses on the side from whence it came. These, at least for several years past, unusually long periods of drought, are sometimes succeeded by sickness; but, fortunately, this has not been the case on this occasion. At Kandy, however, which is only twenty-five miles distant, and in the mountains extending from thence to beyond Kospeta, there had been an abundance of rain; whilst the Seven Korles, Neurecalava, and the country towards the northward, were suffering so direfully from want of it: indeed, so alarmingly, that in almost every temple, the priests were engaged in acts of devotion, in order to appease, as they imagined, some offended deity or devil; and the astounding noises of tom-toms, screaming of pipes, and clashing of cymbals, used in all their religious rites or ceremonies, were to be heard in all directions, night and day, until the rain fell. Then, joy was to be seen pictured in every countenance; for the seed-rice was in the ground, and this province being, in a great measure, the granary of Ceylon, apprehensions were at one time entertained of a famine, as there was no water in the tanks; and, although some of it is still thought to be safe, yet the crops have either been greatly injured or altogether destroyed.

The whole of the flat country, to the northward of the Kandyan mountains, appears to be subject, at times, to these terrible droughts; and nothing can more distinctly shew their effects, than what I copy from Knox's History of Ceylon; who, in speaking of them, says,—"Some eight or nine years, one after another, we followed this trade, going down into the country on purpose to seek to get beyond its inhabitants, and so to run away through the woods to the Hollanders. Three or four years together the dry weather prevented us, when the country was almost starved for want of rain—all which time they never tilled the ground. The wells also were almost all dry; so that in the towns we scarcely could get water to drink, or victuals to eat; which affrighted us at these times from running into the woods, lest we might perish for thirst. All this while upon the mountains, where our dwelling was, there was no want of rain." In his account of one of these attempts to escape, he also says,—"For this northern country being most subject to dry weather, and having no springs, we were fain to drink of ponds of rain-water, wherein the cattle lie and tumble, which would be so thick and muddy, that the very filth would hang to our beards when we drank."

The lake near Kurunagalla, which I have so often mentioned, became during this extraordinary period of drought, a most wonderful sight. There being scarcely any water fit to drink, to be found almost any where else in the neighbourhood, birds of all kinds flocked to it in thousands; so that I might fairly say, the very air, as they arrived, particularly in the evenings, on its shores, was loaded with them; the sporting reader, may therefore imagine, what shooting I must have had; and, how amply my neighbours were supplied with game, or what we reckoned as such. Vast numbers of elephants, buffaloes, deer, hogs, and other animals, were likewise necessitated to repair there, in order to quench their thirst; yet, few of them, excepting elks and deer, were much disturbed or fired at; but of course, during the whole of this period, I took good care to be well supplied with venison, and whatever else was requisite for the table. The danger, however, attending such very superior sport was, from the amazingly increased number of animals, in many instances, very great; indeed so unusually so, that in my eagerness, and sometimes imprudence, when in pursuit of game, I had several very narrow escapes, both from buffaloes and elephants; and, how often then would a determined slayer of the latter have had opportunities of evincing not only his courage, but also his coolness and dexterity!

I have thus attempted—no doubt very imperfectly—to depict the most gloomy and spirit-depressing season which had been experienced since my arrival in Ceylon. My gardens had been almost ruined. My fine melons, upon which I so much prided myself, as well as the splendid shrubs and beautiful flowers which I had taken so much pains to collect, were nearly all dead. As for the several kinds of vegetables which I cultivated, they were of little importance; as I had a good supply of seeds from different parts of the world, and I was, consequently, very soon able to make up for the loss I had sustained.

But, during this period of great drought, and whilst the sufferings to which the people were, in consequence of it, likely to be exposed, became more and more obvious to me, my thoughts were constantly directed, in various ways, to the subject; as I hoped that a palliative, if not a remedy, might be devised. It therefore at last struck me, that a paternal and humane government, which had the happiness and welfare of the people of the whole island at heart, ought surely to take timely measures, so as to be prepared for the recurrence of such emergencies; and to do its utmost to prevent the famines, which occasionally cause such numbers of deaths, and such misery and severe suffering, throughout many parts of the East. Whilst thus turning over the matter in my mind, it became evident to me, that a vast deal might be done, and that too at no great comparative expense, so as to remove even the apprehension of Ceylcn being visited by such calamities, by merely collecting, by means of dams or embankments, and very much according to the ancient Kandyan plan, the waters of the fine Didroo, Kalla, and Weliker rivers, as well as some others, which at present empty themselves, uselessly, into the sea near Putlam and opposite to Calpetyn, and at certain points still farther to the northward. These dams should be formed as near as possible to the sources of the rivers;—for instance, the waters of the Didroo—by far that upon which most reliance could be placed for ample supplies of water—might first be collected where it enters the flat country, somewhere below Beddegammé;—again lower down; and another embankment might be constructed, on scientific principles, and yet upon a moderate and sufficiently efficient scale, not far from a village called Degollé; where the river changes its northerly course to the westward, and from thence flows towards Cehilaw. If the waters of this river alone were thus partially turned out of its old bed, both to the westward and eastward, they might be conveyed, by a judicious and not expensive system of irrigation, over a vast tract of country; much of which, as I have shewn, is now a complete desert; and which would thus be fertilized, and rendered habitable, and all apprehensions of famine, arising from want of water, throughout a considerable part of the north of the island, would be removed. It is, therefore, to be hoped, that the Governor of this valuable island, now rendered doubly so, since so many Chinese ports have been thrown open to British commerce, may be empowered, before long, to employ Her Majesty's Officers of Engineers, in investigating its capabilities in this respect; and, if such a plan as I have presumed to suggest were adopted, there cannot be a doubt, but that Ceylon, in place of being an importing would soon be made an exporting country of grain, and especially of rice, to many other parts of the East. Thus an incalculable benefit would be conferred upon its people; and what would, perhaps, be considered of equal, if not of greater importance, the revenue arising from the amount of tax collected upon corn, (it was formerly about a tenth, and though it appears to have been moderated, I cannot suppose it has been entirely relinquished), would be immensely increased, and become not only available for the wants of the country, and in promoting improvements in the way I have ventured to point out, but also for Government purposes. If, however, the cultivation of the soil were thus extended, it would, perhaps, be deemed good policy, that the tax upon agricultural produce should be considerably reduced; for, it cannot be doubted, that any measure which has a tendency to check, or to become a barrier against, the cultivation of the soil, is an unwise one, and can only end in disappointment to the framers of it, and also in seriously injuring the country whose rulers unwisely and pertinaciously adhere to it; for, does not history teach, and experience shew us, that the only real wealth of a country is that arising from its soil? Every thing else, however it may for a time flourish, is only transient, and cannot be depended upon. But, a Governor of Ceylon, acting cautiously and advisedly, would soon produce great and advantageous changes in the country, its climate, and also in the ideas of its inhabitants; and, he would have the glory of conferring upon them a far greater blessing than that cf a free form of government, which it is impossible that they can understand, and consequently cannot as yet duly appreciate.

How rapidly, since the rains fell in such abundance, had the country recovered its former verdure and loveliness; and with what delight was I induced —as I find by my notes—to revisit my various haunts in the neighbourhood, where once more nature seemed, as it were, to "bound as from her birth!" But, what a part of the world is this, in which to study nature to advantage, and also such works, (though no longer fashionable), as that of "Zimmerman on Solitude," and, amidst the splendidly variegated sylvan shades of which we can completely satiate the feelings, as well as the imagination; for I pity the man whose heart cannot, at times, enjoy its visions! And I think, it will be readily admitted, that such solitary rambles or excursions improve the finer feelings of the heart; and that they tend to rouse the mind to that exalted enthusiasm, which renders man capable of performing noble or praiseworthy actions. The grand and wild scenery into which we can here at all times retire, has many charms for those who can enjoy it; I therefore often, for days together, repair to its wooded retreats, when I find myself disinclined for business, or tired of our very limited society. There, I soon experience that calm and renovating impulse, which renders us fit to play our parts in the common occurrences of life; and I perfectly coincide in opinion with Zimmerman, as to the usefulness of occasional solitude; in which, I may say, we have time to recollect ourselves.

I was thus enjoying myself, a few days ago, in the finely shaded and deeply-worn bed of the Didroo-oya, in which I had been trying whether I had forgotten or not how to swim. It was about two in the afternoon, but, notwithstanding the hour, not a ray of the sun had as yet been able to penetrate into the cool and agreeable recess I was in; which was formed by interwoven branches of trees and runners, that flowered beautifully and tastefully over head, and hung down in long and flaunting festoons. I had brought with me an ample supply of bait, and a few red hackles—all that were left of the fishing tackle which I had brought with me from Ireland. I was hard at work catching good-sized fish, some of which, from their strength and liveliness, afforded really excellent sport. Whilst thus busily and pleasantly engaged in my favourite pastime, and having made up my mind, that in my next letter to a Waltonian friend of mine in England, I would astonish him, by letting him know the exact number and weight of the fish actually basketted on this occasion; I was joined by a young and somewhat corpulent friend, who had come to visit me, and was desirous of being initiated into the delights of Ceylon field sports. He had, all the forenoon, been trying his good gun, fresh from London, upon pea and jungle fowl in the neighbouring forest—when lo! the approach of a solitary, or (as it is called by the natives) rogue elephant, was announced by one of the Malay sentinels; who running up to us, in great haste, recommended, in order that we might be able to get out of his way, that we should instantly cross the river;—this was quickly done at a place close at hand, where it was easily forded. These solitary elephants, as I have before observed, are not to be trifled with; as they are always males, that have been beaten by the others out of the herd. When that is the case, they usually retire to the deepest and most gloomy parts of the jungle; and there, seemingly brooding over their misfortunes, they become desperate, and consequently most dangerous to be met with; so much so, that those acquainted with their habits, try carefully, at such times, to keep out of their way. We therefore very properly and prudently did so in this instance; but he had for that day, most unceremoniously spoiled my sport, and overturned all my calculations ; and, what was worse still, I had, in my hurry to be off, and in making my way through the jungle, broken and almost destroyed my old trusty fishing rod, and had also left my last gut casting line behind me, hanging in a tree. I hoped, however, to be able to mend the former, and, by and by, to recover the latter, as well as my basket of fish ; as I could send back for them, as soon as the huge intruder had taken his departure. But, whilst running off in such an unsportsmanlike manner, I could not help laughing at the idea of the plight in which I should have been, had the elephant made his appearance a little sooner, and when I was bathing! In that case, I should only have had the choice of two evils —that of standing my ground, and trying the effect of a brass ball or two upon his head, or—naked as I was—of taking to my heels, through the close and prickly jungle—far too ridiculous an alternative to be even thought of.

We had, as I supposed, in this instance, managed tolerably well, and had all got safely out of the elephant's way; but I now missed my visitor. At first, I felt no uneasiness about him, as I concluded that he must be following us; but when, a few minutes after, I asked the Malays if they knew what had become of him, one of them told me, that he had seen him climbing up into a large tree, and had requested him to come along with him, but he paid no attention to him; for, he seemed to be eager to have a good view of the elephant, and, he thought it was not unlikely that he wished also to have a shot at him. I now became really uneasy for his safety, and hoped that he had not been so imprudent as to venture to do so alone. I therefore determined to return with the Malays, in order to look for him. As we cautiously went back, we heard some one, whom we instantly concluded must be my young friend, calling out for help. This induced us to quicken our pace; but what should we see, on coming to a small opening, but Mr. C— most strangely suspended! that is to say, his legs were dangling in the air fully four feet from the ground, and he was throwing about his arms, as if trying to lay hold of something behind him; and, what made his situation the more ridiculously laughable, he hung with his back about a yard from a tree, his very red plump face turned towards us; on which was pictured great alarm, and the effects of violent exertion.

It appeared that, after he had seen the cause of our rapid retreat come down into the bed of the river, drink heartily, and even take a cooling roll in the water, the enormous animal, unconscious of a human being having his eye upon his movements, had gone quietly back into the jungle. My friend then thought it would be as well to descend from his concealment in the tree; but, in doing so, and when still some distance from the ground, he turned round and stood upon a branch, with the intention of jumping clear of some brush-wood intermixed with prickly pear that grew around its root. In making a spring from the branch, which happened to be rotten, it suddenly broke; and, to his great astonishment and terror, he found himself caught, by the stump of the broken branch having got up betwixt his coat and waistcoat; so that there he hung, his legs and arms free; but in spite of all his attempts, he found it impossible, from the toughness of his coat, and its being thus greatly tightened at the shoulders, to extricate himself. He, however, as the elephant had retreated, thought that his only chance of being liberated from his alarming situation, was to give tongue; and, I must say, that when we arrived at the spot so opportunely, he was doing so most lustily. But, owing to the irresistible fit of laughter with which I was seized, and in which I was joined even by the habitually grave and respectful Malays, it was some time before I could assist in taking him down. When we had set him upon his legs, he most earnestly entreated that I would upon no account mention to any of his brother subs. what had so untowardly happened; for if they were to hear how ridiculously he had been suspended, it would become, for years, a standing joke against him.

Upon another occasion, about a year before this occurred, an amateur, whom I had taken with me to one of my bungalows, in order to initiate him into jungle field sports, having, by some means or other, parted company from the Malay I had sent with him to pea-fowl shooting, fell in unexpectedly with some buffaloes, (I am inclined to think, as the Malay did, that they were tame, though the amateur said that they ran at him) when he became so much alarmed that he instantly climbed up into a tree, and there remained, terrified out of his wits, and afraid to descend; as he still heard, and indeed at times saw, the large bluish-coloured and dreadfully horned creatures, feeding in the jungle close to him. About 9 A.M., the Malay came in to say, that the gentleman had very unaccountably left him; and that he could nowhere be found. Becoming uneasy at his long and extraordinary absence, I determined, immediately after breakfast, to go in search of him; the Malay, from whom he had gone astray, acting as guide. We looked carefully for him, in every direction, for fully an hour, but all in vain. At last, we thought we would try the effect of hallooing and whistling, in the hope, that if he happened to be near at hand, he might hear and answer us; and, to our surprise, this mighty Nimrod instantly shouted loudly in reply; and, as I calculated, could not have been a quarter of a mile distant from us; indeed, we had passed close to the place where he was, not ten minutes before. We soon found him, in the act of timidly descending, and with difficulty—he being an inexperienced climber—from a very tall tree, among the highest branches of which he had been clinging, in a most doleful plight, for upwards of two wearisome hours. I cannot imagine, what could have put it into the head or heart of this poor man, to venture into the jungle to shoot; or what could have brought him at all into the, by many, so much and absurdly dreaded interior. Perhaps it was, that he might be able to talk of his having been there elephant shooting; at all events, it might well have been said of this valorous sportsman, when up in the tree, that—

> "With him sat Danger, clothed in ragged weed,
> Made of a bear's skin, that him more dreadful made:
> Yet his own face was dreadful . . . ."

The Seven Korles had for several years past been very healthy; but sickness at length made its appearance—at first among the natives, especially in the bazaar, where many strangers, from different parts of the island, had for various purposes now congregated. It, moreover, extended itself before long all over the province, particularly in the flat country, and far to the northward, eastward, and westward. But, as soon as it began to shew itself among the European troops, I took the liberty of recommending, that they should be immediately removed to a distance from the part of the country in which malaria evidently prevailed; and I was glad to find that his Excellency, the Governor, most readily complied with my request; through which precaution I am certain that many lives were saved, and much sickness among the troops was prevented. I became daily more and more convinced that I had acted rightly, in suggesting that they should be removed; for, the people of the country soon became so dispirited and alarmed, on account of the fever, which now raged in all directions, that there could be no reason whatever for us to have any apprehension that they would take advantage of the absence of the British troops and become rebellious.

So many were taken ill, or had gone off, that it became absurd for me to think of holding my usual courts; all business was consequently put a stop to. Even our hard-working surgeon was sick, and I had myself to doctor him; and, when he was fit to be removed, he was sent off to Kandy. I then became chief medical practitioner for the whole country; and being supplied by Dr. Farrell, the head of the medical department in Ceylon, with medicines, but chiefly with a solution of Arsenic, to be given after calomel, I, under Providence, performed wonders in the way of cures, or rather in arresting the progress of disease amongst men, women, and children; crowds of whom attended daily in my long verandah, to receive from my own hand a certain number, according to their ages, of what they now looked upon as my most precious drops; for I could not venture to trust my dangerous and deadly bottle into that of any other person. To those at a distance, or who could not come or be brought to me, I sent daily the proper number of drops in water, in a vessel brought for the purpose. I would, in some cases, have been glad to have given bark;—but, for the number of my patients, all the bark in Ceylon would not have been sufficient. My repeated injunctions to all, however, were, that the moment they felt certain that the fever was checked, they should be off to the mountains, and remain there until they heard of its having subsided in the low lands.

But amidst all this sickness and mortality, I was most wonderfully protected and supported. Never, in any part of the world, had I enjoyed better health, or been in better spirits; which I certainly thought it wise to keep up, by a daily and fair allowance of old Madeira. I soon, however, began to be inconvenienced from the want of my servants, three of whom had gone off ill, or pretending to be so, to Colombo; and I had two others, including my greyhound-like horse-keeper, on my sick-list. At this period, my friend Captain Dawson of the Engineers was brought in to Kurunagalla, having been seized with an exceedingly painful and dangerous ailment, which he bore with his usual fortitude. Our surgeon, as I before remarked, having been sent off to Kandy, I had to do the best I could for him; but, I shall never forget the scene, nor what —assisted by two other officers—I had to perform, and he most reluctantly had to submit to. The remedy, however, had the desired effect, and he was enabled, in a few days, to return to his herculean labours in the mountains, to which he urged me greatly to accompany him; but this I thought it right to decline doing.

When things had come to this alarming pitch, it was most considerately intimated to me, that if I thought fit for a time to leave the district, as all the

Europeans, with the exception of the few officers in charge of the Malays and Caffres had gone off, His Excellency the Governor would sanction my doing so; but, implicitly relying upon Him, who had never amidst many dangers deserted me, I felt it to be my duty to remain at my post, where I was enabled to be useful to so many. My excellent friend, Mr. Newstead, however, stood by me and encouraged me, not only by his example, but also by the cheerfulness of his looks and calmness of his manners. He was at all times indefatigable in his attentions to those who required them, or who would or could be induced to listen to him, when he besought them to look to Him who alone could afford not only present but eternal safety.

During this calamitous period, the sky was particularly serene, and the weather, even at noon, far from being oppressively hot; and, there was no apparent cause whatever for the sickness that prevailed. But, how often did I wish for a thunder-storm; in the hope that it might disperse the malaria, that evidently extended its baneful influence over the country, and cause a beneficial change in the atmosphere. I was now constantly assailed by crowds of Kandyans of all castes, and of both sexes, entreating that I would sanction their having a grand public Devil's dance, and that I would allow other ceremonies to be performed; (the former had been for some time prohibited, and the latter as much as possible discouraged) as they were confident, that, unless the devils were appeased and propitiated, the fever that raged would not cease, so long as there were human beings left to become its victims. Under such circumstances, what could I do? It would have been unfair to consult Mr. Newstead; the people were flying in all directions; and those who remained were unceasingly urgent in their importunities. I, therefore, yet at the same time doing my best to turn such absurdities into deserved ridicule, at last consented, that the people might, for one night only, do as they pleased throughout the country. As soon as this permission was given, such a drumming, piping, clashing of cymbals, and shouting and screeching, were commenced, and most piously kept up, as quickly became quite astounding! But, in spite of all this din and uproar, and sacrifices offered up of cocks, &c. no change or effect whatever was produced; on the contrary, the numbers on my sick list increased rapidly, and the reports I received of deaths became more frequent. My handful of Malays and Caffre troops—a handful when compared with the still remaining population of the province—continued to be, I may say, healthy; especially the latter, about a hundred in number, not one of whom was sick. I must add, that at this time they were employed in improving the new road upon this side of the Kospeta-oya; I also thought it advisable to remove, in turn, most of the former into that part of the country; so that, through this precaution, only a few of them suffered from the effects of malaria.

But, I beg here to observe, that some years ago, when Trincomalie was most awfully visited, (as it too often is,) by fever, many of the European officers and non-commissioned officers belonging to the 3rd Ceylon regiment died of it; as did also numbers of natives, whilst its Caffre soldiers, (five or six hundred,) were perfectly healthy. This, as well as what I have above stated, ought surely to point out to us, that not only a very considerable portion of the troops required to serve in Ceylon, but also in the territories of the East India Company, ought to be Africans.

The entire province remained in this state for some time; and I at length began to find, that my hitherto so much valued *arsenic drops* had not their former beneficial effects. The fever had also now considerably extended itself on the road towards Colombo; and, that beautiful and so much admired station Allow, on the Maha-oya, which I before spoke of as an intended temporary residence of the Governor, became so sickly, that it was no longer safe for any one to remain there for even a single night.

It at last, however, pleased God to put an end to this terrible malady, by which the population of the low lands to the northward had been so much reduced; and even more suddenly than it had commenced. The fever, at once, disappeared, and the whole country became, seemingly and unaccountably, as healthy as it ever had been, and the countenances of all the people again brightened up.

After a delay of a few weeks, therefore, in order to see that the sickness had really subsided, I requested that the European troops might be sent back to the district, to which the Kandyans began to return in crowds.

I gladly took advantage of this improved state of the country, to pay a long promised visit to my friends in Colombo, and elsewhere. I was blamed by many for having, as they thought, very foolishly and unnecessarily exposed myself to jungle fever; and but few gave me any credit for the motives which had induced me to remain in the Seven Korles during such a visitation.

On my return, I found a new garrison of British troops at Kurunagalla; but nearly the same Malays and Caffres remained in the district. I once more opened my courts, and resumed my military duties; and, the reader may be sure, that I did not long defer my delightful sporting excursions, which I recommenced with even greater zest than ever; for which purpose, the weather continued, for a considerable time, to be particularly favourable and agreeable.

I beg leave, here to remark, that I have thought it right to speak, without reserve, of this extraordinary sickness, with which the flat or low lands of the northern part of Ceylon were visited, but from which it had for several years before been spared; because I am anxious to shew Europeans, who may intend to settle in the island, that they can, in almost every instance, avoid what is called jungle fever, by a timely departure from the part of the country, where it has shewn itself, or, rather shewn that malaria prevails there. Malaria must, indeed, be frequently prevalent, so long as so much of the country is covered with jungle, and that swamps are permitted to accumulate; and, I am also desirous of convincing settlers, that they may confidently return, as soon as it is known to have ceased. It ought likewise to be remembered, that there is another half of Ceylon, delightfully situated in point of climate, and which is as healthy as any other part of the world.*

My imprudence, however, in not having acted, as I now recommended others to do, became before long apparent; for, it being requisite that I should go upon some judicial business, which I had to arrange personally with the Commissioners in Kandy, I set off, from Kurunagalla in perfect health, after breakfast, for that purpose; intending to dine and spend the night at Maddewallatené, a most strikingly situated and healthy mountain station upon the road to the Kandyan capital, then in

* In confirmation of the above opinion, Dr. Davy, in speaking of the effects of climate and diseases of Ceylon, says—" In a former part of the work, I have offered the general results of my experience relative to the cause of endemic fever, than which nothing scarcely can be more obscure and mysterious. To escape the disease, the best advice that can be given is to quit for a season the place where it is prevailing; or, if this be not practicable, the next best plan is to take all possible care of the general health, attend to the state of the bowels, be exposed as little as possible to the wind, and avoid the night-air."

charge of Mr. S—, a friend of mine, who was one of the most active and useful officers employed as an agent of Government in the Kandyan provinces.

On arriving at Kospeta, I requested the officer commanding the Caffre company to go back with me about a quarter of a mile, as I wished to point out to him an alteration that should be made in a part of the road, of which he had there the superintendance. Whilst doing so, I felt a slight degree of sickness, as it were, come over me; but, as it seemed to be of no importance, I went on to Maddewallatené. I, as usual, dressed and joined my friends at dinner; but, I had scarcely sat down to it, when I was taken very ill; and had, much against my will, to go off to bed, as, beyond all doubt, I was attacked with fever, the seeds of which, they all, perhaps justly, concluded, had been lurking in me for some time past.

Mr. S—, becoming very uneasy about me, sent a messenger on to Kandy to acquaint Colonel T—, then commanding there, to whom I had intended to pay a short visit, with what had occurred; and the Colonel immediately sent off his surgeon to take charge of me, and have me carried on to Kandy. When I was about half-way to that place,—for which I was still able to start at dawn the following morning,—a faintish feeling having come over me, I left my palanquin for a few minutes, in order to be able to breathe the pure mountain air more freely; but, in returning to it, I found myself so weak, as to be obliged to lie down on a grassy bank, until I should be somewhat stronger. Having done so, I then contrived to get again into the palanquin, and to resume my journey; I had only gone a short way, when I discovered that, when reclining on the grass, I had been assailed by a host of leeches, which were now hard at work enjoying themselves upon my feverish blood. I had, therefore, again to stop the bearers, and to apply chinam and tobacco juice to the leeches' proboscises, which soon made them let go their hold; but, before I could do so, my bed, and almost all my clothes, were stained all over with blood. By the time I reached Kandy, I had become much worse; and was consequently bled over and over again, until I verily believe that not a drop of blood was left in me: in short, the reader will understand, that I was, beyond all doubt, in for jungle-fever; and that, consequently, I became insensible of all that was going on around me.

I have now said more than enough of myself and of this untoward illness, from which, at last, it pleased God to permit me to become convalescent; when, as usual, I was sent off to Colombo. As I left Kandy, on my way to the sea-coast, I felt myself so wonderfully refreshed and strengthened by the almost too cold morning mountain breeze, that when I reached Fort King, where I purposed to spend the day and night with Captain Trydell, who commanded there, and from whom I received much kindness and attention, I was so much better, as to be even able, in the evening, to mount my horse and to look about me. I was now, as at the time I formerly visited this picturesque part of the island, greatly delighted with it, as well as with the charming and magnificent scenery in all directions; and I would, certainly, by all means, direct the attention of settlers to it; as it would be not only a healthy, but also a very desirable part of the country to reside in; for, the soil seemed to be rich and admirably suited for agricultural purposes, and, in many places, there was grass in abundance for cattle.

During the remainder of the journey, I continued to mend; and I was therefore able, occasionally, to mount my horse, in order to enjoy the splendid views over a mountainous country, adorned with the finest trees, and presenting as striking and enchanting scenery, as is to be seen in any part of the world; especially in approaching Ruanwellé; and from thence to Hangwellé, on the road to Colombo. But, on the second day after my arrival there, I had a return of fever; which, after bringing me again to the brink of the grave, ended, as it too often does, in that most annoying of all ailments, fever and ague. On first arriving in Colombo, I was so unfortunate as to be both uncomfortably, and, for an invalid, unsuitably, lodged; as, my old friend the Commandant, to whom I intended to have gone, had not room for me in his house. This was much against my recovery; but, a gentleman and his lady, upon whose hospitality and friendship I had little or no claim, most kindly received me into their charming abode, situated on the sea-shore about three miles from Colombo; and it is to the care and attention of Mr. and Mrs. Marshall that I attribute my temporary recovery. But, unfortunately, intermittent fever, (and I mention the circumstance as a warning to others not to remain, if it can be avoided, in a country in which malaria exists,) had taken too strong a hold of me to be easily eradicated; and, it was therefore at last decided, by the medical gentleman who attended me, that I must go to sea for some months, or I should never be able to get rid of it.

Being fully aware, that there was much judicial business to be attended to in the Seven Korles, I therefore, before I left Colombo, begged leave to acquaint His Excellency the Governor, with the opinion of Dr. Farrell and my other medical attendants; and, with much regret, proffered the resignation not only of my appointment of Commandant, but also that of Judicial Agent of Government. In reply to my letter, I received the following answer, with which, I confess, I was highly gratified; but it only increased the gratitude I already felt for the kindness I had experienced from Sir Edward Paget.

"I have not failed to lay before the Governor, your letter of yesterday's date, submitting the resignation of your command in the Seven Korles on account of illness contracted by a residence there.

"His Excellency directs me to express his deep regret at your being obliged to adopt this measure. His Excellency had every reason to be entirely satisfied with your services in the Seven Korles, and laments exceedingly being thus deprived of them.

"I am farther commanded to assure you, that it will afford his Excellency sincere pleasure to have an opportunity of meeting your wishes, by appointing you to a situation more likely to suit your present state of health, should he have it in his power to do so whilst he remains in command of the forces stationed in this island."

(Signed) G. Marlary,
Military Secretary.

I now set off for Galle, my old and favourite abode, where a ship, on her way to Bombay, was soon expected to touch; and, in her I hoped to be able to proceed to visit that Presidency. Travelling therefore, by easy journeys, in my palanquin, when I arrived at Galle, I found myself so much better, that I began to fancy and hope, that such a long and expensive voyage as that to Bombay might not be necessary.

I was most kindly received by my old friends, Mr. and Mrs. G——, into whose delightfully situated and agreeable mansion I was most heartily welcomed, where I had the pleasure of meeting, and of becoming acquainted with, Mr. and Mrs. S——, who were likewise waiting in expectation of a passage to Bombay in the same ship. But, as she did not make her appearance, I had daily opportunities of seeing many of my kind Singalese friends, and also of visiting some of my old haunts. I was, however, surprised to see the changes which three years, the period that had elapsed since I left Galle for the interior, had made in its appearance. It was now almost without commerce of any kind; the houses, in general, were much in want of repairs; but the inhabitants—mostly the descendants of the Dutch and Portuguese—were too poor to be able to afford them. The number of troops in garrison had been so much reduced, as not to amount to a quarter of what they were when I was Commandant. The trees, that I had planted upon the ramparts and elsewhere, had grown surprisingly; especially the large cuttings or branches from the tulip trees, and already afforded most agreeable shade under their widely spreading branches. Thus here, as everywhere else in the world, the works of man, if neglected, or, if not constructed upon the colossal scale of those of the ancient inhabitants of the Kandyan province, soon perish; whilst the mighty efforts of nature remain always the same; so that her productions are as fine, as beautiful and wonderful today, as they were thousands of years ago.

Having spent three very agreeable weeks at Galle, during which I was more and more confirmed in the opinion I had formed of the healthiness of that charming part of Ceylon; and finding that I had not had, the whole time, a return of ague; and, being besides become quite ashamed of encroaching so long upon Mr. and Mrs. G——'s hospitality, I determined that, if the long looked for ship did not make her appearance in three days, (and I now hoped she would not,) I would return to

Colombo; and, I considered that I should be justified in the eyes of my medical and other friends in doing so, and in ascertaining whether I was not sufficiently recovered, even by this short residence in the neighbourhood of Galle, to make it unnecessary for me to go to sea. Indeed, I confess that I felt, for various reasons, with which it is unnecessary to trouble the reader, but too strongly, the influencing temptation held out to me in the following lines:—

> "But thou, O Hope, with eyes so fair,
> What was thy delighted measure?
> Still it whisper'd promised pleasure,
> And bade the lovely scenes at distance hail!"

At the end of the three days, and contrary to Mr. and Mrs. G—'s and Mr. and Mrs. S—'s advice and warning, I acted upon this, I must admit, unwise decision, and went back to Colombo; when ague again returned; and a voyage of some length being in consequence once more declared to be indispensable, I had now nothing for it, but to submit. I have, however, often regretted, that I had not taken a house, and remained for a much longer time at Galle; for, had I done so, I am convinced, that my cure would have been perfected without going to sea.

CHAPTER XI.

> "Those blazing suns that dart a downward ray,
> And fiercely shed intolerable day;
> Those matted woods where birds forget to sing.
> But silent bats in drowsy clusters cling;
> Where crouching tigers wait their hapless prey."
>
> GOLDSMITH.

EMBARK ON BOARD A FRENCH SHIP, BOUND FOR BOMBAY—THE MALABAR COAST—REMARKS AND REFLECTIONS—BOMBAY, ITS CLIMATE, SOCIETY, ETC. SUPERFICIALLY AND VERY IMPERFECTLY DELINEATED—REMARKS UPON AGRICULTURE IN THE COMPANY'S TERRITORIES, ETC. GIVEN AS USEFUL HINTS TO THOSE INTENDING TO SETTLE IN CEYLON, AS WELL AS TO AFFORD INFORMATION TO READERS IN GENERAL—A YOUNG LADY'S DEBUT IN INDIA—AN ANECDOTE—SOMETHING MORE OF BOMBAY—A LITTLE OF MANGALORE, A STATION AND RUINOUS FORTRESS ON THE MALABAR COAST—RETURN TO CEYLON—VALUABLE DOCUMENTS; SHEWING THE DUTIES CHARGED UPON GOODS EXPORTED FROM AND IMPORTED INTO THE BENGAL AND BOMBAY PRESIDENCIES; TO ADMIT OF A COMPARISON BEING MADE WITH THOSE OF CEYLON.

I MUST now, friendly reader, give you due notice that this chapter scarcely relates to Ceylon; but, chiefly to a part of the sea coast of our Indian empire, to which you may accompany me, or not, as you pléase; the account of the voyage, as well as of what was seen and done there, might, perhaps, have been altogether omitted; but this has not been deemed advisable, as what will be alluded to may, in some measure, enable you to compare the so much extolled Malabar coast with that of the greater part of Ceylon. In this respect it may be useful, though, probably, not very amusing, to the public in general.

A French ship, the Zenobia, bound for Bombay, having touched at Colombo, I took my passage in her, along with two gentlemen, Mr. W— and Captain G—, who were going, *via* Bombay, to England; and, on the 11th of December, left the anchorage with a strong breeze at north-west.

On the 12th, we were off Cape Comorin. Towards evening all sea-sickness—from which I had suffered severely—being gone, I could eat anything put before me; and even enjoyed a glass, or rather nearly a bottle, of vin-de-pays, dignified with the name of claret; such were already the effects of sea air: indeed, I soon began to forget all my ailments; and my companions congratulated me upon the appearance of returning health, indicated in my countenance.

On the 13th, we were close in with the Malabar coast; but, being almost becalmed, we made little or no progress. A long sandy beach, skirted with palm-trees, extending as far as the eye could reach; behind it a flat country, partially wooded, terminated by mountains of considerable height, and of various forms, several of them clad, even to their summits, in that resplendent light or brightness, with which a tropical sun, as it were, gorgeously decks the objects it shines upon; were the most prominent features which Travancore presented to our view. On the 14th, we were off Quillon; which looked tolerably well from sea; and the country still retained the same partly bold and partly tame features; but, inland it was not altogether so mountainous as it had been. It was, certainly, delightful to glide along, so smoothly, upon the surface of the most tranquil sea upon which any of us had ever before sailed; the heat, however, was most oppressive.

It was only on the evening of the 19th, that we arrived at Calicut, having been longer in performing this part of the voyage than we had calculated upon; for, the winds had been light and generally contrary. But, the heat now became quite overpowering; for the sun's rays being brightly reflected by day from the sea, rendered it so unbearably hot, that to escape from its effects we would gladly have fled below, if we could have supported the suffocating and mephitical air which was to be there encountered. The evenings, however, sometimes became more endurable; but it was almost impossible to sleep in bed at night; as we were tormented by the increasing buzzing and biting of myriads of muskitoes, whilst we were stewed in perspiration from the closeness and want of air in our diminutive holes called cabins and state rooms:—A strange part of the world for an unlucky invalid to be sent to, for recovery of health, especially in such a vessel. Although there was occasionally, and when we begged for it, a sort of awning spread over part of the quarter deck, yet the skin was soon literally peeled off our faces and hands; and, in our new suits, we looked as black as half-caste Portuguese. Calicut, however, looked well from where we had anchored. It stands upon a sandy beach; that part of it, which is inhabited by the Natives, being exposed, all day long, to the action of the sun, the heat in it must be unbearable; but the better looking houses, which shew themselves here and there in the midst of groves of palm-trees, seemed as if they were calculated to afford some kind of shelter, comfort, and perhaps coolness, to the unlucky Europeans destined to spend many of their best days on this coast. A long straight line of flat beach, skirted as usual by cocoa-nut trees, still lay before us; something like what many parts of the sea-coast of Ceylon present; but how inferior to them in appearance, from their not possessing that enchanting and lively green, which is every where to be seen and admired on the Ceylonese shore. Close behind Calicut, some high mountains, crowned by a table land, and intersected by deep ravines or fissures, elevate themselves abruptly; and in the distance, there are some variously formed and still more lofty mountains. From the short and imperfect outline which I have given of part of the Malabar coast, the reader may be able to picture to himself the rest; as the features of the country are almost alike from Cape Comorin to far beyond Calicut. I did not land there; as, I considered that it would have been imprudent for me to have done so; but the seafaring people, who came on board, gave us hopes that six days more might suffice to take us to Bombay.

On the 25th of December, we were off Goa, but close to the shore. The winds continued to be light, and those from the sea were so constantly from the northward as to be unfavourable. The country had now become less mountainous, and, at times, it reminded me of several parts of Spain, with its gently undulating hills and extensive plains; and the grass (or what appeared to be so,) had here, as it has there in summer, a scorched or dried up look; in some measure resembling the ripe corn fields of Estremadura. The same want of wood, too, is observable on this part of the coast, as in the country for many miles around Salamanca. How much I already missed and began to long for the bright and perpetual verdure of Ceylon! But, as we sailed slowly along the shore, I thought of the melancholy and degraded state of the Portuguese and native inhabitants; of their blindness and superstition; and of the adventure of the excellent Buchanan in the terrible Inquisition, which is so well and interestingly described in his "Christian Researches." Whilst I was reflecting upon this, and upon what had been for many years going forward in the country now before me, my attention was suddenly called to what I had never seen or heard of before;—that is to say, to what the French Captain and his crew called a "*sea-devil.*" I looked at the monster for nearly two minutes, as it moved about, quite close to the side, and under the stern, of the ship; indeed, at times it was partially on the surface of the sea; yet, I cannot undertake to describe its form with any degree of accuracy. It appeared to me, to be more bulky and larger than any shark I had seen, though not nearly so long; it was of a dirty black and whitish colour; its body seemed to be of an oval shape; and, I fancied that it had a long snout, four curious leg-like fins, and the sailors would have it, that there was a long semicircular claw at the end of each; but this I did not remark: in short, we all admitted, that it was the most extraordinary monster that any of us had ever beheld.

I find among my notes, made at this time, the following remarks.—We are now standing into Bombay, and if the wind lasts which we at present have, we may reach the anchorage this evening. But, I did not expect to find the entrance of the bay by any means equal to what it is in appearance. To the south-east, some high lands, that look like islands, form its limits in that direction. The island of Bombay, covered, apparently, with large houses, is to our left, though still some way off. To the northward is the continent; and in the offing, to the south, is distinctly to be seen a small wooded island. As we thus stood in, the land before us and to our right seemed, as it were, to rise gradually, and become more undulating; but it was almost without wood, and in some places was strongly marked and uneven. The whole of these objects, thus appearing decked in the bright rays of the setting sun, became every instant more strikingly beautiful and splendidly coloured; but, it was the beauty and colouring which usually present themselves, to the surprise of a stranger, in the brilliant, burning clime of the East. The country, however, has still, in some respects, the look of Spain; but, it is Spain under the sky of the torrid zone. Every object has a fiery, golden appearance, doubtless surprisingly attractive; yet, it must impress with apprehension, and even awe, those who have experienced the effects of tropical heat and a tropical climate.

How many a fine young man, the delight of his family and friends; perhaps, the beloved object of a tender heart in his native country, has been sent out, buoyant with hope, to this ungenial clime, to accumulate wealth; and has here, alas! found a long home, far from those who knew his worth, and who must continue to mourn his untimely loss; the family that had sent him forth to a land "whose bright beaming summers exalt the perfume," little aware how few are capable of enjoying the riches they may eventually acquire, if ever they return to Europe, after a residence of years in such a country as India!

The sun has set; but we are still working up the bay. The evening is remarkably fine; and the very light breeze is now become rather more in our favour. But, the moon has just risen over the land, in such unusual brightness, as to shew the objects, an hour ago, so red and fiery, in a more softened, though not in an inferior point of view.

We at last got amongst the shipping, and let go our anchor close to the town. We were now to leave the good ship Zenobia ; and well pleased were we to be delivered from six super-cargoes, each looking sharply after his own venture of stuff, denominated claret,—from her Captain, who had for many years been a prisoner of war in England,—from his officers and noisy crew, several of whom had shared their chief's fate in prison,—from dirty and most confined cabins, and from the sour vin-de-pays, with which we had been amply supplied, we supposed, in order to enable us the more readily to swallow greasy ragouts, boiled beans, seasoned with fetid oil, and such like delicacies, with which the cabin table was daily garnished, and at which we were literally starved, though we had been obliged to pay most extravagantly for our passage and the promise of good entertainment. When we were taking leave of these worthies, Captain G— slyly observed, in not very good French, to their skipper, that, "if all the passengers whom he took on board, had such appetites as he was blessed with, and got as many good things to eat, and such excellent wine to drink, he could make but little by them." To this fair hit, which the Commander of the Zenobia wisely chose to take as a compliment, he proudly and pompously replied, that, "he took passengers on board for the pleasure of their company;—not for what he could make by them."

Day had scarcely dawned, when a boat, sent off by Mr. S—, took me and my servant on shore; and when I arrived at his house, I was received by him and Mrs. S—, with as much kindness and cordiality, as if I had been a much older friend than I was. In the evening, they were good enough to take me with them in their carriage to the esplanade of the fort; which is the usual place of resort of the fashionable world; and though the grass was quite burnt up, and there was scarcely a tree, or any thing else green to be seen; yet, I was pleased, as we drove along, with the effect produced by most of the objects which presented themselves. The tents and temporary bungalows of the civil and military gentlemen, pitched or erected between the road and the sea, the number of people, variously and showily dressed, moving about, or standing in groups amongst them, added greatly to the liveliness of the, to me, unusual scene; for here were congregated carriages of all descriptions, equestrians and pedestrians, as well as crowds of remarkably clean, yet, in our eyes, oddly dressed people; a number of whom were pointed out to me as strangers from various parts of the East; some of them were well mounted on Arab and Persian horses:—in short, there was such a concourse of strikingly attired people, many of them looking grave, some solemn, and others absurdly pompous, who were assiduously attended or waited upon by men whose countenances expressed so many of their national peculiarities or characteristics, that altogether I was much gratified with what I saw, as well as with the novelty of the interesting sights that constantly attracted my attention. My obliging friends considerately ordered their coachman to drive some distance into the country, in order that I might be able to see a little of it; warning me, at the same time, that I was not to expect to see any thing like the scenery in the neighbourhood of Mr. G—'s house at Galle, or upon the sea-coast between that and Colombo; indeed, there could be no comparison; yet, after the periodical rains, the country around Bombay may look better than it does at present.

I was not only disappointed in the appearance of the country, but also in that of the Bombay fashionables; many of whom were pointed out to me the following evening, when the world assembled around a military band upon the esplanade. I had also expected to have seen much Eastern magnificence or showiness in their equipages, &c.; yet I fancied that many of their coachmen, their carriages, harness, &c. reminded me of those belonging to the officers of Cossacks, (several of whose étalages, or turn-outs had been purchased from us,) who cut such a figure, and so much amused us, at the period when the allied armies were assembled around Paris. The fair dames, however, who reclined in eastern state in most of these vehicles, certainly had the look of English women; if being like faded lilies can be said to be a comparison to, or a fair resemblance of, England's bewitching daughters. I must say, however, that even in their wanness they were superior to the pallid beaux who so assiduously endeavoured to attract their attentions, or to win their smiles. But I was assured by my kind friends, that the turn-out, that evening, was most wretched; as most of the first people were then either about to proceed to England, or, for some reason or other, were up the country. I can, however, only judge from what I saw; and, I must, impartially, give the preference, in all respects, to the unpretending equipages of many shapes and fashions, easier and more English-like manners, and much less faded complexions of the ladies, who contrive to make Colombo and a few other stations of Ceylon so agreeable; yet, it ought to be remembered that, in the latter, Europeans are poor indeed, when compared with Bombay Nabobs, or with the servants in general of the Honourable Company.

Mr. S— was good enough to be my bear-leader in the numerous visits, which it was indispensable for me to pay, especially to the great official personages of the Presidency; which ceremony no stranger, with any pretensions to importance, can neglect with impunity, as here, according to etiquette, a new-comer is not called upon; he must, if he wishes to get into society, wait upon all the respectable residents, some of whom, at Bombay, were then certainly curiosities; and, strange enough in such a climate, endued with most frigid manners. I visited, of course, the dock-yard, and was surprised to find that, in this important establishment, every thing was most ably conducted by Parsees. I take a great interest in such establishments, and have had opportunities of inspecting many such in several parts of the world; but, with the exception of Portsmouth, and one or two of our dock-yards, I have nowhere else seen any thing of the kind better conducted. A frigate of forty-six guns was lately launched, and a splendid ship of eighty guns is now building in an excellent and scientific style of workmanship; and numbers of large vessels are also under-going repairs, in the well-constructed and conveniently situated docks.

I had no opportunities of forming an opinion of these most respectable people, the Parsees; but Mr. S—, as well as all those gentlemen who are best acquainted with them, speak in the highest terms of their uprightness, intelligence and industry; and also highly extol their liberality and generosity upon all occasions. I was informed that they are worshippers of one God, according to the tenets of Zoroaster; and that when the religion of Mahommed was established in Persia, their ancestors refused to conform to it, and, in consequence, were obliged to fly from their country; so that it appears they have resided for many years in this part of India; yet, they remain to this day a pure and unmixed race, who pride themselves upon being descended from a once great nation, whose empire extended from the frontiers of India, even to the Mediterranean sea.

I should conclude that these people must, in the Company's territories, be enabled to carry on their various works or undertakings of all kinds to much advantage; for there, as in Ceylon, labour, the great essential, is cheap. No doubt Europeans, possessing considerable capital, can, in many parts of India, avail themselves of this as well as in Ceylon; but, how different are the climates of the two countries, and, in this respect, how superior is the latter to the former; and, how little is the constitution impaired, by a residence of years in the one, to what it is in the other! I must now, however, state that I am aware this has been for some time past extensively attempted in India, and, amongst others, by Mr. Sym, who holds grants of land in Gorackpoor, from the Company, to the extent of 60,000 English acres: he does not state what he pays for this quantity, but for his first grant, of 25,000 English acres, he was liable to a rent of 7,500 rupees. The revenue he has to pay the Company was settled for 50 years;—for the first twenty-five years it is a gradually increasing quit rent; and after that, for the remainder of the term, he is to pay the maximum rent. The crops he cultivates upon the land he holds are wheat and barley, rice and codo, which, like rice, is a crop which requires rain or water; oil seeds of different kinds; rape, mustard, and linseed. His tenants cultivate, but at their own risk, sugar-cane, indigo, and opium. Of the 60,000 acres Mr. Sym (and those concerned with him in the speculation) holds from the Company, he keeps in his own hands but a small proportion, probably 200 acres in sugar-cane, 600 in indigo, and 100 in oats; the rest of the land is let out; and he purchases the cane-juice, sugar, and indigo, from the ryots, his tenants; this, it seems, he prefers doing, to cultivating the land himself, though labour is so cheap. The East India Company, however, reserve to themselves in all such grants, a right to overlook the cultivation in the fifth, tenth, and twentieth years. In the first instance, the company deduct one-fourth of the territorial area as uncultivable; of the remaining three-fourths, Mr. Sym is bound to cultivate one-fourth in five years, half in ten years, and the whole three-fourths in twenty years, on pain of whatever part of the land, that may then be uncultivated, lapsing to Government. It appears that the sugar is worked by Mr. Sym according to the native process. He has no works of any consequence for that purpose; — he has only a cattle-mill, which he bought in India;—he has no steam-engine of any kind, and the sugar (of which he sends home annually about 20,000 maunds of 82 pounds each), is entirely prepared in the native manner. He states, that there is no digging cane-holes by manual labour; but that the canes are planted by the plough. He never cuts the canes for more than three years consecutively; and generally digs them up after the second year. He then goes to a fresh piece of land, and prepares it for sugar-cane by a rotation of crops. He turns up the soil, and lets it have one complete rainy season to cool; as new soil is always a hot soil, and therefore the cane would not grow well in it. To this I particularly call the attention of those who may attempt the cultivation of the sugar-cane in Ceylon, as I am convinced that, owing to this not having been known, most of the failures have taken place. After it has had one rainy season, and has been properly turned up, he sows it with wheat or barley, and after that, perhaps, takes only one crop of sugar, and reverts to grain; but, if he thinks fit, he can, without injury to the land, take more than five crops of sugar-cane in twelve years, and without having recourse to any manual labour except in hoeing.

Mr. Sym also states, that sugar is his most remunerative crop. The natives prefer growing it to any other crop; that is, to tobacco, poppy, or indigo; but the man who grows sugar, grows grain also in rotation; the tenants are not, however, bound in their leases to grow any particular crop,—they are only bound as to payment of rent. In speaking of the land Mr. Sym himself cultivates, he says—it is not the practice in our part of the country to do much by hired labourers;—suppose a farm to be 100 acres, it would require ten men, and boys of twelve years and upwards:—that is, a village community comprising that number of persons, fit to work, may cultivate a farm of 100 acres. Mr. Sym adds, that when the land he has in his own hands requires hoeing, he gives it out to his tenants, paying them a contract price of about four or five annas for a begah, which is two-thirds of an acre; that is, about six-pence English money. He pays these people for ploughing a begah, twice east and west, and, twice north and south, two shillings. The number of ploughings required depends upon what crop it was broken up from;—if it was from wheat land, eight or ten ploughings would be sufficient;—five shillings worth of ploughing would be enough for a begah of sugar-cane land; and for the hoeing of it about two shillings worth. To this there should be added the expense of sugar-cane for seed; but this he does not purchase, as it is generally his own cane that he plants. The planting is, as before remarked, done by the plough, and the expense of it is covered by the five shillings. Mr. Sym charges himself at the rate of two rupees a begah on sugar-land;—thus the cost in all, including a year's rent and the expenses of preparation between the reaping of the wheat and the planting of the cane, (wheat is reaped in March and April, and the cane is planted in the March following) would come to about seventeen shillings a begah. He also says, that, in some situations, water is required for irrigating the sugar-cane land; but, for some reason, which he does not state, this is not necessary upon his. He usually gets off 300 begahs, about 2,000 maunds of sugar only; because his machinery is so imperfect, that a great quantity runs to molasses. He employs hired labourers only in the boiling of the sugar. Head boilers gets six and seven rupees, or fourteen shillings a month; an ordinary workman receives only about four or five pice a day, or from 1½*d.* to 2*d.* a-day. He adds, that these men are his own tenants, who grow enough for themselves to eat—this money-payment is all they receive. The best of Mr. Sym's sugar, in the year 1840, was selling, (including twenty-four shillings for duty) at about seventy shillings the hundred weight—formerly he calculated upon getting at Calcutta, four or five shillings the hundred weight for molasses; but, the market having become glutted, there is no longer any sale there, or elsewhere, for it. As, generally speaking, arrack, which is made from it, as well as from rice, toddy, &c. is forbidden both to the Mahometans and Hindoos by their religion, the former never drink it; but there are some of the latter who do. There are, however, some villages of Roman Catholic Christians, and two or three of Hill coolies, in Mr. Sym's neighbourhood, who drink spirits when they can procure them.

I must also request the further attention of those interested in such matters, to a document, in the Appendix, respecting the cultivation of flax in India; and also to some remarks on free trade.*

I was anxious to have spoken also of silk, as a valuable article of Indian Commerce; but I find that I have already taken up too much space with these remarks. I trust, however, that the information I have thus condensed will be considered to afford useful hints to those who intend to settle in Ceylon; it will, at all events, give readers in

* See Appendix E. & F.

general, a tolerably correct idea of the manner in which agriculture is conducted in the Company's territories. I shall only add, that, at present, land in Ceylon is sold by Government, at five shillings an acre, and the purchaser is, seemingly, unfettered by any conditions.

I have had the pleasure of meeting, and of becoming acquainted with, some agreeable, well-educated, and intelligent persons at Bombay. Yesterday, Mr. and Mrs. S— had a very pleasant dinner-party, when every thing was in good keeping, yet without the slightest ostentation; and though Mr. S— is, I believe, one of the wealthiest men here, yet he had but one course and a dessert; and Madeira and claret were the only wines at his table. But, as he is any thing but penurious, he has no doubt a good reason for thus setting an example of judicious economy, which is here, as in most parts of India, a virtue seldom practised. For such a party in Ceylon, we poor, foolish people, would have had at least two courses and a splendid dessert, with an abundance of champagne, Madeira, sherry, claret, and other French wines, &c.

One evening, I was invited to a large party, and had an opportunity of seeing a poor girl—a fresh arrival from England—exhibited before the company, when she was made to play and sing;—both wretchedly enough. I must say, that she met with much kindness and encouragement: but, God pity the unfortunate girl, if she possesses any feeling, who is thus sent out to India—shall I say—for sale!

I am, however, told that upon their getting, as many of them do, rich and *youthful* husbands, they too often forget, or rather do not wish to remember, the unpleasantness of their debût, and soon are forgetful of kindness, and ungrateful to those who, in the first instance, afforded them hospitality and protection; and, after all, what better can be looked for from girls, probably, fresh from a second-rate boarding-school? I had however, reason to know, that the young lady in question, who had been consigned to the care of a distant relation, was thought, that night, to have made a conquest of a sober-minded civilian, who, I suppose, imagined that it would be a delightful task to win a heart, whilst he taught the young idea how to shoot! Young officers, it must be observed, are as carefully guarded against here, as younger sons, or as they are there termed *scorpions*, are in London: and are as much as possible excluded from their houses by prudent mothers who have daughters to dispose of.

I made, when at Bombay, a memorandum of the following event, and as it is far too good a story to be omitted, I cannot think of withholding it from such readers as may be amused with or curious in such matters.

A General M—, of whom I had previously heard much, is the hero of it. He was well known in the Company's service, and often laughed at on account of his oddities and eccentricities. In very early life, he had served as a volunteer in the Pretender's army, in the rebellion of forty-five; and, as soon as it was suppressed, he left his country, never to return to it, unless—as he then determined—there should be another rising in favour of the exiled family. He was never afterwards known to have drank *the King's health*, as his principles were against his doing so, except in that spirit, or understanding, in which the Baron of Bradwardyne and many others did it. In his ninety-fifth year, he married a young widow of two and twenty. The lady, however, as it may well be supposed, having no great fancy for her youthful spouse, became, as many may think, naturally enough, but very imprudently and inconsiderately, attached to one of the worthy General's staff. The General having some old faithful servants in his establishment, he was, by them, soon informed of what was going forward in it, and was able to lay his plans accordingly; so that the gentleman was one night caught in his house; but, he took good care not to see him, and merely gave orders to his domestics, that he should be tied up to a tree in the garden, and that, at intervals, he should be well flogged *à la militaire;* which was duly done, but so little to the gallant's satisfaction, that he roared and begged most piteously for mercy; whilst the old General sat, apparently, with the utmost nonchalance, smoking his hookah, and drinking brandy-pawny, in his verandah; pretending not to hear, or to be aware of, what was going forward. This he did steadily until day-light, when he went forth to see—merely out of curiosity—the *scoundrel* who had dared to attempt to rob his house.

But, on looking, peeringly, at his aide-de-camp, tied to the tree, he with well-feigned surprise exclaimed, "Eh! B—, is it you, mun?" and pretending great commiseration for what, under such a strange mistake, he had suffered, he had him immediately taken down, and turned out of the garden, and it may well be supposed that he never again ventured to look his offended General in the face. The story, however, got wind, and he was ever after laughed at by every one who knew him.

I have just returned from Parell, the residence of the Governor, which is in many respects a suitable mansion for the head of a Presidency, the importance of which is daily becoming more and more evident. The drawing room is handsomely furnished, and, with the one adjoining, can easily accommodate about three hundred persons. The Governor, Mr. Elphinstone, who is now absent, is much beloved by all classes of people. He has, when at Bombay, a weekly party of about a hundred at dinner; and two hundred more are usually invited in the evening; when the centre part of the rich carpet of the drawing room being removed, they have always dancing, which seems to be as much enjoyed here as in other parts of the East.

There is a small garden attached to the Government house, neatly enough kept; but the grounds are in rather an unseemly state; and there are some most wretched huts, belonging to natives, just under its windows. I am, however, told that his Excellency is far too good natured and compassionate to order them to be removed. It appears that he made his residence what it now is; for, when it was given over to him, by his predecessor, it was nearly a ruin. His own private apartments are still in all respects plain.

A few wild animals are kept at one end of the garden, and amongst them are two wild asses, found somewhere up the country; but, I must say, they appeared to me to be prettily-shaped mules, or animals very like them.

In returning to Bombay, I was obligingly taken by Mr. S—, into Loujee castle; an immense building, belonging to one of the wealthiest Parsee merchants. The rooms are spacious; but as badly finished as furnished, and by no means equal to what I had been led to expect. The walls of many of the rooms are almost covered with Chinese and other pictures;—all of them wretched daubs. As the Loujee family were then residing in Bombay, we were, through Mr. S—'s influence with them, shewn by the servants all over the house, including even the ladies' apartments; but, I saw nothing of that Eastern magnificence and luxury mentioned by Mrs. Graham; nor could I discover any thing worthy of being rated beautiful in the gardens. But, after all, objects often appear to travellers in very different lights: indeed, the associations of ideas, in such cases, usually influence the mind, and cause us to paint scenery, as well as flower-decked parterres, in brighter or more glowing colours than they actually possess. I went one morning into

Mrs. S—'s flower garden in Bombay, in which I was told that I should see some rare flowers and shrubs; but, I found that I had collected, at Kurunagalla, almost every one of them, and many others which are, I suspect, unknown at Bombay; at all events, they were neither in the Governor's garden, nor in that of Loujee castle.

I was induced to go to a ball given here by some gentlemen to Mrs. —, the wife of an officer of rank, who was about to proceed to assume a command in the interior. But, in truth, I cannot even pretend to be an admirer of those who at Bombay are looked upon as fashionables; yet I am by no means, nor had I any reason to be, prejudiced against them. In truth, I looked upon myself, whilst there, as an unconcerned spectator, without the slightest bias one way or other; and, I may therefore observe, I hope without giving offence, that I saw nothing at that grand ball to induce me to change the opinion I had previously formed; or to make me imagine that they could ever have moved in any other world of fashion but their own. With few exceptions, the ladies were either badly or over-dressed; or, I should rather say, that their very expensive dresses were ill made, and generally worse put on; and the profusion of ornaments, which many of them wore, had a very different effect to what was intended; and, I could not but fancy, what a Parisian belle would have thought of most of them! Yet, it must be admitted, that even the English fashionables, who, after Waterloo, went in such crowds to Paris, deservedly excited the amazement, as well as the ridicule, of those admirably dressed pretty trippers. Indeed, our ladies' little silk and straw bonnets, their absurdly long waisted and oddly shaped gowns, and their awkward mode of striding along, too often, I must say, justified the French in exclaiming, —"Mon Dieu!—quelles figures!"

This was the season for the Bombay races, which are, I understand, always well attended. I rode to the course, which is about three miles from the fort, and was both amused and pleased with all I saw. The stand-house is a handsome structure, and well placed, the course excellent, about a mile and a half in circumference, and perfectly level. During the time I remained, there were three well contested races, and the riders did their noble Arab steeds every possible justice: in short, judging from what I saw, I have every reason to speak well of the turf amusements of the Presidency, which appear to be admirably conducted. The crowd of natives, from all parts of the East, was immense; and their, chiefly, white dresses, dark countenances, and many coloured turbans, had really a fine and most striking effect; but, how quiet, orderly and inanimate, they all were; and, how unlike a race-crowd in merry England, or in still more buoyant-spirited Ireland!

Bombay was at this time, as it too often is, unhealthy. His Majesty's 20th Regiment had lost, as I understood, nearly a hundred men, chiefly by fevers, since May last; and such hot weather, at this season, had not been experienced for many years. I really pitied some of the old debilitated looking gentlemen I met with in my morning walks, who, in the months of December and January, always look for cool and renovating weather, which, in some degree, braces and enables them to bear up against the oppressive heat of the rest of the year. But, alas! they had now been altogether disappointed; no cooling breeze had been more than partially felt, and they had no hopes of rain falling before April. What a contrast is this to the delightful climate with which Colombo, Galle, and many other parts of the sea-coast of Ceylon, are blessed; where refreshing showers are so frequent, and where there are almost constantly cooling sea-breezes. Since my arrival at Bombay, I have scarcely seen a cloud; and, it is here that the sun may truly be styled "golden-haired son of the sky!" My having gone to Bombay for the recovery of health, was certainly an absurdity; it was, however, from the effects of sea air that I chiefly expected to be benefited; but, when steam navigation is extended over the Indian ocean, (as it has been since these notes were made), I have no doubt, but that invalids, when they become aware of what a superior climate Ceylon possesses, will be delighted to repair thither for the re-establishment of their health; and I feel confident that they will not often be disappointed in their expectations. But, what would an unlucky wight, who is expiring from heat and exhaustion in the miserable sandy island of Karack in the Persian Gulf, now occupied by the Company's troops, not give to be transported to Horton Plains, or Nuwara-Ellia in Ceylon, where he could breathe not only a cold, but even an English atmosphere! In the unhealthy island of Karack, the thermometer in the shade, for perhaps nine months of the year, is above 100°. Both Europeans and Sepoys stationed there usually sleep out of doors, exposed to the night air, without covering of any kind, for almost the whole year round; as the heat in the houses, expensively built for the soldiers, and in those which the officers are obliged to purchase from each other, is intolerable. These worn-out and emaciated gentlemen, when they are able, mount their horses long before dawn; that is to say, before three in the morning, to ride to the sea-shore to bathe, in the hope of being thereby refreshed, and the better able to support the heat of the day; but, they must be sure to be back and in their houses by seven or eight, at the latest; for, by that time the sun's rays become unbearably scorching. Surely, if it is necessary to overawe Persia, or to ensure the safe navigation of the Persian Gulf, the Euphrates and Tigris, it could be much cheaper and better done, by the occasional appearance on the Persian and Arabian coasts of a few war-steamers, than by occupying, at an enormous waste of human life and treasure, that useless and wretched island.

How well worthy of a traveller's notice, are the famous Pagodas of Elephanta and Salsette: indeed, no one ought, upon any account, to leave Bombay without visiting them I annex a ground plan of

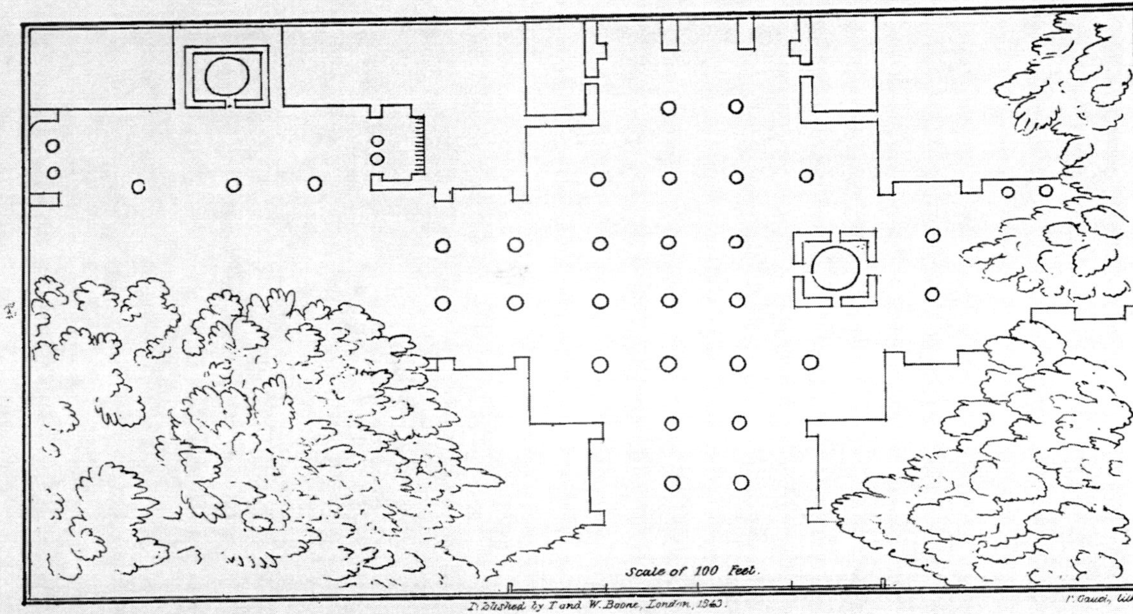
Scale of 100 Feet.
Published by T and W. Boone, London, 1843.
I. Gauci, lith

ELEPHANTA

the former, indifferently executed, but which will give the reader some idea of that wonderful temple ;—he is aware that I have endeavoured to describe those of Dambool in Ceylon, which I look upon as equally if not more extraordinary, and which are also excavated out of the solid rock. Those of Dambool are, however, in a perfect state of repair, and all the colourings retain their original brilliancy; whereas, that of Elephanta is, I may say, a ruin.

I have now, I believe, seen every part of Bombay, and much of its neighbourhood. It is large, and strongly fortified ; but, if ever it were attacked, it would require at least 15,000 men for its defence. The streets are all irregular, most of them narrow and very dirty. The houses are much huddled together, and most of the best of them, especially about Rampart-row, are two or three stories high ; but they have, in general, a mean and comfortless look about them. To my surprise, I found that it is the fashion to purchase, for a considerable number of rupees, temporary bungalows erected on the esplanade of the Fort, not much better than those constructed by officers superintending the road-makers in Ceylon ; and, in these uncomfortable abodes the first people reside for two or three months, at the expiration of which time, according to a Government regulation, they must be pulled down. This strange change of dwelling seems to be much the fashion here, and probably may be pleasant enough to some families ; but I could not understand, how sensible persons, like Mr. and

Mrs. S— would think of leaving a palace, comparatively speaking, to reside in a hovel, merely to be in the fashion. The Black-town, as it is called, outside the walls, is very large and populous, but I have never passed through a more filthy or hotter place; and the houses, in general, are quite as wretched as those in the Petah of Colombo. Beyond the Black-town, there are a number of large and respectable looking houses; in which reside most of the first people, both civil and military. I ought, however, to mention, that the roads in all directions are excellent; and that, consequently, there is no difficulty in having pleasant morning and evening rides and drives.

I accompanied Mr. and Mrs. S— to dine with a friend of theirs, a worthy old Captain of an Indiaman, who had fixed his abode, as I understood for life, in the island of Calaba, which is only separated from that on which Bombay stands by the sea at high water; at ebb-tide, the road across to it is quite dry. Calaba is about two miles long, and a quarter of a mile broad. It is rocky, and has very little soil upon it; yet there is, in some places, sufficient to admit of those residing there to have small gardens, or for the growth of a few trees. There are some private houses upon it, and the Company have allotted part of it, on which there are barracks, for the quarters of an European regiment; I suppose, because it is imagined that they will be there more out of harm's way, than in a station nearer to Bombay. It appeared to me to be a most wretched station for both officers and men; and I have no doubt, but that it seldom fails to create in the minds of the latter those feelings of disappointment, as to anticipated pleasures, which are so often observable amongst them, and, which so frequently render them afterwards the reckless beings we find them. I cannot imagine with what other object such a spot could have been selected for them; and surely it would be much more judicious to push forward troops landing from England at once into the more healthy and mountainous part of the Presidency.—But I have been led away from the excellent dinner to which I had been invited. The old Captain was most hospitable; and I must mention, for the reader's information, that the butcher's meat, especially, was very superior to what can be procured in Ceylon; and, on my account, a great variety of vegetables had been provided,—equal to any to be got in England. Fruits of all kinds were, however, at Bombay, very inferior to those of Ceylon. I find that many of the old Indians, who have spent their best days in this part of the world, and who, from their having at length acquired Eastern habits and Eastern ideas, very wisely consider that they could never be afterwards either happy or comfortable in England, have, therefore, like this gentleman, permanently pitched their tents in or near Bombay; where they are known and respected, and have suitable companions; whereas they know well, that had they returned to their native land, no one would probably remember or care about them, except a few interested and, perhaps, distant relatives; who would, certainly, have an eye to their hardly-earned rupees, and would calculate, each winter, that it must surely be their poor dear cousin the Nabob's last.

Steam navigation makes it now-a-days easy to get from Bombay to Ceylon; but so little intercourse was then kept up between them, that I had begun to fear that I was never to have an opportunity of returning direct to Colombo by sea; and that I should have no alternative but to take a long, and to me, unsuitable land journey towards "Adam's Bridge," and in its neighbourhood endeavour to procure a passage for myself and servant across to Jaffnapatam, in one of the small craft usually to be met with there. At last, however, a vessel called at Bombay on her way to Calcutta, the master of which undertook to land us at Colombo, or Galle.

In closing the few remarks which I have ventured to make upon this part of the world, I shall only add that, notwithstanding the advantages, in point of emolument, which the Company's servants possess over those of Her Majesty, in Ceylon, I must yet say, that I saw nothing in society, or in any respect, to make me give a preference to the Honourable Company's service. In Ceylon fish, fowls, fruit of all kinds, are better than at Bombay; but in the latter almost all other sorts of food are certainly superior. Equal numbers of servants are kept by respectable families and individuals in both, at nearly the same expense. In short, I could see no material difference betwixt the two countries, except in point of climate, in which respect Ceylon has infinitely the advantage over the Bombay Presidency; and indeed—from all I have heard—over any part of the Company's territories in India; and I would much rather remain comparatively poor in the former, than be obliged to run the continual risk of losing health, to which those who reside in the latter are exposed.

In this part of the world, when exposed in an open boat upon the water, to the all-powerful rays of the sun at noon, as I was while proceeding to the vessel, how impressively is the voice of Ossian—the oldest and sweetest of Scotia's bards—felt, when he sublimely exclaims,—"O thou that rollest above, round as the shield of my fathers! Whence are thy beams, O Sun! thy everlasting light? Thou comest forth in thy awful beauty; the stars hide themselves in the sky; the moon cold and pale, sinks in the western wave; but thou thyself movest alone. Who can be a companion of thy course?"—Glad, therefore, was I to find myself under the awning of the good ship Bombay; which, soon after I was on board, spread all sail, to a gentle but propitious breeze, which wafted us on towards Ceylon.

My companions on board were the Captain and his wife, the latter a half-caste Bengali, with two children; a surgeon, married to a Dutch Ceylon lady—they had three squalling children; a large fat lady, with one quiet child; two young gentlemen belonging to the Company's service; and a handsome young widow, who, as I was informed by Mr. S—, had just come into a fortune of £30,000. by the death of her husband, a Lieutenant-Colonel M—, of the Company's service. She was on her way to Calcutta; having determined, as she informed me a few days after, upon visiting some connections she had there; and upon seeing the capital of our Empire in the East, before she returned to Europe. Who can tell what a day may bring forth? She is now, if I mistake not, Lady Macnaghten, and again a widow.

The ship was very clean, our cabins comfortable, and every thing was well and pleasantly managed on board: indeed, on shore we could not have wished to sit down to a nicer table. We breakfasted, dined, &c. on deck, under an awning, which, in such latitudes, is a most desirable plan. But what a contrast was this to our entertainment on board the French ship Zenobia! We had no muskitoes; but, in our cabins, there were thousands of large cockroaches, which always infest what are called country ships; and, how they did gallop over me every night! I, however, felt confident of escaping their bites, by merely taking the pleasant precaution of being particularly cleanly in my person; let those who in such situations neglect this, beware of the consequences.

A fine steady breeze brought the slow sailing old ship off Goa; and in three or four days more we hoped to reach Mangalore, where we are to take in coir; that is, the coarse stuff which surrounds cocoa-nuts, and of which, as I before mentioned, cables, &c. are made. We are then to touch at Cochin, and from thence stand direct for Ceylon.

In due time we anchored off Mangalore, which looks well from the sea; but, as I had brought with me an introduction, or what is here termed a soup-ticket, with which I had been furnished at Bombay, to Colonel M—, the commandant, I therefore hoped to see more of it, if he should be good enough to invite me to his house; for here, as in Ceylon, there are no inns in which strangers can find accommodation. Having received the expected invitation,—for these drafts upon our friends' hospitality are always duly honoured in the East—in the evening I set off for the shore; and was much pleased, as we proceeded towards the landing-place, with what may be considered the harbour of Mangalore, as well as with the appearance of the country around it; for, we rowed pleasantly along, in a boat sent off for me, upon the smooth surface of what I afterwards ascertained to be the junction of two considerable rivers, but which seemed to me to be a lake; the native boatmen, as we glided along, keeping time with the oars to their songs, which, though wild, were on the whole agreeable; and, in some measure reminded me of those I had often heard sung, or well-nigh shouted, by the voyageurs on the Canadian lakes and rivers.

The formations of what are here called back-waters are common along the Malabar coast; and appear to be caused by the rivers, when flooded, encountering the greatly agitated waters of the ocean, during the south-west monsoon; which, at its commencement, rages all along this coast with much violence, when it throws up immense quantities of sand and gravel, which choke the mouths of rivers, and force them to find new and sometimes remote outlets for their waters. Thus, in the course of time, have been formed these sandy reservoirs, or beds of lakes, which are often extensive and of much importance to this country; as it has no regular harbours. At certain periods, evenlarge country vessels, some of which come from the Arabian coast, can enter that of Mangalore. There are similar formations, on some parts of the coast of Ceylon; but they are in size proportionate to the rivers, which are there so much smaller than on the continent.

There was a palanquin waiting for me at the landing place, in which I went about three miles inland, to a very small house, in which Colonel and Mrs. M— were then residing; and I may suppose, with the intention of giving me what many consider there the bcst apartment, I had a tent assigned for my accommodation, which I thought most comfortable. But, in the course of the night, the land-wind sprung up, which is there strong, cold, and dangerous; and to its pernicious effects I was indebted for being confined to Colonel M—'s house on the sea-shore, to which we removed the following morning, a considerable part of the time I was there;—intermittent fever had, alas, returned. I, however, in a few days got over it, and contrived to see a good deal of the country around Mangalore, which is in general pretty, though in some directions it had a somewhat barren appearance;—at all events most of it, at the season I was there, had a withered or burnt-up look. There is not much to be seen deserving the attention of a traveller, excepting the fine rivers which I have mentioned, and the ruins of the old fortress of Mangalore; the fortifications of which were destroyed by Tippoo Sultan, when he took it from the British, after a siege of five months. He then declared, that as it had been so easily taken from his subjects, and had occasioned such a vast loss of time and lives to reduce it with an army of a hundred thousand men, he would take care that it should not plague him again, and he therefore blew it up from its very foundations with gunpowder; so that this once strong fortress now presents only an immense heap of ruins, with scarcely one stone standing upon another.

It appears that, to commemorate this event, Tippoo caused to be erected, upon a projecting point, from whence he usually viewed the operations of the siege, a sort of work which looks like two towers joined by a curtain, which is now a useful object for directing ships to the anchorage; and a stranger, on observing it, is likely to inquire for what purpose it had been built? and may probably learn at once the history of the fallen city, as well as the fate of its conqueror Tippoo. I went one evening to the Sultan's station, and remained there till after sunset, highly pleased with the views from it, over the surrounding country, and over a vast extent of ocean to the westward, which was covered at that season with vessels of all sizes, most of them steering along the coast before the favourable breeze, that blew so gently as scarcely to ruffle its tranquil surface.

Society at Mangalore seemed to me to be both confined and dull; consisting of a few Civil servants, and the officers of a regiment of Sepoys, whose chief amusement, as I understood, was hog-hunting; numbers of these animals being easily found at no great distance from the cantonment.—I left Mangalore impressed with grateful feelings to Colonel and Mrs. M— for all the kindness and attention I had experienced from them.

Again the sails were set, and the ship glided slowly along upon the smooth surface of the ocean. We touched at Cochin; and then stood out from the land, just as "night came down on the sea, and the wan cold moon rose in the east;" but the morning at last dawned, when I again saw "Ceylon rising in all its brightness and loveliness on the eastern wave." But how beautiful it appears in whatever direction it is approached!—what a contrast it presented to the generally burnt up and withered-looking land I had left behind me; and, with what delight I returned to its perpetual verdure, and to valued friends, who were, I knew, expecting me !

The important documents in the Appendix,* shewing the rates of duty charged on goods exported from, and imported into the Presidencies of Bengal and Bombay will, by readers in general, be considered as essential towards a right understanding of several parts of this work ; as Ceylon, from its situation, must always be more or less connected with the East India Company's territories.

* See Appendix, G, H, I, J, K, L.

CHAPTER XII.

"Happy the man who sees a God employ'd
In all the good and ill that chequer life!
Resolving all events, with their effects
And manifold results, into the will
And arbitration wise of the Supreme."—COWPER.

RETURN TO CEYLON—AN ALARMING ACCIDENT CAUSED BY WHITE ANTS—SET OF FOR KURUNAGALLA, BY THE WAY OF NEGOMBO—NEGOMBO AND ITS NEIGHBOURHOOD DESCRIBED, ETC.—ARRIVE IN THE SEVEN KORLES; DOINGS THERE—A LADY'S ADVENTURE WITH A BUFFALO IN THE JUNGLE—OTHER MATTERS—AN EXTRAORDINARY MONKEY AND ITS TRICKS—A LADY STRANGELY ALARMED WHEN AT HER TOILET—A COBRA DE CAPELLO IN A DRESSING ROOM—A DAY'S EXCURSION; ALSO, WHAT SOME MAY THINK TRIFLING YET AMUSING EVENTS—LAND TORTOISES—EXPERIMENTS MADE TO ASCERTAIN, IF SCORPIONS (AS WAS OF OLD SUPPOSED) WHEN SURROUNDED BY FIRE, WILL STING THEMSELVES TO DEATH—SOME OF CEYLON'S FINEST TREES DESCRIBED—THE SEVEN KORLES VISITED BY THE LIEUT.-GOVERNOR, ETC.—RETURN OF INTERMITTENT FEVER—PROCEED TO COLOMBO—DEATH OF BRAN—FINAL DEPARTURE FROM CEYLON TO ENGLAND.

ON my return to Ceylon, I was much gratified to find that, although I had been absent fully two months from it, my command in the Seven Korles, as well as the appointment I had held of Judieial Agent of Government, had been kept vacant for me, in order that I might, if sufficiently reeovered, resume them. I therefore purposed, after spending a few days in Colombo, in making some necessary preparations, to proeeed, once more, into the interior. Whilst thus oecupied, I was one forenoon sitting in a large drawing-room with two ladies and two other gentlemen, conversing upon the usual topics of the day; when, suddenly, we heard a very extraordinary and loud noise over head, which greatly startled us; for, immediately after, the whole of the roof of the large old Duteh house, strange to say, fell all around us!—and there, to our amazement, we sat uninjured; the bright sky above us, and an immense mass of rubbish piled up about us, over whieh, it may be well supposed, we lost no time in scrambling. All the furniture in the several rooms was completely buried under large broken tiles, wood-work, &c.; from whieh arose a dense and suffocating cloud of dust. The reader may easily imagine what a wonderful eseape we all must have had; for, if the immense quantity of materials had fallen upon, in plaee of around us, we must, inevitably, have been erushed to atoms under them. The servants, also, from being, at the moment, in the go-downs or offices, were uninjured; but, the sister-in-law of the Chief Justiee had a most narrow eseape; for she, her palanquin bearers, and the Lascareens, who were in attendance upon her, had just got clear of the large verandah, in front of the house, when the roof fell, chiefly into it; and with such a tremendous crash that it was heard distinctly all over Colombo. So loud was it, indeed, that crowds of people ran from all quarters, in order to ascertain what could have been the cause of such a commotion; many imagining that the sea—as it is said to have done many years before—had again broken into the Fortress. On examining the old materials of the building, it appeared that almost the whole of the large beams and other woodwork, though they looked perfectly sound outside, had been hollowed out by those unseen, but most persevering under-cover labourers, the white ants!

Having a week before sent forward some of my servants with furniture, &c. so as to have the house in readiness for me when I should arrive at Kurunagalla, I set off from Colombo, before dawn of day, for the Seven Korles, by the way of Negombo; as, never having had it in my power to go into the interior by that road, I wished to see the country it passes through; and, for a description of it, as far as Negombo, I must beg the reader's attention to what follows. It is partly taken from Percival's Ceylon, as the account he gives of it is much more minute, and probably more correct, than what I find in my notes; for I had not allowed myself sufficient time to see all I wished or to make inquiries.

The road from Colombo to Negombo is intersected by two broad, deep and rapid rivers, and by several minor ones, over which there are bridges. Those rivers, which add so much to the beauty and richness of the country, have their banks, inland, covered and adorned with most magnificent trees of various kinds; as usual, however, the cocoa-nut tree prevails on the sea-shore; but, the flat and often open country, which a traveller passes through, constantly presents to his view scenery of a very enchanting character. The fields are every where fertile, and clothed with a profusion of productions, which offer a charming variety to the eye. The pastures are of the greenest and richest kind; and the fields are peculiarly well adapted to rice, from there being a constant supply of water; as the whole country is easily inundated during the rainy seasons.

Negombo is situated on the sea-coast, on a most picturesque point; and is accounted one of the healthiest places in the island. Many Dutch families, on that account, reside there; as well as because the necessaries of life are very plentiful and cheap. Their houses and gardens are scattered up and down, in delightful groves of palm and other trees. The Dutch built a fort there for the protection of the cinnamon cutters; as the adjacent country yields a considerable quantity of that spice, of an excellent quality. Negombo is very advantageously situated for carrying on inland trade, particularly with Colombo and its neighbourhood; as a branch of the Muliwaddy river there runs into the sea, and at its mouth there is a harbour, where small craft put in and land their cargoes, which are afterwards conveyed up the Muliwaddy, and then, by canals, which communicate with it, to the lake that skirts Colombo. The country, through which this communication is carried on, is perfectly level in every direction, and has in it several considerable lakes and rivers, which are connected by canals. The banks of these rivers and canals are generally skirted with woods and jungle, which afford to passengers a most agreeable shade from the heat of the sun, and also supply the inhabitants with plenty of fuel; as the rivers do with the greatest abundance of fish; vast quantities of which were formerly exported from Negombo. Besides the produce of the fisheries, (which, like cinnamon, &c. was a Government monopoly), other kinds of traffic are carried on there; for to this port the adjacent country sends such articles as are intended for exportation; the vessels which are to receive them anchor off the harbour, where the goods are put on board and conveyed to their destination.

I have been more minute in describing Negombo and its neighbourhood than I intended; but, I am induced to be so, as it is evidently a part of Ceylon to which the attention of settlers should be drawn: that is to say, if they could find it practicable to obtain land there upon reasonable terms. From its having been long inhabited by Portuguese, Dutch, and natives, I should fear, however, that this cannot be easily or prudently effected. I overtook my palanquin, and a servant who had charge of the bearers and a few coolies carrying light loads, at Negombo, where I remained for the night; and set off for Dambadenia, crossing the Maha-oya, and passing through that well known to be unhealthy village called Giriouli; the country the whole day being beautiful, well, yet not too much, wooded, excepting in a few places where it was covered with thick jungle. At Dambadenia we halted for the night; and, the following morning, went on to Kurunagalla, having breakfasted at Nagahagedra, of which, and its neighbourhood, I have spoken in a former chapter, as being also, at times, very unhealthy.

I once more took charge of the troops in the district, re-opened my long closed court-house, and was soon again immersed in judicial and other business, which confined me more in doors than our judicious surgeon, or I myself, could have wished; though I was now, I may say, in the enjoyment of good health. But, friendly reader, excuse me for observing, that when once a person has suffered so severely from fever as I had done, he cannot afterwards—at least, for a considerable time—expose himself, with impunity, to the noon-day sun; nor can he recklessly persevere in the field-sports of the forest or jungle. Therefore, bearing in mind what I have *so wisely* intimated, I intended for the future to be more moderate than I had formerly been in this respect. But I must give the reader an idea of the kind of sports to which I now more particularly confine myself; and, with that in view, I must beg of him to accompany me to the lake, of which I have so often spoken, and which, I may suppose, we reach about 4 P.M. My two Malay orderlies have the canoe ready for fishing; but, if the fish do not take well, we may amuse ourselves in firing at teal, as well as at those beautiful birds we call water-rails or flamingoes; which, as I before mentioned, are so numerous among the high reeds and flags that in many places extend from the banks of the lake and islets into the water. This does well enough, until the curlews and other water-fowl arrive, and it is then that the real business of the evening commences; for, we usually fire away, knocking down these birds, right and left, until we are tired, or rather till the sport is terminated by the rapidly increasing obscurity of the evening. My large and boisterous dog Bran being always with us on these occasions, he, by his sagacity and eagerness, adds not a little to our noisy amusements. The other evening, whilst thus engaged, and when we were in keen pursuit of one of the large-bodied, long-necked, and sharp-billed ducks I have before spoken of, which I had winged, I made a grasp at it, just as it rose to the surface; but Bran springing also at the same moment at it, between us, we contrived to upset the canoe; when Bran, the two highly-delighted Malays, and my prudent self—gun in hand—were all floundering together in the water. Though fully satisfied that there were no alligators in that part of the lake, yet I felt not quite comfortable, lest one of them might have his eye fixed upon us. Before I was aware of his intentions, Bran had hold of me by the collar of my white jacket; and, in order to make him let go his hold, I had to catch him by the remaining part of one of his ears, and to pull his head under water. The Malays had, in the mean time, righted the canoe, into which, with some difficulty, they managed to get, and paddle for the shore. This was an unlucky dip for one just recovered from ague; but my very light attire was quite dry before I reached home; and I did not afterwards experience any bad effects from it.

I find the greater part of what follows amongst my memoranda;—and though some may perhaps look upon the subjects as unimportant, yet they may amuse, and afford readers in general farther information respecting this charming island, with which, and with the doings of Europeans of old in it, I am anxious to make them still better acquainted before I bring my work to a close: indeed, I consider that those intending to settle in Ceylon, would have been disappointed or dissatisfied, had I not continued to extract from my notes, &c. as I intend doing, in order to bring this work to a conclusion.

I now expected a party of ladies and gentlemen at Kurunagalla upon at least a six weeks' visit; and, as my gardens, and the place altogether, from having been neglected during my absence, were in a very unseemly state, and overgrown with weeds, I amused myself, in the mean time, in putting them in order, and in replacing some of the beautiful flowers and shrubs which had died from want of care and watering. As one of the gentlemen, whose visit I looked forward to, was a keen sportsman, and particularly fond of elephant shooting, I hoped to be able to engage him often in the pursuit of them; and, in order to be prepared to direct him aright, I endeavoured to ascertain, before-hand, where these animals were most numerous; but, I purposed also, though I did not, as yet, like to venture into the wilderness of Neurecalava, to treat them to a battue, somewhere, if I could manage it, in the neighbourhood; and, I had little doubt, but that the country about the head of the lake, which I have so often mentioned, would answer well for the purpose, especially, if we should fancy forcing the deer to take the water, as I did, so successfully, when in the Galle district.

My friends having arrived at Kurunagalla, they seemed to be not only happily occupied, in various ways, but also highly amused and satisfied with my ordinary field-sports, and with our limited society. Both gentlemen were likewise particularly delighted with the superior elephant-shooting;—D— has already bagged five, and S— two very large ones. I therefore hope that they have no intention of leaving this for some time to come. We have constantly gentlemen at dinner; and usually music (the piano) and a rubber of whist in the evening; so that, what with these and other amusements, we usually contrive to get on most agreeably until bed-time. But, let the reader only imagine the commotion caused the other night, by a laughable yet at first seemingly an alarming occurrence.

Mrs. S— had undressed and got into bed; but, in pushing down her feet under the bed-clothes, (here generally only a sheet)—horror of horrors, what should she press them against, but a warm, soft, hairy thing!—in an instant, she sprung out of bed, screaming loudly. This brought into her room all the blacks and whites in the house, most of them as lightly attired as I was. Trembling with terror, she kept pointing at the bed; which, although there was a lamp burning on the floor, she durst not again approach. S— and I, supported by D—, however, did so, cautiously, and with sticks in our hands, ready to kill whatever it might be, that had so unceremoniously presumed to occupy her place in bed: when lo! on our turning slowly down the sheet, what should we see under it, but a poor playful *kitten*, which had snugly ensconced itself there! Mrs. S—, at first, felt somewhat provoked at having made herself so ridiculous, and at the disturbance she had caused; and readily admitted that she deserved to be well laughed at: indeed, it may be supposed that she was neither spared then nor next day. But, such are the common impressions upon the minds of too many persons in Ceylon, that they are constantly, but I must say unnecessarily, keeping themselves in dread of being bitten by snakes, or stung by scorpions, &c.

Almost every morning and evening, excepting

when Mrs. D-- prefers riding with us, the ladies go for some distance in the carriage along the now excellent roads, and always return highly delighted with the scenery in the neighbourhood. Mrs. S—, however, is kept in a continual state of alarm, lest any of us should be killed or maimed by those horrid elephants, buffaloes, and tigers; which, in spite of all she can say or do, we persist in going after. I managed to take her, the other day, through the rocky and thickly wooded country that extends from Kurunagalla towards the northward, by assuring her that she would be delighted with the enchanting sylvan views in all directions; but, as she saw that we, as well as my fierce-looking Malays (as she considers them) were all armed, she asked if there was any danger; and being told by Mrs. D—, for her comfort, that we might, perhaps, fall in with tigers, of which there were several in the wooded crevices of the rocks, her fears were so much increased, that I really pitied her. She did not, however, refuse to accompany us, as she saw that Mrs. D— and I particularly wished her to go; but, her terror was the whole time so great, that she could not admire any of the really fine scenery that I took so much pains to point out to her. All this was very natural in a timid woman; but I have known men, when similarly circumstanced, not more courageous; it, at all events, renders them unnecessarily miserable, and, in a country like Ceylon, deprives them of every enjoyment. I had Mrs. S— carried, on this occasion, in a sort of canopied chair, called a tom-john, which is not unlike a sedan, and to which I would beg the attention of travellers in Ceylon; as in it they are carried along in a much more comfortable and less heating position than in a palanquin; and there is nothing, when the front and side curtains are drawn back, to obstruct the views of the country they are passing through. The one I now speak of formerly belonged to Sir Robert Brownrigg, and was often used by him in his various journeys through the country.

A few evenings ago, Mrs. D— volunteered to accompany me to the far end of the fine lake in this neighbourhood; where, as I have already mentioned, wild beasts are generally numerous; and where, the other day, we had a battue that afforded tolerably good sport, although we could not manage to make any of the deer take water. Mrs. D—, who is fool-hardy enough to attempt any thing, sallied forth upon her sure-footed white Arab, as Mrs. S— remarked, lady-errant-like, in search of adventures, followed by her horse-keeper, and accompanied by S— and me on foot, and also by my two usual attendants, the Malays; Bran also was delighted to be one of the party.

We arrived at the place on the shore of the lake, of which I have spoken as affording the finest views of it, rather sooner than I intended, as I was now better acquainted with the paths; and Mrs. D— being stationed where she could best see the immense flocks of birds flying towards its wooded banks and islets, one of the Malays, who was, as usual, on the look out, came to inform me that there was a large flock of water-fowl swimming about, close to the shore, on the other side of a patch of jungle that extended quite down to the water's edge. I therefore begged of her to remain where she was, as I wished to shoot some of them for next day's dinner. Mr. S— and both the Malays, without my being aware of it, (indeed, we had no apprehension of danger in any shape at the moment), followed me; so that she was left with her horse-keeper only. Mr. S— and I almost immediately after fired at the birds; but, we had no sooner done so, than a large and most fierce-looking buffalo, which, unknown to us, was in the patch of jungle, rushed furiously out of it, and the instant that he saw Mrs. D—, he ran headlong at her and her horse! Fortunately, she did not lose her usual extraordinary presence of mind; but snatching a large umbrella from her horse-keeper, who did not, as might have been expected, run away, she suddenly opened it in the creature's face, which so frightened him that he turned round and fled!—As he was just going off, I made my appearance from the opposite side of the jungle, but only in time to send the dog after him. In place of being alarmed, as any one else would have been, Mrs. D— was apparently delighted with the adventure. I had, however, become so uneasy on her account, especially when I recollected some of my own rencounters there with other animals, that I resolved not again to quit her side, even for a moment, until I got her home in safety. As for poor Mrs. S—, she shook all over, and became faintish, when she was told, on our return, what had happened.

When out walking with both ladies, one fine cool evening, only a short distance from Kurunagalla, and when near the European burying-ground, on the Negombo road, we, by chance, came suddenly upon a buffalo; but, in this instance, though it was a huge dunnish-coloured animal, of terrific appearance, with sharp horns and almost without hair, yet it was a tame one. Wishing, however, to drive her out of the road, I set Bran at her; but she declined to be so polite as to make way even for ladies; he was therefore again made to drive her off, and soon began applying his teeth to her heels; which she, not fancying, turned round, and to the great terror of Mrs. S—, furiously charged the dog, which in an instant seized her by the nose, and held her fast! Bellowing loudly, and making a great effort, she contrived to throw off the powerful dog; but I was glad to see that she did not wait to try the fortune of war a second time. To our surprise, however, Bran, though usually so buoyant-spirited, looked, though victorious, very chop-fallen; and when he came back to us, I observed that some blood was running from his mouth. At first, I thought that it must have come from the buffalo's nose; but when I opened his mouth, in order to ascertain the cause of the continued bleeding, I found that one of the large fangs of the upper jaw was gone;—the sudden and strong jerk of the buffalo, when held by the nose, had, as I supposed, broken it, as part of the stump remained.

Mrs. S—, being a professed botanist and florist, a keen investigator of natural curiosities, and also a conchologist, she had here a very wide field for the study of the three first. For that of the last I could supply her with ample means, for I had been picking up shells ever since my arrival in Ceylon; especially those that are found upon the Trincomalie side of the island, where they are taken out of the sea while the fish in them are alive, and their dwellings are, in consequence, preserved in the most perfect beauty and polish. Let the reader only imagine Mrs. S—'s horror when I informed her how this preservation was usually accomplished. The natives, as taught by some tender-hearted virtuoso, insert a long sort of a hook into the shell, and fix it into the live fish; a piece of cord being attached to the hook, the shell and its cruelly-treated inmate are suspended within a few inches of the ground, and there they hang until the wretched fish dies, shrivels up, and at length comes out; so that the uninjured and now empty shell, in all its beauty, falls on some cotton, placed beneath to receive it, and is thus made, what conchologists call, a *perfect specimen!* The celebrated Dr. Kitchiner, in his well-known "Cook's Oracle," speaks of the delight an oyster experiences while it is tickled to death by the teeth of the piscivorous gourmand in swallowing it! I do not wait to inquire in what way the learned and experienced Doctor made the discovery of an oyster's ticklish propensities; but I suspect that he would have had some difficulty in demonstrating that these dwellers in beautiful mansions have equal pleasure in being suspended alive, and left dangling in the air, with a hook stuck into them!

In my extensive collection are pairs of the rarest and most beautiful shells which could be procured in Ceylon; and I had many others, brought from the Red Sea, Madagascar, the Isles of France and Bourbon, (where the finest of the harp kinds are procured), New Holland, &c.; and having lately got from England Wood's Catalogue, arranged according to the Linnean system, we are able to class them correctly; and in doing so we have all great amusement, as well as much agreeable in-door occupation.

Being in favour with the soldiers, and also with the Kandyans of all castes or degrees, and it being known that I wanted specimens of all kinds of rare flowers, shrubs, air-plants, &c. as well as of curious beasts, birds, and reptiles, for Mrs. S— (who is a general favourite) to examine, they are therefore bringing them in from all parts of the country, in really ridiculous quantities and numbers. Many snakes and a beautiful young tiger soon made their appearance; the former Mrs. S— had turned out immediately, as she could not even bear the sight of them; their glaring eyes, though I assured her that they were not venomous, made her shudder; the latter, brought in a cage, obligingly made on purpose for him by the Kandyans, had been found in the mountains, and from thence carried off, at considerable personal risk, from its greatly enraged and terrific mother. He is now as playful as a kitten, even lying down at our feet to be fondled; but, how long he may continue so is quite another matter, for he will already scarcely eat anything but what he kills himself; and it goes to Mrs. S—'s heart, when she hears that live chickens, ducks, &c. are thrown into his cage, when he instantly tears them to pieces and devours them. As she declared that she would have nothing to say to him, he was given to Mrs. D— as a pet; but even she, handsome as he certainly is, wished soon to get rid of him; she having been told that Mr. W—, one of the civil servants, had brought up two tigers, which followed him, like dogs, wherever he went, to the terror of every one he met with, and which he kept in awe of him and in excellent order, by means of a large club he always carried. One of them, however, on receiving a few unusually hard knocks, for some act of disobedience, suddenly lost his temper and patience, flew upon his fool-hardy master, and had nearly killed him before he could be rescued. Of course, after this, both tigers were walked off; he had had quite enough of such pets!

One of those pretty little spotted deer, we all so much admire, was brought in for Mrs. S— from the jungle. She was quite delighted with it, and desired a servant to put it into a go-down or outhouse, and to give it grass or leaves, or whatever it would eat. But the servant, having at the time something else to do, in an unlucky hour for the gentle creature, he took it into the kitchen, and left it there until he should return. The cook who, naturally enough, considered that it was intended that he should exercise his ingenuity in dressing it, immediately cut its throat, chopped its nicely formed legs off at the knee joints, stuffed it as he would have done a sucking pig, and, to Mrs. S—'s horror and dismay, served it up at dinner, standing on its four stumps, with a small lime in its mouth! I verily believe, that she could almost have cried for vexation, when she found that it was her beautiful pet. She would not touch a morsel of its flesh, though she saw that no one else had the slightest compunction in eating it; and, what was worst of all, she felt that, in the enjoyment of an excellent dish, we neither entered into her feelings, nor sympathized with her on account of her loss.

I had brought in for her an alligator; when, she immediately exclaimed, (as I had been talking of its being likely that it would be excellent eating,) "you may make steaks or soup of him, for what I care; as well as of that other large and horrid looking creature!"—pointing at a cobra coy! I also procured flying foxes and flying squirrels; monkeys with fine beards, which she pronounced to be very like Kandyans; and likewise small greenish ones, of which kind I have one called Pug, as mischievous a creature as ever was seen or heard of; and which, he having taken a great fancy to Mrs. S—, I have made her a present of.

The largest elephant in Ceylon, and therefore, it may be supposed in India, was brought the other day for her to look at. He is well known in the island, and goes by the name of Gomerah. He is at present, being Government property, employed near this, along with another almost as large, in pulling out by the roots, or down, when that is impracticable, good sized trees, and in dragging them out of the way, where they are making a new road. The keepers easily make them understand what is required of them; but, if they do not succeed in their first effort to accomplish any task assigned them, they are seldom made to try again; as they are then apt to become sulky or stubborn, and will, when this is the case, and though usually very gentle and obedient, do only what they please. Gomerah, whilst Mrs. S— was looking in astonishment at his enormous bulk, lay quietly down at her feet; and extending his trunk towards her, slightly touched her arm with it. I then begged of her not to be alarmed, and to give him a pine-apple which was handed to her for the purpose; when, becoming surprised and pleased with his gentleness, she exclaimed, to our great amusement, "Only think of timid me, feeding, perhaps, the largest elephant in the world." With his trunk, much to her delight, he put the pine-apple into his mouth, and cranched it with his teeth; and then again put his trunk on her arm; as much as to say, give me another, which she very willingly did; for she began to fancy him greatly as a pet. Seeing this, I wished her to sit upon one of his turned-up tusks; but this she did not fancy; and, when I, as if in earnest, proposed that she would allow him to lift her up and place her on his great back with his trunk,—which he would have done most carefully,—in order that she might have a short ride, she began to look anxiously around her, and, to Mrs. D—'s great delight, whilst Gomerah, (who was made to get up, as if for the purpose,) was holding out his trunk for another pine-apple, she fairly took to her heels.

In a letter written at this time by Mrs. S—, to a friend in England, which I have lately had an opportunity of seeing, she says,—"It is quite amusing, but still more ridiculous, to witness the proofs of the most tender friendship which subsists between Colonel C—, his cat Goody, and his great dog Bran. Can you imagine that a cat would go with a man and a dog upon their shooting parties? but, so it is;—at least, they usually start together and return together. Goody's usual place, when at home, is the arm of a sofa, upon which her master commonly sits;—Bran lies under it, or more frequently stands staring in his beloved master's face, with his great nose resting on his knee. Master Pug—my pet—does not venture to play his tricks upon either Bran or Goody; but he leads poor Nanny—Goody's daughter—the pretty playful and now nearly grown cat, which was found, as I told you, in my bed, a most miserable life; and in this he is greatly encouraged by your so much admired Mrs. D—. In his devilment, he unexpectedly seizes poor Nanny by the tail, and swings her round and round with astonishing velocity; he chattering with all his might, and she squalling and spitting in such a ridiculous way, that we are often thrown into ungovernable fits of laughter at Pug's performances, which are quite masterly. He thus manages to whirl her round so quickly, and that for minutes together, that she is never able, however willing, to bite or scratch him. Mrs. D—, who takes great delight in teasing and tormenting master Pug, one day helped him most plentifully to some very hot pudding, and then desired a servant to take it from him; but, he instantly grinned, shewed his teeth, and taking up the plate in his two paws or hands, clapped it, hot pudding, sauce and all, in a great rage against his breast; and there he held it, looking defiance at the servant, until the heat made him throw it down on the floor; when he flew around the room, chattering and scolding, in such an absurd way, as completely to convulse with laughter the party at dinner. The poor creature was, however, so much scalded that a good deal of the hair soon after fell off his breast.

"Yesterday evening, accompanied by Colonel C— and other gentlemen on horseback, Mrs. D— and I went in the carriage into the gloomy forest, which extends for a considerable distance, on both sides of the road which leads towards Trincomalie: a horse-keeper led the horse which drew the carriage. We had gone, perhaps, a couple of miles into the dense and over-shadowing woods, and whilst Colonel C— was pointing out to us some objects to which he wished to direct our attention, his strange-looking horse-keeper came up to him, touched his knee gently, and pointed into the jungle, which was there over-topped by some very lofty trees. Neither Mrs. D— nor I knew what had attracted his attention; but the Colonel, I confess to my surprise, made our horse-keeper turn the carriage round and go off at a smart trot; he and Mr. S— remaining behind;—he merely saying to us, that as the sun was setting, it was high time for us to return. This again struck me as odd, as the sun still shone brightly above the trees. But, we had only gone a short way, when we heard the terrific cries, or as it is here called, the trumpeting of elephants, seemingly upon both sides of the road. This accounted, at once, for the sudden manner in which we had been so unceremoniously turned back; but being soon rejoined by the gentlemen, we were assured by them, that we were then quite safe, as the elephants, which were now some way behind us, had not come out of the forest, and it was supposed, from the trumpeting they had set up, that they had smelt the horses, to which, as I was told, they have a great dislike: but, only imagine, our having been in the midst of, probably, a score of wild elephants! I shall at last be afraid to stir out of the house; at all events, though Mrs. D— only laughs at me, they shall not, with my consent, take me again into that horrid gloomy forest.

"I, however, very soon after, had the laugh on my side; and you may well believe, that I was delighted at it. You are aware that Colonel C— is here a Judge, as well as a Commandant. He holds his courts almost daily, which are attended by Kandyans of all classes, some of them very splendidly dressed; but what I admire most are their beards, which give them a truly manly and respectable appearance: but these imposing beards have led me away from what I was going to tell you. It is the custom here, for those who are engaged in law-suits, to make presents to the judge; which, as they consist of mere trifles, he always receives from both parties, in proof of his being unbiassed one way or other. These presents are usually brought to his house in large wooden trays, carried by a number of blacks upon their heads, who have only small pieces of white cotton stuff tied round their waists, which hang down scarcely to their knees. A number of these almost naked men, carrying the presents of a man whose cause was to be heard in the course of the day, arrived just as "Sol through white curtains shot a timorous ray;" and, finding no one in the long verandah, they proceeded some way along it; and seeing a latticed door half open, in they walked, nnperceived and unheard, for they were all unshod. This happened to be Mrs. D—'s dressing-room, who was, at the moment, in the lightest possible attire, occupied at her toilet, and in arranging her dark tresses before a large mirror; so that the first notice which she had of their intrusion, was seeing their figures reflected in the glass; — all of them standing respectfully and in silence behind her, with trays upon their heads. She, naturally enough, started, screamed loudly, and, to the great surprise and alarm of the poor Kandyans, ran to hide herself behind one of the curtains. These much perplexed people, who could not conceive the reason of her terror, but who saw that they had offended her, at once concluded that their master's cause must, by such an untoward occurrence, be certainly lost: none of them had, probably, ever before seen a white lady; at least, in such dishabille. This, of course, caused a great commotion in the mansion; and I declare, that I was not sorry, at thus having an opportunity of exercising a little innocent bantering, and even of practising a sly joke, at her expense. She was asked a few minutes ago,—Why, when she saw the shining crowd around her, (shining from their anointing themselves plentifully with cocoa-nut oil), why she, usually cool and collected, had been so much afraid? and had not, naturally, taken them for a band of Belinda's friendly sprites, despatched to aid her at her toilet, as we are told that:—

> "The busy Sylphs surround their darling care,
> These set the head, and those divide the hair;
> Some fold the sleeve, whilst others plait the gown,
> And Betty's praised for labours not her own."

"I must now tell you what has just occurred. Colonel C—had taken his usual agreeable ride; and, after a few minutes rest on a sofa, in order to cool himself, he went into his dressing room, to prepare for his morning's cold bath, (which we all take here before we dress for breakfast, as we find it strengthens and enables us to support the heat of the day;) when his eye was caught by something waving, as it were, from side to side, under his dressing table;—it was a Cobra de capello!—a most beautiful but exceedingly dangerous snake. He quietly took down from the wall, against which it hung, a large pistol, and loaded it with small shot. He then came to us, and told us that he was going to fire it off, and hoped that we would not be alarmed at the report; but, he did not say what he was going to fire at. Mrs. D— and I—out of mere curiosity—followed him, wondering what he could intend to shoot in the house; when, to our surprise, we saw him go close up to the intruder, which had by this time raised itself considerably, and thereby displayed distinctly the mark upon the back of its neck, that so much resembles a pair of spectacles, and distinguishes it from other snakes; and, aiming at its head, he shot it dead upon the spot. You may well suppose our horror, when we saw what he had killed; *actually under his dressing table;*—it was fully four feet in length!—How it could have got there, or how long it had remained, no one could even imagine; unless it had come in during the

Drawn on Stone by P. Gauci. 9, North Cres[t] Bedf[d] Sq[e]

night at one of the doors, all of which are latticed and open down to the floor. If so, Colonel C— must have, undoubtedly, been within its reach, when dressing by the light of a lamp, before he went out to ride; at all events, his escape was truly miraculous; for, had he again gone up to the table, as was his intention, without seeing this terrible snake, it cannot be supposed that he could possibly have escaped being bitten by it. This event set us all to study Dr. Davy's work upon Ceylon, which Colonel C— had, a short time before, received from England; and, when I had read the accounts he so clearly gives, of his experiments on the poisons of snakes, I could not but shudder, when I thought what must have been the consequences, had this certainly beautiful creature bitten him! He says that, he agrees with Dr. Davy in opinion, that in very few places, are snakes—at all events, those which are venomous—by any means so common in Ceylon as is generally supposed. He had made many remarks upon snakes, and had also pointed out some of their peculiarities, their habits and instincts, which he had noticed since his arrival here; but, having attentively read Dr. Davy's admirable work, he will not allow, even me, to look at his own notes; as, he says, they are worthless, when compared with what Dr. Davy tells us respecting them.

"Before concluding what I have to tell you about snakes, of which most of us make, I believe, a much greater account than is necessary,—but, from what has occurred, I fear I shall even dream of them for some time to come,—I must mention that, a few days ago, the little cat, which affords Master Pug so much exercise and amusement, was playing and skipping about in the shrubbery, in front of my dressing room windows, whilst I was reading, and enjoying the cold breeze, as it occasionally and gently raised the leaves of the passion-flower and jasmine, which have beautifully entwined themselves around the posts that support the verandah, and have even pushed their long tendrils and blossoms into the room; when, all at once, the cat became stationary, with its eyes seemingly fixed upon an object, which I at first supposed to be a bit of stick; but which, to my surprise, began to move, to change its colours, to become brighter, and even lovely!—It was a snake:—its back, or the upper part of its body, grew greenish, and its lower white and something like silver;—next moment, a head was gradually raised; and I saw a pair of very brilliant eyes steadily fixed upon the evidently terrified cat, which became, as it were, fascinated; for, it was actually going nearer and nearer to what I now distinctly perceived to be a small snake. I immediately became greatly alarmed on account of the little playful creature, and called Tomby, the servant who usually waits upon me at table, to come quickly; and pointing to the spot, I asked—"What is that Tomby?"—"Bad snake, ma-am—kill cat."—Out he jumped into the garden, seized a long stick, and then went cautiously up behind the snake, its eyes being still fixed on the trembling cat;—he struck a great blow, and in a moment laid the snake dead on the ground, and thus saved the cat. On examining the snake's teeth, Colonel C— said, that it really was poisonous; and, one of the kind called Carawilla.

"Well may it be observed that, "who can tell what a day may bring forth," for

> "Soon as the morrow fair with purple beams
> Dispersed the shadows of the misty night,"

Mrs. D—and I, escorted by the gentlemen, and—to allay my apprehensions—by a number of Malays, proceeded yesterday morning in a carriage to a beautiful river they call the Didroo, where we were to breakfast, spend the day, and return in the evening to Kurunagalla, in time for dinner, to which some gentlemen had been invited. Having such an escort of armed men with us, and being also assured that we had nothing to fear from wild beasts, my mind was comparatively at ease, and I really think that I never before went upon so delightful an excursion.

"We left the carriage and horses, in charge of their keepers, at some very neatly thatched bungalows, the walls of which were entirely composed of varieties of the fine Ceylon mosses, very tastefully intermixed with the most lovely flowers. Admirable as the fittings up, and charming as the situation selected for these bungalows were, and although they seemed to me to afford every comfort that could be desired in a country and climate like this, yet I found it had before-hand been settled that, for novelty's sake, we were to breakfast at a place about half a mile farther up the river, to which the servants had been sent forward to make the necessary preparations. I was, however, so much enchanted with the bungalows, which had only been finished the night before by the Kandyans, that I would have preferred remaining in them, as it began to be very hot; but, after a pleasant walk, under the shade of some fine thorny cotton-trees with scarlet flowers, and, here and there, some noble ebony-trees and other monarchs of the forest, which almost entirely excluded the sun's rays, we descended into the deep bed of the river; where I was actually overcome with delight and amazement.—I had never before beheld any thing so strikingly beautiful and, at the same time, so surprising! Overhead were immense trees, of various shades of green, brown, or purple foliage, some with pink-coloured flowers; and the iron-tree, with its white blossoms, rose to a considerable height; whilst others grew almost horizontally out of the steep banks, and so widely extended their branches as to reach, in some places, almost across the transparent river, supporting many lovely flowering runners, which formed wreaths around their boughs, and hung down in long festoons, so as, here and there, to touch and even float upon its surface; whilst, at the same time, they had woven above us such a canopy of leaves and flowers, as scarcely to permit a ray of the sun to penetrate to the verdant spot, where breakfast was laid out for us.

"This, it seems, is one of Colonel C—'s favourite retreats, to which he occasionally repairs, attended only by his Malays, for days together; and I do not wonder at his admiration of, and attachment to, such a fairy palace; for, I can fancy that even Calypso's grotto, so well described by the excellent Fenelon, could not have been compared with it, at least in wildness, and in luxuriance of shades or colouring. He had, indeed, told us much of this, his truly enchanting bower; but the realities far surpassed even his enthusiastic descriptions of it, and our highly-raised expectations.

"During breakfast some beautiful birds sung so sweetly, that I could no longer remain prejudiced against them as songsters. I am aware that it is believed by most people that, to compensate for their want of "wood notes wild," nature has adorned the birds in tropical countries with the most splendid plumage; our attention was, however, in this instance, too often and unavoidably distracted from their melodious warblings, and our ears jarred, as it were, by the loud discordant screeching of some birds called toucans, whose bills, seemingly the chief organs of the disagreeable sounds they utter, are fully as large as their bodies, and which had for the time taken up their abode, along with some gaudily-decked parrots, and a few small greenish monkeys, among the trees around us. The gentlemen, in order to drive them away, but contrary to my wishes, shot three of the toucans, which I intend to have stuffed, and if possible preserved, to take with me, should I ever return to England. Colonel C— had made a large collection—such as would have even charmed the heart of a Waterton—of all kinds of birds, as well as of curious insects, &c.; but, during his illness—of which I before told you —from want of care on the part of his servants, the white ants got to them, and destroyed almost the whole of them; and he is now hesitating, whether it will be worth his while or not to make another.

"After breakfast, numbers of beautiful shining fish were caught in the river. I had not seen any of the kinds before, and being desirous of finding out the names by which they are known in Ceylon, I took them down, as correctly as I could, according to the way in which I thought that Tomby pronounced them; but I suspect I have lost the paper on which I made the memorandum. Many very beautiful small birds—some of them the sweet warblers—were, alas! shot, and given to me to examine, and to keep if I pleased; also several fine flowers selected in the woods on both banks of the river, and some very curious air plants; but I found that they had nearly all been collected at Kurunagalla, or transplanted into the gardens there.

"Whilst Mrs. D— and I were thus most agreeably occupied, 'the minutes wing'd their way wi' pleasure ;' for, even in this charming retreat, pleasures, as every where else on earth, are—

> " . . . . like the borealis race
> That flit ere you can point their place,
> Or like the rainbow's lovely form
> Evanishing amid the storm ;"

for, about two o'clock, Colonel C— came to us, in great haste, and requested that we would quit the cool and delightfully shaded bed of the river, as he wished us to look at the sun and the sky, both of which had assumed a very unusual and extraordinary appearance. On ascending the steep bank, we were, indeed, greatly struck with what we beheld ; for, the sun was surrounded by some large connected, or rather blended, circles of various colours, which I at once concluded, were, what I had heard described, as a kind of wonderful solar rainbow ; but, there was likewise, lower down, and, as it seemed, half-way between the sun and the horizon, a brilliant cloud, composed, as it were, of rays of light, which continued to shoot in various directions ; and which are, I believe, something of the nature of what the Kandyans call Boodhoo's rays, and which the priests pretend, never appear but over one of his temples.

" The sky was now, however, so rapidly changing its appearance, and becoming so exceedingly gloomy, that it was decided we had no time to lose in reaching the bungalows, and in starting for home ; which we could scarcely reach before the expected thunder-storm had commenced.

"We consequently went along the road at a good pace, and when we had got about half-way to Kurunagalla, the storm suddenly burst over us, and with such violence that I became greatly alarmed, not only on my own and Mrs. D—'s account—sheltered though we were in the carriage from the torrents of rain that fell,—but, more particularly, lest the gentlemen, or some of the Malays or servants, might be killed. Colonel C—, certainly, did all he could to encourage us, by telling us that he had often been exposed to much worse storms; and that, notwithstanding the flashes of lightning are always so constant and vivid, the thunder so loud, and the rain so heavy, yet that accidents very rarely happened even from forked lightning in Ceylon. I could, however, perceive that the horses, excepting that which the Colonel rode, were becoming every instant more and more frightened, especially the powerful animal which drew the carriage; so much so, that he made great starts or bounds, whenever there came one of those awfully dazzling flashes which, without an instant's pause, was followed by an amazingly loud and truly startling peal of thunder, which seemed, as it were, to shake the world! At such moments, the horsekeeper, even with the help of the gentlemen, could scarcely prevent his running away with the light carriage. This naturally kept me, at all times timid, in the greatest state of alarm, whilst the awfully imposing conflict, which was going on around us, seemed only to delight Mrs. D—: indeed, both she and Colonel C— were constantly, and to my astonishment, expressing their unbounded admiration of the terrific scene!

"At length, and when about half a mile from Kurunagalla, by which time the road had become a deep brown-coloured river, by far the most frightful flash of forked lightning which we had seen, darted just over our heads; and appeared to us all to have shattered to pieces a large projecting point of a wooded rock, which told me, at least, but too plainly and alarmingly, that there must be danger. You may, therefore, suppose how glad I was to find myself, at last, safe and sound, inside my own bedroom; the windows of which, as the storm still continued, I had instantly, and in spite of being laughed at, completely closed; and, there I sat in darkness, notwithstanding all their solicitations, that I would come out to admire the awful sublimity of the scene!

"This terrific storm ceased before six; when, at my request, a person was sent to see what had happened to the rock, which had evidently been struck by lightning as we came along. On his return, we were informed, that considerable parts of it, as well as three large trees, had been literally shivered to atoms. It was also reported, that a dreadful accident had occurred on the Colombo road, and that twenty-two men and women, who were coming towards Kurunagalla, and, though broad as the road is, in the usual Kandyan way, that is, in single file, as soldiers call it, the whole of them talking on the same subject, had all but two been killed by lightning. It was, however, soon after ascertained that, in place of two only being left alive, but two of the twenty-two had been killed: in short, it was at last admitted by every one, that we had been exposed to the violence of one of the grandest and most terrible thunder-storms with which the province had for many years been visited, and the approach of which had been so distinctly indicated by the extraordinary appearance of the sky. I understand that such thunder-storms are not, in this part of Ceylon, confined to any particular season, but are in general most violent at the setting in of the monsoons; you, good people, in England, however, have no idea whatever of the terrific grandeur and sublimity of thunder in the tropics. Here it is more like what might be imagined a breaking up of the ancient barriers assigned to nature; and that the earth, by an omnipotent arm, was about to be hurled, amidst the dread commotion and wreck of elements, into that state in which one may suppose it to have been at the time of the creation, when it "was without form and void."

"Two days ago, Colonel C—, accompanied by most of the gentlemen here, and by others who had come on purpose from the out-stations, went upon another of those hunting excursions of which we hear so much, and like so little; and which took place somewhere in the direction of a province called Matelé, where numbers of elephants and other animals were slain; indeed, so many, that they all declared that they had never had better or more exciting sport! This grand hunt took place some distance from Kurunagalla; for they had gone off, to be in time for it, the evening before, to one of the finest bungalows, where they dined and slept, so as to be ready to set the Kandyans, assembled to drive the monsters before them, to work at dawn of day. On their return, the following evening, Mrs. D— and I happened to be in the verandah; but only think of our surprise, when we saw S—, who was in what had once been a white dress, ride up, spotted all over, something like a piebald horse, with large dark and bloody-looking blotches! We should have been dreadfully alarmed at the accident, which we concluded, must have happened to him, had it not been that they all seemed to be highly amused at the astonishment pictured in our countenances; and, that we also saw that S— sat his horse too firmly to be a dying man. This strange and terrific appearance was, however, soon and satisfactorily accounted for. No wild boar, tiger, or buffalo, had torn or mangled him; but, in waiting for the animals to be driven down to the spot where the gentlemen had placed themselves in readiness to fire at them, as they passed, S— had extended himself upon a grassy bank, under the shade of a tree, to take a comfortable nap; but, whilst agreeably slumbering, he had been assailed by leeches, so that when he awoke he was covered with the blood that had flowed from all parts of his body; and his gory garb was perfected by the bites continuing to bleed profusely, long after the leeches had been forced to let go their holds.

"We have almost all, in turn, and in one way or another, become at different times, and from various causes, ridiculously liable to be laughed at by each other; but, only imagine what has again befallen unlucky me! I was walking most sedately along the verandah, from my own room to that in which breakfast is always laid out, when that rogue Pug, who usually sits on the top of one of the doors watching his opportunity, suddenly pounced upon me, seized my best and handsomely laced morning cap, as well as the hair one which I wear under it, (as I am not quite so young as I was ten years ago,) and was off in an instant with them to the top of the house; dragging his light chain after him, that happened not to be fastened, and leaving me completely bald-pated!—But what considerably augmented the absurdity of my unhappy plight, there stood in the verandah a crowd of Kandyans, and Malay soldiers, &c. waiting to attend Colonel C— to Court; all of them so ridiculously yet respectfully silent, and without the slightest change of countenance, that I verily believe, not even a smile was perceptible among them, when I, covering my bare head with my two hands, ran as fast as I could back to my room. But all the time, high up on the roof sat Master Pug, cap and wig in hand, chattering with delight at his achievement, and picking, as fast as he could, every pin out of the laced cap, and putting them into his chops. The party assembled for breakfast, (six or eight), half dead with trying to smother their laughter, upon hearing of the untoward event, instantly went after Pug. Some of the best Kandyan climbers were sent up on the roof, to recover, if possible, what to a lady, in such a part of the world, are most serious and irreparable losses — but all in vain!—Pug was too much delighted with his prizes to think of giving them up, and was far too nimble to be caught. There was, therefore, as I was told afterwards, nothing for it, as no one could think of shooting him—but to send in for what they call a pellet bow, which they use here with great dexterity and certainty; and, being soon hit with one of the hard clay balls, he in a great rage dropt both cap and wig, which were brought to me by that Job's comforter, Mrs. D—; the former, I cannot say, not a pin the worse, as they were every one taken out; and the latter, I was glad to find, had sustained much less injury than might have been expected. As soon as Pug was caught, even the pins, which fortunately he had not swallowed, were taken out of his chops,—the ready receptacle for every thing he steals. But the ridicule I have to endure, and the annoyances I experience, and must always experience, from the tricks played me by that vile varlet, have determined me, in spite of all Mrs. D—'s solicitations, to part with him; as he now, and upon all occasions, absolutely tyrannises over me."

I must again refer to my own memoranda; and, before doing so, I have to apologise for having introduced what some may be inclined to consider trifling matters; though they, undoubtedly, will tend to shew how we managed to get on of old in Ceylon, and ought, therefore, not to be considered altogether superfluous. I must now, however, and in continuation, beg leave to say that no where else have I seen such tortoises, as are to be met with in this island; and, whatever delicacies they may be considered in Italy, and in some other parts of the world, no one would, under any circumstances, be induced to dine either upon their flesh or eggs, however well dressed or prepared they might be; for here nature, apparently for their defence, has supplied them with the power of emitting such a mephitical odour, as must instantly compel any human being to fly from them, as he would from whatever is most horrid and pestilential. A few days after Mrs. S—'s most ridiculous adventure with the monkey, Mrs. D— and I were out riding, when we observed a tortoise slowly crossing the road a little way before us; and being desirous of taking it home with us, in order that it might be added to the collection of curiosities made by the former, who took such an interest in every thing new and extraordinary, I dismounted, and tying my long lash whip round its shell, at Mrs. D—'s request, and as the most convenient way that struck us of carrying it, I fastened it to the pommel of her side-saddle; and being at the time close to Kurunagalla, we intended to walk our horses quietly there. But we had only gone a few yards, when we were, to our astonishment, completely overcome, as it were, by a most horrid smell. Ascertaining in an instant that it came from the tortoise, I lost not a moment in casting the creature loose; yet, before this could be done, we had both become deadly sick and faintish; and, although we went off as quickly as possible from where it lay, with its head, legs, and tail drawn into the shell, we did not altogether recover from the effects of the pestilential odour for the whole evening. The next day I asked an intelligent Headman if he was aware of land tortoises possessing the horrid power which I have attributed to them; when he told me it was so well known to the people, that they always allowed them to crawl along undisturbed and unprovoked; for, unless they were attacked, they never annoyed any one. At first, he thought that I alluded to the porcupine, about which he entertained the long ago refuted notion of its having the power of darting its quills with great force at an assailant. He, however, assured me that the porcupine is eaten by the Kandyans, and always accounted by them a great delicacy.

I was anxious to ascertain, whether there is any truth, in what seems to be generally believed, that if a scorpion is surrounded by fire, so that it cannot escape, but by running through it, it will sting itself to death. With this view I had two very large black ones brought to me; for they were common enough here, as well as large spiders and centipedes, whose bites are likewise said to be poisonous; but, from what I have seen and heard, I have no doubt, that though their bites, like the sting of the scorpion, are not attended with danger, yet feverish symptoms are often produced, which cannot be safely or prudently neglected. Having, however, the object I have above alluded to in view, I formed on an earthen floor a circle, about a yard in diameter, with ignited charcoal, the fiery redness of which I had kept up, by throwing occasionally upon it dried leaves and bits of wood; and by having three men constantly blowing upon it, all round, through long pieces of hollow bamboo, which answered tolerably well as blow-pipes. Into this circle I put both scorpions, which, after running, for a few minutes, round the inside of it with their tails elevated over their backs, began to fight most furiously, endeavouring to sting each other; but without seeming to care about the heat of the fire by which they were surrounded. I therefore took out one of them, in order to see how the other, when left alone in the circle, would act.

After remaining quiet, for a few minutes, near the middle of the circle, it commenced running round it; evidently looking for an opening through which to escape; but finding none, and the heat of the fire increasing from the continued blowing, it quickened its pace, and ran not only round but across the circle, as if in great terror; all the time with its tail still brandished over its head. Mrs.

S—, as well as Mrs. D—, (whom I had with difficulty got to attend the—I must say—cruël experiment,) and some gentlemen who were present, now expected to witness, its death scene; but to our surprise and disappointment, in place of stinging itself to death, it dashed desperately at the very hottest part of the fire, and got completely through it, with the loss of only a leg, which was burnt off. In order to put it out of pain, it was instantly killed; as its being allowed to live and run about the house were quite out of the question.

Without loss of time, and in order that the fire might not lose any of its still powerful heat, the other scorpion was introduced into the circle. It acted very much as the other had done; but, in endeavouring to make its escape, it perished in the fire. We saw, however, no attempt whatever on the part of either of the scorpions to sting itself to death. But, I have no intention of repeating the experiment; and, although scorpions are known to be very cross-grained, and of a most irritable temperament, and, though no one hesitates to knock them on the head whenever they are met with, yet, I confess, and with not a little compunction, that we have no right whatever to subject them to such a terrible ordeal as that I have described; and, I therefore entreat that none of them may ever again, out of mere curiosity, be exposed to it; for, I suspect, that the result will be found to be muoh the same as in the instances I have given.

I regretted much, on Mrs. S—'s account, that

there were no talipot-trees at this time in flower; but, about four or five miles from Kurunagalla, there were to be seen some very fine teak-trees; and as they were then in blossom, and the ladies and gentlemen were desirous of seeing them, I took them to the spot yesterday evening; when they were much delighted as well as surprised at the magnificence of some of them; which, I think, could not have been under sixty feet in height. Their leaves are of an oval shape, a little indented at their edges; but, what most struck us all, was their being adorned with numerous clusters of small white and sweet-smelling flowers. Every one has heard of the value of teak-wood in ship-building, but, I believe that very few people, in England, are aware of the tree being so beautiful. There were growing amongst them, some very old ebony-trees; their palm-like form, smooth, long, and pointed leaves of a dark hue, and their rough kind of buds, when mingled with the white flowers of the teak, and those of another tree, (the name of which I forget) which had pink blossoms, produced a very striking and extraordinary contrast. I had been struck with this a few evenings before, and it induced me to conduct the party to the spot; when they were all highly gratified at having had an opportunity of examining such perfect specimens of, perhaps, as fine trees of the kinds, as any to be found in the East.

Next day, when in court, I was greatly alarmed by hearing a cry of fire!—my house, as I was told by a messenger, sent to me in all haste, was in a blaze. On hurrying to the spot—not the house, but the whole of the extensive range of adjoining go-downs or offices was on fire. The bugle instantly assembled the troops in garrison. Not a moment was to be lost, if the house itself was to be saved. The burning office, next to it, was soon, according to my direction, pulled down, and the materials removed by upwards of two hundred men; whilst others were gone to the fish-pond to wet in it comblies, or a kind of blankets, to be spread over the exceedingly dry thatched roof of the house. As for the offices, there was no alternative, but to let them burn. My house was thus saved; but the fury with which the very dry materials burned, made it necessary to have carried out into the square, by the active and zealous soldiers, almost the whole of the furniture. Let settlers in Ceylon be on their guard against such accidents; for they cannot possibly call to their aid hundreds of men in extinguishing a fire; and, I must assure them, that during such an operation, no one, who has not been taught by experience, can have a notion of the heat that we were exposed to, not only from a brightly shining noon-day sun, but also from a furiously blazing fire of such an extent: indeed, it was almost unbearable. It was, however, soon over; the combustible matter being all consumed. The furniture, &c. was then carried back to the house; but, what was now to be done?—the Lieut.-Governor (my old 3rd division friend, Sir

James Campbell) and all his attendants, including the head quarter staff, and several civilians, were to dine with me the following day;—there was now no kitchen, the whole of the food, &c. laid in, had been burnt or destroyed, and people cannot here, as in England, go again to market, nor, when such accidents happen, can your intended guests be sent to an inn or hotel.

I had not seen the cook, nor his assistants, since the fire; indeed, they had at once run away, imagining, no doubt, that they would all be punished; at least, they must have thought that they deserved to be so for their carelessness. I sent for my chief artist, who came trembling before me.—"What is now to be done, Master Cokey?"—"Master's dinner this day ready;—plenty time make ready that for him, Governor, to-morrow."—I had then the curiosity to go out, accompanied by the ladies, to see how he and his aides were managing. There they were, roasting, boiling, stewing, frying, upon fires made against the half-ruined outside walls of the offices; coolies were bringing them wood and water; fresh supplies of food were pouring in from all quarters; in short, all was going on as if nothing had happened.

Let the reader only imagine how a French, or any other cook, under such circumstances, could possibly have contrived to prepare a dinner for at least thirty people of the first importance, in the open air, with no other utensils than some earthen chatties or pots, and wooden spits. A French cook would have been completely *au desespoir;* and would, no doubt, have terminated his miserable existence, as the great artist of one of the French Kings of the olden time did, in consequence of having failed in one of his chefs-d'œuvre!

At day-light, the following morning, I went to meet the Lieutenant-Governor, who was coming from Kandy, at Kospeta; where he and his suite were to breakfast; but, what is very extraordinary and unaccountable, although perfectly well when I left home, yet at the very spot where I was originally attacked with fever, and where I had not been for several months, I was again, in an instant, taken ill; and, though I did every thing I possibly could in order to shake of the feverish feeling that had come over me, I could not succeed; neither hot coffee, hot brandy and water, nor any thing I could think of, would warm me. In short, after breakfast, I had to mount my horse, whilst in the last stage of the fit, to accompany the Lieutenant-Governor to Kurunagalla. It has, however, always been incomprehensible to me, why I should have had this sudden return of fever at the very spot where it first assailed me; and that, too, without any apparent cause, as the whole country was at the time, as it had been for months past, perfectly healthy.

As we rode towards Kurunagalla — the fit of ague being soon over—I was able so far to exert myself, as to endeavour to point out to Sir James Campbell, who had not been before in this part of the country, some of the fine scenery and magnificent views; and when we arrived at the cantonment, I found that I could attend to the wants of my numerous guests. At dinner the Lieutenant-Governor, who was aware of my kitchen and other offices being burnt down, expressed to Mrs. D— his surprise at finding such a dinner prepared; and declared, as the other guests also did, that they had not before seen a better in the interior. I however repeat, that I only mention this to shew the reader how we, or rather our cooks, managed matters, at that period, in the Kandyan country. But, I find that, in the present day, it is not unusual for gentlemen travelling, or who go upon shooting or other excursions, to avail themselves of the accommodations offered by Headmen. Such a thing, at the period when I made these notes, would never have been thought of. We then, as I have before mentioned, travelled attended by our own servants, and were therefore quite independent of such hospitality; we then took advantage only of what was always liberally offered by our brother officers, or by Civilians holding Government appointments in the provinces; but, to use a Latin quotation,—"tempora mutantur, et nos mutamur in illis."

By strictly following the advice of my friend Dr. S—, I was before long enabled to attend to business, and even to hold my courts; but, a few weeks after, the horrid ague returned, and with such redoubled violence, that, in spite of all that could be done, he now found it impossible to check its progress; and therefore declared that, to save my life, I must be off immediately for Colombo.

The reader may well suppose that, in quitting the interior, and as I now concluded, for ever, I must have felt not a little cast down. There I lay in my palanquin, a weak helpless creature; unable to walk or ride. My noble steed, led by his old keeper, followed the palanquin; as I wished, should I feel myself better, to mount him occasionally. But, the kind of procession, which I need not particularly describe, in many respects reminded me, from this and other circumstances, of the funeral of an officer of rank; only my boots were not dangling upon the sides of the saddle, nor were my sword and sash laid on the top of the palanquin. Bran, my poor Bran! walked by its side; every now and then peeping in, as I fancied, to look kindly in his beloved master's face. As for his friend Goody, she had been left behind; but, I knew that she would be taken good care of, and handed over, with the house, to whoever might be appointed my successor. Pug, with Judy, his new companion of the same genus, formed part of the cortège, being intended for Mrs. S——. Mrs. D——'s young tiger was likewise in it, and required six coolies to carry him and his cage; but, they all three were ultimately sent to my friend, Captain Hilton, at Mount Lavinia. The doctor, who seemed to think worse of my case than I did myself, was strangely enough, as it struck me at the time, in his proper place in the lugubrious train, that is to say, marching at its head; yet, he came occasionally to the side of the palanquin to ascertain, I supposed, whether I could outlive the journey.

I had taken leave, the night before, but with deep regret, of our excellent and encouraging minister, Mr. Newstead; not, however, as one without hope; for, I still had that firm reliance upon Him, who had never deserted me, that He would order what was best for me; and would likewise protect my friend, in that sphere of great usefulness, in which He had placed him; and in this I was not disappointed.

Upon my reaching Colombo, it was at once decided by Dr. Farrell and my other medical friends, that I must go to England. I had, they said, in the first instance, been too much bled, (though, probably, necessary at the time,) to admit of my remaining afterwards in Ceylon. Whilst I was waiting the arrival at Colombo of a homeward-bound ship, Bran attached himself almost exclusively to Mrs. D—, of whom he had become exceedingly fond when at Kurunagalla; and if he left me on my couch, it was to follow her wherever she went; no matter where it was, he would not be repulsed; indeed, his looks were too terrific for any of the natives to dare to obstruct his passage. In this manner, unknown to her, he followed her to a large evening party, and when she sat down in the midst of the company, Bran placed himself by her, on the Chinese mat, with his eyes watchfully fixed upon her. But, wishing to get rid of him, and to have him taken home, as every one looked alarmed when they approached her and her huge self-constituted protector, she told her servant to try to get him out of the room; but a grin, and slight display of his awe-inspiring teeth, so terrified him, that he would not even venture near him. My Portuguese servant was therefore sent for; and as he knew him, he was induced, but reluctantly, to follow him home.

Next morning, my faithful dog was unaccountably absent. At last he returned; but, to my great distress, a servant ran hastily into the room, exclaiming that Bran was dying! He had been stabbed, seemingly with a bayonet, through the loins, was bleeding profusely, and evidently had not many minutes to live. A surgeon was sent for, who, good-naturedly, came immediately; but he could do nothing for him; and Mrs. D—, on hearing what had happened, had also reached the spot where he lay; and it may well be supposed, was exceedingly distressed about him:—he died licking her hand; and, as if looking for his master, who was unable to be present. We never found out how the accident had occurred:—but, the melancholy fate of my poor companion for so many years, and in so many trying situations, greatly afflicted me; as I fully intended to have taken him with me to England. But, had I been even able to do so, he could not, in the common course of nature, be now alive; yet, I still think of him, in some measure, with that kind of pleasure and regret, with which an old soldier remembers the brave and tried companions of his youth; or rather with those feelings with which the Indian is said to look forward in the hope of finding his faithful dog before him in paradise.

A free-trader having anchored at Colombo, to receive on board a quantity of cinnamon belonging to Government, I took my passage in her for England; and, as I was desired, sent my Portuguese servant and luggage on board, I being to follow the next morning. But in the night a storm arose, that threatened to drive the ship on shore, upon which there ran an awful and overwhelming surf. Embark I must, or lose my passage, my luggage, and my money; for an unfortunate officer, whose health is impaired by the climate of Ceylon, and who cannot possibly remain in it any longer, must go home (and take his family also, if he happens to have one,) at his own expense. Therefore, in the Governor's barge, which was kindly and considerately ordered for me, and followed, (so as to be ready to pick me up in case of an upset, and before a shark could lay hold of me), by one of the small Ceylon boats, or rather canoes, that have out-riggers so constructed and attached to them, as effectually to prevent their being overturned, we proceeded towards the ship, which was pitching and rolling awfully; for, it blew furiously, and there roared and foamed in the roads such a sea, as completely astonished me!—A number of friends, who had just taken leave of me, as well as a crowd of spectators, stood on the ramparts to witness the result of the fearful attempt. A little of my wonted energy, however, returning, from being required to exert it, I steered or directed the steerage of the barge, as I did not altogether like the looks of the half-caste crew or their helmsman; and with much difficulty, and great risk, I at last contrived to get up the side of the ship, which instantly, as she only waited for me, stood out to sea, under a single storm-sail.

Once on the deck of the reeling ship,—for the last time, I cast my eyes towards the verdant shores of Ceylon, which I concluded I should never see again.

CHAPTER XIII.

FUNDAMENTAL ERROR IN OUR COLONIAL SYSTEM—ERRONEOUS IDEAS AS TO THE RIGHTS AND DUTIES OF COLONIES—CONDUCT OF THE UNITED STATES—STRICTURES ON COLONIAL LAND SPECULATORS—DELUSION PRACTISED BY THEM ON EMIGRANTS—ENORMOUS EXPENSE TO BE INCURRED BY EMIGRANTS—CHEAP LABOUR INDISPENSABLE—DISAPPOINTMENTS EXPERIENCED BY EMIGRANTS—PROPER SYSTEM OF EMIGRATION—OVER-MANUFACTURING A MAIN CAUSE OF PAUPERISM—RETIRED HALF-PAY OFFICERS, ETC. NOT CALCULATED FOR EMIGRANTS—AUSTRALIA ENRICHED BY CONVICT LABOUR—DISADVANTAGEOUS CHANGE MADE IN THAT COUNTRY—ADVANTAGES WHICH CEYLON OFFERS TO EMIGRANTS—NATURE OF THE CEYLONESE TERRITORY—POLICY OF INVITING LABOURERS TO EMIGRATE FROM AFRICA TO CEYLON—ABOLITION OF SLAVERY IN CEYLON—WIDE FIELD OPENED, IN CEYLON, FOR THE PRODUCTION OF VARIOUS ARTICLES—NATURALIZATION OF FOREIGN PLANTS IN INDIA AND ENGLAND—SLOW PROGRESS OF CHRISTIANITY IN CEYLON—REMARKS ON THE FRANCHISES ACCORDED TO THE SINGALESE—IMPROVIDENT GRANTS OF LAND TO SPECULATORS—NEW PLAN OF GRANTING LANDS SUGGESTED—LETTER OF DR. CHALMERS—HEAVY BURTHENS BORNE, ESPECIALLY BY LANDED PROPRIETORS—ANTI-CORN LAW LEAGUE CENSURED—CONCLUSION.

When we examine attentively a map of the world, and perceive the many highly important and widely scattered parts of it which belong to Great Britain, our astonishment is naturally excited, and we must be ready to admit, that great indeed is the responsibility which attaches to us, as a Christian and hitherto highly favoured nation! But, that there has long been something fundamentally wrong in our Colonial system, no one who has paid due attention to its workings can deny, and this has always prevented our deriving from our vast possessions that benefit which we might otherwise have had a right to expect. India and her great resources are not, however, here referred to; as the whole of the charges, civil and military, ordinary and extraordinary, including all the expenses incurred on account of the Queen's troops employed in it, are defrayed out of the territorial revenue of that country. The latter item is estimated at nearly £1,400,000 per annum; and, under a recent construction of the law, the Company have agreed to pay for raising and maintaining such farther number of men as may be necessary, in order to keep at all times an effective force of 20,000 men in India; but, under present circumstances, this number of British troops is by no means sufficient. Yet, independent of this and of other considerable outlays, on an average, no less than £3,200,000 derived from India, is expended in this country.

This would appear to be the result of the line of policy pursued by the East India Company, in that immense and populous part of Her Majesty's dominions. But, according to the strange and, it may be inferred, unwise system, which seems to have been rigidly adhered to, for many years past, almost the whole of the expenses of establishing and promoting the welfare and ultimate prosperity of what may be properly denominated our colonies has fallen, it may be said, upon the mother country, and the very idea of their being expected, even in a limited and moderate degree, to contribute towards the expenses of their own colonial Government, naval and military protection, or for almost any other purposes, is now-a-days, looked upon to amount to a kind of tyranny and oppression. The doctrine now upheld by liberals seems to be, that whenever a Colony has reached a certain pitch of greatness and importance, under the protection, and at the expense, of its fostering parent, its independence of her is then readily to be sanctioned and confirmed; and the only return or recompense to be expected, for the mother country's expenditure and care, is, future commercial advantages and preferences, or rather promises of them.

This untoward system, as well as these modern political maxims, have had, we may suppose, their origin in our strange views of colonial management, and in the results of the flagrant ingratitude on the part of the now by so many admired United States of North America towards Great Britain; which had, by every possible means, cherished and protected her trans-atlantic children until they had become sufficiently powerful to despise her authority, and to set her at defiance; and that, too, at a time when she was encompassed with difficulties and dangers. The result of the contest which necessarily ensued is too well known to be here noticed; but, since the period of the acknowledgment of their independence, who can point to a single instance of that gratitude which a child owes to its parent being evinced on the part of the United States? Have not their republican citizens been ever since, and upon all favourable occasions, our most envious, and bitter, though unprovoked enemies; and where are to be found the proofs of preference being given by them to our commerce, as a highly favoured nation? —On the contrary, we only find, as we might have expected, self-interest and jealousy governing all their dealings with us; and the period seems to have arrived, when many of our commercial fellow-subjects may have cause to lament being too closely connected with them; and we may have yet reason to regret that so many of our valuable agricultural population, owing to a want of proper encouragement having been held out to them in our own Colonies, have been induced to join them.

We shall, no doubt, be told that we have nothing but gratitude and brotherly love to look for from the people of the Canadas, from the hour that their independence is acknowledged; but those who can credit or place reliance upon this must know very little of human nature. Yet, do not all our Colonies form, as it were, integral parts of the British Empire?—Why, therefore, when they have become sufficiently wealthy, populous, and important, should not the *British Subjects* who inhabit them, have the option of being, as soon as they wish it, duly represented in our high legislative and other assemblies, and why should they not then be made to contribute, in a moderate and reasonable degree, toward the expenses incurred in the maintenance of their several etablishments, as well as for their government and protection? And, with this in view, surely no dismembering of the Empire, it may justly be imagined, ought upon any pretence, or under any circumstances, to be tolerated; if by force of arms, or otherwise, it can be prevented. Great Britain is, undoubtedly, sufficiently powerful, and her vast resources, if called forth, are more than adequate, to justify her in having it, at least, clearly understood, not only by her own Colonists, (and this would give the well-disposed confidence, whilst it would over-awe the turbulent), but also by the nations of the world, that, under Providence, there shall never again be a dismemberment of her Majesty's dominions in any part of it; and that, whilst her people are governed with strict justice and impartiality, their equal rights and privileges shall be as fully maintained.

It ought now, however, to be mentioned that, in the preceding pages, statements have unavoidably been made, and certain doings brought to notice, which may prove adverse to the views and interests of those who have embarked capital to a large amount in speculations in land in our new colonies; —men whose object it must naturally be to promote, by every means, emigration to them. It has consequently been desirable that, if possible, the work should be freed from this unpleasant and painful dilemma, which is likely not only to be inconvenient, but also embarrassing, to its author; for, if he is not sufficiently explicit, he can have no hope of effecting his object, or of being useful to those infatuated persons, who are daily becoming the victims of their own folly or imprudence, in allowing themselves to be led into speculative undertakings, by the fallacious representations of those who endeavour to have it believed that they are the *great friends* of the people, who talk and write of cheap land, and the fortunes to be easily and rapidly made in the parts of the world where the territory they have acquired is situated. It may, therefore, be necessary to enlarge a little more upon this important subject.

No one can deny, but that an emigrant, possessing capital, may purchase at a cheap rate, either from Government or from speculators, a considerable extent of good land. Let us, however, suppose that he has done so, and taken possession of it: he may then fairly ask what advantage has he gained, or how has he benefited himself by doing so?—the answer, we may suppose will be, that he has acquired and can call *his own*, a large and fine estate, for comparatively a trifling sum of money; but he, no doubt, immediately after discovers that it will take a much larger to enclose, clear, and cultivate it, or even a small part of it. In order, however, to make the best of the emigrant's situation, let us again suppose that he has two or three sons, equally as fit as himself to till the ground; but, still it cannot, we may believe, be expected that they will attempt to cultivate more of the land than their united exertions can bring into a state fit for the plough ; for, no man of common-sense will think of employing hired workmen or labourers to carry out or extend their farming and other operations, or to add to their comforts in such new countries, where they must be paid at the ruinous rates demanded; —for instance, in New Zealand, which we shall take as an example, it being at this moment the part of the world to which emigrants are most desirous of proceeding, and where every hope of success is held out to them. The emigrant and his sons, it is presumed, will soon see, that they must inevitably make up their minds to do everything for themselves and family, however numerous, which can be required of common labourers and mechanics; for, what an immense amount of capital they must have brought out with them, or how great at once must the profits of farming be, to enable them to pay a labourer at the rate of 8*s.* a-day ; a carpenter from 16*s.* to 20*s.*; brick-makers 10*s.*; men-servants £4. per month, and other tradesmen in the same proportion.* But it need not surprise any one that such wages must be required and given in New Zealand, when we find that there, for an unfurnished wooden house, of two small rooms and a kitchen, from £60. to £80. per annum is demanded. For one small unfurnished room 20*s.* per week ; while for board and lodging, without malt or spirituous liquors, and

* See New Zealand, by Charles Terry, Esq. F.R S.; Boone, New Bond Street.

the bed in the room with others, 40*s.* per week must be paid. The prices of articles of food are there also quite as exorbitant as wages. Beef, per pound, 1*s.* 4*d.*; mutton 1*s.*; pork 7*d.*; flour 5*d.*; bread 7*d.*; cheese (English) 2*s.*; butter (Irish) 2*s.* 6*d.*; potatoes, per cwt, 8*d.* &c. &c.

But it may now be asked, have not the tradespeople and labourers been quite as much misled or deceived, in the hopes of advantages held out to them, as the settlers with some capital; for it can only, occasionally, be in their power to procure that employment, without which they must starve; as, the richer class of settlers, who may at first want their help, cannot long continue to pay them at the rates of wages above-mentioned. The result, therefore, too often must be there, as it has been in some of our other colonies, that those who are under the necessity of employing them, must soon be themselves obliged to labour, in order to gain a livelihood, for equally provident and fully as credulous new-comers; so that, in the end, the greater proportion of emigrants are, it may be said, mixed together in an impoverished and confused mass, in which the former grades, which they may have held in society in the United Kingdom, are no longer discernible, but in the greater misery and destitution of those who had before been the best off in the world.

This may be represented and thought, by some, to be an over-drawn picture—and it is sincerely to be wished that it were so—of the fate of many of those unfortunates, who, led away by the enticing prospects of independence, if not of wealth, held out to them, by the ready tools of interested men, were induced, without making due inquiries, or calculating as to what the probable expense of labour in a new colony would be, to expatriate themselves. It seems, also, of late years, to have been altogether forgotten or overlooked that, of old, almost all the settlements of Europeans, in various parts of the world were, in the first instance, formed by slave —that is, cheap labour; and the United States of America, New South Wales, and Van Diemen's Land, are not exceptions; for, what are convicts but slaves, who must labour for the public, or for the individuals to whom they are assigned, and who provide them with food, raiment, and shelter only; and, by the sweat of whose brows, so many fine estates or plantations have been brought into profitable cultivation; but a question is now forcing itself upon public attention, and it is one of vast importance,—can they be kept so by what is termed free labour?

Many emigrants, some possessing small means and others without any, are induced, by the like illusory hopes and fallacious promises to proceed to the United States of America, where they are made to believe that they must soon become rich, substantial citizens, and absurdly enough, important political personages. Part of the trifling means of the former is swallowed up in payment for their own and families' passage out; more of it disappears at the first port where they land; and where, to their dismay, they find that they must take a long and expensive journey into the interior, before they can procure an acre of that cheap land, which they had crossed the Atlantic in search of. Long before they arrive at this Eden, still pointed out, *as only a little way further inland*, their money is entirely gone; and their dreary progess being thus terminated, they have no alternative, but to make up their minds to *slave* for those who have been on the look-out for them, and who soon bring them, by small advances of money, supplies of clothing, shoes, and food, under the necessity, *as debtors*, of submitting to their hard terms. Thus these poor dupes, as well as those who came out destitute of means, continue to toil for their task-masters, until they can scrape together a sufficiency of money (which is there hard to be got, as work of all kinds is chiefly paid for by food and clothing, often charged at exorbitant prices), when those who are able, gladly set off for their native land, or for the Canadas; (as about 6000 of them, chiefly Irish labourers, did last year,) where they are told, that they will be better paid, and infinitely better treated, than in the so much admired and lauded United States, where they too soon had enough of that liberty and equality, of which they had heard so much, and saw so little. But nearly enough has, perhaps, been said of the doings of these, would be, Aristocratic Republicans, as well as of their infatuated dupes; let us, therefore, close this part of the subject, with the following, it may be supposed, almost unnecessary illustration, at least, as far as the United States are concerned.

Extract from a letter received from a gentleman who lately emigrated to New York to a friend in Edinburgh :—" I arrived here from Greenock after a tedious and rather dangerous passage of nearly seven weeks, in the latter end of June last. This place is in a miserably depressed state, as much so as any town in the United Kingdom ; and many emigrants have returned to Europe after staying only a few days. Hundreds of them are returning to this place from the interior also, where they had gone in search of employment, without being able to find it, with the view of returning home. One gentleman (to whom he specially alludes) came here, went 1,500 miles west with his family, where he bought a farm, and after expending nearly £400. in transport from the old country, and up the country here, and on his purchase, is returning to England again to remain,—I have no doubt a more contented individual with things as they are at home than he ever was. The fact is, this is not the sort of place that it has been represented. Thousands come out here buoyed up with most extravagant ideas, in consequence of articles in (here he mentions a well-known periodical, &c. ;) but when they arrive they are disappointed in the extreme. Instead of finding all their hardships are ended by getting to the United States, they find themselves worse than they were at home, surrounded by a population that, I believe, would cheat their own father. Knavery in every shape and form abounds here, and no person, without witnessing it, can have the slightest conception of the coolness and want of shame displayed in perpetrating the grossest acts of fraud. Their laws would seem to have been framed to allow one man to cheat another. Bankruptcy is the order of the day here at present; indeed solvency is the exception, not the rule in New York."

After this exposure (and much more had it been necessary could have been brought forward,) it may now be asked,—ought emigration to be altogether discouraged; and, if so, how can our over-abundant and unemployed, starving population be god rid of?—This, it must be allowed, is a very difficult question to answer; but one thing is certain, that, unless emigration becomes a great national object, and is, as such, taken up by Government, it can neither be desirable nor successful, unless it is in the instances given in the preceding pages; as very few persons who emigrate can possibly afford, for any length of time, to pay in these new countries, the wages or hire necessary to enable labourers and mechanics from the United Kingdom to live; emigration ought therefore, under present circumstances, only to be thought of or attempted by families accustomed to agricultural labour and occupations, and who may possess some capital to begin with; but these are not the description of persons to be got rid of: on the contrary, if we are hereafter to hope for tranquillity at home, such families should, if possible, be retained and employed, so as to render us in future independent of supplies of grain from other countries; but this can only be done by their being able to obtain land (and landlords ought wisely to consider this,) at a moderate rent; and, by agriculture, upon improved principles, being extended and encouraged as it ought to be; for, it surely must be admitted that, there is no real or permanent national wealth, but what arises from a well and judiciously cultivated soil. But, what the country wants to be relieved from by a *Government plan of emigration*, is the maintenance of the multitudes created—it may be said—by the abundance of food produced, for many years past, by over-manufacturing, and who are now, owing to the vast quantities of articles of merchandise of all kinds fabricated by them and by means of machinery, and by which every market still open to us is completely glutted, said to be starving. These constitute the part of our population which it is desirable that the country should, if possible, throw off, as if it were an incubus, which is ready to overwhelm her; and for which purpose the immense sums of money, required to feed and house paupers, might be more wisely expended in enabling them, or a large proportion of them, to emigrate, in a desirable manner, to our Colonies. Yet, it must be allowed, that it is hard upon possessors of land, who are by far the manufacturers' best customers, to be obliged to furnish money for this purpose; as those who ought to do so are the wealthy manufacturers, who, in a work published a few years ago, were asked—" in what " manner the multitudes they had congregated, like " our chiefs of old, around their baronial castles, " (alluding to their factories,) are to be fed in case " of even a temporary stagnation of the trade?" " But, (the author adds) it is beneath them to " think of such matters, and they wisely leave " subjects of this kind to be discussed hereafter by " improvident landlords, who, in consideration of " temporary advantages, have granted leases of " parts of their estates to these *squires*, to enable " them to create cities, towns and villages, the " enormous population of which, if it is to be kept " in tranquillity, must constantly require the pre- " sence of such troops as I have in view."

The following just and judicious remarks made in "The English Chronicle," under the head of " Money Market and City Intelligence," ought, in the minds of all reasonable persons, to settle the question, as to which of the parties—the manufacturers or landholders—should be attributed the present sufferings of the artisan, as well as the labouring classes; for the latter are now, unfortunately, beginning to feel the effects of the diminished value of agricultural produce, and which, notwithstanding the aid farmers may expect hereafter to derive from cheap and portable chymical manures, must, it is to be feared, increase.

" The papers by the Overland Mail, in noticing the state of markets in China, remark on the arrival out at Macao of the John O'Gaunt and Foam with heavy cargoes of manufactured goods, by which the markets, before heavy with stocks on hand, became quite overloaded. It may be feared that the rash spirit of over-adventure, of which the despatch of one of these vessels at least is an example in point, will be followed by worse consequences still when all the ventures now on their way, or despatched since the news of the termination of the war was received, shall reach their destination in the new ports to be opened to trade. The Foam was laid on for China in June last, immediately on receipt of Sir Henry Pottinger's proclamation declaring Hong Kong and Tinghae free ports, and in fourteen days she was already loaded and cleared out, chiefly doubtless with Manchester goods, consigned perhaps in the usual improvident style against advances by consignees either in cash or bills to a certain amount of invoice. If the latter, the accommodation would probably be to full invoice amount, on the understood condition of bill renewals until returns should come to hand from sales realised in China.

"It may be, or not, that such was the character of the adventures by the two vessels named, but, in any case, it is well known that such is the reckless system by which over-production in Lancashire is kept up and disposed of. If the mischiefs infallibly resulting were confined to those immediately concerned, little sympathy would be excited or deserved. But the mischief spreads far wider, and involves the innocent more than the guilty, the honest and careful manufacturers and the working classes still more than the daring and dishonest speculating master manufacturers, who have perhaps little to lose, perhaps even irretrievably insolvent at the very moment when rushing into the most gigantic operations. As at once commentary upon and evidence of the truth, so far only as the working classes, take only the facts asserted in a recent speech of Mr. Henry Ashworth of Bolton, chairman of the day at one of thc revels last week of the Anti-Corn Law people at Manchester. The facts may be true or false, but coming from one of the mouthpieces of thc League, they can hardly be challenged by that body as wanting in authority. The over-production naturally ending in ruinous reductions of prices, the result is visited upon the operatives in the shape of a grinding depreciation of wages, for before the master manufacturers will themselves submit to a curtailment of profits, it is clcar that recourse will bc had to every expedient, and the expedient most easy and most immediately at hand is to fall upon and cut down wages. 'In Preston,' says Mr. Ashworth, 'within the last three ycars the whole amount paid in wages has been reduced 46 per cent., and labourers are willing to work at 1*s.* per day.' Now the League have been liberal in their gibes and exultations over the depressed and degraded condition of agricultural labourers, but surely the 6*s.* per week for a manufacturing operative in 'proud' Preston is not more princely pay than the 7*s.* of the rural workman, who has his cottage and bit of garden to boot perhaps.

'In Saddleworth and the Potteries,' proceeds Mr. Ashworth, 'the reduction (of wages) during the same period was 33 per cent. In Padiham (a place or parish in the north of Lancashire) stonemasons and labourers are working *for meat*, instead of wages.' It is to be observed here, though Mr. Ashworth was cunning enough to suppress the fact, that the people in and about Padiham are chiefly hand-loom calico weavers, whose labour has been invaded and themselves reduced to the most abject pauperism by the cheaper competition of power-loom weaving. 'In Norwich,' says Mr. Ashworth again, 'weavers' wages have been reduced from 12*d.* to 8*d.* (per day of course) since 1839. In Chorley hand-loom weavers have been reduced from 5*s.* 5*d.* to 4*s.* (per week) since 1839.' At 4*s.*, however, the poor Chorley weavers are still magnificently well off compared with their less fortunate brethren at Padiham, who cannot earn the one-half. Now all this deplorable suffering, this oppression, and forced depreciation of the wages of labour is the absolute consequences of manufacturing rapacity, of production enormously stretched for successive years beyond the probable or possible capacity of markets and consumption, and of the insensate rage for amassing hoards and growing suddenly rich by strokes of speculation, instead of rising gradually and contentedly, as manufacturers of the olden time were wont to rise, by the more moral but slower progress of untiring, indefatigable, and personal industry.

"There is not, we tell Mr. Ashworth, a market

on the face of the globe, from whence for successive years the complaints have not been incessant respecting the constant glut, the overpowering imports of British cottons, and the reckless improvidence of Manchester manufacturers. We have ourselves the reports, reports which are derived from foreign official sources, from many score of foreign markets for years past, are still periodically in receipt of them, and not unfrequently giving and observing upon them under this head, and the facts we have stated invariably constitute the more prominent portion of the information. Let Mr. Ashworth mention, if he can, the foreign market where such has not been the case, and we will undertake to meet him on the matter in dispute with such authentic facts and figures as, if he be accessible to conviction, must satisfy his mind that corn-laws have as little to do with manufacturing distress as his cotton-mill, when lighted up, has with Eddystone light-house. The giant evil of low wages and short profits is, and has been, over-production."

It might be supposed (and it is not likely that the present Government are indifferent to such matters) that so fair and unquestionable a statement as this should be made known, by every possible means, throughout the United Kingdom; and then it ought to be left to the acknowledged good sense of the people, whether they will any longer submit to be the dupes of the heartless, most mischievous, and interested Anti-Corn-law League. It is not, however, in Manchester or Lancashire alone, that distress to the extent shewn prevails, for we find that the increase of pauperism and distress in Leeds during the last four years has been truly afflictive. The following is a return of the *relief* given in money and bread to the poor of the township of Leeds, including both the in-door and the out-door paupers, and also of the number of applicants for relief at the workhouse, for the last four years :—

Years.	Relief given in Money and Bread to in-door and out-door paupers.	Number of Applications for relief.
1839	£14,105 1 10	——
1840	14,934 15 5	3,481
1841	17,275 14 8½	7,316
1842	23,358 14 5	14,839

Thus the increase in the amount of relief granted to the poor from 1839 to 1842 is no less than 65 *per cent.*; and the increase in the number of applications for relief from 1840 to 1842 is 326 *per cent.!* We also find, that in the United States of America, the effects of their Tariff has already been to bring down wages 20 *per cent.*; and in order to have it passed in Congress, every thing was promised to the artisans, who are now complaining of having been deceived, and that their wages have been lowered all over the country, whilst they derive no advantage from either the Tariff, or the cheapness and abundance of provisions,—and it may well be asked,—is not this the case also throughout Great Britain?

There is another class of persons besides those already mentioned, who are also cruelly misled by, it is to be believed, the well meant, but erroneous representations of others.—We read in a work just published, that, "exclusive of those accustomed to farming, there are many individuals with certain, yet limited, annual incomes, such as retired half-pay officers, but not possessing tangible capital to any great amount. To such class of persons, with families, New Zealand is particularly adapted; and a few acres around a dwelling, devoted to pasture for the dairy, and rearing of poultry, &c. would abundantly supply all the necessaries of life. A farm of twenty acres, supposing the whole was not cultivated until the sixth year from the date of grant, would only pay altogether £7. 10*s.* of uncultivated tax, or purchase-money,—and the cultivated tax would be only 10*s.* per annum. Such a system of taxation, or rather, payment for land, would be very productive to the revenue,—both for the purposes of emigration of labourers at the expense of Government, if required, and likewise to make good any deficiency of fixed or ordinary revenue to the expenditure."

Now, of all men in the world, half-pay officers, and reduced gentlemen, are the least fitted for emigration; especially to a country where, for the hire of servants, labourers, and trades-people, such enormous sums must, as has been shewn, be paid. Let these gentlemen, if they be wise, stay at home, or else go to Ceylon, as has been already pointed out; but, if they must till the ground, let them, if possible, acquire as much as they want for the purpose, in the United Kingdom; and after providing themselves with neat and comfortable cottages, only try to cultivate it, in strict conformity to a system laid down by a worthy and much to be admired Irish clergyman, who calls himself "Martin Doyle;" and, they may depend upon it, that they will find themselves much better off, than in any of the hitherto so strongly recommended new Colonies; but, above all, let them settle in Ireland, where labour is cheap, and the purchase or rent of twenty acres of land, though not quite so low as in New Zealand, New Holland, or America, is still reasonable. But the truth is,—if people of very small incomes would only condescend, or rather were able to act, *as they must do if they emigrate* to our new settlements—that is to say,—put their hand to the spade or plough, they would be far better off at home than abroad; and they would thus escape the misery too many have brought upon themselves and families, by emigrating to countries of which they knew nothing.

We also hear much of fortunes being easily made by sheep and stock-holders in New South Wales, and in Van Diemen's land. And some persons undoubtedly did so, at first, with the assistance of convicts to look after their stock, which were usually pastured within a certain distance of Sydney; but those who have, of late years, attempted to follow their example, have in very few instances been successful. Being afraid of the aborigines, as well as of the run-away convicts, they did not like to venture into the interior; and therefore hired or employed care-takers to look after their flocks, who, of course, did just as they pleased; and in most instances, swallowed up the greater part of the profits. But, in order to shew the advantages long possessed by New South Wales and by Van Diemen's Land, as Colonies of Great Britain, over all others in point of cheap labour, the Returns are given;* and however objectionable it may—surely erroneously—be considered by some persons to employ convicts as tradesmen, servants, or labourers, it may be presumed, that neither of these countries could possibly have attained their present state of prosperity without them.

Until the year 1822, political economy was seemingly scarcely known by name in New South Wales, far less practically applied; and that with an extent of territory, and a proportion of applicable labour, compared with the consumers of the produce of that labour, far beyond what was to be found in any other part of the world. The strange anomaly presented itself there, that the Government had, up to that period, supported the people, in place of the people the Government; so that the latter were consequently compelled annually to import immense quantities of wheat — viz. from twenty to sixty thousand bushels.

To remedy so flagrant an evil, became an object of the first importance with the then new Governor, who, being aware of the vast disposable means at his command, it was not long before he devised the

* See Appendix, M.

measure of clearing portions of the country for settlers, on their paying into the Government stores five bushels of wheat for each acre so cleared; and notice was given accordingly in the public papers. The result was, that there were soon numerous applications from settlers to have their land cleared. The convicts were divided into gangs of twenty each, under an overseer, who received *3s. 6d.* for each acre cleared by his gang. A thousand convicts were so employed, and it was expected that they would be able to clear at least 7000 acres of land in one year, and of course pay 35,000 bushels of wheat into store. This being but an experiment only 1000 men were employed; and, twelve bushels of wheat being considered the annual consumption of a man, the convicts thus worked for their own livelihood, and the settler was in nowise compromised in the success or failure of his gang. It may, therefore, be easily inferred, that great permanent good was done to the country; that the moral condition of the convicts was improved by their being scattered over it, in place of being, as hitherto, congregated in towns. This seems to have been an excellent plan, and the result was a vast saving of expense to Great Britain; for, not many years before, the then Governor had to draw bills upon the Treasury for £38,000; and, as the number of convicts increased, so did the expenditure, so that in 1821, it amounted to no less than £240,000, independent of £40,000 of colonial revenue. It was no doubt found to be a further improvement, to allow the convicts to go into private service, in place of keeping them in gangs under an overseer; for, we find by the return just given that 19,247 were allowed to do so; and there were besides 3650 who held tickets of leave. This system has recently been changed;—whether wisely or not the following remarks may, perhaps, be allowed to demonstrate. They were published in a Sydney paper, in October, 1841.

"But the faction triumphed, the conciliated faction triumphed with His Excellency's assistance; the Petition of the PEOPLE, unsupported as it was by his brilliant advocacy, failed,—it was thrown aside as a matter of course, and, we are—ruined. Ministers were suffered to believe that when we had no more convicts sent here, free persons would replace them, whereas they should have learned from His Excellency, that it was the advantage we derived from convict labour that alone furnished us with the means of carrying out free men. They should have been told that, when the colonists are pennyless, it will be vain to send out cargoes of pauper operatives, even if means of transport for them were forthcoming. The convicts whose labour we are deprived of, without an effort to prevent it being made by our Governor, (for if there had been, doubtless we should have heard of it from so plain-dealing a man,) were of more worth to us than all the profit of the colonial staple. Did Sir George Gipps tell the ministers this? did he remind them that the cost alone, which themselves allow to be something not much under an annual million, out of the British treasury, on account of these convicts of whom we are deprived, would not be compensated by any advantage to the Mother Country, while it ruined *us?* Did he explain to them, as he was bound to do by his duty to England that was his mistress, and to us whom he should have looked upon as placed under his protection, that this heavy drain was not compensated by a single advantage, that it was depriving *her* of a great and *increasing* market for her manufactures; and though her market might not be closed against *our* wool, we should soon have no wool to send to it; for we cannot continue to keep up our fine flocks if we have not shepherds—we cannot have shepherds without money to pay them,—and we cannot have money when we are deprived of some hundreds of thousands every year, which we gained by convict labour? This is what he should have told them,—this, if it had been explained to the ministers, might have produced such grand and liberal measures of economy as would have proved useful to Great Britain, while they prevented our *ruin.*"

The above causes may have had certain effects; but, we cannot suppose that they have occasioned even half the mischief set forth in the following alarming statement.

"A list of insolvents in Sydney and its neighbourhood, from February 1 to August 4, 1842, a period of six months and four days, has been received. The sheet which they cover is larger than a side of the *Morning Herald*, and on it particulars of each insolvency are arranged under the heads of 'names and calling,' 'residence,' 'trustee's name,' 'date,' 'liabilities,' 'assets,' 'deficiencies,' 'dividends,' &c.

It will scarcely be credited that during this period, 392 persons or firms have been publicly declared insolvent since the new act which came into operation in the colony. The liabilities of some of the estates are very great, surprisingly so for any place save the metropolis of the British empire.

"The following are the amounts for which some of the failures have taken place:—13,696*l.* 16,000*l.* 50,058*l.* 37,750*l.* 20,113*l.* 33,000*l.* 14,000*l.* 34,110*l.* 28,669*l.* 10,086*l.* 175,235*l.* 11,721*l.* 7,143*l.* 5,126*l.* 6,335*l.* 15,819*l.* 34,843*l.* 5,608*l.* 112,697*l.* 30,997*l.* 5,759*l.*

"The total of the liabilities of the 392 insolvents is, in round numbers, one million and a quarter of pounds sterling; many of them, however, shew good assets. We may add that the list is an official one, and signed by H. L. Brabazon, office, King-street, Sydney."

It must now be evident, from what has been said as well as pointed out, that the great and ruinous want that has been experienced of late years, in every part of the world (except in New Holland and Van Diemen's Land) wherein colonization has been attempted, was *moderately priced labour*. Emigrants, especially at first, must dispense with all the elegancies of life, many of the comforts, and most of the articles which tradesmen can supply; or, at least, be content with possessing as few of them as possible; but they cannot accomplish any important object in agriculture, unless they are assisted by *man*, and that at a cheap and reasonable rate;

otherwise, all their exertions and knowledge of cultivation, must inevitably be as fruitless as hopeless.

Putting our vast East Indian possessions out of the question, where large capitalists only can hope to prosper, of all our colonies, Ceylon is the only one, in which free labour can, at present, be calculated upon at a low rate. Food, as well as the few trifling articles required by the labouring portion of the population of that charming island, are very cheap. The native tradesmen work cheaply and well in wood of all kinds; and, equally so in iron and other metals; and they make almost every description of dress or clothing at very moderate charges. Servants' wages are low; and they, at the same time, find themselves with food and clothing; in short, it has been the object of this work, to afford an emigrant, wishing to proceed to that part of the world, such information as will enable him to understand what he is about to undertake, as well as what difficulties he has to contend with; and, he will also be enabled to estimate properly the advantage of settling in Ceylon in preference to any of our other colonies. In Ceylon, land can be purchased either from Government, (at five shillings per acre,) or from the natives at as moderate a price as in any of our new settlements; but, with respect to the parts of it to which emigrants ought to proceed, according to the objects they may have in view, be they agricultural or commercial, it is hoped that this work, while it may interest and amuse readers in general, will at the same time, in some measure, serve as a guide to them, to the most desirable parts of it.

Ceylon, as the reader has been shewn in the preceding pages, is one of the most beautiful islands in the world; rich in vegetation, and valuable on account of its natural productions. Its climate is so mild and agreeable, that, even in ancient times, when it was known by the name of Taprobane, both Diodorus Siculus and Pliny spoke of it in the highest terms; the former remarks, that though under the equinoctial line, it is so temperate, that the inhabitants are but little annoyed by either heat or cold; and that their fruits ripened during the whole year; and the latter observes, that their festivals are devoted to the chase; that they delight most in that of the tiger and elephant. Their fields are in a high state of cultivation. They have no grapes, but abundance of apples; and, it is not uncommon, for them to attain the age of one hundred years.

Major Forbes tells us, in his "Eleven Years in Ceylon," that, according to native chronicles, the ancestors of a people whom Britons long regarded as savages, and for some time treated as slaves, existed as a numerous, and comparatively civilized nation at a period antecedent to the discovery of Great Britain and its semi-barbarous inhabitants. That the ancient and continued annals of the Singalese race have been preserved for upwards of twenty-three centuries, and describe the erection or formation of all those extensive cities, temples, and tanks

—whose ruins (some of which are spoken of in the preceding chapters of this work) and numerous inscriptions, remain to verify the historical records. For a great proportion of that period, the natives of Ceylon, probably, owing, it may be supposed, to their being divided into castes, remained stationary, or rather retrograded in arts and intelligence.

According to Cosmas, an Egyptian merchant, Ceylon had become in the sixth century, or in the time of Justinian, the chief seat of the commerce of the Indian Ocean. Vessels entered its ports from the most remote parts of the East; and the merchants of Ceylon, in their turn, were not deficient in commercial enterprize. In the latter part of the thirteenth century, Ceylon was visited by Marco Polo, a Venetian, who says, that it is the finest island in the world; the king is called Lendernoz; the men and women are idolaters, go naked, save that they cover their loins with a cloth; have no corn but rice; and oil of sesomons, milk, flesh, wine of trees, abundance of brasil, the best rubies in the world, sapphires, amethysts, and other gems. He also states, that a number of pilgrims from remote parts visited Adam's Peak, where some holy reliques were preserved of this great ancestor of mankind: consisting of his fore-teeth and one of his dishes. In the year 1281, the Great Khan of Tartary sent an embassy to Ceylon, and was fortunate enough to succeed in obtaining from the king of the island, two of the above-mentioned teeth, the dish, and a lock of Adam's hair.

In about a century afterwards, Ceylon was visited by Sir John Mandeville, who appears to have been better informed, than preceding travellers, as to the dimensions of the island; the circumference of which he makes to be eight hundred miles, which is not far from the truth. It must then, however, have greatly declined from its former civilization and importance as a commercial country. He mentions also, that it contained a large portion of wilderness, and was infested by serpents, crocodiles, and wild beasts, such as elephants, &c. &c.

Those who wish to be better acquainted with what is related of the monarchs who have reigned in the island, as well as with the religion of Boodhoo, must be referred not only to the history of Ceylon by "Philalethes," but also to Major Forbes's "Eleven Years in Ceylon," in which will be found much interesting information upon both such subjects. But, this fine and valuable island, was from the year 1505 destined to undergo many great and detrimental changes; for, it was at that epoch that the Portuguese, under Laurence D'Almeida, the son of the Viceroy of Goa, first landed on its shores.

The events which took place from that period till the Dutch Admiral Spilbergen arrived at Batticaloa in 1602, and the proceedings of both Dutch and Portuguese until the year 1656, when the latter were driven out of Colombo, and in 1658 finally expelled from the island, are sufficiently detailed in "Philalethes'" History of Ceylon, which has been above alluded to; in which is also given what is necessary to be known of the island whilst the maritime provinces remained under the Dutch, and until their conquest by us in 1796; when they were annexed to the British dominions; the Honourable Frederic North being the first British Governor.

But, what with the constant wars which had been carried on during both the Portuguese and Dutch possession of the sea coast, and the consequent neglect of cultivation, Ceylon had as much decayed from its ancient grandeur and importance, as it had decreased in population. But, after the British conquest, it still remained a weak and unconnected acquisition, with a dangerous, faithless, and hostile kingdom in its centre, until General Sir Robert Brownrigg having deposed the King of Kandy, on account of his cruelties, his dominions were vested in the Sovereign of Great Britain, and the whole island thus became an integral part of the British dominions. The discontents and disappointments, however, of the Kandyan Chiefs, some of whom had hoped to have been put by us upon the throne, in place of the deposed Rajah, rendered our possession, of the naturally very strong and almost impenetrable kingdom of Kandy, exceedingly precarious. The consequence was, that these disappointed Chiefs were able to exercise sufficient influence over the minds of their always subservient followers or dependents, so as to induce them to break out into an open and alarming rebellion—as it was termed—and which was not suppressed until the troops employed had undergone many privations and hardships, and when the reduced population had again been thrown still farther back in civilization.

But, it cannot be properly said, that Ceylon was permanently annexed to the British dominions, until General Sir Edward Barnes, who succeeded Sir Robert Brownrigg in the Government, wisely threw it completely open to the approach of our forces; by forming, at enormous labour, but triflingly comparative expense, excellent highways to its very centre; then indeed, but not till then, there could be no longer a doubt but that, under a humane and just Government, it must once more become in the South-east, what Great Britain is in the North-west, the Queen of Isles; and "the fabled splendour of a descent from the sun, or of a kindred relation to the Lion, may ultimately vanish in the true glory, the real prosperity, and the solid advantages, both commercial, moral, and intellectual, which she will derive from her union with the British crown."

The chief object, as before stated, which has been kept in view in this work, is to point out, to those intending to become settlers, and especially to persons possessing a limited capital, the parts of Ceylon to which they ought to proceed, according to the objects they may have in view. For the surface of the interior varies greatly, and in no part of the world is the distinction between high-land and low-land so obvious. It may be properly divided into flat country, hilly, and mountainous. The mountainous is skirted by the hilly; and the latter is, generally, bounded by flat country. Dividing the island into almost equal parts, by an imaginary line from west to east, the mountainous region will occupy the middle of the southern half. It is difficult to describe, accurately, the boundaries or extent of the hilly division. Perhaps, it may extend from the mountains, from ten to fifteen, and, in some places, to twenty miles. The flat country surrounds what was, of old, considered the Kandyan provinces, with the exception of the western boundary, which is hilly. The features of the three divisions of the interior, are necessarily peculiar: grandeur is the characteristic of the mountainous, beauty of the hilly, and too much sameness of the low country; a defect which even its surprising and surpassing luxuriant vegetation cannot remove.

It ought to be mentioned, that by far the greatest extent, of what may be called the flat country, is to the north and north-east of the mountains, and though in this is included the noble harbour of Trincomalie; yet, it constitutes that portion of the island, to which it would not, for some time to come, be desirable or prudent to call the attention of settlers,—at least, to the greater part of it. There, certainly, much may be done to extend cultivation, which naturally leads to improvement of climate; but, at first, this ought, chiefly, to be under the auspices of Government; as, it would be altogether beyond the power or means of individuals; and, when attempted, it must be with the view of greatly increasing the revenue of the country; and, how this may be judiciously effected, has been already shewn.

Many parts of the great tract of country, spoken of as to the southward of an imaginary line, drawn, it may be supposed, from about Chilaw on the west, to Batticaloa on the east coast, with the exception of Lower Ouvah, as well as a considerable part of the Mahagam-pattas, and most of Wellassé, (three considerable provinces, in most places covered with thick, and occasionally low stunted jungle, and infested with wild beasts,) are those to which it is most desirable that the attention of settlers should be directed; for, there the country is very healthy, and there a variety of rich soils are to be found, which could be made to yield, even by the native system of tillage, all kinds of grain and other productions of the finest tropical countries.*

Mr. Bennett in his "Manual of Useful Information," (to which those intending to settle in Ceylon are particularly referred,) tells us, that, the island abounds with teak, satin-wood, black and white ebony, calamander, iron-wood, red-wood, tulip-wood, and indeed with the most valuable timber in endless variety, and adapted for every domestic and ornamental purpose. He gives the names of ninety species, and adds, — "it is by no means improbable, from what is generally known of the varieties of timber imported into Great Britain, that scarcely one of these varieties of Kandyan trees has ever been seen in the London market." He further observes, that, "too much cannot be said in favour

* See Appendix Q, (Vol. I.) for proof of the healthiness of the district of Galle.

of the fruits of this magnificent country; and very little cultivation is required to improve the several indigenous varieties or to perfect exotics, which, from time to time, have been introduced from various parts of the world."

The capabilities of many parts of India, the fertility of much of its soil, the cheapness of food and labour; and the certainty that the best cotton, sugar, &c. can be produced there; have long been admitted. But, in these, and in many other respects, Ceylon cannot be surpassed by any country of the same extent. Other articles of extensive consumption in the United Kingdom, and elsewhere, have been long exported from India; and we are continually adding new staples to our imports from thence; such as tea from Assam, linseed, tallow, &c. With respect to the tea produced in Assam, the existence there of the tea plant, in a wild state, had for some years been known to the agents of the East India Company; and a correspondence on the subject of its cultivation, had taken place between the Government in India and the Directors in England. Specimens of the tea prepared from the wild plant had been forwarded to Europe, and though they were of a quality inferior to the ordinary teas of China, still they were sufficiently good to justify the belief, that, by cultivation and improved manipulation, a marketable article might be produced. With this view directions were given for the cultivation of the tea plant on a limited scale; and natives skilled in the various processes to which the leaves are exposed were engaged at Canton. Not long ago, a portion of the produce of the establishment arrived in this country. The contents of four chests were gratuitously distributed to various commercial and political departments in the United Kingdom; also to the leading tea-brokers, tea-tasters, &c. with the view of testing the merits of the tea by the opinions of competent judges. The result was extremely favourable; so much so, that the remaining chests were submitted to the trade by auction. But, it is the decided opinion of many, that several parts of Ceylon are also admirably adapted for the growth of the tea-plant; and, with the aid, in the first instance, of a few Chinese to instruct the settlers and natives in the process pursued in its preparation for market, there can be no doubt but that those Europeans who may attempt its cultivation will be successful.

We find that, of East India produce, the article which most decidedly takes the lead in British and European markets, as classed with the same article the produce of other countries, such as our West Indian possessions, and certain parts of America, is Indigo; but, it is only from factories under European management that the fine specimens are obtained; whilst the quality of that which is under native management is very inferior, and said to be always falsely packed; the best being placed at the top of the boxes, whilst the bulk is of little value. That the plant from which indigo is produced could be successfully cultivated in Ceylon, is certain; but the vapour which issues from the fermented liquor is extremely injurious, even to the negroes engaged in the process in the West Indies. It would, therefore, not be advisable to speculate in this valuable article in Ceylon, unless free and hardy labourers, from the south-east coasts of Africa, were induced to emigrate to Ceylon, for this and other purposes; and this is a point deserving the attention of Government; for though the island possesses a considerable and an increasing agricultural and labouring population, the demand for them, if emigration to this fine island were only encouraged as it ought to be, would, in time, exceed the supply, and consequently the price would become so greatly enhanced, as to check if not entirely to put a stop to improvements; for, according to the interesting documents which are given in the Appendix,* slavery will soon terminate in Ceylon. It should, however, be here remarked that, so temperate and excellent is the climate, that even Europeans can, with perfect safety, engage in almost any kind of farm work in Ceylon; but, as they would require to be so much more expensively fed, clothed and lodged, than the natives, no settler could afford to pay them sufficiently high wages, except as assistants or overseers.

By the documents just referred to, it has been shewn that the Ceylon proprietors of slaves were amongst the first to set an example to the world in the abolition of slavery. But, in that island it had for

* See Appendix N.

ages existed in its mildest form; so much so, that it is questionable if the condition of these people will be improved by their emancipation. The Kandyan chiefs, for what seemed to them strong reasons, resisted the measure as long and as much as they thought prudent; but, they are not men who will venture to oppose any measure which they see the Government intend to carry;—they consequently, yet reluctantly, yielded the point. This abolition of slavery and slave trade mania—for it ought to be so termed—has cost the country many millions of money; and yet, after all, the horrid trade is not and cannot be suppressed, and it still remains doubtful if any good has been effected; and, whilst the measure has deprived many of our Colonies of indispensable labourers, it has, at the same time, greatly increased the sufferings and misery of the unfortunate Africans carried on board the slave ships, which, in spite of all our exertions to prevent it, are still employed in the barbarous traffic. And to crown all, we have recently seen the result of the expensive and mad attempt to civilize Africa by dictionaries, model farms, physical sciences, and political economy. By these means—will it be believed?—it was intended (as observed in the "Times") to put down the slave trade at its fountain head, to teach the chiefs that it was their interest to be humane, and to pave the way for the introduction of Christianity; and all this was to have been accomplished with two Government steamers!—Not waiting for the tardy lapse of centuries, as civilization used to do in times of old, but moving at a rail-road pace, within the brief lives of the two great promoters of the scheme, or their still more ephemeral African Civilization Society.

It may here be observed, that sugar can be produced in many parts of Ceylon, in any required quantities, and especially if the system pursued in our West India Colonies were adopted in the cultivation of the canes, their collection when ripe, and conveyance to the mill to be bruised, in order to extract the juice which flows from them into the proper vessels set to receive it; by which means so much labour is saved in the operations of boiling, clarifying, &c. all of which are so well known as to make it quite unnecessary to say more upon the subject; unless it be, that Europeans, who would thus proceed in Ceylon, would have many advantages over the natives and others engaged in producing sugar in the East India Company's territories, where, except it be at Calcutta, neither mechanical nor chemical skill have as yet been introduced.

It should also be known, that the action of the sun, upon the sea water thrown up at a certain time of the year into natural reservoirs upon the south-east coast of Ceylon, forms vast quantities of salt; and far more, by due attention on the part of man, might be obtained; and as salt is no longer, it is concluded, a Government monopoly, profitable speculations in it might be entered into by settlers in that part of the island, for not only supplying the whole country with that necessary of life, but also the many parts of the East, where it is so much wanted.—The duty charged upon its importation into the Company's territories is therefore given in its proper place.

A description not only of the soils to be met with in Ceylon, but also of the various kinds of grain cultivated there, is likewise given in the preceding pages; and it is to be supposed that some of the latter may be usefully brought to the notice of agriculturists in general. These might, in the first instance, be tried on the lofty Horton Plains, and at Nuwara-Ellia, as well as in some of the other elevated situations; and, if they should succeed there, it may be reasonably expected, that some of them might be introduced with advantage, even into Great Britain. It is, however, most gratifying to find, that the attention of those in power in India has been directed to such objects; for in the report of the meeting of the Agricultural Society, in May last, particular notice is taken of the report of the Government Botanical Garden at Saharunpore, by which it appeared, that, in compliance with Lord Auckland's orders, large parties of collectors had been sent early in the seed season of 1839 to the Himalaya, who had made a valuable collection of seeds. In 1838, upwards of 500 species were sent from the Himalayas to England, but most of them were considered unworthy of attention; while in the next year the seeds were selected rather on account of their choice quality, than for the sake of obtaining numerical variety. Nearly all these germinated successfully, and the different kinds of Himalaya pines had flourished, in almost every instance, in the extreme parts of both Great Britain and Ireland, the severity of the winter having left the seedlings uninjured. The lucerne sent from Candahar, and the Affghan clover, had likewise flourished in England; but the latter, which is said to be important on account of its great luxuriance, and the avidity with which it is sought for by cattle, had not as yet attracted sufficient attention.

By the Superintendent of the Botanical Garden, a constant succession of useful seeds, agricultural, vegetable, and medicinal, had been received both from the India House and from other places. The carob-tree, the seeds of which are eaten in Syria, was found to thrive, and expected to prove of great benefit to the poorer classes in India. An experiment had been tried which augured well for the cultivation of cotton. Some specimens of soil from the island of Cheduba had been analyzed, as well as some specimens of American soil, and they were found to be precisely identical. In a few years it was expected not only that that island, but many parts of India, would produce cotton equal to the very best in America. All these facts tend to illustrate the great and progressive development of which our Indian possessions are susceptible, and there is no doubt, but that Ceylon cannot be surpassed, in these respects, by any tropical region on earth; for, where can also be found a climate so temperate and admirably suited for so many kinds of natural productions; such as cinnamon, coffee, and different sorts of spices.

Many may think that it would be presumptuous for any one to say, that it might be questionable, and that time alone can shew, if it was either politic or judicious, to have granted to a people, like the native inhabitants of Ceylon, so suddenly, and before—as many thought—they were prepared for it, such a very liberal form of government, as has been established there: and of which their very confined views, habits of servility, feelings strongly biassed by the influences of castes, attachment to heathenism, as well as strange notions of what we consider morality, rendered them altogether (as the preceding pages have shewn) incompetent to form even an opinion.

Mr. Bennett in his "Manual of Useful Information," (published last year) in speaking of the Church and other Missions, tells us that the whole of the Scriptures and Book of Common Prayer have been translated into familiar Singalese, besides numerous elementary school books and religious tracts. And he adds—"It is, however, a subject of general regret to the Missions, that, although in the immediate neighbourhood of a nominally Christian population, scarcely one native family out of a hundred, unless immediately connected with them, abstains, on religious principles, from the ceremonies and practice of devil worship. When their wizards, astrologers, and conjurors are converted, they will quit the devil practices, by which the native minds are so extraordinarily worked upon, as to render them pliant and subservient victims to the grossest impositions that ever fettered the spirit of man. This may be calculated on as a certain effect of the light of Christianity upon the minds of the *soi disant* Magi, who now hold bodies and souls in perpetual thraldom. But until this grand evil be removed, and by the assistance of a magistracy, whereever it may be needful, in severely punishing all such impostors, the fears of the ignorant natives will not be overcome by merely professing themselves converts to Christianity. The conversion of one greatly dreaded astrologer and devil-worshipper, will do much to reconcile the natives to the power of Christianity over the wiles of the evil one, and tend to reduce their fears of the *Maha Yaka,* or great demon, more than can be hoped for by other means."

"The caste of Seppidiwigie Karayo, or sorcerers, is one of the greatest stumbling-blocks to Christianity that now presents itself, and on its gradual conversion very much depends; for the superstitious natives will never altogether abandon devil worship, so long as its priests have such power over their minds, as to inspire these deluded creatures with the dreadful conviction that both their own bodies and the lives of their cattle, are at their (the sorcerers') command."

"Our missionaries may make proselytes of Singalese and Malabars, but they appear to have little or no chance with any of the many thousands of the followers of Ali and Mahommed, of whom I have not yet heard that they have converted even a solitary individual. And, indeed, amongst the former, the first and most ready converts have been those who anticipated employment in the missionary establishments as the reward of their apostacy from their original faith."—These are, however, the people, who have been suddenly placed (no doubt, to their great surprise!) by a liberal Government—it may be said—on an equality with the intelligent and respectable class of British subjects settled, or about to settle, in Ceylon.

But we are told, in a work written previously, that the result of this great change has been, that the island is already advancing rapidly beyond that barrier of mediocrity, which in Asia seems to have been erected to arrest both mind and manners at a particular point of civilization. It, however, may be asked, how are we to reconcile this opinion with the account given of them, last year, by Mr. Bennett?

Direct taxes on cultivated land have been, most wisely, first moderated, than carefully arranged, fairly levied, and finally redeemed; a whole people have thus passed, in an instant, and, we are told, with perfect safety to the Government, (and who, in these times, could apprehend danger, or anticipate any other result?) from most abject subserviency to complete freedom; and, it is added, that the effects of these measures have already been, a rapid improvement in the face of the country, a most beneficial change in the native character, generally diminished taxation, a rapidly increasing revenue, a prosperous and happy people, and it is not too much to say, an improved climate. These are said to be the fruits of the wise administration of the affairs of Ceylon by its recent Governors. But in their eager attempts to promote the welfare of the people upon modern liberal principles, they, and their admirers, seem to have forgotten, or altogether overlooked, a circumstance, obvious to those acquainted with Ceylon affairs, and which ought to be mentioned; — that the foundation of this so much boasted of prosperity, was chiefly laid, long before, by those enlightened and able men, Sir Robert Brownrigg and Sir Edward Barnes. To their wise and energetic measures, followed up, or in some degree altered, so as to suit the notions of the not always wisely-zealous *philanthropists* of the day, should properly be attributed most of the improvements in agriculture, as well as in the appearance of the country. For, how could these have been effected without the wisely planned and ably executed conquest of the Kandyan kingdom; without establishing in it, what it so much wanted,—that is to say, a judiciously conceived and efficient form of government, suited to the state and ideas of the people; and without throwing it open, at a cheap rate, and in conformity to the ancient laws and customs of the country, by means of high roads, to future improved and intended cultivation, as well as to commercial advantages. On the other hand, their successors in the government, though they had power to alter or improve, appear to have been, in some measure, blind to the best interests of the island; and have continued to exact, as long as they could, and as a source of revenue, ruinous export duties upon insular productions; which, if not removed by our Home Government, will drive (indced, they have all but done so already) at least Ceylon cinnamon out of the British and Foreign markets, and transfer that lucrative branch of trade into the hands of the Dutch. This, surely, it must be admittcd, was, at all events, not a line of policy likely to promote the welfare of a colony, or to benefit the mother country.

But, it should now be observed, that for a trifling consideration, or rather for no consideration whatever, the Home Government, for some years past, apparently influenced by the liberal spirit of the times, has lavished millions of acres of fine land, in our various colonies, upon speculators, or, in general, incompetent and injudicious emigrants. Yet, there does not appear to be any good reason, why a certain but very moderate land or crown rent,—besides the original purchase-money, after a fixed number of years allowed for improvement by cultivation, should not be exacted for all such land. This, in place of retarding (as some theorists have tried to prove) would accelerate and promote cultivation, by exciting actual settlers to exertion; whilst it would, in time, become a source of permanent revenue to the mother country; part of which might be laid out in improvements, such as in making roads, extending inland navigation, &c. as well as for the government and protection of the colonies;

and it would also, in some measure, serve as a desirable check upon those companies, which, taking advantage of this—it is hoped, that it may not be deemed presumptuous in considering—unwisely devised system, have already purchased from Government, enormous tracts of land, for, comparatively, a mere trifle, with the view of disposing of them afterwards, at a certain profit, to incautious, badly informed, and ill-advised emigrants; who very soon, and to their surprise, have found, from the exorbitant price of *labour*, that they cannot possibly attempt to bring their acquisitions into cultivation.

It has now been shewn, that none but these speculators have been benefited; an immense extent of already disposed-of land thus remains, like some of the large grants to individuals, useless and in its natural wildness; as it is only here and there that spots which have passed into the hands of persons accustomed to practical farming, and agricultural labour, are to be found under a system of profitable tillage. When, therefore, the present system of colonization is considered in all its bearings, it must be obvious, that, if emigration is duly encouraged and promoted, it would, perhaps, be more prudent, were Government, in place of disposing of vast tracts of country to speculators, to give small but sufficient portions of it, *gratis*, to families, or to able-bodied individuals, desirous of pushing their fortunes in a foreign land; for, it should again be observed, that as it is deemed necessary to get rid of our redundant population, it at once becomes indispensable, that the individuals, who are said to be starving at home, should be provided by Government, *and by Government only*, (the expense of which would, of course, have to be repaid by the towns, counties, or parishes, to which they might belong,) with a free and sufficiently comfortable passage to the part of the world intended to be colonized; and as the rate-payers would thus, to a certain extent, be relieved from the burthen of daily providing for such numbers of paupers, their being obliged so to contribute, could not be looked upon as a grievance, or as an unreasonable charge. When these emigrants arrive at the place of their destination, it may be supposed, from there being usually abundance of wood in such new countries, that they could be able to find cover for themselves, however severe may be the approaching winter; they would, however, require to be supplied with certain agricultural implements (a preference being given to those suitable for spade cultivation, as that to which the Irish, especially, are most accustomed), also with seed to be sown, as well as with a reasonable allowance of food, until their crops could ripen and become available for their support.

The expense of this could not, properly, and under such circumstances, be expected to be refunded by pauper emigrants; but, at a certain and fixed period, this gratuitously bestowed land—no matter into whose hands it may have passed—should be liable to pay tor ever, or until it is redeemed at a stipulated price, a moderate rent to the Crown, the amount of which should, perhaps, and in order to prevent its being easily sold by improvident persons, be greater than that charged upon land which had been purchased at a regulated price by emigrants of a superior class; who, from possessing capital, had been able to find their own passage, as well as in every other respect to support and supply themselves, without the assistance of the Government agents, who might be appointed to superintend the necessary arrangements, with what should constitute them freeholders or independent settlers; and, for whom, the poorer class of emigrants, sent out at the public expense, would, *in order to get money*, to enable them to purchase indispensable articles of British manufacture, be glad, occasionally, to work, it may be presumed, at reasonable rates of wages. But, as labour must necessarily be allowed to find its own value, and as it might not be advisable for the local government to interfere, if this system cannot keep down its price, it is altogether hopeless to look for prosperity in any new country deprived of slave or convict—that is, of *cheap labour*.

It has been thought advisable, to introduce the following letter from Dr. Chalmers; as it shews, in the strongest manner, how necessary it is that some public measure should be adopted, with a view to assist persons desirous of emigrating; but no society, it is to be feared, can do more, than enable such people to go out, unfortunately, to add to the numbers already in our new colonies, or in the United

States of America, who, from the want of means on the part of those to whom they looked for employment, are now suffering so severely from actual starvation, that hundreds of them are endeavouring to find their way back from the latter to the United Kingdom, as many have done already; and Dr. Chalmers and his charitable friends may rely upon it, that emigration can never be rendered useful or desirable, unless it is attempted under the sanction and with the support of Government.

"Edinburgh, Dec. 29, 1842.

"My dear Sir,—I think I told you some time ago that I had received no less than twenty different applications, from as many Emigration Societies in the west of Scotland, to most, if not all, of which I have given a contribution.

"I resolved when the number had come to twenty that I would make a change in my own treatment of their applications.

"I have since received two additional applications —one by letter subscribed 'Wm. Salmond,' from the Bridgeton District Emigration Society—another by a personal call from two men who appeared in behalf of the 'Glasgow Calton Canadian Village Emigration Society.'

"Now, however painful the necessity for refusing to entertain any more of these specific applications, multiplying upon us by a process of endless subdivision, yet my heart bleeds for the distress which has given birth to them; and I am still willing to make one sacrifice more in behalf of emigration.

"Let a society be formed in Glasgow, which will undertake to examine all the special claims, and to meet them, as far as it is enabled to do, from a general fund, formed by a general subscription from the country at large. Let this society be recommended to public confidence by the guarantee of known and creditable names. Let subscribers at a distance be henceforth protected from the appliance of parties who are perfect strangers to them, and be henceforth relieved from the necessity of ascertaining the merits of each separate application, and I have no doubt but a very large sum may still be had whenever the present system is superseded, by which the patience, though not the wealth, of contributors has been well nigh exhausted.

"Would Government give their countenance to such a society, this additional sanction would stimulate the liberality of all who feel for the distress of their countrymen, and are most desirous of relieving them, if they best knew how to do it effectually.

"I shall most willingly share as a humble contributor towards such an object; and I do think that my compliance with twenty of the bygone applications entitles me at least to make the suggestion, whether it shall be adopted and acted on or not.

"But before I conclude, I must, though you are already aware of it, testify my own opinion of the utter inefficiency of emigration as a lasting expedient of relief for the distress of a redundant or unemployed population. At the most it will but yield a transient and temporary relief from the pressure which is now felt in the manufacturing districts of our country. I cannot see my way to any scheme of permanent amelioration for the working classes, but through the medium of a commensurate parochial system, by which a universal education, both Christian and common, shall be provided for our people. The scheme of a poor law is beginning to look at us in good earnest; and I shall now cease to lament what I hold to be the infatuation of expending a five times greater sum, and doing worse than nothing with it, than would suffice for the establishment and vigorous operation of those moral causes, by which alone the comfort and economic prosperity, as well as the transcendently higher interests, of the common people, can be placed beyond the reach of every fluctuation.

"I have made many an effort for the elevation of that class in society whom I most love —I mean our artisans and our labourers—but my season of effort has now passed away, and I therefore conclude with the expression of every wish, and my most earnest prayers, for a larger sufficiency of this world's comforts and all those spiritual blessings which furnish and prepare for the world to come, in behalf of the common people of Scotland.

"I am, my dear Sir, yours most truly,

"THOMAS CHALMERS.

"To Wm. Collins, Esq., Glasgow."

It is asserted—but this is an extreme case—that in Paisley alone, there are upwards of 5,000 persons desirous of emigrating to the Canadas, and who, from want of means, are unable to go there. From this, as well as from what is known to be the case in all the manufacturing districts, it is evident that, if it were possible to make the expense of their being sent out, in the manner just proposed, fall in some measure upon wealthy manufacturers, who, as already stated, have been the cause of their being thus congregated to starve, it surely ought to be done; as it is well known that numbers of these gentlemen have now, prudently, become money-lenders upon mortgages on land, to improve the cultivation of which, too many landlords, as well as tenants, expecting that agricultural produce would continue remunerative, had unwisely borrowed in various ways and from various sources considerable sums, which were laid out upon its improvement, and in the consequent employment of thousands of agricultural labourers. The following important document will, however, clearly shew that land has contributed far more towards the maintenance of paupers, in the shape of poor-rates, than its fair proportion; and it proves that this, as well as the expense of sending out emigrants, should be made a general charge, or tax, upon all descriptions of property or income.

"An analysis of the various parliamentary returns relative to the poor rates, &c. from 1747 to 1841, a period of 94 years, has been compiled by J. Rowbotham, Esq., at the request of E. Wodehouse, Esq., M.P., which furnishes the following indisputable facts:—With regard to the comparative amount paid by land, and by other descriptions of property, such as dwelling-houses, mills, factories, &c. and manorial profits, which is the only classification that appears to have been laid before Parliament, I have referred to the Appendix E, p. 14, attached to the report from a select committee on poor-rate returns, 1824, (420); to the account of the amount levied by assessment in England and Wales for the year ending 25th March, ordered to be printed 1st March, 1827 (No. 120); and also an abstract of returns for the year ended 25th March, 1833, printed by order of the House of Commons, 27th May, 1834, (No. 355). By computing from the abstracts of returns, for the year ended 25th March, 1833, I find that on poor-rate assessment

Land has paid the sum of	£255,150,063
Dwelling-houses	123,716,217
Mills, factories, &c. . .	16,547,390
Manorial profits, &c. . . .	8,652,285
Total amount of assessment in 94 years	£404,065,955

"Hence it appears that land has paid 106*l.* per cent. more than dwelling-houses, and 1,442*l.* per cent. more than mills, factories, &c. By taking the average on the abstracts of returns for the years 1823, 1826, 1833, it is found that on assessment

Land paid	£269,048,176
Dwelling-houses . . .	112,687,055
Mills, factories, &c. . .	15,589,172
Manorial profits, &c. . .	6,741,552
Total	£404,065,955

"According to these estimates, land has paid 138*l.* per cent. more than houses, and 1,625*l.* per cent. more than mills, factories, &c.; and 99*l.* per cent. more than dwelling-houses, mills, factories, &c., and manorial profits combined, whether on assessment or for relief of the poor. Or, land paid 66·5 per cent.; houses, 27·9; mills, factories, &c., 3·9; and manorial profits, 1·7."

The plan which has above been hinted at, would, as before-stated, unavoidably, in the first instance, be attended with some expense to the towns, counties, or parishes; but, as emigration, according to the letter of Dr. Chalmers, is found to be indispensable, on account of our overwhelming artisan population, there does not appear to be, in the present state of the country, a cheaper or probably a much better mode of proceeding than that which has been suggested. That mode would comparatively, be little burdensome to the public in general; and thus one great cause of the prevailing discontent in the United Kingdom might be removed. For if it were left to the option of pauper families, whether they would reject or embrace the liberal and advantageous offers of Government, of being comfortably and without any expense to themselves, sent to colonies so regulated, or of being compelled, for a maintenance, to go into those hated and unpopular places of confinement, provided at an enormous expense, by or under the authority of poor-law commissioners, there can be no doubt as to which of the two they would prefer. Thus, it is to be hoped, tranquillity, especially in Ireland, where the introduction of the new and unsuitable poor-law is so strongly opposed by all classes of persons, (and there is little doubt, but that it will be equally unpopular, if attempted in Scotland,)—would, in some degree be insured. Thus the present Government would be freed, as they ought to be, from much of the vexatious embarrassment this untoward measure, as well as the attempts of the Anti-Corn-Law League to revive the free trade mania, are now causing, as well as likely still to cause; and, judging from the strange, and as many will think, imprudent sentiments expressed at the late Anti-Corn-Law banquet at Liverpool, Government have yet many difficulties to contend with, before they can hope to tranquillize the minds of a highly excited people. But the greatest difficulty, owing to misrepresentation, must be to prove to artisans in general, as well as to the agricultural labouring classes in Ireland, that the true causes of the present sufferings of the farmer had their origin in ruinous *over-manufacturing*, not only for the British markets, both home and colonial, but also for those of the whole world, in which there is now, unfortunately, so little sale for their wares, that manufacturers no longer deem it prudent to give them that employment without which they must starve; and to both, that they have too long and unwisely submitted to be the dupes and ready tools of interested agitators, who, they may rely upon it, will take good care to conceal from them, that if landlords, tenants, and their work-people, are ruined by low prices for agricultural produce, their own sufferings must thereby be vastly augmented.

The speeches, however, of some of the gentlemen at the Liverpool banquet are so far useful, that they shew the country who are the movers of the crusade in Ireland against landlords and rents, and also, who are those who are unfairly and madly endeavouring to represent our nobility and landed gentry to be, in the present day, as great enemies of the people, as those of France unluckily were, prior to the terrible and bloody Revolution in that country, the very recollection of which makes all good and loyal Frenchmen shudder. To frustrate the views of evil-minded persons, who would be delighted to see similar scenes enacted in the United Kingdom, the best mode of proceeding would probably be for Government to promote, something in the way suggested, an extensive system of emigration, especially from the manufacturing districts, to our Colonies.

The emigration of persons possessing a limited capital or income, to Ceylon, in the manner pointed out in the preceding chapters, is quite distinct from the above; for there, both land and labour, as well as the common necessaries of life, may all be obtained at exceedingly low prices: they can, however, be had equally so, in the territories of the East India Company; but the difference of climate should not be overlooked; and besides, their possession of them,—judging from the fluctuations to which that part of the world has always been liable—seems to be very uncertain; whereas Ceylon must remain an integral, important, and valuable part of Her Majesty's dominions, as long as Britons retain their superiority on the ocean.

APPENDIX.

A.

EXPENSE OF MANUFACTURING SUGAR IN THE EAST INDIES.

		Rupees.
Ten ploughings, at four annas each	.	2 8
Watering once, at one rupee per beegalls	.	1 0
Three ploughings, at five annas each	.	0 15
Fifteen bundles of cane for seed, at five bundles for one rupee . .	.	3 0
Cutting, cleaning, and sowing the above	.	0 6
Watering for two months, three times	.	3 0
Hoeing nine times, at three annas each time		1 11
Manuring . .	.	0 8
Tying the canes in August .	.	0 5
Cutting the canes for manufacturing, including carrying		0 12
Rent of land . .	.	5 8
Expressing the cane, and reducing it to ghoor (or boiled juice) .	.	10 0
		29 9
Expense of manufacturing the ghoor into sugar—thirty maunds of fire wood, at 25 rupees per 100 maunds		7 8
Servants employed		4 0
Sward grass, used for the purpose of claying		1 0
Earthen pans . .	.	0 8
Fire for boiler . .	.	3 0
		45 9

Produce.

7½ maunds fine white benares, at 5 rupees	}	46 8
3 do. grey do at 3 do.	}	
6 do. molasses.		
4½ do. dirt, &c.		

Appendix B.

Periods of Sowing and Reaping the different kinds of Grain throughout the Maritime Provinces of Ceylon.

COLOMBO DISTRICT.

PADDY.

Yalla Harvest. Sown from March 10th to April 30th.
Reaped from July 15th to September 30th

Maha Harvest. Sown in July and August.
Reaped from December 20th to the end of Feb.

Bale Wee Sown from September 15th to November 15th.
Reaped from December 20th to the end of Feb.

Muttches. Sown from December 15th to January 30th.
Reaped from April 10th to May 30th.

FINE GRAINS.

Yalla Harvest. Kurakkan, Meneri and Mun, sown from April 1st to June 15th.
Reaped in 3 months after sowing.

Bada Amu, in a few parts sown in April and May.
Reaped in 4 or 4½ months.

Kurakkan, Meneri, Nun and Kollu.

Maha Harvest. Sown from 15th September to 15th November.
Kurakkan and Meneri in Owittes, sown in Nov. December, and part of January.
Reaped in 3 months after sowing.

Bada Amu, sown from Sept. 15th to the end of Oct.
Reaped in 4 or 4½ months.

Karal Amu, sown in July.
Reaped in 5 or 5½ months.

Mun and Muttches Mey in Owittes, sown in Jan.
Reaped in 3 months.

CHILAW DISTRICT.

PADDY.

Maha Harvest, 1st Crop.	Maha Wee, Hatelie Hamba. Sown from 1st July to 31st August. Reaped in February. Elenkallven, Gotiaran, Handiran, Pode Wee Calocoombele. Sown from 1st September to 31st October. Reaped from 1st January to 5th February. Henety, Ratie Wee, Morunga Wee, Polle-elle Wee. Sown from 15th November to 15th December. Reaped in February.
Yalla Harvest, 2nd Crop.	Ellenkalven, Contiaran, Handiran, Pode Wee Calocoombele, Henety, Ratte Wee, Oolle-elle Wee, Moranga Wee. Sown from 1st April to 31st May. Reaped in August.

FINE GRAINS.

Maha Harvest, 1st Crop.	Natchreen, Meneri, Mun Ammoo, Tanne, Pulloe Oulondoe, Mootsma, Bade Iringo, Cara Iringo, Colle, Talle. Sown from 1st September to 15th October. Reaped in January.
Yalla Harvest, 2nd Crop.	Natchreen, Meneri, Mun, Ammoo, Tanne, Pulloe, Oulondoe, Mootasma, Bade Iringo Caral Iringo, Colle. Sown from 1st April to 31st May. Reaped in July and August.

MANAR DISTRICT.

PADDY.

Paalechederie.	Sown in September Reaped in March.

Ellenkallyen. Karte Ellenkallyen, Panengeallyen, Mootomanican, Kadecalten, Ekichamba, Pondicam be and Hahally.
Sown in October.
Reaped in March.

Norroengan Chienetty and Moroega. Sown in December.
Reaped in March.

Chienetty and Moroega. Sown in May.
Reaped in August.

FINE GRAINS.

Korakkam. Sown in September.
Reaped in December.

Cadecanne. Sown in October.
Reaped in November.

Cambampullo. Koedery Wallie, Tanna.
Sown in October.
Reaped in January.

Gingilie. Sown in March.
Reaped in May.

JAFFNA DISTRICT.

PADDY.

In the four Provinces and Islands is sown in August and Sept.
Reaped in January and February.

At Caretchy
,, Poonreen
,, Polveraucattoe
,, Ilpecadewe
} Sown in September and October.
Reaped in February and March.

In these places except Caretchy, there is sometimes a second crop, but so trivial, as to be scarcely worthy of notice. It is sown in May and June, and principally in the cavities of tanks, &c. &c.

FINE GRAIN.

Warego.	Sown in August		Reaped in	Jan.
Sawny.	Do. in September.		do.	Dec.
Korakhan.	1st sort, sown in May		do.	Aug.
	2nd sort	Oct.	do.	Dec.
	3rd do.	Jan.	do.	March.
Tinnesawmy.	1st do.	April	do.	July.
	2nd do.	July	do.	Oct.

Pannesawmy. 1st sort sown in April		Reaped in July.
2nd do.	July	do. Oct.

A very small portion of dry grain is cultivated at Caretchy, Poonereen, Polverancattoe and Ilpecadewe.

MAHAGAMPATTOO DISTRICT.

PADDY.

1st Sort. Sown in October and November.
Reaped in January and February.

2nd Sort. Sown in October and November.
Reaped in December and January

Indian Corn. Sown in August and September.
Reaped in October and November.

Korakhan. Sown in August and September.
Reaped in November and December.

Tanna. Sown in March and April.
Reaped in June and July.

Moongeh. Sown in October and November.
Reaped in January and February.

N.B.—The natives of the Mahagampattoo seldom venture on sowing any grain (Paddy and Tanna excepted), in the Yalla season.

MATURA DISTRICT.

PADDY.

Maha Harvest. Sown in July.
Reaped in January and February.

Yalla Harvest. Sown in January and February.
Reaped in July and August.

FINE GRAIN.

Sown at the same time with the Paddy, and reaped generally one month before it.

Ammo, Menerie, Tanne, Moong } Sown at all times throughout the year, and do not depend upon the seasons.

GALLE DISTRICT.

PADDY.

Maha Harvest. Ratta Wee Handiram, Kottehandiram, Nandoohandiram and El Wee.

Yalla Harvest. Sown from the 15th Feb. to the 15th April.

Kalookareyal, Ratkareyal, Sooderkareyal Kahattehamba, Soodoo Wee, and Kaharunian. Sown from the 15th of February to the 30th April.

Galpa Wee, Mukelu Wee, Ratkoonde, Tawalvo, Sooderkooro Wee, Poleyel, or Hatiel Katukooro Wec, Roombole, and Danchala—Sown from the 15th of February to the end of May.

The harvest lasts from about the middle of August until the middle of October.

With the exception of Ell Wee, the aforementioned grains are sown for the Maha season—and in addition to them, Mahama Wee Godema Wee and Balema Wee. The sowing time is from the 15th September until the end of October, and the last three sorts between the 15th of July and the end of Scptcmber. They are reaped between January and February following.

FINE GRAIN.

Yalla Harvest. Karukkan, Meneri, Ammo, Tanna } Sown between March and May. Reaped in August and September.

Maha Harvest. They are sown in October and November. Reaped in January and February.

CALTURA DISTRICT.

PADDY.

Moetas. Sown in December and January. Reaped in April and May.

Yalla Harvest. Sown in March, April, and part of May. Reaped in August and September.

Maha Harvest. Sown in July and August. Reaped in January and February.

TRINCOMALEE DISTRICT.

PADDY.

1st Crop. Sown in October and December Reaped in February and April.

2nd Crop. Sown in January and March.

TAMBLEGAM PADDY.

Sown in July ; reaped in October.

DRY GRAINS.

Warrego, Semie and Tanne—sown in November, and reaped in January.

Gingley sown in January, and reaped in April.

WANNY DISTRICT.

PADDY.

Winter Crop. Seeniette sown in November, and reaped in three months.

Manelwarie in four months.

Kartullenkalleen in five months.

Peroenille in 6 months.

Summer Crop. Seeniette, Moeraingew and Patjederoema. } in three months.

DRY GRAINS.

Warego and Natjerry, sown from Nov. to Dec.

BATTICALOA DISTRICT.

PADDY.

Carpoo nillo, or Black Paddy, sown after the middle of October, reaped in 6 months.

Samba. Sown do. do.

Reaped in five months.

Chinety or Hinety. Sown do.

Reaped in 2½ months.

Perianelloo. Sown from 15th January to the 1st May, and till the latter end of July, reaped in four months.

DRY GRAIN.

Payro, planted with Cholom or Indian Corn.	Sown and reaped in 3 months.
Cheropayroo and Porompayroo.	Sown and reaped in 11 weeks.
Na'cherry or Korakan.	Sown and reaped in 14 weeks.

Appendix C.—PRODUCE, STOCK, &c. OF CEYLON, in 1835.

CROPS.—Nature of the Crops, and Number of Acres of Land in each Crop.

Name of the County or District.	Paddy. (a)	Fine Grains. (b)	Coffee. (c)	Pepper. (d)	Mustard (e)	Gram. (f)	Indian Corn (g)	Peas.	Gingely	Cotton (h)	Tobacco. (i)	Pasture. (k)	Total No. of Acres in Crop.	Acres of Uncultivated Land. (l)
Western Province .	185,228	11,822½	9,682⅔	1,251	3½	214	30	..	..	472	2,067½	637	211,408 1/10	1,046,269¼
Southern „ . .	107,166¼	67,682½	6,551¾	215¾	21⅓	60¾	153½	..	9¾	165¾	34⅜	975,078	1,157,140¼	1,182,419⅝
Eastern „ (q)	29,635½	1,606¼	..	..	..	..	913½	16½	7	155½	356	12,820	45,510½	319,530
Northern „ . .	66,848	40,115	..	1	1¼	1,440¼	½	1,396	1,160	496	8,083	104,344	223,88‥	742,171
Central „ (r)	The extent in acres cannot in the present state of the Central Province be filled up with any degree of accuracy, as no general survey has been made.													
Total . . .	388,877¾	121,226½	16,234 7/20	1,467¾	26¼	1,715	1,097⅓	1,402½	1,176¾	1,289¼	10,541¼	1,092,879	1,637,943 17/20	3,290,390

Number of STOCK. — Nature of the PRODUCE, and Quantity of each.

Name of the County or District.	Horses.	Horned Cattle.	Sheep.	Goats.	Paddy. (m)	Fine Grains. (n)	Coffee.	Pepper.	Mustard	Gram.	Indian Corn.	Peas.	Gingely.	Cotton.	Tobacco.
					Bushels.	Bushels.	Bushels.	Bushels.	Bushels.	Bushels.	Bushels.	Bushels	Bushels.	lbs.	lbs.
Western Province .	416	295,750	281	7,960	1,498,700 19/21	81,347⅐	25,558¼	2,605⅜	133⅜	6,495⅐	593 4/7	..	..	99,312	4,412,800
Southern „ . .	136	91,874	55	5,081	1,421,184½	134,679¾	6,417⅓	1,085	293	825	1,441	..	26	20,139	6,267
Eastern „ (q)	56	30,655	367	1,807	351,259⅐	6,603⅜	..	..	..	..	13,654⅐	172	46⅐	6,230	304,823
Northern „ .	92	155,815	39,268	32,730	817,965	272,109	..	28	40	3,215	10	5,326	5,812	111,251	456,705
Central „ (r)	280	105,000	1,100	1,300	1,575,000	186,775	130,000	4,500	550	14,200	2,000	..	1,000	100,000	184,000
Total . . .	980	679,094	41,071	48,878	5,664,109 4/21	681,514 17/28	161,975 11/28	8,218⅜	1,016⅔	24,735⅐	17,699⅐	5,498	6,884⅐	336,932	5,364,595

PRICE OF PRODUCE.

Name of the County or District.	Paddy, per Bushel. (o)	Fine Grains, (p) per Bushel.	Coffee, per Bushel.	Pepper, per Bushel.	Mustard, per Bushel.	Gram, per Bushel.	Indian Corn, per Bushel.	Peas, per Bushel.	Gingely, per Bushel.	Cotton, per lb.	Tobacco, per lb.
	d. s. d.	d. s. d.	s. d. s. d.	s d. s. d.	s. d. s. d.	s. d. s. d	d. s. d.	s.d. s. d	s. d. s. d.	d. d.	d. s. d.
Western Province .	6¾ to 2 9¾	5½ to 3 4½	6 9 to 15 3	4 6 to 31 2	0 8 to 4 6	0 6¾ to 7 0	6¾ to 7 0	..	3 4½ to 4 0	0¾ to 3	1¼ to 0 9
Southern „ . .	7½ „ 1 4½	5 „ 1 4½	8 6 „ 10 0	7 6 „ 16 0	0 9 „ 4 6	1 9 „ 8 6	5¼ „ 1 9	..	1 3 „ 3 0	0¾ „ 4½	1½ „ 1 4
Eastern „ (q)	6 „ 1 1½	5 „ 1 1½	..	..	..	..	4 „ 1 0	0 2½ to 4 0	1 3 „ 2 8½	1 „ 2	1 „ 0 3¾
Northern „ . .	8¼ „ 1 9	6 „ 1 3⅗	..	12s.	1 6 to 3 9	0 11½ to 1 7½	9d.	2 3 „ 3 0	..	1½ „ 2¼	2¼ „ 0 3
Central „ (r)	1s. 6d.	4 „ 2 0	10s.	15s.	4s.	2s. 3d.	1s. 6d.	..	2s.	3d.	4½d.

(a, b) Excepting the 7 Kories (Western Province).
(c, d, e, f, g, h, i) Excepting the 7 and 3 Kories (Western Province).
(k) Excepting the whole of the Western Province (but the 4 and 3 Kories), Matura, (Southern Province) Tamankadda (Eastern Province), and Newerakalawyie (Northern Province).
(l) Excepting the 7 and 4 Kories.
(m, n, o, p) Excepting Newerakalawyie, as regards which the quantities and prices are not specified.
(q) Excepting Bintenne, the information required not being ascertainable.
(r) The "*Produce*" in the Central Province, specified in this statement, is to a considerable degree hypothetical.

Appendix D.

ANALYSIS AND EFFECTS OF WATER IMPREGNATED WITH SULPHURETTED HYDROGEN.

At the Royal Institution, on Friday evening last, Mr. J. F. Daniel read a paper "on the spontaneous evolution of sulphuretted hydrogen in the waters on the western coast of Africa and elsewhere." He commenced by observing, that this subject was now interesting on two accounts—1, because it would recall to the members of that institution the experiments of Sir Humphrey Davy on the subject, and which led him to advise the adoption of ship protectors; and 2, in consequence of the Niger expedition, fitted out to visit and endeavour to introduce civilization on the western coast of Africa. The effect produced on copper sheathing by the presence of sulphuretted hydrogen in the waters on that coast, was, he premised, well known to every one informed respecting vessels visiting it, and it was a fact that a cruise of nine months on the western coast of Africa injured the copper sheathing of a vessel as much as four years' wear in any other part of the world. The lecturer showed a piece of sheathing taken from the bottom of a Government frigate that had not been many months on the African station, and also a piece from the Royal George, sunk at Spithead, and which had been under water 60 years; the former was caten through in very many places, and so thin all over that he might push his thumb through it, while the latter was tough and in excellent condition. His attention had been directed to the subject by the Lords of the Admiralty sending him 10 bottles of water, from as many different places on that coast, extending from 8 deg. north of the Equator to 8 deg. south, to analyse, and to report on the component parts thereof and the accompanying table was the result:—

	Sulphuretted Hydrogen. Cubic. Feet.	Inches.	Saline Matter. Grains.
Sierra Leone, per gallon	6	18	1,696.0
Volta	6	99	2,480.0
Bonny River	1	21	1,788.0
Mooney	..	..	2,104.0
Gaboon	..	..	2,169.0
Lobez-bay	11	69	2,576.0
Congo River (Mouth)	0	67	188.0
Congo River (35 miles inland)	..	..	8.0
Bango	4	35	28,36.0
Lagos	14	75	1,920.0

All the bottles were hermetically sealed, and he had no doubt the water was in every way as good as when taken from the rivers. On drawing the cork, he was immediately struck with the smell of sulphuretted hydrogen, and adopted the general idea that it arose from animal and vegetable decomposition, but it had since appeared to him that such was not entirely the case. The gas extended a distance of 15 or 16 deg., and in some places as far as 40 miles to sea, covering therefore a space of 40,000 square miles. Now what could the origin be? He thought that it arose from the action and reaction of vegetable and animal matter brought from the interior by the rivers upon the sulphates in the sea water. With this idea he gathered last autumn some leaves from a shrubbery and put them into three jars; into one of which he poured some plain New River water, into the second some of the same water in which three ounces of common salt had been dissolved, and into the third the like water, in which some crystallized sulphate of soda was dissolved. To the cover of the jars he fixed inside some litmus paper, and placed them in a cupboard, the temperature of which varied from 70 to 100 or 110°. The effect was, that in the first the litmus paper was perfectly white, and the smell by no means unpleasant; in the second the paper was quite white, and the smell similar to that of a preserve; but in the third jar, in which a sulphate was present, the paper was nearly black, and the stench was horrible and nauseous in the extreme, as every one knew the smell of sulphuretted hydrogen gas to be. Now sea-water contained sufficient sulphates to produce this effect, under peculiar circumstances. But a more interesting part of the subject was the miasma so injurious to life on the marshy shore of Western Africa. Some persons said that if science cannot point out a remedy, it is useless to investigate the causes, but he did not so think; if science could not point out a remedy, still it could point to something as a palliation of the evil. The presence of the injurious gas was easily tested by the roughest hand, so that places in which it abounded could be avoided; and if imperative duty rendered it absolutely necessary to go to those places, then plentiful fumigations of chlorine gas would effectually destroy the sulphuretted hydrogen. The effect of this gas was not only visible on the Western coast of Africa, but in many places elsewhere, although not to so great an extent. Might not the jungle fever of India, the periodical fevers of New York and Charlestown in America, and the minor diseases on the coast of Essex, be traced to be effects of this deleterious gas? It was a well-known fact that the ships in the mouth of the Medway consumed more copper than other ships. Chlorine gas then destroyed the injurious gas, and it was easily made, and the materials very cheap; the Government had plentifully supplied the African Expedition with the materials necessary for the most perfect chlorine fumigations, and he had the pleasure of believing that his report founded on the analysis of the waters submitted to him, and the precautions taken, had imparted confidence not only to the gallant men who composed that expedition, but also to those who had interested themselves in its welfare, and who had been actuated by the most Christian spirit. He hoped its success would be commensurate to its deserts."

It is well known, that in these expectations Mr. Daniels has been sadly disappointed—especially as regards the African expedition; yet, his observations are most useful, and deserve the serious attention of medical gentlemen throughout the world.

Appendix E.

ON THE CULTIVATION OF FLAX IN INDIA.

Mr. Rogers states, that he has factories in India; is an agent here for selling the produce of his factories; and that he is amongst the largest individual holders of indigo factories in India. He (in conjunction with other East India merchants) has tried experiments in flax. "We call ourselves 'The Flax Experimental Society.' We made calculations of the highest produce in Europe of flax per acre; we made calculations also of the greatest average produce of indigo per acre in India. We found in Europe that land produces, at the average, 5 cwts. per acre of flax, which, when sold, yields about £9. for each acre cultivated; and we found in India, taking 5*s* per pound, the average for the last 20 years of the price realized for indigo imported into this country, that we only received £2. 16*s* per acre for the produce of our indigo lands laid down in England. We then assumed, that if we could produce 3 cwts. of flax per acre, which is 2 cwts. less than is produced in Belgium, or in Europe generally, we should realize £6. return for that article imported into this country. We went further into the calculation, in this way: we calculated that, allowing for 1,000 Bengal begahs cultivated in indigo, we received 50 maunds; 50 maunds, if sold at 5*s* a pound, would give us about £825. sterling; if we produced 3 cwts. of flax, and sold it at 40*s* per cwt., which is 4*s* under the average price of Europe flax, it would give us nearly £2,000.; and, deducting for additional freight, would leave us about, £1,625., yielding a very great difference in favour of flax, as contradistinguished from indigo. Upon these calculations I was deputed to go to Belgium, and there engage competent Belgian farmers' men, who have been from their childhood accustomed to the cultivation and preparation of flax. I engaged two, one of them a Mr. De Neef, who turned out a most intelligent man. We purchased flax-seed of the superior qualities which are in use in Europe; we purchased Russian, we purchased American, and we purchased Dantzic flax-seed, and all the different sorts; we also procured samples of flax from Russia; samples of flax from Belgium; samples of flax from Holland; samples of flax from France, and various samples of all the different sorts; we took these in order that we might shew the people of India what flax was, because, though flax has been cultivated for seed from time immemorial in India, though it grows indigenous in that country, the natives, possessing the much easier manufactured article of cotton, have never turned the fibre to usefulness, and they are not aware what flax is; for that reason we thought it necessary to send out samples of the sorts marketable in England. I was then directed to write out a description, with drawings, of all the different models and implements used to prepare flax in the simplest modes used in Europe; not the most difficult modes, with machinery, but the simplest modes. We preferred the simplest modes, because human labour is available in India to an extraordinary degree, and we thought it would benefit the people of India more by employing their labour than by introducing superior machinery, that would deprive them in some degree of work. We sent out the simplest sorts of machinery. I was also directed to have the pamphlet which I published circulated in every bazaar and corner of India, in different languages, in Bengalee, in Hindostanee, and in English, and put into the hands of every indigo planter as well. This was done. We had also directed, previous to sending out the Belgians, that considerable tracts of land in Tirhoot, in Allahabad, near Benares, at Midnapore, in Burdwan, in Jessore, and in Kishnagur, should be cultivated; that no quantity of land less than five English acres, about 15 Bengal begahs, should be cultivated, and that a precise memorandum of the expense of cultivation of each five acres of land should be kept in each separate district. The Belgians went out in the ship Vernon; when they arrived in India there was a very considerable quantity of land, (speaking of it as an experiment,) which had been cultivated, and the plant had arrived to a degree of perfection which is seldom seen in Europe. The Belgian, Mr. Neef, who is a most intelligent man, stated that the flax in Belgium, and on the average in Europe, did not exceed from 24 to 30 inches in height, but much of that in India had attained the height of 36 to 40 inches. He said that he could see no reason whatever why East India flax should not be as good, judging from the appearance of the plant, as any European flax. The reason that East India flax has not hitherto been of value is, that the natives have not cultivated it for fibre, but only for seed, and therefore they have sown it broad-cast and thin, in order that it might throw out lateral branches. Each stem of flax contains exactly the same number of fibres; each lateral branch contains also the same number of fibres branching out from the parent stem; lateral branches conveying out the strength form knots similar to a tree at every junction along the stem, and the consequence is, that when you come to pull it out, like a knotted stick, it snaps off. We directed the seed to be sown thick, in order to make it throw up a single stem, and to throw out no lateral branches whatever, this succeeded to perfection. When the plant had arrived at 36 inches high, there was not a single lateral branch, nor the appearance of one, upon the plant, and it began then to flower. Only one experiment has yet been tried in manufacturing the flax, which is the most important thing, because although the flax may be beautiful in its appearance as a plant, the fibre may be weak, or the nature may be harsh and brittle, and hard to work. That of course we cannot speak of yet. We know the quantity of plant per bundle, but not the quantity of produce of the fibre, which is the thing we want.

Flax is a cold weather crop, and it may be grown in the same year, and upon the same land which has produced indigo.—We gave particular directions that the flax should be sown in the end of September or the beginning of October, or at all events not later than the beginning of November.—It was sown about the middle of October. We sent out 400*l.* sterling worth of seed, which goes a great way; but we lost about 120*l.* worth of the seed, from mismanagement, and want of sufficient care on board ship. It was ripe for pulling about the middle to the end of February; it had actually been pulled at Bowsing, and manufactured before the 6th of March; the seed that was sown in October was in fibre, and the flax in a marketable state, on or about the 1st of March; and it would in no way have interfered with indigo, or with the natives' grain crops: in fact, it would have benefitted them. It was not necessary to manure the soil; the land being inundated by the Ganges annually, the deposit each year is sufficient to grow two crops; it is nothing new to grow two crops; there are always two crops grown of an equally exhausting nature with flax; flax, when pulled green, I do not conceive to be exhausting; when it is allowed to run to seed, I think it is; but when it is taken off green, I do not think it is exhausting.—Mustard, also is grown as a cold weather crop. We have sent home, within these five years, 30,000 tons of linseed for crushing; but they have in Belgium used our East India seed, and grow some flax from seed imported from India within this last year." Mr. Rogers further says that he is not prepared to speak as to where flax succeeds best in India, but adds, "We have not heard yet as to the Upper Provinces, nor from Madras or Bombay; to both of which we have sent seed." He cannot speak distinctly as to whether it would be necessary to manure land not overflowed, but he can say distinctly, that it would require no different mode of cultivation from what is now employed, because the flax is equally now produced upon the lands.—And he adds—" Taking the fibre does not deprive us of the seed, we get the seed also; we do not get the same quantity of seed, for the reason I mentioned, that we do not allow the lateral branches to be thrown out; but then we have more single heads, which in some degree compensate for the lateral branches. —We have heard, from every part of India where it is sown, that the plant appears most promising."

Appendix F.

OBSERVATIONS ON FREE-TRADE.

We hear much of Free Trade, and of a reciprocity system,—that is to say, a desire on the part of manufacturers to injure agriculturists without, they may rely upon it, benefitting themselves, or improving the present unhappy state of the unfortunate artisans; for, until the continental powers of Europe, the United States of America, and other countries, can be got to receive our manufactures on the same terms as it is wished that we should take their produce. it is in vain to talk of reciprocity.

India is the only important part of the world that does so upon any thing like fair terms: indeed, trade with England is much against her. For instance, why should trade with Russia be thought advantageous to us, when she shuts out, by prohibitory duties, the manufactured produce of our industry, whilst Russian produce is admissible here at extremely moderate duties. For example—Untaxed Russian tallow can be introduced into England at a cheaper rate than tallow from India. With Russia the trade is one-sided; she sells, but will not buy; and, therefore, the profit is all on one side. India, on the contrary, is a greater buyer than seller. She takes, at scarcely more than nominal rates of duty, all the products of our industry, even when competing with her own. It may be said, that on an average, every shipment of cottons or woollens to India, realises a profit of not less than twenty per cent.; and the exports of cottons alone to India exceeds, perhaps, the whole amount of imports from that country. To Russia, the exports of cotton, which constitute, probably, three-fourths of the whole exports, amount only to about one-fourth part of the whole imports from that empire; and these exports consist almost entirely of cotton yarns, the profits upon which do not exceed five per cent. It ought, therefore, to follow, that upon a fair balance of trade, we could better afford to pay ten or fifteen per cent. more for Indian than for Russian tallow, although nominally, the first price of Indian tallow was ten per cent. dearer than that of Russia. India is thus shewn to be the cheapest market to buy at, and Russia the dearest of the two;—so much for *reciprocity*, by which we sacrifice some hundreds of thousands of real profits upon Indian trade, and which might be vastly increased, in order to realize, comparatively, a few thousands, the difference between the prices of Indian and Russian tallow. And would not the same principles apply to Free trade in corn?—for, if other countries will not admit, upon equal terms, the produce of our industry, why should our agriculturists be ruined—as they undoubtedly would be—by allowing their grain, cattle, and cured meats to enter our ports duty free? But, it is to be hoped that the agriculturists of the United Kingdom are more than able to supply even our redundant population with corn, though for the present seriously affected by the new price-lowering Tariff, if only due care be taken to prevent what is the produce of the United States of America from being introduced—it may almost be said untaxed, through the Canadas.

Appendix G.

RATES of Duty to be charged on Goods Imported by Sea into any Port of the Presidency of *Fort William*, in *Bengal*, in 1836.

No.	Enumeration of Goods.	When Imported on British Bottoms.	When Imported on Foreign Bottoms.
1	Bullion and coin - -	free - -	free.
2	Precious stones and pearls -	ditto - -	ditto.
3	Grain and pulse - -	ditto - -	ditto.
4	Horses and other living animals - - -	ditto - -	ditto.
5	Ice - - - - - -	ditto - -	ditto.
6	Coal, coke, bricks, chalk, and stones - - -	ditto - -	ditto.
7	Books printed in the United Kingdom, or in any British possession - -	ditto - -	3 per cent.
8	Foreign books - -	3 per cent. -	6 per cent.
9	Marine stores, the produce or manufacture of the United Kingdom, or of any British possession -	3 per cent. -	6 per cent.
10	Ditto, ditto, the produce or manufacture of any other place or country - -	6 per cent. -	12 per cent.
11	Metals, wrought or unwrought, the produce or manufacture of the United Kingdom, or any British possession - - - -	3 per cent. -	6 per cent.
12	Metals, ditto, ditto, excepting tin, the produce or manufacture of any other place - - - - -	6 per cent. -	12 per cent.
13	Tin, the produce of any other place than the United Kingdom, or any British possession - - - -	10 per cent. -	20 per cent.
14	Woollens, the produce or manufacture of the United Kingdom, or any British possession - - - -	2 per cent. -	4 per cent.
15	Ditto, the produce of any other place or country -	4 per cent. -	8 per cent.
16	Cotton and silk piece goods, cotton twist, and yarn, the produce of the United Kingdom, or of any British possession - -	3½ per cent. -	7 per cent.
17	Ditto, the produce of any other place - - - -	7 per cent. -	14 per cent.
18	Opium - - - - -	—24 Rs. per seer of 80 tolas -	— 24 Rs. per seer of 80 tolas.
19	Salt - - - - -	— Rs. 3-4 per Md. of 80 tolas per seer -	—Rs. 3-4 per Md. of 80 tolas per seer.
20	Alum - - - - -	10 per cent. -	20 per cent.
21	Camphor - - - -	10 per cent. -	20 per cent.
22	Cassia - - - - -	10 per cent. -	20 per cent.

No.	Enumeration of Goods.	When Imported on British Bottoms.	When Imported on Foreign Bottoms.
23	Cloves - - - -	10 per cent. -	20 per cent.
24	Coffee - - - -	7½ per cent. -	15 per cent.
25	Coral - - - -	10 per cent. -	20 per cent.
26	Nutmegs and mace - -	10 per cent. -	20 per cent.
27	Pepper - - - -	10 per cent. -	20 per cent.
28	Rattans - - - -	7½ per cent. -	15 per cent.
29	Tea - - - -	10 per cent. -	20 per cent.
30	Vermilion - - -	10 per cent. -	20 per cent.
31	Wines and liqueurs - -	10 per cent. -	20 per cent.
32	Spirits, consolidated duty, including that levied heretofore through the police of Calcutta - - - And the duty on spirit shall be rateably increased as the strength exceeds of London proof, and when imported in bottles, five-quart bottles shall be deemed equal to the Imperial gallon.	—9 As. per Imperial gallon -	—16 As. per Imperial gallon.
33	All articles not included in the above enumeration -	3½ per cent. -	7 per cent.

And when the duty is declared to be *ad valorem*, it shall be levied on the market value without deduction; and if the collector of customs shall see reason to doubt whether the goods come from the country from which they are declared to come by the importer, it shall be lawful for the collector of customs to call on the importer to furnish evidence as to the place of manufacture or production, and if such evidence shall not satisfy the said collector of the truth of the declaration, the goods shall be charged with the highest rate of duty, subject always to an appeal to the Board of Customs, Salt, and Opium.

And upon the re-export by sea of goods imported, excepting opium and salt, provided the re-export be made within two years of the date of import, as per custom-house register, and the goods be identified to the satisfaction of the collector of customs, there shall be retained one-eighth of the amount of duty levied, and the remainder shall be repaid as drawback. And if goods be re-exported in the same ship without being landed (always excepting opium and salt, in regard to which the special rules in force shall continue to apply) there shall be no import duty levied thereon.

Appendix H.

RATES of Duty to be charged upon Goods Exported by Sea from any Port or Place in the Presidency of *Fort William*, in *Bengal*, in 1836.

No.	Enumeration of Goods.	Exported on British Bottoms.	Exported on Foreign Bottoms.
1	Bullion and coin - -	free - -	free.
2	Precious stones and pearls -	ditto - -	ditto.
3	Books printed in India -	ditto - -	ditto.
4	Horses and living animals -	ditto - -	ditto.
5	Opium purchased at Government sales in Calcutta -	ditto - -	ditto.
6	Cotton wool exported to Europe, the United States of America, or any British possession in America -	ditto - -	—8 As. p. Md. of 80 tolas to seer.
7	Ditto, ditto, exported to places other than above -	—As.8 p. Md. of 80 tolas p. seer	— As.16 p. Md. of 80 tolas to seer.
8	Sugar and rum exported to the United Kingdom, or to any British possession -	free - -	3 per cent.
9	Ditto, exported to any other place - - - -	3 per cent. -	6 per cent.
10	Grain and pulse of all sorts	- 1 anna per bag not exceeding 2 Mds. of 80 tolas to the seer, or if exported otherwise than in bags, ½ an anna per Md.	— 2 As. per bag not exceeding 2 Mds. of 80 tolas to the seer, or if exported otherwise than in bags, 1 anna per Md.
11	Indigo - - - - -	- Rs. 3 p. Md. of 80 tolas to the seer - -	— Rs. 6 per Md. of tolas to the seer.
12	Lac dye and shell lac -	4 per cent. -	8 per cent.
13	Silk, raw filature - -	3½ As. p. seer of 80 tolas -	7 As. p. seer of 80 tolas.
14	Silk, Bengal wound - -	3 As. p. seer of 80 tolas -	6 As. p. seer of 80 tolas.
15	Tobacco - - - - -	4 As. p. maund	8 As. p. maund.
16	All country articles not enumerated or named above	3 per cent. -	6 per cent.

And when the duty is declared to be *ad valorem*, the same shall be levied on the market value of the article at the place of export, without deduction.

And in settling for the duties on exports by sea, credit shall be given for payment of inland customs duty, and drawback shall be allowed of any excess of duty paid upon production of ruwanas under the following conditions, until the 1st April, 1837.

1st. That the goods shall be identified, and the destination to the port of export proved in the usual manner.

2nd. That the ruwanas shall bear date before the 1st April, 1836, and the goods shall not have been protected thereby, or by the original thereof, more than two years.

And after the said 1st April, 1837, credit shall not be given, nor shall drawback be allowed, of any inland customs or land frontier duty paid at any custom-house or chokee of the Jumna frontier line, or of Benares, except only upon the articles of cotton wool covered by ruwanas taken out at the custom-houses of the western provinces, and proved to have been destined for export by sea when passed out of those provinces.

Appendix I.

RATES of DUTY to be charged on GOODS IMPORTED by Sea into any Port of the Presidency of *Bombay* in 1838.

No.	Enumeration of Goods.	When Imported on British Bottoms.	When Imported on Foreign Bottoms.
1	Bullion and coin - -	free - -	free.
2	Precious stones and pearls -	ditto - -	ditto.
3	Grain and pulse - -	ditto - -	ditto.
4	Horses and other living animals - - - - -	ditto - -	ditto.
5	Ice - - - - -	ditto - -	ditto.
6	Coal, coke, bricks, chalk, stones, (marble & wrought stones excepted) - -	ditto - -	ditto.
7	Books printed in the United Kingdom, or in any British possession - -	ditto - -	3 per cent.
8	Foreign books - - - -	3 per cent. -	6 per cent.
9	Marine stores, the produce or manufacture of the United Kingdom, or of any British possession -	3 per cent. -	6 per cent.
0	Ditto, the produce or manufacture of any other place or country - - -	6 per cent. -	12 per eent.
11	Metals, wrought or unwrought, the produce or manufacture of the United Kingdom, or any British possession - - -	3 per cent. -	6 per cent.

No.	Enumeration of Goods.	When Imported on British Bottoms.	When Imported on Foreign Bottoms.
12	Metals, ditto, excepting tin, the produce or manufacture of any other place -	6 per cent. -	12 per cent.
13	Tin, the produce of any other place than the United Kingdom, or any British possession. - - -	10 per cent. -	20 per cent.
14	Woollens, the produce or manufacture of the United Kingdom, or any British possession - - -	2 per cent. -	4 per cent.
15	Ditto, the produce of any other place or country -	4 per cent. -	8 per cent.
16	Cotton wool, not covered by certificate of the payment of export duty at any other port of Bombay - -	- - 9 As. per md. of 80 tolas to the seer. -	- - 1 Re. 2 As. per md. of 80 tolas to the seer.
17	Cotton and silk piece goods, cotton twist, and yarn, the produce of the United Kingdom, or of any British possession - -	3½ per cent. -	7 per cent.
18	Ditto, the produce of any other place - - -	7 per cent. -	14 per cent.
19	Opium, covered by a pass -	free - -	free.
20	Ditto, not covered by a pass	24 Rs. per seer of 80 tolas -	24 Rs. per seer of 80 tolas.
21	Salt, not covered by a pass	- - 8 As. per md. of 80 tolas per seer - -	- - 8 As. per md. of 80 tolas per seer.
22	Alum - - - -	10 per cent. -	20 per cent.
23	Camphor - - - -	10 per cent. -	20 per cent.
24	Cassia - - - -	10 per cent. -	20 per cent.
25	Cloves - - - -	10 per cent. -	20 per cent.
26	Coffee - - - -	7½ per cent. -	15 per cent.
27	Coral - - - -	10 per cent. -	20 per cent.
28	Nutmegs and mace - -	10 per cent. -	20 per cent.
29	Pepper - - - -	10 per cent. -	20 per cent.
30	Rattans - - - -	7½ per cent. -	15 per cent.
31	Tea - - - -	10 per cent. -	20 per cent.
32	Vermilion - - -	10 per cent. -	20 per cent.
33	Wines and liqueurs - -	10 per cent. -	20 per cent.
34	Spirits, consolidated duty, including any duties levied heretofore through the police - - - -	9 As. per imperial gallon -	1 Re. per imperial gallon.
	And the duty on spirits shall be rateably increased as the strength exceeds London proof, and when imported in bottles, five quart bottles shall be deemed equal to the imperial gallon.		
35	Tobacco - - - -	- - 1 Re. 8 As per md. of 80 tolas per seer -	- - 1 Re. 8 As. per md. of 80 tolas per seer.
	Which duty shall be the minimum customs' duty		

No.	Enumeration of Goods.	When Imported on British Bottoms.	When Imported on Foreign Bottoms.
	levied on raw Tobacco, and all preparations thereof, in all the ports of the Bombay Presidency; but if at the rate of five per cent, on the actual value, a higher duty than 1 rupee 8 annas per maund should be leviable on any preparation of tobacco, the duty shall be levied *ad valorem* at that rate, if imported on British bottoms, and at 10 per cent. on foreign bottoms. And the customs duty laid upon tobacco shall be allowed in settling for the special duty levied on the import of this article into the Island of Bombay, which special duty shall be levied at the rate of 9 rupees for the Indian maund.		
36	All articles not included in the above enumeration -	3 per cent. -	7 per cent.

And if the collector of customs shall see reason to doubt whether the goods liable to a different rate of duty, according to the place of their production, come from the country from which they are declared to have come by the importer, it shall be lawful for the collector of customs to call on the importer to furnish evidence as to the place of manufacture or production; and if such evidence shall not satisfy the said collector of the truth of the declaration, the goods shall be charged with the highest rate of duty, subject always to an appeal to the Governor in Council at Bombay.

And upon the re-export by sea of goods imported, excepting opium and salt, and all goods of the growth, production, or manufacture of the continent of India, provided the re-export be made within two years of the date of import, as per custom-house register, and the goods be identified to the satisfaction of the collector of customs, there shall be retained one-eighth of the amount of duty levied, and the remainder shall be repaid as drawback.

But no exporter of imported goods shall be entitled to drawback unless the drawback be claimed at the time of re-export, nor shall any payment be made of drawback unless the amount claimed be demanded within one year from the date of entry of the goods for re-export in the custom-house registers.

Appendix J.

RATES of Duty to be charged on Goods Exported by Sea from any Port or Place in the Presidency of *Bombay*, in 1838.

No.	Enumeration of Goods.	Exported on British Bottoms.	Exported on Foreign Bottoms.
1	Bullion and coin - -	free - -	free.
2	Precious stones and pearls -	ditto - -	ditto.
3	Books, maps, and drawings printed in India - -	ditto - -	ditto.
4	Horses and living animals	ditto - -	ditto.
5	Opium, covered by a pass	ditto - -	ditto.
6	Ditto, not covered by a pass	prohibited -	prohibited.
7	Cotton wool exported to Europe, the United States of America, or any British possession in America.	free - -	9 As. per maund of 80 tolas to the seer.
8	Ditto - exported to places other than above - -	9 As. per maund of 80 tolas per seer.	1 Re. 2 As. per maund of 80 tolas to the seer.
9	Salt having paid the excise of 8 annas a maund -	free - -	free.
10	Tobacco - - - -	1 Re. 8 As. per maund of 80 tolas to the seer. - -	1 Re. 8 As. per maund of 80 tolas per seer.
11	All country articles not enumerated or named above.	3 per cent. -	6 per cent.

And upon the re-export to Europe, the United States of America, or to any British possession in America, or from any other port of the Bombay Presidency, of cotton that has been imported under certificate of the payment of the duty specified in this Schedule, provided that the re-export be made in British bottoms within two years from the date of such certificate, and the amount be claimed within one year from the date of re-export, as per custom-house registers, the whole amount of export duty levied at the first place of export shall be refunded.

APPENDIX K.

TABLE OF DUTIES payable on Goods imported into *Ceylon*, and of the Drawbacks to be allowed on the Exportation of such Goods.

	£.	s.	d.
Ale, porter, and all other malt liquors in casks, per gallon	0	0	2½
Do. per dozen quarts, in bottles - - - -	0	0	6
Opium, per lb. - - - - - -	0	1	0
Paddy, per bushel - - - - -	0	0	3
Rice per bushel - - - - - -	0	0	7
Spirits and liquors, per gallon - - - -	0	4	6
Goods, wares, and merchandize, not otherwise charged with duty, and not herein declared to be free of duty, being of the growth, produce, or manufacture of the United Kingdom, or of any of His Majesty's possessions abroad, other than the possessions of the East India Company, for every 100 pounds of the value thereof in this market - - - - - -	4	0	0
Goods, wares, and merchandize, not otherwise charged with duty, and not herein declared to be free of duty, being of the growth, produce, or manufacture of any foreign state, or of the possessions of the East India Company, for every 100 pounds of the value thereof in this market. - - - - - -	10	0	0
Books, printed - - - - - -	free.		
Bullion, coin, pearls, and precious stones - - -	free.		
Garden seeds and plants - - - - -	free.		
Horses, mules, asses, neat cattle, and all other live stock -	free.		
Instruments, scientific - - - - -	free.		
Machinery, implements, and tools, for agriculture and for any kind of manufacture. - - - -	free.		
Maps - - - - - - -	free.		
Regimental clothing and accoutrements - - -	free.		
Timber - - - - - - -	free.		

APPENDIX L.

TABLE OF DUTIES payable on Goods Exported from *Ceylon*.

	£.	s.	d.
Cinnamon, per lb. - - - - - -	0	2	6
Ditto, if assorted as the third sort by the Government assorters, per lb. - - - - -	0	2	0
Cinnamon oil, per oz. - - - - - -	0	1	0
Goods, wares, and merchandize, of the growth, produce, or manufacture of the Island of Ceylon, not being subject to other export duty, nor particularly exempted from export duty, for every 100 pounds of the value thereof - -	2	10	0
Books, printed - - - - - -	free.		
Bullion, coin, pearls, and precious stones - - -	free.		
Horses, asses, mules, neat cattle, and all other live stock -	free.		
Plants and seeds - - - - - -	free.		
Wearing apparel and personal baggage - - -	free.		

N.B.—Thus it appears that in Ceylon the cotton goods of Great Britain are charged with a duty of 5 per cent. only; those of India with duties varying from 10 to 20 per cent. Other goods, the produce or manufacture of the United Kingdom, or of British possessions, are admitted into Ceylon at 4 per cent. And East India goods at 10 per cent.

Appendix M.

Return of the Number of Convicts in New South Wales, on the 31st December, 1835.

Penal Settlements :—	
Norfolk Island - - - - - -	1,062
Moreton Bay - - - - - -	354
Port Macquarie - - - - - - -	531
Hulk - - - - - - - -	208
On the Roads, and Surveyor-General's Department - -	1,080
On the Roads in Irons - - - - - -	1,022
Goat Island - - - - - - -	223
Second Class Convicts, Illawarra - - - -	117
Mineral Surveyor's Department - - - - -	112
Medical Department - - - - - -	123
Commissariat Department - - - - -	58
Hyde Park Barrack - - - - - -	658
Sydney Gaol - - - - - - -	91
Female Factory, Paramatta - - - - -	646
Holding Tickets of Leave - - - - -	3,650
In private Service - - - - - -	19,247
Total - - -	29,182

VAN DIEMEN'S LAND, 1835.

DISTRICTS.	Free Whites.		Military and their Families.		Convicts.		TOTAL.			Persons employed in		
	Males.	Females.	Males.	Females.	Males.	Females.	Males.	Females.	Total.	Agriculture.	Manufactures.	Total.
Hobart Town	5,545	4,446	..	..	2,952	883	8,497	5,329	13,826	600	336	420
Launceston	2,216	1,448	..	..	1,736	335	3,952	1,783	5,735	1,140	226	254
Richmond	1,235	853	..	..	1,364	114	2,599	967	3,566	620	61	38
New Norfolk	517	338	..	..	875	92	1,392	430	1,822	380	..	7
Oatlands	373	225	..	..	665	30	1,038	255	1,293	504	..	109
Campbell Town	682	400	..	..	1,152	86	1,834	486	2,320	2,110	190	20
Norfolk Plains	508	322	..	..	596	38	1,104	360	1,464	454	37	17
Brighton	664	407	..	..	960	51	1,624	458	2,082	734	88	70
Bothwell	260	145	..	..	288	17	548	162	710	686	..	24
Hamilton	313	180	..	..	338	29	651	209	860	530	39	52
Westbury	176	52	..	..	307	10	483	62	545	324	..	110
Great Swan Port	98	59	..	..	157	10	255	69	324	179	..	..
George Town	113	73	..	..	98	4	211	77	288	55	14	..
Circular Head	69	49	..	..	103	2	171	51	222	142	..	7
Tasman's Peninsula	164	46	..	..	1,209	3	1,373	49	1,422	..	..	..
Flinders' Island	8	8	5	7	11	2	24	17	41	..	..	..
" Aborigines	..	..	..	..	..	..	52	59	111	..	..	..
Military in the Island	..	..	779	181	..	..	779	181	960	..	..	..
" Children of	..	..	111	130	..	..	111	130	241	..	..	..
Convicts employed in Road Parties, Chain Gangs, and Houses of Correction	..	..	..	..	2,103	348	2,103	348	2,451	..	..	..
Total	12,940	9,051	895	318	14,914	2,054	28,801	11,482	40,283	..	..	..

Appendix N.

MEASURES TAKEN FOR THE ABOLITION OF SLAVERY IN CEYLON.

To his Royal Highness the Prince of Wales, Regent of the United Kingdom of Great Britain and Ireland, &c. &c. &c.

We, his Majesty's loyal subjects, the Dutch inhabitants and native castes of the maritime settlements in the island of Ceylon, animated with sentiments of sincere and fervent loyalty towards the person and government of his Majesty and your Royal Highness, and emulating the humane and disinterested spirit with which our fellow-subjects in the United Kingdom have moved the Legislature in favour of that unfortunate class of beings placed in the degrading condition of slavery, beg leave to approach your Royal Highness with an humble tender of such tribute on our parts, in furtherance of the same benevolent object, as our circumstances enable us to afford.

In families long settled in this island, of whatever class, the household establishment is usually so much dependent on the service of slaves, that a general discharge of those persons would subject the inhabitants to privations, losses and expense, such as ordinary prudence forbids us to encounter. At the same time we have reason to know, that to great numbers of persons now in our houses in the character of slaves, bred up under our roofs, supported for a course of years with kind and considerate treatment and comfortable subsistence, many of them far advanced in life, the greater part established in habits of attachment, a general emancipation would withdraw the source of their support, without advancing their happiness, or improving their condition.

We therefore humbly incline, both in consideration to them and to ourselves, to adopt the principle sanctioned by the wisdom of British legislation, of a gradual abolition; that which we beg leave to offer being indeed gradual in its progress, but in its issue certain and complete.

We respectfully and dutifully propose, that the era of future freedom to the slaves of this colony shall take its commencement on the auspicious occasion of your Highness's birth-day, the 12th of August in the present year 1816, and we declare all children born of our slaves from that date inclusive, to be free persons.

Some incidental provisions will be perceived to be necessary, with regard to the support and tutelage of these liberated children during their tender years. The leading articles of enactments which appear expedient for this purpose have already been indicated, in Resolutions conveyed by the honourable the Chief Justice for the information of his Excellency the Governor, and we doubt not that these and such other regulations as may be found calculated to place the intended measure on a footing of mutual comfort to the emancipated slaves and their masters, will be distinctly and favourably represented by his Excellency, and receive in substance the gracious acceptance and confirmation of your Royal Highness.

[It is unnecessary to introduce the long list of Subscribers to the address to his Royal Highness the Prince Regent for emancipating Children born of Slaves after the 12th of August, 1816.]

At a Meeting of the Board of Commissioners for the Affairs of the Kandyan Provinces, held in the Hall of Audience at Kandy, this 6th day of December, 1831.

PRESENT:

Colonel Miller Clifford, C. B., commanding the Troops in the Interior.

Henry Wright, Esq., Judicial Commissioner.

George Turnour, Esq., Revenue Commissioner.

The following Chiefs attended according to notice:—

Mollegode, 1st Adikar.
Doolleawe, 2nd Adikar.
Mullegame, 3rd Adikar.
Galagode Desave, of Valapane.
Dunuwile Desave, of Udapalate.
Dehegame Udagabada Nelame.
Kadegemuwe Matra Lekam.
Vattarantenne Nanayak Kare Lekam.
Ganegoda Basnayahe Nelame.
Amunugame Nelame.
Giragame Nelame.
Madugalle Nelame.

A REFERENCE having been made to the chiefs upon the subject of the late Governor Sir Edward Barnes's address to them at his last audience in Kandy, respecting the emancipation of slaves, and the answer received from them appearing to require some further communication with them on this subject, they have been convened for this purpose. After some discussion, in which the views and feelings of government are fully explained, the chiefs express their wish to retire, with the view of consulting together on a matter of so much interest to them and their families, and say that whatever determination they or any of them may come to shall be speedily committed to writing, and presented in the course of this afternoon.

The board accordingly adjourns until five o'clock.

The chiefs return, and present a paper which they have just drawn up, and which is signed by all now present, expressive of the conditions upon which they would consent to a system of progressive emancipation of their slaves, and they likewise request that in submitting this document for the consideration of government, their former representation may be forwarded with it.

The board agrees in the propriety of laying the whole of their proceedings before the Right Honourable the Governor, and in so doing would beg leave to refer to the report on the state of slavery in this country, which was transmitted with its proceedings of the 25th August, 1829.

It will be seen thereby, that slavery in this country is of the mildest possible character, and that the number of slaves is extremely small; considering how recently these provinces have emerged from the barbarism of the despotic rule of a native sovereign, and been brought under the influence of the more enlightened principles of European administration, the feelings evinced by the chiefs on the present occasion are those which might be naturally expected to result from the present state of the society, and of the civilization of the country, and the board would beg to add that, for the same reasons, the concessions they now offer to make appear to them to go as far as might be reasonably expected of them.

By the present offer, though the commencement of the emancipation is deferred for 60 years, yet its operation from that period is certain, and it is to be hoped that the gradual progress of improvement in that interval will afford the means of removing or amending the other stipulations under which the offer is made, excepting the one which requires a pecuniary recompense, as the amount thereof will not be great from the gradually progressive nature of the emancipation.

Under all the circumstances of the case, therefore, the board would venture to suggest, that the proposal now made by the chiefs should be favourably received, and that copies of the second document presented by them should be sent to all the agents of government, in order that the proprietors of slaves residing in their respective districts might be invited to subscribe thercto.

When the wishes of all the Kandyan proprietors of slaves have been thus ascertained, it will then become necessary to consider in what form, and under what stipulations and modifications, a legislative enactment should be passed, conformably with the proceedings adopted in passing the Regulation No. IX. of 1818.

(signed) *Miller Clifford*, Col[l] Comm[g] K. P.
H. Wright, J. C.
George Turnour, R. C.

LETTER to the First and Second Adikars.

WITH reference to the speech delivered by his Excellency Sir Edward Barnes, at the last public audience held in Kandy, in which he proposed a plan for the emancipation of the female children only who may be hereafter born in slavery, we have been directed to ascertain and report what the sentiments of the principal chiefs are upon this subject.

It is obvious that the success of this benevolent measure will greatly depend upon the ready acquiescence of those who, from their rank and station, possess the greatest influence in this country; and as your zeal for the public good has never been questioned, we rely with confidence on your disposition to meet the views of government, so far as you and your family are concerned.

There are various ways in which this object may be accomplished, and that which would prove the least inconvenient to the proprietors would doubtless bè the most acceptable to government.

Any suggestions, therefore, from you, as to the best mode of effecting this object, will be taken into consideration, as well as any difficulties or objections which appear to you to exist, in order that government may adopt suitable measures for removing them.

I have, &c.

(signed) *H. Wright*, Jud. Comm[r].

(True copy.)

(signed) *H. Wright*, J. C.

(Translation.)

Kandy, 22 *November*, 1831.

On the occasion of the last audience given by his Excellency the Governor, Sir Edward Barnes, to the chiefs in Kandy, in the speech then made to us, the chiefs, and to the inhabitants, mention was made of a measure for the enfranchisement of female slaves born hereafter, and we are very sorry that want of time prevented us from submitting the circumstances which we have to urge respecting this before his Excellency's departure from this island. However, in the letter sent by the judicial commissioner to the Adikars, clear and explicit information is called for as to how this measure is to be effected, and what disadvantage will result therefrom to the owners of female slaves.

In the first place, we are clearly informed that government entertains the opinion that it is a good thing to liberate the slaves in this country. If government thus intend prosperity for the slaves, we would also implore government to consider what must be the adversity, loss and disadvantage, the disgrace and the difficulties, which must result to the principal chiefs and the owners of the slaves in consequence of liberating the slaves whom they have inherited from their ancestors.

The most important services rendered to us by our slaves are the following: on the death of a member of any one of our families, the laying out of the corpse, and doing every thing else that is requisite at the funeral, carrying out the corpse, and performing the office of sepulture; whatever may be the amount of the incidental emoluments, none but such slaves will take the same; a free ratta person, of whatever degree, will neither do such service at a funeral, nor accept of the perquisites allotted on the occasion, because such perquisites have been made appropriate to slaves only from ancient times; no people, even of low caste, with the exception of gahaleyas, would accept of such perquisites, and if gahaleyas were to be hired therewith to perform the offices of sepulture, that will involve our families in disgrace.

On the death of a person of a chief s family who possessed no slaves, a relation who has slaves must send them to remove the corpse; amongst ratta people who possess no slaves, the relations themselves bury their dead, but a person of a chief's family cannot do such a thing. In the maritime provinces, in the event of a death in any of the respectable families, respectable appuhamies bear the corpse to the grave, but such a thing is impossible in this country.

The bringing of firewood and water to our walanwes, and various other menial offices and services performed in attendance on the masters and mistresses of respectable families amongst us, can be imposed on none but slaves; no free person of any degree can be so employed. If their slaves were to be liberated, then the masters and mistresses of respectable families will be constrained to do what had been incumbent on their slaves, for none else will submit to be so employed. By this liberation of slaves, we shall suffer other difficulties and distresses which we cannot enumerate.

Moreover, although it is alleged therein that government will consider the prevention of any loss that may accrue to the owners of slaves in consequence of their emancipation, we cannot say what advantage we shall receive to obviate the losses incident on such liberation of slaves.

Therefore we pray government not to inflict on us a distressing loss of the means whereby we maintain the honour and respectability which have devolved to us in this country from ancient times.

Further, we do not exact services gratuitously from these men slaves and women slaves; we allot to them out of our hereditary estates paddy lands and gardens, &c.; and some slaves there are, who, from having been long settled so, have become very rich, and they serve us with much fidelity.

In case of inquiry, we have much more to state touching this matter; if facts were to be fully stated the writing will be extensive, therefore this is written concisely; and we all pray that government will not abolish this usage of the country.

(signed)

Molligodde Maha Nileme.	*Madugalle.*
Dooleywe Maha Nileme.	*Golahella.*
Mullegame Maha Nileme.	*Gonigoda.*
Galagode Walapany Dassawe.	*Angammore.*
Dunneville Dissave.	*Ammurnegama Nileme.*
Dehigamelida Gabeda Nileme.	*Mullegame.*
Waegodapola Lekam.	*Giragama Banda.*
Wattarantenne Nunayakara Lekam.	*Halangoda Lekam.*
Kodigomuwe.	*Kotuwegedere Banda.*

Translated by,

(signed) *J. Armour*, Int^{r}. Jud^{l}. Court.

(Translation.)

Kandy, 1 *December*, 1831.

It was in order that government may be informed of the loss, the detriment and the disgrace consequent on the liberation of slaves in this country, that we lately gave in a statement in writing; however, we have been since informed of Governor Sir Edward Barnes's earnest wish for effecting the liberation of female slaves having been made known to government in England. When his Excellency was governor of this island, he bestowed friendship and conferred honour on persons of the principal respectable families in the Kandyan country, and maintained the institutions and customs in a very proper manner; and on the approach of his Excellency's departure from this island, we were exceedingly sorry thereat; and on account of his Excellency's beneficence, we also evinced to the utmost our fidelity and reverence. How great soever may be the loss resulting to us from this measure which his Excellency wished to adopt, yet if we should counteract his Excellency's wishes, it might seem that all the fidelity and respect which we shewed to his Excellency were a scheme of dissimulation. Therefore we most earnestly pray, that in consideration of our fidelity and attachment to government, this gracious government will also have compassion toward us, and refrain from liberating the female slaves in question for the 60 years ensuing, so that for a short space of time we may continue free from inconvenience; and that it may be so regulated, that female slaves born after the lapse of these 60 years shall be paid for at the rate of 100 ridies (3*l.* 6*s.*) for each, and thus a gradual emancipation of female slaves be effected thenceforth, as his Excellency had suggested; that it may also be ordained, that on the death of a member of our families, the emancipated female slaves shall attend to perform services at the funeral as they (female slaves) now do, receiving the allotted perquisites; or that government may, in regard of this matter, make some other suitable rule that will consist with the customs which have subsisted in this country from ancient times; and that the protection and respect which are at present insured to our religion, and the respect and honours accorded to us and the other ancient and important institutions and usages of this country, may not be abrogated even as the institution in question is sought to be abolished; moreover, we pray that when the plan of emancipating the female slaves born after the ensuing 60 years comes to be made public, it may at the same time be proclaimed by government that the men slaves and women slaves now belonging to us shall continue submissive and obedient as they now are, that the power of enforcing obedience will continue as at present, and that, after the lapse of the 60 years, such slaves as may yet be retained by us must continue under such control.

(signed) *Molligodde Maha Nileme.* *Madugalle.*
Dooleywe Maha Nileme. *Gonigoda.*
Mullegame Maha Nileme. *Angammore.*
Galagode. *Unanbuwe.*
Dunneville Dissave. *Giragama.*
Dehigarne. *Amurnegama.*
Kadigomawe. *Kotuwegedere Bunda.*
Wattarantenne.

Translated by,
(signed) *J. Armour*, Int[r] Jud[l] Court.

Chief Secretary's Office, Colombo, 20th December, 1831.

Gentlemen,

I have laid before the Governor the proceedings of your board at a meeting held at Kandy on the 6th instant, and in reference to your report relative to the proposed emancipation of slaves in the Kandyan provinces, I am directed to acquaint you that his Excellency will take an early opportunity of visiting Kandy, for the purpose of personally entering upon this very important question, with the principal chiefs, and he cannot but hope that, on more mature consideration, they will be inclined to make arrangements for more speedily carrying into effect a measure so highly creditable to themselves, and so much in unison with the wishes of his Majesty's Government.

I have, &c.
(signed) *P. Anstruther*, Dep. Sec.

Colonel M. Clifford, C.B.,
and the Board of Commissioners,
&c. &c. &c.

THE END.

G. NORMAN, PRINTER, MAIDEN LANE, COVENT GARDEN.

LIST OF PLATES TO VOL. II.

MAP OF THE SEVEN KORLES . .	*To face Title Page.*
Ploughing	39
Smoothing the Fields	40
Treading out Rice	42
Historical Painting of the Pastimes of the Kings of Kurunagalla .	79
Historical Painting near Ollagaminé	126
Ditto ditto	126
Ditto at Dambool	186

No. 1.

The King Wessantara, *his Queen, and the two Princes Royal, sitting in the royal palace.*

No. 2.

The white (i. e. the royal) *Elephant of* Kálinza, *together with King* Wessantara, *in the act of bestowing religious charity upon a Bramin, who came to solicit alms, by pouring water into his hands.*

No. 3.

The King Wessantara, *his Queen, and the two Princes, seated in the royal chariot, leaving their country to retire into solitude, for the purpose of becoming religious Ascetics. They are mêt by a Bramin who solicits alms, and the King is pouring water into his hands as an act of religious charity.*

No. 4.

The two Princes, while living in solitude as Ascetics, are visited by an ascetic *Bramin, who comes to solicit alms, and they are in the act of pouring water into his hands as an act of religious charity.*

LIST OF PLATES.

---

* The *Kinduró* are a class of fabulous beings, who, according to *Hindu* Mythology, are the Celestial Musicians and Choristers. They are variously represented in the Temples: sometimes as half man and half bird; at other times as half man and half goat. In this painting the right-hand figure is a male, playing on the *Vina*, or Indian Lute; the other, on the left, is a female, dancing and chanting to the tune of the Lute.